World Archaeoprimatology

Interconnections of Humans and Nonhuman Primates in the Past

Archaeoprimatology intertwines archaeology and primatology to understand the ancient liminal relationships between humans and nonhuman primates. During the last decade, novel studies have boosted this discipline. This edited volume is the first compendium of archaeoprimatological studies ever produced. Written by a culturally diverse group of scholars, with multiple theoretical views and methodological perspectives, it includes new zooarchaeological examinations and material culture evaluations, as well as innovative uses of oral and written sources. Themes discussed comprise the survey of past primates as pets, symbolic mediators, prey, iconographic references, or living commodities. The book covers different regions of the world, from the Americas to Asia, along with studies from Africa and Europe. Temporally, the chapters explore the human–nonhuman primate interface from deep in time to more recent historical times, examining both extinct and extant primate taxa. This anthology of archaeoprimatological studies will be of interest to archaeologists, primatologists, anthropologists, art historians, paleontologists, conservationists, zoologists, historical ecologists, philologists, and ethnobiologists.

Bernardo Urbani is Associate Researcher at the Center for Anthropology of the Venezuelan Institute for Scientific Research, Caracas, Venezuela, and an elected member of the Global Young Academy. Recently, he was selected as a fellow of the Alexander von Humboldt Foundation at the Leibniz Institute for Primate Research/ German Primate Center, Göttingen, Germany. He has received the Martha J. Galante Award of the International Primatological Society and the Early Career Achievement Award of the American Society of Primatologists.

Dionisios Youlatos is Professor of Vertebrate Zoology in the School of Biology of the Aristotle University of Thessaloniki, Greece. He has done field and laboratory research on both extant and extinct primates and other mammals in South America, Europe, East Africa, and South East Asia. His research has been financially supported by both national and international funding. He is the author of more than a hundred articles and book chapters on the ecology, behavior, anatomy, and evolution of mammals.

Andrzej T. Antczak is Associate Professor in Caribbean Archaeology in the Faculty of Archaeology, Leiden University, and Senior Researcher at the Royal Netherlands Institute of Southeast Asian and Caribbean Studies (KITLV-KNAW) in Leiden, the Netherlands. He is co-curator at the Unit of Archaeological Studies, Simón Bolívar University, Caracas, Venezuela, and recently served as chair of the Department of World Archaeology at Leiden University.

Cambridge Studies in Biological and Evolutionary Anthropology

Consulting editors

C. G. Nicholas Mascie-Taylor, University of Cambridge
Robert A. Foley, University of Cambridge

Series editors

Agustín Fuentes, University of Notre Dame
Nina G. Jablonski, Pennsylvania State University
Clark Spencer Larsen, The Ohio State University
Michael P. Muehlenbein, Baylor University
Dennis H. O'Rourke, The University of Kansas
Karen B. Strier, University of Wisconsin
David P. Watts, Yale University

Also available in the series

World Archaeoprimatology

Interconnections of Humans and Nonhuman Primates in the Past

Edited by

BERNARDO URBANI
Venezuelan Institute for Scientific Research

DIONISIOS YOULATOS
Aristotle University of Thessaloniki

ANDRZEJ T. ANTCZAK
Leiden University

CAMBRIDGE
UNIVERSITY PRESS

CAMBRIDGE
UNIVERSITY PRESS

University Printing House, Cambridge CB2 8BS, United Kingdom

One Liberty Plaza, 20th Floor, New York, NY 10006, USA

477 Williamstown Road, Port Melbourne, VIC 3207, Australia

314–321, 3rd Floor, Plot 3, Splendor Forum, Jasola District Centre, New Delhi – 110025, India

103 Penang Road, #05–06/07, Visioncrest Commercial, Singapore 238467

Cambridge University Press is part of the University of Cambridge.

It furthers the University's mission by disseminating knowledge in the pursuit of education, learning, and research at the highest international levels of excellence.

www.cambridge.org
Information on this title: www.cambridge.org/9781108487337
DOI: 10.1017/9781108766500

First published 2022

Printed in the United Kingdom by TJ Books Limited, Padstow Cornwall

A catalogue record for this publication is available from the British Library.

Library of Congress Cataloging-in-Publication Data
Names: Urbani, Bernardo, editor. | Youlatos, Dionisios, editor. | Antczak, Andrzej T., editor.
Title: World archaeoprimatology : interconnections of humans and nonhuman primates in the past / edited by Bernardo Urbani, Venezuelan Institute for Scientific Research, Dionisios Youlatos, Aristotle University of Thessaloniki, Andrzej T. Antczak, Leiden University.
Description: Cambridge ; New York, NY : Cambridge University Press, 2022. |
Series: Cambridge studies in biological and evolutionary anthropology | Includes bibliographical references and index.
Identifiers: LCCN 2022000132 (print) | LCCN 2022000133 (ebook) | ISBN 9781108487337 (hardback) | ISBN 9781108720076 (paperback) | ISBN 9781108766500 (epub)
Subjects: LCSH: Primate remains (Archaeology) | Paleoanthropology. | Ethnozoology. | Animals in art. | Material culture. | Human-animal relationships. | Human ecology–History. | BISAC: SOCIAL SCIENCE / Anthropology / Physical
Classification: LCC CC79.5.A5 W67 2022 (print) | LCC CC79.5.A5 (ebook) | DDC 930.1–dc23/eng/20220303
LC record available at https://lccn.loc.gov/2022000132
LC ebook record available at https://lccn.loc.gov/2022000133

ISBN 978-1-108-48733-7 Hardback

B.U.: To Ana María and Lucía, to my family and students, to the past and present primates. . .

D.Y.: To my late mother Ioanna, to Evangelos Sr. and Jr., and to Alexandra, who patiently supported me.

A.T.A.: With love to Marlena, Konrad and Valeria, and Oliver and Nynke; to all colleagues and students on both sides of the ocean.

Contents

Contributors

Gamini Adikari
Postgraduate Institute of Archaeology, University of Kelaniya, Colombo, Sri Lanka

Aleksa K. Alaica
Department of Anthropology, University of Alberta, Edmonton, Canada

Noel Amano
Department of Archaeology, Max Planck Institute for the Science of Human History, Jena, Germany

Tharaka Ananda
Department of Anthropology, Faculty of Humanities and Social Sciences, University of Sri Jayewardenepura, Nugegoda, Sri Lanka

Tomoko Anezaki
Gunma Museum of Natural History, Tomioka, Japan

Andrzej T. Antczak
Faculty of Archaeology, Leiden University & the Royal Netherlands Institute of Southeast Asian and Caribbean Studies, Leiden, the Netherlands

M. Magdalena Antczak
The Royal Netherlands Institute of Southeast Asian and Caribbean Studies, Leiden, the Netherlands & Unit of Archaeological Studies, Simón Bolívar University, Caracas, Venezuela

Shaw Badenhorst
Evolutionary Studies Institute, University of the Witwatersrand, Johannesburg, South Africa

Massimo Bardi
Department of Behavioral Neuroscience, Randolph-Macon College, Ashfield, Virginia, USA

Lydia Bashford
Department of Ancient History, Macquarie University, Sydney, Australia

Douglas Brandon-Jones
Independent Researcher, Australia

Rubén Cabrera-Castro
Teotihuacan Archaeological Zone, National Institute of Anthropology and History, San Juan Teotihuacán, Mexico

Nicole R. Cannarozzi
Department of Natural History, Florida Museum of Natural History, Gainesville, USA

Lisabeth A. Carlson
SEARCH, Inc., Newberry, Florida, USA

Olivia A. de Carvalho
Department of Archaeology, Federal University of Sergipe, Brazil

Roger H. Colten
Peabody Museum of Natural History, Yale University. New Haven, Connecticut, USA

Raymond Corbey
Faculty of Archaeology, Leiden University, the Netherlands

Raymundo A. C. F. Dijkhoff
Scientific Department, National Archaeological Museum Aruba, Oranjestad, Aruba

Kitty F. Emery
Department of Natural History, Florida Museum of Natural History, Gainesville, USA

Susan M. Ford
Department of Anthropology, Southern Illinois University, Carbondale, USA

Jorge Gamboa
School of Archaeology, Santiago Antunez Mayolo National University, Huaraz, Peru

Debora R. Gilles
Corrientes Biological Station, Centro de Ecología Aplicada del Litoral, CECOAL-CONICET, Argentina

Laurie R. Godfrey
Department of Anthropology, University of Massachusetts, Amherst, USA

Jaap Goudsmit
Department of Epidemiology, Harvard T. H. Chan School of Public Health, Harvard University, Boston, Massachusetts, USA

Songtao Guo
Shaanxi Key Laboratory for Animal Conservation, College of Life Sciences, Northwest University, Xi'an, China & Institute of Wetland and Grassland, Shaanxi Academy of Forestry, Xi'an, China

Gang He
Shaanxi Key Laboratory for Animal Conservation, College of Life Sciences, Northwest University, Xi'an, China & Institute of Wetland and Grassland, Shaanxi Academy of Forestry, Xi'an, China

Hitomi Hongo
School of Advanced Science, Graduate University for Advanced Studies, Hayama, Kanagawa, Japan

Rong Hou
Shaanxi Key Laboratory for Animal Conservation, College of Life Sciences, Northwest University, Xi'an, China

Xiduo Hou
Shaanxi Key Laboratory for Animal Conservation, College of Life Sciences, Northwest University, Xi'an, China

Michael A. Huffman
Wildlife Research Center, Kyoto University, Japan

Thomas Ingicco
Department of Prehistory, National Museum of Natural History & Department of Man and Environment, University of Perpignan, Paris, France

Xueping Ji
Kunming Natural History Museum of Zoology, Kunming Institute of Zoology, Chinese Academy of Sciences, Kunming, China

Nelum Kanthilatha
Department of Anthropology, Faculty of Humanities and Social Sciences, University of Sri Jayewardenepura, Nugegoda, Sri Lanka

William F. Keegan
Department of Natural History, Florida Museum of Natural History, Gainesville, USA

Martín M. Kowalewski
Corrientes Biological Station, Centro de Ecología Aplicada del Litoral, CECOAL-CONICET, Argentina

Michelle J. LeFebvre
Department of Natural History, Florida Museum of Natural History, Gainesville, USA

Baoguo Li
Northwest University, Xi'an, China & International Centre of Biodiversity and Primate Conservation Centre, Dali University, Dali, Yunnan, China

Anne-Marie Moigne
Department of Prehistory, National Museum of Natural History & Department of Man and Environment, University of Perpignan, Paris, France

Charmalie A. D. Nahallage
Department of Anthropology, Faculty of Humanities and Social Sciences, University of Sri Jayewardenepura, Gandodawila, Sri Lanka

Ndukuyakhe Ndlovu
South African National Parks, Pretoria, South Africa and Department of Anthropology and Archaeology, University of Pretoria, South Africa

Dennis C. Nieweg
Naturalis Biodiversity Center, Leiden, the Netherlands

Yuichiro Nishioka
Museum of Natural and Environmental History, Shizuoka, Japan

Ruliang Pan
Shaanxi Key Laboratory for Animal Conservation, College of Life Sciences, Northwest University, Xi'an, China, International Centre of Biodiversity and Primate Conservation Centre, Dali University, Yunnan, & School of Human Sciences and Centre for Evolutionary Biology, The University of Western Australia, Perth, Australia

Edithe Pereira
Section of Archaeology, Emilio Goeldi Museum, Belém, Brazil

Nimal Perera
Central Cultural Fund of Sri Lanka & Department of Philosophical and History Inquiry, Faculty of Arts and Social Sciences, The University of Sydney, Australia

Roberta R. Pinto
Laboratory and Museum of Archaeology, Catholic University of Pernambuco, Brazil

Albérico N. de Queiroz
Department of Archaeology, Federal University of Sergipe, Brazil

R. Florencia Quijano
Corrientes Biological Station, Centro de Ecología Aplicada del Litoral, CECOAL-CONICET, Argentina

Damián Ruíz-Ramoni
Regional Center for Scientific Research and Technological Transfer of Anillaco, CONICET, La Rioja, Argentina

Anne-Marie Sémah
Department of Prehistory, National Museum of Natural History & Department of Man and Environment, University of Perpignan, Paris, France

François Sémah
Department of Prehistory, National Museum of Natural History & Department of Man and Environment, University of Perpignan, Paris, France

Carlos Serrano-Sánchez
Institute of Anthropological Research, National Autonomous University of Mexico, Mexico City, Mexico

Truman Simanjuntak
Indonesian Baptist Theological College, Semarang, Indonesia

José de Sousa e Silva Júnior
Department of Zoology, Emilio Goeldi Museum, Belém, Brazil

Katherine E. South
Department of Language & Cultural Studies, Anthropology, and Sociology, Eastern Kentucky University, Richmond, USA

Jan Štefka
Institute of Parasitology, Biology Centre, Czech Academy of Sciences & Faculty of Science, University of South Bohemia, České Budějovice, Czech Republic

Marcos Such-Gutiérrez
Department of Classical Philology, Autonomous University of Madrid, Spain

Masanaru Takai
The Kyoto University Museum, Kyoto University, Kyoto, Japan

Bernardo Urbani
Center for Anthropology, Venezuelan Institute for Scientific Research, Caracas, Venezuela

Raúl Valadez-Azúa
Institute of Anthropological Research, National Autonomous University of Mexico, Mexico City, Mexico

Alexandra A. E. van der Geer
Department of Geology, National and Kapodistrian University of Athens, Zografos, Greece & Naturalis Biodiversity Center, Leiden, the Netherlands

Natalie Vasey
Department of Anthropology, Portland State University, Oregon, USA

Marco Vespa
Department of Classical Studies, The Hebrew University of Jerusalem, Israel

Thomas A. Wake
Cotsen Institute of Archaeology, University of California, Los Angeles, USA & Smithsonian Tropical Research Institute, Panama City, Panama

Haitao Wang
Shaanxi Key Laboratory for Animal Conservation, College of Life Sciences, Northwest University, Xi'an, China

Dionisios Youlatos
Department of Zoology, School of Biology, Aristotle University of Thessaloniki, Greece

He Zhang
Shaanxi Key Laboratory for Animal Conservation, College of Life Sciences, Northwest University, Xi'an, China

Foreword

The last few decades have witnessed a surge of interest in human–animal relations under headers such as Human–Animal Studies, Animal Studies, and Animal Ethics. Symptomatic was the founding of a slew of new journals, for example, *Anthrozoös* (1987), *Society & Animals* (1993), *Humanimalia* (2008), *Animal Studies Journal* (2011), *Relations: Beyond Anthropocentrism* (2012), and *Politics and Animals* (2014).

Most of these journals are associated with new learned societies, websites, conferences, research, and teaching programs. Such convergent initiatives were intent on moving beyond strictly life-sciences perspectives, stressing humanities and human science approaches instead, in an effort to overcome narrow anthropocentric paradigms in all fields of knowledge, such as, ecology, economics, ethnography, ethics, and philosophy. The appearance of the present volume, devoted to the archaeology of human–nonhuman primate interfaces and interdependencies, fits this broad development. As such it is certainly timely; perhaps even, being a first, it is a bit overdue.

One root of the new interest in (nonhuman) animals since the late twentieth century is the addition of the topic "species" to the 1970s triad race–class–gender as foci of research into stereotypes, inequality, and discrimination against various "others." Another root is ethnozoology. This traditional subdiscipline of anthropology ethnographically addresses the broad variety of ways in which particular ethnolinguistic groups categorize and use animals around them – as prey, pets, symbols, for work, etc. At the dawn of the twenty-first century this was given a twist in multispecies ethnography. Instead of continuing, in too anthropocentric a manner, to see nonhuman animals as just part of the local ecological backdrop or as expressing human meanings, this approach stresses the subjectivity and agency of these animals, and the ways their lives are entangled with those of other species, including the human one.

The broader canvas against which the abovementioned developments – including archaeoprimatology as a burgeoning multidisciplinary field – can be situated was a shift in climate of opinion in the Western world, including academia. This shift has perhaps most clearly been visible in philosophy since the 1970s. The anthropocentrism of both the Christian metaphysical tradition and the humanistic "Modern," that is, Enlightenment, discourse on politics and ethics was criticized by post-Modern, post-colonialist, post-humanist, and other approaches. The latter often took inspiration from French thinkers who were no longer under the sway of Immanuel Kant, that champion of the Enlightenment, but under the influence of, among others, Friedrich Nietzsche, the iconoclastic *Philosoph mit dem Hammer* (philosopher with a hammer) who secularized human primates by situating them in instead of above nature.

In a different but convergent way, human specialty assumptions were increasingly undermined by the ever-increasing influence of the sciences on public opinion. Evolutionary biology and cognitive neuroscience show how profoundly natural humans are as just another "unique" species, while the ecological disciplines address the daunting challenges of environmental sustainability in the Anthropocene, emphasizing interdependencies between humans and other species.

The present volume's editors, Andrzej Antczak (a colleague at Leiden University), Bernardo Urbani, and Dionisios Youlatos, asked me to contribute this foreword because as a philosopher I worked on the roots of this cluster of profound changes. I was also privileged to be able to closely follow ethno-/archaeozoological research by the Caribbean archaeology group of which Andrzej is part. The present volume on archaeoprimatology converges with a 2018 special issue of the journal *Environmental Archaeology* on archaeo-ornithology which for me, next to the present volume, was another exciting read. What Katrin Cost and Shumon Hussain, the editors of that issue, another first, write fully applies to the present volume as well: among other things, archaeology "offers a unique deep-historical perspective on the animal part in the human story and is capable of investigating human-animal dynamics on varying timescales – some available exclusively for archaeological analysis."

The deep time perspective and the stress on interdependencies between humans and other species in these publications is of particular importance in the Anthropocene, the present era of unprecedented transformation of an entire planet by a single primate (*sic*) species to suit its own needs. The present volume also provides considerably more time depth to a series of multidisciplinary studies which, since the late 1990s and under the header "ethnoprimatology," have explored the multifarious relations between indigenous peoples and alloprimates. Furthermore, multispecies studies also inspired a 2011 volume entitled *Ethnozooarchaeology* (edited by Umberto Albarella and Angela Trentacoste) which sets out to move faunal analysis in archaeology beyond the division of processual and post-processual approaches.

Finally, ethno- and archaeozoological studies on primates in particular also have epistemological relevance. The term "epistemology" is sometimes used in a rather loose manner, but here it refers not so much to the analysis of data itself but of the ways data is handled theoretically. Anthropology partly developed from, and arguably partly still is, European ethnozoology (Christian, secularized, and folk perceptions of and dealings with the animal world), in particular European ethnoprimatology (perceptions of and dealings with apes and monkeys). Consequently, anthropology as a discipline, here, in a reflexive manner, also ponders itself, its own roots, the cultural backgrounds of the ways it handles its data.

Here is what I mean. The history of primatology, primate taxonomy, and palaeoanthropology since the eighteenth century shows how human primates which usually deemed themselves uniquely elevated above the rest of living nature, both cognitively and morally, had much trouble classifying themselves, their own "apish" ancestry, and other primates. Unlike, for example, birds, other primates in many cultural settings, including some studied in this volume, had a special position because they are so uncannily similar to humans. Other primates are thus categorially ambiguous with respect to the strong classificatory boundary between humans and (other) animals in western worldviews. Other primates were hard to classify, and as such often had a strong, usually either negative or positive, symbolic and moral load. They were often vilified and seen as grotesque, in particular in the European tradition. Precisely this created problems when scholars of the day started to realize the close affinity of humans with other primates (Linnaeus) and, subsequently, their own "apish" ancestors (Darwin).

Therefore ethno-/archaeoprimatological research is of epistemological interest as well: it contributes to reflection on the anthropological disciplines as wrestling with their own roots in European anthropocentric perceptions of sovereign, privileged humans versus (extant or extinct) apish others. This too, next to reflection on the role of that anthropocentrism, and of one primate species in particular, in the coming about of the Anthropocene, is part of the promise of the present volume on archaeoprimatology as a burgeoning field of research.

Raymond Corbey
Professor of Philosophy of Science and Anthropology,
Leiden University, the Netherlands

Acknowledgments

First, we want to express our special gratitude to all the authors for dedicating their intellectual time to write the excellent pieces that comprise this volume, as well as for their responsiveness and patience during all editorial stages, especially throughout the uncertain times of the global pandemic. We are grateful to Karen Strier (University of Wisconsin at Madison, USA), primatological editor of the Cambridge Studies in Biological and Evolutionary Anthropology, for her support in this endeavor and to the staff at Cambridge University Press, namely Olivia Boult, Dominic Lewis, Aleksandra Serocka, and especially Jenny van der Meijden, for their dedication at the different stages of this project. During the copy-editing and production phases, thanks to Franklin Mathews Jebaraj from Straive and Vicki Harley. We appreciate the contribution of Raymond Corbey (Leiden University) in preparing the foreword of this edited volume: his words are highly welcome when looking retrospectively at all steps taken and challenges faced in making this book possible. Moreover, we would like to thank all the scholars who kindly shared their time and expertise to serve as external reviewers (in alphabetical order): Joaquín Arroyo-Cabrales (National Institute of Anthropology and History, Mexico), Alessandra Caputo-Jaffé (Alfonso Ibañez University, Chile), Vérène Chalendar (College of France), Susan deFrance (University of Florida), Arati Deshpande-Mukherjee (Deccan College Post-graduate and Research Institute, India), Dominique Gommery (National Museum of Natural History, France), Adrian Paul Harrison (University of Copenhagen, Denmark), Terry Harrison (New York University, USA), Erica Hill (University of Alaska Southeast, USA), Tsuyoshi Ito (Kyoto University, Japan), Chiori Kitagawa (Johannes Gutenberg University, Mainz, Germany), R. Barry Lewis (University of Illinois at Urbana-Champaign, USA), Daniel Loponte (National Institute for Anthropology and Latin American Thoughts, Buenos Aires, Argentina), Andrzej Niwiński (University of Warsaw, Poland), Jacqueline Phillips (University of London, UK), Alfred L. Rosenberger (City University of New York, USA), Matteo Scardovelli (University of Quebec, Canada), Ashley Sharpe (Smithsonian Institution, USA), Kay Tarble de Scaramelli (Central University of Venezuela), Samuel Turvey (Zoological Society of London, UK), Fabio Tutrone (Research University of Palermo, Italy), Scott A. Williams (New York University, USA), and Sarah Zohdy (Auburn University, USA). Our appreciation to Segundo Jiménez (Venezuelan Institute of Scientific Research) for getting the cover image of the book set, and the Metropolitan Museum of Art of New York for openly sharing it. Bernardo Urbani received the institutional support of the Venezuelan Institute for Scientific Research, Dionisios Youlatos of the Aristotle University of Thessaloniki, and Andrzej T. Antczak's contribution is possible through the European Union's Seventh Framework Programme, FP7/2007-2013 (ERC Grant Agreement No. 319209), under the direction of Professor Dr. C. L. Hofman. Last but not least, our thankfulness to our families for their patience during the many home hours devoted to this editorial project. To all of you, once again, thanks so much!

World Archaeoprimatology

An Introduction

Bernardo Urbani, Dionisios Youlatos, & Andrzej T. Antczak

Archaeoprimatology – a term originally coined by one of the editors – explores the interface between humans and nonhuman primates (hereafter referred to as 'primates') in antiquity. Hence, archaeoprimatology embraces, both theoretically and methodologically, the disciplines of archaeology and primatology. Archaeoprimatological research is still relatively limited despite its significant implications that range from the art history realm of past iconographic identification of primates to a better grasp of current primate conservation issues. Archaeoprimatology is a discipline that offers multiple perspectives to understand the roots of our perception and apprehension of our own taxonomic group, the order Primates. The edited volume in your hands –the first fully devoted to this discipline – is thus intended to serve as an effort to promote and expand archaeoprimatological studies.

The 21 chapters examine different regions of the globe, from the valley of Teotihuacan in Mexico, through the Aegean islands, to Jomon period Japan (Fig. I.1; Table I.1). The book covers a time span starting millions of years ago until the past century, encompassing information from early hominin sites in South Africa to perceptions on primates in the narratives of Roman rhetoricians, as well as to the relatively recent oral traditions of Madagascar. It explores a variety of past societies, in relation to their interconnections with primates, including, among others, ancient Taíno, Arawakans, and Caribans of the circum-Caribbean region; Mayans; pre-Columbian lowland South American peoples; Mesopotamians; and Buddhists and Hindu from the Indian subcontinent. Eight chapters refer to Neotropical settings, six to Asia, five to Africa, and two to Europe, and the volume is arranged according to these geographical divisions. There are pairs of chapters devoted to different archaeoprimatological topics of four countries: Brazil, Peru, Egypt, and South Africa. Twenty-nine percent of the studies focus on primate remains in the zooarchaeological record, 38% on material culture with primatomorphic depictions, and the remaining 33% combines multiple approaches including written and oral sources with information about primates. Sixty-six researchers from around the world share their expertise to build this editorial endeavor. Thirty-nine percent of them are women, and 59% are nationals of the countries where the studies were conducted. The determination of the authors in completing their chapters was especially inspiring considering that the last phase of this project was marked by an unusual year signed by the global turmoil derived from the COVID-19 pandemic. This made their efforts in working on their manuscripts not only challenging but also more significant than ever before. The diversity of the authors with multiple cultural and academic

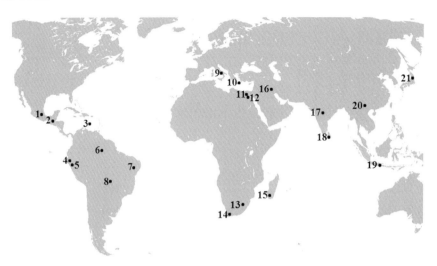

Figure I.1. Location of the archaeoprimatological studies present in this edited volume. See numbers in Table I.1. (Image by B. Urbani, after an open access base map from San Jose, 2006. Wikimedia Commons-CC BY).

backgrounds can be fully perceived through the pages of this book. In addition, to promote and enhance inclusivity, the abstracts of the chapters are presented in the native languages of the countries where the studies focus. This is the first time they have been included in the Cambridge Studies in Biological and Evolutionary Anthropology Series. We consider that it is a modest but yet significant step toward fulfilling the goals of the 'Joint commitment for action on inclusion and diversity in publishing' to which Cambridge University Press is a signatory.

Regarding the content of the chapters, Bernardo Urbani and collaborators examine the material culture and skeletal remains of primates recovered in Teotihuacan that is one of the largest pre-colonial urban areas of today Mexico. Portable objects and murals that depict monkeys were recovered in different areas of Teotihuacan. Monkeys and their depictions with the symbolic value attached, circulated in Teotihuacan, especially between ~200 CE and 550 CE (the Classic period). Remains of spider monkeys were reported from the Pyramid of the Moon, the Plaza of the Columns, and from inside the structure in Xalla. The authors argue that, possibly, primates reached Teotihuacan through interconnections with peoples from distant regions, such as those from the Mayan area and the Oaxacan region. The authors argue that the presence and use of primates may be attributed to the elite ruling Teotihuacan and may also include individuals of other adjacent societies. Also, in Mesoamerica, Katherine South and Susan M. Ford provide an evocative example on how to encompass the use of phenotypic attributes of primates and ancient iconography with primatomorphic depictions for identifying primate taxa that interacted with past societies. In doing so, and using an ample iconographic dataset, they explore the relationship between Mayans and spider monkeys, howlers, and possibly capuchin monkeys. The results show that primates have different roles in this society ranging from scribal functions to dancers.

Table I.1. Synopsis of the archaeoprimatological studies present in this edited volume

# in Fig. I.1	Ancient society	General focus	Country/region	Chapter author(s)
1	Teotihuacan	Material culture and zooarchaeology	Mexico	B. Urbani, C. Serrano-Sánchez, R. Valadez-Azúa, D. Ruiz-Ramoni, & R. Cabrera-Castro
2	Maya	Material culture	Guatemala	K. E. South & S. M. Ford
3	Taino, Arawak (Barrancoid/Saladoid), Cariban	Zooarchaeology, Material culture and written sources	Circum-Caribbean region	B. Urbani, A. T. Antczak, M. M. Antczak, N. R. Cannarozzi, R. H. Colten, K. F. Emery, R. A. C. F. Dijkhoff, T. A. Wake, M. J. LeFebvre, L. A. Carlson, W. F. Keegan, & D. C. Nieweg
4	Chimú, Lambayeque, early Colonial	Material culture	Peru	J. Gamboa
5	Moche	Material culture	Peru	A. K. Alaica
6	Lowland South American peoples	Material culture	Brazil	E. Pereira & J. de Sousa e Silva Júnior
7	Caatinga dwellers	Zooarchaeology	Brazil	A. N. de Queiroz, O. A. de Carvalho, & R. R. Pinto
8	Indigenous peoples	Zooarchaeology	Neotropics (general)	R. F. Quijano, D. R. Gilles, J. Štefka, & M. M. Kowalewski
9	Roman	Written sources and material culture	Italy	M. Vespa
10	Minoan	Material culture	Greece	B. Urbani & D. Youlatos
11	Old Kingdom Egyptian	Material culture	Egypt	L. Bashford
12	Late Dynastic Egyptian	Zooarchaeology	Egypt	D. Brandon-Jones & J. Goudsmit
13	San	Material culture	South Africa	N. Ndlovu

Table I.1. (cont.)

# in Fig. I.1	Ancient society	General focus	Country/ region	Chapter author(s)
14	Hominins	Zooarchaeology and material culture	South Africa	S. Badenhorst
15	Island indigenous peoples	Zooarchaeology and oral sources	Madagascar	N. Vasey & L. R. Godfrey
16	Mesopotamian	Written sources and material culture	Iraq/Iran	M. Such-Gutiérrez
17	Buddhist/Hindu	Material culture	India	A. A. E. van der Geer
18	Island Indigenous peoples	Zooarchaeology	Sri Lanka	M. A. Huffman, C. A. D. Nahallage, T. Ananda, N. Kanthilatha, N. Perera, M. Bardi, & G. Adikari
19	Island Indigenous peoples	Zooarchaeology	Indonesia	N. Amano, T. Ingicco, A-M. Moigne, A.-M Sémah, T. Simanjuntak, & F. Sémah
20	Hominins	Zooarchaeology, written sources, and material culture	China	G. He, H. Zhang, H. Wang, X. Ji, S. Guo, B. Li, R. Hou, X. Hou, & R. Pan
21	Jomon	Zooarchaeology	Japan	Y. Nishioka, M.Takai, H. Hongo, & T. Anezaki

In their chapter on pre-Hispanic primates in the circum-Caribbean region (300–1500 CE), Bernardo Urbani and colleagues provide a comprehensive review of the interface between the indigenous peoples of the area and primates before and at early European contact. The analysis of the zooarchaeological record, portable crafted material, alleged rock art, and written documentary sources suggest that interactions between native Caribbean human populations and monkeys existed deep in time with profoundly rooted connections, confirming a close, extended, intricate, and multipurpose interface.

Moving to South America, two chapters illustrate the past interconnections of peoples from the northern desert of Peru with monkeys from lowland South America. In this direction, Jorge Gamboa presents how primates were culturally configured by the Chimú and Lambayeque societies. By using the zooarchaeological record and an iconographic dataset, Gamboa studies the depiction of primates in clay and wooden figurines of these cultures to explore their significance in the context of corporality and symbolism. The cover of this volume embodies the relationship between the Chimú and monkeys as examined in this chapter. In her study, Aleksa K. Alaica claims that monkey images in Moche iconography of northern Peru are well-known and monkey remains have also been excavated in burial sites but, she argues, that limited systematic research has been carried to explore their function in this society. With this premise in mind, she explores monkey representations among the Moche, their characteristics, the contextual information, and their role in purportedly legitimizing authority. Because primates were considered as imitating humans in Moche iconography, they likely have an ancestral connection with elites and ritual practices. Both Gamboa and Alaica contextualize monkey depictions in the Peruvian arid region as key agents of alterity of living subjects from tropical lands.

Two chapters are dedicated to Brazil. In the first, Edithe Pereira and José de Sousa e Silva Júnior explore 29 petroglyphs with representations of primates, from 15 different archaeological sites in Brazilian Amazonia. The examination of taxonomic diagnostic characters, along with features related to life history, behavior, and geographic distribution results in the identification of nine different taxa at species level, one taxon at genus level, and one at family level. All the identified taxa are endemic to Amazonia, three are currently considered vulnerable to extinction, and two are allochthonous to the areas of their representations. These findings probably suggest displacements of ancient human communities in those regions or shrinkage of prior larger, more extended distributions. In the second Brazilian chapter, Albérico N. de Queiroz and colleagues focus on two unusual samples of cranial bones of tufted capuchin monkeys recovered in archaeological excavations at the Furna do Estrago site in the state of Pernambuco in northeastern Brazil. These scarce samples with anthropic modifications allow a reflection on biocultural aspects of the presence of primates in human funerary environments. Thus, they most likely highlight a possibly symbolic or ritual status and their rarity perhaps supports their function as hierarchical indicators within a social group.

To finish with the Neotropics, R. Florencia Quijano and coauthors explore the potential cost of monkeys as hunting game or pets by examining the presence of lice in howlers. After review of the existing scholarly reports, they concentrate on the presence of lice (*Pediculus mjobergi*) in three species of howler monkeys in order to determine possible data on louse host switch between humans and primates. They argue that paleontological as well as genetic data suggests that an exchange of genetic material between howler lice and humans happened during interactions related to subsistence activities (e.g. hunting) and/or having monkeys as pets. The authors further suggest this could happen early when modern humans migrated from Africa and later went into the Americas.

Europe is represented by two chapters. Romans and their narrative practices about primates are studied by Marco Vespa. In this study, the author proposes that this society perceived these animals differently than many other European peoples. For example, Romans performed a set of descriptors to interpret the relation of monkeys with them. These descriptors considered not only observable traits but also behavioral features that particularly distinguished them from other animals. Vespa complements his text by adding information on remains of monkeys and primatomorphic representations from the Roman archaeological record. In the Aegean region, Bernardo Urbani and Dionisios Youlatos thoroughly re-examine the depictions of primates on material evidence such as figurines, seals/sealings, and frescoes left by the Minoan civilization from Crete and Santorini. Their analyses that incorporate expertise in archaeology and primatology strengthen previous reports and confirm a vast cultural exchange between Minoans and Egyptians. They also argue that while the depictions of vervet monkeys were related to a more naturalistic context, the baboons were largely part of ritual contexts. Judging from the paintings of detailed narratives the authors state that Minoans were first-hand observers of monkeys.

Lydia Bashford discusses primate behavior in ancient Egypt and presents the iconography of monkeys in the Old Kingdom. During this period, monkeys were allochthonous in Egypt and were traded from southern lands. However, Bashford suggests that the persistence of the depiction of monkeys in this and later Egyptian periods is due to special religious reasons. In another context, particularly in representations related to humans, they display jokily, emulating humans, or performing their natural behavior. In the second chapter on Egypt, Douglas Brandon-Jones and Jaap Goudsmit suggest that Late Dynastic Egyptians macerated and wrapped primates in Saqqara. Almost 200 corpses of, mostly, Anubis baboons were deposited in the animal catacombs of this site. The authors found evidence of malnutrition, as well as a higher ratio of male individuals that might suggest breeding practices. This chapter stands as an interesting and detailed case study on the mummification of primates in ancient Egypt.

From South Africa, Ndukuyakhe Ndlovu summarizes the depiction of chacma baboons on the rock. These primates are less represented than other animals, and some of them were fused with human shapes to create therianthropic images that merge both baboons and humans. Still in South Africa, but from a different viewpoint, Shaw Badenhorst presents a systematic revision on the relationship between chacma baboons and hominins during three million years of co-existence. He argues that although in the late Plio-Pleistocene, both taxa might have been under the same predation pressures, later, during the Middle Stone Age, humans possibly hunted baboons, as well as samago monkeys and vervets.

In their chapter, Natalie Vasey and Laurie R. Godfrey evaluate the human impacts on *Pachylemur* extinction, some 500 years ago, combining evidence from current hunting practices, Madagascar's oral history, and archaeological and paleontological records. The detailed analysis of such diverse data indicates that this large lemur was a high forest specialist and coexisted with humans for a long time. This evidence suggests that both habitat degradation and hunting played significant roles in the extinction of the, once widespread, *Pachylemur*.

Moving to western Asia, Miguel Such-Gutiérrez argues that the paucity of evidence about primates in Mesopotamia during the third millennium BCE, is due to the fact that they were allochthonous in this region. The earliest mentions of monkeys in Mesopotamia are found on depictions during the Early Dynastic period (*c.* 2600–2340 BCE) and in the documents, they are mentioned from the Ur III period onwards (*c.* 2100–2000 BCE). Likely, they were brought in from western-central Asia, or from the Indus Valley. Monkeys show a "ludic character" and, arguably, were pets. In these texts, primates often used to tease the enemies of Sumer and, according to Such-Gutiérrez, this is how the word 'monkey' started, and until now, it bears this humorous and pejorative character. East of Mesopotamia and centuries later, Alexandra A. E. van der Geer explores the ample repertoire of primatomorphic depictions in the religious architecture of India. Monkeys, especially macaques and langurs, have different attributes among Buddhist and Hindu representations, ranging from symbols of beauty and cleverness to foolish individuals, as well as erotic characters. Rhesus macaques are predominantly represented in northern India, while langurs (mostly as Hanuman) in the south of this subcontinent. This review also includes an integrative summary that serves to trace the performative representation of this animal group is this large Asian region.

In South East Asia, Michael A. Huffman and collaborators examine the subfossil primate remains yielded in the Sigiriya Potana cave of Sri Lanka. Three primate species, still native to the island, were found with burning evidence that suggests their consumption in the cave between *c.* 6000 and 3700 BCE. These monkeys are toque macaques, tufted gray langurs, and purple-faced langurs. As it is also the case at other sites in Sri Lanka, monkeys appeared as relevant sources of protein in this location. In Indonesia, Noel Amano and colleagues explore the patterns of primate exploitation in the Early to Mid-Holocene in the Eastern Javan Braholo Cave. The majority of primate remains is represented by cercopithecids, particularly langurs, and was most likely processed on-site, with further use of skeletal elements (e.g., ulnae) for bone tool manufacture. This evidence points to complex human and primate interactions in this site. The authors further argue that it is very likely that primate populations may have not been severely affected by hunting pressures, probably because of relatively low human population densities or because hunter gatherer communities moved across the landscape throughout the year.

Figure I.2 Archaeoprimatological loci in present-day quotidian life. (a) photographer in front of the Minoan fresco with vervets at the Museum of Prehistory in Santorini, Greece; (b) metro rider of Mexico City at the Pino Suárez station in front of a large poster of an Aztec clay figure of Ehécatl-Ozomatli (monkey) at the place where this piece was discovered; (c) seated baboon, god Thoth, with tourists behind at the yards of the Egyptian Museum in Cairo. (Photographs by B. Urbani).

In the province of Yunnan, China, Gang He and colleagues, after conducting a broad literature review, explore the biogeographical importance of this region, on the relationships between primates and archaic and modern humans. The archaeological record indicates a strong tendency of coexistence and currently, the province hosts the largest number of ethnic groups (26 of 56) as well as primate species (21 of 25) in China. Although primates were inspiration for significant contributions to arts, culture, social life, and medical research, they suffered greatly in recent Chinese history, particularly since the second half of the last century. In Japan, macaques were present long before the arrival of humans. As reported by Yuichiro Nishioka and coauthors, the interactions occurred during the Holocene with the rise of the Jomon culture. Remains of primates have been found in shell middens. The zooarchaeological evidence impressively appears to suggest the presence of Japanese macaques in archaeological locations at around 200 sites dispersed along the island.

The collection of chapters in this volume – with an ample diversity of cultures from different regions of the world – provides firm foundations upon which the discipline of archaeoprimatology can be solidly built. In effect, a thorough look through these pages reveals that archaeoprimatological research has multiple perspectives and ways of exploring the past interactions of humans with other primates. Archaeoprimatological research envisioned as an interdisciplinary field that poses novel research questions and employs new techniques is expected to untangle the long-lasting quests on defining humans before the appearance of the Anthropocene and explore new ways of conceiving human–animal relations and ethics related to these phenomena. Once again, we hope that this volume will help pave the intellectual challenge and explore, among others, theories of posthumanism and postanthropocentrism, as well as approaches to indistinction. In the meanwhile, factual archaeoprimatological references will be present to remind us that this endeavor is still open (Fig. I.2).

Part I

The Americas

1 Monkeys in the City of Gods

On the Primate Remains and Representations in Teotihuacan, Central Mexico

Bernardo Urbani, Carlos Serrano-Sánchez, Raúl Valadez-Azúa,
Damián Ruíz-Ramoni, & Rubén Cabrera-Castro

Monos en la Ciudad de los Dioses: Sobre los restos y representaciones de primates en Teotihuacán, México central

Resumen

Los primates son mamíferos con gran importancia cultural en las sociedades pasadas. El objetivo de esta investigación es explorar la cultura material y los restos biológicos de los primates hallados en Teotihuacán, una de las áreas urbanas prehispánicas de mayor tamaño en México. Se encontraron restos de monos araña mesoamericanos (*Ateles* cf. *A. geoffroyi*) en la Pirámide de la Luna, Plaza de las Columnas y Xalla. Cultura material que representa a primates se recuperó en varias partes de Teotihuacán, pero principalmente en Tetitla y La Ventilla. A su vez, se encontraron murales con representaciones de monos en estos dos últimos sitios de Teotihuacán. Posiblemente, los primates llegaron a Teotihuacán a través de relaciones con pueblos de tierras más lejanas, como la región maya y la provincia oaxaqueña gobernada por Monte Albán. El aumento de la presencia de primates en Teotihuacán ocurrió durante el período Clásico (~200-550 d.C.); sin embargo, es relativamente escaso teniendo en cuenta el gran tamaño de la ciudad y el largo período de tiempo en que Teotihuacán había sido estudiado. Sin embargo, la existencia de monos en Teotihuacán, ya sea como animales exóticos o como objetos portátiles, también parece indicar que fueron diseminados dentro de diferentes partes de la ciudad. Así, los primates vivos y sus representaciones circulaban con su valor simbólico en Teotihuacán, particularmente entre los miembros de la élite gobernante, y probablemente entre miembros de otras sociedades mesoamericanas vecinas.

Palabras clave

Arqueoprimatología – cerámica – Maya – Oaxaca – osteoarqueología – período clásico – Puebla – primatología

Abstract

Primates are mammals with high cultural significance in ancient societies. The objective of this research is to explore the material culture and biological remains of primates found in Teotihuacan, one of the largest pre-Hispanic urban areas of Mexico. Remains of Mesoamerican spider monkeys (*Ateles* cf. *A. geoffroyi*) were found in the Pyramid of the Moon, Xalla, and the Plaza of the Columns. Portable material culture that resembles primates was recovered elsewhere within Teotihuacan, but mostly in Tetitla and La Ventilla. Murals with representations of monkeys were found at these last two Teotihuacan sites. Possibly, primates reached Teotihuacan because of relationships with peoples from more distant lands such as the Mayan region as well as the Oaxacan province ruled by Monte Albán. The rise of the presence of primates in Teotihuacan occurred during the Classic period (~200–550 CE); however, it is relatively scarce considering the large size of the city and the long period of time in which Teotihuacan had been researched. Nevertheless, the existence of monkeys in Teotihuacan, either as exotic animals or as portable objects, does also seem to indicate that they were disseminated within different parts of the city. Thus, living primates and their representations circulated with their symbolic value in Teotihuacan, particularly among members of the ruling elite, and likely among members of other neighboring Mesoamerican societies.

Keywords: Archaeoprimatology, Classic period, Maya, Oaxaca, Osteoarchaeology, Pottery, Primatology, Puebla.

1.1   Introduction

Teotihuacan was the largest city in ancient Mexico (Manzanilla, 2017a; Fig. 1.1). Teotihuacan is also the archaeological site of pre-Hispanic Mexico and has been studied for the longest time: a century of formal archaeological research (Matos-Moctezuma, 2017). It has been proposed that the city was administered by a corporate government of four rulers who maintained order and control over five centuries (Manzanilla, 2017a). Between 100 and 200 CE, many structures were built, such as the pyramids of the Sun and the Moon and the Temple of Quetzalcoatl. The control that Teotihuacan had over the area's obsidian mines led not only to its exploitation, but also to the presence of multiple workshops where this volcanic glass was converted into instruments and objects that were distributed throughout Mesoamerica (Carballo, 2011). The productive system of the Teotihuacan valley turned it into a city that quickly extended its power and influence in four directions (Cowgill, 1997). We know that in the interior of the city there were neighborhoods and sectors where groups of different ethnic origins coexisted with the purpose of maintaining relationships and communication between the central government and its regions of origin (Manzanilla, 2015, see also Meza-Peñaloza, 2015). This development reached its highest level during the Xolalpan period (350–550 CE), when the city also reached its largest extension and population size, around 150,000 inhabitants, and likely one of the major cities in the world at that time (Valadez, 1992). Despite the great development, within this urban area there were strong social tensions which led to moments of violence at the city's fall. Although control was recovered, its power was reduced to the degree that the central government practically disappeared and the control of resources ended in the hands of other peoples (Manzanilla, 2017b).

Archaeoprimatology is an interdisciplinary research area that links primatology and archaeology (Urbani, 2013). Archaeoprimatological studies explore the interface between humans and nonhuman primates in the past, where the liminality of this relationship is examined over a long chronological period (Urbani, 2013). In doing so, archaeoprimatological research scrutinizes primate remains from archaeological sites and the material culture that depicts primates. This chapter examines the representation and actual presence of nonhuman primates in one of the largest

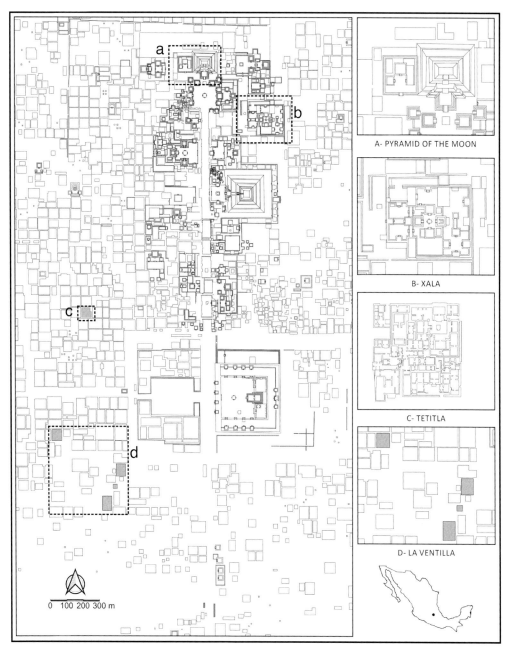

Figure 1.1 The city of Teotihuacan in central Mexico, with details of the Teotihuacan sites commonly referred in the text: (a) Pyramid of the Moon, (b) Xalla, (c) Tetitla, and (d) La Ventilla. (Courtesy of L. Manzanilla and G. Jiménez-Delgado).

pre-Hispanic cities of Mesoamerica. Therefore, the goals of the present research are to review existing information on primates in the Teotihuacan culture. To achieve this, it is proposed (a) to describe biological remains of primates found in Teotihuacan, (b) to present information on Teotihuacan material culture where monkeys are represented, (c) to evaluate the contexts of the archaeological material in order to infer the possible roles of nonhuman primates in the Teotihuacan society, and (d) to review the extent of the interface between the Teotihuacan society and its primates with other non-Teotihuacan Mesoamerican archaeological regions.

1.2   The Presence of Monkeys in Teotihuacan

1.2.1   Osteological Remains

Focusing on Teotihuacan, there have been several occasions when, either by personal communication or by comments in various publications (N. Sugiyama, 2014; Valadez and Childs-Rattray, 1993), the discovery of osteological remains of monkeys in various sectors of the city has been reported. An example of purported reports of primate remains refers to a monkey femur at the site of Oztoyahualco in the Teotihuacan periphery (García del Cueto, 1989), but without indicating the exact location or its temporality (as reviewed by Valadez and Ortiz, 1993). Thus, these mentions have been discarded, and currently only three examples of primate biological material are fully known in Teotihuacan contexts.

It was almost a century ago when Gamio (1922) presented commentaries on Teotihuacan animal skeletal remains. Subsequently, in the 1970s, Starbuck (1987) reported no primates in the first large-scale zooarchaeological survey in Teotihuacan. As well as the sites of Xalla (Rodríguez, 2002) and the Pyramid of the Moon (N. Sugiyama, 2014; N. Sugiyama et al., 2014, 2017) that have ample zooarchaeological research and evidence of primate remains, other zooarchaeological studies have been carried out at specific Teotihuacan localities such as Teopancazco (Manzanilla and Valadez, 2017; Rodríguez, 2006, 2010, 2017; Valadez et al., 2017), Quetzacoalt pyramid (Valadez et al., 2002), and Oztoyahualco (Valadez, 1993) and no primates have been found. For example, in the Teotihuacan site of Oztoyahualco, a total of 45 different animals have been found, mostly mammals, mainly dogs and leporids (Valadez, 1993). The vast majority of the sample is from the Xolalpan phase (450–650 CE), when most of the representation of primates were made (see Table 1.2), but no primate was found at this site. This site was a residential area located in the northwestern area of the Teotihuacan valley (Manzanilla, 1993). Also, a preliminary assessment of the archaeofauna at the Teotihuacan site of La Ventilla (excavation seasons 1992–1994, sectors 1–3) was conducted by D. Ruiz-Ramoni and B. Urbani (2018, pers. obs.). Remains of dogs and coyote (*Canis familiaris* and *C. latrans*), felids (cf. *Leopardus*), rabbits (Lagomorpha), sheep (Caprinae), and vultures (Cathartidae), were frequently observed at this site. However, there were no primate remains. Information will now be presented with the only three confirmed specimens of primates registered in Teotihuacan.

1.2.1.1 Primate of the Moon Pyramid

Family Atelidae Gray, 1825
Subfamily Atelinae Gray, 1825
Genus *Ateles* Geoffroy, 1806
Ateles geoffroyi (after/cf. by N. Sugiyama, 2014)

Referred material: a left proximal ulna and a left distal humerus of a single individual (MNI=1, incomplete) (N. Sugiyama, 2014; N. Sugiyama et al., 2015).

Description and comparison: because of "the small size of the elements in question suggested that we are dealing with an immature individual" (N. Sugiyama, 2014: 115); thus, "likely [the remains are] from a young individual considering its relatively small size" (N. Sugiyama, 2014: 206). No further descriptive and comparative information was provided.

Context: the Pyramid of the Moon was an uninterrupted construction of several structures, seven buildings built throughout the history of Teotihuacan (N. Sugiyama, 2014). Throughout this process, various ceremonial events took place that included the sacrifice of humans and animals under very different schemes. After the completion of Phase 5 and before the creation of Phase 6 of the Pyramid of the Moon, *Entierro 5* (Burial 5) was made, in which the bones of a Geoffroy's spider monkey (*Ateles geoffroyi*) were found (N. Sugiyama, 2014). These primates and other animal remains were isolated objects in ceremonial secondary deposits. In these cases, it is considered that the fundamental symbolic value of these pieces is related to the particularity of the objects themselves. The two primate remains were found in very poor condition. Unfortunately, no other feature was obtained that would help interpret the original placement and use of the deposited material.

Burial 5 (6 × 4 × 3.5 m) was discovered in 2001 and dated approximately at 350–400 CE, likely during the late Tlamimilolpa period (Cabrera-Castro, 2012; Sugiyama and López-Luján, 2006a, b). Looking toward the West, three adult individuals (>40 years of age) were found seated in "lotus flower" positions as in Mayan elite burials (Sugiyama and López-Luján, 2006a); this is a rare arrangement of the Classic Mesoamerican chronology, and similar to those of the Mayan area of Kaminljuyú and Uaxactum (Cabrera-Castro, 2012; Sugiyama and López-Lujan, 2006a). The hands were crossed in front of the individuals and two of them were superimposed on skulls of animals. Complete animals were placed in front of each of the three individuals and scattered remains of rattlesnakes and other animals like the monkey, were found throughout the space, close to wolves, eagles, and cougars (probably related to the military orders), that were chosen by the Teotihuacan government as basic actors in their ceremonies and the main species as victims of appropriate sacrifices (Sugiyama, 2014; Sugiyama and Cabrera-Castro, 2004). These burials are associated with shell earflaps decorated with jadeite and pectorals of green stone similar to those of the Mayan area. The jadeite of this burial comes from the Motagua valley in Guatemala. This kind of material culture is found in Mayan elite burials (Sugiyama and López-Luján, 2006a). A pectoral was found with an

X-shaped design that is typical of representations associated with the Mayan elite (Cabrera-Castro, 2012). In addition there are other objects made of green stone that represent humans in similar position to the buried individuals., There are obsidian statues and snails as well as obsidian objects representing serpents and knives that were associated with the three bodies (Sugiyama and López-Luján, 2006b). These objects seem to follow an ordered pattern (Sugiyama and Cabrera-Castro, 2004). There are also remains of grasses in this burial. Perhaps one of the buried characters was from the highest Teotihuacan elite, and accompanied by other two Mayan elite subjects (Cabrera-Castro, 2012; Sugiyama and López-Luján, 2006a). There is no other funeral niche like Burial 5 in Teotihuacan in terms of configuration and its Mayan association (Cabrera-Castro, 2012; see also Manzanilla and Serrano, 1999).

Remarks: "two [monkey] bones, along with some unidentified irregular and flat bone, were deposited just to the east of the sacrificed wolf. This was an extraordinary discovery which represents the second instance of this species ever reported at Teotihuacan... Unfortunately, this secondary burial of the forelimb did not provide any surface features to interpret how they were utilized or what the final product would have look like... Most likely, this forearm was brought into Teotihuacan and deposited bare" (N. Sugiyama, 2014: 206). "Whether these elements reached the city center as skeletal parts or as live individuals is uncertain, but it certainly suggests fauna products moved across long distances" (N. Sugiyama, 2014: 115).

Material: The specimen from the Pyramid of the Moon is deposited at the Pyramid of the Moon Project facility in San Juan Teotihuacan, Mexico (S. Sugiyama, 2018: pers. comm.). No further observations and morphometric comparisons were made with postcranial material of current Mesoamerican primates in order to fully determine the genus (*Ateles, Alouatta,* or eventually *Cebus*).

1.2.1.2 Primate of Xalla

Family Atelidae Gray, 1825
Subfamily Atelinae Gray, 1825
Genus *Ateles* Geoffroy, 1806
Ateles cf. *A. geoffroyi* (Fig. 1.2; Table 1.1)

Referred material: LP-IIA-UNAM 43271; a fragmented hemimandible with the incomplete coronoid process, and the horizontal branch lacking the distal end at the level of p2 (symphysis absent) (Fig. 1.2a, b); lower premolars (p3–p4) and first lower molar (m1) are present but not erupted (Fig. 1.2c, d). A second lower molar (m2) without the root developed is associated with this hemimandible (Fig. 1.2e).

Description and comparison: LP-IIA-UNAM 43271 is a platyrrhine because it has three lower premolars, p3 (Fig. 1.2a, b, d) (Table 1.1). It corresponds to an infant individual because molars are not fully erupted (Fig. 1.2c, d). In p3 and p4, only one main cusp, as well as an accessory one in p3 is present. Molars cuspids are sharp unlike those in Cebids. Also, molars are quadrangular (Fig. 1.2d, e), as in most of the platyrrhines except *Alouatta*, characterized by a more rectangular shape with a narrow area between the trigonid and talonid. The m1size coincides with that of

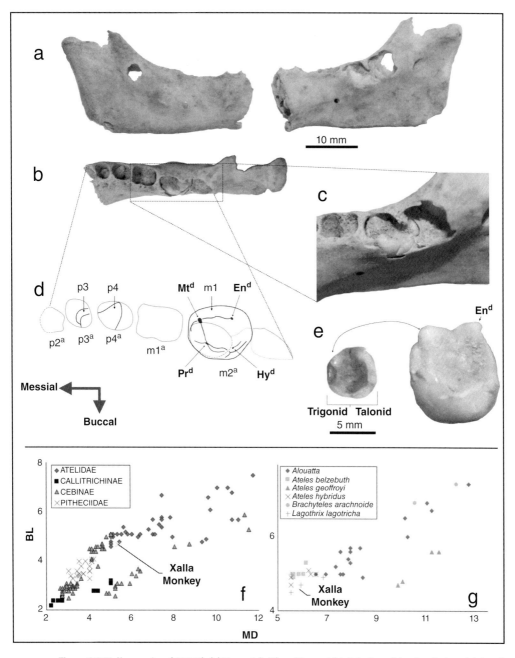

Figure 1.2 Xalla monkey (43271). (a) lingual (left) and buccal (right) view; (b) oclusal view; (c) detail (in buccal view) of unerupted dm1; note that this tooth is displaced posteriorly and located under the m2 alveolus; (d) diagram of the occlusal view; the m1 dental topology is highlighted; (e) m2 in occlusal view (left) and semi-lateral (right); (f) scatter plot showing the position of the Xalla monkey in relation to buccolingual (BL) and mesiodistal (MD) m1 values (in mm) with comparative sample of platyrrhines; (g) scatter plot showing the position of the Xalla monkey in relation to BL and MD m1 values of members of the family Atelidae. *Abbreviations*: p, premolar; m, molar; Pr^d, protoconid; Mt^d, metaconid; En^d, entoconid; Hy^d, hypoconid. (Photographs by D. R.-R.).

Table 1.1. Xalla monkey (LP-IIA-UNAM 43271) dental measurements

p2	p3		p4		m1		m2	
W	L	W	L	W	L	W	L	W
2.59[a]	2.39[a]	2.82[a]	3.00[a]	2.53[a]	4.29[a]	3.15[a]	4.79	5.15
					5.34*	4.59*		

Measurements: mesiodistal [MD] and buccolingual [BL] dimensions of premolars and molars in mm. *Abbreviations*: p, premolar; m, molar; L, length; W, width; [a], alveolus; *; measures taken at m1 without erupting.

the family Atelidae (Fig. 1.2f). Within this family, it is one of the smallest, certainly excluding the larger *Ateles*, *Alouatta*, and *Brachyteles* (Fig. 1.2g); however, the size of this m1 is close to *Ateles hybridus* and *Lagothrix lagotricha*, used as non-Mesoamerican control primates. 43271 has a notch in front of the protoconid and metaconid that it is well-differentiated for the genus *Ateles*. This dental morphology is also repeated for m2 (Fig. 1.2e). The m2 has the entoconid and hypoconid more separated (bucco-lingually) than the other observed *Ateles*. As expected for an infant, the mandibular angle is underdeveloped, and correspond to that of an *Ateles* (Fig. 1.2a).

Context: Xalla is a government palace of Teotihuacan (Manzanilla, 2017a, b) and dates from with the Late Classic period (300–700 CE). The hemimandible appeared in a pit (activity area 43), as part of the workshops of the so-called *Plaza 5* (Pérez, 2005; Rodríguez, 2002), which was intentionally dug in the *tepetate* (yellowish stone used in construction for floors) of the plaza in the southern sector of Xalla. It mainly contained wasted ceramics, polished lithics, and projectile tips, as well as slate and mica, some of them wasted as ritual and offerings materials. Various ceramics were identified, from *cajetes* (clay bowls) to a seal, a zoomorphic figurine, a flute, obsidian, projectile tips, remains of various tools, a polished lithic, a mortar, a *metate* hand stone, green stone, a fragment of metal in its natural state, mica, a worked slate, and two seashells. In addition there is an association with other zooarchaeological material such as a needle made of deer bone (*Odocoileus virginianus*) and a smooth bone plate from a turtle (*Trachemys scripta*), as well as human bone chisels, an *omichicahuaztli* (musical instrument made on human long bone with slits for the purpose of generating sound when brushed with a rod), and a fragment of a human bone engraved with several lines. For example, in the Teopancazco neighborhood of Teotihuacan, the inhabitants had a tradition of placing waste materials or materials still in use, in places such as pits or fills, where they remained as a testimony of their activities in specific spaces of the neighborhood (Manzanilla et al., 2011; Manzanilla and Valadez, 2017).

Remarks: The material corresponds to an infant monkey, as evidenced by the low development of the mandibular angle. Although this material corresponds to an infant of a small *Ateles*, there are not enough diagnostic characters in this specimen to fully identify it at the species level. The only *Ateles* in the region of Mexico is *A. geoffroyi*, but the size of m1 differs with respect to this species: it appears to be an exception in this single specimen. It is important to note that the material shows porosity around the alveolus (Fig. 1.2b, c), which is also observed in sick and captive mammals (D. Ruiz-Ramoni, pers. obs.).

Material and methods: The specimen from Xalla (43271) described here is deposited at the Laboratory of Paleozoology of the Anthropological Research Institute at the National Autonomous University of Mexico (LP-IIA-UNAM), Mexico City, Mexico. Observations and morphometric comparisons were made with material from living Platyrrhini collections deposited at the Museo de la Estación Biológica Rancho Grande (MEBRG) in Maracay, Venezuela, and the Museo de Historia Natural La Salle (MHNLS) in Caracas, Venezuela. Measurements were taken using a digital caliper (± 0.1 mm, max. 150 mm; Mitutoyo™).

1.2.1.3 Primate of the Plaza of the Columns

Recent news releases reported the presence of a spider monkey recovered in an offering (*Ofrenda D4*) of the Plaza of the Columns (Anonymous 2018, 2019; Paz-Avendaño, 2019; Salinas-Cesáreo, 2018). This monkey remain is "particularly interesting because his hands are tied behind its back" (Paz-Avendaño, 2019) and "it is the first time that the complete body of a monkey has been found [in Teotihuacan] that was surely brought from abroad, from the Gulf, the Pacific Ocean or the Mayan zone" as indicated by S. Sugiyama (Salinas-Cesáreo, 2018). It is associated with other faunal remains such as rattlesnakes, a cougar cranium, and a golden eagle as well as shells (Anonymous 2018, 2019; Paz-Avendaño, 2019). The associated material culture included green stones and obsidian artifacts (Anonymous, 2018). In addition, in another part of the plaza, there are multiple bone remains of adult human individuals; among them are three crania resembling those with modifications that are typical of the Mayan area (Anonymous, 2019). At this location, the chronological record of the possible interactions between people of Teotihuacan and the Mayan region ranged between 300 CE and 450 CE (Anonymous, 2019).

1.2.2   Material Culture

Within the Teotihuacan iconographic universe, mural painting has received most attention from researchers (e.g. de la Fuente, 1996a; Langley, 1986; Miller, 1973). In contrast, however, it has undoubtedly been the small figures of animals made from clay that have not yet been examined in detail within the Teotihuacan realm (but see, e.g. Gamio, 1922; Séjourné, 1959). The reasons for the lack of further characterization of Teotihuacan zoomorphic representations are mainly its small size, fragmented conditions, being normally found in landfills and therefore difficult to contextualize. In this section, existing information on primate representations in the material culture of the Teotihuacan valley and its zones of influence is presented (Tables 1.1 and 1.3).

1.2.2.1 Pottery

During the pre-Classic (1500–300 BCE), at the site of Tlapacoya-Zoapilco of the Tlatilco culture, in the valley of Mexico, López-Austin (1996 in Nájera-Coronado, [2015]) reported a primate-like head that seems to be associated with the representation of the wind. The Tlapacoya, among others, were ancestors of the Teotihuacans (Vargas, 1978). Later, chronologically, the first historical archaeoprimatological reference to Teotihuacan – and possibly to Mexico – was provided by a pioneer of Mexican archaeology, Manuel Gamio (1883–1960). In a monumental work, Gamio (1922) compared three primatomorphic clay pieces with the photograph of a spider monkey from the former Museum of Natural History in charge of the Directorate of Biological Studies of the early twentieth century (Fig. 1.3a). In these images, the frontal crests, rounded eyes, facial prognathism, and monkey "masks" can be seen. Later, excavations carried out by the Italian-Mexican archaeologist Laurette Séjourné (1911–2003) in the 1950s, mostly in the so-called Tetitla Palace, obtained numerous artifacts; some coming from burials and offerings and others from the fills (Séjourné, 1966a–c). It highlights a collection of zoomorphic figures in small format (~5 cm), many of them made from molds. The collection consists of 114 pieces, 7 of which can be identified as representations of monkeys (Valadez, 1992). The criteria used for their recognition as images of monkeys are the body position with visible caudal bases (Fig. 1.3b, c), the bulging on the forehead (Fig. 1.3d, f, g), and the prognathous face (Fig. 1.3e, g, h). Figure 1.3h has an expression similar to a monkey vocalizing. In the images of complete monkeys from Tetitla, the base of the tail of the monkey can be seen (Fig. 1.3b, c). Similar to these monkey figurines, there are also others with no tails from the same site and time, which clearly represent humans (see Childs-Rattray, 2001: 541, figs. 133a, a). Figure 1.3h of the L. Séjourné collection resembles the one reported by Childs-Rattray (2001: 550, fig. 146i, j; Fig. 1.4a in this chapter) at the base of a vessel and apparently was made with a production mold. Photographs of Séjourné's ceramic collection with primatological features of the Tetitla architectural complex are fully published here for the first time (Fig. 1.3b–h) (Table 1.2).

L. Séjourné also presents a broad illustrative review of primates represented in the material culture of Teotihuacan, predominantly Tetitla as explained in the previous paragraph. Séjourné (1966c) shows a large plate where there are multiple illustrations of alleged primates in Teotihuacan (e.g. Fig. 1.4b), including some that are difficult as to identify with certainty as monkeys. Séjourné (1966c) suggests that unlike the representation of birds and canids, those of primates also have complementary elements, such as necklaces and mouth plates. Séjourné (1959) also indicates that at the site of Zacuala, some primates have pectorals (e.g. Fig. 1.4c), as well as pronounced bellies, frontal masks, and earflaps, and the number of representation of primates is only lower than that of canids. The frontal masks look like that of *Ehécatl* (God of the Wind) and the earflaps are similar to the *oyohualli*, typical earflaps of the Post-classic period of the central valley of Mexico.

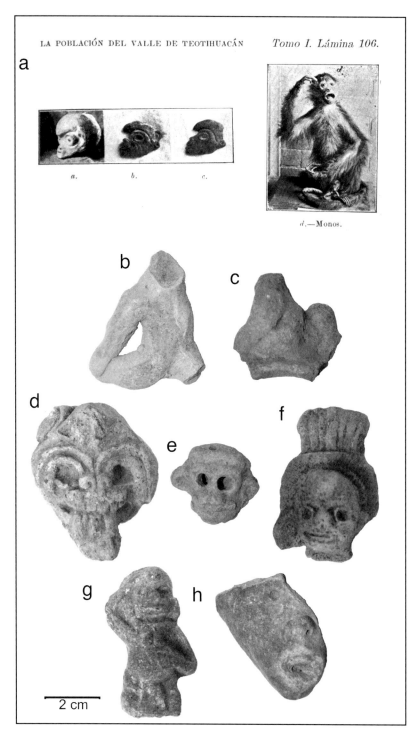

Figure 1.3 Primate representations from the historical collections of Manuel Gamio (a), and Laurette Séjourné (b–h). (Gamio, 1922 [public domain] and pieces from L. Séjourné collection deposited at the Paleozoology Laboratory, Institute for Anthropological Research, UNAM. Photographs by B. U.).

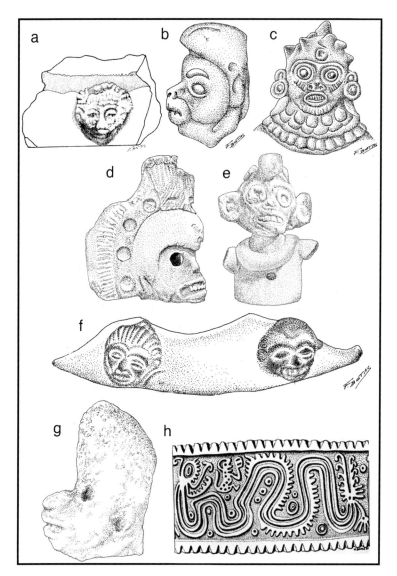

Figure 1.4 Primates from different locations of Teotihuacan. (Images not to scale; sources in Table 1.2. Illustrations by F. Botas).

In addition, something that had remained elusive in the characterization of Teotihuacan zoomorphic clay material is the presence of primate representations in the collection of the Mexican artists Frida Kalho (1907–1954) and Diego Rivera (1886–1957). Kalho's interest in primates is known, as she had a pet spider monkey (Cormier and Urbani, 2008). For example, in the museum designed by Rivera to house his collection of archaeological artifacts there is a primate with a monkey "mask" and a nose that has platyrrhine features (Fig. 1.4d). In this collection there is also a figurine (Fig. 1.4e) that has some similarity to that of Teotihuacan influence found in

Table 1.2. Primate representations in clay and stone from the Teotihuacan valley

Objects	Location	Date	Repository	Figure	References
Primate adornos	Teotihuacan valley	–	–	1.3a	Gamio (1922: Plate 106)
Primate figurines	Tetitla	Classic undetermined, possibly Tlamimilolpa or Xolalpan (200–550 CE).	Laboratorio de Paleozoología, Instituto de Investigaciones Antropológicas, Universidad Nacional Autónoma de México. Mexico city, Mexico	1.3b–c	L. Séjourné collection (R. Valadez-Azúa and B. Urbani pers. obs.)
Primate adornos	Tetitla	Classic undetermined, possibly Tlamimilolpa or Xolalpan (200–550 CE).	Laboratorio de Paleozoología, Instituto de Investigaciones Antropológicas, Universidad Nacional Autónoma de México. Mexico city, Mexico	1.3d–h	L. Séjourné collection (R. Valadez-Azúa and B. Urbani, pers. obs.)[a]
Primate head adorno	Tlajinga	Late Xolalpan (~500–550 CE)	–	1.4a	Childs-Rattray (2001: 550, fig. 146j)[b]
Primate adorno	Teotihuacan valley	–	–	1.4b	Séjourné (1966c: fig. 179)
Primate head in figurine	Zacuala	–	–	1.4c	Sénourjé (1959: 105, fig. 82A)
Monkey head from pottery	Teotihuacan valley	100 BCE–700 CE	Museo Diego Rivera Anahuacalli. Mexico city, Mexico	1.4d	Hall 9, Diego Rivera Anahuacalli Museum
Monkey figurine	Teotihuacan valley	100 BCE–700 CE	Museo Diego Rivera Anahuacalli. Mexico city, Mexico	1.4e	Hall 9, Diego Rivera Anahuacalli Museum
Two monkey in pottery sherd	Teotihuacan valley	–	Museo Casa Estudio Diego Rivera y Frida Kahlo. Mexico city, Mexico	1.4f	Main Studio, Diego Rivera y Frida Kahlo House–Studio Museum

Table 1.2. (cont.)

Objects	Location	Date	Repository	Figure	References
Monkey head from pottery	Neighborhood of the Merchants	Late Xolalpan (500–550 CE)	–	1.4g	Valadez (1992); Valadez and Childs-Rattray (1993: 225, Photograph 2)
Cylindrical *pintadera*	Neighborhood of the Merchants	Early Xolalpan (350–400 CE)	–	1.4h	Valadez (1992); Valadez and Childs-Rattray (1993: 226–227, Photographs 3 and 4)
Monkey head from pottery	Teotihuacan valley		Museo de Sitio Teotihuacán. Teotihuacan, Mexico	1.5a	Social and Economic Organization Hall, Teotihuacán Site Museum
Monkey head from pottery	Teotihuacan valley		Museo de Sitio Teotihuacán. Teotihuacan, Mexico	1.5b	Aesthetic Manifestation Hall, Teotihuacán Site Museum
Monkey head from pottery	Cosotlan		–	1.5c	Sullivan (2007: 21, fig. 14E)[c]
Monkey body with loincloth	Teotihuacan valley		National Museums and Galleries on Merseyside (44.3.27). Liverpool, UK	1.5c	Scott (2005: 25, Plate 94)[d]
Whistle vase with primatomorphic figure	La Ventilla, Structure 1, Burial 2 (season 1963)	Classic-Xolalpan (~350–550 CE)	Museo Nacional de Antropología (Inv. #10-80673). Mexico city, Mexico	1.5e	INAH (2017); Solís (2009: 348, fig. 167a),
Whistle vase with primatomorphic figure	Teotihuacan valley	Classic undetermined, possibly Xolalpan (~350–550 CE)	Museo Nacional de Antropología. Mexico city, Mexico	1.5f	Teotihuacan Hall, National Anthropological Museum

Globular monkey figurine	Teotihuacan valley	Classic (200–900 CE)	Museo de Sitio Teotihuacán. Teotihuacan, Mexico	1.5g	Religion Hall, Teotihuacán Site Museum
Monkey head	Teotihuacan valley		Museo de Sitio Teotihuacán. Teotihuacan, Mexico	1.5h	Flora and Fauna Hall, Teotihuacán Site Museum, Manzanilla (2016)[e]
Monkey on double-chambered vase	Teotihuacan valley	300–500 CE	Los Angeles County Museum of Art, Los Angeles, USA (AC1992.134.10)	1.7a	Peterson (1994)

[a] A similar object to the one represented in Fig. 1.3d is deposited at the British Museum (Am2002,11.5). It is indicated with the "Production place: Teotihuacan," and reported to be found in the cathedral of Mexico City. Another one is located at the American Museum of Natural History (30/3347) as part of the objects collected during the expedition of the Norwegian archaeologist Carl Lumholtz (1851–1922).

[b] There is also a modeled monkey-like piece in a Teotihuacan pottery base border from the period Late Xolalpan (~500–550 CE) (Childs–Rattray, 2001: 550, fig. 146j).

[c] A similar object was found in the Great Pyramid of Cholula (Tlachihualtepetl) in Puebla. It is deposited in the Pitt Rivers Museum at Oxford University (1886.1.1061).

[d] Two similar pieces (30.0/1837, 30.1/7979) are deposited in the anthropological collection of the American Museum of Natural History, one of them labeled as "Teotihuacan V?" and found at Santiago Ahuitzotla, Mexico City. The other was found at Atzcapotzalco, also in Mexico City.

[e] This object was made in stone. The other objects in this table are made of clay.

Puebla (see Fig. 1.6e). In another collection owned by these artists, a border of a clay vase appears to have two monkeys with faces with nasal-mouth configuration similar to platyrrhine primates, as well as forehead hairs (Fig. 1.4f).

A couple of objects with primatological depictions had been found in the *Barrio de los Comerciantes* (Neighborhood of the Merchants). They are apparently related to societies from the Gulf of Mexico, which suggests the traffic of these objects from that region or that they were produced by people from these regions in the valley of Teotihuacan (Valadez, 1992). A head that appears to represent a monkey has a frontal crest and facial prognathism that seems distinctive to atelines (Fig. 1.4g; Valadez, 1992; Valadez and Childs-Rattray, 1993) as in some pieces found in Tetitla. The second object is a cylindrical ceramic stamp (Fig. 1.4h), possibly for corporal or textile use, with the representation of a snake, with a tail resembling a bouquet, apparently a rattle and an appendage at its base, perhaps its hemipenis (D. Ruíz-Ramoni, 2018: obs. pers.). The monkey appears on one side of the head of the snake, in profile and is recognizable by its forelock, forelimbs, and long tail, hands bulging but representing large size with long fingers, body upright, and hind limbs forward. The materials referred to in this neighborhood were found in a fill, while the seal was discovered under the floor of a room, suggesting it been buried on purpose and seems to indicate that it had a differential treatment.

There is a piece in the Teotihuacan Site Museum, similar to one in the collection of L. Sejourné. This is an adornment with mask head and monkey pompadour as well as a narrow nasal configuration (Fig. 1.5a). The outline and eyes have diffuse reddish orange slip. In this collection there is another example of a monkey (Fig. 1.5b). It shows a primatomorphic mask, hair on the forehead, smiling face, with exposed tongue and earflaps, similar to those that are observed later in the Post-classic period of the central valley of Mexico, in Mexica representations of primates with *oyohualli* earflaps. Sullivan (2007) reports another monkey with the characteristic primate mask and pronounced front (Fig. 1.5c). Noguera (1965) and Rivera-Dorado (1969) indicate that monkeys represented in Teotihuacan are clearly made with molds. An example of this type of production, including a monkey, is part of the historical collection excavated by the Swedish archaeologist Sigvald Linné (1899–1986) (Scott, 2005). The monkey from this collection has a protuberance on the forehead, a primatomorphic mask, and prominent and rounded eyes as in other Teotihuacan representations of primates in addition to a pronounced belly, rounded eyes earflaps, and a loincloth (Fig. 1.5d).

There is a primatomorphic whistling vessel (14.2 × 11.9 × 17.7 cm) with a monkey with crossed arms, common in spider monkeys kept in captivity (B. Urbani, pers. obs.). It also has a tail, a prognathous face, a platyrrhine aligned nose, a protuberant belly, and bangs on the forehead (Fig. 1.5e). This object is deposited at the National Anthropological Museum. It was found in the Teotihuacan area of La Ventilla which is a complex that included a temple, institutional buildings, and an extended household area of highly specialized artisans who inhabited this complex between 300 CE and 650 CE (Gómez-Chávez, 2000a, b; Serrano-Sánchez et al., 2003). Another similar vessel, also with the characteristic Teotihuacan orange slip, and deposited in the same museum, has similar characteristics, and in this case a more visible tail (Fig. 1.5f). A globular figurine in orange slip (12.3 × 19.5 × 11.3 cm), held at the Teotihuacan Site Museum, is a seated deity and depicts a monkey. This object also displays an element that seems to be observed in archaeological material of the Post-classic Aztec period: a protruding mouth that resembles the characterization of *Ehécatl* (Fig. 1.5g). Finally, it should be noted that in Teotihuacan, families in multi-ethnic complexes worshiped gods such as the god of the storm, as well as the monkey or the rabbit (Manzanilla, 2016). The monkey, possibly "9 Monkey" as a deity, is represented in a rock sculpture (Fig. 1.5h).

Outside the central valley of Mexico, there is ceramic material with representation of primates of clearly Teotihuacan characteristics (Table 1.3). A couple of primate-like adornos were found in Cerro de la Estrella, today's south Mexico city (Fig. 1.6a, b). From the Mexican eastern region, specifically from the center of the state of Veracruz, there is a tripod vessel of Teotihuacan style (Fig. 1.6c; 12.2 cm × 11.7 cm), with a seated monkey inside looking at the horizon (Escobedo-Gonzalbo, 2017); a vessel with a monkey in a similar posture was found in Teotihuacan (Fig. 1.7a). In the same region of the Gulf, Matos-Moctezuma (2009) reports the presence of material of Teotihuacan influence in *Cerro de los Monos* (The Monkeys' Mountain) located in the middle section of the Balsas River basin. A primatomorphic vase of San Martín Texmelucan, Puebla (16 × 20.8 × 13.8 cm, Fig. 1.6d) shows the Teotihuacan orange slip that seems to indicate mobility of this material from the metropolis to the south. This vessel was likely a ceremonial object (Solís, 2009), and also represents a monkey with protuberant belly, prognathic face, and pronounced forehead. Another figure from the state of Puebla that used to belong to a private collection, now held at the Regional Museum of Cholula, shows some features that are reminiscent of the face of a primate, as a protuberance on the forehead, prognathic face, and a monkey "mask" (Fig. 1.6e). The region of Cholula had influence from Teotihuacan, as in the large pyramidal base of this Pueblan city (Marquina, 1972). Furthermore, in Teteles de Santo Nombre, a pre-Classic/Classic site in the state of Puebla, a polished green stone that resembles a primate head has been found (INAH, 2018); however, it might be a stylized human head. Cook de Leonard (1957) reports two whistling vessels with primatologi-cal representations made from Teotihuacan orange slip and found in Ixcaquixtla, Puebla. In both vessels the monkeys have rounded eyes, pronounced foreheads, crossed arms on the chest, prognathic face, and nose with a line like a septum that separates the nostrils (Fig. 1.6f, g). One of them seems to have a rope around its neck that is held in the hand of the monkey (height: 16.5 cm; Fig. 1.6f), while the other has a prehensile tail visible on its right side (height 11.5 cm; Fig. 1.6g). On the other hand, there is another whistling vessel of doubtful provenance indicated as possibly from Mitla in the state of Oaxaca (Kidder et al., 1946). This object is located in the Field Museum of Natural History of Chicago (Fig. 1.6h) and is extremely similar to those of Teotihuacan and Puebla. It has a pronounced forearm and belly, a prognathic face, rounded eyes, and arms resting on its folded legs. Another example of an orange-slipped whistling vase with a similar monkey was found in Escuintla, Guatemala (Fig. 1.7b).

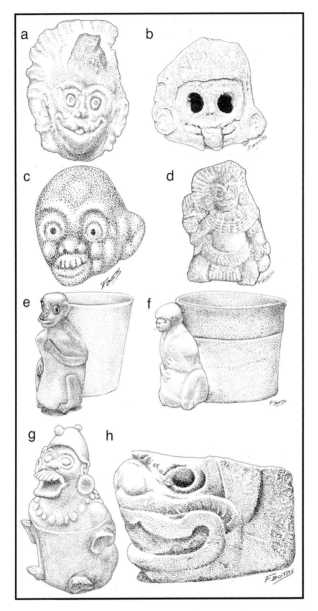

Figure 1.5 Representation of primates from Teotihuacan, mainly in Mexican national collections. (Images not to scale; sources in Table 1.2. Illustrations by F. Botas).

1.2.2.2 Murals

The murals of Tetitla are characterized by presenting animal profiles, with the peculiarity of being located on the wall edges and near the ground (Miller, 1973). From that corpus of mural paintings, Langley (1986) includes in his compendium of Teotihuacan notational signs, the design of a head that looks like a primate, indicating that it "bears a resemblance to depictions of animals identified as monkeys"

Table 1.3. Primatomorph pottery with Teotihuacan influence found south of the Teotihuacan valley

Object	Location	Date	Repository	Figure	References
Monkey head from pottery	Cerro de la Estrella, Iztapalapa, Mexico valley.	–	Museo Fuego Nuevo. Mexico city, Mexico	1.6a	Rafael Álvarez Pérez Hall, New Fire Museum
Monkey head from pottery	Cerro de la Estrella, Iztapalapa, Mexico valley.	–	Museo Fuego Nuevo. Mexico city, Mexico	1.6b	Rafael Álvarez Pérez Hall, New Fire Museum
Tripod base with a "watching monkey"	Center of Veracruz, state of Veracruz	Early Classic (200–600 CE)	Museo del Amparo (Sala 6, Arte, forma y expresión), Puebla, Mexico	1.6c	Escobedo-Gonzalbo (2017: n/p)
Whistle vase with primatomorphic figure	San Martín Texmelucan, state of Puebla (Tlaxcala)	Classic-Xolalpan (~350–550 CE)	Musée du quai Branly (ex-Pinart, former Boban, 71.1878.1033), Paris, France	1.6d	Solis (2009: 348, fig. 167b)
Vase with alleged monkey	Cholula region, state of Puebla	–	Museo Regional de Cholula (Coll. Ángel Trauwitz and Museo José Luis Bello y González), Cholula, Mexico	1.6e	Cultures of the Area of Teotihuacan Hall, Regional Museum of Cholula
Large whistle vase with primatomorphic figure	Ixcaquixtla, state of Puebla	–	–	1.6f	Cook de Leonard (1957: fig. 55a, b)
Small whistle vase with primatomorphic figure	Ixcaquixtla, state of Puebla	–	–	1.6g	Cook de Leonard (1957: fig. 55b)
Whistle vase with primatomorphic figure	"said to be from Mitla" (Kidder et al., 1946: fig. 197) in "Oaxaca (?)"(Kidder et al., 1946: 191, fig. 78)	–	Field Museum of Natural History, Chicago, USA	1.6h	Kidder et al. (1946: fig. 197)[a]
Whistle vase with monkey	Escuintla, Guatemala	450–650 CE	Los Ángeles County Museum of Art, Los Angeles, USA (M.2010.115.800)	1.7b	O'Neil (2018)

[a] Next to the illustration of this whistling vessel, Kidder et al. (1946: 191, fig. 78) presents another illustration of a seated monkey from Las Colinas, state of Tlaxcala, Mexico. However, it does not indicate its style or associated culture.

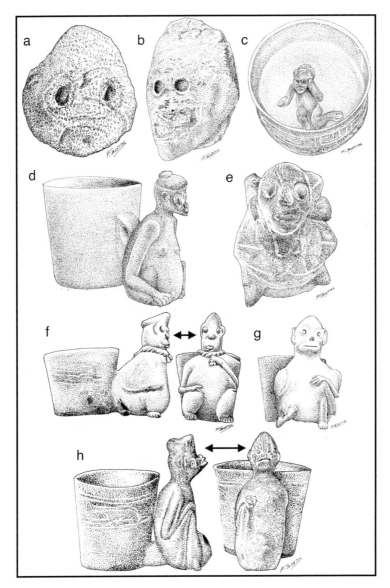

Figure 1.6 Pottery of Teotihuacan influence with primate representations from sites south of the Teotihuacan valley. Images not to scale; sources in Table 1.3. (Illustrations by F. Botas).

(Langley, 1986: 265). In doing so, the author refers to Miller's work (1973: 148, fig. 310). The representation of the monkey has a prognathous face, a platyrrhine nose, pronounced forehead, a rounded eye and a primatomorphic "mask." The mural with the aforementioned monkey is called the "Goddess of Jade" or *Tláloc Verde* [Green Tlaloc] and is located in the northern side of the complex in the portico 11 of the structure 2 of Tetitla (de la Fuente, 1996b). Figure 1.8a presents a panoramic view of the mural and the small representation of the primate found there. The image of

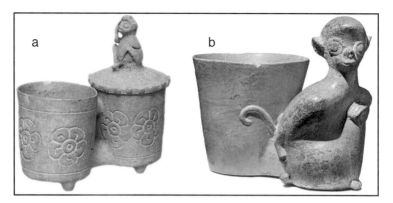

Figure 1.7 Depictions of (a) a seated monkey on a double vase from Teotihuacan and (b) orange slipped Teotihuacan-like whistling vessel with a monkey from the Mayan region). ©Los Angeles County Museum of Art, Los Angeles. Public domain-CC BY.

the goddess with the monkey is at the far right of the whole fresco – from the perspective of the observer – in the building where four similar goddesses were painted (Fig. 1.8a). A detail of the fauna represented and falling from the left hand of the studied goddess shows the outline of the head of a monkey (Fig. 1.8b). Figure 1.8c shows the head of the monkey which is now degraded: only its outline can be seen today without the internal delineations that represent the monkey's face. Figure 1.8d shows the same photograph as in Figure 1.8c but with our digital reconstruction of the face of the primate superimposed as photographed in February 1971 by Miller (1973: 148, fig. 310).

At La Ventilla, Cabrera-Castro (1996) reported two representations of monkeys on the floor of the structure known as the *Plaza de los Glifos* [Plaza of the Glyphs]. The floor area (7.5 × 11.7 m) is decorated with more than 40 glyphs in red paint on a reticulated area. This is a rare context for painted glyphs to be found but has been found in a few other places in Tetitla and La Ciudadela (Cabrera-Castro, 1996). The first is a monkey profile with a felid nose and mouth as well as "flames" emanating from its head (Fig. 1.8e; Cabrera-Castro, 1996). This representation is relatively similar to a stone carving found in Teotihuacan (Fig. 1.5h) and the so-called 9 Monkey from Oaxaca (Fig. 1.9c). A second painting is an apparent monkey profile with an earflap and rounded eye (Fig. 1.8f; Cabrera-Castro, 1996). The two paintings are found at similar positions in opposite corners of the room.

1.3   Discussion

Among the elements that suggest the representation of monkeys in the Teotihuacan material culture are the presence of prehensile tail, prominent forehead, primato-morphic "masks," superciliary arches, prominent belly, noses with separated nostrils, and prognathous face. Primate species are difficult to be full determined in these representations, although, those depicted in whistle vases are similar to spider

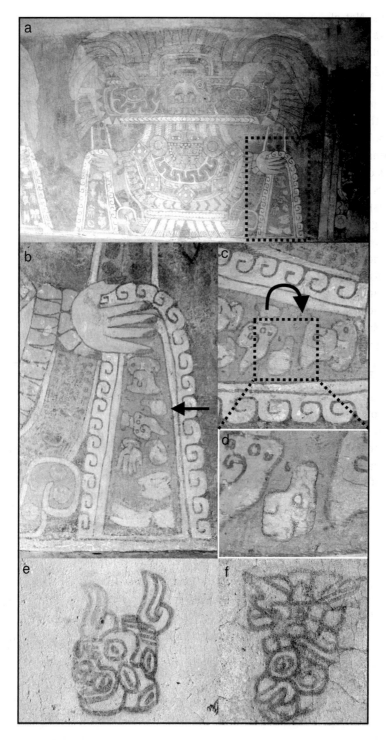

Figure 1.8 Teotihuacan frescos with monkey representations. (a) mural with a Jade goddess from Tetitla; (b) detail of the right side of the Jade goddess; (c) current detail of the monkey

monkeys. Not all representations of primates in Teotihuacan have been found as offerings or in symbolic contexts. However, Séjourné (1966c) suggests that unlike the representation of birds and canids, that primates seems to have a symbolic meaning, including the association with Quetzacoatl (Feathered Serpent), the god of wind, fertility, light, and wisdom. One of the discoveries of primate remains was in a burial in the Pyramid of the Moon which is related to individuals of possible Mayan origin. The primate found in the Plaza of the Columns might also be related to the Mayans. The other confirmed primate element was found in Xalla, an area used for governing the city of Teotihuacan. There are characteristics that link the primate remains of spider monkeys: (1) two were incomplete buried individuals, but isolated elements (Xalla and Pyramid of the Moon), and an entire skeleton (Plaza of the Columns); (2) in the case of Xalla and the Pyramid of the Moon, they were captured as young animals in regions with wild populations or bred in captivity (generally pet *Ateles* are more viable than *Alouatta*); (3) they had ritually oriented use – possibly the bones themselves had such cultural values; and (4) they were linked to the ruling elite. This link is also supported by the fact that the representations of primates in the region and the largest collection of primatomorphic material culture found in a Teotihuacan site were in the vicinity of the Tetitla Palace.

The Mayan and Zapotec cultures began their historical development almost simultaneously in tropical zones: the first in the extreme southeast and the second in the southern zone (Clark et al., 2014; Wiesheu, 2014). In Teotihuacan, there are elements of material culture (frescoes and ceramics) that resemble features from Tlaxcala, Chupicuaro, as well as Puebla, Oaxaca, and the Mayan region (Angulo-Villaseñor, 2002; Gomez-Chávez, 2002). In addition, outside the Teotihuacan valley, Kolb (1987) refers to the exchange with the coastal areas of the Gulf of Mexico as well as the Pacific region. Daneels (2002) reviews Teotihuacan elements in Gulf sites such as Matacapan (a commercial enclave), in addition to other localities, such as the river basins of Nautla (Pital), Tecolutla (El Tajin), Papaloapan (Cerro Las Mesas), Coaxtla (La Joya), and Los Tuxtlas (Matacapan). Primatomorphic objects were found in the Neighborhood of the Merchants which is related to the peoples of the Gulf region (Fig. 1.4g, h), as well as a Teotihuacan tripod with a primate, in present-day state of Veracruz. Paddock (1972) also suggests the presence of Teotihuacan elements in the Monte Albán region and the Maya area of Uaxactún. Chronologically, it is during the Xolalpan period (450–650 CE) that Teotihuacan is perceived as a valley of great influence in the center of Mexico and surrounding regions (Matos-Moctezuma, 1990). Based on this, it is understandable that many of the animal icons that formed the basis of their religion were typical from the tropics: jaguars (N. Sugiyama, 2014)

Figure 1.8 (*cont.*) head profile, turned to the right for a better appreciation, without the internal delineation of the monkey face (photograph taken on June 15, 2018); (d) previous photograph's digital reconstruction of the monkey face after Miller (1973: 148, fig. 310. Illustration by F. Botas); (e) monkey with "flames" from La Ventilla; (f) possible monkey with earflap from La Ventilla. (Photographs by B. U. [Tetitla] and R. C.-C. [La Ventilla]).

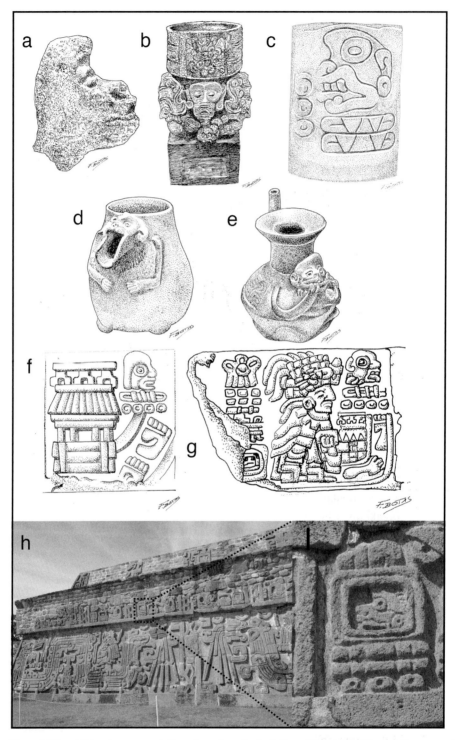

Figure 1.9 (a–g) Primate representations in archaeological sites of the state of Oaxaca (Images not to scale; sources in the text. Illustrations by F. Botas); (h) Monkey in Xochicalco's Temple of the Quetzacoatl, Morelos state; (i) Detail of Xochicalco's monkey. (Photographs by Bernardo Urbani).

and quetzals (Aguilera, 2002; Kubler, 1972a), as well as others like the monkeys. The concentration of these cultural foci in the southern parts of the Mexican territory did not prevent their influence from reaching places like the center, as in Teotihuacan. Teotihuacan inherited characteristics of the preceding societies and those that contemporaneously shared with it the Mesoamerican territory. So the basic guidelines on their relationship with nature did not change fundamentally; however, it is clear that human–animal interactions occurred with adjustments depending on the region where the city was located, and the cultures with which it was related. Starting from these bases, it is clear that within the Teotihuacan pantheon of animals there were many from tropical habitats with symbolic relevance as is the case of monkeys. Moreover, there seems to be a notion of the similarity and liminality among Teotihuacans as can be inferred from the similarity of representation of nonhuman primates and humans in Tetitla (as in two primates from the L. Séujourné collection [Figs. 1.3b, c in this study] and Childs-Rattray [2001: 541, figs. 133a, b]).

The representation of primates in Mesoamerica, and particularly among the Maya, has generated special interest since the beginning of the last century (Preuss, 1901) until the present (Baker, 1992, 2013; Nájera-Coronado, 2012, 2013, 2015, 2016; Rice and South, 2015; South, 2005). It was suggested that monkeys were partially represented in the Classic Maya period (300–900 CE). They have been studied with the aim of determining which species of primate has been represented in the Maya archaeological iconography (Baker, 1992, 2013; Rice and South, 2015; South, 2005). Nájera-Coronado (2012, 2015) also suggests that in the Maya society, primarily in the Late Classic (550–900 CE), primates played a fundamental role in their association with cocoa, which is possibly the most revered botanical item after corn. Monkeys might have a fundamental role in the framework of mythical Mayan thought. Nájera-Coronado (2013, 2016) locates the primates on the edge of humans with animals. The monkey is an animal that provides symbolic meanings, such as its association with the sun and wind, libido, and writing. In addition, primates were characterized by their particular intelligence up to their role as an entity that represents fertility (Braakhuis, 1987; Bruner and Cucina, 2005). As for pre-Hispanic osteoarchaeological remains of primates in the Mayan area, there are elements from the Yucatan peninsula in Itzamkanac (a humerus, Terminal Classic, 900–100 CE) and Yaxuná (an ulna, Pre-Postclassic 500 BCE to 1600 CE) (Valadez, 2014). In both cases, postcranial remains, attributed to *Ateles geoffroyi*, are represented in food waste deposits (Valadez, 2014). Looking further south, Pohl (1976) indicates the presence of Postclassic locations in Flores and Tikal, as well as spider monkeys in Tikal (Post-classic) and in Seibal (late Classic). In Tikal, a complete skeleton of a spider monkey was found in an early Classic *chultun* tomb (Moholy-Nagy, 2004). In the Guatemalan site of Seibal, Pohl (2004) also reports howler monkeys (*Alouatta*) and spider monkeys (*Ateles*) in its late Classic deposits. On the other hand, remains of howler monkeys have been found in the Mayan site of Selín Farm in the Ulúa valley in Honduras (Henderson and Joyce, 2004). Emery and Thornton (2008) indicated that colorful birds, large felids, and primates might have been particularly prized among the Mayan.

In Mayan regions, such as Piedras Negras, there is evidence of the relationship of the Teotihuacan people and their Tlaloc with prominent members of the Peten Maya on a lintel (Angulo-Villaseñor, 2002). The relations between Teotihuacan and the sites of Kaminaljuyu, Copán and Tikal appear in the Early Classic period (Fash, 2002). Sugiyama and López-Lujan (2006a) refers to a strong connection between the ruling elites of Teotihuacan and the Mayan, at least from the fourth century CE. In research that explores the relationship between Teotihuacan and the Mayan region, Laporte-Molina (1989) indicates that Uaxactun was ruled by the Ma'Cuch lineage by 380 CE, and also had a relationship with Tikal (Coe, 1972). As remarked by Sugiyama and López-Lujan (2006b), Kaminajuyu is a site with links with Teotihuacan and has elite "lotus flower" burials. In this sense, the sites of Kaminajuyu and Uaxtactun present burials that resemble Burial 5 of the Pyramid of the Moon, in the treatment of their ruling elites. Burial 5 is the site where postcranial remains have been found, as in the Mayan sites of the Yucatán Peninsula.

Laporte-Molina (1989) reviews the presence of material culture from the Mayan area in Teotihuacan, and indicates the existence of Mayan pottery in La Ventilla A and Xolalpan burials as well as in the site of the so-called Mayan Murals of Tetitla with Mayan-like jade pieces. For instance, Tetitla is located 600 m west of the Street of Death that links both Teotihuacan pyramids (Taube, 2004). Tetitla is the structure that preserves more paintings southwest of Teotihuacan. Green goddesses are represented in this complex (Ruiz-Gallut, 1999), one of them with a monkey representation. Taube (2004) indicates that Tetitla cannot be considered a Mayan neighborhood, although it presents evidence of material culture, such as murals and movable objects, as well as Maya phonetic texts suggesting interactions of particular relevance. The murals of Tetitla have "foreign" features according to Ruiz-Gallut (2002). A primatomorphic vessel was found at the Mayan-related site of La Ventilla (Fig. 1.5e) as well as paintings on the floor structure (Fig. 1.8e, f). For this vessel it was suggested that "a cylindrical duct connects the simian character to the vase; the body of the monkey being hollow, when filling the vase of water, this last passes through this conduit and flows into the animal, which causes a hissing. The monkey is associated with the divinity of the Wind; this type of vase was probably used during ceremonies related to this phenomenon" (Solís, 2009: 348). A vessel from Escuintla, Guatemala (Fig. 1.7b) is similar to others found in the Teotihuacan valley and surrounding central Mexican regions (Figs. 1.5e–f; 1.6d, f–h). This represents an example of the circulation of Teotihuacan primate imageries in the Mayan region. Therefore, the presence of primates in Teotihuacan could be, in part, related to the presence of populations of Mayan origin in the City of the Gods. Primates are present in elite burials (such as Burial 5 of the Pyramid of the Moon), the only primates in Teotihuacan murals (Tetitla and La Ventilla), the largest collection of primatomorphic Teotihuacan pieces – also recovered in Tetitla – and the alleged evocation of the divinity of the wind in of the vessel from La Ventilla (Solís, 2009). The latter is a characteristic that has been associated with primates and their connection with the Maya (e.g. Nájera-Coronado, 2015).

Not only Uaxactun and localities of southern Guatemala (Zaxualpa, Amatitlan, and Kaminaljuyu) had relationships with areas of influence of Teotihuacan but also

Monte Albán as well as other sites in present-day state of Oaxaca (Matos-Moctezuma, 1990). There is a clear relation of Oaxacans and the Zapotecs of Monte Alban with Teotihuacan; stylistic similarities existed in the material culture, as in the case of urns, particularly between 500 BCE and 700 CE (Berlo, 1984). On the other hand, in the Oaxacan Neighborhood of Teotihuacan, Zapotec-style pottery made with local clay was found (Taube, 2004). Winter et al. (2002) reviewed existing information on the relationship of Monte Albán and Teotihuacan, and commented on the shared elements of the Oaxacan neighborhoods of Teotihuacan with the Oaxacan Preclassic localities, as follows: (1) the material culture of the Oaxacan Cerro de la Minas has a clear Teotihuacan influence; (2) excavations on the Monte Albán platforms shows Teotihuacan cultural elements; (3) there are stelae on the southern flank of the Monte Albán platform where the Teotihuacan–Oaxaca relationship is recorded; (4) there is possible Zapotec archaeoastronomic linkage with the configuration of Teotihuacan; and (5) there are possible similarities in the configuration of red discs in Zapotec and Teotihuacan buildings. Regarding archaeoprimatological aspects, Kubler (1972b) lists monkeys as one of the 22 animal motifs represented in Teotihuacan iconography in dated ceramics and describes Teotihuacan zoomorphic representations as more austere than those of the Mayan region, and at the same time, they represent an additional element that links them with those of Monte Albán.

Considering this information, in the state of Oaxaca, figurines representing monkeys have been found at Carrizal, a site located near Ciudad Ixtepec, a region where natural populations of *A. geoffroyi* are closely located (Ortiz-Martínez and Rico-Gray, 2005). Also in the Oaxacan site of San José Mogote, figures identified as spider monkeys, with frontal crests, rounded eyes, and prognathic faces, have been reported (Fig. 1.9a; Marcus, 1998). At the same site, a skull of a spider monkey with red pigment cover has been recovered (Marcus, 1998). The "spider monkey skull had been placed (as an offering) under the plaster floor of a 'men's house' [*Casa de Varones*]. That [small] ritual building [on Mound 1] had been largely destroyed by later buildings constructed above it. There were many meters of heavy earth above the skull. The skull was crushed by the enormous weight. [They were] bone fragments coated both in (ritual) red pigment and white lime plaster (from the floor). Only when we began to clean the fragments in the laboratory did we see its teeth and realize that it was an exotic animal" (J. Marcus, 2018: pers. comm.). Thus, it is relevant to notice that the primate element from Xalla was also recovered under a plaster floor. On the other hand, there is also a Ñuiñe urn (now deposited in the Regional Museum of Huajuapan) with a representation of a seated monkey holding a bowl (Fig. 1.9b). This urn/censer comes from the Cerro de la Minas in the Lower Mixteca, is classified as typical of the Epiclassic period (600–900 CE);, and has stylistic similarities to those urns of Teotihuacan. Ortiz-Maciel and Serrano-Rojas (2016) indicate that this ancient society seems to have followed the representative characteristics of Teotihuacan and Monte Albán.

In Monte Albán, state of Oaxaca, there are also three pieces of particular Teotihuacan interest, now deposited in the National Museum of Anthropology. The first is a vase from Atzompa (Monte Albán IIIA, early Classic) dated from 200 to 500 CE. This piece represents "13 Monkey," typical of the calendar system of central Mexico (Fig. 1.9c). This monkey is similar to the one found in Teotihuacan and considered a deity (Fig. 1.5h). Also, from the early Classic period there are ceramics that look like similar to the ones of the Teotihuacan style within the territory ruled by Monte Albán (Fig. 1.9d, e). In this Oaxacan pre-Hispanic city, Marcus (2008; see also: Acosta, 1958–1959; Piña-Chan, 1993) referring to one of the main structures of the Monte Albán complex, comments that:

The Stela 1, in the northeast corner of the platform, shows the ruler 12 Jaguar sitting on his throne; it is wearing a jaguar suit and carries a spear. The associated hieroglyphic text refers to his divine ancestry, his pilgrimages and his divinations. Hidden on the underside of Stela 1 are representations of four ambassadors, one of which (called '9 Monkey') appears coming out of a temple decorated in the style of several Teotihuacan temples. This scene has been interpreted in the sense that '9 Monkey' traveled from Teotihuacan. There is a more elaborate version of this 'diplomatic' scene engraved on the underside of another stela, the 'Estela Lisa' (in the northwest corner of the platform). In both Stela 1 and Lisa Stela the ambassador who appears retreating from a Teotihuacan-style temple bears the name 9 Monkey.

Marcus (2008) also pointed out that the Teotihuacan ambassadors may have participated in the dedication of the Southern Platform. This reference shows not only the close relationship between Monte Albán and Teotihuacan during the Classic period but also reveals the presence of the name of a monkey as part of the Teotihuacan diplomatic entourage at Monte Albán. That is to say, the primatological referent was implicit in the denomination of a diplomatic agent of the Teotihuacan elite, who traveled from a region without autochthonous populations of primates to another that does harbor primates. Furthermore, Marcus (1983) commented that the structures associated with the 9 Monkey in the lower part of Stela 1 (Fig. 1.9f) and the Stela Lisa (Fig. 1.9g) of Monte Albán are similar to those of the Tetitla site in Teotihuacan (see Fig. 1.8e, f). In this connection, Marcus (1983: 179) suggests that it "seems reasonable to propose that the individual 9 Monkey came from Teotihuacan, if not from the actual Tetitla precinct, which lies only 2 km from the Oaxaca barrio at Teotihuacan." It should be noted that in Xalla, an area used by the ruling elite and located on an esplanade just between the pyramids of the Sun and the Moon of Teotihuacan, there is not only the presence of artisans destined to produce for the rulers, but also of large quantity of mica plates brought from Oaxaca (Manzanilla, 2017a, b).

As for the allochthonous Teotihuacan animals, such as jaguars (*Panthera onca*) (Valadez, 1992) or red brocket deers (*Mazama americana*) (Valadez et al., 2017), appear as isolated elements, in most cases, even with characteristics that indicate that they are not just "bones that survived time," but as objects that were intentionally prepared to be used in that way (Manzanilla and Valadez, 2017; Rodríguez, 2010; Rodríguez and Valadez, 2014; Valadez, 1992, 1993). Under this perspective, the idea of the use of the symbolic force of a species is strongly supported. This could be the case for the primate bone remains at the Pyramid of the Moon, which could have a ritual meaning as inferred by its location and contextualization. On the other hand, the partial mandible of Xalla, displays porosity that seems similar to that observed in captive animals, and it was from a juvenile spider monkey, suggesting it might have been captured to be kept as a pet linked to the ruling elite (also a possible monkey pet with a rope in a Teotihuacan-style whistle vase from Puebla: Fig. 1.6f). In addition, the primate remains from Teotihuacan have a possible emblematic value as being buried with members of the Teotihuacan elite (e.g. Valadez, 2014). As indicated by López-Austin (1984), for the Postclassic period, infants were considered relevant supernatural resources that had the ability to communicate with the gods. The author also pointed out that the arm was considered as a body part related to executional and manipulative capabilities, with the left arm having special supernatural leverage and authority. The fact that primates associate with places linked to foreign human communities, such as the people of the Gulf (Merchants' Quarter), Mayan people (Burial 5 of the Pyramid of the Moon, Plaza of the Columns, Tetitla, and La Ventilla), or the Oaxaca region (Xalla), could be supportive of the argument that monkeys were adopted as symbolic "commodities" in the central metropolis of Teotihuacan. On the other hand, the presence of primatomorphic cultural material produced in Teotihuacan artisan neighborhoods, allowed the mobility of these pieces and images within the city, and may have had a figurative meaning among the inhabitants of this valley. Considering the foregoing, it is clear that primate remains and material culture are scarce considering the extent of the city and the long period when it has been archaeologically studied. However, it was of particular interest to explore how primates circulated and were appropriated in the City of Gods, particularly among the ruling elite (Pyramid of the Moon, Xalla, Plaza of the Columns, Tetitla, La Ventila, Zacuala), as well as looking at how they arrived in this valley from distant lands, and overall how they also travelled with their burden of aesthetic and cultural values to other distant regions with Teotihuacan influence and relations such as present-day Puebla, Oaxaca, and distant Guatemala. To conclude, after the fall of the City of Gods, during the Epiclassic (560–900 CE), peoples from Teotihuacan, as well as the Mayan and coastal regions might have inhabited the city of Xochicalco, in modern Morelos state (e.g. Litvak-King, 1970; Webb, 1978). In this city, the main structure, the Temple of Quetzacoatl, bears a conspicuous primate engraving in a central position (Fig. 1.9h, i) – a signal of the past role of primates in ancient central Mexican societies.

Acknowledgments

Thanks to the personnel of the libraries of the National Anthropological Museum, Institute of Anthropological Research of the National Autonomous University of Mexico (UNAM), Institute of Aesthetic Research-UNAM, Joint Earth Science Library-UNAM, National School of Anthropology and History, and Harvard University as well as the staff of the Teotihuacan Archaeological Zone, Xochicalco Archaeological Zone, Teotihuacan Site Museum, Tetitla Palace Site, National Anthropological Museum, Diego Rivera Anahuacalli Museum, Diego Rivera and

Frida Kahlo House-Studio Museum, Regional Museum of Cholula, National Palace Museum, Rancho Grande Biological Station Museum (Venezuela), and La Salle Natural History Museum (Venezuela). We appreciate the support of Jessica Garrido-Guzmán at the Osteology Laboratory of the Institute of Anthropological Research-UNAM, Alejandra Martínez-Melo at the "María del Carmen Perrilliat M." Museum of the Institute of Geology-UNAM, Liliana Cortés-Ortiz at the University of Michigan, and Segundo Jiménez and Yoly Velandria at the Center for Anthropology of the Venezuelan Institute of Scientific Research. We also thank the communication and support of Joyce Marcus (University of Michigan) and the cooperation of Sergio López-Alonso (National Institute of Anthropology and History-Oaxaca). Thanks to Saburo Sugiyama (Aichi Prefectural University, Arizona State University, and Pyramid of the Moon Project) and Mariela Pérez-Antonio (Pyramid of the Moon Project). Our appreciation to Linda Manzanilla and Gerardo Jiménez-Delgado at the Institute of Anthropological Research-UNAM for sharing the base map of Teotihuacan used in this study, and the former for her comment on the text. Thanks to Robbi Siegel (Art Resource, Inc.) as well as the anonymous persons in the photographic department of Los Angeles County Museum of Art for openly sharing images of their collection. Special thanks to Omar Mauricio (SOS Recovery, Caracas) for his excellent technical support at a final stage of the manuscript preparation. Last, but not least, we would like to sincerely thanks Fernando Botas (Institute of Anthropological Research-UNAM), pioneer of Mexican archaeological illustration, for the fantastic figures specially made for this chapter. It is a real honor to have the aesthetics and works of F. Botas in this piece of research. Thanks to D. Youlatos, A. T. Antczak and the external reviewer for the constructive comments. D. R. R. was supported by a DGAPA-POSDOC-UNAM postdoctoral fellowship and B. U. by a DGAPA-PREI-UNAM visiting scholar fellowship as well as supports from the Posgrado de Antropología-UNAM and the Coordinación de Humanidades-UNAM during their research stays at the National Autonomous University of Mexico between October 2017 and June 2018 when most of this chapter was written.

References

Acosta, J. A. (1958–1959). Exploraciones arqueológicas en Monte Albán, XVIII Temporada. *Revista Mexicana de Estudios Antropológicos*, 15, 7–50.

Aguilera, C. (2002). Los quetzales de Teotihuacán. In M. E. Ruiz-Gallut, ed., *Ideología y política a través de materiales, imágenes y símbolos. Memoria de la Primera Mesa Redonda de Teotihuacán*. Mexico: Universidad Nacional Autónoma de México and Instituto Nacional de Antropología e Historia, 399–410.

Angulo-Villaseñor, J. (2002). Formación del estado teotihuacano y su impacto en los señoríos mayas. In M. E. Ruiz-Gallut, ed., *Ideología y política a través de materiales, imágenes y símbolos. Memoria de la*

Primera Mesa Redonda de Teotihuacán. Mexico: Universidad Nacional Autónoma de México and Instituto Nacional de Antropología e Historia, 359–329.

Anonymous (2018). Élite maya residió en Teotihuacan, revelan hallazgos en la Plaza de las Columnas. *Boletín de la Dirección de Medios de Comunicación del Instituto Nacional de Antropología e Historia*, 335 (September 22), 1–3.

Anonymous (2019). Nuevos hallazgos en Teotihuacan revelan relación con mayas entre 350 y 450 d.c. *Boletín de la Dirección de Medios de Comunicación del Instituto Nacional de Antropología e Historia*, 175 (June 13), 1–4.

Baker, M. (1992). Capuchin monkeys (*Cebus capucinus*) and the ancient Maya. *Ancient Mesoamerica*, 3, 219–228.

Baker, M. (2013). Revisiting capuchin monkeys (*Cebus capucinus*) and the ancient Maya. *Revue de primatologie*, 5, document 67.

Berlo, J. C. (1984). *Teotihuacan Art Abroad: A Study of Metropolitan Style and Provincial Transformation in Incensario Workshops. Part I*. Oxford: BAR Publishing, 199 (i).

Braakhuis, H. E. M. (1987). Artificers of the days: Functions of the howler monkey gods among the Mayas. *Bijdragen tot de Taal-, Land-, en Volkenkunde*, 143, 25–53.

Bruner, E., & Cucina, A. (2005). *Alouatta*, *Ateles*, and the Mesoamerican cultures. *Journal of Anthropological. Sciences*, 83, 111–118.

Cabrera-Castro, R. (1996). Caracteres glíficos teotihuacanos en un piso de La Ventilla. In B. de la Fuente, ed., *La pintura mural prehispánica en México. I. Teotihuacán*. Mexico: Instituto de Investigaciones Estéticas de la Universidad Nacional Autónoma de México and Instituto Nacional de Antropología e Historia, 402–427.

Cabrera-Castro, R. (2012). Secuencia constructiva y entierros-ofrenda descubiertos en las excavaciones de la Pirámide la Luna, Teotihuacán. *Temas de antropología mexicana*, 17, 109–133.

Carballo, D. M. (2011). *Obsidian and the Teotihuacan State: Weaponry and Ritual Production at the Moon Pyramid*. Pittsburgh: University of Pittsburgh Press.

Childs-Rattray, E. (2001). *Teotihuacan: Ceramics, Chronology, and Cultural Trends*. México: CONACULTURA and Universidad de Pittsburgh.

Clark, J., Hansen, R., & Pérez, T. (2014). La zona maya en el Preclásico. In L. Manzanilla, & L. López, eds., *Historia antigua de México. Volumen I, en México antiguo, sus áreas culturales, los orígenes y el horizonte Preclásico*. Mexico: Editorial Porrúa, Consejo Nacional para la Cultura y las Artes, Instituto Nacional de Antropología e Historia, and Instituto de Investigaciones Antropológicas de la Universidad Nacional Autónoma de México, 437–509.

Coe, W. R. (1972). Cultural contact between the lowland Maya and Teotihuacan as seen from Tikal, Peten, Guatemala. In Anonymous, ed., *Teotihuacán. XI mesa redonda*. Mexico: Sociedad Mexicana de Antropología, 257–271.

Cook de Leonard, C. (1957). El origen de la cerámica Anaranjado delgado. Master's thesis, Escuela Nacional de Antropología e Historia.

Cormier, L., & Urbani, B. (2008). The ethnoprimatology of the spider monkeys (*Ateles* spp.): from past to present. In C. J. Campbell, ed., *Spider Monkeys: Behavior, Ecology and Evolution of the Genus Ateles*. Cambridge: Cambridge University Press, 377–403.

Cowgill, G. L. (1997). State and society at Teotihuacan, México. *Annual Review of Anthropology*, 26, 129–61.

Daneels, A. (2002). Presencia de Teotihuacán en el centro y sur de Veracruz. In M. E. Ruiz-Gallut, ed., *Ideología y política a través de materiales, imágenes y símbolos. Memoria de la Primera Mesa Redonda de Teotihuacán*. Mexico: Universidad Nacional Autónoma de México e Instituto Nacional de Antropología e Historia, 655–683.

de la Fuente, B. (1996a). *La pintura mural prehispánica en México. I. Teotihuacán*. Mexico: Instituto de Investigaciones Estéticas de la Universidad Nacional Autónoma de México and Instituto Nacional de Antropología e Historia.

de la Fuente, B. (1996b). *Tetitla*. In B. De la Fuente, ed., *La pintura mural prehispánica en México. I. Teotihuacán*. Mexico: Instituto de Investigaciones Estéticas de la Universidad Nacional Autónoma de México and Instituto Nacional de Antropología e Historia, 259–312.

Escobedo-Gonzalbo, P. (2017). *Vaso trípode con mono que mira*. Puebla: Museo del Amparo. Available at: http://museoamparo.com/colecciones/pieza/473/vaso-tripode-con-mono-que-mira (Accessed December 18, 2017)

Emery, K. F., & Thornton, E. K. (2008). Zooarchaeological habitat analysis of ancient Maya landscape changes. *Journal of Ethnobiology*, 282, 154–178.

Fash, W. L. (2002). El legado de Teotihuacán en la ciudad maya de Copan, Honduras. In M. E. Ruiz-Gallut, ed., *Ideología y política a través de materiales, imágenes y símbolos. Memoria de la Primera Mesa Redonda de Teotihuacán*. Mexico: Universidad Nacional Autónoma de México and Instituto Nacional de Antropología e Historia, 715–729.

Gamio, M. (1922). *La población del valle de Teotihuacán*. Mexico: Dirección de Talleres Gráficos del Departamento de la Secretaria de Educación Pública.

García del Cueto, H. (1989). Acerca de la connotación simbólico-ritual del mono en la sociedad prehispánica (Altiplano Central). In A. Estrada, & López- R. Wilchis, eds., *Primatología en México: Comportamiento, ecología, aprovechamiento y conservación de primates. Memorias del Primer*

Simposio Nacional de Primatología. Mexico: Universidad Nacional Autónoma de México and Universidad Autónoma Metropolitana, 144–159.

Gómez-Chávez, S. (2000a). La Ventanilla. Un barrio de la antigua ciudad de Teotihuacán. Tomo I. Honor thesis, Escuela Nacional de Antropología e Historia.

Gómez-Chávez, S. (2000b). La Ventanilla. Un barrio de la antigua ciudad de Teotihuacán. Tomo III. Honor thesis, Escuela Nacional de Antropología e Historia.

Gómez-Chávez, J. (2002). Presencia del occidente de México en Teotihuacán. Aproximación a la política exterior del estado teotihuacano. In M. E. Ruiz-Gallut, ed., *Ideología y política a través de materiales, imágenes y símbolos. Memoria de la Primera Mesa Redonda de Teotihuacán*. Mexico: Universidad Nacional Autónoma de México and Instituto Nacional de Antropología e Historia, 563–625.

Henderson, J., & Joyce, R. A. (2004). Human use of animals in prehispanic Honduras. In K. F. Emery, ed., *Maya Zooarchaeology: New Directions in Method and Theory*. Los Angeles: University of California at Los Angeles, 223–236.

INAH (2017). Vasija silbadora. Museo Nacional de Antropología. Mexico: Dirección de Mediateca-Instituto Nacional de Antropología e Historia. Available at: http://mediateca.inah.gob.mx/islan dora_74/islandora/object/objetoprehispanico% 3A18508 (Accessed December 17, 2017)

INAH (2018). Cabeza de mono. Museo de sitio de Teteles de Santo Nombre. Mexico: Dirección de Mediateca-Instituto Nacional de Antropología e Historia. Available at: http://hool.inah.gob.mx:1147/es/ museos-inah/museo/museo-piezas/15052-15052-cabeza-de-mono.html?lugar_id=472&item_lugar= 14640&seccion=lugar (Accessed July 3, 2018)

Kidder, A. V., Jennings, J. D., & Shook, E. M. (1946). *Excavations at Kaminaljuyu, Guatemala*. State College: Pennsylvania State University Press.

Kolb, C. C. (1987). *Marine Shell Trade and Classic Teotihuacan, Mexico*. Oxford: BAR Publishing.

Kubler, G. (1972a). Los pájaros de Quetzalpapalotl. In Anonymous, ed., *Teotihuacán. XI mesa redonda*. Mexico: Sociedad Mexicana de Antropología, 87–101.

Kubler, G. (1972b). La iconografía del arte teotihuacano. Ensayo de análisis configurativo. In Anonymous, ed., *Teotihuacán. XI mesa redonda*. Mexico: Sociedad Mexicana de Antropología, 69–85.

Langley, J. C. (1986). *Symbolic Notation of Teotihuacan*. Oxford: BAR Publishing.

Laporte-Molina, J. P. (1989). Alternativas del clásico temprano en la relación Tikal-Teotihuacán. Grupo 6

C-XVI, Tikal, Peten, Guatemala. PhD thesis, Universidad Nacional Autónoma de México.

Litvak-King, J. (1970). Xochicalco en la Caída del Clásico: Una hipótesis. *Anales de Antropología*, **7**, 131–144.

López-Austin, A. (1984). *Cuerpo humano e ideología*. *Vol. 1*. Mexico: Universidad Nacional Autónoma de México.

Manzanilla, L. R., & Serrano, C. (1999). *Prácticas funerarias en la Ciudad de los Dioses*. Mexico: Dirección General de Asuntos del Personal Académico-Universidad Nacional Autónoma de México.

Manzanilla, L. R. (ed.) & Valadez, R. (coord) (2017). *El uso de los recursos naturales en un centro de barrio de Teotihuacán: Teopancazco*. Mexico: Dirección General de Asuntos del Personal Académico, Instituto de Investigaciones Antropológicas de la Universidad Nacional Autónoma de México.

Manzanilla, L. R. (1993). Introducción. In L. Manzanilla, ed., *Anatomía de un conjunto residencial teotihuacano en Oztoyahualco. I. Las excavaciones*. Mexico: Instituto de Investigaciones Antropológicas, Universidad Nacional Autónoma de México, 15–30.

Manzanilla, L. R. (2015). Cooperation and tensions in multiethnic corporate societies using Teotihuacán, Central Mexico, as a case study. *Proceedings of the National Academy of Sciences of the United States of America*, **112**(30), 9210–9215.

Manzanilla, L. R. (2016). *Los secretos de Teotihuacán*. *Capítulo 4*. Mexico: TV UNAM Available at: www .youtube.com/watch?v=l9C9Bv2ZIWM

Manzanilla, L. R. (2017a). *Teotihuacán. Ciudad excepcional de Mesoamérica*. Mexico: Opúsculos, El Colegio Nacional.

Manzanilla, L. R. (2017b). The Xalla Palace in Teotihuacan. In M. Robb, ed., *Teotihuacan, City of Water, City of Fire*. Los Angeles: Fine Arts Museums of San Francisco de Young y University of California Press, 118–123.

Manzanilla, L. R., Rodríguez, B., Pérez, G., & Valadez, R. (2011). Arqueozoología y manufactura de vestimentas rituales en la antigua ciudad de Teotihuacán, México. *Arqueología*, **17**, 221–246.

Marcus, J. (1983). Teotihuacán visitors on Monte Albán monuments and murals. In K. V. Flannery, & J. Marcus, eds. *The Cloud People. Divergent Evolution of the Zapotec and Mixtec Civilizations*. New York: Academic Press, 175–181.

Marcus, J. (1998). *Women's Ritual in Formative Oaxaca. Figurine-Making, Divination, Death and the Ancestors*. Ann Harbor: Memoirs of the Museum of Anthropology University of Michigan, Number 33.

Marcus, J. (2008). *Monte Albán*. Mexico: Colegio de México and Fondo de Cultura Económica.

Marquina, I. (1972). Influencia de Teotihuacán en Cholula. In Anonymous, ed., *Teotihuacán. XI Mesa redonda*. Mexico: Sociedad Mexicana de Antropología, 241–243.

Matos-Moctezuma, E. (1990). *Teotihuacán. La metrópolis de los dioses*. Madrid: Lunwerg Editores S.A.

Matos-Moctezuma, E. (2009). *Teotihuacán*. Mexico: Colegio de México and Fondo de Cultura Económica.

Matos-Moctezuma, E. (2017). *Historia de la arqueología del México antiguo I*. Mexico: El Colegio Nacional.

Meza-Peñaloza, A. (2015). *Afinidades biológicas y contextos culturales en los antiguos teotihuacanos*. México: Instituto de Investigaciones Antropológicas-Universidad Nacional Autónoma de México.

Miller, A. G. (1973). *The Mural Paintings of Teotihuacan*. Washington: Harvard-Dumbarton Oaks.

Moholy-Nagy, H. (2004). Vertebrates in Tikal burials and caches. In K. F. Emery, ed., *Maya Zooarchaeology: New Directions in Method and Theory*. Los Angeles: University of California at Los Angeles, 193–222.

Nájera-Coronado, M. I. (2012). El mono y el cacao: La búsqueda de un mito a través de los relieves del grupo de la serie inicial de Chichén Itzá. *Estudios de Cultura Maya*, **29**, 133–172.

Nájera-Coronado, M. I. (2013). Un acercamiento al simbolismo del simio entre los grupos mayas. In L. Millones, & A. López-Austin, eds., *Fauna fantástica de Mesoamérica y los Andes*. Mexico: Instituto de Investigaciones Antropológicas, Universidad Nacional Autónoma de México, 211–252.

Nájera-Coronado, M. I. (2015). *Dioses y seres de viento en los antiguos maya*. Mexico: Instituto de Investigaciones Filológicas-Universidad Nacional Autónoma de México.

Nájera-Coronado, M. I. (2016). El mono y el cacao: a la búsqueda de un mito. In M. H. Ruz-Sosa, eds.,*Kakaw, oro aromado. De las cortes mayas a las europeas*. Mexico: Instituto de Investigaciones Filológicas-Universidad Nacional Autónoma de México.

Noguera, E. (1965). *La cerámica arqueológica de Mesoamérica*. Mexico: Universidad Nacional Autónoma de México.

O'Neil, M E. (2018). *Forces of Nature: Ancient Maya Arts from the Los Angeles County Museum of Art*. Beijing: Shenzhen Museum-LACMA.

Ortiz-Maciel, D., & Serrano-Rojas, G. (2016). Exposición "John Paddock y la identificación del estilo ñuiñe. Indagaciones en el pasado de la Mixteca Baja." Oaxaca: Fundación Alfredo Harp Helú. Available at: http://fahho.mx/blog/2016/09/07/exposicion-john-paddock-y-la-identificacion-del-estilo-nuine-inda gaciones-en-el-pasado-de-la-mixteca-baja/ (Accessed June 5, 2018)

Ortiz-Martínez, T., & Rico-Gray, V. (2005). Monos araña (*Ateles geoffroyi*) habitando una selva baja caducifolia en el distrito de Tehuantepec, Oaxaca Mexico. *Programa y libro de resúmenes del II Congreso Mexicano de Primatología*: n/p.

Paz-Avendaño, R. (2019). Hallan restos de mono araña en una ofrenda de Teotihuacán. *La Crónica Diaria* (crónica.com.mx). Available at: www.cronica.com .mx/notas-hallan_restos_de_mono_arana_en_una_ ofrenda_de_teotihuacan-1122246-2019

Paddock, J. (1972). Distribución de rasgos teotihuacanos en Mesoamérica. In Anonymous, ed., *Teotihuacán. XI mesa redonda*. Mexico: Sociedad Mexicana de Antropología, 223–239.

Pérez, G. (2005). El estudio de la industria del hueso trabajado: Xalla, un caso teotihuacano. Honor thesis, Escuela Nacional de Antropología e Historia.

Peterson, J. F. (1994). *Sacred Gifts: Precolumbian Art and Creativity*. Santa Barbara: Santa Barbara Museum of Art.

Piña-Chan, R. (1993). *El lenguaje de las piedras. Glífica olmeca y zapoteca*. Mexico: Fondo de Cultura Económica.

Pohl, M. D. (1976). Ethnozoology of the Maya: An analysis of fauna from five sites in the Peten, Guatemala. PhD thesis, Harvard University.

Pohl, M. D. (2004). The ethnozoology of the Maya: Faunal remains from five sites in Peten, Guatemala. In G. R. Willey, ed., *Excavations at Seibal. Department of Peten, Guatemala*. Cambridge, MA: Peabody Museum of Archaeology and Ethnology, 143–174.

Preuss, K. T. (1901). Der Affe in der mexikanischen Mythologie. *Ethnologisches Notizblatt*, **2**, 66–76.

Rice, P. M., & South, K. E. (2015). Revisiting monkeys on pots: a contextual consideration of primate imagery on classic lowland Maya pottery. *Ancient Mesoamerica*, **26**(2), 275–294.

Rivera-Dorado, M. (1969). Las figuritas teotihuacanas y la colección del Museo Antonio Ballesteros. *Revista de Antropología Americana*, **4**, 93–111.

Rodríguez, B. (2002). *Fauna del proyecto Xalla 2001–2002*. Unpublished report, Instituto de Investigaciones Antropológicas de la Universidad Nacional Autónoma de México.

Rodríguez, B. (2006). El uso diferencial del recurso faunístico en Teopancazco, y su importancia en las áreas de actividad. Master's thesis, Universidad Nacional Autónoma de México.

Rodríguez, B. (2010). Captura, preparación y uso diferencial de la ictiofauna encontrada en el sitio arqueológico de Teopancazco, Teotihuacán. PhD thesis, Universidad Nacional Autónoma de México.

Rodríguez, B. (2017). Capítulo 4. Los recursos animales costeros. In L. Manzanilla, ed., & R. Valadez, (coord.) *El uso de los recursos naturales en un centro de barrio de Teotihuacán: Teopancazco*. Mexico: Dirección General de Asuntos del Personal Académico, Instituto de Investigaciones Antropológicas de la Universidad Nacional Autónoma de México, 185–273.

Rodríguez, B., & Valadez, R. (2014). Recursos Costeros en la Ciudad de los Dioses. In Ch. Götz, & K. Emery, eds., *La arqueología de los animales de Mesoamérica*. Atlanta: Lockwood Press, 51–82.

Ruiz-Gallut, M. A. (1999). Teotihuacán a través de sus imágenes pintadas. In B. De la Fuente, ed., *Pintura mural prehispánica*. Barcelona: Lunweg Editores, 41–66.

Ruiz-Gallut, M. E. (2002). Imágenes de Tetitla: De disfraces y vecinos. In M. E. Ruiz-Gallut, ed., *Ideología y política a través de materiales, imágenes y símbolos. Memoria de la Primera Mesa Redonda de Teotihuacán*. Mexico: Universidad Nacional Autónoma de México and Instituto Nacional de Antropología e Historia, 315–329.

Salinas-Cesáreo, J. (2018). Descubren en Teotihuacán cuatro grandes depósitos arqueológicos. *Periódico La Jornada*, Sept. 22, p. 2. Available at: www.jornada .com.mx/2018/09/22/cultura/a02n1cul

Scott, S. (2005). *Las figurillas de terracota de las excavaciones de Sigvald Linné en Teotihuacán*. Mexico: Foundation for the Advancement of Mesoamerican Studies, Inc.

Séjourné, L. (1959). *Un palacio en la ciudad de los dioses. Exploraciones en Teotihuacán, 1955–1958*. Mexico: Instituto Nacional de Antropología e Historia.

Séjourné, L. (1966a). *Arquitectura y pintura en Teotihuacán*. Mexico: Editorial Siglo XXI.

Séjourné, L. (1966b). *Arqueología de Teotihuacán. La cerámica*. Mexico: Fondo de Cultura Económica.

Séjourné, L. (1966c). *El lenguaje de las formas*. Mexico: Editorial Siglo XXI.

Serrano-Sánchez, C., Rivero de La Calle, M., & Yépez-Vázquez, R. (2003). La deformación cefálica intencional en los habitantes prehispánicos del barrio teotihuacano de La Ventilla. In C. Serrano-Sánchez, ed., *Contextos arqueológicos y osteología del barrio de*

La Ventilla (Teotihuacán (1992–1994). Mexico: Instituto de Investigaciones Antropológicas, Universidad Nacional Autónoma de México, 103–113.

Solís, F. (2009). *Teotihuacan, Cite des Dieux*. Paris: Somogy éditions d'art.

South, K. E. (2005). Monkeying around the Maya region: A four-field look at primate iconography and the Maya. Master's thesis, Southern Illinois University.

Starbuck, D. R. (1987). Faunal evidence for the Teotihuacan subsistence base. In E. McClung de Tapia, & E. Childs-Rattray, eds., *Teotihuacán. Nuevos datos, nuevas síntesis, nuevos problemas*. Mexico: Instituto de Investigaciones Antropológicas, Universidad Nacional Autónoma de México, 76–90.

Sugiyama, N. (2014). Animals and sacred mountains; How ritualized performances materialized state ideologies at Teotihuacan, Mexico. PhD thesis, Harvard University.

Sugiyama, N., Pérez, G., Rodríguez, B., Torres, F., & Valadez, R. (2014). Animals and the State: The Role of Animals in State-Level Rituals in Mesoamerica. In B. S. Arbuckle, & S. A. McCarty, eds. *Animals and Inequality in the Ancient World*. Boulder: University Press of Colorado, 11–13.

Sugiyama, N., Somerville, A. D., & Schoeninger, M. J. (2015). Stable isotopes and zooarchaeology at Teotihuacan, Mexico reveal earliest evidence of wild carnivore management in Mesoamerica. *PLoS ONE*, 10(9), e0135635.

Sugiyama, N., Valadez, R., & Rodríguez, B. (2017). Faunal acquisition, maintenance, and consumption: how the Teotihuacanos got their meat. *Archaeological and Anthropological Sciences*, **9**, 61–82.

Sugiyama, S., & Cabrera-Castro, R. (2004). *Voyage to the Center of the Moon Pyramid. Recent Discoveries in Teotihuacán*. Mexico: CONACULTURA-IHAH and Arizona State University.

Sugiyama, S., & López-Lujan, L. (2006a). Sacrificios de consagración en la Pirámide de la Luna. In S. Sugiyama, & L. López-Lujan, eds., *Sacrificios de consagración en la pirámide de la Luna*. Mexico City: CONACULTURA-INAH, 25–52.

Sugiyama, S., & López-Luján, L. (2006b). Simbolismo y función de los entierros dedicatorios de la Pirámide de la Luna en Teotihuacán. In L. López-Luján, D. Carrasco, & L. Cué, eds., *Arqueología e historia del centro de México: Homenaje a E. Matos Moctezuma*. Mexico City: Instituto Nacional de Antropología e Historia, 131–151.

Sullivan, K. (2007). *Haciendo y manipulando el ritual en la ciudad de los dioses: producción y uso de figurillas en Teotihuacán*. Mexico: Foundation for the Advancement of Mesoamerican Studies, Inc.

Taube, K. A. (2004). Tetitla and the Maya presence at Teotihuacan. In G. E. Braswell, ed., *The Maya and Teotihuacan. Reinterpreting Early Classic Interaction*. Austin: University of Texas Press, 273–314.

Urbani, B. (2013). Arqueoprimatología: Reflexión sobre una disciplina y dos localidades antropoespeleológicas venezolanas. *Boletín de la Sociedad Venezolana de Espeleología*, **45**, 66–68.

Valadez, R. (1992). Impacto del recurso faunístico en la sociedad teotihuacana, PhD thesis, Universidad Nacional Autónoma de México.

Valadez, R. (1993). Macrofósiles faunísticos. In L. Manzanilla, ed., *Anatomía de un conjunto residencial teotihuacano en Oztoyohualco, Vol. II*. Mexico: Instituto de Investigaciones Antropológicas de la Universidad Nacional Autónoma de México, 729–813.

Valadez, R. (2014). Monos y jaguares en el universo prehispánico. In A. Sandoval-Hoffmann, A. Sandoval-Martínez, & L. I. Saínz, (coord.), *Los artistas responsables en defensa de la fauna*. Mexico: Vínculos, Comunidad y Cultura A.C., 296–321.

Valadez R., & Childs-Rattray, E. (1993). Restos arqueológicos relacionados con primates encontrados en la antigua ciudad de Teotihuacán. In A. Estrada, E. Rodriguez-Luna, R. Lopez-Wilchis, & R. Coates-Estrada, eds., *Estudios Primatológicos en México, Vol. 1*. Mexico: Biblioteca Universidad Veracruzana, 215–232.

Valadez, R., & Ortiz, E. (1993). Apéndice 2. Representaciones zoomorfas en algunos objetos arqueológicos de Oztoyohualco. In L. Manzanilla, ed., *Anatomía de un conjunto residencial teotihuacano en Oztoyohualco, Vol. II*. Mexico: Instituto de Investigaciones Antropológicas de la Universidad Nacional Autónoma de México, 826–831.

Valadez, R., Rodríguez, B., Cabrera, R., Cowgill, G., & Sugiyama, S. (2002). Híbridos de lobos y perros (tercer acto): hallazgos en la pirámide de Quetzalcoatl de la antigua ciudad de Teotihuacán. *Revista de la Asociación Mexicana de Médicos Veterinarios Especialistas en Pequeñas Especies*, **13**(5–6), 165–176, 219–231.

Valadez, R., Rodríguez, B. Christian, J., & Silva. A. F. (2017). Arqueofauna de Teopancazco, dinámicas de uso y cambios en el tiempo. In L. Manzanilla, & R. Valadez, eds., *El uso de los recursos naturales en un centro de barrio de Teotihuacán: Teopancazco*. Mexico: Dirección General de Asuntos del Personal Académico, Instituto de Investigaciones Antropológicas de la Universidad Nacional Autónoma de México, 39–130.

Vargas, E. (1978). Transición del Clásico al Postclásico a través de Ojo de Agua y Teotenango. Honor thesis, Escuela Nacional de Antropología e Historia.

Webb, M. C. (1978). The significance of the 'Epiclassic' period in Mesoamerican prehistory. In D. I. Browman, ed., *Cultural Continuity in Mesoamerica*. The Hague: Mouton Publishing, 155–178.

Wiesheu, W. (2014). La zona oaxaqueña en el preclásico. In L. Manzanilla, & L. López, (coord.) *Historia antigua de México. Volumen I, en México antiguo, sus áreas culturales, los orígenes y el horizonte Preclásico*. Mexico: Editorial Porrúa, CONACULTURA, Instituto Nacional de Antropología e Historia, and Instituto de Investigaciones Antropológicas de la Universidad Nacional Autónoma de México, 407–136.

Winter, M., Martínez-López, C., & Herrera-Muzgo T. A. (2002). Monte Albán y Teotihuacán: Política e ideología. In M. E. Ruiz-Gallut, ed., *Ideología y política a través de materiales, imágenes y símbolos. Memoria de la Primera Mesa Redonda de Teotihuacán*. Mexico: Universidad Nacional Autónoma de México and Instituto Nacional de Antropología e Historia, 627–644.

2 Monkeys and the Ancient Maya

Using Biological Markers and Behavior for Primate Species Identification in Maya Iconography

Katherine E. South & Susan M. Ford

Los monos y los antiguos mayas: Uso de marcadores biológicos y comportamentales para la identificación de especies de primates en la iconografía maya

Resumen

Comprender cómo una cultura clasifica y asigna significado a la naturaleza puede proporcionar información clave sobre esa cultura. Los antiguos mayas usaban imágenes de monos de muchas maneras. Este estudio explora si las especies individuales de monos pueden identificarse en las imágenes mayas y, de ser así, si los mayas usaron imágenes de diferentes especies de maneras únicas y separadas o asociadas con diferentes actividades «humanas». Identificamos nueve características que podrían discriminar entre los tres géneros encontrados en el área Maya (*Alouatta*, *Ateles* y *Cebus*) y obtuvimos 106 imágenes de primates de cerámica maya. La mayoría de las imágenes fueron identificables como *Ateles* (65%), 9% identificables como *Alouatta*, y algunas identificadas tentativamente como *Cebus*, habiendo un 22% de monos genéricos no identificados. *Ateles* se asociaron más con la actuación, el baile y el manejo del cacao, mientras que *Alouatta* se representó más en las actividades de los escribanos. Los resultados indican que los mayas distinguieron entre los géneros en niveles simbólicos, asociándolos con diferentes comportamientos y actividades.

Palabras clave

Interacción humanos-primates no-humano – Maya – simbolismo de primates – platirrinos – Mesoamérica – Neotrópico

Abstract

Understanding how a culture classifies and assigns meaning to nature can provide key insight into that culture. The ancient Maya used images of monkeys in many ways. This study tests whether individual species of monkeys can be identified in Maya imagery and, if so, whether the Maya used images of different species in unique and separate ways or associated with different "human" activities. We identified nine features that could discriminate between the three genera found in the Maya area (*Alouatta*, *Ateles*, and *Cebus*) and scored 106 primate images from Maya pottery. Most images were identifiable as *Ateles* (65%) with 9% identifiable as *Alouatta*, a few tentatively identified as *Cebus*, and 22% unidentified generic monkeys. *Ateles* were associated more with performance, dancing, and cacao handling, while *Alouatta* were depicted more in scribal activities. Results indicate that the Maya distinguished between the genera on symbolic levels, associating them with different behaviors and activities.

Keywords: Human–nonhuman primate interaction, Maya, Primate symbolism, Platyrrhine, Mesoamerica, Neotropics

2.1   Introduction

Iconographic elements and primate imagery provide important clues in understanding the ways primates were viewed by the ancient Maya. When the individual species can be identified, this information is critical in considering how people classified and assigned meaning to what they encountered in nature. The ancient Maya inhabited a region that extends from what is presently southern Mexico, just east of the Isthmus of Tehuantepec, into the western sections of El Salvador and Honduras (Sharer and Traxler, 2006). There are three species of monkeys currently found throughout the Maya region: *Alouatta pigra* (the Yucatán black howler), *Alouatta palliata* (the mantled howler), and *Ateles geoffroyi* (the black-handed spider monkey) (see Fig. 2.1). In addition, *Cebus capucinus* (the white-faced capuchin) ranges just to the south of the Maya region, encroaching slightly in a southeastern corner of known Maya area (Rylands et al., 2006) (see Fig. 2.2). This study tests whether specific monkey taxa can be identified in Maya imagery from the Classic period and whether different monkey taxa are associated with different types of activities in these images.

Contact between the Maya and primates is well documented within the archaeological, ethnographic, and linguistic records. Direct evidence of monkeys is comparatively rare in the archaeological record of the Maya region, with as few as ten primate skeletons identified in published reports (Boileau et al., 2020; Emery, 2007). As a result, what we know about primate symbolism in the prehistoric Maya world is limited to images left primarily on Classic period pottery vessels and portable carvings. These small-scale media frequently displayed mythological episodes that, unlike larger-scale monumental art at the time, directly connected the viewer to mythical figures (Mazariegos, 2017). The frequency of monkey representations suggests that the animals were meaningful members of the Maya symbol set; however, their cultural meaning is not spelled out in the surviving codices. Monkeys play roles

Figure 2.1 (a) *Alouatta pigra* (photograph by Chris Wolf); (b) *Ateles geoffroyi* (photograph by Michelle Raponi), and (c) *Cebus capucinus* (photograph by Michelle Raponi). All photographs are sourced from Pixabay.com (Public Domain-Pixabay License).

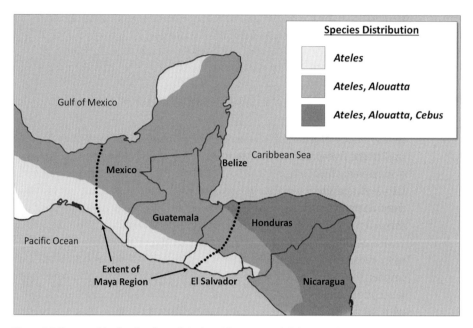

Figure 2.2 Geographic distribution of *Ateles*, *Alouatta*, and *Cebus* in relation to the Maya culture area (set off by dotted lines). Map by Nate Meissner.

in many of the different creation stories told by Maya cultural groups, and they played important roles in the *Popol Vuh*, the K'iche' creation story (Coe, 1973, 1977; Thompson 1970). In this story, the Hero Twins transform their unpleasant older brothers into monkeys, stranding the brothers in tall trees and transforming their dangling loin cloths into tails (see Tedlock, 1985). The brothers (now monkeys) became recognized as patrons of the arts and music, as the brothers were apparently flautists, singers, writers, carvers, jewelers, and crafters (Coe, 1977; see also Benson, 1994). A repeated theme of monkeys being flawed relatives or precursors to human beings is found among modern Maya, including the Mam Maya of Santiago Chimaltenango, Guatemala (Thompson, 1970), and the Chamula (Gossen, 1974) and Zinacantán (Hunt, 1977) of Chiapas, Mexico. Other Mesoamerican stories portray monkeys as survivors of catastrophic events, including great floods and windstorms (Benson, 1994; Bricker, 1973; Nicholson and Quiñones Keber, 1983; Perera and Bruce, 1985; Thompson, 1970).

Many discussions about monkeys in Maya culture highlight the role of the monkey as a scribe (Baker, 1992; Benson, 1994; Coe, 1977, 1982; Mock, 1997; Milbrath, 1999; Ringle, 1988; Schele and Miller, 1986). Painted pottery from the Late Classic period provides examples of monkey scribes with their toolkit of scribal accessories. Although humans and rabbits are also depicted as scribes, monkeys are commonly shown associated with the act of writing (Miller and Taube, 1997). Monkey characters tend to be shown with a stylized deer's ear in place of the regular ear and/or a set of three spots on the cheek (Coe, 1977; Milbrath, 1999; Miller and Taube, 1997). The deer's ear element is seen on both human and monkey scribes, leading Coe (1977) to suggest it is diagnostic of scribes. Other scribal accessories include inkpots, pens, codices in hand, a "folded napkin" headdress, a sacrificial scarf tied around the shoulders or neck, and "death collars" sometimes decorated with disembodied eyes (Benson, 1994; Coe, 1977; Reents-Budet, 1994).

Modern Maya groups portray monkeys as dancers, usually in ritual events and festivals. Men in Chiapas, Mexico, dress in monkey costumes and include military items to evoke warrior images (Benson, 1994; Bricker, 1973; LaFarge and Byers, 1931). In the village of Chamula, "monkey" dancers fight battles (Morris, 1987). There is a traditional five-day period at the end of the year corresponding to the five "lost days" occurring each year in the Maya calendar, which in Chiapas is celebrated as a *fiesta* of Carnival and characterized by drunkenness, licentiousness, and obscenity, freedom from normative behavior. In Chamula, it is the monkeys that take over the earth for these five days, and there are portrayals of monkeys as licentious and lascivious creatures, often jokingly threatening to seize people by wrapping them in their costume tails, partaking in debauchery, and making sexual advances at women (Bricker, 1973). Bricker (1973) argued the Chamula Maya behavior during Carnival typifies their perception of monkeys as being pleasure-seeking clowns, and it also serves as a social warning about uncontrolled behavior that falls outside cultural norms.

In addition to playing roles in the arts and ritual activity, monkeys are also associated with Underworld imagery. From the ethnographic record, the Zinacantán of Chiapas believe that the Underworld is inhabited by monkeys and other products of failed attempts to make human beings (Vogt, 1976). This association with the Underworld is also referenced in the archaeological record, where monkeys are depicted as passengers or escorts on the journey into the Underworld (Schele and Miller, 1986). The link between monkeys and death is often depicted in quite literal images, with monkeys associated with the act of death and sacrifice. Monkeys are frequently shown with death symbols, including a scarf associated with sacrifice by decapitation, paper wristlets and anklets, and death-eye collars (Benson, 1994). This association with death can also be understood through the Maya cosmic diagram, in which the sun's rising and setting is analogous to birth and death. Monkeys are often connected to the sun, moon, and various planets such as Mars and Jupiter (Bruce, 1979; Milbrath, 1999; Tedlock, 1985). Monkeys directly represent a celestial body in some cases but are simply companions in others. According to Milbrath (1999), howler monkeys may be tied to the Morning Star, which is visible before dawn. This association may reflect the behavior of the animals, which tend to emit loud calls to one another in the early hours of morning. Spider monkeys may take a role that is similar to the sun but only as a substitute for it after it sets; therefore, the count of days for the spider monkey symbol would begin at dusk.

Hieroglyphs representing monkeys have been found in both inscriptions and calendars (Ringle, 1988; Stross, 2008). Logograms depicting a monkey head appear throughout the span of the Maya writing system, attesting to its embeddedness in language use (Ringle, 1988). Contextually, the monkey-head variants are associated with *k'ul* (Yukatek) and *ch'ul* (Ch'olan), translated as "holy," "sacred," or "divine" (Milbrath, 1999; Ringle, 1988). The monkey-head variant is also found within Maya calendar inscriptions that reference information about lunar phases or dusk (referred to as "the monkey's moon"), leading Ringle (1988) to posit that these head variants depict spider monkeys. Linguistically, modern Mayan language groups distinguish between howler monkeys (*batz'*) and spider monkeys (*maax*), and the earliest Mayan language groups contain glosses for both howler and spider monkeys (Coe, 1977; Kaufman and Norman, 1984; Milbrath, 1999; Ringle, 1988; Stross, 2008). This indicates an acknowledged separation between the two species of monkey early in Mayan language development.

The abundance of primate symbols in both the Maya past and present reinforces the notion that the Maya have been interacting with their primate neighbors for thousands of years, observing them and incorporating them into their mythological, linguistic, and artistic traditions. However, past work on Maya monkey images has lumped them into a single "monkey" category or simply assumed a species with little biological justification (e.g. Baker, 1992; Coe, 1973, 1977).

Comparing the physical features of monkey images to the diagnostic characteristics of each species may provide insight into which attributes were significant to cultural groups. Many studies of animal representations discuss the animal image aesthetically, but few venture into biological correlates between the artistic representation and the real, living animal (see Saunders, 1994, 1998). In this study, we tested whether specific monkey taxa are identifiable in Maya imagery and, when they are, if specific monkey taxa are associated with specific types of behaviors, generally human-type behaviors (such as scribal or dancing/performance activities). We examined both the physical features of the monkey images and the attributes associated with them within the scene, comparing design features to the known characteristics of monkey species found in the region. If the Maya did indeed distinguish between species, one would expect this to be reflected in the monkey images that are illustrated on high-status items such as polychrome painted pottery, which were the source of images examined here.

2.2   Materials and Methods

Diagnostic attributes of each genus known in or near the Maya area that might be visible in Maya imagery were identified, including pelage color and features, hand morphology, facial markings, limb length and proportion, tail length, positional behavior, and facial prognathism. No features that might discriminate between the two species of howler monkeys in pottery images were identified.

Alouatta has a smaller body size than *Ateles* and shows marked sexual dimorphism (Kinzey, 1997; Nisbett, 1995). Morphologically, howler monkeys have extended hyoid bones to enable their distinctive call, low foreheads, and the most prognathic faces of the three genera discussed here (Baker, 1992; Kinzey, 1997). While all three genera have prehensile tails, *Alouatta* largely uses it for support during suspension (Bergeson, 1996; Emmons and Feer, 1997). The highly folivorous diet of howlers requires elongated colons and a slow rate of food passage. As a result, howlers have more restricted day ranges and tend to prefer rest using hunched sitting postures for up to 75% of the day (Bergeson, 1996; Chapman, 1988; Nisbett, 1995). Both *Alouatta pigra* and *Alouatta palliata* have dark bodies with paler bellies and dark masks around the eyes; their heavier hair surrounding a naked face lends the appearance of a beard (Baker, 1992). *Alouatta palliata* exhibits a fringe or saddle of yellow, brown, or buff hair on its lower back (Emmons and Feer, 1997; Rylands et al., 2006).

Ateles geoffroyi is characterized by long and thin limbs, flexible shoulders, elongated tails, and a protruding belly, and their hands have curved, elongated fingers with a vestigial thumb, giving a hook-like appearance (Bergeson, 1996; Cant, 1986; Eisenberg and Kuehn, 1966). Spider monkeys have a more frugivorous diet and spend more time actively moving through their day ranges (Cant, 1986; Strier, 1992). They are forelimb-dominated climbers that frequently use suspensory positions and brachiation for locomotion, as well as bridging, leaping, and inverted bipedal postures (Bergeson, 1996). Spider monkeys use their prehensile tails to grip supports both during locomotion and to aid in suspension while foraging for fruit on terminal branches (Bergeson, 1996; Cant, 1986). Spider monkeys in the Maya area have dark dorsal areas and white, pale brown, or buff underparts on the abdomen, forearms, lower legs, and feet, and a distinctive pale mask of light skin surrounding the eyes and nose (Emmons and Feer, 1997).

Cebus capucinus has a current range largely outside the boundaries of the Maya region but only marginally. Rylands et al. (2006) report that there are no records of capuchin monkeys in Mexico or El Salvador, but there are unconfirmed reports of capuchins being seen in both southern Belize and northeastern Guatemala. Capuchins are much smaller than both howler and spider monkeys (approximately a third to a fourth the size), and they are sexually dimorphic (Emmons and Feer, 1997). They have pseudo-opposable thumbs on their hands and prehensile tails that they tend to hold curled over their bodies. *Cebus capucinus* has a distinctive appearance, with a black body except for the neck, shoulders, and upper arms, which are white or buff; the head is yellow with a black, V-shaped cap on the crown (Emmons and Feer, 1997).

Maya imagery of primates generally has few detailed features and is not carefully realistic, with primates often anthropomorphized to some extent. The most distinctive features in images include pelage color patterns, skull shape, limb length, presence or absence of a beard, hand morphology, and tail length. Each of the three primate genera has some distinguishing traits for one or more of these attributes (see Table 2.1). Additionally, posture and locomotor behavior may be good indicators of species identity: *Alouatta* often sits in a hunched position; *Ateles* frequently uses suspensory postures and often uses the prehensile tail for support during both postures and locomotor behavior; and *Cebus* often coils its prehensile tail over its back in both postures and locomotion. These are all examples of attributes that can be seen in illustrations.

Using both painted and incised images on Maya pottery dating largely to the Classic period (250–800 CE), we identified the species depicted, when possible, by scoring whether diagnostic attributes were discernible on the monkey images. The pottery images in this study were collected from multiple sources, including the Maya

Table 2.1. Diagnostic attributes of primate genera in the Maya region

Attribute	Alouatta	Ateles	Cebus
Black head cap			X
Pale face mask		X	
Pronounced facial prognathism	X		
Beard	X		
Pale underbelly		X	
Pseudo-opposable thumb			X
Elongated limbs, esp. forelimb		X	
Elongated tail		X	
Extended positional behavior / suspension		X	
Body hunched, sitting	X		
Tail coiled over back			X

Table 2.2. Image sources used in the study

Maya Vase Database Kerr Images		Other Image Sources
K0505	K3637	ADS001 (Adams, 1971; fig. 34d)
K0626	K4947	CLH001 (Mock, 1997; fig. 4)
K0774	K4963	CLH002 (Mock, 1997; fig. 7)
K1180	K4992	CLH003 (Mock, 1997; fig. 8)
K1181	K5010	CLH004 (Mock, 1997; fig. 9)
K1203	K5070	CLH005 (Mock, 1997; fig. 10)
K1208	K5744	RB001 (Reents-Budet, 1994; fig. 6.7)
K1211	K6738	TIK001 (Culbert, 1993; PD. 134c)
K1491	K6765	TIK002 (Culbert, 1993; PD. 134d)
K1558	K7007	TOP001 (Wurster, 2000; fig. 151)
K1809	K7152	UAX001 (Smith, 1955; fig. 2f)
K1811	K7525	UAX003 (Smith, 1955; fig. 11)
K2010	K7993	
K2249	K8234	
K3038	K8575	
K3060	K8640	
K3413	K8733	
K3433		

Vase Database sponsored by the Foundation for the Advancement of Mesoamerican Studies, Inc. (FAMSI) and published excavation reports (see Table 2.2). The sample is a total of 106 separate primate images. After assigning a species identification when possible, the associated behaviors of the monkey images were also recorded. Behaviors were initially described in detail but were later lumped in the following four categories for analysis: "scribal activity," "ritual activities associated with offerings," "processions often incorporating dancing and musical instruments," and the "handling of cacao pods," this last appearing as a unique set of behaviors not readily grouped into the others. A full presentation of the details of analysis as well as the images analyzed is presented in South (2005; see also Rice and South, 2015). Possible correlations between monkey species and specific behaviors were examined using chi-square correlations.

2.3   Results

The majority of monkey images (65%) were identified as spider monkeys (*Ateles*) (see Fig. 2.3). These identifications were largely based on the presence of pale face masks and pale undersides. Limb and tail proportions were also recorded based on body proportion, but pelage markings were the most reliable physical attribute. Of the remaining monkey images, 9% were identified as howler monkeys *(Alouatta)*, 4% were very tentatively identified as capuchins *(Cebus)* (see Fig. 2.4), and the remaining 22% were unknown/generic "monkey" (see Fig. 2.5).

Behaviors associated with the primate images were grouped into four broad categories: scribal activities, ritual activities associated with offerings, processions often incorporating dancing and musical instruments, and the handling of cacao pods. Chi square (χ^2) testing indicated that statistically significant associations exist between scribal activities and howler monkeys and also between spider monkeys and rituals, processions with dancing and instruments, and cacao handling ($p = 0.0003$) (see Fig. 2.6). These results suggest that different behavioral patterns were assigned to the different genera by the Maya, perhaps as a reflection of observed behaviors characteristic of each. Activity levels of each species may be an important contributing factor in these behavioral choices, particularly the more lethargic habits of the

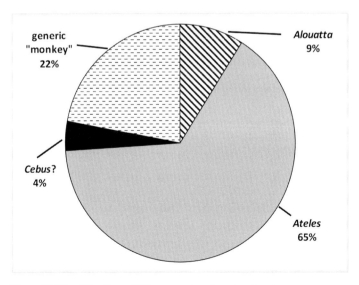

Figure 2.3 Identification of Maya monkey imagery by genus.

Figure 2.4 Primate images tentatively identified as *Cebus capucinus*: (a) crouching monkey with compact body, pale abdomen, and round head gestures to possible codex while wearing headdress, wristlets, and anklets (K0626); (b) central, adorned figure in procession with compact body, capped marking on forehead, and tail curling toward monkey's back (K1211); (c) two seated monkeys in profile, pale faces, black capped pattern on head, holding possible shells and balancing tail bundles (K8640). Images by Justin Kerr-Public Domain.

folivorous howlers (see Fig. 2.7) as opposed to the more energetic, frugivorous spider monkeys (see Figs. 2.8 and 2.9).

2.4   Conclusions

Contrary to prior work, it is apparent that Maya images do often clearly differentiate between primate genera. In the majority of cases, genus identification was primarily based on pelage features. The majority of images (65%) were identified as *Ateles geoffroyi* (black-handed spider monkeys). The two howler monkey species present in the region, *Alouatta pigra* and *Alouatta palliata*, could not be differentiated in Maya imagery, but "howler monkeys" (*Alouatta)* were clearly identifiable in 9% of the

Figure 2.5 Unidentified or generic primate images: (a) seated monkeys with pale bodies and dark faces showing little prognathism, wearing bracelets, and carrying jars and tail bundles (K8642); (b) seated monkey without adornment, arms and legs splayed, pronounced thumbs on both hands (K4599); (c) squatting monkey in upper register with fully pale head in profile, wears wristlet and other unidentified adornments (K1491). Images by Justin Kerr-Public Domain.

images examined. The remaining images were generic, with only a few (4%) very tentatively identified as possibly capuchins (*Cebus capucinus*). Many monkey images were humanized greatly, increasing the difficulty of identifying the possible underlying monkey model.

With the identification of the genus of monkey in Maya images (particularly as a spider or howler monkey), for the first time, it became possible to examine if the

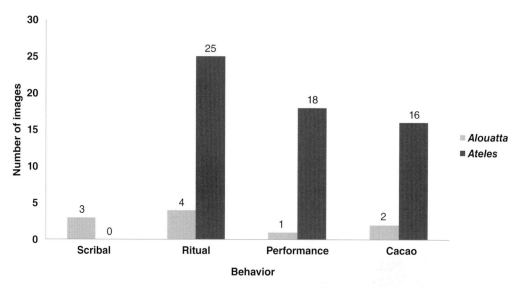

Figure 2.6 Association of behaviors with identified genus (*n = 106*).

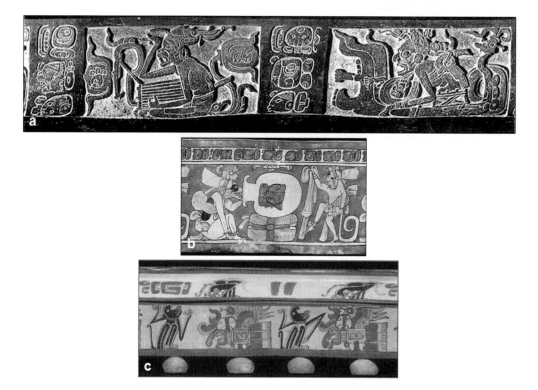

Figure 2.7 Primate images identified as *Alouatta*: (a) seated scribe with facial prognathism, hunched over an open codex and wearing a deer's ear (K0954); (b) dancing "Monkey-Man" figure with facial prognathism and short beard, wearing "napkin" headdress and other accessories, carrying scarf (K0505); (c) abstract seated monkeys with black faces, elongated arms gesturing (K6765). Images by Justin Kerr-Public Domain.

Figure 2.8 Primate images identified as *Ateles geoffroyi*: (a) seated monkey wearing a scarf, a deer's ear, and a tail bundle while holding a turtle shell drum (K1181); (b) dancing monkey wearing a collar (K1208); (c) repeated monkeys in motion surrounded by stylized cacao pods (K8234). Images by Justin Kerr-Public Domain.

Maya used particular monkeys in different contexts. The different settings, behaviors, and associations with howler and spider monkeys were statistically significant. Howler monkeys were more frequently used in association with scribal attributes such as pens, codices, and the deer's ear, while spider monkeys were not found in these iconographic contexts. Although howler monkeys were also depicted in ritual settings associated with offerings, spider monkeys were shown more than five times as often in ritual settings, the most frequent setting for spider monkeys. In addition, spider monkeys were used far more frequently than howler monkeys in performance-related scenes and in processions, including dancing and holding objects such as musical instruments, and also in situations where they are holding or handling cacao pods. They frequently wore accessories associated with death, including sacrificial scarves, death-eye collars, and offering bundles that contained long bones, hands, and disembodied eyes in what Robicsek and Hales (1981) refer to as triadic bowl offerings.

These results suggest the Maya saw a duality in monkey roles, indicating a cultural distinction between howler monkeys and spider monkeys. This may have reflected an understanding of the different energy levels exhibited by these monkeys in the wild,

Figure 2.9 Additional images identified as *Ateles geoffroyi*: (a) line drawing of ceramic plate illustrating two monkeys in dynamic poses, wearing wristlets and anklets, carrying bundles, and reaching with hook-shaped hands (K3637); (b) three seated monkeys with pale faces and undersides holding a shell or cacao pod in right hands, wearing death collars and possible scarves (K1789); (c) monkey with pale face, elongated limbs, and hook-shaped hands leads procession carrying a deer while wearing wristlets, anklets, and a death collar (K7152). Images by Justin Kerr-Public Domain.

where the frugivorous spider monkeys are far more energetic and active through the daytime than the more folivorous howler monkeys. But it is possible that the differing use of these primates in Maya imagery may reflect some other understanding or interpretation of them by the Maya, reflecting their general appearance, other aspects of their behavior, or myths and stories that the Maya may have developed in association with these monkeys. As Saunders (1994, 1998) suggests, when examined through the cultural lens, the animal is a bundle of attributes and meanings defined by the culture group. As this study reveals, recognizing the physical and behavioral differences in species leads to the development of different bundles of meaning.

The nature of this study provides an exciting opportunity for using primate studies in tandem with archaeological and ethnographic data. Recent studies in ethnoprimatology concerning the species discussed here (Cormier and Urbani, 2008; Urbani and Cormier, 2015) bolster our understanding of the interconnectedness between humans and primates, in both the past and present. Focusing on primate symbolism provides insight into how the Maya interacted with animals living in their natural environment, what they understood of the monkeys' behavior, and the ways in which symbolism was transmitted through the representation of these animals.

Acknowledgments

We wish to thank Prudence Rice and C. Andrew Hofling for their comments and support. We are grateful to Nate Meissner for creating Fig. 2.2 and Albert Allen for his assistance with image formatting.

References

Adams, R. E. W. (1971). The ceramics of Altar de Sacrificios. *Papers of the Peabody Museum of Archaeology and Ethnology*, **63**(1). Cambridge: Harvard University.

Baker, M. (1992). Capuchin monkeys (*Cebus capucinus*) and the ancient Maya. *Ancient Mesoamerica*, 3, 219–228.

Benson, E. P. (1994). The multimedia monkey, or, the failed man: the monkey as artist. In V. Fields, ed., *The Seventh Palenque Round Table, 1989*. San Francisco: The Pre-Columbian Art Research Institute, 137–143.

Bergeson, D. (1996). The positional behavior and prehensile tail use of *Alouatta palliata*, *Ateles geoffroyi*, and *Cebus capucinus*. Unpublished PhD thesis, Washington University.

Boileau, A., Delsol, N., & Emery, K. F. (2020). Human-animal relations in the Maya world. In S. R. Hutson, & T. Ardren, eds., *The Maya World*. New York: Routledge, 164–182.

Bricker, V. R. (1973). *Ritual Humor in Highland Chiapas*. Austin: University of Texas Press.

Bruce, R. D. (1979). *Lacandon Dream Symbolism*. Mexico City: Ediciones Euroamericanos.

Cant, J. G. H. (1986). Locomotion and feeding postures of spider and howling monkeys: Field study and evolutionary interpretation. *Folia Primatologica*, **46**(1), 1–14.

Chapman, C. A. (1988). Patterns of foraging and range use by three species of neotropical primates. *Primates*, **29**(2), 199–194.

Coe, M. D. (1973). *The Maya Scribe and His World*. New York: The Grolier Club.

Coe, M. D. (1977). Supernatural patrons of Maya scribes and artists. In N. Hammond, ed., *Social Process in Maya Prehistory*. London: Academic Press, 327–347.

Coe, M. D. (1982). *Old Gods and Young Heroes: The Pearlman Collection of Maya Ceramics*. Jerusalem: The Israel Museum.

Cormier, L. A., & Urbani, B. (2008). The ethnoprimatology of spider monkeys (*Ateles* spp.): from past to present. In C. J. Campbell, ed., *Spider Monkeys: Behavior, Ecology, and Evolution of the Genus Ateles*. Cambridge: Cambridge University Press, 377–403.

Culbert, T. P. (1993). *The Ceramics of Tikal—Vessels from the Burials, Caches, and Problematical Deposits: Tikal Report 25A (Vol. 81)*. Philadelphia: University of Pennsylvania Museum of Archaeology.

Eisenberg, J. F., & R. E. Kuehn. (1966). The Behavior of *Ateles geoffroyi* and Related Species. Smithsonian Miscellaneous Collections.

Emery, K. F. (2007). Assessing the impact of ancient Maya animal use. *Journal of Nature Conservation*, 15 (3), 184–195.

Emmons, L. H., & Feer, F. (1997). *Neotropical Rainforest Mammals: A Field Guide*. Chicago: University of Chicago Press.

Gossen, G. H. (1974). *Chamulas in the World of the Sun: Time and Space in a Maya Oral Tradition*. Cambridge, MA: Harvard University Press.

Hunt, E. (1977). *The Transformation of the Hummingbird: Cultural Roots of a Zinacantecan Mythical Poem*. Ithaca, NY: Cornell University Press.

Kaufman, T. S., & Norman, W. M. (1984). An outline of Proto-Ch'olan phonology, morphology, and vocabulary. In J. S. Justeson, & L. Campbell, eds., *Phoeneticism in Mayan Hieroglyphic Writing, Institute for Mesoamerican Studies, no. 9*. Albany: State University of New York at Albany Press, 77–166.

Kerr, J. (2019). The Maya Vase Database. Available at: www.famsi.org, Los Angeles: Los Angeles County Museum of Art. Electronic database, Available at: http://research.mayavase.com/kerrmaya.html (Accessed August 28, 2019)

Kinzey, W. G. (1997). *New World Primates*. New York: Aldine de Gruyter.

La Farge, O., & Byers, D. S. (1931). *The Year Bearer's People. Middle American Research Institute Publication, no 3*. New Orleans: Tulane University.

Mazariegos, O. C. (2017). *Art and Myth of the Ancient Maya*. New Haven: Yale University Press.

Milbrath, S. (1999). *Star Gods of the Maya: Astronomy in Art, Folklore, and Calendars*. Austin: University of Texas Press.

Miller, M. E., & Taube, K. (1997). *An Illustrated Dictionary of the Gods and Symbols of Ancient Mexico and the Maya*. London: Thames and Hudson.

Mock, S. B. (1997). Monkey business at Northern River Lagoon: a coastal interaction sphere in Northern Belize. *Ancient Mesoamerica*, 8, 165–183.

Morris, W. F. (1987). *Living Maya*. New York: Henry N. Abrams.

Nicholson, H. B., & Keber, E. Q. (1983). *Art of Ancient Mexico: Treasures of Tenochtitlan*. Washington, D.C.: National Gallery of Art.

Nisbett, R. A. (1995). The functional ecology of howling monkey positional behavior: proximate effects of habitat structure, tree architecture, phenopause, and body size upon *Alouatta palliata* foraging in discrete forest and crown types. PhD dissertation, University of Iowa.

Perera, V., & Bruce, R. D. (1985). *The Last Lords of Palenque: The Lacandon Mayas of the Mexican Rain Forest*. Boston: Little, Brown Publishers.

Reents-Budet, D. (1994). *Painting the Maya Universe*. Durham, NC: Duke University Press.

Rice, P. M., & South, K. E. (2015). Revisiting monkeys on pots: a contextual consideration of primate imagery on Classic lowland Maya pottery. *Ancient Mesoamerica*, 26(2), 275–294.

Ringle, W. M. (1988). *Of Mice and Monkeys: The Value and Meaning of T1016, The God C Hieroglyph. Research Reports on Ancient Maya Writing 18*. Washington, DC: Center for Maya Research.

Robicsek, F., & Hames, D. M. (1981). *The Maya Book of the Dead: The Ceramic Codex*. New Haven, CT: Yale University Press.

Rylands, A. B., Groves, C. P., Mittermeier, R. A., & Cortés-Ortiz, L. (2006). Taxonomy and distributions of Mesoamerican primates. In A. Estrada, P. A. Garber, M. S. M. Pavelka, & L. Luecke, eds., *New Perspectives in the Study of Mesoamerican Primates: Distribution, Ecology, Behavior, and Conservation*. New York: Springer Press, 29–79.

Saunders, N. J. (1994). Predators of culture: jaguar symbolism and Mesoamerican elites. *World Archaeology*, 26(1), 104–117.

Saunders, N. J. (1998). *Icons of Power: Feline Symbolism in the Americas*. London: Routledge.

Schele, L., & Miller, M. E. (1986). *The Blood of Kings: Dynasty and Ritual in Maya Art*. Fort Worth, TX: Kimbell Art Museum.

Sharer, R. J., & Traxler, L. P. (2006). *The Ancient Maya*. Palo Alto: Stanford University Press.

South, K. E. (2005). Monkeying around the Maya region: a four-field look at primate iconography and the Maya. MA thesis Southern Illinois University Carbondale.

Smith, R. E. (1955). *The Ceramic Sequence of Uaxactún, Guatemala. Middle American Research Institute Publication No. 20*. New Orleans: Tulane University.

Strier, K. B. (1992). Atelinae adaptations: behavioral strategies and ecological constraints. *American Journal of Physical Anthropology*, 88(4), 515–524.

Stross, B. (2008). K'U: the divine monkey. *Journal of Mesoamerican Languages and Linguistics*, 1(1), 1–34.

Tedlock, D. (1985). *Popol Vuh: The Definitive Edition of the Mayan Book of the Dawn of Life and the Glories of Gods and Kings*. New York: Simon and Schuster.

Thompson, J. E. S. (1970). *Maya History and Religion*. Norman: University of Oklahoma Press.

Urbani, B., & Cormier, L. A. (2015). The ethnoprimatology of the howler monkeys (*Alouatta* spp.): from past to present. In M. Kowalewski, P. Garber, L. Cortés-Ortiz, B. Urbani, & D. Youlatos, eds., *Howler Monkeys*. New York: Springer, 259–280.

Vogt, E. Z. (1976). *Tortillas for the Gods: A Symbolic Analysis of Zinacanteco Rituals*. Cambridge, MA: Harvard University Press.

3 Monkeys on the Islands and Coasts of Paradise

Pre-Hispanic Nonhuman Primates in the Circum-Caribbean Region (300–1500 CE)

Bernardo Urbani, Andrzej T. Antczak, M. Magdalena Antczak, Nicole R. Cannarozzi, Roger H. Colten, Kitty F. Emery, Raymundo A. C. F. Dijkhoff, Thomas A. Wake, Michelle J. LeFebvre, Lisabeth A. Carlson, William F. Keegan, & Dennis C. Nieweg

Monos en las islas y costas del Paraíso: Primates no-humanos prehispánicos en la región circum-caribeña (300–1500 d.C.)

Resumen

Este capítulo presenta una revisión exhaustiva de la interacción de los pueblos indígenas del circum-Caribe con los primates no-humanos antes y durante el primer contacto europeo. Llena vacíos significativos en la literatura académica contemporánea al proporcionar una historia arqueológica actualizada de los roles sociales y simbólicos de los monos en esta región. Se inicia describiendo el registro de restos zooarqueológicoas de primates en los sitios arqueológicos cerámicos insulares y costeros del circum-Caribe. Además, a partir de las últimas investigaciones arqueológicas que utilizan métodos y técnicas novedosas, también revisamos otras pruebas biológicas de existencia de monos. Igualmente, recopilamos las imágenes de material portátil hechas por indígenas y revisamos el arte rupestre que presuntamente representa primates en el Caribe. Trascendiendo 1492, la investigación se complementa con la adición de fuentes documentales escritas, específicamente, información etnoprimatológica de fuentes etnohistóricas tempranas sobre las múltiples interacciones entre humanos y monos en las primeras sociedades coloniales. Finalmente, destacamos ciertos patrones que habrían caracterizado las relaciones entre humanos y monos en las sociedades pasadas de la región circum-caribeña (300-1500 d.C.) y, de esta manera, abrimos caminos para futuras investigaciones sobre este tema.

Palabras clave

Arqueología costera e isleña – arqueoprimatología – Grandes y Pequeñas Antillas – período cerámico – Saladoide – Taíno – Isla de Trinidad – Venezuela

Abstract

This chapter presents a comprehensive review of the interaction between circum-Caribbean indigenous peoples and nonhuman primates before and at early European contact. It fills significant gaps in contemporary scholarly literature by providing an updated archaeological history of the social and symbolic roles of monkeys in this region. We begin by describing the zooarchaeological record of primates in the insular and coastal circum-Caribbean Ceramic period archaeological sites. Drawing from the latest archaeological investigations that use novel methods and techniques, we also review other biological evidence of the presence of monkeys. In addition, we compile a list of indigenously crafted portable material imagery and review rock art that allegedly depicts primates in the Caribbean. Our investigation is supplemented by the inclusion of written documentary sources, specifically, ethnoprimatological information derived from early ethnohistorical sources on the multifarious interactions between humans and monkeys in early colonial societies. Finally, we illustrate certain patterns that may have characterized interactions between humans and monkeys in past societies of the circum-Caribbean region (300–1500 CE), opening avenues for future investigations of this topic.

Keywords: Archaeoprimatology, Ceramic period, Greater and Lesser Antilles, Island and coastal archaeology, Saladoid, Taíno, Trinidad, Venezuela

3.1   Introduction

In this chapter we describe and analyze the archaeological material culture, indigenous depictions, and documentary sources of nonhuman primates (hereafter referred as to 'primates') in the circum-Caribbean region between circa one millennium before European conquest into early colonial times. Several scholars examined the primate fossil record of the Caribbean, including Ford (1990), Gutiérrez-Calvache and Jaimez-Salgado (2007), Horovitz and MacPhee (2012), MacPhee and Horovitz (2002), and Silva-Talboda et al. (2007). Wing (2012) has listed some archaeological sites with pre-Hispanic remains of primates from this part of the world. However, a recent history of the archaeological presence of monkeys in the Caribbean is lacking in scholarly literature. We aim to fill this gap and present a comprehensive review of the interactions of Caribbean indigenous peoples with primates. Therefore, the objective of this study is to: (a) describe the available osteological remains – and other biological evidence – of primates from insular and coastal Ceramic Age archaeological sites; (b) compile information on material culture that depicts primates; (c) discuss ethnoprimatological information from ethnohistorical sources of the region; and (d) characterize patterns of interactions between humans and monkeys in the circum-Caribbean region.

3.2   The Bioarchaeology of Primates in the Circum-Caribbean Region

This section explores the biological presence of primates in the Caribbean. It mostly encompasses osteological remains as well as biological evidence, such as DNA extracted from human coprolites and a hair sample. Determining taxonomic identification is based on the closer local populations of monkeys, either primates currently inhabiting archaeological sites or the nearest primate populations to the sites with allochthonous primate samples. Figure 3.1 presents the distribution of those archaeological sites. No primate osteological remains have been found at island and coastal Mayan archaeological sites (see Valadez, 2014; Chapter 1).

3.2.1   Osteological Evidence

Herein, we present data on cranial and postcranial remains of monkeys in archaeological sites from four Caribbean islands and three northern South American

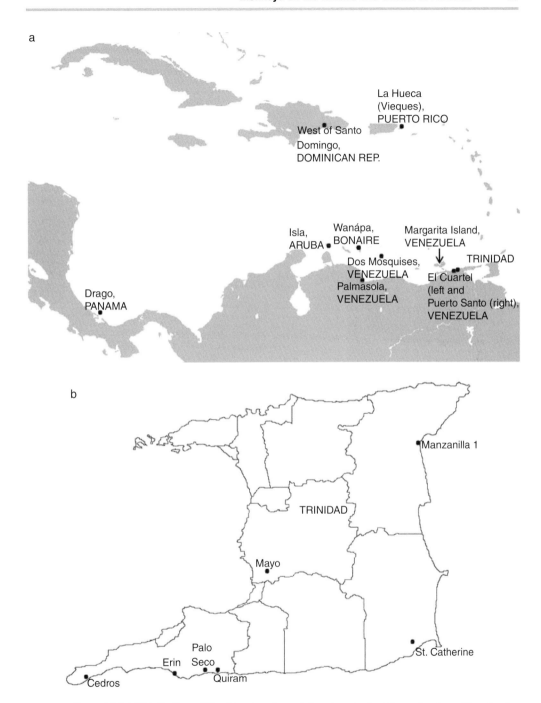

Figure 3.1 (a) Distribution of the island and coastal archaeological Ceramic sites with primate remains in the circum-Caribbean region. (b) Distribution of osteological remains of primates in archaeological sites on the island of Trinidad. (Base maps from Wikimedia Commons-CC BY. Creators: San Jose, 2006, and Guettarda, 2006, respectively).

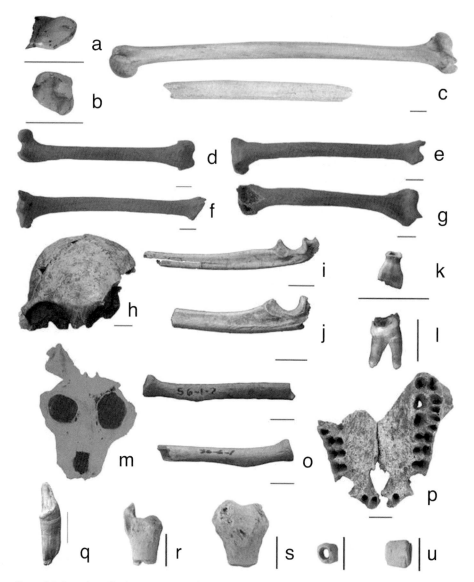

Figure 3.2 Samples of primate remains from Ceramic sites of the circum-Caribbean region. See text for localities, descriptions, and contexts. The bars equal 1 cm. Photographs by T. A. Wake (a, b, c]) B. Urbani (d, e, f, g, h, i, j, k, l, n, o), I. Vargas-Arenas (1979, plate 58) (m), N. R. Cannarozzi (p), D. C. Nieweg (q), and L. A. Carlson (r, s, t, u).

locations as well as the island of Trinidad (Fig. 3.2). The information presented is from the Panamanian Island of Colón in the southwestern Caribbean, Bonaire, Aruba, and the island of Dos Mosquises in Los Roques Archipelago of Venezuela, located in the middle of the southern part of this region (Fig. 3.2). Three sites on the coast of mainland Venezuela are also listed, and the account finishes with the island of Trinidad (Fig. 3.2). The latter island has the greatest number of sites with primate remains. Primate species found at these archaeological sites included various species of spider, howler, and capuchin monkeys.

3.2.1.1 Drago Site, Colón Island, Northwestern Panama

Site Description and Dating

Sitio Drago is strategically located on the northwestern-most point of Isla Colón at the westerly passage into the Bocas del Toro Archipelago, in northwestern Panama. The site covers approximately 18 ha and consists of a cluster of low earthen mounds located on a stabilized beach ridge with a mortuary mound near its center. The archaeological deposits are up to 2 m in depth in the excavated mounds and near 50 cm–1m deep in the spaces between them. As of 2016, some 61 one square meter excavation units have been excavated to between 0.3 m and 1.5 m in depth. The project has emphasized excavation of the most conspicuous low earthen mounds visible at the site, Mounds 1, 6, 10, and 15 (the mortuary mound). A suite of 55 radiocarbon dates indicate that Sitio Drago was occupied for approximately 750 years between 700 CE and 1450 CE (Wake and Martin, 2016). Specifically, the radiocarbon dates related to the excavated primates are 870–1050 CE or 1050 ± 60 BP (Unit 1N; Beta-182651, howler monkey); 870–1150 CE or 1050 ± 70 BP (Unit 1N; Beta-182655, spider monkey); and 990–1210 CE or 960 ± 60 BP from Unit 2 (Beta-196143, spider monkey). The recovered material is currently held in the University of California, Los Angeles (UCLA) Zooarchaeology Laboratory (first report in this study). The comparative reference specimens used are held in the comparative osteological collection in the Zooarchaeology Laboratory of the UCLA Cotsen Institute of Archaeology, the UCLA Dickey Natural History Collection and the University of California, Berkeley, Museum of Vertebrate Zoology.

Description of the Primates

The monkey specimens recovered from archaeological contexts at Sitio Drago include the crown of one deciduous right upper incisor (I^1) identified as a young adult of *Alouatta* cf. *A. palliata* from Unit 1N, Level 10–20 cm below surface (buccolingual length: 3.66 mm; Fig. 3.2a), the crown of a recently erupted right upper M^2 identified as a young individual of *Ateles* cf. *A. geoffroyi* from Unit 2, 40–50 cm bs (buccolingual length: 7.19 mm: Fig. 3.2b), and one left humerus proximal shaft fragment bearing cut marks identified as an adult *Ateles* cf. *A. geoffroyi* from Unit 1N, 90–100 cm bs (maximum length: 113.61 mm; Fig.3. 2c). The cut marks visible on the spider monkey humerus shaft fragment suggest processing for consumption. Two diurnal monkey species, the white-faced capuchin (*Cebus capucinus*) and the mantled howler monkey (*Alouatta palliata*), and one nocturnal species (*Aotus zonalis*) currently inhabit Isla Colón (Urbani, 2003). Spider monkeys (*Ateles geoffroyi*) are still present in mainland Bocas del Toro, but not on any of the islands in the archipelago. No monkey specimens have been previously reported from the Bocas del Toro region (Grayson, 1973, 1978; Linares and White, 1980).

Context and Associated Archaeological Material

Unit 1N was placed in one of the largest mounded structures at the site (Mound 6) and Unit 2 in a large, low mound 100 m north of Mound 6, termed Mound 10. Distinct stratigraphic levels are difficult to distinguish in the deposits at Sitio Drago due to the overall consistent dark sandy soil matrix, so arbitrary 10 cm levels were used in all excavated units. The soil matrix across the site consists of a dense, dark artifact- and ecofact-rich anthrosol. Where sterile levels have been encountered an abrupt shift from the rich anthrosols to light yellow sterile coralline beach sand is obvious. Artifacts recovered include numerous ceramic fragments, including diagnostic sherds representing vessels originating from several hundred kilometers away in central Panama, Pacific coastal Chiriquí, and northwest Costa Rica, and various locally produced wares with appliqued human, marine and terrestrial invertebrates, fish, birds, and mammals on (Wake, n.d.). Other artifacts include sculptural and metate fragments, basalt axes, chisels, and projectile points, shell beads, and ornaments, and a few bone tools, (Wake et al. 2021; Wake and Martin, 2016; Wake et al., 2004, 2012, 2013). The white beach sand parent soil facilitates excellent preservation of organic materials, resulting in the collection of large samples of molluscan and vertebrate faunal remains as well as a wealth of carbonized plant remains (see Martin, 2015; Wake 2006; Wake et al., 2013).

3.2.1.2   Isla Site, Island of Aruba

Site Description and Dating

The Isla site is located in southwest Aruba approximately 900 m from the shore. It consists of various limestone terraces and a seaward dipping top surface. Predominantly sandy soils are present at the Isla site (De Buisonjé, 1974; Grontmij & Sogreah, 1968). Isla is 67 to 70 m a.s.l. Weathering has formed several gullies around the site. The gully Rooi Lamoenchi runs from Isla toward the southwest coast and empties into a *saliña* (salt lake) at Pos Grandi which connects to the sea. Isla has dense xerophytic vegetation and there are a number of small and large limestone rock shelters (abris) present. Human burials were first found at the site in 2000 (abri 1) as well as in 2002 (abri 2), both located some 30–40 m a. s. l. The abri 1 burial also contained bones of a nonendemic monkey. Isla is located within the site catchment area of the Ceramic Age (900/1000–1515 CE) village of Savaneta (Sabaneta). The human bones were recovered in a secondary burial context and are not robust like those of Aruba's Archaic Age (1500 BCE to 900/1000 CE) inhabitants, suggesting Ceramic Age or maybe Early Historic Age burials. Three radiocarbon dates from Savaneta place its main occupation between 950 and 1250 CE, but evidence shows that Amerindians were still living there when the Spaniards arrived in the early 16th century (Dijkhoff, 1997; Mickleburgh, 2013; Oliver, 1989, 1997).

Description of the Primates

Four primate postcranial elements are identified from the Isla site (Urbani, 2016a). These elements include a complete right femur (maximum length: 113.89 mm; Fig. 3.2d), a complete left tibia (maximum length: 110.46 mm; Fig. 3.2e), a complete right tibia (maximum length: 109.75 mm; Fig. 3.2f), and a partial left humerus (maximum length: 98.8 mm; Fig. 3.2g). There is no evidence of cut marks or burning. The bones are fully developed. The femur lacks the medial inclination as in *Homo* (D. Ruiz-Ramoni, pers. obs.) and appears to be primate. A fifth incomplete bone may represent an ulna (Urbani, 2016a; M. L. P. Hoogland, pers. obs., 2020). The sample is identified as *Cebus* cf. *C. brunneus*, after considering the closest capuchin populations in the northern Venezuelan coast. These remains are part of the collection of the National Archaeological Museum Aruba (NAMA) located in Oranjestad (first published in this study). The osteological remains from Aruba and Venezuela (see Sections 3.2.1.2 and 3.2.1.4–3.2.1.7) were compared with Neotropical primate samples stored in the Museo de Ciencias de Caracas and the Museo de Zoología of the Instituto de Zoología y Ecología Tropical at the Universidad Central de Venezuela in Caracas. In the latter, the primatological collection from the region of Barlovento, Miranda state, Venezuela, was used for comparative purposes as it includes individuals of different sexes and ages (see Cordero-Rodríguez and Boher, 1988).

Context and Associated Archaeological Material

Surveys were carried out at Isla in 2000, 2002, 2004, and 2006. When the bones in abri 1 were found, they were removed by the discoverer and the police, destroying the exact anatomical context of this burial. Preliminary analysis indicated that it must be a secondary burial. Cranial bones, a mandible, and two mastoid processes of a young adult woman (17–25 years) and a few unfused long bones and a maxilla of a child (8 ± 2 years) were identified. The other bones correspond to a monkey. Furthermore, some stones, probably red limestone or manganese, were found in the contents of abri 1 (Dijkhoff, 2001). A red dye may have been purposely placed on the outside and inside parts of some of the cranial bones, while the mandible also has some of this dye on it. The monkey, identified as C. cf. brunneus, represents the first zooarchaeological evidence of a primate found in Aruba (Urbani, 2016a). Isla is also the first site on the island with a secondary burial in an abri and a human burial with an animal. Furthermore, the Isla find is only the second human burial located outside of the village. The other site is located at Budui at the northeast coast. The buried individuals were probably of high status based on the site's exceptional location and association with the Santa Cruz village (site catchment area) and may be from the Ceramic Age or Early Historic period (Tacoma and Versteeg, 1990; Versteeg, 1990). During Aruba's Ceramic Age, the island was occupied by sedentary, ceramic-producing agriculturalists, archaeologically known as the Dabajuran people and historically known as the Caquetío. Aruba belonged to the core area of the Coastal Caquetío Polity, which was socio-politically organized into a paramount chiefdom (Dijkhoff and Linville, 2004; Oliver, 1989, 1997).

Abri 2 is located at a distance of 21.40 m of abri 1 in a 20° northwest direction. As with abri 1, human bones became exposed on the surface as a result of postdepositional erosional processes. These included bones and teeth of at least one adult and a child. The remaining deposit was left in place for future investigation. Much farther from these two abris, a third large abri (no. 3) was found to contain a few shell artifacts. Surveys yielded artifacts in the vicinity of the abris, including a few ceramic Ordinary Ware sherds, some stone tools, a few pieces of red limestone or manganese, colonial glass and shell, including shell tools. The paucity of archaeological material together with the contents of the two abris do not suggest intensive use or long-term activities at Isla. The site could have had a ceremonial function, possibly associated with high status people.

3.2.1.3 Wanápa Site, Island of Bonaire

Site Description and Dating

The Wanápa site (B-016) is the largest Ceramic Age permanent settlement in the central-eastern part of the island of Bonaire, which lies to the north of the coast of western Venezuela, in the southeastern Caribbean. The site is located *ca* 1 km inland from the mudflats and mangrove thickets of Lac Bay, which is connected to the open Caribbean Sea. The terrain is relatively flat, and the soils have drainage suitable for indigenous horticulture including manioc and maize. Subsistence of the Wanápa inhabitants was based on horticulture and complemented by fishing, mollusk gathering and hunting. Fresh water, lithic and clay sources are available nearby (Haviser, 1991: 127–128, fig. 49 and table V). This site was excavated by H. R. van Heekeren in 1960 and by J. Haviser in 1987 (Haviser, 1991: 123–124, 149, fig. 54; van Heekeren, 1960, 1963; see also du Ry, 1960). The Wanápa site was inhabited longer than any other archaeological site on Bonaire with an initial Archaic Age date of 2975 ± 45 or 1025 BCE obtained from a shell sample. The Ceramic Age strata of this site are dated by charcoal samples to between 1480 ± 25 BP (470 CE), 885 ± 45 BP (1065 CE), and 505 ± 35 BP (1445 CE) (Haviser, 1991: 51, fig. 27).

Description of the Primate

In 1990, Elizabeth Wing in personal communication with Jay Haviser (1991) suggested that the monkey remains recovered at the Wanápa site represent a juvenile individual of *Cebus* sp. She further suggested that they "were of sufficient number to possibly suggest that the whole animal was brought to the site" (Haviser, 1991: 159). Wing concluded that the remains of nonlocal mammals in this site, including these monkey bones, may indicate that they were used as either food items or were traded from beyond Bonaire (Haviser, 1991). The remains of this monkey are curated in the Environmental Archaeology Program collections at the Florida Museum of Natural History of the University of Florida in Gainesville, USA (FM-EAP). Considering Wing's identification and the closest capuchin population in Venezuela, the sample is preliminarily identified as *Cebus* cf. *C. brunneus*.

Context and Associated Archaeological Material

The bones identified by Wing as *Cebus* sp. were recovered in the living or residential area (Area B) of the Wanápa site, where the remains of an indigenous house structure were found (Haviser, 1991). The ulna of an ocelot (*Felis pardalis*) was also found there suggesting that this bone was brought to the site as a special object (Haviser, 1991). The zooarchaeological sample also contains remains of various indeterminate rodents including vesper mice (*Calomys* sp.). The most abundant vertebrate remains represent diverse reef fish and marine turtles (Haviser, 1991). Abundant potsherds, lithic, stone, shell and bone artifacts and body adornments pertaining to the Dabajuroid archaeological culture were also recovered at the Wanápa site.

3.2.1.4 Dos Mosquises Site, Los Roques Archipelago, Venezuela

Site Description and Dating

A skull of a howler monkey was recovered in 1983 during systematic archaeological excavations on Dos Mosquises island (DM/A site), in the Los Roques Archipelago, Venezuela in Trench B in cultural strata between 20 and 40 cm below the surface (Antczak, 1999; Antczak and Antczak, 2006). The site has been interpreted as a multifunctional temporary campsite pertaining to the Valencioid culture from the north-central region of mainland Venezuela. These Valencioid peoples navigated dugout canoes across the 135 km of open sea that separate the mainland from the oceanic islands of Los Roques. Economic targets of these voyages were the dense populations of queen conch (*Lobatus gigas*) and other marine resources such as turtles, fish, other molluscs, and salt. Valencioid peoples (see e.g. Cruxent and Rouse, 1958; Rouse and Cruxent, 1963) are the descendants of the Arauquinoid Cariban-speaking migrants who arrived in the Lake Valencia Basin from the Middle Orinoco area circa 800 CE (Antczak et al., 2017a). An absolute carbon-14 date was obtained from charcoal extracted from one of the Valencioid hearths in Trench B is 490±80 BP or 1460 CE (sample LR/DM/A/B/9 sample, # I-16,294, Teledyne Isotopes). The monkey skull itself has not been directly dated. All archaeological material recovered in the DM/A site, including the monkey skull, is curated in the Unidad de Estudios Arqueológicos of the Instituto de Estudios Regionales y Urbanos at the Universidad Simón Bolívar (USB), Caracas.

Description of the Primate

The sample (Inv. # 1156, Fig. 3.2h) is a cranial vault with a partial occipital area around the condyles and foramen magnum flanked with a partial temporal auditory bulla. This piece presents a conspicuous broken frontal part along with the two parietals. The right parietal, near the bregma, has a second small fracture in the anterior half and the left anterior corner is absent. Even though nasal bones are missing, the nasion landmark remains. The supraorbital ridge of the left side is missing. The lack of both temporal crests in the vault but the presence of full closures of the sutures seem to point into a young adult individual of undetermined sex. The first identification of this specimen was made by Omar Linares (USB) who referred to it as a "subadult female" representing *Alouatta seniculus* (Antczak, 1995). The absence of temporal crests as seen in mature male individuals might have helped Linares to determine the age and sex of this individual. Antczak and Antczak (2006) provided an opposite three-quarter view of this piece and Urbani (2021) presented a lateral view. Following current taxonomic nomenclature, the animal is identified as *Alouatta* cf. *A. arctoidea*.

Context and Associated Archaeological Material

The monkey skull was found in a so-called cache deposit in the DM/A site. It was associated with diverse nonperishable objects made of pottery, stone, bone, and shell. The deposition of small, solid pottery figurines together with mammal mandibles, oleoresin fragments, land snail (*Labyrinthus plicatus*) pendants, shell and micro vessels was initially observed at an Ocumaroid campsite in Domusky Norte Island, adjacent to Dos Mosquises. This site dates to the first two centuries after 1000 CE and appears related to the Arawakan-speaking bearers of the Ocumaroid pottery (Antczak, 2000). At the later Valencioid campsite in Dos Mosquises, this initial patterning continues, with ceramic pipes, bone flutes, mammal skulls (feline and monkey), mineral ochre, oleoresin and ceramic ocarinas and burners being added (Antczak and Antczak, 2017). The recovery of these objects together suggests that the assemblages of practice related to ritual activities presided over by shamans (Antczak and Antczak, 2006; Antczak and Beaudry, 2019). Various ecofacts were also recovered from Trench B including *Lobatus gigas* and other shells, bird bones, turtle and fish bones and otoliths (Antczak et al., 2017b). The monkey skull was included into the category of unmodified bones recovered from the DM site. Trench B also yielded cranial vaults and mandibular fragments of wild cats (*Felis wiedii, Leopardus pardalis*) (Antczak, 1999). Isotopic analyses of the feline bones demonstrate that they came from the Lake Valencia Basin on the mainland. This region possesses the variation in geochemical conditions to account for the isotopic diversity of all the analyzed exotic tooth specimens at the site and is closest to Los Roques Archipelago (Laffoon et al., 2016). The combined isotopic and archaeological data demonstrate that some of mammal bones originated within the Valencioid Interaction Sphere that linked various communities within Lake Valencia and surrounding regions between 1200 CE and European Conquest (Antczak and Antczak, 1999, 2006). Based on the archaeological evidence, we suggest the howler monkey skull is derived from the same region.

3.2.1.5 Palmasola Site, North-Central Venezuelan Coast

Site Description and Dating

Palmasola is located near the town of Morón, in the Venezuelan state of Carabobo, on the country's north-central coast. The site has been excavated by Sýkora (2006) between 1995 and 2001 with the occasional participation of M. M. Antczak and A. T. Antczak. Palmasola was a permanent settlement whose inhabitants obtained, processed, and consumed diverse food resources but focused on marine fish and molluscs. They crafted local pottery, basketry, tools, and body adornments in stone, bone, and shell. The site also shows evidence of ritual activities, especially related to mortuary practices. Sýkora (2006) suggests that the origin of Palmasola pottery is stylistically related to that of the Coastal Saladoid archaeological culture (see Rouse and Cruxent, 1963) that were extending their influence from the east. Absolute dating of Palmasola archaeological site is lacking. The relative dating proposed by Sýkora (2006) was based on the analysis of pottery and other materials recovered in Palmasola and its interrelationship with other phenomena detected in adjacent regions. Accordingly, the human occupation of Palmasola started *circa* 200 CE and continued uninterrupted until European Conquest. The site was likely still inhabited during the early colonial times (Sýkora, 2006). Much of the archaeological material from this site is currently deposited at the Unidad de Estudios Arqueológicos at USB.

Description of the Primates

"Bone remains of a capuchin monkey (*Cebus olivaceus* [Schomburgk, 1848]) were found at Palmasola in Level 3 (number of identified specimens [NISP] = 1) and Level 2B (NISP=2); but were most numerous in Level 2A (NISP = 5), accounting for MNI [minimum number of individuals] = 1 out of a total MNI of 74 and an NISP of 1527" (Sýkora, 2006: 506, 517–518). Sýkora (2006: 633) identified an adult primate "right auditive bulla with its parietal [part]" referred to *Cebus olivaceus* (=*C. brunneus*). The author also reported harpoon points with different thin and curved points (38–55 mm) made of diaphyses of small mammals such as *Didelphis marsupialis* and *Cebus brunneus* (Inv. PPPAY11), among others. Sýkora (2006) also identified a radius of a capuchin monkey (Inv. PIUPMV41) which finally seems to be an ulna of a young animal according to the published photograph (B. Urbani, pers. obs.) that was described as an object that has a slightly modified distal section, possibly rounded by the action of use. The *Cebus* radius measures 60.3 mm in length (Sýkora, 2006).

These three elements were lost in the previous institutional repository. Additional primate osteological material was found in the current collection held at UEA-USB in Caracas. This material was identified preliminarily by A. Sýkora and later revisited by B. Urbani. This new material is reported for the first time in this chapter. The sample consists of: a partial left ulna (F22–2A, trochlear notch length: 8.34 mm; Fig. 3.2i); a partial right ulna with apparent cut marks (F10–26, trochlear notch length: 8.82 mm; Fig. 3.2j); and an upper right incisor, I_1 (F23–20, buccolingual length: 2.95 mm; Fig. 3.2k). They are all recognized as juvenile *Cebus* cf. *C. brunneus* by Sýkora and confirmed by Urbani in this study. Sýkora also recognized two capuchin premolars that remain to be precisely identified, as they may represent some other terrestrial mammal. An additional tooth is identified as a lower left molar, M_2, of an adult ursine howler monkey (*Alouatta* cf. *A. arctoidea*, FR-3, buccolingual length: 6.29 mm; Fig. 3.2l).

Context and Associated Archaeological Material

The indigenous inhabitants of Palmasola (*Palmasolenses*) are considered representatives of the Saladoid-Ocumaroid culture (makers of Saladoid and Ocumaroid pottery, as defined by Cruxent and Rouse [1958]; Rouse and Cruxent [1963]). Monkey remains had no specific spatial/depositional association at the Palmasola site. They were found in habitational refuse areas, in secondary contexts that may have been affected by trampling, bioturbation, redeposition and many other postdepositional taphonomic processes all occurring in a matrix of sandy beach soil. Zooarchaeological remains from this site include skeletal elements of tapir (*Tapirus terrestris*), manatee (*Trichechus manatus*), peccary (*Tayassu pecari*), deer (*Mazama* sp. and *Odocoileus virginianus*), diverse rodents and porcupines, a rabbit, and a squirrel.

3.2.1.6 El Cuartel Site, Eastern Venezuelan Coast

Site Description and Dating

A single monkey specimen was recovered from the site of El Cuartel located in the coastal city of Carúpano, Sucre state, eastern Venezuela. This site consists of mounded ceramic deposits covering an area of 25,000 m^2 (Vargas-Arenas, 1979). The layer (S1.9.3) where the monkey specimen was found dates to 1055 CE, 895 ± 90 BP (IVIC SI854) (Vargas-Arenas, 1979). The El Cuartel material is currently held in the archaeological collection of the School of Anthropology at the Universidad Central de Venezuela; however, the primate specimen in question was not encountered when this collection was visited.

Description of the Primate

A large fragment of a howler monkey cranium was reported by Vargas-Arenas (1979: Plate 58a), originally identified by O. Linares (M. Sanoja, pers. comm.) (Fig. 3.2 m). The partial right side of the frontal area is exposed and shows a marginal temporal crest that is characteristic of *Alouatta*. Although the left zygomatic arch is broken both bony orbits are present. The nasofrontal, internasal, and nasomaxillary sutures are visible. In addition, the exposed maxillary and nasal areas remain intact. Unfortunately, no measurements are presented, nor does the original photograph include a graphic scale. However, after a closer observation of the photograph, it appears to represent a young adult individual (B. Urbani, pers. obs.). The primate is identified here as *Alouatta* cf. *A. arctoidea*.

Context and Associated Archaeological Material

Ceramic material from the El Cuartel site appears related to the Saladoid tradition. The Saladoid were likely sedentary horticulturists. Some 230 (MNI) animals were recovered and the howler monkey cranium is associated with other animal food remains (Vargas-Arenas, 1979). Vargas-Arenas (1979) reported the presence of fishes, tortoises, crabs, birds, deer, and a sloth in the same layer (S1.9.3; 0.3–0.6 m) where the howler monkey cranium was found. Stone tools, potsherds, and burned shells were also recovered. This is one of the two layers with the largest amounts of animals (MNI: 34, each layer).

3.2.1.7 Puerto Santo Site, Eastern Venezuelan Coast

Site Description and Dating

The site of Puerto Santo (S6) is located in a narrow valley close to the road on the small El Morro peninsula, between the coastal towns of Carúpano-Río Caribe-Güiria (Vargas-Arenas, 1978, 1979). The material was recovered in two 2 × 2 m units during a first field season. During a second field season, an additional 13 units were excavated (Vargas-Arenas, 1978). These excavations were conducted in mounds yielding ceramic material, shells, and animal remains (Vargas-Arenas, 1978). The author reported a charcoal sample dating to 425 CE or 1525 ± 80 BP (Teledyne I-9729). The zooarchaeological remains of this site are held in the archaeological collection of the School of Anthropology at the Universidad Central de Venezuela. This is a new archaeological primate record.

Description of the Primates

Distal fragments of two different adult howler monkey (*Alouatta* cf. *A. arctoidea*) radii were recovered from the site. One is a partial left radius (S6–1-2; length: 6.44 cm; Fig. 3.2n), and the other is a right radius fragment (S6–6-1; length: 6.33 cm; Fig. 3.2o).

Context and Associated Archaeological Material

Shell remains are abundant at this site, particularly *Donax* spp. and *Tivela* spp. (Vargas-Arenas, 1978). Ash lenses were found in the excavation units as well as black earth with abundant sherds. Evidence of a household floor, with postholes, pressed earth, and domestic fire was found in four units (Vargas-Arenas, 1978). Red-slipped sherds from the site are similar to those observed in collections from Puerto Rico and the Lesser Antilles (Vargas-Arenas, 1978). The author also noted the presence of incisions on some pottery sherds that resemble Barrancoid style pottery. In fact, Vargas-Arenas (1978) suggested that this site has a relationship with both Barrancoid and Saladoid peoples with influence from the Orinoco River. She suggested that the people at this coastal site had a mixed subsistence system based on fishing, mollusk gathering, hunting, and agriculture.

3.2.1.8 Archaeological Sites in the Island of Trinidad

Site Description and Dating

Seven Ceramic sites from Trinidad for which primate remains are curated in various institutions are presented in this section. Manzanilla (SAN-1) was excavated by Dutch archaeologists in the last two decades, and St. Catherine was excavated by

L. A. Carlson in 2004. Wing (1962: 41) indicates that she identified red howler monkey (*Alouatta seniculus*) at five Ceramic sites excavated by the Yale expedition: Mayo, Cedros, Erin, Palo Seco, and Quinam. Vertebrate faunal material from the sites of Mayo, St. John, Cedros, Erin, Palo Seco, Chagonaray, Quinam, Mayaro, and St. Joseph was included in Wing's (1962) dissertation, a pioneering work on archaeozoology in the Caribbean region. Most of the zooarchaeological material studied by Wing was acquired during the Rouse and Goggin excavations conducted in 1946 and 1953, although bones from other excavations and additional sites are also included in her analysis (Wing, 1962). The Rouse and Goggin faunal materials came from seven Ceramic sites including the previously mentioned, St. Joseph and the pre-Ceramic St. John site. These sites were excavated in arbitrary levels and the soil was searched for artifacts and other cultural material. Additional faunal material later excavated by James A. Bullbrook at Erin and surface collected bones acquired by H. G. Kugler at Cedros were also included in Wing's analysis. In 1959, Wing visited Palo Seco, Mayaro (St. Bernard), Mayo, and St. John, as well as the sites of Chagonaray and Guayaguayare, and collected faunal material (Wing, 1962).

For reasons currently unclear, most of the collections from these excavations, along with Rouse's field documents, are curated at the Yale Peabody Museum Division of Anthropology, while a portion of the vertebrate material that Wing analyzed is curated at FM-EAP. The Trinidad collections curated in the FM-EAP include some of the faunal remains analyzed by Wing in her dissertation (Wing, 1962) and some likely analyzed by her students in later years. The entirety of the zooarchaeological collections analyzed by Wing and students from the Trinidad sites of Cedros, Palo Seco, Quinam, and Erin have been returned to the Yale Peabody Museum while a portion of the fauna from the sites of St. John, Mayo, St. Joseph, Chagonaray, and Mayaro remain in the FM-EAP collections. The Yale Peabody Museum and its collections were closed due to major restoration at the time this chapter was written. Since Wing's dissertation focused on the mammalian fauna in these sites, she did not report on the fauna of other taxonomic classes and these have not been sorted or analyzed, so they are also not reported here. No other cultural material from these sites is curated in the FM-EAP. The following descriptions for these sites are summarized from Boomert et al. (2013). As indicated above, apart from the sites described by Wing (1962), this piece also covers the information from the site of Manzanilla 1 (SAN-1) which is located in northeastern Trinidad and St. Catherine in the southeastern side of the island.

Mayo site

This site is a Spanish-Amerindian mission in the western portion of the Montserrat Hills in the southwestern part of Trinidad, about 6 km inland from the coast. The site includes a Roman Catholic church and a shell midden containing Amerindian pottery mixed with European colonial artifacts (Boomert et al., 2013). Rouse and Goggin excavated at the site in 1953. Boomert et al. do not list any radiocarbon dates for this site.

Cedros site

This is a Ceramic age site located in the southwestern part of Trinidad that includes a series of shell midden deposits. This is the type site for the Cedrosan subseries ceramics of the Saladoid series. Irving Rouse, Fred Olsen, and José M. Cruxent visited the site in 1969 to collect samples for radiocarbon dating (Boomert et al., 2013). The older of the two dates from the site is 2140 ± 70 BP, or 352–356 cal BCE (Boomert et al., 2013).

Erin site

This is another Ceramic, multicomponent shell midden located along the southern coast of Trinidad. Rouse excavated two trenches in the site in 1946. Artifacts from these excavations pertain to the Palo Seco and Erin complexes. Boomert et al. (2013) do not list any radiocarbon dates for this site.

Palo Seco site

This site is located along the southwestern coast of Trinidad. This multicomponent Ceramic site is the type site of the Palo Seco complex of the Cedrosan subseries, Saladoid series. The site includes several small distinct shell midden deposits. The site was initially excavated by J. A. Bullbrook in 1919, and I. Rouse returned to the site in 1946, excavating a large trench. The deposit included Cedros complex ceramics, as well as ceramics transitional between Cedros and Palo Seco. I. Rouse, F. Olsen, and J. M. Cruxent visited the site in 1969 to collect samples for radiocarbon dating (Boomert et al., 2013). Radiocarbon dates from the site range from 2130 ± 80 BP to 1480 ± 70 or cal 469–650 CE (Boomert et al., 2013).

Quinam site

This is a multicomponent Ceramic site located on the south shore of Trinidad. Quinam, like the other sites discussed here, is composed of several discrete shell midden deposits. Rouse excavated at the site in the summer of 1946, including a series of auger holes and five trenches. Most of the pottery from the site represents the Palo Seco and Erin complexes, and Boomert et al. (2013) do not list any radiocarbon dates for this site.

Manzanilla 1 (SAN-1) site

This site is located on Cocos Bay coastline close to the town of Lower Manzanilla in the County of St. Andrew, central-eastern Trinidad (Dorst et al., 2003). It is a 200 × 250 m flat plateau that drains to the Atlantic through the Nariva river basin (Dorst et al., 2003). In terms of ceramic styles, two ceramic complexes belonging to two different series are recognized at the Manzanilla 1 site. The material collected in the trench where the monkey specimen was recovered corresponds to the Cedrosan Saladoid series is represented by the Late Palo Seco complex (300–650 CE) (Harris, 1977). This coastal site was excavated over the last couple of decades by Dutch archaeologists under the auspices of the Archaeological Committee of Trinidad and Tobago. The archaeological material recovered from SAN-1 is currently curated in the University of the West Indies and the Muséum National d'Histoire Naturelle in Paris and the reference comparative collection is located at the Naturalis Biodiversity Center at Leiden, the Netherlands.

St. Catherine (MAY-17) site

The site is located on the southeastern coast of Trinidad and approximately 1 km inland from Mayaro Bay, in the Hilaire river basin of Mayaro county. The site is on a Petrotrin petroleum company property (Harris, 1972). Excavation was carried out in 2004. Units A–F formed a trench that proved unproductive after 30 cm, although later excavations in the trench by Peter Harris (pers. comm.) encountered a deeper Cedrosan Saladoid deposit. Units Q, R, S, and T yielded Saladoid and Barrancoid pottery, stone tools, and an incomplete diorite bead, but few faunal remains. Units W, X, Y, and Z (Z was laid out but not excavated) were located further into the site on higher ground in a midden deposit that contained thousands of *Donax* sp. shells and many vertebrate faunal remains. Boomert (2010) mentions two components to the St. Catherine's site, with the deeper component (I) characterized by Cedrosan Saladoid pottery (Palo Seco style, 800 BCE). St. Catherine's I is one of two Saladoid sites on Trinidad with the fine-lined incised Mount Irvine style pottery from Tobago, which is related to the Río Guapo style in coastal Venezuela. St. Catherine's II dates to around 500 CE (Barrancoid) (Boomert, 2013). Observations made during 2004, indicate that the excavations were conducted in the late Saladoid-Barrancoid component (St. Catherine's II).

Description of the primates

A descriptive list of the primate remains recovered in Trinidad's Ceramic sites surveyed during the Yale Expedition, and originally reported on by Wing (1962), as well as those from the project in Manzanilla 1 and former L. A. Carlson's zooarch-aeological research on St. Catherine is presented in Table 3.1. The archives of the FM-EAP also provided additional details on the *Alouatta* skeletal element specimen counts for the various sites analyzed by Wing (1962). Thus, identifications are listed in Table 3.1 and reflect not only Wing (1962) but also original identification data in the FM-EAP archives and recent reanalysis. In addition, FM-EAP personnel reassessed the primate specimens from the Mayo and St John sites originally identi-fied by Wing and students. This provided additional information on the taxonomy, life stages, and element representation of red howler monkeys from these two sites. Verifications and new observations on Wing's (1962) identifications (by N. R. Cannarozzi) were made using specimens cataloged in the Florida Museum Mammals collection. No review was done of the material from the other Wing-analyzed sites. Access to this larger collection permitted the revision of two speci-mens originally identified as *Alouatta* (a femur and a canine tooth), to *Tamandua* sp. and Mammalia, respectively. These specimens were included in the NISP of the original analysis but have been excluded from calculations in this analysis. Wing's early identifications were presented at the species level as *Alouatta seniculus*. The

Table 3.1. Howler monkeys identified from archaeological Ceramic sites on Trinidad

Osteological element	Mayo[1]	Cedros	Erin	Palo Seco	Quinam	St Catherine	Manzanilla 1[a]
Maxilla	1L,1R maxilla+premaxilla, 1 anterior (L), 1 complete (R) (Fig. 3.2p)	–	–	–	–	–	–
Mandible	–	–	2L,1R	–	–	1L, 1R	–
Canine	1R[1], 1 canine[1], complete; 1L mandibular C1, complete; 1L,1R maxillary C1, complete	–	–	1	–	–	1R (Fig. 3.2q)
Premolar	1L mandibular P1, complete	–	–	–	–	–	–
Molar	1R maxillary M1, complete; 1L maxillary M2, complete	–	–	–	–	–	–
Humerus	2L[1], 1 proximal[1], 1 distal (fused)	–	1L-distal	–	–	–	–
Radius	–	–	1L,1R,1 (side not recorded)	1-proximal	–	–	–
Femur	–	1L,1R	1L-distal	1L,1R-proximal	1L- proximal	–	–
Podials	–	–	–	–	1 Phalanx	–	–
Total NISP	12	2	8	4	2	2	1
Percent cranial	86	0	29	25	0	100	100
Percent postcranial	14	100	71	75	100	0	0

Note: [a]Elements from Mayo whose identifications that have not been verified and are not curated at the FM-EAP; [2]Delsol & Grouard (2015) reported the presence of 7 individuals (MNI) of red howler monkey, *Alouatta seniculus* (= *Alouatta. A.* cf. *macconnelli*)

sample from these Ceramic sites are more likely from Trinidad's endemic howler population (*Alouatta* cf. *A. macconnelli*, using current taxonomy).

We report a total of 28 primate specimens (NISP) based on Wing's original identifications and the recently reanalyzed material from the Ceramic sites including Mayo, Cedros, Erin, Palo Seco, and Quinam; however, MNI could not be verified because not all specimens are curated in the FM-EAP, and therefore this count could not be evaluated. Without access to the full assemblage for verification, roughly half of these data can only be reported as listed in the archives. Nonetheless, combined, these provide a more robust dataset. In one of the two reanalyzed sites (Mayo, ceramic), cranial elements are more prevalent than post-cranial elements representing 86% of the NISP of red howlers. Cranial elements are represented exclusively by fragmented mandibles and maxillae, including both articulated and disarticulated teeth (e.g. Fig. 3.2p). The opposite is true for specimens reported in the FM-EAP archives by Wing and students in which postcranial elements are most prevalent. Femora are most frequently identified postcranial elements (NISP=6).

In the case of the site of Manzanilla 1, the faunal remains from Trench 3 include several elements from a non-feature context. One of these specimens is the canine (lower right mandibular) tooth of a howler monkey (buccolingual length: 6.40 mm, Fig. 3.2q) that is attributed to *Alouatta* cf. *A. macconnelli* (by D. C. Nieweg.; first report in this study). Delsol and Grouard (2015) mention that nine Cebidae individuals were recognized at Manzanilla 1 site, including seven red howler monkeys, *Alouatta seniculus* (*Alouatta* cf. *A macconnelli*) and two capuchin monkeys, *Cebus albifrons*. No primate remains were recovered during the later campaigns at the Manzanilla site; however, most of the animal bones from these campaigns remain unanalyzed.

At St. Catherine, Carlson (2005, 2007) reported a red howler monkey (*Alouatta* cf. *A. macconnelli*) and white-fronted capuchins (*Cebus albifrons*) represented by two individual bone specimens per species. The red howler specimens include the left and right portions of a mandible and represent a single animal (Unit W, Level 6). These elements do not exhibit any evidence of anthropogenic modification. In contrast, the only capuchin specimens present in the samples are modified elements: one distal end of a left tibia (Unit X, Level 3. Fig. 3.2r), and one distal end of a right femur (Unit W, Level 4. Fig. 3.2s). The specimens occurred in spatially distinct test units and levels and may represent two individuals. The distal epiphyses of both specimens are fully fused and the proximal portions of both showed evidence of the diaphysis (shaft) being cut and snapped off. The diaphysis ends of the capuchin femur and tibia specimens are consistent with discard from bead manufacture. Furthermore, four beads made from mammal long bone diaphyses are present and were recovered within the same two units as the capuchin specimens. Although the modified specimens are only identifiable to mammal, they are commensurate in size, shape, and texture with the capuchin femur and tibia, suggesting use of capuchin long bones for bead manufacture (Figs. 3.2t, u). We suggest further analysis and testing because it is difficult to taxonomically identify modified bone specimens and finished artifacts. Unlike the red howler monkey, no unmodified capuchin specimens were identified at the site.

Context and associated archaeological material

As reported by Wing (1962), the primatological sample from the Ceramic sites of Mayo, Cedros, Erin, Palo Seco, and Quinam (MNI=14) represents 1.58% of the total number of identified individual mammals from those sites. Wing (1962) analyzed vertebrate faunal samples from the Rouse excavations and other collections now curated at the FM-EAP. She summarized her analysis of vertebrate fauna from several Trinidad sites as MNI by taxon and site in a single table (Wing, 1962). Wing reports red howler monkey as present in six of the nine sites in her table, but it is only 1.58 percent of the total MNI across sites. More abundant taxa include white-lipped peccary, agouti, collared peccary, paca, nine-banded armadillo, and opossum. These are the only data in the archaeological portion of her dissertation and therefore we cannot assess numbers of identified specimens (NISP), or element or age distributions, from that publication. At Quinam, Cedros, Erin, and Palo Seco; however, the sample size is much smaller in these sites compared to the Mayo site. None of the bones shows evidence of consumption, such as butchery marks or burning. It is unclear how these animals may have been used and if the differences in elemental distribution patterns reflect changes in use over time.

Of the sites not presented by Wing (1962), Manzanilla 1 is probably a food refuse deposit that includes animals such as tapir (*Tapirus* sp.), West Indian manatee (*Trichechus manatus*) vertebrae as well as reptile bones. The faunal remains were recovered from midden contexts at St. Catherine's. The red howler and capuchin monkey specimens contribute to the dominance of terrestrial mammals within the vertebrate assemblage. Terrestrial mammals contribute 72% of the total bone weight (1432.5 g) and approximately 42% of the minimum number of individual animals represented (n = 146) (see Carlson, 2005 for more detail). Table 3.2 shows detailed information on the context and associated material from the Ceramic period sites of Trinidad.

3.2.2 Other Biological Evidences

There are two other bioarchaeological materials of archaeoprimatological interest in the Caribbean region (Fig. 3.1). From La Hueca, one of the Saladoid and Huecoid localities on the Sorcé Estate in the island of Vieques in Puerto Rico, pre-Columbian human coprolites were found. Radiocarbon dates shows a chronological span from 1300 CE to 220 CE (Rivera-Pérez et al., 2015 [Beta Analytic]). Using metagenomic ancient DNA, Rivera-Pérez et al. (2015) studied the coprolites and the proviral sequences found in Huecoid and Saladoid diets, confirming the presence of endogenous marmoset retrovirus (Rivera-Pérez et al., 2015). The authors stated that "the presence of retroviral DNA from marmoset New World monkeys may support the hypothesis of ancient organic trade between Caribbean and South American cultures" (Rivera-Pérez et al., 2015: 7). As no marmoset is present in the circum-Caribbean region, and simian foamy viruses are common in New World primates (see Ghersi et al., 2015; Santos et al., 2019), we propose that the reported marmoset

Table 3.2. Context and associated zooarchaeological material from archaeological Ceramic sites of Trinidad

Site name	Context	Associated zooarchaeological material
Mayo	Tr1a, 1st coll, surface and unknown proveniences, context undescribed	Zooarchaeological materials (from Wing, 1962): *Dasypus novemcinctus* (14), *Tamandua longicaudata* (3), *Coendu prehensilis* (2), *Agouti paca* (12), *Dasyprocta aguti* (5), *Canis* (1), *Pecari tajacu* (17), *Mazama americana* (8)
Cedros	Excavation 1, Section A-5, Level 0.00–0.20 m	Zooarchaeological materials (from Wing, 1962): *Didelphis marsupialis* (5), *Dasypus novemcinctus* (15), *Tamandua longicaudata* (2), *Agouti paca* (16), *Dasyprocta aguti* (14), *Proechimys guyannensis* (1), *Canis* (3), *Procyon cancrivorus* (2), *Herpestes auropunctatus (4), Pecari tajacu (14), Mazama americana* (23), *Bovidae* (1), *Trichechus manatus* (2)
Erin	Excavation 1, Section A-4, Level 1.20–1.40 m; Excavation 1, Section B-2, Level 1.20–1.40 m	Zooarchaeological materials (from Wing, 1962): *Didelphis marsupialis* (18), *Caluromys philander* (2), *Dasypus novemcinctus* (10), *Tamandua longicaudata* (2), *Sciurus granatensis* (1), *Nectomys squamipes* (1), *Coendou prehensilis* (4), *Agouti paca* (14), *Dasyprocta aguti* (59), *Echimys armatus (2), Proechimys guyannensis (2), Canis* (1), *Procyon cancrivorus* (1), *Lutra enudris* (1), *Felis pardalis* (2), *Herpestes auropunctatus* (1), *Pecari tajacu* (11), *Mazama americana* (61), *Trichechus manatus* (1)
Palo Seco	Excavation 2, Section G-5, Level 0.20–0.40 m; Excavation 2, Section G-2, Level 0.20–0.40 m, Excavation 2, Section G-3, Level 0.40–0.60 m	Zooarchaeological materials (from Wing, 1962): *Didelphis marsupialis* (14), *Dasypus novemcinctus (18), Tamandua longicaudata* (2), *Coendu prehensilis* (6), *Agouti paca* (41), *Dasyprocta aguti (47), Proechimys guyannensis* (2), *Felis pardalis* (1), *Pecari tajacu* (26), *Mazama americana* (76), *Bovidae* (1), *Tapirus* (1), *Trichechus manatus* (1), *Cetacean* (1)
Quinam	Excavation 1, Section A-2, Level 0.40–0.60 m; Excavation 1, Section A-3, Level 0.20–0.40 m	Zooarchaeological materials (from Wing, 1962): *Didelphis marsupialis* (4), *Dasypus novemcinctus (10), Tamandua longicaudata* (2), *Agouti paca* (16), *Dasyprocta aguti (26), Lutra enudris* (1), *Felis pardalis* (2), *Pecari tajacu* (3), *Mazama americana* (27)

Table 3.2. (cont.)

Site name	Context	Associated zooarchaeological material
Manzanilla 1	Several units and one trench (T.3) were excavated. Most from a 2 × 2 m unit called small unit 6 (SU 6). Faunal remains from trench 3 (T.3; 22 × 2.5 m) and units 2 and 3 (LU2, LU3). Trench 3 at the so-called plaza area and a hypothetical third house area which is suggested by the presence of a large posthole and several burials	*Tayassu tajacu* (25.1%), *Mazama americana americana* (11.4%), *Agouti paca* (7.9%), *Dasyprocta agouti* (5.7%)
St Catherine	Fourteen 1 m^2 test units by 10 cm arbitrary levels (see site description)	Carlson (2005, 2007) provides a full zooarchaeological description of this site. Prevalent mammals are *Dasypus novemcinctus* (8%), *Dasyprocta leporina* (8%), *Mazama americana* (6.4%), Echymyidae (6.4%), and *Tayassu tajacu* (4.8%). Among other vertebrates, *Boa constrictor* (2.4%), *Caiman sclerops* (1.6%) *Tupinambis teguixin* (1.6%), *Rhysoprionodon porosus* (1.6%), and fishes like *Caranx hippos* (8.8%) and *Arius felis* (5.6%). Beads made with skate (Rajiformes) and requiem shark (Carcharhinidae) bones.

Comment: All taxonomic identifications from Elizabeth Wing in 1962 are presented as they were published by her with counts of minimum number of individuals. The information from Manzanilla 1 St. Catherine is based on current mammal taxonomy as identified by D. C. Nieweg and L. A. Carlson. Counts for these sites are based on percent of minimum number of individuals

retrovirus might has been present in atelids or cebids from Mesoamerica or northern South America trafficked to and consumed in this Caribbean island before the contact with the Europeans

Another bioarchaeological element of primate origin was recovered within the Turin Taíno cotton *cemí* (1439±1522 CE) (Ostapkowicz and Newson, 2012). Found in a cave located west of Santo Domingo, in the Dominican Republic, this *cemí*, included a sample of hair representing an undetermined Neotropical primate. This cut reddish-brown hair with diameter 34–35 μm. It was also described as having a regular, unicellular, and uniserial ladder covered by a mosaic/imbricated cuticle (Ostapkowicz and Newson, 2012). The comparative hair sample used by Ostapkowicz and Newson (2012) was from a squirrel monkey (*Saimiri sciureus*).

Finally, in the Venezuelan island of Margarita, there is an endemic subspecies of tufted capuchin monkeys (*Sapajus apella margaritae*) (Fig. 3.3). Today, this capuchin

Figure 3.3 Margarita tufted capuchin monkey (*Sapajus apella margaritae*).
(Photograph by Natalia Ceballos-Mago).

taxon is critically endangered (Ceballos-Mago et al., 2010). Linares (1998: 120) claimed that the absence of tufted capuchins from the Orinoco delta and the northern mountain range of Venezuela and the existence of exchange networks between societies of the Lesser Antilles and the Orinoquia "strongly suggest that the insular population [of capuchin monkeys] was established from tamed individuals transported by indigenous peoples from the Orinoco River." Linares (1998) also suggested that the close similarity of insular and continental capuchin individuals and the lack of primates in the zooarchaeological record of the island seem to rule out a relatively recent introduction. Ceballos-Mago (2010, 2013) also proposed a possible eastern origin of this insular tufted capuchin population, such as the Guiana Shield in present-day Surinam, Guyana, and French Guyana. Close to the island of Margarita, a species of white-fronted capuchin monkey (*Cebus trinitatis*) –part of the South American white-fronted capuchin (*albifrons*) group – is reported on the island of Trinidad (Pusch, 1941). This primate taxon has the status of a critically endangered species (Phillips and Jack, 2016). Hershkovitz (1949: 350) indicated that "[*Cebus*] *trinitatis* is completely cut off from its relatives by the northern portion of Venezuela [and] may have been introduced into Trinidad from Brazil or from the interior of Venezuela or Colombia." He also pointed out that the closer populations of white-fronted capuchin monkeys are located in the "upper Orinoco region (*albifrons*) and in the Lake Maracaibo (*adustus*)" and were likely "introduced into the island through human agency" (Hershkovitz, 1949: 380).

3.3   Depictions of Primates in the Circum-Caribbean Region

In this section, we focus on evidence of a dozen primates depicted or allegedly depicted in Caribbean material culture (for conceptual connotations behind the terms 'depiction' and 'representation' used here, see Antczak, 2000). Figure 3.4 shows the locations of the sites where confirmed depictions of primates are found.

Figure 3.4 Distribution of island and coastal archaeological sites of the circum-Caribbean region with depictions of primates in portable objects. (Base map from Wikimedia Commons-CC BY. Creator: San Jose, 2006).

3.3.1 Confirmed and Alleged Portable Objects Depicting Primates

There are seven confirmed depictions of primates in the circum-Caribbean region (Fig. 3.5). In the Greater Antilles, the best known artifact bearing a primate motif was recovered in the Dominican Republic (Fig. 3.5a). The description on the collection file card at the Museo del Hombre Dominicano reads: "Extremely stylized monolithic cruciform axe. At the apex, there is a possible depiction of a monkey, with the hands on the sides of the face. The final part of the axe is the representation of a foot. It has a flange that divides the handle from the rest of the piece" (Olsen-Bogaert, 1981). This Taíno piece is an axe that measures approx. 35 cm long (Inv. # MHD-A000405–24-L) (Jorge Ulloa, pers. comm.), with symmetrical sides (García-Arévalo, 2019: 134). This axe probably represents a Taíno ceremonial artifact (Montás et al., 1983). The depiction of the primate is located in the upper part of the piece (Rimoli, 2010), measuring *c.* 6 × 6 cm without the tail. It was carved in a supine position, with both hands on the ears, flexed hindlimbs, and extended tail, and with a pronounced fringe and prognathic lower facial area. Also, Lovén (1935: Plate XI) presented a photograph of a different axe with an animal face that resembles a primate (former Mus. du Trocadéro Inv. # 2.331) (Fig. 3.5b). The piece measures 23 cm high and 11 cm wide (current Inv. # 71.1884.4.1, Musée du Quai Branly 'Jacques Chirac') (B. Urbani, pers. obs.). It was found in San Tomás de Jánico, near Santo Domingo, Dominican

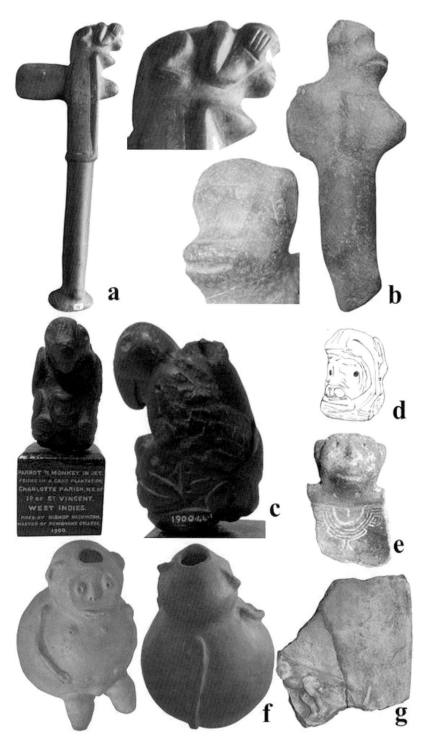

Figure 3.5 Portable objects with primate depictions from archaeological sites of the circum-Caribbean region. See text for localities, descriptions, and contexts. Images not to scale. Photographs

Republic (Lovén, 1935). The head is rounded with a facial mask composed of a large brow ridge with lateral globular ears, and a prognathic lower part. This last morphological attribute is common to both axes with primate motifs and is different from the depictions of human faces in Taíno axes. In both cases, the faces depicted are similar to cebine or ateline primates.

In the Lesser Antilles, Ostapkowicz (2018) reported a small carving of a parrot-like bird and a primate (height: 8.6 cm, width: 5.3 cm) forming a composite snuff tube (Fig. 3.5c). This piece was excavated before 1870 from a plantation in Charlotte Parish on the northeastern part of the island of Saint Vincent (Ostapkowicz, 2018; Fig. 3.4c). Ostapkowicz (2018) found similarity with black carvings reported from the Arauca River in the Venezuelan Middle Orinoco basin by Arroyo et al. (1971). She also suggested that it a possible import from the Lower Orinoco region of Venezuela (Ostapkowicz, 2020). Additionally, Ostapkowicz (2018) presents a three-quarters photograph of this carving. The unknown species of monkey is in a squatting position and displays a light facial mask and a relatively prognathic face. It is currently held in the Pitt Rivers Museum of the University of Oxford (Inv. # 1900.44.1). Recently, Ostapkowicz (2020) indicated that it might be related to the Orinoco's Barrancoid style; however, after a review of Barrancoid primatomorphic depictions (e.g. Urbani and Rodríguez, 2021), this insular object appears to depart from the stylistic repertoire of this ceramic group. Waldron (2009, 2011, 2016) illustrates Saladoid monkey imagery from Grenada, Tobago, and Barbados and states that depictions of primates are rare in indigenous material culture and are mainly concentrated in the southern part of the Lesser Antilles. Waldron (2009, 2011) illustrates a Saladoid adorno (modeled decoration attached to a pot) (250 BCE–650 CE) from Mount Irvine on the island of Tobago that resembles a primate. It has a primate-like prognathic face, lateral nostrils, rear-positioned ears, and frontal mask (Fig. 3.5d). This adorno (2.5 × 5 cm) is now in the Tobago Museum and is similar to examples found in the Orinoco River basin of Venezuela (e.g. Osgood and Howard, 1943; Sanoja, 1979; Urbani and Rodríguez, 2021; see also Waldron, 2016, fig. 4.11 of Barrancoid/Saladoid adorno from Saladero, Venezuela). A Saladoid vessel fragment (5 × 9 cm) from the Chancery Lane site on Barbados held in the Florida Museum of Natural History in Gainesville also merits attention (Fig. 3.5e). Its upper part bears resemblance to a howler monkey (Waldron, 2016: 73–74, fig. 4.12), although the pointy nose and rounded facial area of this adorno may instead indicate a human being. The geometric decoration on the lower part of this same vessel shows a possible necklace and may be related to the ontological liminality between humans and monkeys so visible in the late precolonial Valencioid imagery and purported burials of monkeys with necklaces from the Lake Valencia Basin in north-central Venezuela. Despite this evidence, Waldron is cautious about identifying primates in indigenous imagery considering that "several possible monkey

Figure 3.5 (*cont.*) by J. Ulloa (a), B. Urbani (b, f), Pitt Rivers Museum, Oxford University (c), Florida Museum of Natural History (e), and T. A. Wake (g). Made by B. Urbani based on image from Waldron (2011: 6, fig. 15) (d).

adornos were ambiguous enough to be anthropomorphous, especially when accounting for Saladoid stylizations" (Waldron, 2016: 73).

A monkey-like ceramic vessel exhibited at the Museo de Antropología e Historia de Maracay, Aragua state, Venezuela is allegedly from the north-central Venezuelan town of Ocumare de la Costa in Aragua State (Sýkora, 2006; B. Urbani, pers. obs.) (Fig. 3.5f). The Ocumaroid series spans from 250 CE to 1500 CE (Antczak and Antczak, 1999). The globular vessel has a primate-like facial mask and a rounded tail. Populations of *Cebus brunneus*, *Alouatta arctoidea*, and *Ateles hybridus* currently live near these archaeological sites. In Bocas del Toro, Panama, a monkey is depicted on the exterior surface of a large ceramic rimsherd from Sitio Drago (Fig. 3.5g). The Bocas brushed-pinched ceramic complex consists primarily of small to large necked globular vessels with outflaring red-painted rims. The external rims of these vessels are often decorated with applied figures representing a variety of marine and terrestrial vertebrates and invertebrates (Linares and White, 1980; Wake, n.d.). The illustrated sherd represents the rear half of a monkey hanging below a tree branch by its tail. External sexual organs are depicted in a way that suggests the monkey could represent a female spider monkey. Four monkeys are found in the region (*Alouatta palliata*, *Aotus zonalis*, *Ateles geoffroyi*, and *Cebus capucinus*), with two, mantled howlers and white-faced capuchins, currently found on Isla Colón. In regard to material culture from coastal and island Mayan sites (e.g. Tulum, San Gervasio), there are no known primatomorphic representations to our knowledge. Based on the information available, the objects illustrated in Fig. 3.5 represent the only confirmed depictions of primates on portable objects in the circum-Caribbean region.

There are alleged images of primates in circum-Caribbean material culture that can be traced back for over more than a century. They are reported here as relevant to historical backgrounds of archaeoprimatological interest for this region. For example, pottery adornos in Cuban Taíno sites that were originally described as resembling primates are currently redescribed as bats and owls (Jiménez-Vásquez, 2015). Poey (1855a: 12) indicated that a figurine found at the site of Junco, in Barbacoa, eastern Cuba (Fig. 3.6a):

represents an idol in squatting position on its hindquarters. The front legs are crossed over the abdominal region, without the sculpture making any indication of the genital organs. Behind the head is an eminence like rings without any visible perforation. The idol's features are rude, but his expression is more mocking than fierce. In the position of the front legs, there is a certain lubricity that is peculiar to the monkeys of Guinea, and especially to the *papion* (genus *cynocephalus* [sic]; or dog's head); position that perhaps was imitated of intent. (2). I owe this indication to my father, Mr. Felipe Poey, director of the Natural History Museum of Havana... (2) The black girdle of the visage depicts the face of Walton's monkey similar *simia apella* than the capuchin [in Buffonian terms]. Amans are very close species. (Cuvier, Rein An I.: 102.)

The previous report was later complemented with this comment: "My father, who is perhaps the person who has done more extensive research than any other naturalist in Cuba, nor me, we have not been able to have the slightest news of the existence

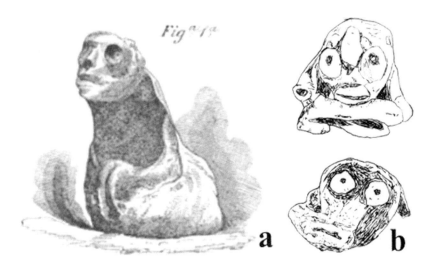

Figure 3.6 Portable objects with alleged primate depictions from archaeological sites of the circum-Caribbean region. See text for localities, descriptions, and contexts. Images not to scale. (From Poey (1855a: Lám. 3) (a), made by B. Urbani based on image from Sýkora (2006: 789, fig. 20–223; 806, fig. 20–261-A.) (b).)

of monkeys, or of the finding of a [monkey] skeleton on the Island" (Poey, 1855b: 26). A current evaluation of the image cited by Poey (Fig. 3.6a) shows that it does not resemble a primate but this was likely the first attempt to interpret a potential depiction of a primate in the pre-Hispanic Caribbean material culture. Later, Harrington (1921) also indicated the inclusion of monkey heads as part of Cuban Taíno pottery adornos. In sum, in Cuba, there is no material culture that depicts monkeys (see also Jiménez-Vásquez, 2015) and even the fact that some Taíno adornos found in the eastern Cuban fields of Maisí are locally named "monitos [little monkeys]" (Rivero de la Calle and Borroto-Páez, 2012: 365).

By 1869, a set of pre-Hispanic adornos and vessel handles collected in Puerto Rico by the former US Consul in San Juan, George C. Latimer, were later deposited and cataloged as "monkey faces" at the US National Museum of Natural History (USNHM-Smithsonian Institution, accession numbers: A17123–0 and A17124–0). Latimer's collection was used by the American archaeologist Jesse W. Fewkes (1850–1930) for writing a pioneering book on Puerto Rican archaeology (Alegría, 1996). In this work, Fewkes (1907: plates LXXIV and LXXV) presented images of archaeological sherds similar to the ones placed in the Smithsonian Institution by Latimer, but indicated that they were found in Santo Domingo, Dominican Republic. Fewler (1907: 181) anticipated the possible misidentification of the "clay heads" and wrote when referring to the images reproduced in both plates that "the general cast of many of the specimens suggests monkey heads, but this resemblance is uninten-tional, being due rather to the method of working clay into faces adopted by the ancient potters. It is impossible to identify the great majority of these figurines, and they may be regarded as simply fantastic forms used for decorative purposes, having no further import or meaning." After a closer examination of a pair of photographs of the ceramic assemblage deposited in the Smithsonian Institution (online images of USNHM A17123-0 and A17124-0) as well as the two plates published by Fewkes (1907), these pieces do not show attributes to describe them as primate depictions. In addition, Fewkes (1907: plate XLIa, a') presented a Taíno three-cornered stone with a face that he identified as a monkey. Unfortunately the image lack quality for proper identification; however, the profile of the object shows a very prognathic facial area that differs from that of a primate (e.g. Fig. 3.5a, b).

Similarly, in the north-central Venezuelan coastal site of Palmasola, Sýkora (2006) reported the existence of pottery attachments that to him resemble monkeys (Fig. 3.6b); nevertheless, after closer examination, they do not present diagnostic attributes that allow us to identify them as primates. Recently, Nortje Wauben (2018: 90, fig. 25) initially considered that certain ceramic adornos from Dominican Republic (El Flaco site, 13th–15th Century) may depict monkeys but finally identified them as "human faces [depicted] with exaggerated mouths." We concur with her identification of them as non-monkey faces.

3.3.2   Alleged Primate Depictions on Rock Art

Systematic study of rock art depicting primates on Caribbean coasts and islands is lacking. This is most likely due to the fact that no primate images are mentioned in the major reviews on rock art research from Trinidad, the Lesser Antilles, and the Virgin Islands (Dubelaar, 1995), the islands of Aruba, Curacao, and Bonaire (Wagenaar-Hummelinck, 1991), Cuba (Nuñez-Jiménez, 1975), the Dominican Republic (Atiles-Bidó, n.d.; DuVall 2011; Pagán-Perdomo, 1978), Puerto Rico (Dubelaar et al., 1999), and Venezuela (e.g. Valencia and Sujo-Volsky, 1987). Hayward et al. (2009) do not mention monkey or monkey-like images among several animals depicted in insular Caribbean rock art. Neither Pérez de Barradas (1941) nor Costa et al. (2015) report indigenous pictographs of primates from the Caribbean coast of Colombia or Central America. In the central mountain range that reaches the Venezuelan Caribbean coast, there is a large rock art panel called Piedra de los Indios depicting petroglyphs of primate-like animals in San Esteban National Park in the state of Carabobo, Venezuela (Valencia and Sujo-Volsky, 1987). In the same mountain range at the site of Camaticaral in the state of Vargas, there are also animal depictions similar to primates (Rojas and Thanyi, 1992; see also Antczak and Antczak, 2007); however, some of these depictions have dots on their bodies that might indicate that they are instead felines.

Although images of primates are generally lacking in the Greater Antilles, there are three cases that deserve further examination. Cueva Número 4 de Borbón at El Pomier, San Cristóbal Province in the Dominican Republic (Atiles-Bidó, n.d.), displays a panel that shows animals with primate-like prehensile tails on what is likely a hunter's carrying rod (Fig. 3.7a). This depiction is associated with a person playing a

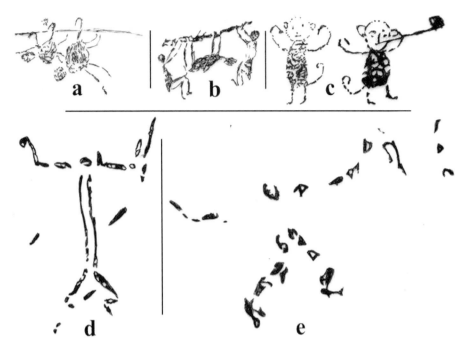

Figure 3.7 Depictions of alleged primates from rock art sites of the circum-Caribbean region. See text for localities, descriptions, and contexts. Images not to scale. Made by B. Urbani based on images from Rivero de la Calle and Borroto-Páez (2012: 364, fig. 4) (a), Atiles-Bidó (n.d) (b), Nuñez-Jiménez (1973: 104, fig. 2) (c), Arrendondo and Varona (1983: 10, fig. 1) (d), Jiménez-Vásquez (2015: 36, fig. 4) (e).

flute. Similar animals, without the tails, are present in the Dominican Cueva Hoyo de Sanabe (Pagán-Perdomo, 1978; Rivero de la Calle and Borroto-Páez, 2012). Apart from hutias, this depiction has been also described as edentates or even Hispaniolan primates on a branch (L. T. Suárez, pers. comm. in Rivero de la Calle and Borroto-Páez, 2012) (Fig. 3.7b). Similarly, in Cuba, Nuñez-Jiménez (1973, 1975) reports animals with primate-like prehensile tails related to "totemic" events depicted in the Cueva de Matías in the Sierra de Cubitas, Camaguey Province (Fig. 3.7c). Nuñez-Jiménez (1973, 1975) provides a more parsimonious suggestion of what might have been depicted: Desmarest's hutias (*Capromys pilorides*). In the Dominican Republic, likewise, the animals might be Hispaniolan hutias (*Plagiodontia aedium*). In both cases, according to the authors, these depictions are possibly related to ritual events.

In Cuba, there has been controversy over a charcoal "archaic" rock painting of an alleged large primate (Jiménez-Vásquez, 2015) (Fig. 3.7d, e). This image is 10 cm height and was discovered in 1981 in Cueva Ciclón (pictography # 1) of the Gato Jíbaro Cavern in the Bellamar Karst System in the Matanzas Province of Cuba (Jiménez-Vásquez, 2015; Rivero de la Calle and Borroto-Páez, 2012). As reviewed by Jiménez-Vásquez (2015), a reconstruction of this image was published by

Pérez-Orozco (1982) as shown in Fig. 3.7d. Arredondo and Varona (1983) imply that it depicts an ateline primate, suggesting its former presence in Cuba. In words of Arredondo and Varona (1983: 10), it is "a true spider monkey (*Ateles*). With its long arms, the small sunken head within the shoulders, in the characteristic position of these platyrrhines as they bipedally move on the ground... [made by] a pre-Agro-Columbian culture of Cuba." Jiménez-Vásquez (2015) requested the original photograph from Pérez-Orozco in order to reexamine the original source (Fig. 3.7e). It was found that the photograph was taken from below, but even so, it is strikingly different than the published version in Pérez-Orozco (1982) and Arredondo and Varona (1983) (Fig. 3.7d). As observed in Fig. 3.7e, the depiction more likely represents a human being. Bruner and Cucina (2005), after republishing Fig. 3.7d, indicated that it represents a pre-Columbian spider monkey even though only Miocene-Pleistocene primates related to *Alouatta* (*Paralouatta*) are found in the Cuban fossil record. In sum, to our knowledge, no confirmed rock art depictions of primates are known from the circum-Caribbean region.

3.4   Early Historical Ethnoprimatology of the Circum-Caribbean Region

Herein, we explore fifteen to seventeen century European chronicles providing ethnoprimatological information of archaeoprimatological interest for the Caribbean (see Urbani 1999, 2011, 2015, 2016b; Urbani and Rodríguez, 2021). Hernando Colón (1488–1539), son of the Genovese admiral Christopher Columbus, in a posthumous text, known by 1571, presented the first account of a monkey seen on his father's landing in Trinidad. The event occurred at present-day Galeota Point, Trinidad, on August 1st, 1498, four days before the first European contact with the American *terra firme* [i.e. Peninsula of Paria, northeastern Venezuela]. This is the first ethnoprimatological record from the Neotropics (Urbani, 2011, 2015). The text reads: "they found many animal footprints that looked like goats, and also bones from one, but, since the head did not have horns, they believed it was a *gato paúl*, or monkey, later they knew that it was, since they saw many *gatos paúles* in Paria [present-day Paria Peninsula, Venezuela]..." (H. Colón, 1932: 132, translation from Urbani [2011]). These bones of monkeys found along the beach may have been deposited by indigenous peoples. Urbani (2011, 2015) identified these primates as Trinidadian *Cebus albifrons trinitatis* or *Alouatta macconelli*; most likely the second, as the term *gatos paúles* was normally used to designate howler monkeys during that period. In 1595, these Trinidadian monkeys were reported to be called *howa* by the indigenous peoples (Dudley, 1899; Urbani, 2004). During his fourth voyage (1502–1504), Columbus reported primates along the Caribbean coast of Central America, likely in Nicaragua or Honduras (Urbani, 1999, 2016b). He wrote that, "A crossbowman hunted an animal, which resembled a cat, except that it is much larger and has the face of a man; it has an arrow between the breasts and the tail, and because he was fierce, he cut off an arm and a leg... threw the tail through the snout and he tied it very tightly and with his remaining hand he slashed it down the top like an enemy" (Colón, 1984: 326). It is not clear if this account refers to a hunter of Spaniard or

Amerindian origin. If the latter, this represents active primate hunting by indigenous peoples in the Neotropics; however, he was most likely a Spaniard. By 1504, the assistant to the Venetian ambassador to the Spanish Crown, Angelo Trevisan, wrote the narrative of the expedition of Pedro Alonso-Niño (1469–1502) in 1499. Alonso-Niño indicated that while "entering the island [refers to *terra firme* = Peninsula of Paria], they saw forests with the tallest dense trees, from where voices of animals filled the country with strange howls. But they saw that there were no dangerous animals, because the local inhabitants of those forests walked quietly, without fear, with their bows and spears" Trevisan (1989: 151, translation from Urbani [2011]). This report relates an unusual account of the indirect interaction of indigenous peoples with likely howler monkeys while sharing the same forest.

By 1516, the Piedmontese chronicler Peter Martyr d'Anghiera (1457–1526) recorded that in the site of Cariai in the western Venezuelan coast "one of our archers shot [a monkey] with an arrow" (Anglería, 1965: 321–322). Once again, unfortunately, it is not possible to know if the hunter was a Spaniard or an Amerindian. Later at the western Venezuelan coast locality of Chichiriviche, he wrote: "That land was raised by wild cats [monkeys]: the mother, carrying them hugging, snakes through the trees and must be wounded to take the offspring. They keep these animals for their entertainment, like us the *cercopitecos* or monkeys, from which they differ greatly, according to the friars putting ties to the banks of the rivers" (Anglería, 1965: 693). The way the text is written appears to indicate that indigenous peoples not only hunted monkeys but also kept them as 'pets'. These primates possibly are *A. arctoidea* and/or *C. olivaceus* (Urbani, 2011, 2015). When discussing the "customs" of the peoples of Cumaná, the Spanish historian Francisco López de Gómara (1511–1566) refers to howler monkeys living near that town along the coast of northeastern Venezuela in 1552. He said that "[they] flee the hunters, take the arrow off and throw it gracefully at the one who threw it" (López de Gómara, 1979: 122). This information is later replicated in 1601 by the Spanish historian Antonio de Herrera y Tordesillas (1601: 160–161) and the friar Pedro Simón (1963: 109) in 1627. These primates likely are *A. arctoidea* and/or *Cebus brunneus* (Urbani, 2015, 2016b). The Milanese traveler Girolamo Benzoni (1519 to 1566–1572?) reported by 1561 that the Amerindians eat monkeys in the Paria region of Venezuela (Benzoni, 1989).

During the seventeen century two Spanish chronicles from the northeastern Venezuelan coast refer to the interaction of indigenous peoples and primates. Between 1672–1708, the Spanish friar Matias Ruiz Blanco (1643–1708) reported that in the coastal town of Píritu, local "indians hunt them, and so they take them. There is a species that are large, very vermilion and have beards in the manner of males. These are what the Indians eat. They go to hunt them and bring their body parts roasted" (Ruiz Blanco, 1965: 24–25). In that region, Ruiz-Blanco also indicated that the *piaches* (shamans) of the Cumanagoto people "were recognized by certain aspects [among others]. . . they bring a sitting idol in the form of a monkey, which they say is their God" (Ruiz Blanco, 1965: 41). These primates are likely *A. arctoidea*. Later in 1786–1789, the Spanish-Ecuadorian historian Antonio de Alcedo y Bejarano

(1735–1812) reported from the same coastal town and the Venezuela Guayana that "indians prefer the meat [of howlers] rather than other animals because they say it is very delicate" (Alcedo, 1988: 152). The previous Spanish chronicles ethnoprimatologically stand as early sources on the use of howlers as 'pets' and as hunted game by the indigenous societies of the northern South American coastal Caribbean.

3.5   Discussion and Conclusions

The relationship between humans and primates in the Neotropics is complex, deeply-rooted in time, and contextually bounded (see Urbani and Cormier, 2015). After examining the osteological evidence of primates from the circum-Caribbean, different patterns can be observed. In most archaeological sites, mainly those from Trinidad, the Venezuelan coast and islands, and Panama, primates appeared to be associated with food related discard contexts. In many of these sites, juvenile or young adult individuals are identified, indicating the possible selection of them by age (Drago, Wanápa. Palmasola, El Cuartel, Trinidadian sites), or being the by-product of hunting adult females (see Urbani, 2005). While few, some of these monkey specimens present direct evidence of processing in the form of cut marks on the bones (Drago, St. Catherine, and Palmasola). The ethnohistorical record also supports the contention that primates in general and howler monkeys in particular, were hunted in the region. This pattern appears to be similar to that observed in lowland South America where howlers figure prominently in subsistence practices of contemporary indigenous societies (Urbani, 2005). Trinidad is interesting because multiple sites on a single large island are reported to have primates as hunted game (including modified bones from Mayaro and St. Catherine sites). These also align with the conspicuous first historical record of likely human-discarded remains of howler monkeys on the island. The data presented here illustrate that howler monkeys were being used in consecutive precolonial periods through the colonial Mission period. A prevalence of cranial remains similar to that seen at the Mayo site in Trinidad is also reported in the El Guácharo cave, Dos Mosquises, and the El Cuartel sites in Venezuela (Urbani and Rodríguez, 2021; Antczak and Antczak, 2006; Urbani and Gil, 2001; Vargas-Arenas, 1979), and the Moraes site in Brazil (Plens, 2010). Plens (2010) posits that this pattern may be due to the increased taphonomic survivability of teeth. This pattern could also reflect a preference for keeping certain skeletal elements involved in particular cultural practices such as cranial parts of the monkeys. In Trinidad, the modification of bones at St. Catherine might imply a special significance of monkeys to the site's inhabitants, e.g. aesthetic or symbolic value, or both. In the vast canon of stories of South American indigenous peoples, monkeys are often presented as tricksters that act in ways inverse to those of humans, but they are often the founders of 'humanity' and ease communication with 'ancestors' (Paulsen, 2019; Waldron, 2016). On the other hand, at Palmasola, capuchins appeared to be the preferred primates. It is also possible that the scarcity of primate material at this site, according to Sýkora (2006), might be related to possible food taboos, although he also indicated that hunting of primates may have increased, as capuchins are currently abundant in the region (assuming similar abundances). Indigenous narratives also inform us that certain species of monkeys are considered huntable game with edible flesh while other monkeys (mainly those with nocturnal habits) are perceived as nonedible spirits, although the latter is not frequent (Paulsen, 2019). The presence of spider monkey specimens at Drago, Panama, may indicate the past local presence of this species on Isla Colón, or possibly importation from the mainland as howlers represent the only ateline species currently present on the island.

In Aruba, the Isla site burial reflects a possible mother–child relationship, while the capuchin monkey could have been a 'pet', a (funerary) gift, a trade item, or maybe an animal with symbolic value to the buried individuals. Similarly, the monkey from Bonaire, was possibly a 'pet.' Other than this sample, no material culture depicting a monkey, or any artifact made of monkey bone has been found in Aruba. It is relevant here to point out that an early chronicle from Chichiriviche, part of the Venezuelan coast fronting the Dutch Antilles, recorded the use of primates as 'pets' by indigenous people (see, chronicler P. M. d'Anghiera in Section 3.4). At Dos Mosquises, the monkey specimen is associated with a food discard (domestic trash) context, although the skull might represent a 'hunting trophy' or may have been an offering. The presence of primates on Bonaire, Aruba, and, perhaps, at Dos Mosquises, may imply the circulation of live animals from mainland central Venezuelan coasts. This pattern of zooarchaeological evidence supports the interconnection of these islands between 25 km and 135 km from *terra firme*. Monkeys as 'pets' and laden with symbolic value may have been transported by the Dabajuroid to Aruba and Bonaire and by Valencioid peoples to Dos Mosquises. It is noteworthy that Giovas (2018) reported the presence of nonnative deer species from South America in archaeological sites of the Lesser Antilles between 500 BCE and 1500 CE (see also Newsom and Wing, 2004). Giovas et al. (2011) reported the exchange of exotic fauna such as peccaries, opossums, agoutis, and armadillos from the continent to Carriacou, a relatively close Lesser Antillean island.

The material from Bonaire, Aruba, and Dos Mosquises (the first two of possible Arawak affiliation, and the latter of Carib linguistic association) represent a continuum of tradition related to the liminal interaction of primates and humans in northern South America. Marcano (1971 [1889]) reported monkey remains recovered at a site on the eastern shore of the Lake of Valencia. Alfredo Jahn excavated monkey remains with a shell necklace in a ceramic urn burial in the same region (Falci et al., 2017; Steinen, 1904). In 1943 Osgood (1943) reported a mound excavated at the site of Tocorón in the early 1930s that yielded a burial of a child or a monkey with shell beads. At nearby Los Cerritos, Peñalver (1981) reported that excavated mounds yielded several burials that include remains of monkeys and associated offerings. This suggests that monkeys were of particular symbolic relevance among the late Caribs of north-central Venezuela as they are repeatedly associated with urn burials and may represent 'pets.' The virtual absence of monkey bones in nonburial contexts in north-central Venezuela, despite their remarkable natural abundance in the region (see Antczak, 1999), suggests that a taboo might have been imposed on hunting them. Unfortunately, apart from the insular Dos Mosquises site, the monkey specimens recovered from these Carib-related sites on the northern Venezuelan mainland could not be relocated and were not reexamined. In the same Valencia region, a worked cranial specimen recovered from the Barrancoid site of La Culebra was relocated (Urbani and Rodriguez, 2021). This site represents an Arawakan occupation of Orinocan traders that reached the area around 200–c. 800 CE (see chronology in Antczak and Antczak, 1999), previous to a second later expansion of Caribs from the same lowland South American region (Antczak et al., 2017a).

The above-referenced osteological material signals the ritual value of primates among the Arawakans of northern Venezuela, and may suggest that ultimately, this tradition may have an Orinocan origin associated with spread of Barrancoid and Saladoid pottery makers (Urbani and Rodriguez, 2021). The sites of El Cuartel and Puerto Santo are Saladoid settlements and this association continues in the region from the time from the first Arawakan occupation to the more recent occupation by Carib-speaking peoples (Urbani and Rodriguez, 2021). In the case of Aruba and Bonaire, this implies an actual connection and influence between Dabajuroid pottery makers of Arawak origin, and the Valencioid people of Carib origin, as has been suggested by a number of authors (Antczak and Antczak, 2006; Bongers, 1963; Boomert, 2003; Dijkhoff, 1997; Dijkhoff and Linville, 2004; Sterks, 1982; Van Heekeren, 1963). Finally, it worth mentioning that the osteological remains of primates are geographically located along the most meridional part of the circum-Caribbean region.

The report of a simian foamy virus in human coprolites from the island of Vieques (Puerto Rico) may indicate contact of peoples of Mesoamerica or northern South America with native populations of cebids and atelids suggesting that long-distance trade may have been occurring between these *terra firme* regions and the island of Vieques in the Greater Antilles. This is not entirely unlikely when considering that confirmed long-distance early maritime connections related to the exchange of variscite existed between the Tairona of northeastern Colombia, and the Los Roques archipelago just off the north-central Venezuelan coast (Acevedo et al., 2016). Even more, pre-Hispanic jadeite artifacts recovered in St. Eustatius and Antigua and dated to ~230–890 CE– the period when this contact occurred with cebids or atelids – appear to confirm a circum-Caribbean exchange network between the Lesser Antilles and present-day Guatemala, Costa Rica, Panama, and Colombia (García-Casco et al., 2013). The green stones and monkeys may represent highly esteemed commodities to indigenous peoples of the circum-Caribbean region.

Compared with closer capuchin populations in northern South America, the very disjunct distribution of capuchin monkeys present in two Caribbean islands (Margarita and Trinidad) appear to suggest the action of humans in the past movement of living individuals of these primate taxa. Regarding the Margarita capuchin monkeys, if the hypothesis of Linares (1998) is correct, then, these primates are living examples of pre-Hispanic mobility of monkeys by indigenous peoples from northern South America to a Caribbean island. Thus, the concentration of archaeological sites with primate remains related to Arawakan peoples (Saladoids) on the Venezuelan coast facing Margarita Island and on the closer island of Trinidad, as reported in this chapter, appears to support this contention. In addition, there are Saladoid sites in the Guianas and the Upper Orinoco that overlap the distribution of the closer *terra firme* populations of tufted capuchin monkeys (*Sapajus apella*). For instance, the Saladoid site of Wonotobo Fall in western Surinam (Boomert, 1983) is on the western limit of tufted capuchins in the Guianas (Lehman, 2006), and Arawakan-related sites are found in the Upper Orinoco River (Zucchi, 1999), where the other closer continental population of *Sapajus apella* is distributed (Linares, 1998; Urbani and Portillo-Quintero, 2018) Today, in this Venezuelan region, peoples of Arawakan linguistic affiliation recognize a tufted capuchin taxon (B. Urbani, pers. obs.). Even more, the connection of the Orinocan sites with Barrancoid/Saladoid primatomorphic depictions with northern Venezuelan Saladoid/Barrancoid sites with primate remains (Urbani and Rodríguez, 2021) seems to reinforce the argument that, if of pre-Hispanic origin, the monkeys of Margarita were not only possibly transported by indigenous peoples, but also likely by Arawakans. Referring to Trinidadian white-fronted capuchin monkeys, Hershkovitz (1949) proposed that the nearest inland populations of white-fronted capuchin monkeys are in the Venezuelan Orinoquia and around Maracaibo Lake. He also proposed that the capuchins of Trinidad might have been transported to this island by humans. If this contention is correct and likewise occurred during pre-Hispanic times in a Trinidadian territory occupied by Saladoid/Barrancoid porters that interacted with monkeys (see Section 3.2.1.8), then the cultural connection with Arawakans also appears more plausible. The nearest region with *albifrons* capuchins is located in the Middle Orinoco River basin (Linares, 1998; Urbani and Portillo-Quintero, 2018), right where one of the most dynamic precolonial exchange and trading centers of multicultural dimension (Arawakan [Saladoid, Barrancoid] and Cariban [Valloid, Arauquinoid, related to coastal Valencioid]) existed in northern lowland South America: the Átures Rapids (e.g. Antczak et al., 2017a; Gassón, 2002; Lozada-Mendieta et al., 2016). Even the Middle Orinoco region is the most conceivable source area for the Trinidadian capuchin taxon, if the alternative of northwestern Venezuela is also considered: there peoples of Arawakan linguistic affiliation (e.g. see Oliver, 1989) overlapped the distributional range of a northern-most *albifrons* form (*Cebus leucocephalus*) (Boubli et al. 2021).

The portable artifacts that depict primates recovered from Taíno sites on two localities on Hispaniola (the Dominican Republic) is striking evidence considering the great distance between those islands and continental primate populations. However, there is confirmed evidence on the presence of Taíno artifacts – and possibly Taíno traders – near the coast of northern South America as found in archaeological surveys on the island of Carriacou, in present-day Grenadian territory (Fitzpatrick et al., 2014). The identification of a hair sample of the Turin Taíno cotton *cemí* requires further attention. Unfortunately, the hair used for comparison is from *Saimiri* spp., a primate taxon with a natural distribution distant from the Caribbean, compared to other cebid genera such as *Cebus* spp. and *Sapajus* spp. (Mittermeier et al., 2012). Other primate species that might be used for comparanda include night monkeys (*Aotus zonalis*), spider monkeys (*Ateles geoffroyi*, *A. fuscipeps*, *A. hybridus*), howler monkeys (*Alouatta palliata*, *A. pigra*, *A. arctoidea*, *A. macconnelli*), and tamarins (*Saguinus oedipus*, *S. geoffroyi*). If the primate hair from the *cemí* of Turin is actually from a squirrel monkey, then it might indicate Taíno exchange with the Guianas, the Middle and Upper Orinoco in present-day Colombia and Venezuela, or perhaps even the Pacific coast of Panama and

Costa Rica where populations of *Saimiri oerstedi* exist. Thus, it is relevant to point out that not only imageries about primates, not depicted in the Caribbean rock art, but also primates or primate parts arrived in the Dominican Republic.

In sum, interaction between native Caribbean human populations and primates has existed since the Archaic Age (e.g. Steadman and Stokes, 2002). In addition, extinct Antillean primates species, such as *Antillothrix bernensis* in the Hispaniola or *Xenothrix mcgregori* in Jamaica, may have also coexisted with indigenous peoples who contributed to their extinction in late Holocene times (Cooke et al. 2017; Gutierrez-Calvache and Jaimez-Salgado, 2006, 2007; MacPhee and Flemming, 1999; MacPhee and Rivero de la Calle, 1996). It was not until the Ceramic Age (300–1500 CE) that diverse sites along the southern circum-Caribbean region show ample osteological evidence as well as material culture indicating deep-rooted connections between indigenous peoples and primates. Early historical records appear to confirm an extended, intricate, and multipurpose interaction between humans and primates. With the development of European maritime trade routes in the Atlantic world, primates from Brazil (*Callithrix* spp.) and Africa (*Chlorocebus aethiops sabaeus* and *Cercopithecus mona*) reached the Caribbean region in the sixteenth and seventeenth centuries (Dore, 2017; Glenn, 1998; Sade and Hildrech, 1965; McGuire, 1974; Urbani, 2019; B. Urbani, pers. obs.) and probably interacted with local indigenous peoples as well. Additionally, for instance, Kemp et al. (2020: 6–7) recently suggested "that the introduction of the yellow fever virus and its mosquito vector, *Anopheles aegypyti* – directly tied to the slave trade – shaped the political fortunes of colonial powers in the Caribbean. . . As monkeys can serve as natural reservoirs for this virus, the Late Holocene extinction of native monkeys from the Greater Antillean islands might have lessened potential local impacts, whereas the introduction of feral monkey populations across the Lesser Antilles may have exacerbated them." The findings presented in this chapter serve not only as a background for future research into human-primate interactions in the circum-Caribbean region but also incentivize comparative studies of interactions between humans and primates on wider spatial scales.

Note Added in Proof

Due to the COVID-19 pandemic, the primate specimen from the Wanápa Site (Island of Bonaire) held at the Florida Museum of Natural History at the University of Florida was unavailable for examination. The absence of this specimen's description does not modify the conclusions of this chapter.

Acknowledgments

Thanks go to Luis Molina for access to the archaeological collection of the Escuela de Antropología at the Universidad Central de Venezuela (UCV) as well as Hyram Moreno (Museo de Ciencias de Caracas) and Carmen Ferreira (Museo de Zoología, Instituto de Zoología y Ecología Tropical, UCV) for the access to the reference primatological collections under their care, James L. Patton (University of California, Berkeley, Museum of Vertebrate Zoology) for access to Berkeley's primate specimens, Cathy Molina and Jonathan Marcot (University College Los Angeles) for access to the James R. Dickey Bird and Mammal primate specimens. Special thanks to Iraida Vargas-Arenas (UCV) for granting permission to publish her photograph from El Cuartel. Segundo Jiménez (Instituto Venezolano de Investigaciones Científicas, IVIC) cooperated in the preparation of Figs. 3.2 and 3.4. To Omar Linares (Universidad Simón Bolívar, USB) for his earlier identifications of primates from Venezuelan archaeological sites. In Caracas, we also appreciate the support of Mario Sanoja (UCV), Luis Lemoine (USB), Lilliam Arvelo (IVIC), Erika Wagner (IVIC), Ascanio D. Rincón (IVIC), Andrej Sýkora, Flor Pujol (IVIC), Juan Carlos Navarro (UCV), and the personnel of the libraries of IVIC and the Venezuelan Speleological Society. In Leiden and Oranjestad, we also appreciate the cooperation of Corinne L. Hofman and Menno L. P. Hoogland. Our gratitude to Damián Ruiz-Ramoni (Centro Regional de Investigaciones Científicas y Transferencia Tecnológica de Anillaco, La Rioja-Consejo Nacional de Investigaciones Científicas y Técnicas), Johan Rodríguez (History Flight, Inc.), and Paul A. Garber (University of Illinois at Urbana-Champaign), for their professional advice in primate identification, and to Dionisios Youlatos and the external reviewer for the constructive comments on an early draft of this chapter. Thanks to Peter O'B. Harris† and Keith Laurence (Trinidad and Tobago National Archaeological Committee) for his support at St. Catherine and Manzanilla. Thanks to Marc Dorst (Leiden) for providing additional information about the Manzanilla 1 site. *Gracias* to Jorge Ulloa at the Museo del Hombre Dominicano for the photograph of Fig. 3.5a and its director Cristian Villanueva for authorizing its reproduction; *thanks* to Laura van Broekhoven, Julia Nicholson, and Chris Morton at the Pitt Rivers Museum in Oxford University for permitting the use of the image of Fig. 3.5c; and *merci* to Paz Núñez-Regueiro, Steve Bourget and Yves Le Fur at the Musée du quai Branly 'Jacques Chirac' for allowing the use of the photograph of Fig. 3.5b, and nicely share their time during the collection visit in Paris (Bernardo Urbani). Bernardo Urbani also appreciates the courtesy of Raymundo A. C. F. Dijkhoff and Harold J. Kelly during his visit at the National Archaeological Museum Aruba in Oranjestad, and during the fieldtrip to Isla site along with Franco Urbani (UCV). For their cooperation, we thank the support of Jay B. Haviser (St. Maarten Archaeological Center) and Oliver Antczak (University of Cambridge) as well as Emperatriz Gamero (IVIC) and Natalia Ceballos-Mago (Fundación Vuelta Larga-University of Montana); the latter also share the photograph of Fig. 3.3. The contribution of Andrzej T. Antczak and M. Magdalena Antczak is the result of the European Union's Seventh Framework Programme, FP7/2007–2013 (ERC Grant Agreement No. 319209), under the direction of Prof. Dr. C. L. Hofman. Lisabeth A. Carlson was supported in the field by Petronin (St. Catherine). We appreciate the institutional support of the Instituto de Patrimonio Cultural (Venezuela), Departamento Nacional de Patrimonio Histórico of the Instituto Nacional de Cultura de Panamá, Smithsonian Tropical Research Institute in Panama, Trinidad and Tobago National Archaeological Committee, and University of the West Indies.

References

Acevedo, N., Weber, M., García-Casco, A., Proenza, J., Sáenz, J., & Cardona, A. (2016). A first report of variscite Tairona Artifacts (A.D. 1100-1600) from the Sierra Nevada de Santa Marta, Colombia, and its implications for Precolumbian exchange networks in the region. *Latin American Antiquity*, 27(4), 549-560.

Alcedo, A. de. (1988). *Diccionario geográfico histórico de las Indias Occidentales o América (1786-1789)*. Caracas: Fundación de Promoción Cultural de Venezuela, Colección Viajes y Descripciones p. 11.

Alegría, R. E. (1996). Archaeological research in the scientific survey of Porto Rico and the Virgin Islands and its subsequent development on the island. *Annals of the New York Academy of Sciences*, 776, 257-264.

Angleria, P. M. de (1965). *Décadas del Nuevo Mundo (1530)*. México DF: Ediciones Porrúa.

Antczak, A. T. (1995). Mammal bone remains from the late prehistoric Amerindian sites on Los Roques Archipelago, Venezuela: An interpretation. In *Proceedings of the 16th International Congress for Caribbean Archaeology*. Basse Terre, Guadeloupe: Conseil Régional de la Guadeloupe, 83-99.

Antczak, A. T. (1999). Late prehistoric economy and society of the islands off the coast of Venezuela: A contextual interpretation of the non-ceramic evidence. Unpublished PhD dissertation. University College London.

Antczak, A. T., & M. M. Antczak (1999). La esfera de interacción Valencioide. In M. Arroyo, L. Blanco, & E. Wagner, eds. *El Arte Prehispánico de Venezuela*. Caracas: Fundación Galería del Arte Nacional, 136-154.

Antczak, A. T., Urbani, B., & Antczak, M. M. (2017a). Re-thinking the migration of Cariban-speakers from the Middle Orinoco river to North-Central Venezuela (AD 800). *Journal of World Prehistory*. 30(2), 131-175.

Antczak, M. M. (2000). "Idols" in exile: Making sense of prehistoric human pottery figurines from Dos Mosquises Island, Los Roques Archipelago, Venezuela. Unpublished PhD dissertation. University College London.

Antczak, M. M., & Antczak, A. T. (2006). *Los ídolos de las Islas Prometidas: arqueología prehispánica del Archipiélago de Los Roques*. Caracas: Editorial Equinoccio.

Antczak, M. M., & Antczak, A. T. (2007). *Los mensajes confiados a la Roca*. Caracas: Editorial Equinoccio.

Antczak, M. M., & Antczak, A. T. (2017). Making beings: Amerindian figurines in the Caribbean. In T. Insoll, ed., *The Oxford Handbook of Figurines*. Oxford: Oxford University Press, 195-220.

Antczak, M. M., Antczak, A. T., & Lentino, M. (2017b). Avian remains from late pre-colonial Amerindian sites on islands of the Venezuelan Caribbean. *Environmental Archaeology*, 24, 161-181

Antczak, K. A., & Beaudry, M. (2019). Assemblages of practice. A conceptual framework for exploring human–thing relations in archaeology. *Archaeological Dialogues*, 26(2), 87-110.

Arredondo, O, Varona, L. S. (1983). Sobre la validéz de *Montaneia anthropomorpha* Ameghino, 1910 (Primates: Cebidae). *Poeyana*, 255, 1-25.

Arroyo, M. G., Cruxent, J. M., & Pérez Soto de Atencio, S. (1971). *Arte prehispánico de Venezuela*. Caracas: Fundación Mendoza.

Atiles Bidó, J. G. (no date). Panorama histórico de los estudios del arte rupestre en República Dominicana. Rupestreweb. Available at: www.rupestreweb.info/panorama.html

Bennett, W. C. (1937). *Excavations at La Mata, Maracay, Venezuela*. New York: Anthropological Papers of the American Museum of Natural History 36, part II.

Benzoni, G. (1989). *Historia del Nuevo Mundo*. Madrid: Alianza Editorial-Quinto Centenario.

Berry, E. W. (1939). Geology and palaeontology of Lake Tacarigua, Venezuela. *Proceedings of the American Philosophical Society*, 81(4), 547-552.

Bongers, H. P. (1963). *Aantekeningen over de archeologie van de Indianen op Aruba*. Manuscript on file, *Archaeological Museum Aruba*. Oranjestad: Aruba.

Bonvicino, C. R., Fernandes, M. E. B., & Seuánez, H. N. (1995). Morphological analysis of *Alouatta seniculus* species group (Primates, Cebidae). A comparison with biochemical and karyological data. *Human Evolution*, 10(2), 169-176.

Boomert, A. (1983). The Saladoid occupation of Wonotobo Falls, western Suriname. *Proceedings of the 9th International Congress for the Study of the Pre-Columbian Cultures of the Lesser Antilles, Montreal*. 97-120.

Boomert, A. (2003). Agricultural societies in the continental Caribbean. In J. Sued-Badillo, ed.*General History of the Caribbean, Vol. 1 Autochtonous Societies*. Paris, London and Oxford: UNESCO Publishing and Macmillan Publishers Ltd, 134-194.

Boomert, A. (2009). Between the mainland and the islands: The Amerindian cultural geography of

Trinidad. *Bulletin of the Peabody Museum of Natural History*, **50**(1), 63–73.

Boomert, A. (2010). Crossing the Galleons' passage: Amerindian interaction and cultural (dis)unity between Trinidad and Tobago. *Journal of Caribbean Archaeology* **10**, 106–121.

Boomert, A. (2013). Gateway to the Mainland: Trinidad and Tobago. In W. F. Keegan, C. L. Hofman, & R. Rodríguez-Ramos, eds., *The Oxford Handbook of Caribbean Archaeology*. New York: Oxford University Press, 141–154.

Boomert, A., Faber-Morse, B., & Rouse, I. (2013). *The 1946 and 1953 Yale University Excavations in Trinidad*. New Haven: Yale University Press.

Boubli, J. P., Urbani, B., & Lynch-Alfaro, J. W. (2021). Cebus leucocephalus (amended version of 2019 assessment). The IUCN Red List of Threatened Species 2021: e.T70333164A191707856.

Bruner, E., & Cucina, A. (2005). *Alouatta, Ateles,* and the ancient Mesoamerican cultures. *Journal of Anthropological Sciences*, **83**, 111–117.

Buisonjé, P. H. de (1974). *Neogene and Quaternary Geology of Aruba, Curaçao and Bonaire*. Utrecht Uitgaven: Natuurwetenschappelijke Studiekring voor Suriname en de Nederlandse Antillen 78.

Carlson, L. (2005). *Zooarchaeological Analysis of the 2004 Season of Excavations at the St. Catherine's Site, Trinidad*. Report prepared for the National Archaeological Committee Trinidad and Tobago.

Carlson, L. (2007). Cursory versus complete: Contrasting two zooarchaeology data analysis approaches at the St. Catherine's Site (MAY-17) in Trinidad. In R. Basil, H. Petitjean Roget, & A. Curet, eds., *Proceedings of the Twenty-first Congress of the International Association for Caribbean Archaeology*. St. Augustine, Trinidad: University of the West Indies, 445–458.

Ceballos-Mago, N. (2010). The Margarita Capuchin Cebus apella margaritae: A critically-endangered monkey in a fragmented habitat on Isla de Margarita, Venezuela. Unpublished PhD dissertation. University of Cambridge.

Ceballos-Mago, N. (2013). A critically-endangered capuchin (*Sapajus apella margaritae*) living in mountain forest fragments on Isla de Margarita, Venezuela. In L. K. Marsh, & C. A. Chapman, eds., *Primates in Fragments: Complexity and Resilience*. New York: Springer, 183–195.

Ceballos-Mago, N., González, C. E., & Chivers, D. J. (2010). Impact of the pet trade on the Margarita capuchin monkey *Cebus apella margaritae*. *Endangered Species Research*, **12**, 57–68.

Civrieux, M. de (1980). Los Cumanagoto y sus vecinos. In A. Butt Colson, ed., *Los aborígenes de Venezuela*, vol. I. Caracas: Fundación La Salle de Ciencias Naturales, 27–241.

Colón, C. (1984) [1502–1504]. Relación del Cuarto Viaje. In C. Valero, (comp.) *Cristóbal Colón. Textos y documentos completos*. Madrid: Alianza Editorial, 316–330.

Colón, H. (1932). *Historia del Almirante Don Cristóbal Colón por su hijo Don Hernando (Tomo Primero)*. Madrid: Librería General de Victoriano Suárez.

Cooke, S. B. , Mychajliw, A. M. Southon, J., & MacPhee, R. D. E. (2017). The extinction of Xenothrix mcgregori, Jamaica's last monkey. *Journal of Mammalogy*, 98, 937–949.

Cordero-Rodríguez, G. A., & Boher, S. (1988). Notes on the biology of *Cebus nigrivittatus* and *Alouatta seniculus* in northern Venezuela. *Primate Conservation*, 9, 61–66.

Costa P., Künne, M., & deBatres L. (2015). Recent rock art studies in Eastern Mesoamerica and Lower Central America, 2005–2009. *Rock Art Studies News of the World*, 4, 11–42.

Cruxent, J. M., & Rouse, I. (1958). *Arqueología Cronológica de Venezuela*, 2 vols. Caracas: Armitano Editores.

DaRos, M., &. Colten, R. H. (2009). A history of Caribbean archaeology at Yale University and the Peabody Museum of Natural History. *The Bulletin of the Peabody Museum of Natural History*, **50**(1), 49–62.

Delsol, N., & Grouard, S. (2015). Comments on Amerindian hunting practices in Trinidad (West Indies): Tetrapods from the Manzanilla site (Late Ceramic Age 300–900 AD). *The Journal of Island and Coastal Archaeology*, **11**, 385–410.

Dijkhoff, R. A. C. F. (1997). Tanki Flip/Henriquez: An early Urumaco site in Aruba. Unpublished Master's thesis. Leiden University.

Dijkhoff, R. A. C. F. (2001). Salvage excavations and accidental finds in Aruba: 1996–2001. *Nineteenth International Congress for Caribbean Archaeology*, Aruba.

Dijkhoff, R. A. C. F., & Linville, M. S. (2004). Aruba, "Island of Shells." In R. A. C. F. Dijkhoff, & M. S. Linville, eds., *The Archaeology of Aruba: The Marine Shell Heritage*. Oranjestad: Publication of the Archaeological Museum Aruba, 10, 1–8.

Dore, K. M. (2017). Navigating the methodological landscape: Ethnographic data expose the nuances of 'the monkey problem' in St Kitts, West Indies. In

K. M. Dore, E. P. Riley, & A. Fuentes, eds., *Ethnoprimatology: A Practical Guide to Research at the Human-Nonhuman Primate Interface.* Cambridge: Cambridge University Press, 219–231.

Dorst, M. C., Nieweg, D. C., Baetsen, S. (2003). Manzanilla 1 (SAN 1) An excavation of an Amerindian habitation area, September 2001. Typescript excavation report.

Dubelaar C. N. (1995*). The Petroglyphs of the Lesser Antilles, the Virgin Islands and Trinidad.* Amsterdam: Natuurwetenschappelijke Studiekring voor het Caraibisch Gebied.

Dubelaar, C. N., Hayward-Merkling , M. H., & Cinquino-Argana, M. A. (1999). *Puerto Rican Rock Art: A Resource Guide.* Buffalo: Panamerican Consultants for Puerto Rico State Historic Preservation Office.

Dudley, R. (1899). Robert Dudley's voyage to the West Indies, 1594–1595, narrated by Himself. In G. F. Warner ed., *The Voyage of Robert Dudley, Afterwards Styled Earl of Warwick and Leicester and Duke of Northumberland, to the West Indies, 1594–1595, Narrated by Capt. Wyatt, by Himself, and by Abram Kendall, Master.* London: The Hakluyt Society, 67–79.

Dupony, W. (1946). La fauna de la Provincia de Venezuela según las relaciones geográficas del siglo XVI. *Memoria de la Sociedad de Ciencias Naturales La Salle,* 6(15), 45–55.

DuVall, D. (2011). *Rock Art Imagery of the Dominican Republic: An Introduction.* Santo Domingo: Editorial Búho.

Du Ry, C. J. (1960). Studies on the archaeology of the Netherlands Antilles: I, Notes on the pottery of Aruba, Curaçao and Bonaire. *Nieuwe West-Indische Gids/New West Indian Guide,* 40(1), 81–102.

Falci, C. G., Antczak, M. M., Antczak, A. T., & Van Gijn A. L. (2017). Recontextualizing bodily ornaments from north-central Venezuela (AD 900–1500): The Alfredo Jahn collection at the Ethnologisches Museum Berlin. *Baessler-Archiv,* 64, 87–112.

Fewkes, J. W. (1907). *The Aborigines of Porto Rico and Neighboring Islands.* Washington, DC: Government Printing Office-Bureau of American Archaeology of the Smithsonian Institution.

Fitzpatrick, S. M., Kaye, Q., Kappers, M., & Giovas, C. M. (2014). A decade of archaeological research on Carriacou, Grenadine Islands, West Indies. *Caribbean Journal of Science,* 48, 151–161.

Ford, S. M. (1990). Platyrrhine evolution in the West Indies. *Journal of Human Evolution,* 19, 237–254.

García-Arévalo, M. A. (2019). *Taínos, arte y sociedad.* Santo Domingo: Banco Popular Dominicano.

García-Casco, A., Knippenberg, S., Ramos, R. R., et al. (2013). Pre-Columbian jadeitite artifacts from the Golden Rock Site, St. Eustatius, Lesser Antilles, with special reference to jadeitite artifacts from Elliot's, Antigua: implications for potential source regions and long-distance exchange networks in the Greater Caribbean. *Journal of Archaeological Science,* 40, 3153–3169.

Gassón, R. (2002). Orinoquia: The archaeology of the Orinoco basin. *Journal of World Prehistory,* 16, 237–311.

Ghersi, B. M., Jia, H., Aiewsakun, P., et al. (2015). Wide distribution and ancient evolutionary history of simian foamy viruses in New World primates. *Retrovirology,* 12, 89.

Giovas C. M. (2018). Continental connections and insular distributions: Deer bone artifacts of the pre-columbian West Indies – A review and synthesis with new records. *Latin American Antiquity,* 29, 27–43.

Giovas C. M., LeFebvre, M. J., & Fitzpatrick, S. M. (2011). New records for prehistoric introduction of Neotropical mammals to the West Indies: evidence from Carriacou, Lesser Antilles. *Journal of Biogeography,* 20, 1 12.

Glenn, E. (1998). Population density of *Cercopithecus mona* on the Caribbean island of Grenada. *Folia Primatologica,* 69, 167–171

Grayson, D. K. (1973). On the methodology of faunal analysis. *American Antiquity,* 38(4), 432–439.

Grayson, D. K. (1978). Minimum numbers and sample size in vertebrate faunal analysis. *American Antiquity,* 40(1), 53–65

Grontmij, & Sogreah (1968). *Water and Land Resources Development Plan for the Islands of Aruba, Bonaire and Curaçao.* Grenoble: De Bilt.

Gutiérrez-Calvache, D. A., & Jaimez-Salgado E. J. (2006). El problema del Ateles cubano. Situación actual y perspectivas. *Boletín del Museo del Hombre Americano,* 40, 7–31.

Gutiérrez-Calvache, D. A., & Jaimez-Salgado E. J. (2007). *Introducción a los primates fósiles de las Antillas. 120 años de paleoprimatología en el Caribe insular.* Santo Domingo: Universidad Autónoma de Santo Domingo.

Harrington, M. R. (1921). *Cuba before Columbus.* New York: Heye Foundation-Museum of American Indians.

Harris, P. O. B. (1972). *Notes on Trinidad Archaeology.* Trinidad and Tobago Historical Society, South Section. Unpublished report, on file.

Harris, P. O. B. (1977). *A Revised Chronological Framework for Ceramic Trinidad and Tobago. Proceedings of the 7th International Congress for the study of Pre-Columbian Cultures of the Lesser Antilles.* Caracas, Venezuela, 47–57.

Haviser, J. B (1991). *The First Bonaireans.* Curaçao: Reports of the Archaeological-Anthropological Institute of the Netherlands Antilles, No.10.

Hayward, M. H., Atkinson L-G., & Cinquino, M. A. (2009). *Rock Art of the Caribbean.* Tuscaloosa: The University of Alabama Press.

Heekeren, H. R. van (1960). Studies on the archaeology of the Netherlands Antilles: II, A survey of the non-ceramic artifacts of Aruba, Curacao and Bonaire. *Nieuwe West-Indische Gids/New West Indian Guide,* **40**(1), 103–120.

Heekeren, H. R. van (1963). Studies on the Archaeology of the Netherlands Antilles: III, prehistorical research on the islands of Curaçao, Aruba and Bonaire. *Nieuwe West-Indische Gids/New West Indian Guide,* **43**(1), 1–24.

Herrera y Tordesillas, A. (1601). *Historia general de los hechos de los castellanos en las Islas y Tierra Firme del mar Océano. Década Tercera.* Madrid: Imprenta Real.

Hershkovitz, P. (1949). Mammals of northern Colombia. Preliminary report No. 4: Monkeys (Primates) with taxonomic revisions of some forms. *Proceedings of the United States National Museum,* **98**, 323–427.

Holly Smith, B., Crummett, T. L., & Brandt, K. L. (1994). Ages of eruption of primate teeth: a compendium for aging individuals and comparing life histories. *American Journal of Physical Anthropology,* **37** (S19), 177–231.

Horovitz, I., & MacPhee, R. D. E. (2012). The primate fossil record of the Greater Antilles. In R. Borrote-Páez, C. A. Woods, & F. E. Sergile, eds., *Terrestrial Mammals of the West Indies.* Gainesville: Florida Museum of Natural History and Wacachoota Press, 305–336.

Humboldt, A. von (1941). *Viaje a las regiones equinocciales del Nuevo Continente.* Caracas: Biblioteca Venezolana de Cultura.

Humboldt, A. von (1956). *Viaje a las regiones equinocciales del Nuevo Continente,* vols. 1–5. Caracas: Biblioteca Venezolana de Cultura.

Jahn, A. (1927). *Los Aborígenes del Occidente de Venezuela; Su Historia, Etnografía y Afinidades Lingüísticas.* Caracas: Litografía y Tipografía del Comercio.

Jahn, A. (1932). Los cráneos deformados de los aborígenes de los Valles de Aragua. *Actas y trabajos científicos del XXV Congreso Internacional de Americanistas,* **1**, 59–68.

Jahn, A. (1940). Estudio sobre el Lago de Valencia. *Boletín de la Academia Nacional de la Historia,* **33** (91).

Jiménez-Vásquez, O. (2011). Los monos extintos. In R. Borroto-Páez, & C. A. Mancina, eds., *Mamíferos en Cuba.* Vaasa: UPC Print, 44–49.

Jiménez-Vásquez, O. (2015). Sobre la coexistencia de los aborígenes precolombinos y los primates en Cuba. *Cuba Arqueológica,* **8**, 33–40.

Kemp, M. E., Mychajliw, A. M., Wadman, J., & Goldberg, A. (2020). 7000 years of turnover: historical contingency and human niche construction shape the Caribbean's Anthropocene biota. *Proceedings of the Royal Society B,* **287**, 20200447.

Kidder, A. (1944). *Archaeology of Northwestern Venezuela.* Papers of the Peabody Museum of American Archaeology and Ethnology 26(1). Cambridge, Massachusetts: Harvard University.

Laffoon, J. E., Sonnemann, T. F., Antczak, M. M., & Antczak A. T. (2016). Sourcing nonnative mammal remains from Dos Mosquises Island, Venezuela: new multiple isotope evidence. *Archaeological and Anthropological Sciences,* **10**, 1265–1281.

Lehman S. M., Sussman R. W., Phillips-Conroy J., & Prince W. (2006). Ecological biogeography of primates in Guyana. In S. M. Lehman, & J. G. Fleagle, eds., *Primate Biogeography.* New York: Springer, pp. 105–130.

Linares, O. (1998). *Mamíferos de Venezuela.* Caracas: Sociedad Conservacionista Audubon de Venezuela.

Linares, O. F., & White, R. S. (1980). Terrestrial fauna from Cerro Brujo (CA-3) in Bocas del Toro and La Pitahaya (IS-3) in Chriqui. In O. F. Linares, & A. J. Ranere, eds., *Adaptive Radiations in Prehistoric Panama., Report 16. Peabody Museum monographs,* No. 5. Cambridge, MA: Harvard University. 181–193.

López de Gómara, F. (1979). *Historia General de las Indias.* Caracas: Biblioteca Ayacucho.

Lovén, S. (1935). *Origins of the Tainan Culture, West Indies.* Gothenburg: Elanders Bokfryckeri Akfiebolag.

Lozada-Mendieta N., Oliver O., & Riris P. (2016). Archaeology in the Átures Rapids of the Middle Orinoco, Venezuela. *Archaeology International,* **19**, 73–77.

MacPhee, R., & Rivero de la Calle, M. (1996). Accelerator mass spectrometry 14C age determination for the alleged Cuban spider monkey, *Ateles* (=*Montaneia*) *anthropomorphus. Journal of Human Evolution,* **30**, 89–94.

MacPhee, R. D. E., & Flemming, C. (1999). Requiem Æternam. The last five hundred years of mammalian species extinctions. In R. D. E. MacPhee, ed., *Extinctions in Near Time. Advances in Vertebrate Paleobiology*, vol 2. Boston, MA: Springer, 333–372.

MacPhee, R. D. E., & Horovitz, I. (2002). Extinct Quaternary platyrrhines of the Greater Antilles and Brazil. In W. C. Hartwig, ed., *The Primate Fossil Record*. Cambridge: Cambridge University Press.

Marcano, G. (1971) [1889–1891]. *Etnografía Precolombina de Venezuela*. Caracas: Instituto de Antropología e Historia, Universidad Central de Venezuela.

Martin, Lana S. (2015). Forests, gardens, and fisheries in an ancient chiefdom: Paleoethnobotany and zooarchaeology at Sitio Drago, a Late Ceramic phase village in Bocas del Toro, Panama. Unpublished PhD dissertation. University of California at Los Angeles.

McGuire, M. T. (1974). *The St. Kitts Vervet*. Basel: S. Kargel.

Mickleburgh, H. L. (2013). Reading the dental record. a dental anthropological approach to foodways, health and disease, and crafting in the pre-Columbian Caribbean. Published PhD dissertation. Leiden University.

Mittermeier, R., Rylands, A. B., & Wilson, D. E., eds., (2012). *Handbook of the Mammals of the World. 3: Primates*. Barcelona: Lynx.

Montás, O., Borrel, P. J., & Moya-Pons, F. (1983). *Arte taíno*. Santo Domingo: Banco Central de La República Dominicana.

Newsom, L. A., & Wing, E. S. (2004). *On Land and Sea: Native American Use of Biological Resources in the West Indies*. Tuscaloosa: The University of Alabama Press.

Nieweg, D. C. (2003). The faunal remains from the SAN-1 site, Trinidad, Phase III, 2003. Unpublished type report for the University of the West Indies (UWI) and The Archaeological Committee of Trinidad and Tobago.

Nuñez-Jiménez, A. (1973). La Cueva de Matías. Estudio de sus dibujos indocubanos. In Panoš, V. ed., *Proceedings of the 6th International Congress of Speleology*. Paper of the Section of Spelo Archaeology. Olomouc (Czech Republic), 101–112.

Nuñez-Jiménez, A. (1975). *Cuba: Dibujos rupestres*. La Habana: Editorial de Ciencias Sociales.

Oliver, J. R. (1989). The archaeological, linguistic and ethno-historical evidence for the expansion of Arawakan into Northwestern Venezuela and Northeastern Colombia. Unpublished PhD dissertation. University of Illinois at Urbana-Champaign.

Oliver, J. R. (1997). Dabajuroid archaeology, settlements and house structures: An overview from mainland Western Venezuela. In A. H. Versteeg, & S. Rostain, eds., *The Archaeology of Aruba: The Tanki Flip Site*. Aruba & Amsterdam: Archaeological Museum Aruba 8/Foundation for Scientific Research in the Caribbean Region, 363–428.

Olsen-Bogaert, H. (1981). Hacha monolítica cruciforme. Código MHD-A 000405-24-L. Época Prehispánica. Cultura Taina. Museo del Hombre Dominicano, Colecciones Arqueológicas. Inventario General (Museum file card by Harold Olsen Bogaert. August 8, 1981).

Osgood, C., & Howard, G. (1943). *An Archaeological Survey of Venezuela. Yale University Publications in Anthropology 27*. New Haven: Yale University Press.

Osgood, C. (1943). *Excavations at Tocorón, Venezuela*. New Haven: Yale University Press.

Ostapkowicz, J., & Newson, L. (2012). "Gods . . . adorned with the embroiderer's needle": The materials, making and meaning of a Taino cotton reliquary. *Latin American Antiquity*, 23, 300–326.

Ostapkowicz, J. (2018). New wealth from the Old World: glass, jet and mirrors in the late fifteenth to early sixteenth century indigenous Caribbean. In, D. Brandherm, E. Heymans, & D. Hofmann, eds., *Gifts, Goods and Money Comparing Currency and Circulation Systems in Past Societies*. Oxford: Archaeopress, 154–193.

Ostapkowicz, J. (2020). Conduits to the supernatural: Bifurcated snuff tubes in the pre-Columbian Caribbean. *Journal of Caribbean Archaeology*, 20, 45–67.

Pagán-Perdomo, D. (1978). *Nuevas pictografías en la Isla de Santo Domingo. Las Cuevas de Borbón*. Santo Domingo: Ediciones del Museo del Hombre Dominicano.

Paulsen, E. (2019). Everything has its Jaguar: A narratological approach to conceptualising Caribbean Saladoid animal imagery. Unpublished PhD dissertation. Leiden University, the Netherlands.

Peñalver Gómez, H. (1981). *Adornos y atavíos: Protectores genitales de los pobladores precolombinos que habitaron la cuenca del Lago de Valencia, Venezuela*. Maracay: Grafindustrial.

Peñalver, J. (1969). *Deformaciones maxilo dento facial en los indios de la cuenca del Lago Tacarigua*. Valencia: Instituto de Antropología del Estado Carabobo.

Pérez de Barradas, J. (1941). *El arte rupestre en Colombia*. Madrid: Instituto Bernardino de Sahagún, Consejo Superior de Investigaciones Científicas.

Pérez-Orozco, L. (1982). Hallazgos arqueológicos en el sistema de Bellamar. *Boletín del Grupo Espeleológicos Norbert Casteret*, 3, 1–4.

Phillips, K. A., & Jack, K. M. (2016). Trinidad white-fronted capuchin. In N. Rowe, & M. Myers. eds., *All the World's Primates.* Charlestown: Pogonas Press, 216–217.

Plens, C. R. (2010). Animals for humans in life and death. *Revista do Museu de Arqueologia e Etnologia*, 20, 31–52.

Poey, A. (1855a). Arqueología americana. Memoria presentada por D. Andrés Poey a la Sociedad Arqueológica Americana sobre "Antigüedades Cubanas" (1). *Revista de La Habana, periódico quincenal, de ciencias, literatura, artes, modas, teatros, & con litografías y grabados*, 4, 12–13.

Poey, A. (1855b). Arqueología americana. Memoria presentada por D. Andrés Poey a la Sociedad Arqueológica Americana sobre "Antigüedades Cubanas" (2) (continuación). *Revista de La Habana, periódico quincenal, de ciencias, literatura, artes, modas, teatros, & con litografías y grabados*, 4, 25–27.

Raguet-Schofield, M., & Pavé, R. (2014). An ontogenetic framework for *alouatta*: infant development and evaluating models of life history. In M. M. Kowalewski, P. A. Garber, L. Cortés-Ortiz, B. Urbani, & D. Youlatos, eds., *Howler Monkeys: Adaptive Radiation, Systematics, and Morphology.* New York: Springer, 289–316.

Requena, R. (1932). *Vestigios de la Atlántida.* Caracas: Tipografía Americana.

Rimoli, R. O. (2010). Presencia de monos entre los taínos. *La Voz del Pueblo Taíno*, 2, 3.

Rivera-Pérez, J. I., Cano R. J., Narganes-Storde Y., Chanlatte-Baik L., & Toranzos G. A. (2015). Retroviral DNA sequences as a means for determining ancient diets. *PLoS ONE*, 10, e0144951.

Rivero de la Calle, M., & Borroto-Páez, R. (2012). Land mammals in indigenous art in the West Indies. In R. Borrote-Páez, C. A. Woods, & F. E. Sergile, eds., *Terrestrial Mammals of the West Indies.* Gainesville: Florida Museum of Natural History and Wacachoota Press, 363–368.

Rojas, A., & Thanyi, L. (1992). *Arte rupestre del Municipio Vargas.* La Guaira: Fondo Editorial El Tarmeño.

Rouse, I. (1947). Prehistory of Trinidad in relation to adjacent areas. *Man* 103, 93–98.

Rouse, I. (1953). Indian sites in Trinidad. In J. A. Bullbrook ed., *On the Excavation of a Shell Mound at Palo Seco*, Trinidad, B.W.I. New Haven: Yale University Press, 94–111.

Rouse, I., & Cruxent, J. M. (1963). *Arqueología Venezolana.* Caracas: Tipografía Vegas.

Ruiz Blanco, P. M. (1965). *Conversión de Píritu.* Caracas: Academia Nacional de la Historia. Fuentes para la Historia Colonial de Venezuela 78.

Sade, D. S., & Hildrech, R. W. (1965). Notes of the green monkeys (*Cercopithecus aethiops sabeus*) on St. Kitts, West Indies. *Caribbean Journal of Science*, 5, 67–79.

Sague-Machiran, M. A. (2008). The Ceremonial Taino petaloid hatchet and its relation to the Maya hatchet god Kawil. Available at: https://indigenouscaribbean.ning.com/profiles/blogs/p-styletextalign-leftimg?overrideMobileRedirect=1

Sanoja, M. (1979). *Las Culturas Formativas del Oriente de Venezuela. La Tradición Barrancas del Bajo Orinoco. Vol. 6.* Caracas: Biblioteca de la Academia Nacional de la Historia.

Sanoja, M. (1969). *La Fase Zancudo. Investigaciones Arqueológicas en el Lago de Maracaibo.* Caracas: Instituto de Investigaciones Económicas y Sociales, Universidad Central de Venezuela.

Sanoja, M. (1970). Análisis zooarqueológico de los restos de una fauna excavados en el sitio Caño Grande, Distrito Colón, Estado Zulia. *Revista de la Facultad de Ciencias Económicas y Sociales de la UCV*, 3, 21–25.

Santos, A. F., Cavalcante, L. T., Muniz, C. P., Switzer, W., & Soares, M. A. (2019). Simian foamy viruses in Central and South America: A New World of discovery. *Viruses*, 11, 967.

Silva-Talboda, G., Suárez-Duque, W., & Díaz-Franco, S. (2007). *Compendio de los mamíferos terrestres autóctonos de Cuba, vivientes y extinguidos.* La Habana: Museo Nacional de Historia Natural.

Simón, Fray P. (1963). *Noticias Historiales de Venezuela. Tomo II.* Caracas: Academia Nacional de la Historia. Fuentes para la Historia Colonial de Venezuela 67.

Steadman, D. W., & Stokes, A. V. (2002). Changing exploitation of terrestrial vertebrates during the past 3000 years on Tobago, West Indies. *Human Ecology*, 30, 339–367.

Steinen, K. von den (1904). Ausgrabungen am Valenciasee. *Globus*, 86(7), 101–108.

Sterks, W. B. J. (1982). Het Archeologisch Aardewerk van Aruba, Curaçao en Bonaire met als Uitgangspunt de Van Heekeren Collectie. Unpublished Master's thesis. Utrecht University.

Sýkora, A. (2006). Manejo de Recursos Faunísticos por los Pobladores del Sitio Prehispánico en Palmasola, Estado Carabobo, Venezuela. Unpublished Master's thesis. Central University of Venezuela.

Tacoma, J., & Versteeg, A. H. (1990). *Skeletmateriaal van de Sites Budui, Malmok, en Canashitu-5 op Aruba.* Intern Rapport Archeologisch Museum Aruba no. 7.

Trevisan, A. (1989). Libretto de tutta la nauigationes de Re de Spagna de le isole et terreni nuouamente trouati. In M. Vannini de Gerulewicz, ed., *El Mar de los Descubridores.* Caracas: Fundación de Promoción Cultural de Venezuela (Colección Viajes y Descripciones, 111–158.

Urbani, B. (1999). Nuevo mundo, nuevos monos: sobre primates neotropicales en los siglos XV y XVI. *Neotropical Primates,* 7(4), 121–125.

Urbani, B. (2003). Utilización del estrato vertical por el mono aullador de manto (*Alouatta palliata,* Primates) en Isla Colón, Panamá. *Antropo,* 4, 29–33.

Urbani, B. (2004). Further information on Neotropical monkeys reported in the XVI century. *Neotropical Primates,* 12(3), 146–147.

Urbani, B. (2005). The targeted monkey: a re-evaluation of predation on New World primates. *Journal of Anthropological Sciences,* 83, 89–109.

Urbani, B. (2011). Further information on Neotropical monkeys reported in the XVI century, Part 3. *Neotropical Primates,* 18, 62–64.

Urbani, B. (2015). Historia de la primatología en Venezuela, Parte 1: Siglos XV y XVI. *Memoria de la Fundación La Salle de Ciencias Naturales,* **175–176,** 125–146.

Urbani, B. (2016a). Nonhuman Primate Samples from the National Archaeological Museum of Aruba, Final Report – Zooarchaeological Collection. Manuscript on file, Instituto Venezolano de Investigaciones Científicas, Caracas, Venezuela.

Urbani, B. (2016b). De *gatos monillos, bogios* y otras *simias* americanas: Los primates neotropicales en la crónica hispano-lusa del siglo XVI. *Anartia,* 26, 71–135.

Urbani, B. (2019). Primates in the Caribbean: Monkeys' Histoire in a 16th-century French manuscript. *Journal of the National Museum (Prague), Natural History Series,* 188, 81–88.

Urbani, B. (2021). Archaeoprimatology, the longue durée interface between humans and nonhuman primates. *Annual Review of Anthropology,* 50, 379–401.

Urbani, B., & Gil, E. (2001). Consideraciones sobre restos de primates de un yacimiento arqueológico del oriente de Venezuela (América del Sur): Cueva del Guácharo, estado Monagas. *Munibe Antropologia-Arkeologia,* 53, 135–142.

Urbani, B., & Cormier, L. A. (2015). The ethnoprimatology of the Howler Monkeys (*Alouatta* spp.): From

past to present. In M. M. Kowalewski, P. A. Garber, L. Cortés-Ortiz, B. Urbani, & D. Youlatos, eds., *Howler Monkeys: Behavior, Ecology, and Conservation.* Springer, New York, 259–280.

Urbani, B., Portillo-Quintero, C. (2018). Consideraciones sobre la distribución y estado de conservación de los primates de la Guayana venezolana. In B. Urbani, M. M. Kowalewski, R. Grassetto Texeira da Silva, S. de la Torre, & L. Cortés-Ortiz, eds., *La primatología en Latinoamérica 2 / A primatologia na America Latina 2. Tomo II. Costa Rica-Venezuela.* Ediciones IVIC, Instituto Venezolano de Investigaciones Científicas, Caracas, 677–689.

Urbani, B., & Rodríguez, J. (2021). Pre-Hispanic howler monkeys from two sites of northern Venezuela and the Orinocan connection: An archaeoprimatological study. *International Journal of Osteoarchaeology,* 31, 325–338.

Valadez, R. (2014). Monos y jaguares en el universo prehispánico. In A. Sandoval-Hoffmann, A. Sandoval-Martínez, & L. I. Saínz, eds., *Los artistas responsables en defensa de la fauna.* Mexico: Vínculos, Comunidad y Cultura A.C., 296–321.

Valencia, R. de, & Sujo-Volsky, J. (1987). *El diseño de los petroglifos venezolanos.* Caracas: Fundación Pampero.

Vargas-Arenas, I. (1978). Puerto Santo: Un nuevo sitio arqueológico de la costa oriental de Venezuela. Actes du Septieme Congres International d'Etudes des Civilisations Precolombiennes des Petites Antilles, 211–229.

Vargas-Arenas, I. (1979). *La Tradición Saladoide del Oriente de Venezuela. La Fase Cuartel.* Caracas: Academia Nacional de la Historia.

Versteeg, A. H. (1990). *Resultaten Voorlopig Onderzoek van het Budui terrein. Intern Rapport Archeologisch Museum Aruba 6.* Oranjestad: Aruba.

Versteeg, A. H. (1997). Pre-Columbian houses at the Santa Cruz site. In L. Alofs, W. Rutgers, & H. E. Coomans eds., *Arubaans Akkoord, Opstellen over Aruba van voor de komst van de olieindustrie.* Stichting Libri Antilliani, Kabinet van de Gevolmachtigde Minister van Aruba, Bloemendaal, 89–101.

Pusch, B. von (1941). Die Arten der Gattung Cebus. *Zeitschrift für Säugetiere,* 16, 183–237.

Wagenaar-Hummelinck, P. (1991). *De Rotstekeningen van Aruba.* Utrecht: Uitgeverij Presse-Papier.

Wagenaar-Hummelinck, P. (1992). *De Rotstekeningen van Bonaire en Curaçao.* Utrecht: Uitgeverij Presse-Papier.

Wake, T. A. (2006). Prehistoric exploitation of the swamp palm (*Raphia taedigera*: Arecacae) at Sitio Drago, Isla Colón, Bocas del Toro, Panamá. *The Caribbean Journal of Science*, **42**, 11–19.

Wake, T. A. (no date). A Pre-European archaeology of Greater Bocas del Toro, Western Caribbean. In C. Dennett, & V. Lyall, eds., *El Mar Caribe: The American Mediterranean*. Denver: Denver Art Museum.

Wake, T. A., De Leon, J., & Fitzgerald, C. (2004). Prehistoric Sitio Drago, Bocas del Toro, Panamá. *Antiquity* Project Gallery **78** (300). Available at: www.antiquity.ac.uk/projgall/wake300/

Wake, T. A., Doughty, D. R., & Kay, M. (2013). Archaeological investigations provide Late Holocene baseline ecological data for Bocas del Toro, Panama. *Bulletin of Marine Science*, **89**(4), 1015–1035.

Wake, T. A., & Martin, L. S. (2016). Proyecto Arqueológico Sitio Drago: Sociedad y Subsistencia Prehistórica en el Caribe Noroccidental de Panamá: Comprendiendo el Comportamiento Ritual Pasado, Fase 2: Pruebas Adicionales en el Sitio Drago (BT-IC-1), Isla Colón, Bocas del Toro, Panamá. Report on file, Departamento Nacional de Patrimonio Histórico, Instituto Nacional de Cultura, Panamá.

Wake, T. A., Martin, L. S., & Mendizábal T. E. (2021). Sitio Drago (Isla Colón, Bocas del Toro, Panamá): Un Aldea y Centro de Intercambio en el Caribe Panameño. In J.-G. Martín, T. E. Mendizábal, & R. G. Cooke, eds., *Más que un puente terrestre: Nuevos datos sobre la vida aldeana en Panamá*. Panamá: Editora Novo Art.

Wake, T. A., Mojica, A. O., Davis, M. H., Campbell, Ch. J., & Mendizábal, T. E. (2012). Electrical resistivity surveying and pseudo three-dimensional tomographic imaging at Sitio Drago, Bocas del Toro, *Panama. Archaeological Prospection*, **9**(1), 49–58.

Waldron, L. (2011). *Geographic distributions of zoomorphic motifs in Saladoid ceramics. Actes du 24e Congress de l'AIAC. Martinique.* 450–466.

Waldron, L. (2009). Whiskers, claws and prehensile tails: Land mammals' imagery in Saladoid ceramics. *Proceedings of the 23rd Congress of the International Association of Caribbean Archaeology, Antigua.* Unpublished presentation.

Waldron, L. (2016). *Handbook of Ceramic Animal Symbols in the Ancient Lesser Antilles.* GainesvilleUniversity of Florida, Florida Museum of Natural History: Ripley Bullen Series.

Wauben, N. (2018). Expressive and performative material culture: investigating the social roles of ceramic adornos from the Site of El Flaco (13th–15th century) in the Northwestern Dominican Republic. Unpublished RMA thesis. Leiden University.

Werbata, J. (1913). *Topografische kaart van Aruba.* [triangulation J. J. Beaujon, R. J. Beaujon en L. Lens, 1904–1909, terrain surveying W. A. Jonckheer 1909–1911]. The Hague: Lith J. Smulders & Co.

Wilson, D. E., & Reeder, D. M., eds., (2005). *Mammal species of the World: a Taxonomic and Geographic Reference.* Vol. 1. Baltimore: Johns Hopkins University Press.

Wing, E. (1962). Succession of mammalian faunas on Trinidad, West Indies. PhD dissertation. University of Florida, USA.

Wing, E. (2012). Zooarchaeology of West Indian land mammals. In R. Borrote-Páez, C. A. Woods, & F. E. Sergile, eds., *Terrestrial Mammals of the West Indies.* Gainesville: Florida Museum of Natural History and Wacachoota Press, 341–356.

Zucchi, A. (1999). El Alto Orinoco. In M. Arroyo, L. Blanco, & E. Wagner, eds., *El arte prehispánico de Venezuela.* Caracas: Fundación Galería del Arte Nacional, 22–33.

4   Mirroring Desert Societies with Monkeys

Primates in the Late Pre-Hispanic and Early Colonial North Coast of Peru, Central Andes (c. 900–1600 CE)

Jorge Gamboa

Un reflejo de la sociedad: Las imágenes prehispánicas tardías y coloniales tempranas del mono en la costa norte de Perú, Andes centrales (*circa* 900-1600 d.C.)

Resumen

A pesar de la distancia geográfica, la costa norte de Perú nunca estuvo desvinculada de las tierras boscosas orientales y la cuenca del Amazonas. Una evidencia de la interacción entre esas regiones es la presencia en el registro arqueológico e iconográfico norcosteño de uno de los habitantes más característicos del bosque amazónico: el mono. En esta contribución se examina la presencia de primates en las sociedades prehispánicas Lambayeque y Chimú. En ambas encontramos representaciones visuales de monos llevados por portadores humanos, monos hamaqueros y monos con frutos. Asimismo, se identifica una imagen cerámica colonial temprana mostrando a un mono junto a un felino. La revisión de la información zooarqueológica e iconográfica permite explorar el simbolismo de los primates para las poblaciones indígenas del norte de la costa peruana durante el tiempo abarcado en esta contribución. Ese ejercicio conduce a reconocer al mono como un signo de relaciones existenciales y jerarquías sociales incorporado tempranamente en las sociedades Andinas, pero a la vez sujeto, como en los casos presentados, a múltiples formas de construcción de significados en torno a su corporalidad, alteridad y conducta.

Palabras clave

Andes – Perú – costa norte prehispánica – período colonial – primates

Abstract

Although the North Coast of Peru and the Amazon basin are separated by hundreds of kilometers and a massive cordillera, they were never worlds completely apart. Imagery of monkeys, one of the most conspicuous inhabitants of the South American tropical forest, provides evidence of interaction among those regions. This chapter examines the presence and meaning of monkeys in the Lambayeque and Chimú cultures, two Late pre-Hispanic societies that developed on the North Coast between 900 CE and 1450 CE. The focus is in particular on figurative depictions of monkeys carried by humans, bearing litters, and holding fruits. A peculiar indigenous early Colonial depiction has also been identified wherein a monkey is portrayed pulling the ear of a roaring feline. A review of zooarchaeological and visual data permits an exploration of the symbolism of monkeys for the Late pre-Hispanic and early Colonial indigenous populations of the northern Peruvian coast. This interpretative exercise leads us to recognize the monkey as both a living sign of dependent relationships and hierarchies and a captive being subject to the construction of meanings based on its corporality, otherness and behavior.

Keywords: Andes, Peru, pre-Hispanic North Coast, Colonial period, primates, iconography.

4.1   Introduction

The *Manuscrito de Huarochirí*, written in Quechua around 1608 in the highlands of Lima, contains a paragraph that speaks of monkeys from a land destined to disappear: "*Chaymanta chay pachataqsi kay Llantapa urqumanta huk pullao sutiyuq chay huk urqu Huichoca ñisqawan hapinakurqan arcohina. Chay Pullao ñisqas ancha hatun saca karqan. Chaysawas **kusillupas** caquipas ima hayka rikchaqkuna pisqukunapas tiyakuq karqan. Chaykunaktawansi tukuy hinantinta qucaman aparqan*" [There was also in that time a pullao tree that grew in this hill of Llantapa and it was linked with another (tree) that grew on a hill named Huichoca; together (their branches) formed an arch. This pullao was a very large tree. Upon its branches there were to be found **monkeys**, caquis and all manner of birds. All were dragged to the sea] ([Tomás?] [1608] 2008: 40–41). This famed indigenous narrative was recorded in a territory unsuited for the natural reproduction of monkeys. The North Coast of Peru is another Andean region lying beyond the natural habitat of South American primates where visual representations and cultural traditions were also elaborated around those tropical forest animals.

   Within academia, the wooden sculptures from the site of Huaca de la Luna in the valley of the Moche River are some of the best known Chimú artifacts of this genre with a secure provenance (Uceda, 1997). Two of those miniature models, which we will refer to more extensively below (see Section 4.6.1.1), present the carved effigies of a man carrying a monkey. These images serve as a point of departure for examining the role of primates in the pre-Columbian ideology of the North Coast of the Central Andes, particularly in the Late pre-Hispanic Chimú and Lambayeque societies (900–1532 CE). The exploration of the varied and complex relationship between Andean societies and the animal world also includes an example from the early Colonial period (1532–1600). This study on the meaning of primates in the Andes also considers relevant data from other regions and periods.

4.2   Relations between Human Society and the Animal World

The existences of *Homo sapiens* and nonhuman primates are deeply and complexly interwoven. A useful perspective for examining this field of mutual interaction is the theoretical stance known as multispecies ethnography defined by Kirksey and Helmreich (2010: 545). They maintain that the human–animal relationship is best understood from a perspective that recognizes the latter as beings with agency. Further, they argue that there is a need to pay greater attention on one hand to the *other*, in this case the animal species, and the consequences of the interaction between human society and nature, on the other. From this viewpoint, primates are recognized as social actors that respond to and initiate change in human socio-economic contexts (Haraway, 2008; Van Dooren et al., 2016). The ontological turn at the center of these propositions evolved out of earlier proposals of Viveiros de Castro (1992, 1998) and Descola (2005). The perspectivism of Viveiros de Castro and the consideration of animism by Descola certainly were crucial in the beginning of the research on ideological systems that place humans in a dynamic environment of corporalities, agencies and hierarchies, intertwined with other animated bodies constantly sought, desired, and interpreted.

The visual rendering of monkeys from the Peruvian North Coast should be examined as part of a larger set of cultural traditions distributed along the Andes and the lowlands of South America. These regions shared similar, but not identical, conceptions and established relations of hierarchy, domination and asymmetrical predation among human beings and a nondomesticated fauna ordered through anthropic categories and interests (Fausto, 2000, 2012). Following Fausto's proposal, the anthropomorphization, iconical and descriptive, of animals would reflect a schema of mutual "predation" negotiated through gestures of commitment aimed to propitiate the hunting of animals (including primates) and legitimate the role of humans as protectors, enemies and inhabitants of the forest.

Understanding of those imagined links as "reciprocal" (or mutual) in terms of negotiation, appropriation, and surrendering can be complemented with the proposals on the conceptual making of humans and animals based in pragmatism. Recently, Servais (2018: 2, 8–9) remarked the need to comprehend these relationships and dependences from situational contexts and the recognition of the forms through which the persons make sense (using their own perceptions) of animal behavior. The dynamism and variability of human–animal interaction was highlighted by this author, who stated "animal status can change abruptly, in a rapid process that challenges the whole definition of the situation" (Servais, 2018: 8). These issues are especially useful to avoid interpretations based in the simple projection of human properties to other (nonhuman) animal beings.

4.3   North Coast, Sierra, and *"Montaña*

The North Coast of Peru – the territory of the Lambayeque and Chimú peoples – is a desert region that extends from Piura to the coast of Ancash and is transected by river valleys that begin in the Andean cordillera. Agriculture in the area depends mostly on complex systems of artificial irrigation. The Peruvian northern coast experienced a notable demographic growth in Late pre-Hispanic times and a population decline in the early Colonial period. The region consists of two main areas. The northern portion between the Alto Piura and Jequetepeque belongs to the southern extreme of the *equatorial forest* region (Brack, 1986; Delavaud, 1984, 2001: 39–34; Hocquenghem, 1991); Late pre-Columbian languages spoken there were Muchik, Sec, and Colán. The southern area forms part of the *Pacific desert* region (Brack, 1986), and encompasses the territory between the Chicama and Huarmey Valleys; Quignam and the Pescadora were two pre-Colonial languages reported for the zone. Inca influence was felt in both areas from 1450 to 1532.

There is no evidence of wild monkey populations on the Peruvian North Coast in the paleontological and archaeological records during the Pleistocene and Holocene periods (Hocquenghem, 2001: 41–43; Jean-Noël Martinez pers. com. 2020). The geographical context of the northern coastal peoples cannot be understood without mentioning the neighboring regions to the north and east. The northern limit of the Peruvian coast constitutes an ecosystem dominated by mangroves and estuaries with beaches and wet and dry woodlands inland that begin on the coast of Ecuador and continue southward to Tumbes and the Chira valleys. To the east, the wooded highlands of Huancabamba and Ayabaca (Piura) and Jaén and San Ignacio (Cajamarca) form corridors linking the northern part of the North Coast with the lower basin of the Marañón River, which serves as a frontier and route to the cloud forests and warm valleys – the *selva alta* – of the Utcubamba River and Chachapoyas (Pulgar Vidal, 1989). The northern and north-central *selva alta*, extends from San Ignacio and Chachapoyas in the north to the Monzón Valley at Huánuco in the south, and serves as a gateway to the vast plainfields and navigable rivers of the lower Amazon Basin (Fig. 4.1).

4.4   Monkeys: Species and Distribution

Wild primate populations of the northern lowlands of South America occupy the rainy regions of the Amazon and Orinoco Basins and some parts of the woodlands to the west of the equatorial Andes. In this section, I will highlight the more abundant primate species occupying the areas proximate to the territory of the Chimú and Lambayeque societies and their neighbors in the northern Peruvian highlands (Fig. 4.2).

Howler monkeys (*Alouatta*) are classified into a number of species. The upper, central, and lower sections of the Amazon are inhabited by *Alouatta palliata*, the black howler, whose range extends far beyond Peru to Mexico in the north. Another species, *A. seniculus* or reddish howler is found from Venezuela to the central high jungle of Peru and the northwest part of Brazil. Similarly, *A. juara, A. puruensis*, and *A. sara* inhabit some parts of these regions. Howler monkeys are found beyond the Amazon Basin as well. The *A. palliata aequatorialis* has been recorded in Amotape (Tumbes), Guaquillas, Machala, and Loja (Hocquenghem, 2001: 43; Hurtado et al., 2016: 153, table 2). *A. seniculus* is present in the forests of Huancabamba, in Piura's sierra (Manchay and Ramírez, 2014) and Jaén-San Ignacio, at Cajamarca (Aquino et al., 2014). The existence of howler monkeys in those areas shows the importance of natural corridors connecting the North Coast with the eastern cloud forest.

Extremely agile in their arboreal habitat, *Ateles* or spider monkeys are recognized by their dark fur and a tuft of hair over the forehead (Rosenberger et al., 2010). The Peruvian and Ecuadorian jungles are home to *A. belzebuth* and *A. chamek*. The black-headed spider monkey *A. fusciceps fuscicepsis* occupies the tropical regions to the west of the Andes in coastal Ecuador. Belonging to a different genus, the

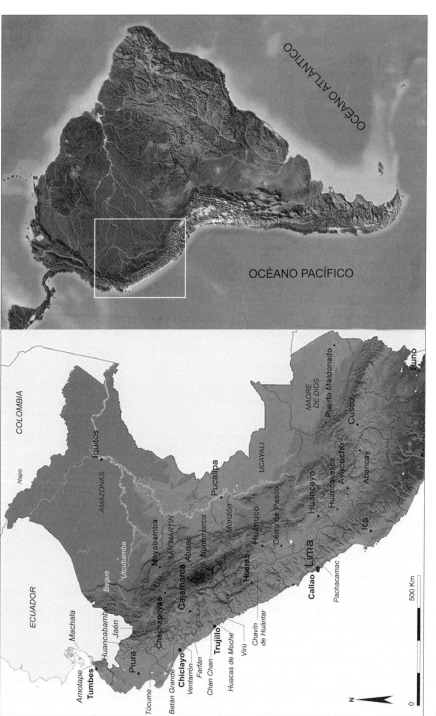

Figure 4.1 Central Andes and sites mentioned in the text. (Based on data from https://solargis.info/). Map by Hoover Rojas in cooperation with Jorge Gamboa.

Figure 4.2 Ceramic representation of a monkey from Nunamarca.
(Pataz, La Libertad, Alto Marañón Basin). Photograph by Federico Mosna, 2018.

Figure 4.3 *Sapajus apella* monkey. Photograph by Shane Hawke
(hawkephotography.com).

yellow-tailed *Lagothrix flavicauda*, a species endemic to the north-eastern Peruvian Andes, is found in the Abiseo River, the Cordillera de Colán, and the Alto Mayo and Alto Nieva valleys.

Forming an extensive family with two genera and 17 species, the highly social capuchin monkeys are the nonhuman primates with widest distribution in the Neotropics (Fragaszy et al., 2004). The genus *Cebus* includes the species that occupy the north and west sections of the Amazon Basin; the genus *Sapajus* refers to species originally found over the south and east parts of that region (Fig. 4.3). With whitish head and shoulders, *C. albifrons*, known as the machín monkey, inhabits the upper and central Amazon, the Caribbean coast of Colombia, the lower western lands of Ecuador (Albuja and Arcos, 2007: 63, 65), and the northern extreme of the Peruvian coast.

C. albifrons aequatorialis is found at Amotape as well as *A. palliata* (Jack and Campos, 2012: 175, 183). Natural populations of *C. albifrons (yuracus)* have been reported at San Ignacio, Cajamarca (Aquino et al., 2014).

In the coastal and upper forest, *Cebus* were not the only capuchin monkeys within reach of the pre-Hispanic northern populations. *Sapajus macrocephalus*, or black tufted capuchins, extends from Colombia to the Juruá and Purús Rivers, and lives in the Marañón, Huallaga, Ucayali, and Alto Amazonas Basins (Aquino et al., 2017: 28–29; Wright et al., 2015: fig. 1), where it shares habitats with *C. albifrons*. *Sapajus apella* occupies the Lower Amazon Basin. Most of the species described are threatened by deforestation, hunting, and international networks involved in the illicit trading of exotic animals.

4.5   Archaeozoological Evidence of Primates in the North and Central Coast of Peru

In comparison with the archaeozoological record of primates in Mesoamerica, where remains of *Alouatta pigra*, *Ateles geoffroyi*, and *Cebus capucinus* have been identified in the Maya lowlands, Teotihuacan, and Veracruz (Baker, 1992; Rice and South, 2015: 278, table 1; Valadez, 2014: 293), the number of remains of those animals in archaeological sites from the Central Andes appears scarce. However, some of the earliest evidence for raising and caring for monkeys in the Western Hemisphere comes from Late pre-ceramic period (3000–1800 BCE) settlements in the North and Central Coasts of Peru. The first of these finds was recorded from the Paloma site, a fishing settlement at Chilca, south of Lima, where a femur of *Ateles* spp. was reported in a burial of a young adult male (Reitz, 2003: 78). The second find belongs to the Pre-ceramic site of Ventarrón, at Lambayeque, where a *C. albifrons*, apparently complete, was buried within a ceremonial building (Alva, 2013: 141, fig. 181); the site also yielded remains of guacamayo (*Ara ararauna*), yaguarundí (*Felis yagouar-oundi*), and an otter (*Lutra felina*). Dating to the same period, the ceremonial center of Caral, in the Supe valley, was a religious complex where people used bone flutes incised with designs of animals identified as howler monkeys (Shady and Leyva, 2003: 291). Archaeozoological evidence of monkeys in "Formative" (1800–100 BCE) northern coastal sites, surprisingly (given the previous data), is elusive.

The physical remains of primates are absent from the archaeological record of wild animals raised in captivity during the Moche period (200–800/850 CE; see Goepfert, 2012). Notwithstanding hard data, Moche style witnessed a "revolution" regarding artistic representations of monkeys. For the Moche, primates (especially *Cebus*) would become liminal beings that lent their features to trading partners and enemies from the warm coca-producing valleys of the northern sierra (Wołoszyn, 2014). The visual culture and materiality of Moche settlements also indicates this coastal society had access to a wide variety of Amazonian plants and animals: ishpingo (*Nectandra* spp.), ulluchu (*Guarea* spp., see Bussmann and Sharon, 2009), toucans, guacamayos (*Ara* spp.), jaguars, and ocelots.

Remains of primates in Chimú and Lambayeque sites (800–1532 CE) are not abundant. Topic (1977, pers. com. 2019) did not report remains of these animals from excavations in middens, commoner residences, and workshop zones of Chan Chan, the Chimú capital. Recently, the project conducted by Gabriel Prieto at Huanchaco, a shore settlement near Chan Chan, identified the body of a monkey in a Chimú context. The Lambayeque cultural area shows a similar situation, with a lack of published reports on the presence of nonhuman primates. A third physical line of evidence that demonstrates access of Central Andean populations to Neotropical primates comes from the central coast. The Templo del Mono at Pachacamac, south of Lima, presented among its foundational offerings the funerary bundle of a *C. albifrons* wrapped in textiles, with a shell placed beside its head. A platform and residential patio dating to the Yschma period (1100–1400 CE) and used in celebrations were built over the burial's level (Eeckhout, 2002, 2004: 438, 441). This architectural space also contained child burials and offerings of coca (*Erythroxylum coca*), Guinea pigs (*Cavia porcellus*) and ishpingo seeds.

4.6   The Monkey in Chimú and Lambayeque Societies

Subsistence on the North Coast during pre-Columbian times depended in large part on the construction and maintenance of irrigation canals. Late pre-Hispanic and early Colonial indigenous rulers – including women in Lambayeque and Piura – controlled the communal workforce necessary for cultivation of lands through norms of reciprocity and, eventually, coercion. Part of the northern coastal population was dedicated to craft production; goods elaborated by those groups were used in local and regional exchange networks. The material culture of popular and ruling Lambayeque and Chimú classes exhibited common features inherited from the Moche and the period of interaction with the Wari society during the Middle Horizon (700–900 CE). The main Lambayeque settlement was Batán Grande (800–1100 CE); later, the political authority of the area shifted to Túcume and other sites. The Chimú political center was located in Chan Chan, in the lower Moche Valley. From Chan Chan, the Chimú extended their control to the rest of the region, extending their domain or influence in around 1300 CE from Piura and Lambayeque in the north to Casma in the south. At approximately 1450 CE the north coast was incorporated into the Inca realm. One of the favored means of reproducing hierarchical and socioeconomic structures throughout this time frame centered on the brewing and distribution of maize *chicha*, an activity that took place both in domestic spaces and public settings (Moore, 1989).

Ceramics were a principal medium for the graphic representation of primates on Peru's ancient North Coast. An exhaustive and detailed study of the number and variety of the Chimú and Lambayeque ceramic images of monkeys, however, is a task yet to be undertaken. Nonetheless, the number of ceramic vessels of both styles with representations of primates appears to be high. These vessels were used as mortuary offerings or as household artifacts. A Chimú ceramic category closely related to the figure of the monkey is the greyware stirrup spout bottle, often with a small monkey at the base of the spout. These same pieces sometimes show the entire figure of a primate on the vessel chamber. Another ceramic category depicting monkeys is jars with everted necks and ovoid bodies, the last provided with a three-dimensional head of a primate and extremities and tail modeled in relief on the vessel wall. In the Lambayeque style we find ceramic images of monkeys on bottles (with one or two spouts as well as on jars). Monkey figures on bowls and figurines appear to be less common in these regional styles.

The Chimú introduced ceramic forms typical of the first tradition described above into the Lambayeque area around 1100–1200 CE. Further south in the Casma area (between the Chao to Huarmey Valleys), the Casma style also featured ceramic images of monkeys in ceremonial and utilitarian pots and jars (Gamboa, 2020). The Inca period on the northern coast of Peru did not produce radical changes in the ceramic forms produced in the territory controlled by the Chimú; rather, that time witnessed continuity in the manufacture of cooking, storage, and ritual vessels. Additional examples of representations of monkeys on Chimú and Lambayeque ceramics can be found in the works of Narváez (2014a, 2014b) and Shimada (1995: 76). Further, Mackey and Nelson (2020) published a large set of Chimú-Inca vessels found in context at the site of Farfán in the Jequetepeque Valley. The cases presented in the following sections include renderings of primates in ceramics and other materials.

4.6.1   Images of Primates in the Chimú and Lambayeque Styles

4.6.1.1 Porters Bearing Monkeys

Each of the Chimú wooden models with monkey effigies from Huaca de la Luna showed the processional transportation of closed bundles (Uceda, 1997: 159). The similarity of the bundles and their human porters with scenes rendered on Chimú ceramics featuring the transport of extended human bodies invites comparison between the two groups of images. But do they depict living individuals or corpses? Processions of high-ranking personages borne in litters and hammocks were common in late pre-Hispanic/early Colonial times. Similarly, Moche iconography showed the use of those conveyances as symbols of status and memory for the living and the dead (Makowski, 2001: figs. 1, 3a). At Guadalupito (600–800 CE), in the Lower Santa Valley (100 km to the south of Chan Chan and Huaca de la Luna), archaeologists documented the burial of a Moche male wrapped in textiles and tied to a long wooden pole that could serve to transport his corpse (C. Chapdelaine, pers. com. 2008).

The rear parts of the Huaca de la Luna's Chimú scenes were completed by three male characters: two holding jars over their heads and, in the middle, an individual carrying a monkey (Figs. 4.4 and 4.5). Primates appear climbing directly over the back of their porters, holding onto his head and shoulders with their feet and hands. The absence of cords to secure the animals is a trait that deserves attention; notably, the position of each animal and their porters suggests that these wooden sculptures depict living monkeys exhibited in real situations. Ahead of the men with vessels and animals, we encounter a woman with a child on her back, the funerary bundle porters, and men transporting diverse objects.

Figure 4.4 Chimú wooden model from Huaca de la la Luna. Courtesy of Dr. Ricardo Morales, Director of Huacas del Sol y de la Luna Project.

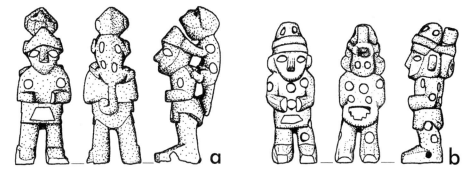

Figure 4.5 Porters carrying monkeys (a) and jars (b) in Chimú wooden model from Huaca de la Luna. (Based on images from Uceda, 1997: figs. 83, 89).

A sample of 53 Chimú wooden sculptures from two other Moche Valley sites, Huaca Tacaynamo and Huaca El Dragón, produced depictions of men carrying jars with lids but no representations of monkey porters (Jackson, 2004). However, there are two additional examples of Chimú (or late pre-Hispanic) renderings of primates being carried by a human; both are in the Museo Larco collection (which brings together archaeological materials collected during the first part of the twentieth century from the southern part of the North Coast). The first piece (ML100461) is a silver pin that repeats in part the design of the Huaca de la Luna carvings; in this artifact the man takes one of the monkey's hands in a gesture of indeterminate meaning apparently related to the manipulation of a sphere or fruit. A second example (ML21088) corresponds to a ceramic jar in which the primate stands over the shoulder of an adult male, with a cord around its neck, illustrating a modality of captivity not seen in the previous examples. This vessel could be an elaboration inspired by a Moche model.

4.6.1.2 Monkeys in Chimú Vessels

Chimú vessels were made with molds (a factor we should always remember when contemplating the frequency of this motif). A common type of Chimú ceramic

Figure 4.6 Chimú stirrup spout bottles depicting monkeys. Museo Larco, Lima (ML021778, ML021781). Drawings by Jorge Gamboa.

artifact was the stirrup spout bottle, a vessel used in different functional ways (such as mortuary offerings, kitchen utensils, or household ritual objects). On those vessels it is common to find a small effigy of a monkey placed between the spout and the handle, a position that, if we follow De Bock's (2012) suggestion, signaled the encounter of opposed pairs. These bottles have been recorded at Huaca de la Luna (Tufinio, 2006: 60–61, 2013: 83). Chimú vessels including monkey motifs were also reported at El Brujo (Chicama Valley), where Bennett (1939: fig. 17a, b, d) excavated bottles with the monkey on the stirrup handle, jars with appliqued sculptural heads of a monkey, and vessels with the figure of a primate holding fruit.

Other Chimú and Chimú-Inca vessels feature large quadrupedal monkeys with a cord around their waist; in these examples, a diminutive monkey occupies the spout's base (Narváez, 2014a: fig. 339). At Farfán the monkey on the handle was replaced during the Inca period by an ornament in the likeness of a bird (Mackey, 2003: 336, fig. 13a, 23); the Chimú-Inca jars of Complex VI at the same site frequently showed the head, extremities, and tail of a primate (Mackey, 2003: fig. 19). On the stirrup spout bottles of monkeys on all fours the animal was depicted looking attentively ahead with its tail coiled downward (a position usual in capuchin monkeys); in some examples, the head of those primates also reveal the features of *Cebus* or *Sapajus* (Fig. 4.6). The position and morphology of the monkey's body in the described bottles are similar to those of vessels representing a quadruped feline. The affinity between monkeys and felines in compositional images of the Middle Horizon from the central coast of Peru has been also noted by Karadimas (2016: fig. 6).

A different category of Chimú visual representation shows the primates eating a pacay (*Inga feuillei*), a fruit of the warm coastal and sierra lands, or exhibiting their genitalia. The effigy of a monkey with pacay crowns a second pin in the Museo Larco (Narváez, 2014a: 259). Primates could be also represented eating the "pepino" (*Solanum muricatum*) or sweet cucumber. A bottle in the Museo de América de

Figure 4.7 Hamaquero monkeys in Lambayeque vessel. Museo Nacional Brüning. Photograph by Jorge Gamboa.

Madrid shows this kind of image (Martínez, 1986: fig. 7). At Pachacamac, a small silver spoon, possibly used for extracting the lime employed in the chewing of coca, was decorated with the figure of a monkey with a maize cob (Pozzi-Escot and Uceda, 2015: 46–47). Those images could indicate the perception of the monkey as an animal able to manifest sensuality and satisfaction, a theme that will be examined later. Northern images of monkeys eating and carrying fruits were produced until the Inca period. The excavations of Luis E. Valcárcel (1946: 181) in Sacsayhuaman (Cusco) produced a vessel in the Chimú style representing a monkey with two pacay fruits.

4.6.1.3 The Lambayeque "Hamaquero" Monkey

The northern section of the region was occupied from the eight century CE onwards by the Lambayeque (or Sicán) populations. From 900 to 1200 CE the ceremonial center of Batán Grande established political and economic links with the coast and highlands of Ecuador, the Chimú area, and the Cajamarca sierra. As mentioned above (see Section 4.6), Túcume and other sites took the lead in the following centuries. The Lambayeque style included depictions of monkeys in the role of litter and hammock porters. A Late Lambayeque bottle now in the Museo Brüning illustrates this motif (Fig. 4.7): two monkeys of different size transport a hammock in which a smaller and less humanized primate rests. Asymmetry in the dimension of the porters seems related to other Lambayeque scenes with pairs of large and small monkeys associated with a crescent-shaped object (Narváez, 2014a: 172). It should be noted that hammocks take the form of a crescent, which supports the existence of a link between both designs. That kind of affinities could include the pacay fruit, whose pods may take a crescent form.

Chotuna-Chornancap was another main Lambayeque settlement. A complex female burial excavated at the site presents an outstanding assembly of Lambayeque, Chimú, Cajamarca, and Ecuadorian materials. Among the offerings were vessels decorated with monkeys holding pacay fruit placed around the funerary bundle (Wester, 2016: 188–189, fig. 104). The Chornancap tomb incorporated

Figure 4.8 Chimú architectural vessel with monkey and a type of roof frequently found in Lambayeque area. Museo Nacional Brüning. Photograph by Jorge Gamboa.

another instance of primate imagery: a miniature scenic group that shows the transport of a chief on a litter (Wester, 2016: 326). Porters of the litter are four humanized monkeys of similar size. Distinct from his servants, the personage carried on high presented fully anthropomorphized features and possesses earspools and a headdress.

4.6.1.4 Primates in Architectural Settings

The Chimú ceramic corpus includes images of monkeys within architectural models (Fig. 4.8). Sometimes, primates stand in a central position of the built, and presumably, sacred space. That placement would have marked the association between the animal, the edifice, and the ritual activity taking place there; nevertheless, the exact meaning of this kind of depiction is still unknown. Monkeys could be employed as a token alluding to the religiosity and ceremonies of death – something suggested by the Huaca de la Luna wooden scenes and the Chotuna-Chornancap's data. The northern association of precincts, primates, and mortality recalls the Templo del Mono's case at Pachacamac (Eeckhout, 2004), the building dedicated with the burial of a *C. albifrons* monkey.

4.6.1.5 Chimú-Inca Ceramics

The Chimú-Inca period (1450–1532 CE) seems to have been one of continuity, if not of increase, of the range of meanings attributed to monkeys by the northern coastal populations. With their political center in Cusco, in the southern highlands, the Incas

Figure 4.9 Colonial indigenous vessel with monkey and feline. Museo Nacional Brüning. Photograph by Jorge Gamboa.

had an elaborate conception of the forested lands and their inhabitants. At Farfán and Túcume (Levine, 2011; Mackey, 2003), two administrative and religious Inca centers on the North Coast, tombs have been recorded with ceramic vessels decorated with images of a monkey with a cord around the waist. Jars molded in the form of a primate were also integrated into the offerings of a Chimú-Inca female burial at Huaca Curaca, in the rural hinterland of Chan Chan (Donnan and Mackey, 1978: 369, 371). The Andean Late Horizon (1450–1532 CE) included a particular type of artifact: the *pacchas*, a recipient with a spout used for pouring water or chicha in rituals of fertility; some *pacchas* adopted the design of the monkey jars popular in Farfán and Túcume (Carrión Cachot, 2005: plate 21y).

4.6.1.6 Early Colonial Representation

We now turn to the appearance of primates in the indigenous material culture of the colonial North Coast. The early Colonial period was for the region a time of profound political and economic change, disruption of native cultural patterns, and demographic decline. The Museo Brüning of Lambayeque preserves a Colonial vessel that shows an improbable couple: a monkey grabbing a roaring feline by the ear (Fig. 4.9). This double-chamber bottle belongs to the ceramic type that Van Valkenburgh et al. (2015) calls "indigenous lead-glazed." The primate exhibits long arms – in literal and allegoric senses – and a triangular forehead. The feline lacks spots and therefore might depict a puma (*Puma concolor*). The vessel morphology makes reference to opposed dualities expressed both in its compositional form and the figurative encounter depicted on one of its parts.

4.7   Routes of Interregional Traffic

While primates were clearly important to the native peoples of the North Coast, where craftsmen imbued representations of simians with a variety of meanings, the actual physical remains of primates in Chimú and Lambayeque settlements are surprisingly uncommon. A possible explanation is that the real number of monkeys in the Chimú and Lambayeque settlements was always low; another option is that their bodily remains were subject to special treatments that make difficult their identification. Clearly, tropical products, both from the Amazon basin and the Ecuadorian coast, were, as evidences of the Preceramic to the Inca periods demonstrate, important during millennia for the political economies of northern coastal polities. Further study is needed to determine the pre-Hispanic routes of long-distance exchange that gave inhabitants of the North Coast access to primates; this will have important implications for understanding wider patterns of trade, exchange and transcultural contacts in South America. For the moment, I propose the following points of origin for monkeys introduced into the North and North-central coastal sections of the Central Andes:

4.7.1   Tumbes and the Coast of Ecuador

When one considers the provenance of monkeys brought to the coast and sierra of Peru in pre-Hispanic times and more recently, usually the Amazon Basin is the first focus. However, the sources of those animals may have been more diverse than assumed. *C. albifrons aequatorialis* occupies Amotape, where it coexists with *A. palliata aequatorialis*. The Lambayeque and Chimú maintained contact with Tumbes and Guayaquil (McEwan and Delgado, 2008; Shimada, 1995: 87, 89, 158). The Amotape area also presents Inca state installations (Vílchez, 2015). The latter zone and some parts of the Ecuadorian coast (as Machala and Guayas) could, in this perspective and following the route of the *Spondylus* shell traffic from Ecuador to the Central Andes, have provided of specimens of *C. albifrons* to the North Coast.

4.7.2   Forested Sierra of Piura-Cajamarca

The identification of *A. seniculus* in the highlands of Piura (Manchay and Ramirez, 2014) and *Cebus* and other primates in the northern provinces of Cajamarca (Aquino et al., 2014) suggests that there may have been more options for North Coast peoples to acquire primates. In this case, capuchin monkeys could have been taken in the forested Sierra of Piura and Cajamarca and transported to the west through the corridors that connect the Huancabamba-Jaén-San Ignacio area with the coast of Piura and the northern part of Lambayeque.

4.7.3   Chachapoyas and Bagua

Some *Cebus* and *Sapajus* monkeys introduced into the North Coast could have originated in the *selva alta* of Chachapoyas and the nearby zones of Bagua, Chiriaco (Imaza) and Condorcanqui. The Chachapoyas area was in contact with the northern coast and sierra from the Formative period onwards (Guengerich and Church, 2017:

316–319; Guffroy, 1992). The arrival of the north-oriental *Cebus* at the coast could be one component in the circulation of a larger set of goods – ishpingo, ulluchus, selected varieties of coca, medicinal herbs, gold, and Amazonian birds – in demand for distinct coastal and highlands groups.

4.7.4   Alto Marañón and Huallaga Basins

The potential *tumbesino* or northeastern origin of primates brought to the North Coast should not lead us to ignore other possible pre-Hispanic routes of commerce. For example, the high jungle of the La Libertad to Huánuco area was accessible from the north-central sierra, the meridional Chimú territory, and the north-central coast. The main routes of that interregional system would have included natural corridors like Abiseo-Pataz-Tablachaca-Santa and, to the south, Monzón-Alto Marañón-Chavín de Huántar-Fortaleza. Presently, the Mishollo, Tocache, Crisnejas, Chontayacu, and Monzón (San Martín and Huánuco) forests, 30–70 km to the east of the Marañón River, are inhabited by a high diversity of primates, including *Cebus yuracus* and *S. macrocephalus* (Aquino et al., 2017: table 3).

4.8   Interpretations

4.8.1   Food and Subsistence

The monkey is represented in the indigenous iconography of the Peruvian coast as a "thirsty" being. In Moche ceramics monkeys were depicted directing themselves to the mouth of the jars or attached to that part of the vessel (occasionally leaving aside a bag with ulluchus). In other cases, they were dressed as religious officiants or are shown firmly holding, with all four paws, a jar. The Early Chimú (800–1000 CE) potters placed monkey effigies with ropes around their waists on the neck of jars; those images have been found in Huacas de Moche (Rojas and Mejía, 2013: 394, fig. 23) and Virú (Bennett, 1939: fig. 9g). The pepino, a sweet fruit that stores substantial amounts of water, illustrates the association among wet fruits, monkeys, and the management of liquids in the late pre-Hispanic ritual dramas. Something similar can be said of images of the pacay, another favorite food of the northern monkey. The Chimú-Inca *pacchas* in the form of pacays are not rare (Carrión Cachot, 2005; Joyce, 1922: fig. XI.4); in these cases, the pacay was shown complete, without a monkey about to devour it. The pacay fruit is usually bigger in seasons of abundant water. The act of feeding and being fed (Ramirez, 2005) would have found an appropriate reference in the figurative presentations of the monkey holding a fruit, a motive that probably became an implicit allusion to the life cycle.

4.8.2   A Symbol of Distant Lands

Monkeys appear to have been identified as living signs of the east, the direction of their places of origin and the daily sunrise. However, as described above (see 4.5), the origin of primates raised in captivity on the North Coast could comprise a wider set of regions extending from Tumbes to the Alto Marañón. Economic and political inter-actions articulating the North Coast, Cajamarca, and the Marañón Basin were firmly established from the second millennium BCE (Alva, 2013; Kaulicke, 1998; Shady, 2011). The late pre-Hispanic North Coast's engagement with Tumbes and Machala reveal, for its part, a complexity that defies simple models of conquest or hegemonic domination (Hocquenghem, 1993; Moore, 2008). During the Spanish Colonial period, the monkey continued to be a symbol of eastern lands, but it also became an index of its potential dangers. In the thirteenth century, a water colorist painter working for Baltazar Martínez de Compañón, Trujillo's bishop, painted an *omeco-machacuai* serpent as a bicephalous, hairy being that wound its body around a *catahua* tree while devouring a primate and a deer (Trever and Pillsbury, 2011: 246–247).

4.8.3   A Sign of Human Hierarchies

It is necessary to return our attention to the jar porters in Chimú sculptures. In the Huaca Tacaynamo carvings, the jars shown with lids were considered by Jackson (2004: 314, 316) to be containers filled with chicha. Vessels carried on high at the end of the Chimú processions could serve as a visual and performative reference to the distribution of chicha. The chicha beer, or *kotso* in the Muchik language (Schaedel, 1988: 118), was a drink of varying alcoholic content produced in both specialized and domestic kitchens. The distribution of chicha was sponsored by rulers, who used it in acts of reciprocity required for securing the collaboration of local chiefs and farmers. That kind of social contract remained active until at least 1566 (Rostworowski, 1975: 122).

The Lambayeque scenes of *hamaquero* monkeys do not speak only of a form of comportment and ordering of bodies in the physical landscape. The early colonial *parcialidades* (labor groups based on descent) of hammock carriers in Lambayeque and Trujillo had a special status related to their proximity, and sometimes, kinship with noble lineages. The hamaqueros were subject to internal diversity, having leaders in charge of their organization and performance: an example from the first decades of the Colonial period was the curaca Chiquiamanaque (or Chicama Anaque), "jefe de los hamaqueros del Chimú Capac [chief of the litter porters of the Chimú ruler]" (Netherly, 1990: 475, 480; Rostworowski, 1976).

The presence of the monkey in north coastal ceremonial and public spaces also reflects relations of hierarchy and reciprocity between unequal pairs. A modern relational complex found in Quechua oral literature from the southern sierra portrays the fox and the puma as *compadres* or fictive brothers, a link created through the norms of kinship and categorization particular to human communities. In these narratives the fox is also a young and subordinated relative –*niñucha* or *lari/tayu* (*cuñado*) – of the feline (Harris, 2000: 156; Urton, 1985: 260). A comparable type of asymmetrical relationship could involve felines and monkeys as well.

4.8.4   Metaphor and Social Satire

Daily and ritual humor is a topic rarely explored in pre-Colonial and Colonial Andean societies. The anthropomorphization of animals, in this context, should be understood not only in terms of their figurative transformation; animals could also become signs of the errors and weaknesses of mankind. The projection of anthropomorphic qualities to animals use to open the door to expressions of social critique. We are reminded of the action in the colonial bottle of the Museo Brüning: the monkey grasping the ears of a feline (that shows its fangs, but does not attack its daring companion), while touching the puma's flank with his other hand. In this image, the monkey exercises an apparent or momentary domination over the feline, a symbol of the *curacas* and their political authority (Zuidema, 1983). Here I propose that this vessel materialized through visual metaphor a narrative on diverse indigenous socioeconomic segments, making mention in the tone of derision or mockery of power disputes (or contradictions) between those groups.

To whom could this reference have been directed? The early colonial *hamaqueros* – the human counterpart of the hammock-carrying Lambayeque monkeys – were subject to both indigenous and European critiques. The affirmation, perhaps biased, of Gonzales de Cuenca to those personages in the town of Jayanca, in 1566, presented them as guilty of "juntar y ençerrar las yndias solteras doncellas y biudas del repartimiento [gathering and locking up the indigenous single girls and widowed women of the area]" (Rostworowski, 1975: 141). The early Colonial period was a time of changing dynastic lines and political progress for individuals of previously minor status. An example of the ascent to power is provided by the careers of Don Christobal and Pedro Ocxaguaman, curacas of the lower Moche Valley (Netherly, 1990: 472) and son and grandson of Canocachay – a minor rank relative and "prenzipal de los chicheros" [leader of the chicha brewers] of the last Chimú rulers (Zevallos, 1994). Although promoted because of the interests of Colonial authorities, the elevation of these personages also reflected the tensions and rivalries within local native populations.

A second interpretation of this remarkable vessel is that it depicts a healing ceremony; however, the absence of any implement used in those rituals (Gareis, 1994) does not tend to support that interpretation. The motif of the monkey pulling the ear of a feline can be seen as an artistic and narrative trope pointing to the changes in social positions in the early Colonial period. The indigenous popular literature of the northern coast in the sixteenth and seventeenth centuries is little known. The monkey appears in the modern oral stories of Lambayeque, in which it is presented as the animal transformation of *curanderos* (healers) considered to be linked to the pre-Hispanic world, the natural forces, and, given the demonization of indigenous religions in colonial and republican periods, the devil. An example comes from Túcume; in that narrative, the monkey, a respected and feared healer, has human behaviors – a taste for chicha, snoring while sleeping, and stealing maize from the farmers – and is skillful in descending from mamey (*Pouteria sapota*) trees (Narváez, 2014b: 289–290).

4.8.5   Monkeys and Sensuality

Rural traditions of the Peruvian north portray the monkeys as sweet toothed, and avid eaters of pacays, pepinos, and maize. That attribution can also be seen in the pre-Hispanic iconography. Pozzi-Escot and Uceda (2015) interpret the metallic effigy of a monkey with a maize cob as the depiction of an act of offering. There is a complementary possibility. Those images could make reference to the observation of the rules of commensality between human and nonhuman purveyors of sustenance, but also could show the satisfaction of the animal depicted. Today, fruits like the mamey, the chirimoya, and the papaya are used in the northern coast and sierra as allegories of the female sexuality evoked and desired. Despite the advances in the study of the discursive relation between eating and sexuality in the Andes and Amazon Basin (Allen, 2012: 271; Rossi, 1999), the links between eating, the satisfaction of senses, and sex in both regions should be seen as an extensive field of meanings still only partially explored.

4.9   Final Comments

The links created by humans to make sense of, and legitimize, their relationships with animals place the latter in situations of otherness, subalternity, and inferiority – something visible even in those societies where wild beings have a marked religious and political symbolism. In the late pre-Hispanic and early Colonial periods of the Andes, primates would have been perceived as beings ontologically different and "inferior" to humans. In Colonial times that position was the product of a major event. In the narratives of Con and Pachacamac from the central coast of the sixteenth and seventeenth centuries, monkeys were presented as descendants of a primal human population wiped out for their persistent failure to show gratitude toward their creators (Duviols, 1983). That imperfect mankind, described as "unfinished" by Alva (2013: 141), became transformed into monkeys, felines, and other animals. Becoming in monkeys was presented in those narratives (apparently marked by Western precepts on sin and fall) as a necessary prelude of the process that led to the formation of true humanity. The weight of the Christian ideology in these indigenous versions of the origin of society and nature is an issue yet unresolved.

In a more recent complex of beliefs, monkeys are the by-product of a socialization process that allowed some animals to become humans. For the inhabitants of the Napo River basin, cutting off the long tail possessed by Secoya or Huitoto ancestors marked the appearance of the true anthropomorphic beings; for its part, the severed tails gave rise to the capuchins, spider monkeys, and howlers (Casanova, 1990). The incomplete condition of the Secoya ancestor was demonstrated by "its" inability to produce a true *masato* – the fermented drink of yucca – or cook correctly the fruit of the *pihuayo*. The desire for a well prepared *masato* acted as final impulse that led the ancient settlers to abandon the interior of the earth; the primate's tail was reaffirmed in that transition as testimony of the alterity attributed to the animal world. Here it is

Figure 4.10 "Monkey seated with chain" by Hendrick Goltzius, c. 1597. Rijksmuseum. (https://commons.wikimedia.org/wiki/File:Seated_Monkey_on_a_Chain.jpg) Public Domain.

worth noting the existence of differences and continuities in the pre-Hispanic and Colonial indigenous perspectives on similar subjects and objects. A comparison of Andean indigenous reflections on primates also reveals points of divergence and commonalities with the European, medieval, and modern, viewpoints on monkeys (Fig. 4.10) – among them, the emphasis on the subaltern nature of the animal body and its integration into the social life of its captors and owners (Urbani, 2014; Veracini and Martins-Teixeira, 2017).

An analysis informed by a broad historical and anthropological framework, but not less rigorous for its breadth, helps to clarify the meanings of pre-Hispanic and Colonial Andean indigenous images of the monkey. On the pre-Colonial Peruvian North Coast, primates were appreciated as beings of human likeness associated with burial ceremonies and public celebrations. At the same time, those animals served as a conventional symbol for distant regions important in the religious and political coastal order. Early Colonial narratives from the sierra and central coast on imperfectly formed versions of humankind surviving in monkeys should not be immediately extended to the northern groups and ideologies, where primates may have been perceived differently. Within even a single region, there emerge temporal and zonal differences in the ontological construction of the monkey. Among the Moche, we find images of naturalistic monkeys, humanized primates, and humans with monkey features; the late pre-Hispanic primate was, on the contrary, less often transmuted into a human hybrid. Chicha and social stratification were co-essential to all of those conceptions of primates.

The pre-Columbian and early Colonial images of the monkey on the North Coast of Peru resist the formulation of a generalizing theory. Rather than being mutually exclusive, the interpretative possibilities presented above can be seen as part of the multiplicity of meanings attributed to primates in the Andes and the Peruvian north. Departing from a pragmatist viewpoint (Servais, 2018), it can be assumed that the entanglement of the Chimú and Lambayeque peoples with monkeys was also mediated by situational conditions and everyday relationships that produced a number of perceptions and practical actions larger than those visually indexed. The condition of a well-fed and revered monkey coexisted with the one of the manipulated and imprisoned primate, with each instance producing convergent forms of delight, astonishment, annoyance, or compromise.

This research revealed the value of extending the analysis and perspectives on the indigenous management of wild animals beyond the boundaries established for the time of contact among the Andes, the Amazon, and Europe. For the late pre-Hispanic populations of the North Coast, monkeys were popular symbols of the captive, subaltern, and, possibly, incomplete body. The early Colonial vessel – a piece belonging to one of the last episodes of this history – could present in metaphorical terms the tensions particular to a cycle of alteration of the Andean structures of authority and power. Neotropical primates are yet subject to discipline and routine by their human masters, who in turn find themselves under diverse forms of normalization and control of their own behavior. The making of those relationships reflects a constant desire for extending (and imposing) the parameters of human conduct to and upon certain animals. These anxieties and reflections are, as this essay has sought to demonstrate, inherent to coexisting with a being as similar and different from ourselves.

Acknowledgments

Shane Hawke kindly provided the photograph of a *Sapajus* monkey included in the chapter. Hugo Iván Chávez (Ministerio de Cultura de El Salvador), Ingrid Coronado (Universidad Nacional Pedro Ruiz Gallo, Lambayeque), Karina Garrett (Universidad Nacional de La Plata), Jean-Noël Martínez (Instituto de Paleontología, Universidad Nacional de Piura), Robert Markens (Instituto de Investigaciones Estéticas, Sede Oaxaca, Universidad Nacional Autónoma de México), Federico Mosna (Pontificia Universidad Católica del Perú), Verónica Ortega (Instituto Nacional de Antropología e Historia -Teotihuacán), Enrique Plasencia, Gabriel Ramón (Pontificia Universidad Católica del Perú), Hoover Rojas (Universidad Nacional de Trujillo), Sarahh Scher (Salem State University), Raquel Soriano (Escuela Nacional de Antropología e Historia, Mexico), Edward Swenson (University of Toronto), and Eladio Terreros (Instituto Nacional de Antropología e Historia, Mexico) collaborated with references and questions. David Pacifico (University of Wisconsin Milwaukee) generously shared valuable data on the late pre-Hispanic societies from the coast of Ancash and, with Robert Markens, helped to translate this chapter.

References

Albuja, L., & R. Arcos. (2007). Evaluación de las poblaciones de *Cebus albifrons* cf. *aequatorialis* en los Bosques Suroccidentales Ecuatorianos. *Politécnica*, 27(4) *Biología*, **7**, 58–67.

Allen, C. (2012). *Foxboy: Intimacy and Aesthetics in Andean Stories*. Austin: University of Texas Press.

Alva, I. (2013). *Ventarrón y Collud. Origen y auge de la civilización en la costa norte del Perú*. Lima: Ministerio de Cultura and Proyecto Naylamp.

Aquino, R., Charpentier, E., García, G., Arévalo, I., & López, L. (2014). Reconocimiento de primates y amenazas para su supervivencia en bosques premontano y montano de la Región Cajamarca, Perú. *Neotropical Primates*, 21(2), 171–176.

Aquino, R., García, G., Charpentier, E., & López, L. (2017). Estado de conservación de *Lagothrix flavicauda* y otros primates en bosques montanos de San Martín y Huánuco, *Perú. Revista Peruana de Biología*, 24(1), 25–34.

Baker, M. (1992). Capuchin monkeys (*Cebus capucinus*) and the ancient Maya. *Ancient Mesoamerica*, 3(2), 219–228.

Bennett, W. (1939). *Archaeology of the North Coast of Peru. An Account of Exploration and Excavation in Viru and Lambayeque Valleys*. New York: American Museum of Natural History.

Brack, A. (1986). Las ecorregiones del Perú. *Boletín de Lima*, **44**, 57–70.

Bussmann, R., & Sharon, D. (2009). Naming a phantom – The quest to find the identity of *Ulluchu*, an unidentified ceremonial plant of the Moche culture in Northern Peru. *Journal of Ethnobiology and Ethnomedicine*, 5, 8.

Carrión Cachot, R. (2005). *El culto al agua en el Antiguo Perú*. Lima: Instituto Nacional de Cultura.

Casanova, J. (1990). El mito de los ancestros Secoya. Origen de los humanos y los monos. *Amazonia Peruana*, 19, 89–98.

De Bock, E. (2012). *Sacrificios humanos para el orden cósmico y la regeneración. Estructura y significado en la iconografía Moche*. Trujillo: Ediciones Sian.

Delavaud, C. (1984). *Las regiones costeñas del Perú septentrional*. Lima: Centro de Investigación y Promoción del Campesinado and Pontificia Universidad Católica del Perú.

Descola, P. (2005). *Beyond Nature and Culture*. Chicago: University of Chicago Press.

Donnan, C., & Mackey, C. (1978). *Ancient Burial Patterns of the Moche Valley, Perú*. Austin: University of Texas Press.

Duviols, P. (1983). El*Contra Idolatriam* de Luis de Teruel y una versión primeriza del mito de Pachacámac-Vichama. *Revista Andina*, 1(2), 385–392.

Eeckhout, P. (2002). Hallazgo y desenfardelamiento de un bulto funerario de Pachacamac. In V. Solanilla, ed. *Actas de las II Jornadas Internacionales sobre textiles precolombinos*. Barcelona: Universitat Autonoma de Barcelona, Departament d'Art, 135–152.

Eeckhout, P. (2004). Relatos míticos y prácticas rituales en Pachacamac. *Boletín IFEA*, **33**(1), 1–54.

Fausto, C. (2000). Of enemies and pets: Warfare and shamanism in Amazonia. *American Ethnologist*, **26**(4), 933–956.

Fausto, C. (2012). Too many owners: Mastery and ownership in Amazonia. In M. Brightman, V. Grotti, & O. Ulturgasheva, eds., *Animism in Rainforest and Tundra: Personhood, Animals, Plants and Things in Contemporary Amazonia and Siberia*. Oxford: Berghahn, 29–47.

Fragaszy, D., Visalberghi, E., & Fedigan, L. (2004). *The Complete Capuchin: The Biology of the Genus Cebus*. Cambridge University Press.

Gamboa, J. (2020). Un personaje elusivo: Los monos en el estilo cerámico Casma de la costa norcentral de Perú (ca. 800–1350 dC). *Chungará*, 52(2), 285–303.

Gareis, I. (1994). Una bucólica andina: curanderos y brujos en la costa norte del Perú (siglo XVIII). In L. Millones, & M. Lemlij, eds. *En el nombre del señor. Shamanes, demonios y curanderos del norte del Perú*. Lima: Seminario Interdisciplinario de Estudios Andinos, 211–230.

Goepfert, N. (2012). New zooarcheological and funerary perspectives on Mochica culture (100–800 AD), Peru. *Journal of Field Archaeology*, 37(2), 104–120.

Guengerich, A., & Church, W. (2017). Una mirada hacia el futuro: Nuevas direcciones en la arqueología de los Andes Nororientales. *Boletín de Arqueología PUCP*, **23**, 313–334.

Guffroy, J. (1992). Las tradiciones culturales formativas en el Alto Piura, In D. Bonavia, ed. *Estudios de Arqueología Peruana*. Lima: FOMCIENCIAS, 99–122.

Haraway, D. (2008). *When Species Meet*. Minneapolis: University of Minnesota Press.

Harris, O. (2000). *To Make the Earth Bear Fruit: Ethnographic Essays on Fertility, Work and Gender in Highland Bolivia*. London: University of London, Institute of Latin American Studies.

Hocquenghem, A. M. (1991). Frontera entre 'Áreas culturales' nor y centroandinas en los valles y la costa del extremo norte peruano. *Boletín IFEA*, **20**(2), 309–348.

Hocquenghem, A. M. (1993). Rutas de entrada del Mullu en el Extremo Norte del Perú. *Boletín IFEA*, **22**(3), 701–719.

Hocquenghem, A. M. (2001). Una historia del bosque seco. *Debate Agrario*, **33**, 39–60.

Hurtado, C., Serrano-Villavicencio, J., & Pacheco, V. (2016). Population density and primate conservation in the Noroeste Biosphere Reserve, Tumbes, Peru. *Revista Peruana de Biología*, **23**(2), 151–158.

Jack, K., & Campos, F. (2012). Distribution, abundance, and spatial ecology of the critically endangered Ecuadorian capuchin (*Cebus albifrons aequatorialis*). *Tropical Conservation Science*, **5**(2), 173–191.

Jackson, M. (2004). Chimú sculptures of Huacas Tacaynamo and the Dragon. *Latin American Antiquity*, **15**(3), 298–322.

Joyce, T. (1922). The "paccha" of ancient Peru. *Journal of the Royal Anthropological Institute of Great Britain and Ireland*, **52**(1), 141–149.

Karadimas, D. (2016). Monkeys, Wasps and Gods: Graphic perspectives on Middle Horizon and later pre-Hispanic painted funerary textiles from the Peruvian coast. *Nuevo Mundo. Nuevos Mundos*. Available at: https://doi.org/10.4000/nuevomundo.69281

Kaulicke, P. (1998). El periodo Formativo de Piura. *Boletín de Arqueología PUCP*, **2**, 19–36.

Kirksey, S. E., & Helmreich, S. (2010). The emergence of multispecies ethnography. *Cultural Anthropology*, **25**(4), 545–576.

Leo, M. (1989). Biología y conservación del mono choro de cola amarilla (*Lagothrix flavicauda*), especie en peligro de extinción. In C. Saavedra, R. Mittermeier, & I. Santos, eds. *La Primatología en Latinoamérica*. Washington, DC: World Wildlife Fundation, 23–30.

Levine, A. (2011). A case for local ceramic production in the Jequetepeque Valley during the Late Horizon. In C. Zori, & I. Johnson, eds., *From State to Empire in the Prehistoric Jequetepeque Valley, Peru*. Oxford: BAR Publishing, 169–177.

Mackey, C. (2003). La transformación socioeconómica de Farfán bajo el gobierno Inka. *Boletín de Arqueología PUCP*, **7**, 321–353.

Mackey, C., & Nelson, A. (2020). *Life, Death and Burial Practices during the Inca Occupation of Farfán on Peru's North Coast. Andean Past Special Publications*, **6**. Available at: https://digitalcommons.library.umaine.edu/andean_past_special/6

Makowski, K. (2001). Ritual y narración en la iconografía mochica. *Arqueológicas*, **25**, 175–203.

Manchay, J., & Ramírez, S. (2014). Registro de dos poblaciones de «mono aullador» *Alouatta seniculus* (Linnaeus, 1766) en la provincia de Huancabamba,

región Piura, Perú. *Revista Biodiversidad Neotropical*, **4**(1), 49–54.

Martínez, M. C. (1986). Temas iconográficos de la cerámica Chimú. *Revista Española de Antropología Americana*, **16**, 137–152.

McEwan, C., & Delgado, F. (2008). Late Pre-Hispanic polities of coastal Ecuador. In H. Silverman, & W. Isbell, eds., *Handbook of South American Archaeology*. New York: Springer, 505–525.

Moore, J. (1989). Pre-Hispanic beer in Coastal Peru: Technology and social context of prehistoric production. *American Anthropologist*, **91**(3), 682–695.

Moore, J. (2008). El Periodo Intermedio Tardío en el Departamento de Tumbes. *Revista del Museo de Arqueología de la Universidad Nacional de Trujillo*, **10**, 155–175.

Narváez, A. (2014a). *Dioses de Lambayeque. Introducción al estudio de la mitología tardía de la north coast de Perú*. Chiclayo: Ministerio de Cultura and Proyecto Naylamp.

Narváez, A. (2014b). *Dioses, encantos y gentiles. Introducción al estudio de la tradición oral Lambayecana*. Chiclayo: Ministerio de Cultura and Museo Túcume.

Netherly, P. (1990). Out of many: The organization of rule in the north coast polities. In M. Moseley, & A. Cordy-Collins, eds., *The Northern Dynasties: Kingship and Statecraft in Chimor*. Washington DC: Dumbarton Oaks, 461–485.

Pozzi-Escot, D., & Uceda, C. (2015). *Museo Pachacamac*. Lima: Ministerio de Cultura.

Pulgar Vidal, J. (1989). *Análisis geográfico de la Región Nororiental del Marañón*. Lima: Instituto Nacional de Fomento Municipal.

Ramirez, S. (2005). *To Feed and Be Fed: The Cosmological Bases of Authority and Identity in the Andes*. Stanford: Stanford University Press.

Reitz, E. (2003). Resource use through time at Paloma, Peru. *Bulletin of Florida Museum of Natural History*, **440**, 65–80.

Rice, P., & South, K. (2015). Revisiting monkeys on pots: A contextual consideration of primate imagery on Classic Lowland Maya pottery. *Ancient Mesoamerica*, **26**, 275–294.

Rojas, C., & Mejía, J. (2013). Plataformas funerarias menores oeste del núcleo urbano Moche. In S. Uceda, & R. Morales, eds., *Proyecto Arqueológico Huaca de la Luna. Informe Técnico 2012*. Universidad Nacional de Trujillo, 363–422.

Rosenberger, A., Halenar, L., Cooke, S., & Hartwig, W. (2010). Morphology and evolution of the spider monkey, genus *Ateles*. In C. Campbell, ed., *Spider*

Monkey: The Biology, Behavior and Ecology of the Genus Ateles. Cambridge University Press, 19–49.

Rossi, P. (1999). Cuando los amantes se transforman en tunches: Sexo y moral en las sociedades nativas en transformación. *Amazonia Peruana*, 13(26), 211–254.

Rostworowski, M. (1975). Algunos comentarios hechos a las ordenanzas del Doctor Cuenca. *Historia y Cultura*, 9, 119–154.

Rostworowski, M. (1976). El señorío de Changuco. *Boletín IFEA*, 5(1–2), 97–147.

Schaedel, R. (1988). *La etnografía muchik en las fotografías de H. Brüning 1886–1925*. Lima: Ediciones COFIDE.

Servais, V. (2018). Anthropomorphism in human-animal interactions: A pragmatic view. *Frontiers in Psycholog*, 9, 1–10.

Shady, S. (2011). Sociedades Formativas de Bagua-Jaén y sus relaciones andinas y amazónicas. In P. Lederberger, ed., *Formativo Sudamericano. Una reevaluación.* Quito: Abya-Yala, 201–211.

Shady, R., & Leyva, C. (2003). *La ciudad sagrada de Caral-Supe.* Lima: Instituto Nacional de Cultura.

Shimada, I. (1995). *Cultura Sicán. Dios, riqueza y poder en la costa norte del Perú.* Lima: Banco Continental y Edubanco.

[Tomás?] (2008 [1608]). *Ritos y Tradiciones de Huarochirí.* G. Taylor,ed., Lima: Instituto de Estudios Peruanos, IFEA y UNMSM.

Topic, J. (1977). The lower class at Chan Chan. A qualitative approach. PhD thesis. Harvard University.

Trever, L., & Pillsbury, J. (2011). Martínez de Compañón and his illustrated 'Museum'. In D. Bleichmar, & P. Mancall, eds., *Collecting Across Cultures: Material Exchanges in the Early Modern Atlantic World.* Philadelphia: University of Pennsylvania Press, 236–253.

Tufinio, M. (2006). Excavaciones en el Frontis North y Plaza 1 de Huaca de la Luna. In S. Uceda, & R. Morales, eds., *Proyecto Arqueológico Huaca de la Luna. Informe Técnico 2005.* Universidad Nacional de Trujillo, 41–77.

Tufinio, M. (2013). Excavaciones en Fachada Norte y Plaza 1: Resultados de la temporada 2004. In S. Uceda, E. Mujica, & R. Morales, eds., *Investigaciones en la Huaca de la Luna 2004.* Trujillo: Proyecto Huacas del Sol y de la Luna, 57–90.

Uceda, S. (1997). Esculturas en miniatura y una maqueta en madera. In S. Uceda, E. Mujica, & R. Morales, eds., *Investigaciones en Huaca de La Luna 1995.* Universidad Nacional de Trujillo, 151–176.

Urbani, B. (2014). De *gatos monillos*, *bogios* y otras *simias americanas*: Los primates neotropicales en la crónica hispano-lusa del siglo XVI. *Anartia*, **26**, 71–135.

Urton, G. (1985). Animal metaphors and the life cycle in an Andean community. In G. Urton, ed., *Animal Myths and Metaphors in South America.* Salt Lake City: University of Utah Press, 251–284.

Valadez, R. (2014). Monos y jaguares en la cosmovisión prehispánica. In A. Sandoval, & L. Sáinz, eds., *Los artistas responsables en defensa de la fauna.* México DF: Grupo Turín SA, 289–313.

Valcárcel, L. (1946). Cusco archaeology. In J. Steward, ed., *Handbook of South American Indians.* Washington, DC: Smithsonian Institution, 177–182.

Van Dooren, T., Kirksey, S. E., & Münster, U. (2016). Multispecies studies. Cultivating arts of attentiveness. *Environmental Humanities*, 8(1), 1–23.

Van Valkenburgh, P., Kelloway, S., Dussubieux, L., Quilter, J., & Glascock, M. (2015). The production and circulation of indigenous lead-glazed ceramics in northern Peru during Spanish colonial times. *Journal of Archaeological Science*, **61**, 172–185.

Veracini, C., & Martins-Teixeira, D. (2017). Perception and description of New World nonhuman primates in the travel literature of the fifteenth and sixteenth centuries: A critical review. *Annals of Science*, **74**(1), 25–63.

Vílchez, C. (2015). *El camino Inca de la costa en el Parque Nacional Cerros de Amotape, Tumbes.* Lima: Ministerio de Cultura.

Viveiros de Castro, E. (1992). *From the Enemy's Point of View: Humanity and Divinity in an Amazonian Society.* Chicago: University of Chicago Press.

Viveiros de Castro, E. (1998). Cosmological deixis and Amerindian perspectivism. *Journal of the Royal Anthropological Institute*, 4(3), 469–488.

Wester, C. (2016). *Chornancap. Palacio de una gobernante y sacerdotisa de la cultura Lambayeque.* Chiclayo: Ministerio de Cultura.

Wołoszyn, J. (2014). *Wróg – Inny – Sąsiad. Obraz obcego w kulturze Moche. (Enemies – Strangers – Neighbours. Image of the Others in Moche Culture).* Warsaw: Instytut Archeologii Uniwersytetu Warszawskiego.

Wright, K., Wright, B., Ford, S., et al. (2015). The effects of ecology and evolutionary history on robust capuchin morphological diversity. *Molecular Phylogenetics and Evolution*, 82, 455–466.

Zevallos, J. (1994). *La crónica de Ocxaguaman.* Trujillo: Fundación Alfredo Pinillos.

Zuidema, T. (1983). The lion in the city. Royal symbols of transition in Cuzco. *Journal of Latin American Lore*, 9(1), 39–100.

5 Alterity, Authority, and Ancestors

Exploring Monkey Images in Moche Iconography of North Coast Peru

Aleksa K. Alaica

Alteridad, autoridad y ancestros: Exploración de las imágenes de monos en la iconografía moche de la costa norte del Perú

Resumen

Los primates no-humanos en la región de los Andes de América del Sur han sido excavados en contextos de enterramiento y se representan comúnmente en la cerámica. Las imágenes de monos en la iconografía moche son bien conocidas, pero se han realizado pocos análisis sistemáticos para aproximar su papel y significado en actividades sociopolíticas y rituales. Este capítulo investiga la variación en las representaciones de primates no-humanos de la cultura moche para determinar el uso de imágenes de monos por parte de élite por su valor simbólico y significado ritual en la árida región de la costa norte del Perú actual. Al examinar sus características compartidas, su asociación con especies clave de plantas amazónicas y su uso para legitimar la autoridad, contextualizo las representaciones de los monos moche como agentes clave de alteridad debido a su origen no-local. Sostengo que la asociación de primates no-humanos con tocados, vasijas de servicio y rituales funerarios indica que los monos eran percibidos como afines no-locales en la sociedad moche que ejercían un poder considerable en las prácticas políticas y ceremoniales. En la Iconografía moche, los monos no eran simplemente aditivos estéticos, sino que formaban parte de un grupo seleccionado de seres no-humanos con agencia social que derivaba de su origen amazónico no-local y su relación con potentes sustancias rituales. Se reconoció que los monos, que se asemejaban a sus parientes humanos, tenían roles ancestrales que legitimaban la autoridad de las élites involucradas en actividades ceremoniales relacionadas con el sacrificio, la fertilidad y la renovación.

Palabras clave

Amazonia – desierto costero – interacción interregional – monos – ritual – *ulluchu* – *ishpingo*

Abstract

Nonhuman primates in the Andes region of South America have been excavated in burial contexts and are commonly depicted in ceramic art. Monkey images in Moche iconography are well-known but few systematic analyses have been conducted to approximate their role and meaning in sociopolitical and ritual activities. This chapter investigates variation in nonhuman primate depictions from the Moche culture to determine the elite use of monkey images for their symbolic value and ritual significance in the arid desert north coast region of present-day Peru. By examining their shared features, their association with key Amazonian plant species and their use in legitimizing authority, I contextualize Moche monkey depictions as key agents of alterity because of their nonlocal origin. I argue that the association of nonhuman primates with headdresses, serving vessels, and funerary rituals indicate that monkeys were perceived as nonlocal affines in Moche society that wielded considerable power in political and ceremonial practices. In Moche iconography, monkeys were not simply aesthetic additives but formed part of a selected group of nonhuman beings with social agency that derived from their nonlocal, Amazonian origin and their relationship to potent ritual substances. Monkeys, resembling their human relatives, were recognized to have ancestral roles that legitimized authority for elites involved in ceremonial activities related to sacrifice, fertility, and renewal.

Keywords: Monkeys, Amazon, Interregional interaction, Desert coast, Ritual, *ulluchu*; *ishpingo*

5.1   Introduction

Evolution links human and nonhuman primates through their shared anatomical features and common social collective dwelling. Yet, nonhuman primates exist apart from the human world because of their differing cognition, communication capacity, and their predominantly arboreal lifeways. Representations of nonhuman primates are found throughout the world (Langdon, 1990; Pareja, 2017; Pareja et al., 2020; Urbani, 2005). Shifting landscapes changed the contexts of interaction between human communities and other primate populations in the past (Masseti, 2015; Rice and South, 2015). In regions that are inhabited by nonhuman primates, there are economic, political, and religious factors that account for why these animals may have been traded, ritually deposited in the mortuary contexts, or depicted in iconography (Haraway, 2003). It is not possible to know if these communities were aware of their own genetic closeness to other primates, but the anatomy and behavior of nonhuman primates clearly fascinated past human societies.

Monkey species in the Neotropics are distributed based on long-term factors involving environmental change, interspecies competition, and human predation. Hunting monkeys placed considerable pressures on different species in their subsistence activities, group interactions, and overall survival. The depth of interactions between humans and monkeys may stem to over 11,000 years ago, with recent research suggesting that humans are dominant predators of monkeys alongside harpy eagles and jaguars in Amazonia (Urbani, 2005). Humans and monkeys coevolved in the Neotropics creating a set of interactions that allowed for people to begin depicting and imagining monkeys in their artwork and incorporating them as part of their cultural practices. It is significant to find monkeys outside of their tropical habitats as it attests to their long-distance trade acquisition and prestige value. The way that monkeys are used in iconography can indicate the meaning behind their origin, their liminal role in elite practices and legitimizing authority.

The Andes region has a deep history of interregional interaction, where exchange occurred between the Amazonian lowlands and the Pacific desert coast for many millennia. Monkeys are not indigenous to the desert coast of the Andes region in South America since arid conditions are not conducive to their habitation. Nevertheless, artisans during the Moche period (200–900 CE) depicted these animals in ceramic, metal, bone, and textile artifacts (Benson, 1997; Goepfert, 2008, 2011, 2012). There are hundreds of representations of monkeys climbing fruit trees, dressed with elite status marks, and as figures molded on vessel spouts. The discovery of interments of complete monkey skeletons also suggest that these animals were brought from the Amazonian lowlands as pets or prestige items (Benson, 1997; Eeckhout, 2013). My analysis of monkeys in the Moche iconographic record points to the importance of nonhuman primates as emblems of the exotic origin and as symbols of alterity. I argue that examining monkey representations provides a medium to understand Moche ideologies of Otherness (vis-à-vis Helms, 1998) and constructions of nonlocal, ancestral affiliation to legitimize elite authority. In the end, monkeys symbolized fertility, regeneration, and elite status as evinced in representations of monkeys serving liquids, collecting fruit, and participating in sacrificial rites.

5.2   Contextualizing Monkeys on the Arid Coast

Moche cultural material from the North Coast of Peru is an ideal assemblage of artifacts to explore the variation of animal iconography. Moche designates a sphere of sociopolitical and religious influence that spans the desert North Coast of Peru from Nepeña in the south to the Piura Valley in the north (Fig. 5.1) (Bawden, 1996; Benson, 1985, 2012; Castillo, 2001, 2010; Castillo and Holmquist, 2000; Cordy-Collins, 2001; Swenson, 2007, 2008, 2018; Uceda, 2010; Uceda et al., 2016). Moche influence in this region persists from the middle Early Intermediate Period and into the early Middle Horizon (200–900 CE). Highly specialized artisans producing ceramics, metals, and textiles incorporated nonhuman animal images to communicate elite narratives on their origins, the scale of their influence and the legitimacy of their authority.

The naturalism of Moche visual culture affords an unrivalled opportunity to understand the symbolism and ontological status of monkeys in Andean society (Billman, 2002; Bourget, 1994, 2001a, 2001b, 2006; DeMarrais et al., 1996; Donnan, 1978, 1992; Trever, 2019). The finite number of scenes and repeated characters attest to specific narratives about supernatural and elite individuals (Donnan, 1978, 2007; Quilter, 1997). Rice and South (2015) emphasize that representations of animals in art vary in terms of naturalism, abstraction, and stylization. Features that are displayed further reveal "something about the way it [an animal] was conceived of and understood through parts represented and contexts in which it is included" (Morphy, 1989: 2; Saunders, 1994: 103–105, 1998: 20). The artistic style and iconography of a culture are symbolically coded, which forms a visual mode of communication through which a community structures experience and perceptions of social realities and the cosmos (Munn, 1966). Monkey depictions in Moche iconography can shed light on indigenous conceptions of nonlocal, Amazonian species and the role of such animals in exchange of exotic plants and animals, ceremonial practice, and as a marker of elite identity. Moche leaders commonly

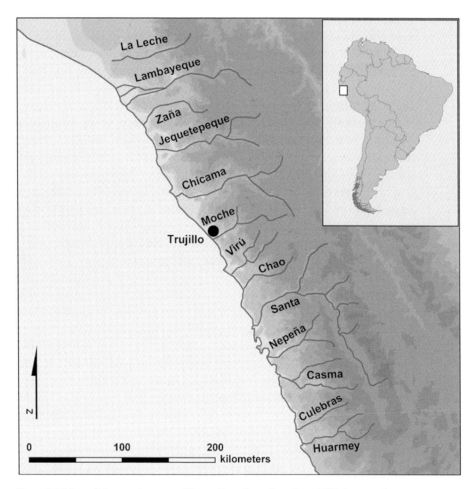

Figure 5.1 Map of the north coast of Peru. (Based on data from Millaire, 2010).

received tribute and offerings from their communities and trading partners with many items derived as far afield as the Amazon Basin (Benson, 2012; Topic and Topic, 1983; Van Buren, 1996).

The actual exchange of monkeys between the Amazon and the coast would have been difficult across most of the Andean mountain range, except for key locations. It so happens that the narrowest and lowest part of the Andean highlands is situated in the department of Piura of present-day Peru, an area known as the Huancabamba deflection (Reynel et al., 2013). This point of exchange is located along the northern frontier of Moche influence and it may have been used in early Pleistocene exchange networks (Kaulicke, 2020). The plant and animal species from the Amazon would have been traded with the coast since this early contact, permitting the distribution of subsistence, medicinal, and ritual plant and animal taxa for daily and ceremonial activities.

The presence of monkey images on the coast indicates that individuals may have travelled to the Amazon Basin, where they saw monkeys first-hand. One of the most well-known coastal images of a monkey derives from the Nasca Lines (500 BCE–500 CE) of the south coast, a remarkable geoglyph that measures 110 km long. The spiral tail of this glyph, along with its thin front limbs, likely depict a spider monkey. In the early twentieth-century, María Reiche, hypothesized that images like the Nazca monkey functioned as an astronomical device and thus held cosmological significance. Johan Reinhard later suggested that there was insufficient evidence for alignment with constellations: rather these lines were associated with deities and faunal and flora depictions were meant to ensure the availability of water. In addition, on the south coast, at the site of Paloma, Chilca (5800–2700 BCE), the tomb of a young man was excavated and found to contain the femur of a spider monkey (*Ateles* sp.) (Reitz, 2003: 78). Evidence suggests that the remains of this monkey originated from a pet, as marine animals constituted the bulk of subsistence for the community at Paloma (Gamboa, 2020).

On the central coast, archaeologists have documented early evidence of nonhuman primate images in the material culture of Caral and Aspero (3000–1800 BCE), with bone ornaments and flutes depicting monkeys (Shady and Leyva, 2003: 291). Later, the physical remains of monkeys were placed as dedicatory offerings. At the site of Pachacamac, the Temple of the Monkey dates to the middle of the Late Intermediate Period (1250–1450 CE) of the Ychsma cultural phase. This structure contains offerings of sacrificed animals, exotic seeds, and textiles. In a central posthole in the temple, a child was placed with a funerary bundle of a white-fronted capuchin monkey (*Cebus albifrons*) (Eeckhout, 2013). At the southern end of the temple, archaeologists unearthed offerings of the mummy of a woman and a bundle of almost a thousand Amazonian *Nectandra* sp. (*ishpingo* or *amala*) seeds. These offerings were sealed beneath a floor and they probably corresponded to final occupation of the temple (Eeckhout, 2013; Eeckhout and Lawrence, 2015). Capuchin monkeys and *ishpingo* seeds uncovered together emphasizes the intentional use of different Amazonian species for mortuary practices and to potentially reinforce the elite identity of the female burial.

On the northcentral coast, Casma style ceramics also depict monkeys (800–1350 CE). The monkey figures appear on the body of a *cántaro* (serving vessel), often grasping the ears of the human face depicted on the neck. These figures have characteristic heads, rounded and prominent ears, similar to a white-fronted capuchin, or *machín*. Gamboa (2020: 15) suggests that monkey figures around the heads depicted on *cántaros* could be understood as part of a visual metaphor and narrative originally associated with "listening" to or "hearing" Casma leaders. The representation of monkeys in Casma-style ceramics exhibit some similarities with monkey images in Moche and earlier cultural sequences of the North Coast (Gamboa, 2020). Other contemporaneous objects depicting monkeys originate from Castillo de Huarmey (800 CE); a female weaver that accompanied an adult man was interred with wood earspools decorated with monkey images (Giersz, 2016: 251, fig. 25).

Archaeologists have also confirmed the interment of a monkey at the early pre-ceramic North Coast ceremonial site of Ventarrón (3000–1600 BCE), a center associated with important nonlocal trade items. The complete skeleton of a white-fronted capuchin was interred within a bench of the central enclosure, and the offering commemorated an architectural renovation event associated with the third phase of construction (Alva 2013: 141). In addition, a blue-and-yellow macaw (*Ara ararauna*) was recovered at Ventarrón from the central enclosure and dated to the second phase. The offerings of nonlocal trade items indicate sustained contact with the Amazon Basin millennia before the emergence of the Moche. Kaulicke (2020) emphasizes the important role of Ventarrón as an important point for interregional exchange but also the concentration of ritualized power during an early phase of cultural development on the North Coast.

5.3   Contextualizing Monkeys in the Americas

Primate species such as howler monkeys (*Alouatta* spp.), spider monkeys (*Ateles* spp.), and capuchins (*Cebus* spp.) are common in the archaeoprimatological record of the ancient Americas (Benson, 1997; Rice and South, 2015; Urbani, 2015). In Maya material culture, Rice and South (2015) identify spider monkeys, capuchins, and two species of howlers. These species have wide variation in prognathism, the opposability of the thumb, prehensile tails, and diet. Some of the distinguishing features among these nonhuman primates include the thick "beard" of adult howler males, the long thin limbs of spider monkeys, and fur patterning of capuchins with black upperparts and pale undersides. Locomotion also distinguish these species; for instance, spider monkeys spend more time on the ground than howlers (Bergeson, 1996; Cant, 1986) and capuchins move through quadrupedal walking and leaping aided by their hind legs (Gebo, 1992; Janson and Boinski, 1992). Many species have different levels of resistance to disease, such as the yellow fever that commonly afflicts howlers but with greater resistance among spider monkeys and capuchins (Bryant et al., 2007; Galindo and Srihongse, 1967: 152–153). The use of different monkey taxa can suggest the perceived role of monkeys in the cosmological order of past worldviews.

Among some indigenous groups of the Americas, many oral histories describe monkeys as failed attempts to create mankind or as a former human race transformed into monkeys as punishment for disobeying the gods (Benson, 1997; Rice and South, 2015). In the Maya *Popul Vuh*, the half-brothers of the Hero Twins Hunahpu and Xbalanque are transformed into monkeys: a howler (*b'atz'*; Hun Batz) and a spider monkey (*chuen*, Hun Chuwen) (Rice and South, 2015). Interestingly, today there are homophones in various Mayan languages that reveal the association of monkeys with artisans as well as writing, music and entertainment (Barrera Vásquez 1991: 110; Stross, 2008: 10). Also, Classic Maya hieroglyphic script includes the depiction of monkeys meaning artist/scribe, day/sun and human lord/ruler (Macri and Looper, 2003: 70–72). The interchanging role of monkey images for a ruling individual, an artisan, and even a celestial figure attests to the versatility of the primate form to signify political preeminence and ritual authority.

In the Amazonian lowlands of South America, there are various origin stories that link monkeys with celestial entities. In the Miraña myth of Colombia, monkeys embody stars that interact with other nonhuman figures (Karadimas, 2016). Night-Aster is a figure that represents the Moon and takes a Kinkajou-woman as his wife. Jealous of the union, the four Night-Monkey brothers of this Kinkajou-woman steal her and engage in incest. Night-Aster chases these monkeys to a hollow tree, where they cut off his head, which falls into the underworld (Land of the Fishes). Day-Aster (or Sun) is born to the Kinkajou-woman, whose placenta becomes a Stingray creature; a figure from incestuous relationship with the four Night-Monkeys. When Day-Aster is grown, he kills the four monkeys with his father's blowgun and then proceeds to eat them, placing each skull on four central pillars (Karadimas, 2016). The Day-Aster takes his wife from the fish people, but the woman he chooses is already the wife of the Stingray. They fight and the Day-Aster kills the Stingray with a lance to the heart. Other pre-Columbian cultures in the Nariño and Carchi regions have iconography on ceramics that also relate monkeys and stars.

Monkeys have been documented to serve important roles in rites of passage ceremonies. Among the Zo'é, a Tupi-lingustic group that live close to the Cuminapanema River in Pará in northeast Brazil, all juvenile and adult members wear wooden lip plugs, which are elongated cylinders that are placed in the lower lip after perforation. Boys and girls receive their first lip plug around the age of eight (Garve et al., 2017). They recount the origin of this practice from their ancestor *Sihié'abyr*, who demonstrated how to use the first lip plugs. Following hours of dancing to induce a trance state, the father of each child pierces the lip of initiates with the tibia of a spider monkey, where a tiny '*m'berpót* (a small lip plug) is inserted. As these children grow, larger plugs are inserted (Garve et al., 2017). Highly significant, the Zo'é explain that lip plugs are inserted to make a person a true human being and they serve as diacritical markers of ethnic individuals. Indeed, the Zo'é categorize individuals without plugs as 'Kirahé' (or foreigner) or enemies (Garve et al., 2017).

We know that monkeys are nonhuman primate relatives, but they would have been representatives of foreign landscapes from the Moche point of view, whose own arid coastal environment was far removed from the Amazonian lowlands. Architectural renovation and ritual reinforced ancestral power at important Moche centers (Uceda, 2001). The death of key elites and priests were consecrated through ceremonial events that incorporated prestigious and long-distance traded items. Ancestors were venerated through interactions in mortuary practices and post-depositional revisitation (Hill, 2016). Depicting monkeys in relation to integral ritual items reinforces their association to sacrifice, reciprocity and renewal controlled by elites.

The use and meaning of monkeys differs depending on the cultural context. Despite this variation, there can be common material correlates that indicate the importance of nonhuman primates. Zedeño (2009) emphasizes that archaeologists must fully consider the context and relationship between individual objects (and other nonhuman beings) to properly interpret the function and meaning of assemblages. The relational taxonomy of objects and beings creates dependent associations that can vary in quotidian and ritual contexts. Relational taxonomies can incorporate nonhuman primates using their likeness as symbols of nonlocal origin and in relation to other Amazonian plant and animal species. This is argued by Helms (1998: 31) who considers how the "distinctive treatment of another type of bones bespeaks links with animals, a category of Others that conceptually may well have preceded the idea of ancestors." The presence of monkeys in the order of celestial bodies, in rites of passage and in the legitimization of power in other cultures of the Americas highlights the potential significance of monkeys for the Moche. Furthermore, it has been shown elsewhere (notably Sahlins, 2008) that nonlocal origin is an important part of identity politics among figures of authority.

5.4   Monkey Images in Moche Iconography

Moche iconography depicts a diversity of animals that include birds, fish, felines, and nonhuman primates (Benson, 1997). Archaeologists and art historians have interpreted key figures in the iconographic record as central characters in specific themes and narratives (Donnan, 1978, 1992, 2007; Donnan and McClelland, 1979; Quilter, 1997). Benson (1997) has classified monkeys in Moche vessels as anomalous species. Despite the lack of systemic analysis of monkey remains, previous scholarship has connected the depiction of monkeys to transporting coca in bags (Benson, 1997; Eeckhout, 2013). Monkeys and coca both derive from the Amazonian lowlands, but it can also be grown in the *chaupiyunga* (~500 masl) near the Pacific. Therefore, coca was not exclusive obtained through trade with the Amazonian lowlands. Benson (2012: 64) contends that "there was probably an origin myth that linked monkeys and coca." This creation myth is associated with monkeys commonly appearing at the juncture of the spout and the stirrup on Chimú (1000–1400 CE) vessels. Some Chancay and Casma (1100 CE) vessels from the central coast depict monkeys on the shoulders of vessels that depict human figures (Gamboa, 2020). This form may allude to a creation story or may portray the high places where monkeys travel (Benson, 1997). In order to understand Moche perceptions of monkeys, I examined their images from ceramic, metal, and bone material culture.

I analyzed monkeys in Moche iconography on an assemblage of vessels and two metal artifacts from the Larco Museum in Lima, Peru, and the Dumbarton Oaks Research Collection and Library in Washington DC, USA. The Larco assemblage contains 349 objects depicting monkeys accessed through the Online Researchers' Catalogue. I accessed the Dumbarton Oaks assemblage through the online Moche Archives, and it includes 17 images drawn by Donna McClelland. In total, there are 366 objects that depict 462 monkeys in figurative form and as fineline drawings. The analysis of artwork permits the assembling of different communities, exclusion of certain parts of society and the negotiation of power relations (DeMarrais and Robb, 2013). There are five key characteristics that I used to make identifications of monkeys: (1) prognathism; (2) prehensile tail; (3) elongated limbs; (4) long canine teeth; and (5) rounded ears. I analyzed the artifacts with three principal criteria in mind: (1) natural versus anthropomorphic; (2) vessel type: feasting, serving or storage; and (3) role of the monkey: on headdress, as a pet, or collecting fruit. Based on these characteristics, I interpret the role of monkeys as nonlocal symbols but also significant to elite and ritual practice.

Monkey images are most often depicted in natural form, such as sculpted figures, fineline representations, and in low relief (315/366 = 86%). The anthropomorphized monkey images have the combination of human hands, legs and heads, and curled monkey tails (51/366 = 14%). Monkey depictions in natural form (255/366 = 70%) are portrayed with realistic head with prognathism, rounded ears, elongated limbs, and tail (210/366 = 57%). The depictions of nonhuman primates derive mainly from bichrome ceramic vessels (192/366 = 53%), blackware (14/366 = 4%), beige slip (132/366 = 36%) and with a red hue of the clay paste (26/366 = 7%) (Fig. 5.2). Most of the vessels that depict monkeys are stirrup jars that have two spouts that join to form a single opening (258/366 = 71%). Serving vessels (*cántaros*) (82/366 = 22%), bowls (5/366 = 2%), single-spout jars (7/366 = 2%), and whistles (6/366=2%) are less common in this assemblage. I only recorded two examples of miniature *cántaros* and trumpets depicting monkeys, while there are single examples of a figurine, pendant, sceptre, and miniature sculpture.

Monkeys in these depictions most often form the figure of vessels (143/366 = 39%). The whole body of the monkey with limbs and tail compose the main chamber of these vessels with some variation of the head in figurative form and the body in relief or fineline on the base (Fig. 5.3a). There are also depictions of monkeys holding fruit and bags with their heads in figurative form and the hands in fineline (Fig. 5.3b). Monkeys commonly adorn the headdresses of anthropomorphize figures, supernatural beings, and even zoomorphic figures, such as crabs (80/366 = 22%) (Fig. 5.3c). The fact that monkeys are depicted on identifying headdresses suggest their role as a marker of status or group affiliation. There are other aquatic-related depictions of monkeys with the bodies of shells (Fig. 5.3d). The rest of the monkey images from this assemblage grasp stirrup spouts (61/366 = 17%), assume a subsidiary figure in fineline scenes (33/366 = 9%), or are crafted into the base of vessels (25/366 = 7%), neck (13/366 = 4%), and handles of vessels (11/366 = 3%). Finally, depictions of monkeys on the bodies of stirrup jars and *cántaros* appear to wear belts and have ropes fastened around their waists. In one case, a monkey is tied to a post and eating, which suggests their role as pets (Fig. 5.3e, f).

Most monkey images do not hold any objects (261/366 = 71%), but several examples are associated with net bags (39/366 = 11%) and *cántaros* (18/366 = 5%) (Fig. 5.4a). The net bags are often depicted in fineline on the globular base of vessels where the hands of monkeys are also represented. Fruit or seeds are often painted in these bags. There are also depictions of monkeys emerging from tubers (Fig. 5.4b). *Cántaros* are held by monkey figures tilting their head toward the opening, indicating the association of monkeys with decanting liquids (Fig. 5.4c,d). The representation of

Figure 5.2 The vessels with monkey depictions include: (a) spout-vessel with the monkey on the handle (ML002442); (b) *cántaro* with a monkey in relief on the body (ML005494); (c) stirrup jar with monkey in relief and bichrome pigment (ML008166); (d) stirrup jar with monkey in fineline on base (ML008174); (e) stirrup jar with *ulluchu* tree in relief and monkeys with figurative heads (ML008208); (f) *cántaro* with monkey on neck with belt and earrings (ML009857). (Museo Larco, Lima).

monkeys on a scepter head manufactured from copper also shows various monkeys involved in pouring and sharing beverages (Fig. 5.4e). A *cántaro* vessel was discovered with a monkey image from the Late Moche ceremonial center of Huaca Colorada (600–850 CE) in the southern Jequetepeque Valley (Fig. 5.4f). It was uncovered below a ramp leading to the main ceremonial precinct of the site and possibly served as a foundation offering to animate or protect the ramp (Swenson and Seoane, 2019). The vessel could have been interred with *chicha* (or corn beer) or another important ritual beverage, but residue analysis is required to test this hypothesis. These types of *cántaro* vessels are well-known in the Moche period with depictions of human heads with earspools (King of Assyria vessels), however there are many examples of animal heads that have not been given the same research attention.

Other Moche vessels depict monkeys eating or holding fruits or seeds (Fig. 5.5a,b). Archaeologists have identified the ovoid-shaped fruit commonly depicted with monkeys as '*ulluchu*' (Benson, 1997; Bourget, 2006). The specific species related to the identity of '*ulluchu*' is still contested, but recent research contends it was used in ritual practices (Bussmann and Sharon, 2009; Wassén, 1987). Some of these depictions also portray ovoid-shaped objects that I posit represent seeds (contrasting with Benson, 1997: 65, who interprets them as maize ears). Others have documented that *Nectandra* sp. seeds (*ishpingo*) from the Amazon were consumed for their analgesic,

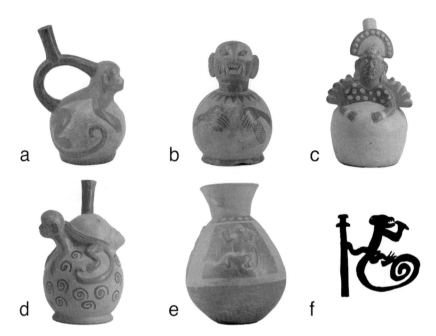

Figure 5.3 Variation in monkey depictions: (a) stirrup jar with monkey figure on base (ML008284); (b) stirrup jar with head of monkey in figurative form and hands holding fruit and net bag in fineline (ML008432); (c) stirrup jar with an anthropomorphic crab with monkey on headdress (ML003214); (d) stirrup jar of monkey with shell body (ML003876); (e) *cántaro* with monkey in relief with and rope around waist (ML012213) (Museo Larco, Lima); (f) fineline image of monkey tied to a pole (drawing by Donna McClelland) (Image ID 17341739). (Dumbarton Oaks Research Library and Collection).

psychotropic, and lethal properties in ritual practices (Eeckhout, 2006; Montoya, 2004; Toyne, 2015). At the site of Tecapa (750–1000 CE), adjacent to Huaca Colorada, excavations recovered a fragment of a blackware handle depicting a person holding a tunic with four *ishpingo* seeds along the handle (Fig. 5.5c). Swenson and Seoane (2019) associate this finding with a similar handle found on a stirrup jar from San José de Moro, from the priestess tomb M-U1525 (Mauricio and Castro, 2007: 134, fig. 35) and in the M-U1242 tomb in area 34 (Carpio Perla and Delibese Mateos, 2004: 132), similar to fragments from area 35 (Prieto and Cusicanqui, 2007: 61). The same disc protrusions decorate the bridge of the vessel in the priestess tomb, which Castillo and Quilter (2010) have interpreted as *ishpingo* seeds. These medicinal seeds were frequently deposited inside bottles with a bridge handle. The body of the ceramic from San José de Moro represents the scene of monkeys exchanging *Spondylus* (thorny oyster) for *ulluchu* and this theme was possibly represented in the lost body of the vessel from Tecapa (Swenson and Seoane, 2019: 335).

Archaeologists have also documented several depictions of monkeys holding shells of the Strombidae family and panpipes that link musical activities to simians (Fig. 5.6a). One of these representations includes the figures of two skeletonized monkeys, with one monkey playing the panpipes (Fig. 5.6b). There are also whistles

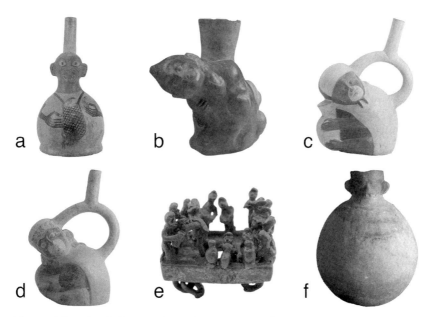

Figure 5.4 Associated objects with monkey depictions: (a) stirrup jar with monkey holding a bag of *ulluchu* fruit (ML008322); (b) *cántaro* depicting a tuber with the head of a monkey holding a fruit emerging from one end (ML007265); (c) stirrup jar with monkey holding a *cántaro* (ML004158); (d) stirrup jar with monkey holding a *cántaro* with *ulluchu* fruit depicted on head wrapping (ML004089); (e) scepter head depicting monkeys serving beverages in *cántaros* (ML100706) (Museo Larco, Lima); (f) *cántaro* from Huaca Colorada found below a ramp (Swenson and Seoane, 2019).

Figure 5.5 Fruits and seeds depicted with monkeys: (a) stirrup jar of monkey holding a seed (ML008193); (b) *cántaro* with a monkey in relief eating fruit (ML012225) (Museo Larco, Lima); (c) handle of a person exchanging textiles and *ishpingo* seeds. (Swenson and Seoane, 2019).

that depict two monkey heads (Fig. 5.6c). Wołoszyn and Piwowar (2015) have interpreted some of these depictions as same-sex relationships in Moche art and society.

A few depictions of monkeys on headdresses of anthropomorphized or supernatural figures hold weapons, such as *tumi* knives, clubs, or shields (9/366 = 3%). Most

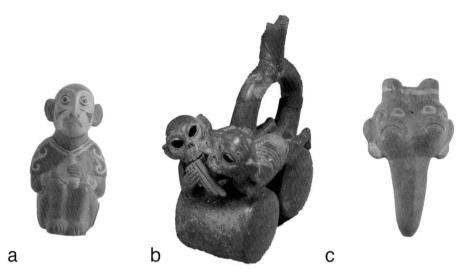

a   b   c

Figure 5.6 Monkeys in musical instruments in Moche iconography: (a) seated monkey holding a strombus shell (ML004083); (b) two monkeys on their stomachs with touching tongues, one playing a panpipe (ML004325); (c) two-monkey head whistle (ML014375). (Museo Larco, Lima).

depictions with monkeys are in scenes of harvesting fruit and serving liquids. These associations underscore that nonhuman primate images may have held specific meaning for ceremonial practice related to fertility and renewal. Gamboa (2020: 15) emphasizes that pre-Colonial Andean ideologies presented primates like symbols of authority, fertility, and alterity, converting them, at the same time, into animate beings that held roles in in social memory and legitimizing spatial (or temporal) origin.

Taxonomic identification of monkey species in this material culture is not always possible. Artisans used generalized monkey features to associate figures in iconography with monkeys but specific Moche monkey depictions focus on capuchins and spider monkeys based on fur patterns and elongated limbs. There is no clear indication that the Moche depicted howler monkeys, as the diagnostic 'beards' are not explicitly portrayed. There are occasional depictions of squirrel monkeys; however, the most common monkeys in Moche iconography appear to be capuchins and spider monkeys based on the capuchin coat patterns and the long tail of the spider monkeys. The use of general primate features in most cases attests to the use of monkeys as emblems of nonlocal origin, without species-specific characteristics. This may further indicate that monkey images were important to depict for universal understandings of Amazonian contact, but not specific traits to identify species that most Moche elites and other community members would not have seen firsthand.

5.5   Discussion: Ancestors, Origins, and Authority

The images of monkeys consistently relate to the exchange of vital substances and liquids. Their depictions both in scenes making use of *cántaros* and as part of *cántaro* themselves highlight that monkeys were intimately associated with potent, mind-altering substances. These vessels may have contained *chicha* or psychoactive compounds from *ulluchu* fruit and *ishpingo* seeds. Both groups of liquids induce inebriation or hallucinogenic states that possibly accompanied sacrificial rituals (Hill, 2016). The way that monkeys are depicted in different types of material culture creates and transforms new ways of imaging nonlocal entities. Gamboa (2020) also addresses the closeness between monkeys and *cántaros* in Andean art for Casma artifacts. Common representations of dressed primate priests on all fours may have served as allegories of sentient animals consuming liquids and *chicha* for Casma iconography (Gamboa, 2020: 13).

The common depiction of monkeys with *ulluchu* attests to the importance of nonhuman beings with ritual activities. Although, it not clear whether *ulluchu* is always the fruit depicted or whether it ever existed, Bussmann and Sharon (2009) posit that it likely derives from the genus *Guarea*, a lowland tropical evergreen tree. The seeds of *Guarea*, when ingested, increases a person's heartbeat, elevating blood pressure, and even causing erections (Bussmann and Sharon, 2009: 6). The physiological effects of the compounds in these seeds would make it much easier to extract sacrificial blood and may even have induced short-term hallucinations (Bussmann and Sharon, 2009). The sacrificial and erotic activities facilitated by *ulluchu* parallels the iconographic association between monkeys and supernatural figures. For example, a repeated scene in low-relief on various stirrup jars depict a copulation scene between a fanged deity and a woman, where an *ulluchu* tree is growing above the copulating figures with monkeys holding bags and harvesting *ulluchu* fruit (Fig. 5.7a,b). *Ishpingo* seeds are also present in the center-left of the scene, above the anthropomorphized iguana and fox figures (Fig. 5.7a). There are various examples of monkeys with erect penises with net bags around their necks, presumably containing *ulluchu* fruit (Scher, 2012) (Fig. 5.7c). Benson (1997) has highlighted that the behavior of living in trees and eating fruit links monkeys to vegetation as well as with the sky and sun. A monkey depicted in a Moche stirrup vessel, possibly of a common squirrel monkey (*Saimiri sciureus*), holds fruit or maize, reinforcing the symbolic role of monkeys in agricultural fertility and renewal (Benson, 1997: 65, fig. 46).

The depiction of monkeys in Moche iconography parallels aspects of origin stories and myths that are recorded from the tropical lowlands. These common tropes emphasize cross-cultural significance of monkeys and their shared meaning. It is interesting that the uncles of the Maya Hero Twins, One Monkey and One Artisan, are linguistically associated with weaving, writing, and celestial beings. At Huaca Colorada, a bone weaving sword was recovered from one of the principal production zones that depicts a Chavin-style monkey in profile (Burger, 1992; Swenson and Seoane, 2019) (Fig. 5.8a,b). The body of this implement appears worn and polished, suggesting it was used in the crafting of textiles, and not solely for aesthetic purposes. This connection between monkey images, textiles, and origin stories is further highlighted by the representation of a stingray and four spirals on the tunic of a man with a monkey headdress in a Moche *cántaro* vessel (Fig. 5.8c). These details parallel the Miraña myth of Colombia where the stingray is the incestuous offspring of four Night-Monkeys and their sister. These depictions are also present in Chimu

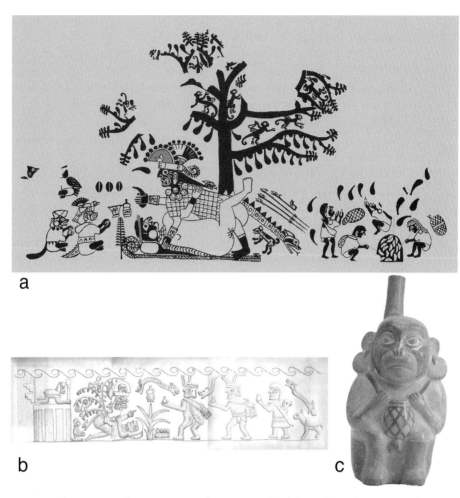

Figure 5.7 There are copulation scenes and erect genitalia: (a) ritual copulation scene (ID 18887645) (drawing by Donna McClelland) (Dumbarton Oaks Research Library and Collection); (b) roll-out drawing of ritual copulation scene (ML004359); (c) stirrup jar of seated monkey with net bag around neck, earrings and erect penis (ML004144). (Museo Larco, Lima).

textiles, where geometric spots and spirals have been argued to play the role of the four monkeys (Karadimas, 2016). Miraña communities still today say that the night-monkey is a "jaguar" with its common name being *mono-tigre* (tiger [jaguar]-monkey). This affiliation with a feline is connected to the way that night-monkey eyes shin like stars at night. Karadimas (2016: 21) highlights how the depiction on Chimu textiles metaphorically relate feline and monkey forms to represent night-monkeys. Feline and primate composite figures in textiles, ceramics and even embedded in myth that suggest a relational understanding of the natural world. Communities may have recognized the common environment inhabited by monkeys and jaguars celebrated for their predatory and powerful perspectives. This relates to the Amazonian concept of perspectivism that different beings can be agentive

Figure 5.8 Weaving associations with monkeys among the Moche: (a) weaving sword from Huaca Colorada; (b) close-up of weaving sword from Huaca Colorada depicting a Chavin-style monkey in profile; (c) *cántaro* of male figure with monkey headdress with a stingray and four spirals on tunic (ML002752). (Museo Larco, Lima).

subjects, with distinct bodies (Viveiros de Castro, 1998, 2004). Human communities both in the Amazon and the arid north coast would have valued nonhuman primates as agentive beings in their own environments.

In the end, the way that monkeys are depicted in Moche iconography attests to the important role of exchanging ideas, things, and human and nonhuman persons. There are fascinating consistencies in monkey depictions that attest to their role in collecting powerful ritual substances and participating in ceremonial activities. For Ventarrón, Alva (2013: 141) posits that monkeys could represent the alter ego or totem of the powerful elite. As important ancestors, following 'the myth of the ages', monkeys were the attempt of an unfinished humanity (Alva, 2013). It is apparent that the monkey image was part of identifying headdress among Moche elites, supernatural figures and ritual specialists. The argument for a primate totem does not seem to apply to Moche monkey depictions; instead, monkeys are symbolic figures for the procurement and use of psychoactive substances for transforming some groups of people into sacrificial offerings and select elites into sacrificial priests and ancestors. Primate images are not, therefore, solely about representing an 'incomplete humanity' but symbols for potent nonhuman beings that can transform some individuals into valuable offerings for new architectural renovations, funerary practices and the renewal of the cosmos.

5.6   Conclusions

The examination of nonhuman primate images in Moche material culture indicates that these animals were associated with important ritual substances and practices of renewal. Monkeys are depicted trading and collecting *ishpingo* (*Nectandra* sp.) and *ulluchu* (*Gurarea* sp.). The medicinal and sacrificial use of these plants highlights their possibly embedded cultural significance (Bussman and Sharon, 2006). Furthermore, the copulation between humans and deities represented on various vessels highlights the symbolic meaning of fertility that encompasses the aid of monkeys and the plant species from their landscape of origin. The common representation of monkeys in headdresses of anthropomorphic characters, deities, and composite beings indicates that the affiliation of these individuals with elite status and of nonlocal, Amazonian origin. This status symbol was not necessarily a literal origin to the tropical lowlands but an implication of connections to valued resources, such as coca, *ulluchu*, and *ishpingo*, which facilitated the formation of power relations between competing members of society (Helms, 1998).

The monkey form evokes a liminal state, where people can identify common features between themselves and nonhuman primates, but at the same time the distinct traits of these animals relegated them to alterity. For Gamboa, (2020: 16) the monkey of the Peruvian northcentral coast was in a liminal position, originating from the tropical forests but adapted, to a certain degree, to human settlements. It has been recognized that the Moche may have understood the animal world within categories of 'wild' and 'domestic', or those animals that were closer or further away from human communities (Alaica, 2018). However, the anthropomorphizing of these animals from a natural state converted monkeys to unique entities that were possibly neither wild or domestic (Gamboa, 2020). The malleability of primate characteristics was recognized among Moche artisans and elites and utilized to reinforce connections with the landscape of the lowland tropics that transplanted both the meaning and resources of this environment to the arid desert of the north coast.

Among the Moche, monkey depictions were key identifiers for Amazonian contact, a foreign landscape that held symbolic significance. As agents of nonlocal origin, monkeys were potent beings that had the capacity to legitimize Moche elites during events of cosmological renewal and political reciprocity. In the end, the monkey form in Moche iconography indicates nonhuman beings were capable of corporeal metamorphosis that transformed the primate body and mind for ceremonial activities.

Acknowledgments

Museo Larco in Lima, Peru granted permission to examine primate ceramic vessels and images. Special thanks to Giannina Bardales for selecting and sharing the images published here. Dumbarton Oaks Collections and Research Library provided permission to use online images for this chapter. Special thanks to Alyson Williams for arranging these permissions. The Jatanca-Huaca Colorada-Tecapa Archaeological

Project authorized the use of artifact photos for this chapter. Luis Manuel González La Rosa and Edward Swenson provided important feedback on the contents and interpretations. Special thanks to Luis Manuel for his time in preparing the figures. This research was funded by the Social Sciences and Humanities Research Council of Canada (#752-2014-2431) and the University of Toronto, Department of Anthropology Doctoral Fellowships.

References

Alaica, A. K. (2018). Partial and complete deposits and depictions: Social Zooarchaeology, iconography and the role of animals in Late Moche Peru. *Journal of Archaeological Science: Reports*, **20**, 864–872.

Alva, I. (2013). *Ventarrón y Collud. Origen y Auge de la Civilización en la Costa Norte del Perú*. Lima: Ministerio de Cultural del Perú, Proyecto Especial Naylamp Lambayeque.

Bawden, G. (1996). *The Moche*. Oxford: Blackwell.

Benson, E. P. (1985). The Moche moon. In D. Peter Kvietok, & D. H. Sandweiss, eds., *Recent Studies in Andean Prehistory and Protohistory*. Ithaca: Latin American Studies Program, Cornell University, 105–144.

Benson, E. P. (1997). *Birds and Beasts of Ancient Latin America*. Gainesville: University Press of Florida.

Benson, E. P. (2012). *The Worlds of the Moche on the North Coast of Peru*. Austin: University of Texas Press.

Bergeson, D. (1996). The positional behavior and prehensile tail use of *Alouatta palliata*, *Ateles geoffroyi*, and *Cebus capucinus*. Unpublished PhD thesis, Washington University.

Barrera Vásquez, A. (1991). *Diccionario Maya*, 2nd ed. Mexico City: Editorial Porrúa.

Billman, B. R. (2002). Irrigation and the origins of the Southern Moche state on the north coast of Peru. *Latin American Antiquity*, 13(4), 371–400.

Bourget, S. (1994). Los Sacerdotes a la Sombra del Cerro Blanco y del Arco Bicéfalo. In *Revista del Museo de Arqueología, Antropología e Historia* No. 5, Trujillo: Facultad de Ciencias Sociales, Universidad Nacional de Trujillo, 81–125.

Bourget, S. (2001a). Rituals of sacrifice: Its practice at Huaca de la Luna and its representations. In J. Pillsbury,ed., *Moche Art and Archaeology in Ancient Peru*. New York: Yale University Press, 89–110.

Bourget, S. (2001b). Children and ancestors: Ritual practices at the Moche Site of Huaca de la Luna, North Coast of Peru. In P. Benson, & A. G. Cook, eds., *Ritual Sacrifice in Ancient Peru*. Austin: University of Texas Press, 93–118.

Bourget, S. (2006). *Sex, Death and Sacrifice in Moche Religion and Visual Culture*. Austin: University of Texas Press.

Bryant, J. E., Holmes, E. C., & Barrett, A. D. T. (2007). Out of Africa. A molecular perspective on the introduction of yellow fever virus into the Americas. *PLoS Pathogens*, 3(5), 375.

Burger, R. L. (1992). *Chavin and the Origins of Andean Civilization*. London: Thames and Hudson.

Bussmann, R. W., & Sharon, D. (2006). Traditional medicinal plant use in Northern Peru: Tracking two thousand years of healing culture. *Journal of Ethnobiology and Ethnomedicine*, 2(47), 1–18.

Bussmann, R. W., & Sharon, D. (2009). Naming a phantom – the quest to find the identity of the *Ulluchu*, an unidentified ceremonial Plant of the Moche culture in Northern Peru. *Journal of Ethnobiology and Ethnomedicine*, 5(8), 1–6.

Cant, J. (1986). Locomotion and feeding postures of spider and howling monkey: Field study and evolutionary interpretation. *Folia Primatologica*, **46**, 1–14.

Carpio Perla, M., & Delibes Mateos, R. (2004). La Cámara Funeraria M-U1242 del Área 34. L. J. Castillo Butters, ed., *Programa Arqueológico San José de Moro, Temporada de 2004*. Lima: Pontificia Universidad Católico del Perú, 126–139.

Castillo, L. J. (2001). The Last of the Mochicas: A view from the Jequetepeque Valley. In *Moche Art and Archaeology in Ancient Peru*, J. Pillsbury, ed., New Haven: Yale University Press, 307–328.

Castillo, L. J. (2010). Moche politics in the Jequetepeque Valley: A case for political opportunism. In J. Quilter, & L. J. Castillo, eds., *New Perspectives on Moche Political Organization*. Washington DC: Dumbarton Oaks Research and Collection, 83–109.

Castillo, L. J., & Homquist, U. (2000). Mujeres y Poder en la Sociedad Mochica Tardia. In N. Henriquez, ed., *El Hechizo de las Imágenes: Estatus Social, Género y Etnicidad en la Historia Peruana*. Lima: Fondo Editorial de la Pontificia Universidad Católica del Perú, 13–34.

Castillo, L. J., & Quilter, J. (2010). An overview of past and current theories and research on Moche political organization. In J. Quilter, & L. J. Castillo, eds., *New Perspectives on Moche Political Organization.* Washington DC: Dumbarton Oaks Research and Collection, 1–16.

Cordy-Collins, A. (2001). Blood and the moon priest-esses: *Spondylus* shell in Moche ceremony. In E. P. Benson, & A. G. Cook, eds., *Ritual Sacrifice in Ancient Peru.* Austin: University of Texas Press, 35–54.

DeMarrais, E., & Robb, J. (2013). Art makes society: An introductory visual essay. *World Art*, 3(1), 3–22.

DeMarrais, E., Castillo, L. J., & Earle, T. (1996). Ideology, materialization, and power strategies. *Current Anthropology*, 37(1), 15–31.

Donnan, C. B. (1978). *Moche Art of Peru: Pre-Columbian Symbolic Communication.* Los Angeles: Museum of Cultural History, University of California.

Donnan, C. B. (1992). *Ceramics of Ancient Peru.* Los Angeles: Fowler Museum of Cultural History, University of California.

Donnan, C. B. (2007). *Moche Tombs at Dos Cabezas.* Los Angeles: UCLA, Cotsen Institute of Archaeology.

Donnan, C. B., & McClelland, D. (1979). *The Burial Theme in Moche Iconography. Studies in Pre-Columbian Art and Archaeology* No. 21. Washington, DC: Dumbarton Oaks Research Library and Collection.

Eeckhout, P. (2006). Semillas Sadradas: El Ishpingo (Nectandra sp.) en Pachacamac, Costa Central del Perú. In D. E. Olivera, & H. D. Yacobaccio, *Change in the Andes: Origins of Social Complexity, Pastoralism and Agriculture.* Oxford: BAR Publishing, 201–210.

Eeckhout, P. (2013). Change and permanency on the coast of Ancient Peru: The religious site of Pachacamac. *Archaeology of Religious Change*, 45(1), 137–160.

Eeckhout, P., & Owens, L. S. (eds). (2015). *Funerary Practices and Models in the Ancient Andes.* Cambridge: Cambridge University Press.

Galindo, P., & Srihongse, S. (1967). Evidence of recent jungle yellow-fever activity in Eastern Panama. *Bulletin of the World Health Organization*, 36, 151–161.

Gamboa, J. (2020). Un Personaje Elusivo: Los Mono en el Estilo Cerámico Casma de la Costa Norcentral de Perú (ca. 800–1350 DC). *Chungara Revista de Antropología Chilena*, 52, 285–303.

Garve, R., Garve, M., Türp, J. C., & Meyer, C. G. (2017). Labrets in Africa and Amazonia: Medical implications and cultural determinants. *Tropical Medicine and International Health*, 22(2), 232–240.

Gebo, D. (1992). Locomotor and positional behavior in *Alouatta palliata* and *Cebus capucinus. American Journal of Physical Anthropology*, 26, 277–290.

Goepfert, N. (2008). Ofrendas y sacrificio de animals in la cultura Mochica: El ejemplo de la Plataforma Uhle, Complejo Arqueológico Huacas del Sol y de la Luna. In *Arqueológia Mochica: Nuevos Enfoques. Actas del Primer Congreso Internacional de Jóvenes Investigadores de la Cultura Mochica, Lima, 4-5 de Agosto de 2004.* Lima: Institut Français d'Études Anides-Fondo Editorial de la Pontificia Universidad Católico del Perú, 231–244.

Goepfert, N. (2011). *Frayer la route d'un monde inversé. Sacrifice et offrandes animals dans la culture Mochica (100-800 apr. J.-C.), côte nord du Pérou.* Paris Monographs in American Archaeology 28. Oxford: BAR Publishing.

Goepfert, N. (2012). New zooarchaeological and funerary perspectives on Mochica culture (A.D.100–800), Peru. *Journal of Field Archaeology*, 37(2), 102–120.

Haraway, D. (2003). *The Companion Species Manifesto: Dogs, People, and Significant Otherness.* Chicago: Prickly Paradigm Press.

Helms, M. (1998). *Access to Origins: Affines, Ancestors and Aristocrats.* Austin: University of Texas Press.

Hill, E. (2016). Images of ancestors: Identifying the revered dead in Moche iconography. In E. Hill, & J. B. Hageman, eds., *The Archaeology of Ancestors: Death, Memory, and Veneration.* Gainesville: University of Florida Press, 189–212.

Janson, C., & Boinski, S. (1992). Morphological and behavioral adaptations for foraging in generalist primates: The case of cebines. *American Journal of Physical Anthropology*, 88, 483–498.

Karadimas, D. (2016). Monkeys, wasps and gods: Graphic perspectives on middle horizon and later Pre-Hispanic painted funerary textiles from the Peruvian Coast. *Nuevo Mundo Mundos Nuevos.* Available at: https://journals.openedition.org/nuevo mundo/69281 (Accessed July 1, 2020)

Kaulicke, P. (2020). Early social complexity in Northern Peru and its Amazonian connections. In A. J. Pearce, D. G. Beresford-Jones, & P. Heggarty, eds., London: UCL Press, 103–114.

Langdon, S. (1990). From Monkey to man: The evolution of a geometric sculptural type. *American Journal of Archaeology*, 94(3), 407–424.

Macri, M. J., & Looper, M. G. (2003). *The New Catalog of Maya Hieroglyphs. Volume 1. The Classic Period Inscriptions*. Norman: University of Oklahoma Press.

Masseti, M. (2015). The early 8th century AD zoomorphic iconography of the wall decorations in Qasr al-Amra Hashemite Kingdom of Jordan. *Anthropozoologica*, **50**(2), 69–85.

Mauricio, A. C., & Castro, J. (2007). *Informe Técnico de las Excavaciones en el Área 42 de San José de Moro-Temporada de 2007*. In L. J. Castillo, ed., *Programa Arqueológico San José de Moro, Informe de Investigaciones Temporada de 2007*. Lima: Pontificia Universidad de Católica del Perú, 102–161.

Millaire, J.-F. (2010). Primary state formation in the Virú Valley, north coast of Peru. *Proceedings of the National Academy of Sciences of the United States of America*, **107**(14), 6186–6191.

Montoya, M. (2004). Estudio Fitoquímico y Bioquímico de Semillas Prehispánicas de Nectandra sp. *ECIPERU: Encuentro Científico Internacional*, **1**(1), 1–5.

Morphy, H. (1989). Introduction. In H. Morphy, ed., *Animals into Art*. London: Unwin Hyman, 1–20.

Munn, N. (1966). Visual categories: An approach to the study of representational systems. *American Anthropologist*, **68**, 936–950.

Pareja, M. N. (2017). Monkey and ape iconography in Minoan Art. Unpublished PhD dissertation, Temple University.

Pareja, M. N., McKinney, T., Mayhew, J. A., Setchell, J. M., Nash, S. D., & Heaton, R. (2020). A new identification of the monkeys depicted in a Bronze Age Wall Painting from Akrotiri, Thera. *Primates*, **61**, 159–168.

Prieto, G., & Cuiscanqui, S. (2007). Informe Técnico de la Excavaciones en el Área 35-Temporada 2007. In L. J. Castillo Butters, ed., *Programa Arqueológico San José de Moro, Informe de Investigaciones Temporada de 2007*, Lima: Pontificia Universidad Católico del Perú, 36–79.

Quilter, J. (1997). The narrative approach to Moche iconography. *Latin American Antiquity*, **8**(2), 113–133.

Reitz, E. (2003). Resource use through time at Paloma, Peru. *Bulletin of Florida Museum of Natural History*, **440**, 65–80.

Reynel, C., Pennington, R. T., & Särkinen, T. (2013). *Cómo Se Formó la Diversidad Ecológica del Perú*. Lima: Jesús Bellido.

Rice, P. M., & South, K. E. (2015). Revisiting monkeys on pots: A contextual consideration of primate imagery on classic lowland Maya Pottery. *Ancient Mesoamerica*, **26**, 275–294.

Sahlins, M. (2008). The stranger-king or, elementary forms of the politics of life. *Indonesia and the Malay World*, **36**(105), 177–199.

Saunders, N. J. (1994). Predators of culture: Jaguar symbolism and Mesoamerican elites. *World Archaeology*, **26**, 104–117.

Scher, S. (2012). Markers of masculinity: Phallic representation in Moche art. *Boletín Instituto Frances de Estudios Andinos*, **41**(2), 169–196.

Shady, R., & Leyva, C. (eds.). (2003). *La Ciudad Sagrada de Caral-Supe*. Lima: Instituto Nacional de Cultura.

Stross, B. (2008). *K'u*: The divine monkey. *Journal of Mesoamerican Languages and Linguistics*, **1**, 1–34.

Swenson, E. (2007). Adaptive strategies or ideological innovations? Interpreting sociopolitical developments in the Jequetepeque Valley of Peru during the Late Moche Period. *Journal of Anthropological Archaeology*, **26**, 253–282.

Swenson, E. (2008). San Ildefonso and the "Popularization" of Moche Ideology in the Jequetepeque Valley. In L. J. Castillo Butters, H. Bernier, G. Lockard, & J. R. Yong, eds., *Arqueologia mochica: Nuevos Enfoques*. Lima: Fondo Editorial Pontificia Universidad Católica del Perú, 411–431.

Swenson, E. (2018). Sacrificial landscapes and the anatomy of Moche biopolitics: (AD200–800). In J. Jennings, & E. Swenson, eds., *Powerful Places in the Ancient Andes*. Albuquerque: University of New Mexico Press, 247–286.

Swenson, E., & Seoane, F. (2019). *Proyecto de Investigación Arqueológica Jatanca-Huaca Colorada-Tecapa Valle de Jequetepeque-Temporada 2018*. Lima: Ministry of Culture.

Topic, J. R., & Lange Topic, T. (1983). Coast-highland relations in Northern Peru: Some observations on routes, networks, and scales of interaction. In R. Leventhal & A. Kolata, eds., *Civilization in the Ancient Americas*. Albuquerque: University of New Mexico, 237–259.

Toyne, J. M. (2015). The body sacrificed. *Journal of Religion and Violence*, **3**(1), 137–172.

Trever, L. S. (2019). A Moche riddle in clay: Object knowledge and art work in ancient Peru. *The Art Bulletin*, **101**(4), 18–38.

Uceda, S. (2001). Investigations at Huaca de la Luna, Moche Valley: An example of Moche religious architecture. In J. Pillsbury, ed., *Moche Art and Archaeology in Ancient Peru*. Washington, DC: Yale

University Press, New Haven, CT, and National Gallery of Art, 47–67.

Uceda, S. (2010). Theocracy and secularism: Relationships between the temple and urban nucleus and political change at the Huacas de Moche. In J. Quilter, & L. J. Castillo, eds., *New Perspectives on Moche Political Organization*. Washington, DC: Dumbarton Oaks Research Library and Collection, 132–158.

Uceda, S., Morales, R., & Mujica, E. (2016). *Huaca de la Luna. Templos y dioses Moche*. Lima: Fundación Backus & World Monument Fund.

Urbani, B. (2005). The targeted monkey: A re-evaluation of predation on New World primates. *Journal of Anthropological Sciences*, 83, 89–109.

Van Buren, M. (1996). Rethinking the vertical archipelago: Ethnicity, exchange, and history in the south-central Andes. *American Anthropologist*, 98(2), 338–351.

Viveiros de Castro, E. B. (1998). Cosmological deixis and Amerindian perspectivism. *Journal of the Royal Anthropological Institute*, 4(3), 469–488.

Viveiros de Castro, E. B. (2004). Exchanging perspectives: The transformation of objects into subjects in Amerindian ontologies. *Common Knowledge*, 10(3), 463–484.

Wassén, S. H. (1987). "Ulluchu" in Moche iconography and blood ceremonies: The search for identification. *Årstryck*, 1985/1986, 59–85.

Wołoszyn, J. Z., & Piwowar, K. (2015). Sodomites, Siamese twins, and scholars: Same-sex relationships in Moche art. *American Anthropologist*, 117(2), 285–301.

Zedeño, M. N. (2009). Animating by association: Index objects and relational taxonomies. *Cambridge Archaeological Journal*, 19(3), 407–417.

6 Representations of Primates in Petroglyphs of the Brazilian Amazonia

Edithe Pereira & José de Sousa e Silva Júnior

Representações de primatas em gravuras rupestres da Amazônia brasileira

Resumo

Vinte e nove gravuras rupestres localizadas em 15 sítios arqueológicos na Amazônia brasileira previamente selecionadas como possíveis representações de primatas foram analisadas em detalhe à procura de traços ou posturas que pudessem ser utilizados para identificar os táxons. O procedimento de identificação foi baseado no pressuposto de que cada artista retratou a fauna local. Após a identificação dos gêneros foram examinadas as distribuições geográficas das respectivas espécies na região. Foram identificadas nove espécies, além de uma identificação no nível da família e outra no nível do gênero. Na literatura arqueológica que trata da representação de animais, verifica-se que grande parte das publicações omite na metodologia os procedimentos utilizados para identificação dos grupos taxonômicos. Um procedimento mais refinado envolve um exame dos caracteres diagnósticos dos táxons e do conhecimento sobre o modo de vida dos mesmos, além das respectivas áreas de distribuição geográfica. Todos os táxons observados são endêmicos da Amazônia. Entre as espécies identificadas, três são atualmente consideradas vulneráveis à extinção. Além disso, duas espécies foram representadas em sítios localizados em áreas geográficas onde tais espécies aparentemente não ocorrem, sugerindo a necessidade da realização de inventários faunísticos mais refinados e estimulando a pesquisa sobre os movimentos das antigas comunidades humanas naquelas regiões.

Palavras Chave

Arte rupestre – arqueologia – zoologia – morfologia – comportamento

Abstract

Twenty-nine petroglyphs found in 15 archaeological sites in Brazilian Amazonia, previously selected as possible representations of primates, were analyzed in detail in search of shapes or postures that could be used for identifying taxa. Identification was based on the assumption that each artist would have depicted local fauna. After genera had been determined, geographic distribution of the respective species in the region was examined. This method allowed for the identification of nine species, in addition to one animal at genus level and another to family level. Archaeological publications dealing with representations of animals often disregard methodological procedures used for taxon identification. A more refined procedure would include examining taxon diagnostic characters, life history and behavior, and geographic distribution. All observed taxa are endemic to Amazonia. Among the identified species, three are currently considered vulnerable to extinction. Two species were found to be represented in sites located in geographic areas where they supposedly do not occur, which suggest the need for more thorough faunal inventories and should stimulate research on the displacements of ancient human communities in those regions.

Keywords: Rock art, Archaeology, Zoology, Morphology, Behavior

6.1   Introduction

With its almost eight million square kilometers, Amazonia has the Amazon river as its main axis into which several tributaries converge; these, in turn, collect the waters of thousands of streams that contribute to form an immense hydrographic grid over the region. On the rocks and stony walls flanking the rivers and waterfalls that establish the transition from the Amazonian plains to the Guiana Shield to the north, and to the Brazilian Central Plateau to the south, there are hundreds of sites with rock engravings.

Rivers were and continue to be the main ways traversed by Amazonian peoples, and this is possibly the reason why most information on rock engravings in the region is found along them. However, studies carried out in the past few decades have demonstrated that sites with rock engravings also do occur in places farther from water courses, such as in mountain ranges and inside caves and natural shelters.

News of the existence of rock engravings date from the eighteenth century, through the reports of clergymen and travelers (Pereira, 2006). Some mentioned the engravings as mere curiosities, with no further information on them. Others only cared to record or describe what they saw, and there were still others who did record and study them, such as Hartt (1871), Koch-Grünberg (1907, 2010), Stradelli (1900), and Wallace (1979), between the mid-1800s and early 1900s.

However, from the late 1950s on, when systematic archaeological research began in Amazonia, the study of rock paintings and engravings was neglected. This was the result of a theoretical orientation of archaeological research towards ceramics as the most important kind of vestiges, capable of providing information that could identify migratory and dispersal routes, and of establishing sequences of cultural development for the region (Meggers, 1985). Thus, a considerable gap between the knowledge on rock art and that on ceramics in the region was established. This gap only began to narrow from the mid-1980s on, when the earliest studies of rock art were published (Consens, 1988, 1989; Corrêa, 1994; Pereira, 1990; Ribeiro et al., 1986, 1987, 1989, 1996). However, research about the groups of animals represented in both rock art and ceramics, remained undeveloped. The difficulties in identifying zoological groups in these two sources are of similar magnitude. Navarro and Silva-Júnior (2019) have reported the difficulties they faced in their attempt to identify mammals on ceramic objects dating from c. 1300 years found in a flooded area of the eastern Amazon. While the drawings observed in the rock engravings show only a general body plan, the observed ceramic sculptures lack this general frame, depicting body parts which are often simplified and out of proportion. Today, there has been a significant increase in the quantity of archaeological studies on rock art in Brazilian Amazonia. Nevertheless, this research is still limited considering the vastness of the region. Such studies have been conducted in specific, restricted areas in the states of

Amazonas (Cavallini, 2014, 2015; Valle, 2010), Rondonia (Oliveira, 2013), Tocantins (Berra, 2004, 2015; Braga, 2015; Pereira, 2008), Pará (Pereira, 2004, 2012), and Mato Grosso (Migliacio, 2017), and already give an idea of the quantity of sites and of the diversity of techniques and motifs represented. This research has already defined a series of styles for rock paintings and engravings in continental Amazonia, as summarized by Cavallini (2014).

Still, very few published articles deal with the characteristics of certain motifs engraved or painted on rocks. Among the handful of papers on specific themes of Amazonian rock art are Cavallini (2014), Greer (1995), Greer and Greer (2006), Pereira (2000a), and Urbina Rangel (1994, 2004) for anthropomorphic figures, and Greer (2001) and Urbina Rangel (2015) for representations of animals. This chapter is the first attempt to gather together the array of information available on the representation of monkeys (Primates) in rock engravings in Brazilian Amazonia. These are, of course, interpretations based on certain anatomical features that, in our eyes, bear similarity with characteristics specific to certain primate taxa. These interpretations, however, remain hypothetical, and we will hardly be able to prove them, since the authors – the bearers of the real meaning of the figures – no longer exist. The examples presented here are obviously but a small sample of what really exists in the region, as information is limited by the scarce dissemination of images of rock art sets that would provide the groundwork for the identification of monkey figures. Far from being exhaustive, what we present here is specific information on the places where they were found, and the forms ancient indigenous peoples used to represent monkeys.

6.2   Methodology

Zoomorphic motifs observed in rock engravings in Amazonia are usually very schematic, making it very hard for a genus, or species, level identification of the represented animals. Notwithstanding, some figures show certain features that are diagnostic characters of given taxa, helping their identification.

Rock figures observed in seven archaeological sites in the State of Pará were pre-sorted for the identification of primate images. Few general traits that define a primate (*sensu* Pough et al., 2005) could be observed in the schematic drawings of the rock engravings. However, it was possible to select the figures which represented primates through the combination of certain specific traits such as the shape of the head, the proportional size of the head (large, to hold an equally large brain) and, for the limbs, the position of the feet and, specifically regarding New World primates, the length and position of the tail. Figures lacking representation of the tail were considered anthropomorphic and therefore discarded, since there are no tailless nonhuman primates in the Neotropics. Twenty such images were selected representing the basic body plan of a monkey. Morphological characters in the figures were compared to morphological data of primate genera in Amazonia according to Hill's anatomy manuals (Hill, 1960, 1962) and to studies by Silva-Júnior (2001) and Lynch-Alfaro et al. (2012). Species identification was based on the assumption that each artist would have represented the local fauna around them. Thus, after genus identification, the geographic distribution of the respective species was examined (Boubli et al., 2008; Gregorin, 2006; Hershkovitz, 1984, 1985, 1987; Kellogg and Goldman, 1944; Mercês et al., 2015; Mourthé et al., 2015; Rylands and Régis, 2015; Silva-Júnior et al., 2013, to which the localization of the archaeological site was overlapped. When only a single species of a given genus occurred in the region under study, positive species-level identification could be achieved. Identification of species of *Saimiri*, *Chiropotes*, and *Ateles* was supported by behavioral features depicted in engravings and described by Baldwin and Baldwin (1981), van Roosmalen et al. (1981), van Roosmalen and Klein (1988), and Veiga and Ferrari (2013). The nine illustrations from the works of Koch-Grünberg (2010), Rauschert (1959), and Valle (2012, 2014) were also re-evaluated for an attempt at a more refined identification of the taxa represented. Figure 6.1 shows the location of each archaeological site with the studied engravings.

6.3   Representations of Monkeys in Rock Engravings in the Brazilian Amazonia

From a total of 29 examined engravings, six species of primates were identified in archaeological sites in Pará and three others in the illustrations available in published writings. This makes up for a total of nine species belonging to six genera and three families (Fig. 6.2). All identified species are endemic to Amazonia. Among the images taken from Koch-Grünberg (2010), one was positively identified at the species level (although the picture was partially the result of adverse weather over the rock and not an intentional representation of a monkey), two only as primates, while further two could not be ascribed with certainty to that order. As for the images from archaeological sites in Pará, one could be identified at the genus level (a site located at the border between the geographic distribution areas of two species), two simply as primates, and one could not be positively determined as a monkey.

Few authors have identified monkey figures in Amazonian rock art. In the early twentieth century, Theodor Koch-Grünberg documented several rock engravings in the Negro River basin; among the rocks of the many waterfalls he traversed, he identified the image of a monkey:

In the midst of some illustrations, these partially destroyed, a chunk of the rock surface came off, so the resulting figure greatly resembled the image of a monkey running wild, and for this reason it is called "monkey" by the natives. Trunk and head of the animal are formed by the flaw caused by the cracking of the rock, while the coiled, raised tail results from a portion of a figure in the shape of a swirl, and the legs, in turn, are the effect caused by other figures whose initial appearance cannot be recognized anymore. (Koch-Grünberg, 2010, p. 62, translated from the Portuguese edition).

Figure 6.3 from Koch-Grünberg (2010) can be associated with a real animal, although its face is distorted, as is the proximal part of its tail. Comparing the body shape with the ten primate genera occurring in the Negro River region, the animal

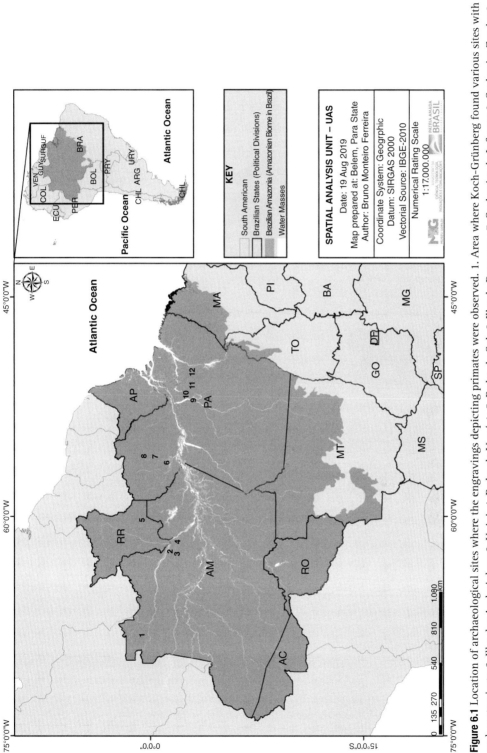

Figure 6.1 Location of archaeological sites where the engravings depicting primates were observed. 1. Area where Koch-Grünberg found various sites with rock engravings; 2. Ilha das Andorinhas; 3. Unini; 4. Pedra da Vovó 1; 5. Pedra do Sol; 6. Ilha do Descanso; 7. Cachoeira do Inferno; 8. Cachoeira Zoada; 9. Nameless waterfall, lower Rio Xingu; 10. Pedra das Arraias; 11. Pedra das Macacos; 12. Pedra do Reis. Map by Bruno Monteiro Ferreira, 2019.

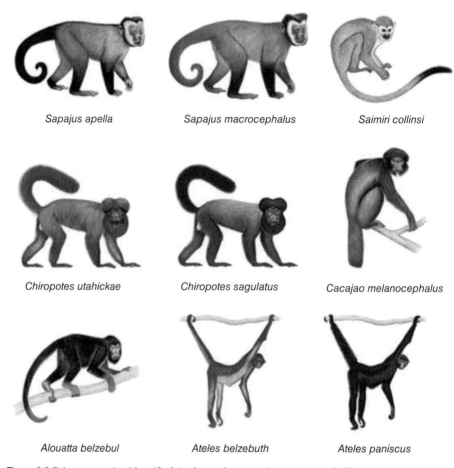

Sapajus apella   *Sapajus macrocephalus*   *Saimiri collinsi*

Chiropotes utahickae   *Chiropotes sagulatus*   *Cacajao melanocephalus*

Alouatta belzebul   *Ateles belzebuth*   *Ateles paniscus*

Figure 6.2 Primate species identified in the rock engravings examined. Illustrations copyright 2013 Stephen D. Nash / IUCN SSC Primate Specialist Group. Used with permission.

represented was determined to be a robust capuchin monkey (genus *Sapajus*). Silva-Júnior (2001) and Lynch-Alfaro et al. (2012) observed that monkeys of this genus can be recognized by their short and stocky body and short limbs. A semi-prehensile tail of mid-size length relative to body length is also another feature of the group. According to Silva-Júnior (2001), the only species of *Sapajus* occurring in the Upper Negro River region is *S. macrocephalus*, whose conservation status is considered as "least concern" (LC) (Martins et al., 2015).

In addition to the image on Fig. 6.3, Koch-Grünberg (2010) further mentioned other alleged monkey representations in the engravings found in Caiari-Uaupés (Fig. 6.4a), Tiquié (Fig. 6.4b), and Curicuiari (Fig. 6.4c, d), all rivers in the Rio Negro basin. In those images, the feature that Koch-Grünberg used to identify a monkey was the presence of a long tail. Indeed, the presence of the tail added to the morphology of the limbs and the rounded head recalls the basic body design of a monkey in Figs. 6.4c and 6.4d. However, such association was not possible for Figs. 6.4a and 6.4b.

Figure 6.3 Monkey representation described by Theodor Koch-Grünberg (1907). (Public domain).

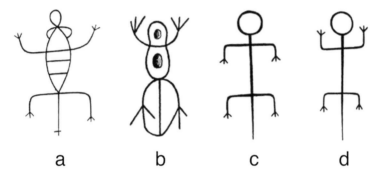

a   b   c   d

Figure 6.4 Representations of monkeys as interpreted by Theodor Koch-Grünberg (1907). (Public domain).

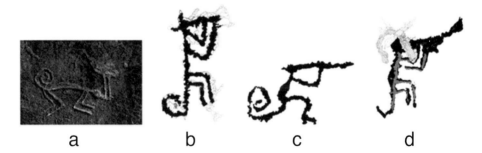

a   b   c   d

Figure 6.5 (a) Representation of monkey in the Unini 4 site; "flute-playing monkey" in (b) Ilha das Andorinhas; (c) Pedra da Vovó 1; (d) Pedra do Sol. Photograph and drawings based on images from Valle (2014). Courtesy of Raoni Valle.

At the site named Unini 4 (panel 2), located at the second waterfall of Unini River, a right-hand tributary of the lower Negro River (01°41′50.86″S, 61°50′06.03″W), Valle (2012, 2014: 348) identified a monkey (Fig. 6.5a). Some details of the depicted animal recall the image of a spider monkey (*Ateles* spp.): an elongated upper body and a relatively small head are typical of the genus (Hill, 1962; Kellogg and Goldman,

1944). In spite of an exceedingly short tail – spider monkeys have particularly long tails that function as a fifth limb – one can notice that the appendage was drawn as a prehensile tail, bent backwards, with a highlighted tip that suggests a hairless area. The presence of *Ateles* in the Unini River region is still a subject of debate. Updated information on geographic distribution (Mourthé et al., 2015) suggests *A. belzebuth* as the most probable species in the area. This species was not recorded in the inventory by Iwanaga et al. (2014), but the representation in the engraving favors a confirmation of the hypothesis of Barnett et al. (2002) on the possible reduction of the species original distribution. Barnett et al. (2002) also stated that the species can further be found at the Jaú National Park. *Ateles belzebuth* is classified as "vulnerable" (VU) (Mourthé et al., 2015).

In the region of the lower Negro River and its left-bank tributary, Jauaperi River, Valle (2012, 2014: 342) identified a quite peculiar figure at three archaeological sites, and described one of them as: "A zoomorph resembling a primate, in profile, its hand in a upturned arm holding a rectilinear object, which would compel us to interpret it as a flute, raising it to its head much like it were playing a musical instrument." Valle (2014) called this kind of figure a "flute player" (Fig. 6.5b–d), taking into account the importance of sacred flutes in the ritual-myth of Jurupari in the upper course of the Negro River (Mello, 2013) – aimed at male initiation rites and forbidden to women - and searched for evidence that allowed to relate the rock figure of the "flute player" to the said ritual-myth (Valle, 2012, 2014). Furthermore, considering the anatomy of the figures, the author identified them as howler monkeys (*Alouatta* spp.), a genus that is frequent in the region of the rock engravings and is characterized by its loud vocalizations. This vocal ability is due to the morphology of the monkeys' hyoid bone (Gregorin, 2006; Hill, 1962), which works as a sounding board for loud calls used mainly for territory demarcation (Neville et al., 1988). Although an association of howler monkey vocalizations with the sounds of a musical instrument may seem tempting, none of the three engravings feature morphological attributes typical of the genus *Alouatta*. The image on Fig. 6.5b was observed at Ilha das Andorinhas (01°23′58.74″S, 61°44′59.82″W), an island in a canal at the right bank of Negro River, in the Negro-Solimões-Japurá interfluvium. The animal in question has a more "generalistic" body shape, similar to that of a capuchin monkey (genera *Sapajus* and *Cebus*). The relevant species whose distribution overlaps with the location of the archaeological site are either *Sapajus apella* or *Cebus albifrons*. The engraving in Fig. 6.5c was observed at the Pedra da Vovó 1 archaeological site (01°33′07.87″S, 61°28′22.87″W), located on a small island in the southernmost canal of Jauaperi River, next to its confluence with Negro River, in the Branco-Negro-Trombetas interfluve. The elongated arms and tail suggest a spider monkey, and the species that occurs in the region is *Ateles paniscus* (Kellogg and Goldman, 1944; Mourthé et al., 2015).

Figure 6.5d shows an image observed at the Pedra do Sol archaeological site (0°51′13 ″N, 60°07′55 ″W), in the upper Jauaperi River region, in the same interfluve mentioned above. The depicted animal most likely resembles a uakari (*Cacajao* spp.), the only New World primate with a short tail. The pose of the figure bears a remarkable resemblance to the illustration of *Cacajao melanocephalus* (then named *Simia melanocephala)* made by Aimé Bonpland in Humboldt (1811). However, according to Boubli et al. (2008), Hershkovitz (1987), and Silva-Júnior et al. (2013), the genus *Cacajao* does not occur in the Jauaperi River region. The uakari species found closest to that site is indeed *C. melanocephalus*, located in the Negro-Solimões-Japurá interfluve (Boubli et al., 2008). The possible representation of *Cacajao* at Pedra do Sol could be related to ancient displacements of human populations between the regions of the upper Jauaperi River and both banks of the lower Negro River, if we consider that migrations of indigenous populations were frequent in the past (Zucchi, 2010) and are still common in the present. In terms of conservation status, Bezerra (2015) classifies *C. melanocephalus* as "least concern" (LC). It is also possible that the depicted animal is not a *Cacajao* after all, and the shorter tail may be the carver's perception of the anatomy of regional species. A different hypothesis was proposed by Valle (2014: 404), who presented the interpretation of a representative of the Tatuyo people, from Pira-Paraná River, in Colombia, for whom the figure depicts the 'hunter monkey' holding a blowpipe and not a flute.

In the State of Pará, monkey representations appear at sites in different regions (Fig. 6.1). In the municipality of Oriximiná, in northeastern Pará, monkey depictions appear in at least two sites along Erepecuru River, in the Trombetas-Jari interfluve. These sites are located in waterfall rocks and the engravings can only be seen from time to time, when the water volume lowers and they are exposed. In one of the first waterfalls on the Erepecuru River, there is a series of engravings with different motifs are spread across the rocks that form an island called Ilha do Descanso (1°3′35.57″S, 56°2′53.20″W). Primate representations appear in three panels. In two of them, the images are isolated (Fig. 6.6a, b), while in the other one they show a group of animals in a single row, facing in the same direction (Fig. 6.6c). Among the isolated images, the first (Fig. 6.6a) resembles the body shape of a bearded saki (*Chiropotes* spp.). Although the "beard" typical for this monkey is not represented, the large, round head seems an indication of the presence of temporal bulbs; the thick, non-prehensile tail may be held in a dangling position over the dorsum. According to Silva-Júnior et al. (2013), the species of *Chiropotes* that occurs in the Erepecuru River region is *C. sagulatus*, considered as "least concern" (LC) (Azevedo and Veiga, 2015). Another possibility is that the animal represented is not, indeed, *Chiropotes*, but *Sapajus* (in this case, *S. apella*). The dangling tail over the dorsum could be the result of the carver's perception about the behavior of the species. The animal represented in Fig. 6.6b can be identified as a spider monkey (*Ateles* spp.) because of its elongated body, proportionally small head, and relatively long forelimbs, seemingly suspended from its long, prehensile tail. According to Kellogg and Goldman (1944) the spider monkey species of the region is *Ateles paniscus*, classified as "least concern" (LC) (Rylands and Régis, 2015). The animals in Fig. 6.6c have the same body shape as that of Fig. 6.6a, and can thus be determined either as bearded sakis (*C. sagulatus*) or capuchin monkeys (*S. apella*), typically walking on all fours. These monkeys usually form large social groups (van Roosmalen et al., 1981; Veiga and Ferrari, 2013).

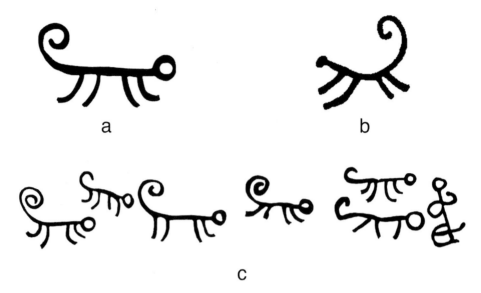

Figure 6.6 Representations of monkeys in the Ilha do Descanso site: (a) *Chiropotes sagulatus*; (b) *Ateles paniscus*; (c) line-up of monkeys in a common scenic representation of *Chiropotes sagulatus*. Based on data from Pereira (1996).

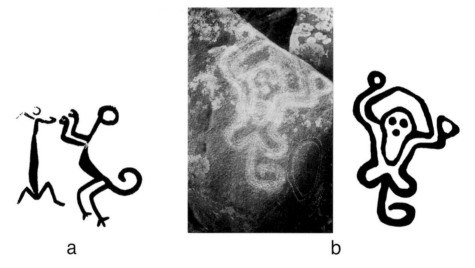

Figure 6.7 Rio Erepecuru: (a) representation of *Ateles paniscus* (at right), Cachoeira do Inferno site; (b) representation of *Ateles paniscus*, Cachoeira Zoada site. Based on data from Pereira (1996); photograph from Rondon (1953) (public domain).

At Cachoeira do Inferno (56°4′46.31″W, 0°59′42.35″S), a waterfall in the course of rio Erepecuru, Manfred Rauschert (1959) illustrated many petroglyphs. In one of them there is the representation of a standing monkey, viewed in profile, at the side of another subject (Fig. 6.7a). The image at left recalls a human figure, sitting on the ground with flexed legs, next to an animal pet, to its right, which in spite of the exceedingly large head and short tail, was depicted in the typical attitude of a spider monkey when walking on its hindlimbs, with its arms and tail lifted. The spider monkey that occurs in the region of Cachoeira do Inferno is *Ateles paniscus*. Still along Erepecuru River, there is a clear representation of a moving monkey engraved between the rocks of Cachoeira Zoada waterfall (55°54′41.11″W, 0°21′17.92″N) (Fig. 6.7b). The image displays a mixture of *Ateles* and *Alouatta* traits. Some traits such as the facial morphology, the long forelimbs with extremities recalling hooks (suggesting arm-swinging locomotion), the slightly flexed hindlimbs, and the prehensile tail, allow for its identification as a spider monkey (*Ateles paniscus*). On the other hand, despite that arm swinging locomotion is not usual for howler monkeys, the area just below the face suggests the presence of a large hyoid, a typical feature of adult male *Alouatta*. According to Gregorin (2006), the howler species in the area is *A. macconnelli*, and its conservation status is considered as "least concern" (LC) (Rylands and Santos, 2015).

In the southeast of the State of Pará, in the municipalities of Anapu, Pacajá (Xingu-Tocantins interfluve) and Vitória do Xingu (Xingu-Tapajós interfluve), monkey representations occur at four archaeological sites – one located in the Rio Xingu waterfalls, and the other three in areas close to the Transamazônica highway, the 4,223 km-long highway that traverses seven Brazilian states. In the lower course of Rio Xingu, at a waterfall with no name (51°38′31.06″W, 3°15′27.90″S), where the rocks are exposed only during the dry season (Fig. 6.8a), there is the representation of a monkey at the side of a subject that seems to be an anthropomorphic figure (Fig. 6.8b). The features of the depicted primate are similar to those observed in the engravings of Ilha do Descanso (Fig. 6.6). In addition, the typical 'beard' of the bearded saki (*Chiropotes* spp.) is well represented. The site is located exactly at the border of the distribution range between two species of *Chiropotes*, established by Rio Xingu: *C. utahickae* occurs in the Tocantins-Xingu interfluve, on the right bank of Rio Xingu, while *C. albinasus* is found in the Xingu-Tapajós interfluve, on the left bank of Rio Xingu. This

a   b

Figure 6.8 (a) View of the waterfall in the dry season, where the rocks with engravings are exposed; (b) representation of *Chiropotes* in an engraving in Rio Xingu. Photographs of Leandro Valle.

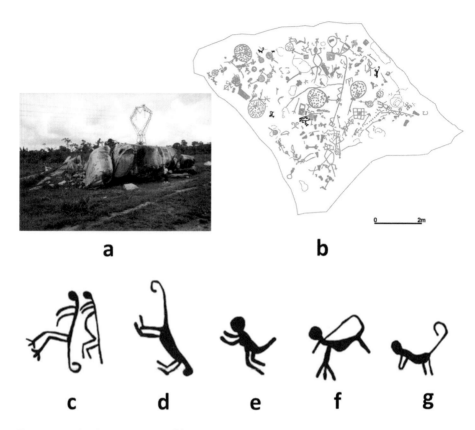

Figure 6.9 Pedra das Arraias site: (a) engravings are located on the top portion of this granite outcrop; (b) main panel with the monkey representations in black, showing their position within the panel; (c–g) Monkey representations at the Pedra das Arraias site. Photograph and illustrations by E. Pereira, based on data from Pereira (2000).

engraving reinforces the assumption that the images in Fig. 6.6 represent bearded sakis, since *Sapajus apella* does not have a prominent beard.

In the area of the Transamazônica highway, between the municipalities of Anapu and Pacajá, in the Xingu-Tocantins interfluvium, three sites show rock engravings representing monkeys. The Pedra das Arraias site (51°31′47.42″W, 3°11′54.13″S) was established during the deforestation process prior to the implementation of a transmission line called Tramo-Oeste (Fig. 6.9). The rock paintings at this site are located on three granite boulders lying on the route of this transmission line. Positioned horizontally on the top part of a large granite outcrop (Fig. 6.9a), there is the main panel (Fig. 6.9b), characterized by numerous engraved subjects (Pereira, 2000b). Forty-five representations of animals were identified on this panel, among which snates, lizards, birds, and monkeys. Most of these animals are apparently shown in isolated form, and there is no indication of a scene composition involving them. Five engravings that resemble monkeys were selected from this site. In Fig. 6.9c, despite the fact that the presence of a tail consistent with the shape of the limbs and the (round) head could suggest the basic form of a primate, the other features do not suggest any character that resembles those of any primate genus in the region. They could vaguely recall capuchin monkeys (*Sapajus* spp.), although the tail in one of the depicted individuals is curled on the wrong side and is incomplete on the other. The individual in Fig. 6.9d is hanging down by means of its semiprehensile tail, which works as a simple hook, quite like in a *Sapajus* capuchin monkey. The *Sapajus* species that occurs in that area is *S. apella*, whose conservation status is deemed as "least concern" (LC) (Alves et al., 2015). An alternative interpretation would eventually be that of a howler monkey *(Alouatta)* with an incomplete prehensile tail end. The howler monkey found in the area is *A. belzebul*, considered "vulnerable" (VU) (Valença-Montenegro et al., 2015). On the other hand, the animal in Fig. 6.9e could not be determined. The sketch indicates movement, as if the creature were jumping: the body shape recalls only vaguely a primate, with no identifiable features. Its tail is short and thick, a trait not found in any primate in eastern Amazonia. As for Fig. 6.9f, the animal depicted could be a squirrel monkey (*Saimiri* spp.) because of its elongated head (Hill, 1960) and the long, nonprehensile tail; however, the illustrated stance would be unusual for this genus. The *Saimiri* species found in the region is *S. collinsi*, considered as "least concern" (LC) (Silva-Júnior et al., 2015). Finally, in Fig. 6.9g one can identify a howler monkey (*Alouatta belzebul*), with a long and truly prehensile tail, which is shown curled around a branch in a rock crack, its body hanging down. Just as for Fig. 6.9d, an alternative interpretation could be that of a capuchin monkey (*Sapajus apella*).

Pedra dos Macacos (51°27′15.95″ W, 3°13′31.87″ S), that evocatively translates as the "Rock of the Monkeys", is a site with rock engravings in the open, next to the border between a farm and a secondary road known as Km 96 of the Transamazônica highway (direction Altamira to Marabá), in the municipality of Anapu. The engravings are on one of the vertical faces of a large granite boulder and on six other rocky outcrops around the larger one. Among the several motifs in the site, 13 are animal representations and 10 of those are of primates. Figure 6.10a shows the boulder with the engravings of the main panel and the reproduction of the drawings with the monkeys highlighted (Fig. 6.10b). In the upper part of the rock one can see a group of monkeys in movement that seems to have been engraved deliberately over a crack, suggesting locomotion over a substrate in the tree canopies. Body and tail shape, as well as their stance in movement, hint at squirrel monkeys (*Saimiri* spp.). Figure 6.10c supports this notion, indicating a group of many primate individuals where the animals are moving in a single line, a behavior observed in *Saimiri* when crossing a discontinuity in the forest canopy (Baldwin and Baldwin, 1981). The image further evokes the presence of more individuals than shown in the engraving. In this scene, a female carries an infant on her back (among squirrel monkeys, only females carry infants). The *Saimiri* species that occurs in that area is *S. collinsi*. This set of animals aligned in a row is the only recognizable group scene at this site: the other representations of monkeys appear beside other subjects, but without any trace of a relationship between them. Images in Fig. 6.10d–f also show features of *S. collinsi*. The one on Fig. 6.10d is shown performing a jump, with extended forelimbs and a tail

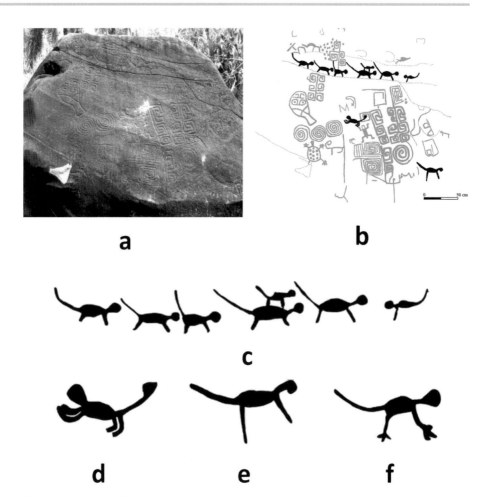

a

b

c

d   **e**   **f**

Figure 6.10 Pedra dos Macacos: (a) Rock with the main panel; (b) reproduction of the images on the panel, with the monkey representations in black; (c–f) the monkey representations. Photograph and illustrations by E. Pereira.

(with the tail 'brush' typical to *Saimiri*) functioning as a rudder. In addition to the representations here mentioned, there is another, located on the smaller rocks next to the main panel (Fig. 6.10f), which can also be identified as *S. collinsi*.

The Pedra do Reis site (50°38′38.58″ W, 3°44′43.98″ S) is located in the grazing area of a farm in the municipality of Pacajá. It is a granite block with engravings on all its faces, but some of the figures were destroyed by the detachment of part of the rock by fire action (Fig. 6.11a). Among the several images forming the panel with rock art in Pedra do Reis, four representations of monkeys could be detected (Fig. 6.11b). All images appear isolated and do not resemble scene compositions. The traits of the animal in Fig. 6.11d are similar to those of Fig. 6.9c, although in the former the tail of the creature has a rounded tip. Likewise as in Fig. 6.9c, the drawing has no features that could be associated to any of the monkey genera occurring in the region, although it faintly resembles a capuchin monkey. The

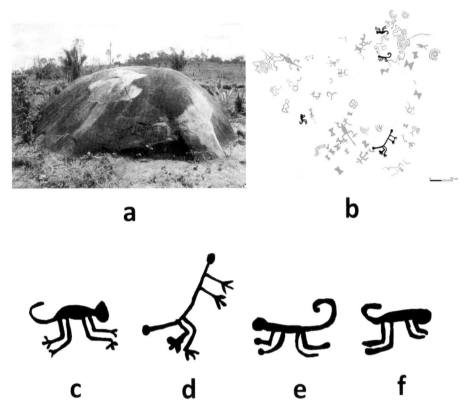

Figure 6.11 Pedra dos Reis: (a) Rock with engravings at the site; (b) reproduction of the petroglyphs, highlighting the monkey representations; (c–f) the monkey representations. Photograph and illustrations by E. Pereira.

subjects on Fig. 6.11c, e, f are reminiscent of bearded sakis (*C. utahickae*) and the hair tufts on their head suggest they have a very large and rounded head top. Bearded sakis adopt a similar stance while moving. *C. utahickae* is considered a 'vulnerable' species (VU) (Alonso and Carvalho, 2015).

6.4   Conclusions

Representations of animals are quite common in the prehistoric iconography of Amazonia. It is manifested in rock art, in ceramics, in stone artefacts such as *muiraquitãs*, and polished stone figurines (idols) representing anthropomorphic and zoomorphic figures individually or in association, and other fantastic figures (Porro, 2010).

The choice of a given animal to be represented could be related to the role it is ascribed in the mythology of the diverse peoples who lived in the region. Ethnographic studies demonstrate the complexity and subjectivity of the relationships between humans and animals in current indigenous societies. Temporal distance and what little was left from the culture of ancient Amazonian peoples do not allow us to investigate thoroughly the reasons that led to the selection of a given animal as a representation, let alone to hazard a guess at any interpretation of its meaning.

We will confine ourselves to analyzing the form represented, which in our own views, impregnated by the Western references around us, manages to identify traits that resemble those of some particular animal groups. Keen observers of nature, the authors of rock engravings recorded anatomical or behavioral details that allowed for a more specialized examiner to identify traits that are typical of a given species. Among the primates identified in this study, three (*Chiropotes utahickae, Ateles belzebuth* and *Alouatta belzebul*) are currently considered vulnerable to extinction. In addition, two species (*Cacajao melanocephalus* and *Ateles belzebuth*) were represented in sites located in geographical areas where they do not occur now, which suggests the need for more thorough faunal inventories, and encourages research on the displacements of ancient human communities in those regions or shrinkage of prior more extended distributions. This enhances the importance of collaborative work involving experts in different fields of knowledge.

In many publications in the archaeological literature dealing with the representation of animals in ceramics or in rock engravings, the methodology for taxonomic group identification is omitted. Furthermore, the animals are often referred to only through their popular names. The way they are represented, be it with an anatomical detail or displaying a given stance, often helps in the identification of a genus or a species. The location of the archaeological site, where the images are found, also provides information on the past distribution of a given species, which should be compared to its current distribution. All in all, a more refined procedure would involve the identification of diagnostic characters for given taxa, the knowledge of their life histories, and of their respective areas of geographic distribution.

Acknowledgments

The authors thank Bernardo Urbani, Dionisios Youlatos, and Andrzej T. Antczak for their invitation to participate in this volume; Stephen D. Nash for the permission to use the images of Fig. 6.2; Leandro Valle for the photographs illustrating Fig. 6.8; Raoni Valle for the images of Fig. 6.5; Horácio Higuchi and Cristiana Barreto for the English translation. The authors also thank the two anonymous reviewers who contributed with valuable suggestions.

References

Alonso, A. C., & Carvalho, A. S. (2015). *Avaliação do Risco de Extinção de Chiropotes utahickae (Hershkovitz, 1985) no Brasil. Processo de Avaliação do Risco de Extinção da Fauna Brasileira.* Brasilia: ICMBio.

Alves, S. L., Buss, G., Ravetta, A. L., Messias, M. R., & Carvalho, A. S. (2015). *Avaliação do Risco de Extinção de Sapajus apella (Linnaeus, 1758) no Brasil. Processo de Avaliação do Risco de Extinção da Fauna Brasileira.* Brasilia: ICMBio.

Barnett, A. A., Borges, S. H., Castilho, C. V., Neri, F. M., & Shapley, R. L. (2002). Primates of the Jaú National Park, Amazonas, Brazil. *Neotropical Primates,* 10(2), 65–70.

Berra, J. C. A. (2015). As Pinturas Rupestres Pré-Históricas de Contorno Aberto na Serra do Lajeado – TO: Similaridades e Diversidades com as Pinturas de Contorno Aberto no Parque Nacional Serra da Capivara. PhD dissertation, Universidade Federal de Pernambuco.

Berra, J. C. A. (2004). As Pinturas Rupestres na Serra do Lajeado – Médio Curso do Rio Tocantins. MSc dissertation, Universidade de São Paulo.

Bezerra, B. M. (2015). *Avaliação do Risco de Extinção de Cacajao melanocephalus (Humboldt, 1811) no Brasil. Processo de Avaliação do Risco de Extinção da Fauna Brasileira.* Brasilia: ICMBio.

Boubli, J. P., Da Silva, M. N. F., Amado, M. V., Herbk, T., Pontual, F. B., & Farias, I. (2008). A taxonomic reassessment of black uakari monkey, *Cacajao melanocephalus*, Humboldt (1811), with the description of two new species. *International Journal of Primatology*, 29, 723–741.

Braga, A. (2015). Paisagens e Técnicas Distintas, Motivos Semelhantes: a Dispersão da Arte Rupestre no Rio Tocantins, o Caso de Palmas e Lajeado – TO, Brasil. PhD dissertation, Universidade de Trás-Os-Montes e Alto Douro.

Cavallini, M. S. (2014). As Gravuras Rupestres da Bacia do Baixo Rio Urubu: Levantamento e Análise Gráfica do Sítio Caretas, Itacoatiara, Estado do Amazonas. Uma Proposta de Contextualização. MSc dissertation, , Universidade de São Paulo.

Cavallini, M. S., Stampanoni Bassi, F. S., & Gallo, D. L. R. (2015). Petróglifos do rio Urubu. Rumo à contextualização de uma arte rupestre amazônica. *Arkeos*, 37, 567–588.

Consens, M. (1988). First rock paintings in the Amazon basin. *Rock Art Research*, 5 (1), 69–72.

Consens, M. (1989). Arte rupestre no Pará: análise de alguns sítios de Monte Alegre. *Dédalo*, 1 (special issue), 265–278.

Corrêa, M. V. M. (1994). As Gravações e Pinturas Rupestres na Área do Reservatório da UHE-Balbina - AM. MSc dissertation, Universidade Federal do Rio de Janeiro.

Greer, J. (1995). Rock art chronology in the Middle Orinoco Basin of Southwestern Venezuela. Unpublished PhD dissertation, University of Missouri.

Greer, J. (2001). *Lowland South America. Handbook of Rock Art Research*. D. S. Whitley, ed., New York: Altamira Press, 665–706.

Greer, J., & Greer, M. (2006). Human figures in the cave paintings of Southern Venezuela. *1994 IRAC Proceedings, Rock Art-World Heritage.* American Rock Art Research Association, 155–166.

Gregorin, R. (2006). Taxonomia e variação geográfica das espécies do gênero *Alouatta* Lacépède (Primates, Atelidae) no Brasil. *Revista Brasileira de Zoologia*, 23 (1), 64–144.

Hartt, C. F. (1871). Brazilian rock inscriptions. *American Naturalist*, 5 (3), 139–147.

Hershkovitz, P. (1984). Taxonomy of squirrel monkeys, genus *Saimiri* (Cebidae, Platyrrhini): A preliminary report with description of a hitherto unnamed form. *American Journal of Primatology*, 6, 257–312.

Hershkovitz, P. (1985). A preliminary taxonomic review of the South American bearded saki monkeys, genus *Chiropotes* (Cebidae, Platyrrhini), with the description of a new subspecies. *Fieldiana: Zoology, n.s.*, 27, 1–46.

Hershkovitz, P. (1987). Uacaries, New World monkeys of the genus *Cacajao* (Cebidae, Platyrrhini): A preliminary taxonomic review with the description of a new subspecies. *American Journal of Primatology*, 12, 1–53.

Hill, W. C. O. (1960). *Primates, Comparative Anatomy and Taxonomy. Vol. IV - Cebidae, Part A.* Edinburgh: Edinburgh University Press.

Hill, W. C. O. (1962). *Primates, Comparative Anatomy and Taxonomy. Vol. V - Cebidae, Part B.* Edinburgh: Edinburgh University Press.

Humboldt, A. (1811). *Recueil d'Observations de Zoologie et d'Anatomie Comparée, Faites dans l'Océan Atlantique dans l'Interieur du Nouveau Continent et dans la Mer du Sud Pendant les Années 1799, 1800, 1801, 1802 et 1803 par Al. Humboldt et A. Bonpland. 2ème Volume.* Paris Levrault Schoell.

Iwanaga, S. (2004). Levantamento de mamíferos diurnos de médio e grande porte no Parque Nacional do Jaú: resultados preliminares. In S. H. Borges, S. Iwanaga, C. C. Durigan, and M. R. Pinheiro, eds., *Janelas para a Biodiversidade no Parque Nacional do Jaú: uma Estratégia para o Estudo da Biodiversidade na Amazônia.* Brazil, Amazonas, Manaus: Fundação Vitória Amazônica, 195–207.

Koch-Grünberg, T. (1907). *Südamerikanische Felszeichnungen.* Berlin: Ernest Wasmuth.

Koch-Grünberg, T. (2010). *Petróglifos Sul-Americanos.* Transl. J. B. Poça da Silva, org. E. Pereira. Brazil, Belém/São Paulo: Museu Paraense Emílio Goeldi / Instituto Socioambiental.

Kellogg, R., & Goldman, E. A. (1944). Review of the spider monkeys. *Proceedings of the United States National Museum*, 96, 1–45.

Martins, A. B., Calouro, A. L., & Ravetta, A. L. (2015). Avaliação do Risco de Extinção de Sapajus macrocephalus (Spix 1823) no Brasil. Processo de Avaliação do Risco de Extinção da Fauna Brasileira. ICMBio. Available at: www.icmbio.gov.br/portal/bio diversidade/fauna-brasileira/estado-de-conserva cao/7276-mamiferos-sapajus-macrocephalus-macaco-prego.html

Meggers, B. (1985). Advances in Brazilian archaeology, 1935-1985. *American Antiquity*, 50(2), 153-158.

Mello, G. B. R. (2013). *Yurupari – o Dono das Flautas Sagradas dos Povos do Rio Negro: Mitologia e Simbolismo*. Brazil, Belém: Pakatatu.

Mercês, M. P., Lynch-Alfaro, J. W., Ferreira. W. A., Harada, M. L., & Silva-Júnior, J. S. (2015). Morphology and mitochondrial phylogenetics reveal that the Amazon River separates two eastern squirrel monkey species: *Saimiri sciureus* and *S. collinsi*. *Molecular Phylogenetics and Evolution*, 82(B), 426-435.

Migliacio, M. C. (2017). Pedra Preta de Paranaíba: arte rupestre na ocupação do Alto Tapajós, Amazônia Mato-grossense. *Cadernos de Ciências Humanas – Especiaria*, 17(30), 173-201.

Mourthé, I., Muniz, C. C., & Rylands, A. B. (2015). Avaliação do Risco de Extinção de *Ateles belzebuth* (E. Geoffroy Saint-Hilaire, 1806) no Brasil. Processo de Avaliação do Risco de Extinção da Fauna Brasileira. ICMBio. Available at: www.icmbio.gov.br/portal/biodiversidade/fauna-brasileira/lista-de-espe cies/7189-mamiferos-ateles-belzebuth-macaco-aranha.html

Navarro, A. G., & Silva-Júnior, J. S. (2019). Cosmologia e Adaptação Ecológica: o caso dos apliques-mamíferos das estearias maranhenses. *Revista Anthropologicas*, 30(2), 203-233.

Neville, M. K., Glander, K. E., Braza, F., & Rylands, A. B. (1988). The howling monkeys, genus *Alouatta*. In R. A. Mittermeier, A. B. Rylands, A. F., Coimbra-Filho, & G. A. B. da Fonseca, eds., *Ecology and Behavior of Neotropical Primates. Vol. 2*. Washington DC: World Wildlife Fund, 349-453.

Oliveira, M. C. (2013). *Arte Rupestre em Rondônia*. Brazil, Rondônia: Presidente Médici.

Pereira, E. (2000a). As representações antropomorfas nas gravuras rupestres de Prainha, Pará, Brasil. *Revista CLIO. Série Arqueológica*, 14, 39-54.

Pereira, E. (2000b). Salvamento e resgate do Sítio Pedra das Arraias, Senador José Porfírio. Technical Report. Brazil, Belém: Museu Paraense Emílio Goeldi.

Pereira, E. (2004). *Arte Rupestre na Amazônia - Pará*. Brazil, Belém/São Paulo: Museu Paraense Emílio Goeldi / Universidade Estadual Paulista.

Pereira, E. (2006). Historia de la investigación sobre el arte rupestre en la Amazonía brasileña. *Revista de Arqueología Americana*, 24, 67-98.

Pereira, E. (2008). Arqueologia na região da Serra das Andorinhas. In P. S. S. Gorayeb, ed., *Parque Martírios-Andorinhas: Conhecimento, História e Preservação*. Brazil, Belém: Universidade Federal do Pará.

Pereira, E. (2012). *A Arte Rupestre de Monte Alegre, Pará, Amazônia, Brasil*. Brazil, Belém: Museu Paraense Emílio Goeldi.

Porro, A. (2010). Arte e Simbolismo Xamânico na Amazônia. *Boletim do Museu Paraense Emílio Goeldi, Série Ciências Humanas*, 5(1), 129-144.

Pough, F. W., Janis, C. M., & Heiser, J. B. (2005). *Vertebrate Life*. 7th ed. New York: Pearson.

Rauschert, M. (1959). Felszeichnungen am unteren Erepecuru. *Zeitschriff für Ethnologie*, 84(1), 110-123.

Ribeiro, P. A. M., Ribeiro, C. T., Guapindaia, V. L. C., Pinto, F. C. B., & Félix, L. A. (1986). Projeto Arqueológico de Salvamento na Região de Boa Vista, Território Federal de Roraima, Brasil - Segunda Etapa de Campo (1985) - Nota prévia. *Revista do Centro de Ensino e Pesquisas Arqueológicas da Universidade de Santa Cruz do Sul*, 13(16), 5-48.

Ribeiro, P. A. M., Machado, A. L., & Guapindaia, V. L. C. (1987). Projeto Arqueológico de Salvamento na Região de Boa Vista, Território Federal de Roraima, Brasil - Primeira Etapa de Campo (1985). *Revista do Centro de Ensino e Pesquisas Arqueológicas da Universidade de Santa Cruz do Sul*, 14(17), 1-81.

Ribeiro, P. A. M., Ribeiro, C. T., & Pinto, F. C. B. (1989). Levantamentos arqueológicos no Território Federal de Roraima - Terceira Etapa de Campo (1987). *Revista do Centro de Ensino e Pesquisas Arqueológicas da Universidade de Santa Cruz do Sul*, 16(19), 5-48.

Ribeiro, P. A. M., Guapindaia, V. L. C., Ribeiro, C. T., & Machado, A. L. (1996). Pitture rupestri nel Territorio di Roraima – Brasile. *Bollettino del Centro Camuno di Studi Preistorici*, 29, 151-154.

Rondon, C. M. S. (1953). *Indios do Brasil do Norte do Rio Amazonas*. Rio de Janeiro: Conselho Nacional de Proteção aos Indios.

Rylands, A. B., & Régis, T. (2015). *Avaliação do Risco de Extinção de Ateles paniscus (Linnaeus, 1758) no*

Brasil. Processo de Avaliação do Risco de Extinção da Fauna Brasileira. Brasilia: ICMBio.

Rylands, A. B., & Santos, M. (2015). *Avaliação do Risco de Extinção de Alouatta macconnelli Elliot, 1910 no Brasil. Processo de avaliação do risco de extinção da fauna brasileira.* Brasilia: ICMBio.

Silva-Júnior, J. S., Figueiredo-Ready, W. M. B., & Ferrari, S. F. (2013). Taxonomy and geographic distribution of the Pitheciidae. In L. M. Veiga, A. A. Barnett, S. F. Ferrari, & M. A. Norconk, eds., *Evolutionary Biology and Conservation of Titis, Sakis and Uacaris.* Cambridge: Cambridge University Press, 31–42.

Silva-Júnior, J. S., Ravetta, A. L., Alfaro, J. W. L., & Valença-Montenegro, M. M. (2015). *Avaliação do Risco de Extinção de Saimiri collinsi Osgood, 1916 no Brasil. Processo de Avaliação do Risco de Extinção da Fauna Brasileira.* Brasilia: ICMBio.

Stradelli, E. (1900). Iscrizioni indigene della regione dell'Uaupés. *Bolletino della Società Geografica Italiana, ser.* **4**, 1(37), 457–483.

Urbina Rangel, F. (1994). El hombre sentado: mitos, ritos y petroglifos en el río Caquetá. *Boletín del Museo del Oro,* **36**, 67–111.

Urbina Rangel, F. (2004). *Dïijoma. El Hombre-Serpiente-Águila. Mito Uitoto de la Amazonía.* Colombia, Bogotá: Convenio Andrés Bello.

Urbina Rangel, F. (2015). Perros de guerra, caballos y vacunos en el arte rupestre de la serranía de la Lindosa, Río Guayabero, Guaviare, Colombia. In Rupestreweb. Available at: www.rupestreweb.info/serranialindosa.html

Valença-Montenegro, M. M., Fialho, M. S., Carvalho, A. S., et al. (2015). *Avaliação do Risco de Extinção de Alouatta belzebul (Linnaeus, 1766) no Brasil. Processo de Avaliação do Risco de Extinção da Fauna Brasileira.* Brasilia: ICMBio.

Valle, R. (2010). Gravuras rupestres no Rio Negro: Panorama Preliminar. In E. Pereira & V. L. C. Guapindaia, eds., *Arqueologia Amazônica, Vol. 1.* Brazil, Belém: Museu Paraense Emílio Goeldi, 317–340.

Valle, R. (2012). *Mentes Graníticas e Mentes Areníticas Fronteira Geo-Cognitiva nas Gravuras Rupestres do Baixo Rio Negro, Amazônia Setentrional, Volumes I e II.* Tese, Programa de Pós Graduação em Arqueologia, Museu de Arqueologia e Etnologia da Universidade de São Paulo.

Valle, R. (2014). Arte Rupestre do Juruparí? Explorando relações iconográficas entre gravuras rupestres e o complexo mito-ritual do Jurupari no baixo rio Negro, Amazônia. In S. Rostain, ed., *Antes de Orellana – Actas del 3er Encuentro Internacional de Arqueologia Amazónica. Col. Actes et Mémoires de l'Institut Français d'Études Andines,* 37. Peru, Lima: Instituto Francés de Estudios Andinos, 339–345.

van Roosmalen, M. G., & Klein, L. L. (1988). The spider monkeys, genus *Ateles.* In R. A. Mittermeier, A. B. Rylands, A. F. Coimbra-Filho, & G. A. B. da Fonseca, eds., *Ecology and Behavior of Neotropical Primates, Vol. 2.* Washington, DC: World Wildlife Fund, 455–537.

van Roosmalen, M. G., Mittermeier, R. A., & Milton, K. (1981). The bearded sakis, genus *Chiropotes.* In A. F. Coimbra-Filho & R. A. Mittermeier, eds., *Ecology and Behavior of Neotropical Primates, Vol. 1.* Brazil, Rio de Janeiro: Academia Brasileira de Ciências, 419–441.

Veiga, L. M., & Ferrari, S. F. (2013). Ecology and behavior of bearded sakis (genus *Chiropotes*). In L. M. Veiga, A. A. Barnett, S. F. Ferrari, & M. A. Norconk. eds., *Evolutionary Biology and Conservation of Titis, Sakis and Uacaris.* Cambridge: Cambridge University Press, 240–249.

Wallace, A. R. (1979). *Viagem pelos Rios Amazonas e Negro.* Brazil, Belo Horizonte: Itatiaia.

7 Nonhuman Primates in the Archaeological Record of Northeastern Brazil

A Case Study in Pernambuco State

Albérico N. de Queiroz, Olivia A. de Carvalho, & Roberta R. Pinto

Primatas não humanos na arqueologia do nordeste brasileiro: Um estudo de caso no estado de Pernambuco

Resumo

Dentre os diversos materiais recuperados em escavações arqueológicas no Brasil, os remanescentes zooarqueológicos têm sido foco de estudos sobre a biodiversidade, sustentabilidade e relações entre humanos e não humanos no passado, desde o Pleistoceno ao Holoceno. Neste artigo apresentamos amostras de ossos cranianos de primatas, um dos quais cuja diagnose aponta para a espécie *Sapajus libidinosus* (Spix, 1823) com modificações antrópicas intencionais (corte, perfuração, polimento), e outra amostra com marcas semelhantes a anterior e características morfológicas que indicam pertencer aos Primatas, os quais foram recuperados em escavações arqueológicas no sítio "Furna do Estrago" (SFE), um abrigo sob rocha granítica, localizado no município de Brejo da Madre de Deus, estado de Pernambuco, na região Nordeste do Brasil. Esses achados permitem uma reflexão sobre os aspectos bioculturais envolvendo as relações entre humanos e não humanos, particularmente os primatas do Novo Mundo.

Palavras Chave

Zooarqueologia – arqueoprimatologia – sítio arqueológico Furna do Estrago - Pernambuco – Nordeste – Brasil

Abstract

Among the various materials recovered from archaeological excavations in Brazil, zooarchaeological remains have been the focus of studies on biodiversity, sustainability and relations between humans and nonhumans in the past, from the Pleistocene to the Holocene. In this chapter we present samples of primate cranial bones recovered in archaeological excavations at the Furna do Estrago site, a granitic rock shelter located in the city of Brejo da Madre de Deus, state of Pernambuco, in the Northeast region of Brazil. One sample with anthropic modifications (cutting, perforation, polishing), has been identified as *Sapajus libidinosus*; another sample with marks similar to the previous one has morphological characteristics that point more broadly to (nonhuman) Primates. These findings allow a reflection on biocultural aspects of the relations between humans and nonhumans, particularly the primates of the New World.

Keywords: Zooarchaeology, Archaeoprimatology, Furna do Estrago archaeological site, Pernambuco, Northeast, Brazil

7.1   Introduction

In recent years, researchers have increasingly recognized the interpretive potential of faunal remains among the materials recovered from archaeological sites in several Brazilian regions. In the Northeast region, a growing number of studies on the vertebrate archaeofauna have contributed to the formation of new generations of archaeologists in the country. This research has shown a great diversity of animals in interaction with humans from the Pleistocene as mentioned by Bélo (2012), Bélo (2017), Dantas (2012), Dantas et al. (2012), Guérin (1991), Guérin et al. (1993, 1996a, 1996b), Hadler et al. (2018), Locks et al. (1993, 1997), and Peters and Oliveira (2019). Archaeofaunal remains found in many sites have included fossilized megafauna, mainly specimens of *Eremotherium* sp. (Dantas et al., 2012), *Hippidion* sp. (Bélo & Oliveira, 2013), and *Mylodonopsis ibseni* (Prous, 1992). Nonfossilized Holocene fauna have also been recovered at various archaeological sites, as presented by Carvalho et al. (2019), Lima (1988, 1991, 1992), Locks et al. (1995), Queiroz (1994a, 1994b, 2001), Queiroz and Cardoso 1995/1996), Queiroz and Carvalho (2008), Queiroz and Chaix (1999), Queiroz et al. (2018), Lima (2012), and Simon et al. (1999). These assemblages are mostly comprised of rodents (*Kerodon rupestris*, *Galea spixii*), cervids (*Mazama* sp.), lizards (*Salvator merianae*), and birds (*Rhea americana*) and show some evidence for anthropogenic modifications (cutting, burning, scraping). The bones of these taxa were present in the stratigraphic layers, but some animal bones were also found in association with human burials. Differentiated marks (polishing and perforations) were observed on specific parts of these bones, which has been interpreted as their use as funerary ornaments (Queiroz et al., 2018), as well as evidence for ritual practices (Queiroz et al., 2017).

The Brazilian zooarchaeological literature still lacks information about the occurrence of nonhuman primates in funerary contexts, especially in the Northeast region of the country. An explanation of the very small quantity of these animals in archaeological samples throughout Brazil could be related to the low rate of preservation of bone remains due to the action of natural taphonomic agents (Queiroz & Carvalho, 2008). This is also the case for other vertebrates that have been also recovered in some very particular funerary contexts, in which only a few anatomical parts were intentionally modified, with cutting, polished edges and perforation marks. Sometimes, they are even partially buried closed to human burials, probably representing a complex funerary ritual (Queiroz et al., 2014, 2017, 2018; Silva et al., 2014). The very few samples of nonhuman primates occur in stratigraphic profiles in the excavations, probably as part of human food according to Silva (2013). Caatinga capuchins have also been associated with the use of lithic tools in the processing of indigenous cashew nuts, as reported by Haslam et al. (2015). This chapter is the first report on the occurrence of intentionally modified bone elements from nonhuman primates recovered in excavations at the necropolis known as the archaeological site Furna do Estrago (SFE), located in Brejo da Madre de Deus county at Pernambuco state (Fig. 7.1).

Figure 7.1 Location of Pernambuco State in Brazil and the Brejo da Madre de Deus county. Based on image from Lima (2012)/Museu de Arqueologia e de Ciências Naturais-UNICAP.

7.2   Brejo da Madre de Deus County, Pernambuco, Brazil

The county of Brejo da Madre de Deus (36°22′15″W, 8°09′00″S) is located in the Agreste physiographic zone of the state of Pernambuco, an intermediate area between the humid forest (Tropical Forest) and the Semi-Arid area called Sertão, in the Microregion of Vale do Ipojuca (see Lima, 1985, 1986). The relief and vegetation range from depressions, slopes, and steep slopes, to flat areas with wide valleys and predominance of Caatinga vegetation, which presents strong degradation due to anthropic interventions like agropastoral activities. The lithological ensemble dates from the Precambrian and consists of granite rocks. There are three types of climate in the municipality, and according to the classification of Köppen (Lima, 1985, 1986) they include Bsh (hot semiarid, predominant climate in the Caatinga area), As′ (hot humid, with autumn–winter rains, in a limited area close to the altitude swamp), and Csa (wet mesothermal, microclimate restricted to mountainous forest of Bituri). In addition, according to Lima (1985), the average annual temperature is around 20.4°C, with maximum of 29.6°C (in November and December), and minimum of 16.6°C (in July and August). Rainfall ranges from 500 to 1100 mm per year.

7.2.1   Furna do Estrago Archaeological Site (Rock Shelter)

As described by Lima (1985, 1986), the Furna do Estrago site (36°28′14″W, 08°11′36″S) is a shelter under a granite rock and is located on the northern slope of Serra da Boa Vista, popularly known as Serra do Estrago (Fig. 7.2). It is found at 650 m asl, approximately 1 km from Brejo da Madre Deus, and it is 280 m away from the highway near Serra do Estrago.

Initial archaeological investigations at this site took place in 1983 and again in 1987, when seven trenches were excavated, with trench 7 being positioned at the bottom of the shelter under rock and considered as the best stratigraphic parameter

Figure 7.2 Serra do Estrago, Brejo da Madre de Deus, Pernambuco, Brazil, showing the Furna do Estrago archaeological site (rock shelter) (circle). Modified from Queiroz (1994). (Photograph of the author).

Figure 7.3 Outside view of Furna do Estrago archaeological site (granitic rock shelter). (From Bodega da História – WordPress.com (bodegadahistoria.wordpress.com-Open access).

(Figs. 7.3 and 7.4). In addition, 88 human burials were exhumed from all seven trenches. Each burial was recorded with the abbreviation "FE" plus a sequential number.

The chronology for the Furna do Estrago was determined through radiocarbon dating by carbon-14 at the Smithsonian Institution, Washington DC, USA, from the charcoal fragments recovered from structured fires, which can be seen in the ash lenses collected in the stratigraphic profile of the excavated area (Lima, 1985, 1986, 2001, 2012). The dates indicate the earliest occupation at $11,060 \pm 90$ BP (SI 6298). The chronological sequence is approximately $9,150 \pm 90$ BP (SI 6297), $8,495 \pm 70$ BP

Figure 7.4 Inner view of Furna do Estrago archaeological site showing the excavated area and the stratigraphic profile (trench 7). (Based on image from Lima (2001)/Museu de Arqueologia e de Ciências Naturais-UNICAP).

(SI 6269), 1,860 ± 50 BP (Beta 145954), 1,730 ± 70 BP (Beta 149749), and 1,610 ± 70 BP (Beta 145955), with a superficial level dated at 1,040 ± 50 BP (SI 6295). This range of dates allows us to consider different phases of human occupation, settlement, and inhumation practices in the area. Lima (2012) proposed the following chronological sequence of human occupation and funerary practices at Furna do Estrago: Ancient: 1,860 ± 50 BP (Beta 145954), Medium: 1,730 ± 70 BP (Beta 149749), and Recent: 1,610 ± 70 BP (Beta 145955).

7.2.2   Archaeoprimatological Samples from Furna do Estrago

In the excavations carried out at Furna do Estrago, five mammal cranial fragments were recovered in the layers close to human burials. Two of them in the same layer as the FE 22 human burial (Lima, 2012), as shown in Figs. 7.5a,b and 7.8, and three others in different layers but close to those of the human burials. Morphological characteristics and bone proportions, despite the fragmentation, confirmed that these fragments are those of nonhuman primates. Three fragments had no diagnostic structures to allow deeper taxonomic identification at family, genus, or species levels. In this work, we focus on the two cranial fragments that showed a lower degree of fragmentation, allowing for a better diagnostic assessment of their their taxonomic identification.

It is important to note that, in addition to the occurrence of these cranial elements in a funeral context with other structures, such as vegetable mats, as reported by Lima (2001, 2012), the specimens also had intentional perforations, which were observed macroscopically. These perforations are not naturally present on the skull, and their location and morphology indicate that they result from anthropic intervention. Beyond macroscopic observation, a more accurate traceological study with the use of optical equipment (stereomicroscope and digital microscope) would allow for the visualization of striations and other details related to the perforation process.

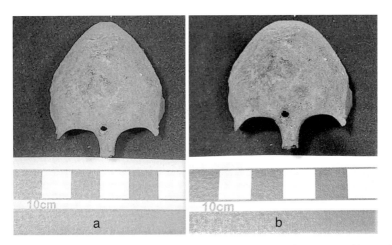

Figure 7.5 Primate skulls of *Sapajus libidinosus* (Spix, 1823): top view (a) and front view (b) with anthropogenic modifications (cutting at the level of the coronalis suture and artificial circular perforation in the glabella region) recovered from the FE 22 human burial (female, adult) at Furna do Estrago archaeological site, Brejo da Madre de Deus, Pernambuco, Brazil. (Based on photograph from the Museu de Arqueologia e de Ciências Naturais-UNICAP).

These two fragments are in the archaeofaunal collection and on display at the Museum of Archaeology and Natural Sciences of the Catholic University of Pernambuco (UNICAP), Brazil. The two nonhuman primate specimens are fragments of the frontal bones cut longitudinally at the level of the coronalis suture (Figs. 7.5a, b; 7.6a,b). They also show a regular and artificial circular perforation in the glabella, certainly intentionally, since it is not a natural anatomical feature, as mentioned above. The cranial diagnostic morphological characteristics point to the species *Sapajus libidinosus* (Spix, 1823) (bearded capuchin), whose geographical range is in the Northeastern region (Martins et al., 2019). The diagnostic morphological characteristics include a regularly rounded orbital roof and a slightly depressed and elongated rostrum (part of the frontal and nasal bones). In these samples, nasal bones are absent due to the state of preservation. Lima (2012) suggested that one of them is a pendant, recovered from the FE 22 human burial, an adult female from the medium chronological period (1.730 ± 70 BP - Beta 149749), as shown in the plan of human burials presented by the author (Fig. 7.7). Lima (2012: 45) describes the ornaments found with the human individuals buried in this archaeological site: "The bone pendants were presented with a neat finish; two elaborated on skull bones of small primates, measured $44 \times 33 \times 1$ mm, with perforation of 3 mm in diameter." Due to the cranial dimensions of these skulls we believe the author is probably referring to both as belonging to the species *S. libidinosus*, the specimens from which also have the same perforation in the glabella; however, the second specimen has no indication of the burial it came from.

The second nonhuman primate sample is a portion of the parietal bone (Fig. 7.8) whose fragmentation did not allow identification to a more specific taxonomic level.

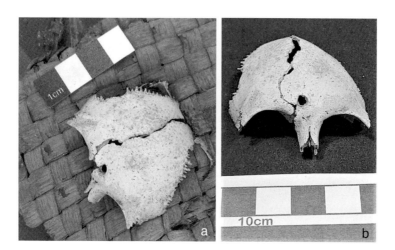

Figure 7.6 Primate skulls of *Sapajus libidinosus* (Spix, 1823): top view (a) and front view (b) with anthropogenic modifications (cutting at the level of the coronalis suture and artificial circular perforation in the glabella region) recovered from FE 11 human burial (male, adult) at Furna do Estrago archaeological site, Brejo da Madre de Deus, Pernambuco, Brazil. (Based on photograph from the Museu de Arqueologia e de Ciências Naturais-UNICAP).

However, the pronounced degree of concavity and curvature of the bone, in addition to the smooth internal ornamentation, are consistent with its identification as a nonhuman primate skull fragment. Regarding intentional changes, this specimen also shows an artificial circular perforation that is morphologically different in proportion and location than that of a natural nutritional foramen. This sample was also recovered from the FE 22 burial, measured 57 × 38 × 1 mm.

7.3   Discussion and Final Considerations

The records of vertebrates recovered from pre-Hispanic archaeological sites in Northeastern Brazil point to different scenarios concerning the relations between humans and nonhumans, including past biodiversity, sustainability (Lima, 1988), paleoenvironmental reconstruction (Guérin et al., 1996a), and funerary and symbolic function (Queiroz et al., 2017, 2018; Simon et al., 1999).

Investigations on these relationships, particularly between humans and nonhuman primates, also known as archaeoprimatology, contribute to the knowledge of several biocultural repercussions in South America (Silva, 2013; Urbani, 2013; Urbani & Gil, 2001). The remains from the archaeological site Furna do Estrago presented here represent the first record of nonhuman primates in Pernambuco. Although this is a small sample, it allows for some observations about the occurrence of these animals in human funerary environments. These are the absence of

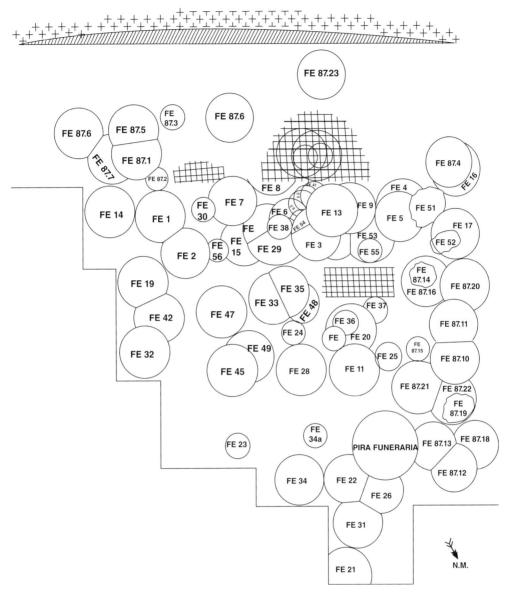

Figure 7.7 General plan of the distribution of human burials in the excavated area at Furna do Estrago Archaeological Site, Brejo da Madre de Deus, Pernambuco, Brazil, showing FE 11 and FE 22 (framedoutlines in black) from where cranial elements of nonhuman primates were recovered. Based on image from Lima (2012).

whole skulls and post-cranial bones, as well as details of the manufacturing process of the pieces, particularly the longitudinal cuts at the height of the coronal suture and smoothly polished perforations that are likely a result of continuous circular perforating movements. This intentional postmortem treatment of the

Figure 7.8 Undetermined primate nonhuman skull with anthropogenic modification (perforation) recovered from FE 22 human burial (female, adult) at Furna do Estrago archaeological site, Brejo da Madre de Deus, Pernambuco, Brazil. (Based on photograph from the Museu de Arqueologia e de Ciências Naturais-UNICAP).

crania indicates that these animals could have a different status, possibly symbolic or ritual, as the markings are similar to those observed on other kind of adornments produced on cervid long bones and on canid and felid teeth found in some human burials within necropolises in Northeastern Brazil (Carvalho et al., 2019; Lima, 2012; Queiroz et al., 2018; Silva et al., 2014). It is very likely these ornaments would have been used in life by individuals, perhaps as hierarchical indicators within a social group, as they did not occur in many burials at this site, as observed and postulated by the archaeologist Jeannette Maria Dias de Lima (1939–2002) in her many published works (Lima, 1985, 1986, 1991, 2001, 2012). This work is dedicated to her memory and pioneering work.

Acknowledgments

We would like to express our deepest thanks to the Museum of Archaeology and Natural Sciences of Catholic University of Pernambuco (UNICAP) and the Brazilian National Council for Scientific and Technological Development (CNPq) for access to the zooarchaeological information and financial support respectively, and also to Sarah Whitcher Kansa for important help with the manuscript English review.

References

Bélo, P. S. (2012). Alterações antrópicas em restos fósseis da megafauna: tafonomia do sítio arqueológico e paleontológico "Toca da Janela da Barra do Antonião", área arqueológica do Parque Nacional da Serra da Capivara, Piauí, Brasil. Unpublished Master's dissertation, Universidade Federal de Pernambuco.

Bélo, P. S. (2017). Extinção e a interação homem-megafauna no final do Pleistoceno e início do Holoceno, nos estados de Pernambuco e Pauí, Nordeste do Brasil. Unpublished Doctoral thesis, Universidade Federal de Pernambuco.

Bélo, P. S., & Oliveira, É. V. (2013). Análise tafonômica de marcas em restos esqueletais de *hippidion*, sítio Toca da Janela da Barra do Antonião, Piauí, Brasil. *Estudos Geológicos*, 23(2), 59–79.

Carvalho, O. A., Etcheverne, C. A., & Queiroz, A. N. (2019). Associação de Vasos Cerâmicos e Ossos de Animais: Ritual Funerário ou Resto de Cozinha em Populações do Passado Provenientes da Região Nordeste do Brasil? *Revista Etnobiología*, 17, 76–88.

Dantas M. A. T. (2012). Contribuição ao conhecimento da Megafauna Pleistocênica da região intertropical brasileira. Unpublished Doctoral thesis, Universidade Federal de Minas Gerais.

Dantas, M. A. T., Queiroz, A. N., Santos, F. V., & Cozzuol, M. A. (2012). An anthropogenic modification in an *Eremotherium* tooth from northeastern Brazil. *Quaternary International*, 253, 107–109.

Guérin, C. (1991). La faune de vertébrés du Pléistocène supérieur de l'aire archéologique de São Raimundo Nonato (Piauí, Brésil). *Comptes rendus de l'Académie des Sciences de Paris*, 312(2), 567–592.

Guérin, C., Curvello, M. A., Faure, M., Hugueney, M., & Mourerchauvire, C. (1993). La faune pléistocène du Piauí (Nordeste du Brésil): implications paléoécologiques et biochronologiques. *Quaternaria Nova*, 3, 303–341.

Guérin, C., Curvello, M. A., Faure, M., Hugueney, M., & Mourerchauvire, C. (1996a). A fauna pleistocênica do Piauí (Nordeste do Brasil): Relações paleoecológicas e biocronológicas. *Anais da Reunião Internacional sobre o Povoamento das Américas, São Raimundo Nonato 1993, Fumdhamentos*, 1(1), 51–111.

Guérin, C., Galindo Lima, M., & Parenti, F. (1996b). La transition Pléistocène/Holocène à Conceição das Creoulas (Pernambuco, Brésil): Mégafaune disparue et industries lithiques. *Proceedings of the XIII International Congress of Prehistoric and Protohistoric Sciences*, 5, 339–343.

Hadler, P., Mayer, E. L, Motta F., & Ribeiro, A. M. (2018). Fossil bats from the Quaternary of Serra da Capivara, northeast Brazil. *Quaternary International*, 464, 411–416.

Haslam, M., Falótico, T., Luncz, L. V., & Ottoni, E. (2015). Archaeological investigation of capuchin monkey (*Sapajus libidinosus*) cashew processing sites at Serra da Capivara National Park, Brazil. *Folia Primatologica*, 86, 235–386.

Lima, J. M. D. (1985). Arqueologia da Furna do Estrago, Brejo da Madre de Deus - PE. *Clio - Revista do Curso de Mestrado em História*, 3, 97–111.

Lima, J. M. D. (1986). Arqueologia da Furna do Estrago, Brejo da Madre de Deus – Pernambuco. Master's dissertation, Universidade Federal de Pernambuco.

Lima, J. M. D. (1988). Alimentação do homem préhistórico na região da caatinga. *Revista de Arqueologia*, 5(1), 103–114.

Lima, J. M. D. (1991). Dois períodos de subsistência no Agreste Pernambucano: 9.000 e 2.000 A. P. *CLIO, Série Arqueológica (Número extraordinário dedicado aos Anais do I Simpósio de Pré-História do Nordeste Brasileiro)*, 4, 57–60.

Lima, J. M. D. (1992). Estudos zoo e fitoarqueológicos em Pernambuco. *Symposium*, 34(2), 146–179.

Lima, J. M. D. (2001). El sitio Furna do Estrago – Brasil en una perspectiva antropológica y social. Unpublished Doctoral thesis, Universidad Autónoma de México.

Lima, J. M. D. (2012). A Furna do Estrago no Brejo da Madre de Deus, PE. *Antropologia*, 69, 1–159.

Locks, M., Beltrão, M. C., & Cordeiro, D. (1993). Região arqueológica de Central – Bahia - Brasil: N° 2 – Abrigo da Lesma: Os mamíferos. *CLIO, Série Arqueológica*, 1(9), 69–75.

Locks, M. Beltrão, M., & Amorim, J. (1995). Região arqueológica de Central, Bahia, Brasil: Dasypodidae sub-recente (Mammalia-Edentata). *Anais V Congresso da Associação Brasileira de Estudos do Quaternário*, 46–51.

Locks, M., Beltrão, M., Soares, A. A., & Ribeiro, S. (1997). Região arqueológica de Central, Bahia, Brasil: associação bioestratigráfica de mamíferos fósseis e sub-recentes. *Boletim de Resumos 15° Congresso Brasileiro de Paleontologia*, 118, São Paulo.

Martins, A. B., Bezerra, B., Fialho, M., Jerusalinsky, L., Laroque, P., Lynch Alfaro, J., Melo, F., & Valença Montenegro, M. 2019. *Sapajus libidinosus. The IUCN Red List of Threatened Species* 2019: e. T136346A70613454.

Peters, E. T., & Oliveira, E. V. (2019). Marcas em fósseis de Megafauna do sitio Conceição das Creoulas, Pleistoceno Superior-Holoceno, Salgueiro, Pernambuco. *Estudos Geológicos*, **29**(2), 31–39.

Prous, A. (1992). *Arqueologia Brasileira*. Brasília: Ed. Universidade de Brasília.

Queiroz, A. N. (1994a). A presença do *Tupinambis teguixin* (Linnaeus, 1758) nos restos alimentares do homem pré-histórico na região do Agreste de Pernambuco, *Brasil. Biociências*, **2**(1), 149–157.

Queiroz, A. N. (1994b). Fauna reptiliana de Brejo da Madre de Deus, Pernambuco, Brasil, com a identificação de restos alimentares do sítio arqueológico Furna do Estrago. Unpublished Master's dissertation, Pontifícia Universidade Católica do Rio Grande do Sul.

Queiroz, A. N. (2001). Contribution à l'étude archéozoologique des vertébrés de cinq sites préhistoriques de trois régions du Brésil. Unpublished Doctoral thesis, Université de Genève.

Queiroz, A. N., & Cardoso, G. M. B. (1995/1996). Nota prévia sobre a fauna holocênica de vertebrados do sítio arqueológico "Pedra do Alexandre", *Carnaúba dos Dantas-RN, Brasil. CLIO, Série Arqueológica*, 1 (11): 137–140.

Queiroz, A. N., & Chaix, L. (1999). Os vestígios faunísticos provenientes dos sítios arqueológicos: Uma visão geral – A fauna arqueológica do sítio Justino. In C. Simon, O. A. Carvalho, A. N. Queiroz, & L. Chaix, eds., *Enterramentos na Necrópole do Justino – Xingó*, Projeto Arqueológico de Xingó, Convênio PETROBRAS/CHESF/UFS, Aracaju, SE: Universidade Federal de Sergipe, 49–55.

Queiroz, A. N., & Carvalho, O. A (2008). Problems in the interpretation of Brazilian archaeofaunas: different contexts and the important role of taphonomy. *Quaternary International*, **18**, 75–89.

Queiroz, A. N., Carvalho, O. A., Silva, J. A., & Cardoso, C. E. (2014). Whole vertebrates and invertebrates related to human burials from Xingo Region, Sergipe, and Alagoas States, Northeastern Brazil.

Cuadernos del Instituto Nacional de Antropología y Pensamiento Latinoamericano, **1**, 122–128.

Queiroz, A. N., Cardoso, C. E, & Carvalho, O. A. (2017). Animais como psicopompos nas sepulturas do sítio arqueológico Justino? (Canindé de São Francisco – Sub-região de Xingó – Sergipe, Brasil). *Antípoda. Revista de Antropología y Arqueología*, **28**, 57–73.

Queiroz, A. N., Guérin, C., Silva, J., Faure, M., & Carvalho, O. A. (2018). Os adornos em osso de *Mazama* na sepultura 118, cemitério B, sítio arqueológico Justino, Canindé de São Francisco, Sergipe, Brasil. *Clio Arqueológica*, **33**(1), 10–25.

Silva, R. R. N. (2013). Predação de primatas não humanos pelo homem do Holoceno na região do sítio arqueológico Pedra do Alexandre – Rio grande do Norte. Anais do II Congresso Latino Americano e XV Congresso Brasileiro de Primatologia. Recife: Sociedade Brasileira de Primatologia, 142.

Silva, J. A., Carvalho, O. A., & Queiroz, A. N. (2014). A Cultura Material Associada a Sepultamentos no Brasil: Arqueologia dos Adornos. *Clio. Série Arqueológica*, **29**, 45–82.

Simon, C., O. A. Carvalho, A. N. Queiroz, L., & Chaix L. (1999). *Enterramentos na Necrópole do Justino- Xingó*, Projeto Arqueológico de Xingó, Convênio PETROBRAS/CHESF/UFS. Aracaju, SE: Universidade Federal de Sergipe.

Teixeira-Santos, I., Sianto, L., Araújo, A., Reinhard, K. J., & Chaves, S. A. M. (2015). The evidence of medicinal plants in human sediments from Furna do Estrago prehistoric site, Pernambuco State, Brazil. *Quaternary International*, **377**, 112–117.

Urbani, B. (2013). Arqueoprimatología: reflexión sobre una disciplina y dos localidades antropoespeleológicas venezolana. *Boletín del Sociedad Venezolana de Espeleología*, **45**, 66–68.

Urbani B., & E. Gil. 2001. Consideraciones sobre restos de primates de un yacimiento arqueológico del Oriente de Venezuela (América del Sur): Cueva del Guácharo, estado Monagas. *Munibe (Antropologia- Arkeologia)*, **53**, 135–142.

8 Lice in Howler Monkeys and the Ancient Americas

Exploring the Potential Cost of Being Past Pets or Hunting Games

R. Florencia Quijano, Debora R. Gilles, Jan Štefka, & Martín M. Kowalewski

Piojos en monos aulladores desde la América pretérita: Explorando el costo potencial de haber sido sujetos de subsistencia o mascotas

Resumen

Los piojos son ectoparásitos altamente específicos, en primates particularmente la mayoría de las especies de piojos se encuentran en una sola especie hospedadora. Los piojos se encuentran en prosimios, primates del Nuevo Mundo, primates del Viejo Mundo y simios. El género *Pediculus* se encuentra naturalmente en humanos (*Homo sapiens*), bonobos y chimpancés (*Pan*), monos aulladores (*Alouatta*), monos araña (*Ateles*) y monos caí (*Cebus*). Este capítulo se concentra principalmente en la presencia de *Pediculus* spp. en los monos aulladores para proporcionar información sobre el posible cambio de huésped entre los piojos humanos y de primates neotropicales. A pesar de que los estudios sobre piojos en primates del Nuevo Mundo son escasos y se encuentran desactualizados, hemos encontrado reportes de *P. mjobergi* en 3 especies de aulladores: *Alouatta caraya, Alouatta guariba* y *Alouatta belzebul*. La evidencia paleontológica y genética sugiere que se produjo un intercambio de material genético entre los piojos de los humanos y los aulladores durante encuentros casuales por ejemplo por caza o mascotismo, probablemente cuando los humanos modernos partieron de África y entraron a las Américas, y que *P. mjobergi* puede ser un linaje evolutivo de *P. humanus*.

Palabras clave

Piojos – *Pediculus* – *Alouatta* – cambio de hospedador – poblamiento de las Américas – monos neotropicales

Abstract

Sucking lice are highly host-specific ectoparasites, particularly on primates with most lice species occurring only on a single species of host. Lice are found on prosimians, New World monkeys, Old World monkeys, and apes. The genus *Pediculus* is found naturally on humans (*Homo sapiens*), bonobos and chimpanzees (*Pan*), howler monkeys (*Alouatta*), spider monkeys (*Ateles*), and capuchin monkeys (*Cebus*). This chapter concentrates mainly on the presence of *Pediculus* spp. in howler monkeys to provide information on the potential louse host switch between humans and Neotropical primates. Although studies on lice in New World monkeys are very scarce and outdated, after a thorough review we found *P. mjobergi* reports for three species of howlers: *Alouatta caraya, Alouatta guariba*, and *Alouatta belzebul*. Genetic and paleontological evidence suggest that an interchange of genetic material between humans and howler lice occurred during encounters for example for subsistence or pets, probably when modern humans moved out of Africa and entered the Americas, and that *P. mjobergi*, may be an evolutionary lineage of *P. humanus*.

Keywords: Lice, *Pediculus*, *Alouatta*, Host-switch, Peopling of the Americas, New World primates

8.1   Introduction

Parasites often exhibit host specificity which may lead to co-speciation with their hosts (Page 1993; Ricklefs et al., 2004; Vienne et al., 2013). As a result, the parasite evolutionary history often parallels the history of its host. If disagreements between the host and parasite histories are found these are usually attributed to host switches, that is horizontal transfer of a parasite to a new host (Johnson & Clayton, 2004) but see Johnson et al. (2003) for other sources of incongruence. Parasites were found to serve as convenient predictors of host population demographic history and, particularly, lice may give us hints into host evolutionary history when fossils are not easily found or when the evolutionary events of interest are too recent (e.g. Light et al., 2010; Light & Reed, 2009; Linz et al., 2007; Štefka et al., 2011; Whiteman & Parker, 2005).

Traditionally, lice (order Phthiraptera) are divided into two main groups: sucking lice belonging to the suborder Anoplura and chewing lice to suborders Amblycera, Ischnocera, and Rhynchophthirina (Durden, 2019). Sucking lice are obligate ecto-parasites that complete their entire life cycle on the body of the host; they cannot survive more than a few hours or days off the host (Durden, 2019; Takano-lee et al., 2003; Wall & Shearer, 2001). The more diverse chewing lice include species that are obligate associates of birds, marsupials, or placental mammals (Durden, 2019), whereas all sucking lice are hematophagous ectoparasites of eutherian mammals (Kim & Ludwig, 1978), and there are no native sucking lice of marsupials or monotremes (Wall & Shearer, 1997). Over 532 species of sucking lice (Durden & Musser, 1994), and 4,464 species and subspecies of chewing lice – 422 of them parasitize mammals – (Price et al., 2003) have been described. The sucking lice have conical short heads with mouthparts modified for piercing and sucking blood: a small proboscis, armed with small denticles and two stylets of hypopharyngeal and labial origin retracted within the trophic pouch (Kim & Ludwig, 1978). Another distinguishing feature is that sucking lice also possess strongly developed legs, with delicate modification of tibia and tarsus with a strong claw for effective grip to the hairs of their hosts (Kim & Ludwig, 1978).

Most species of lice are highly host-specific (Clayton, 1990; Clayton et al., 1992; Zuo et al., 2011). Many mammalian sucking lice are closely tied to their hosts in both ecological (Reed & Hafner, 1997) and evolutionary time (Hafner et al., 1994). These highly specialized blood-sucking insects modify their saliva to facilitate blood ingestion by containing various substances, such as anticoagulants (Mumcuoglu et al., 1996). These components of the louse's salivary glands may have undergone a long process of adaptation to the host's immune system (Reed et al., 2007; Volf, 1994; Waniek 2009). Transmission of sucking lice between conspecific hosts is most commonly brought about by close physical contact between individuals for instance by grooming, huddling, mating, biting, during suckling, or nest sharing (Cohn, 2017; Durden, 2019; Wall & Shearer, 1997).

The lice described from primates are also generally host specific, with most louse species occurring only on a single host species (Durden & Musser, 1994). Chewing lice are found on hosts such as prosimians (*Indri, Propithecus, Eulemu, Nycticebus*) and New World monkeys (*Alouatta, Aotus, Brachyteles*). They include the genera *Felicola, Trichophilopterus, Aotiella*, and *Cebidicola*. There are no reports of chewing lice infestations involving great apes and humans (Price et al., 2003). In contrast, there is a larger number of primate host species parasitized by sucking lice, including prosimians (*Lepilemur, Eulemur, Avahi, Galago, Microcebus, Cheirogaleus*), New World monkeys (*Alouatta, Ateles, Cebus*), Old World monkeys (*Macaca, Trachypithecus, Cercocebus, Lophocebus, Chlorocebus, Papio, Colobus, Procolobus, Presbytis, Piliocolobus, Cercopithecus, Miopithecus, Erythrocebus*), great apes (*Pan, Gorilla*), and humans (*Homo*). They include the genera *Pedicinus, Pediculus, Phthirpediculus, Lemurpediculus, Lemurpthirus*, and *Pthirus* (Durden & Musser, 1994). Lice of the genus *Pediculus* are found naturally on humans (*Homo*), chimpanzees (*Pan*), howler monkeys (*Alouatta*), spider monkeys (*Ateles*), and capuchin monkeys (*Cebus*) (Durden & Musser, 1994). This chapter concentrates mainly on the presence of *Pediculus* spp. in howlers to provide some information on the potential louse host switch between humans and a widely distributed Neotropical primate.

Only three species of *Pediculus* are currently recognized: *Pediculus schaeffi, Pediculus mjobergi*, and *Pediculus humanus*, which has two subspecies (or morphotypes), *P. humanus humanus* (body louse) and *P. humanus capitis* (head louse) (Barker et al., 2003). Historically, disagreement regarding the taxonomic status of *Pediculus* lice of cebid and atelid monkeys has occurred. For example, Ewing (1938) recognized *P. atelophilus, P. chapini, and P. lobatus* as distinct species; Ferris (1951) recognized only *P. mjobergi*; and Kim and Ludwig (1978) listed only *P. humanus* for the genus *Pediculus*. The genus *Pediculus* possesses an unbalanced host and geographical distribution with *Pediculus humanus* occurring globally, *P. schaeffi* living on chimpanzees in tropical Africa, and *P. mjobergi* found on howler monkeys (and other neotropical primates) in South and Central America. No other hosts of *Pediculus* lice are known throughout the global range of the genus. This interesting pattern of distribution is not easily explained by co-evolution from a common ancestor. Thus, the most probable explanation for the distribution of the three *Pediculus* species is evolution of *P. humanus* and *P. schaeffi* from a common ancestor in Africa, followed by spread of *P. humanus* around the globe with its human host. Finally, after reaching the South American continent a host-switch from modern humans to American primates (howler monkeys and possibly other taxa) may have occurred. Archaeological evidence shows that the peopling of the Americas by humans was very rapid and took place in several waves in a direction from north to south with the latest and most massive migration between 17,000 to 15,000 years ago (Kitchen et al., 2008; Potter et al., 2018; Schurr & Sherry, 2004).

8.2   The Genus *Alouatta* as Pets

Alouatta, one of the four genera of the family Atelidae, is composed of nine species (*A. paliatta, A. pigra, A. seniculus, A. sara, A. macconelli, A. caraya, A. belzebul, A. nigérrima,* and *A. guariba*). Three more cryptic taxa may acquire the species category *A. nigerrima, A. ululata,* and *A. discolor,* and a number of potential subspecies exists (Cortés-Ortiz et al., 2015; Groves, 2001; Rylands et al., 1995; Rylands & Rodriguez-Luna, 2000). The genus *Alouatta* has the widest geographic distribution of Neotropical primates, extending from southern Veracruz in Mexico in the north, through central America, and as far south as the province of Santa Fe in Argentina, inhabiting a wide range of environments, the most diverse within the Neotropical primates (Cortés-Ortiz et al., 2003; Crockett & Eisenberg, 1987; Zunino et al., 2001). Urbani and Cormier (2015) presented an extensive review on the interactions of indigenous societies and howler monkeys across the Americas, mainly for subsistence. Although compiling these data is difficult, they presented data from several countries including (from North to South): Mexico, Belize, Nicaragua, Costa Rica, Colombia, Venezuela, Surinam, Ecuador, Peru, Brazil, and Paraguay. Based on these data, they suggested that when humans initiated their early colonization of the tropical Americas, there was an increase in parasite exchange between *Homo* and *Alouatta* populations. The use of howlers for subsistence allowed the incorporation of these primates as pets. For example, sometimes, infants were not consumed but reared as family pets to be consumed later, kept for companionship, or released later (e.g. Hill & Hawkes, 1983; Lizarralde, 2002; Rival, 1993, 2006; Shepard, 2002; Smole, 1976). Coincidentally, howlers are the most common host reported for *Pediculus* in the New World, but it remains unclear when this host switching has occurred.

8.3   Relations between Social Strucure and Lice Infestation

Social structure in animal populations may affect levels of infestation by parasites. Eley et al. (1989) have reported the presence of louse nits (eggs) in *Papio anubis*, with the juvenile age category having with most infected individuals, and among adults, nits were found more frequently in low rank females, thus suggesting some costly relationship between low ranking position and the degree of infestation. Sanchez-Villagra et al. (1998) reported that in captured wild *Alouatta seniculus* (Hato el Frio, Venezuela) louse nits and lice were confined to the beard with no differences among age or between sex classes in ectoparasitic loads. They captured between 8 and 22 animals in 1991, 1993, and 1994, and the proportions of infested animals were 24%, 14%, and 40 % respectively. Although their data support a primarily social versus hygienic function for allogrooming, in 1992 they reported that two of the infested animals were solitary males, and they presented the most severe infestations compared to other captured *A. seniculus* in the study. Thus, although anecdotal, the situation of these males represents a potential cost of louse infestation if these animals are not incorporated into social groups, a cost that both females and males may confront when dispersing.

Studies on lice in New World monkeys are very scarce and outdated, in many of them the parasite species are undetermined, and in some cases, the lice were extracted from a single individual host. Being the genus with the widest distribution in the Americas, we reviewed lice found in different species of the genus *Alouatta*. We also explore the possibility of hosts switching from humans to howlers, as howlers were potentially treated as pets. Finally, we suggest new directions for this research program.

8.4   Methods and Results

We reviewed all published articles, book chapters, and unpublished dissertations available through Primate Lit, Google Scholar, and The Global Mammal Parasite Database up to May 2020 that focused on the relationship of *Pediculus* spp. and *Alouatta* spp. The results of this review are shown in Table 8.1, which provides the following data: host species, ectoparasite, study site, year of sample collection, number of samples collected, number of individuals sampled (hosts), condition of the hosts (wild, captive, museum, other), habitat type (remote, rural, fragmented, and continuous) and the referenced literature. It was not possible to include descriptions of the morphology or genetics of the lice specimens, since the vast majority of the reviewed works did not have this information. We considered remote sites, the sites with no permanent human presence, and rural sites where the forest fragments are embedded in a matrix of grassland with cattle ranching and agricultural practices. We also constructed a map with the collection sites of New World monkeys' lice reported in Table 8.1 using Free and Open Source QGIS (Fig. 8.1).

We have found *P. mjobergi* reports for only four species of howlers: *A. caraya*, *A. guariba*, *A. seniculus*, and *A. belzebul*. *Cebidicola* spp. (a chewing lice) was reported to be also present in these species and in *A. ursina* (*A. arctoidea*). Table 8.1 also shows the presence of *P. mjobergi* in other primate species including *Ateles* sp., *Brachyteles* sp., and *Cebus* sp. For all howler species reported in Table 8.1, *P. mjobergi* was recovered from wild animals. However, for most of the non-howler species in Table 8.1, lice were recovered from museum skins and captive individuals. *Alouatta caraya* was the most sampled species, and although data are still scarce *P. mjobergi* is found both at remote sites characterized by continuous forests, and at rural and fragmented forests suggesting that there is no specific ecological association between the presence of lice and forest structure and composition. For this comparison we considered forest as either rural-fragmented or remote-continuous (based on the definition provided in Marsh, 2003). As such, fragments are defined as small (1–10 ha), medium (10–100 ha), and large (100–1,000 ha). Rural-fragmented sites are composed of small and medium fragments.

Table 8.1. Review of lice on New World primates

Host species	Ectoparasite species	Study site	Year of sample collection	Number of collected samples	Number of individual sampled (hosts)	Condition of the host	Habitat type	References
Alouatta caraya	*Pediculus mjobergi*	Bella Vista, Corrientes, Argentina.	–	–	300	Wild	Rural-fragmented	Pope (1966)
Alouatta caraya	*Pediculus mjobergi*	Northeast Argentina (Corrientes and Misiones - National Park Iguazú-)	1993	6	2	Wild	Remote-continuous	Drali et al. (2016)
Alouatta caraya	*Pediculus mjobergi*	San Cayetano, Corrientes, Argentina (27°30' S, 58°41' W)	–	–	21	Wild	Rural-fragmented	Santa Cruz et al. (2000)
Alouatta caraya	*Pedicinus mjobergi*	Paraná River, Chaco, Argentina (27°30' S)	–	–	–	Wild	Rural-fragmented	Coppo et al. (1979)
Alouatta caraya	*Cebidicola semiarmatus*	Sao Paulo; and Mato Grosso, Brazil	–	–	–	–	–	Werneck (1950)
Alouatta seniculus	*Cebidicola semiarmatus*	–	–	–	–	Apparently wild	–	Hopkins (1949)
Alouatta seniculus	*Cebidicola semiarmatus*	San Fernando de Apure, Apure, Venezuela	–	–	–	–	–	Stafford (1943)
Alouatta seniculus	*Cebidicola extrarius*	Mirimiri, Falcon; El Rosario, Zulia; and Hato mata de Bejuco; Monagas, Venezuela	–	–	39	Apparently wild	–	Emerson & Price (1975)
Alouatta guariba clamitans	*Pediculus mjobergi*	Santa Catarina, Brazil.	2005	–	35	Captive. A single host individual exhibited the lice	–	Souza Junior (2007)
Alouatta guariba clamitans	*Cebidicola semiarmatus*	Santa Catarina, Brazil.	2005	–	35	Captive and wild	–	Souza Junior (2007)
Alouatta guariba clamitans	*Cebidicola semiarmatus*	Matias Barbosa, Minas Gerais, Brazil (21°52'S 43°19'W)	2015	30	1	Wild	–	Nascimento et al. (2018)
Alouatta guariba	*Cebidicola semiarmatus*	Espírito Santo and Sao Paulo, Brazil	–	–	–	–	–	Werneck (1950)
Alouatta belzebul	*Pediculus mjobergi*	–	–	–	–	Museum skin	–	Hopkins (1949)

Host	Louse	Location	Year	Nits	Lice	Status	Contact	Reference
Alouatta belzebul	*Cebidicola semiarmatus*	–	–	–	–	Apparently wild	–	Hopkins (1949)
Alouatta belzebul	*Cebidicola semiarmatus*	Rio Tocantins, Brazil	–	–	–	–	–	Werneck (1950)
Alouatta arctoidea	*Cebidicola semiarmatus*	–	–	–	–	Apparently wild	–	Hopkins (1949)
Ateles paniscus chamek	*Pediculus mjobergi*	Santa Cruz, Bolivia (13°35'S, 60°54'W)	1995	1	8	Wild. A single host individual presented the lice.	Remote-continuous	Karesh et al. (1998)
Ateles paniscus	*Pediculus mjobergi*	–	1922	Many	3	Captive. Museum skin	–	Ewing (1926)
Ateles paniscus	*Pediculus mjobergi*	–	–	–	–	Captive and wild	–	Hopkins (1949)
Ateles geoffroyi	*Pediculus mjobergi*	–	–	6	1	Captive	–	Hinman (1931)
Ateles geoffroyi	*Pediculus mjobergi*	–	1933	at least 7	at least 3	Captive	–	Ewing (1938)
Ateles geoffroyi	*Pediculus mjobergi*	–	1909	1	1	Captive. Museum skin	–	Ewing (1926)
Ateles fusciceps rufiventris	*Pediculus mjobergi*	–	1930	4	–	Apparently wild	–	Ewing (1938)
Ateles geoffroyi vellerosus	*Pediculus mjobergi*	–	–	1	–	Museum skin	–	Ewing (1926)
Ateles hybridus	*Pediculus mjobergi*	–	–	lice nits	–	Captive	–	Ewing (1938)
Cebus (Sapajus) apella	*Pediculus mjobergi*	–	–	–	–	Captive	–	Hopkins (1949)
Cebus capucinus	*Pediculus mjobergi*	–	–	–	–	Captive	–	Hopkins (1949)
Brachyteles arachnoides	*Cebidicola armatus*	–	–	–	–	Apparently wild	–	Hopkins (1949)
Pithecia monachus	*Pediculus mjobergi*	–	1930	Many	1	Captive. Museum skin	–	Ewing (1938)
Cacajao calvus rubicundus	*Pediculus mjobergi*	–	1930	Many	–	Captive	–	Ewing (1938)

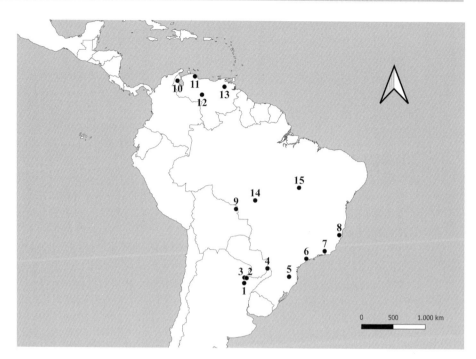

Figure 8.1 Collection sites of New World monkey's lice. Based on data from 1. Bella Vista, Corrientes, Argentina (Pope, 1966). 2. San Cayetano, Corrientes, Argentina (Santa Cruz et al., 2000). 3. Paraná River, Chaco, Argentina (Coppo et al., 1979). 4. Iguazú, Misiones, Argentina (Drali et al., 2016). 5. Santa Catarina, Brazil (Souza, 2007). 6. Sao Paulo, Brazil (Werneck, 1950). 7. Matias Barbosa, Minas Gerais, Brazil (Nascimento et al., 2018). 8. Espirito Santo, Brazil (Werneck. 1950). 9. Santa Cruz, Bolivia (Karesh et al., 1998). 10. El Rosario, Zulia, Venezuela (Emerson and Price, 1975). 11. Mirimire, Falcón, Venezuela (Emerson and Price, 1975). 12. San Fernando de Apure, Apure, Venezuela (Stafford, 1943). 13. Monagas, Venezuela (Emerson and Price, 1975). 14. Mato Grosso, Brazil (Werneck, 1950). 15. Tocantins River, Brazil (Werneck, 1950).

8.5   Discussion

We have found scarce data on the presence of *P. mjobergi* in *Alouatta* across their range. This fact does not reflect the absence of these lice in the rest of howler species, but probably the lack of sampling, difficulty in sampling lice, seasonal changes in louse prevalence, or absence of specific projects designed to collect lice in wild howlers and other neotropical primates. Besides, the limited availability of morphological and genetic characterizations of *P. mjobergi* makes its recognition difficult. As shown in Table 8.1, lice were found in *Alouatta caraya* at both remote and rural sites characterized by continuous and fragmented forest, respectively (Kowalewski & Zunino, 2004). Different forest structure and composition allow different social organization of howlers, for example continuous forests result in 70–80% group home range overlap, high frequency of intergroup encounters, high proportion of multimale groups, and social interactions that maintain group stability (Kowalewski, 2007; Kowalewski & Garber, 2015; Kowalewski & Zunino, 2004). On the other hand, more fragmented forests (up to 15 ha) are characterized by one-two groups per fragment, lower home range overlap, lower frequency of intergroup encounters, high proportion of unimale groups, and a different type and degree of social interactions to maintain group cohesion (Kowalewski et al., 2019; Kowalewski & Zunino, 2004; Raño, 2016). Despite these differences, lice seem to infest howlers at multiple sites. We also found, across the years (through different projects) in our study site (Estación Biológica Corrientes, Corrientes, Argentina; 27°30'S, 58°41'E), that individual *A. caraya* were more infested with lice nits during winter than summer seasons, where winter temperature may reach 0°C and summer 40°C, suggesting a seasonal difference in louse prevalence. However, more research needs to be done in this direction.

Humans can be infested with *P. h. capitis or P. capitis* (head louse) and *P. h. humanus* or *P. humanus* (body louse), two ecotypes that spread globally when modern humans have moved out of Africa over the past 100,000 years (Ascunce et al., 2013). Based on the sequences of mitochondrial (mt) genes for cytochrome oxidase subunit 1 (cox1), cytochrome b (cytb), and 12S ribosomal RNA (12S) (Amanzougaghene et al., 2019; Drali et al., 2015; Reed et al., 2004) human lice have been divided in six haplogroups denominated with letters A to F. Haplogroup A occurs globally and was confirmed to be already in the pre-Columbian America by a genetic analysis of lice from Peruvian mummies (Raoult et al., 2008). This group is older than haplogroup B (Light & Reed, 2009; Reed et al., 2004), the second most common haplogroup, found in the Americas, Western Europe, Australia, and North Africa (Boutellis et al., 2014), whereas the other haplogroups (C–F) are more geographically restricted (Amanzougaghene et al., 2019; Boutellis et al., 2014). Head lice were associated with all six haplogroups whereas body lice belong only to haplogroups A and D. The neotropical *P. mjobergi* has been found also in other primates different from howlers, such as, *Ateles* spp., *Cebus* spp., and *Pithecia* sp. (Table 8.1).

Drali et al. (2016) compared four adult lice samples of *P. mjobergi* collected from one *Alouatta caraya* from Iguazu National Park, Argentina, and two lice samples from one individual from Corrientes, Argentina, and compared them against 19 head lice samples from humans from a remote Amazonian region in French Guiana. The phylogenetic analyses performed for four mtDNA markers (cytochrome b [*cytb*], cytochrome oxidase subunit 1 [*cox1*], 16S ribosomal RNA, and NADH dehydrogenase subunit 2 [*nad2*]), showed that *P. mjobergi* sequences are divided into two haplogroups that corresponded to haplogroups A and B haplotypes, whereas the Amazonian head lice only have haplogroup B haplotypes. Moreover, the analysis of the *cox1* gene revealed that *P. mjobergi* has a unique haplotype that is part of a subgroup of haplogroup B that contains haplotypes from Argentina, Mexico, and Amazonia. Similarly, for the *cytb* gene, the haplotype of one of the *P. mjobergi* lice was closely related to a haplotype unique to Amazonian head lice, which only differ in five nucleotides that result in a single amino acid difference.

The authors also found that lice were morphologically similar among them, supporting previous studies (Ewing, 1938; Maunder, 1983), and their genetic analysis indicated an interchange of genetic material between human and howler lice, specially, the evidence that lice sequences were characterized by having two different genetic lineages of lice (haplogroup A and B). The host switch was suggested to have occurred during casual encounters, for example for subsistence (Urbani & Cormier, 2015) or pets (Horwich, 1998). Subsequently, using more genetic data, Amanzougaghene et al. (2019) indicated that *P. mjobergi* belongs to haplogroup F specific to human samples from Argentina, Mexico, and Amazonia. Such tight genetic linkages suggest that *P. mjobergi* is an evolutionary lineage of *P. humanus* (following Drali et al., 2016 who suggested that *P. mjobergi* may have switched from humans to nonhuman primates when humans entered the Americas).

Furthermore, it is possible that another genus of sucking lice, *Pthirus*, has switched from gorillas to humans. *Pthirus pubis* and *Pthirus gorillae* parasite *Homo sapiens* and *Gorilla gorilla* respectively. Reed et al. (2007) and Light and Reed (2009) perform phylogenetic analyses indicating that this is the most parsimonious evolutionary model, and the divergence between *P. pubis* and *P. gorillae* is much younger than their hosts' divergence. It is unknown how this host switch occurred, but it could have resulted from habitat sharing, predation, or other forms of contact between archaic hominids and gorillas.

Lice have been associated with humans for millions of years and dispersed throughout the world by early human migrants (Ascunce et al., 2013). *P. humanus* shows genetic evidence of population expansion from Africa approximately 100,000 years ago, which is consistent with the host evolutionary history because humans originated in Africa (Reed et al., 2004, 2007) and dispersed to four continents within the past 80,000 years (Forster, 2004; Light et al., 2008). In this regard, Araujo et al. (2000) found the first evidence of ancient human lice (10,000 years old) east of the Andes and suggests that the lice arrived with the first human migrants to enter the New World, and possible past contact between humans and monkeys. Theoretically, the earliest peoples of the Americas could have brought lice during migration to the New World, where lice remained in situ for thousands of years (Raoult et al., 2008).

Finally, we found few data available on the relationship between lice and howler monkeys (limited number of samples collected from wild animals, and genetic sequences available for analysis across the Americas). However, these limited data suggest that at some point lice probably switched from humans to howlers, possibly during a scenario where howlers were kept as family pets. On the other hand, we suggest that future research focus on the influence of lice infestation on the dispersal options of primates since the available data show that louse infestation of solitary howlers may be a burden for these individuals and, especially during low temperatures in more seasonal environments, this may result in a decrease in individual fitness if these individuals do not find a social group to live with. Therefore, louse infestation may be considered as a cost of dispersal for the species, especially in highly seasonal environments.

8.6   Future Research

The study of the relationship of lice distribution and neotropical nonhuman primates is a promising field to explore. We still need to disentangle the morphological and genetic differences between these lice in humans and primates to deepen our understanding in how and when host switches may have occurred. The limited volume of faunistic and genetic data available up to date does not allow for an estimate of the age of the host switch or its possible recurrence. Particularly, whole genome data collected from *P. mjobergi* and human louse samples and analyzed with coalescent simulations may help to understand dates of the earliest time of the human to howler monkey host switch and obtain archaeology-independent data on the colonization of South America by modern humans. The approach of using parasites to date important events in human history was also employed in a study analyzing genetic divergence between head and body louse forms to provide more accuracy to the archaeological estimates of the origin of clothing in humans (Reed et al., 2015; Toups et al., 2011). Moreover, understanding the dynamics and evolutionary history of these lice would also help to understand the dynamics of certain diseases where lice act as pathogen vectors, such as *Rickettsia prowazekii* (typhus), *Bartonella quintana* (trench fever), *Borrelia recurrentis* (relapsing fever), and possible *Yersinia pestis* (plague) (Amanzougaghene et al., 2019; Blanc & Baltazard, 1941; Drali et al., 2015; Houhamdi et al., 2006; Piarroux et al., 2013; Raoult & Roux, 1999). Finally, we suggest a coordinated collaboration of researchers across the world to put together a standardized protocol of collection and analyses of lice.

Acknowledgments

We are very grateful to the anonymous reviewer for the valuable input. We thank Bernardo Urbani for helpful comments during the development of this manuscript. MK thanks Bruno K who has never had lice yet. MK and FQ are members of CONICET.

References

Amanzougaghene, N., Fenollar, F., Davoust, B., et al. (2019). Mitochondrial diversity and phylogeographic analysis of *Pediculus humanus* reveals a new Amazonian clade "F." *Infection, Genetics and Evolution*, 70, 1–8.

Araújo, A., Ferreira, L. F., Guidon, N., et al. (2000). Ten thousand years of head lice infection. *Parasitology Today*, 16(7), 269.

Ascunce, M. S., Toups, M. A., Kassu, G., Fane, J., Scholl, K., & Reed, D. L. (2013). Nuclear genetic diversity in human lice (*Pediculus humanus*) reveals continental differences and high inbreeding among worldwide populations. *PLoS ONE*, 8(2), e57619.

Barker, S. C., Whiting, M., Johnson, K. P., & Murrell, A. (2003). Phylogeny of the lice (Insecta, Phthiraptera) inferred from small subunit rRNA. *Zoologica Scripta*, 32(5), 407–414.

Blanc, G., & Baltazard, M. (1941). Recherches expérimentales sur la peste. L'infection du pou de l'homme, Pediculus corporis de Geer. *Comptes Rendus de l'Académie Des Sciences*, 213, 849–851.

Boutellis, A., Abi-Rached, L., & Raoult, D. (2014). The origin and distribution of human lice in the world. *Infection, Genetics and Evolution*, 23, 209–217.

Clayton, D. H. (1990). Host specificity of *Strigiphilus* owl lice (Ischnocera: Philopteridae), with the description of new species and host associations. *Journal of Medical Entomology*, 27(3), 257–265.

Clayton, D. H., Gregory, R. D., & Price, R. D. (1992). Comparative ecology of Neotropical bird lice (Insecta: Phthiraptera). *Journal of Animal Ecology*, 61(3), 781–795.

Cohn, D. L. (2017). Lice. In A. Fuentes, ed., *The International Encyclopedia of Primatology*. Hoboken, NJ: John Wiley and Sons Inc., 1–2.

Coppo, J. A., Moreira, R. A., & Lombardero, O. J. (1979). Parasitism in the primates of CAPRIM. *Acta Zoologica Lilloana*, **35**, 9–12.

Cortés-Ortiz, L., Bermingham, E., Rico, C., Rodríguez-Luna, E., Sampaio, I., & Ruiz-García, M. (2003). Molecular systematics and biogeography of the Neotropical monkey genus, Alouatta. *Molecular Phylogenetics and Evolution*, **26**(1), 64–81.

Cortés-Ortiz, L., Rylands, A. B., & Mittermeier, R. A. (2015). The taxonomy of howler monkeys: Integrating old and new knowledge from morphological and genetic studies. In M. M. Kowalewski, P. A. Garber, L. Cortés-Ortiz, B. Urbani, & D. Youlatos, eds., *Howler Monkeys: Adaptive Radiation, Systematics, and Morphology*. New York: Springer, 55–84.

Crockett, C. M., & Eisenberg, J. F. (1987). Howlers: variations in group size and demography. In B. B. Smuts, D. L. Cheney, R. M. Seyfarth, R. W. Wrangham, & T. T. Struhsaker, eds., *Primate Societies*. Chicago: University of Chicago Press, 54–68.

Drali, R., Shako, J.-C., Davoust, B., Diatta, G., & Raoult, D. (2015). A new clade of African body and head lice infected by *Bartonella quintana* and *Yersinia pestis*–Democratic Republic of the Congo. *The American Journal of Tropical Medicine and Hygiene*, **93**(5), 990–993.

Drali, R., Abi-Rached, L., Boutellis, A., Djossou, F., Barker, S. C., & Raoult, D. (2016). Host switching of human lice to new world monkeys in South America. *Infection, Genetics and Evolution*, **39**, 225–231.

Durden, L. A. (2019). Lice (Phthiraptera). In G. R. Mullen, & L. A. Durden, eds., *Medical and Veterinary Entomology*. 3rd ed., London: Academic Press, 79–106.

Durden, L. A., & Musser, G. G. (1994). The mammalian hosts of the sucking lice (Anoplura) of the world: a host-parasite list. *Bulletin of the Society for Vector Ecology*, **19**(2), 130–168.

Eley, R. M., Strum, S. C., Muchemi, G., & Reid, G. D. F. (1989). Nutrition, body condition, activity patterns, and parasitism of free-ranging troops of olive baboons (*Papio anubis*) in Kenya. *American Journal of Primatology*, **18**(3), 209–219.

Emerson, K. C., & Price, R. (1975). Mallophaga of Venezuelan mammals. *Brigham Young University Science Bulletin, Biological Series*, **20**(3), 1–77.

Ewing, H. E. (1926). A revision of the American lice of the genus *Pediculus*, together with a consideration of their geographical and host distribution. *Proceedings of the United States National Museum*, **68**(2620), 1–33.

Ewing, H. E. (1938). The sucking lice of American monkeys. *The Journal of Parasitology*, **24**(1), 13–33.

Ferris, G. F. (1951). The sucking lice. *Memoirs of the Pacific Coast Entomological Society*, **1**, 1–130.

Forster, P. (2004). Ice Ages and the mitochondrial DNA chronology of human dispersals: a review. *Philosophical Transactions of the Royal Society of London. Series B: Biological Sciences*, **359**(1442), 255–264.

Groves, C. (2001). *Primate Taxonomy*. Washington, DC: Smithsonian Institution Press.

Hafner, M. S., Sudman, P. D., Villablanca, F. X., Spradling, T. A., Demastes, J. W., & Nadler, S. A. (1994). Disparate rates of molecular evolution in cospeciating hosts and parasites. *Science*, **265**(5175), 1087–1090.

Hill, K., & Hawkes, K. (1983). Neotropical Hunting among the Aché of Eastern Paraguay. In R. B. Hames, & W. T. Vickers, eds., *Adaptive Responses of Native Amazonians*. New York: Academic Press, 139–188.

Hinman, E. H. (1931). *Pediculus (Parapediculus) atelophilus* Ewing 1926 from the red spider monkey, Ateles geoffroyi. *Parasitology*, **23**(4), 488–491.

Hopkins, G. H. E. (1949). The host-associations of the lice of mammals. *Proceedings of the Zoological Society of London*, **119**(2), 387–604.

Horwich, R. H. (1998). Effective solutions for howler conservation. *International Journal of Primatology*, **19**(3), 579–598.

Houhamdi, L., Lepidi, H., Drancourt, M., & Raoult, D. (2006). Experimental model to evaluate the human body louse as a vector of plague. *The Journal of Infectious Diseases*, **194**(11), 1589–1596.

Johnson, K. P., & Clayton, D. H. (2004). Untangling coevolutionary history. *Systematic Biology*, **53**(1), 92–94.

Johnson, K. P., Adams, R. J., Page, R. D. M., & Clayton, D. H. (2003). When do parasites fail to speciate in response to host speciation? *Systematic Biology*, **52**(1), 37–47.

Karesh, W. B., Wallace, R. B., Painter, R. L. E., et al. (1998). Immobilization and health assessment of free-ranging black spider monkeys (*Ateles paniscus chamek*). *American Journal of Primatology*, **44**(2), 107–123.

Kim, K. C., & Ludwig, H. W. (1978). The family classification of the Anoplura. *Systematic Entomology*, **3**(3), 249–284.

Kitchen, A., Miyamoto, M. M., & Mulligan, C. J. (2008). A three-stage colonization model for the peopling of the Americas. *PLoS ONE*, **3**(2), e1596.

Kowalewski, M. M. (2007). Patterns of affiliation and cooperation in Howler Monkeys: An alternative model to explain social organization in non-human primates. PhD dissertation, University of Illinois.

Kowalewski, M. M., & Garber, P. A. (2015). Solving the collective action problem during intergroup encounters: the case of black and gold howler monkeys (*Alouatta caraya*). In M. M. Kowalewski, P. A. Garber, L. Cortés-Ortiz, B. Urbani, & D. Youlatos, eds., *Howler Monkeys: Behavior, Ecology, and Conservation*. New York: Springer, 165–189.

Kowalewski, M., & Zunino, G. E. (2004). Birth seasonality in *Alouatta caraya* in Northern Argentina. *International Journal of Primatology*, **25**(2), 383–400.

Kowalewski, M. M., Pavé, R., Fernández, V. A., Raño, M., & Zunino, G. E. (2019). Life-history traits and group dynamic in black and gold howler monkeys in flooded forests of Northern Argentina. In A. A. Barnett, I. Matsuda, & K. Nowak, eds., *Primates in Flooded Habitats: Ecology and Conservation*. Cambridge, UK: Cambridge University Press, 263–269.

Light, J. E., & Reed, D. L. (2009). Multigene analysis of phylogenetic relationships and divergence times of primate sucking lice (Phthiraptera: Anoplura). *Molecular Phylogenetics and Evolution*, **50**(2), 376–390.

Light, J. E., Toups, M. A., & Reed, D. L. (2008). What's in a name: The taxonomic status of human head and body lice. *Molecular Phylogenetics and Evolution*, **47**(3), 1203–1216.

Light, J. E., Smith, V. S., Allen, J. M., Durden, L. A., & Reed, D. L. (2010). Evolutionary history of mammalian sucking lice (Phthiraptera: Anoplura). *BMC Evolutionary Biology*, **10**(1), 292.

Linz, B., Balloux, F., Moodley, Y., et al. (2007). An African origin for the intimate association between humans and *Helicobacter pylori*. *Nature*, **445**(7130), 915–918.

Lizarralde, M. (2002). Ethnoecology of monkeys among the Barí of Venezuela: perception, use and conservation. In A. Fuentes, & L. D. Wolfe, eds., *Primates Face to Face: The Conservation Implications of Human-Nonhuman Primate Interconnections*,. 85–100.

Marsh, L. K. (2003). The nature of fragmentation. In L. K. Marsh, ed., *Primates in Fragments: Ecology and Conservation*, Boston: Springer, 1–10.

Maunder, J. W. (1983). The appreciation of lice. *Proceedings of the Royal Institution of Great Britain*, **55**, 1–31.

Mumcuoglu, K. Y., Galun, R., Kaminchik, Y., Panet, A., & Levanon, A. (1996). Antihemostatic activity in salivary glands of the human body louse, *Pediculus humanus humanus* (Anoplura: Pediculidae). *Journal of Insect Physiology*, **42**(11), 1083–1087.

Nascimento, R. M. do, Maturano, R., Oliveira, M. de, & Daemon, E. (2018). First record of *Cebidicola semi-armatus* (Phthiraptera: Trichodectidae) on the red howler monkey, *Alouatta guariba clamintans* (Primate: Atelidae) in Brazil. *Revista Colombiana de Entomología*, **44**(1), 129–131.

Page, R. D. M. (1993). Parasites, phylogeny and cospeciation. *International Journal for Parasitology*, **23**(4), 499–506.

Piarroux, R., Abedi, A. A., Shako, J. C., et al. (2013). Plague epidemics and lice, Democratic Republic of the Congo. *Emerging Infectious Diseases*, **19**(3), 505–506.

Pope, B. L. (1966). Some parasites of the howler monkey of Northern Argentina. *The Journal of Parasitology*, **52**(1), 166–168.

Potter, B. A., Baichtal, J. F., Beaudoin, A. B., et al. (2018). Current evidence allows multiple models for the peopling of the Americas. *Science Advances*, **4**(8), eaat5473.

Price, R. D., Hellenthal, R. A., Palma, R. I., Johnson, K. P., & Clayton, D. H. (2003). *The Chewing Lice: Word Checklist and Biological Overview*. Illinois Natural History Survey Special Publication.

Raño, M. (2016). *Reproductive strategies of female black and golden howler monkeys (Alouatta caraya) in Northeast Argentina*. University of Buenos Aires.

Raoult, D., & Roux, V. (1999). the body louse as a vector of reemerging human diseases. *Clinical Infectious Diseases*, **29**(4), 888–911.

Raoult, D., Reed, D. L., Dittmar, K., et al. (2008). Molecular identification of lice from Pre-Columbian mummies. *The Journal of Infectious Diseases*, **197**(4), 535–543.

Reed, D. L., & Hafner, M. S. (1997). Host specificity of chewing lice on pocket gophers: A potential mechanism for cospeciation. *Journal of Mammalogy*, 78(2), 655–660.

Reed, D. L., Smith, V. S., Hammond, S. L., Rogers, A. R., & Clayton, D. H. (2004). Genetic analysis of lice supports direct contact between modern and archaic humans. *PLoS Biology*, 2(11), e340.

Reed, D. L., Light, J. E., Allen, J. M., & Kirchman, J. J. (2007). Pair of lice lost or parasites regained: the evolutionary history of anthropoid primate lice. *BMC Biology*, 5(1), 7.

Reed, D. L., Allen, J. M., Toups, M. A., Boyd, B. M., & Ascunce, M. S. (2015). The study of primate evolution from a lousy perspective. In B. R. Krasnov, D. T. J. Littlewood, & S. Morand, eds., *Parasite Diversity and Diversification: Evolutionary Ecology Meets Phylogenetics*, 202–214.

Ricklefs, R. E., Fallon, S. M., & Bermingham, E. (2004). Evolutionary relationships, cospeciation, and host switching in avian malaria parasites. *Systematic Biology*, 53(1), 111–119.

Rival, L. (1993). The growth of family trees: Understanding Huaorani perceptions of the forest. *Man*, 28(4), 635–652.

Rival, L. (2006). Amazonian historical ecologies. *Journal of the Royal Anthropological Institute*, 12, S79–S94.

Rylands, A. B., & Rodriguez-Luna, E. (2000). An assessment of the diversity of New World primates. *Neotropical Primates*, 8(2), 61–93.

Rylands, A. B., Mittermeier, R. A., & Rodriguez-Luna, E. (1995). A species list for the New World primates (Platyrrhini): Distribution by country, endemism, and conservation status according to the Mace-Land system. *Neotropical Primates*, 3, 113–160.

Sánchez-Villagra, M. R., Pope, T. R., & Salas, V. (1998). Relation of intergroup variation in allogrooming to group social structure and ectoparasite loads in red howlers (*Alouatta seniculus*). *International Journal of Primatology*, 19(3), 473–491.

Santa Cruz, A. C. M., Borda, J. T., Patiño, E. M., Gomez, L., & Zunino, G. E. (2000). Habitat fragmentation and parasitism in howler monkeys (*Alouatta caraya*). *Neotropical Primates*, 8(4), 146–148.

Schurr, T. G., & Sherry, S. T. (2004). Mitochondrial DNA and Y chromosome diversity and the peopling of the Americas: Evolutionary and demographic evidence. *American Journal of Human Biology*, 16(4), 420–439.

Shepard, G. H. (2002). Primates in Matsigenka subsistence and world view. In A. Fuentes, & L. D. Wolfe, eds., *Primates Face to Face: The Conservation Implications of Human-nonhuman Primate Interconnections*. Cambridge, UK: Cambridge University Press, 101–136.

Smole, W. J. (1976). *The Yanoama Indians. A Cultural Geography*. Austin: University of Texas Press.

Souza Junior, J. C. (2007). *Perfil sanitário de bugios ruivos, Alouatta guariba clamitans (Cabrera, 1940) (Primates: Atelidae): um estudo com animais recepcionados e mantidos em perímetro urbano no município de Indaial, Santa Catarina – Brazil*. Universidade Federal de Santa Catarina.

Stafford, E. W. (1943). Some Venezuelan Mallophaga. *Boletin de Entomologia Venezolana*, 2, 35–58.

Štefka, J., Hoeck, P. E., Keller, L. F., & Smith, V. S. (2011). A hitchhikers guide to the Galápagos: co-phylogeography of Galápagos mockingbirds and their parasites. *BMC Evolutionary Biology*, 11(1), 284.

Takano-lee, M., Yoon, K. S., Edman, J. D., Mullens, B. A., & Clark, J. M. (2003). In vivo and in vitro rearing of *Pediculus humanus capitis* (Anoplura: Pediculidae). *Journal of Medical Entomology*, 40(5), 628–635.

Toups, M. A., Kitchen, A., Light, J. E., & Reed, D. L. (2011). Origin of clothing lice indicates early clothing use by anatomically modern humans in Africa. *Molecular Biology and Evolution*, 28(1), 29–32.

Urbani, B., & Cormier, L. A. (2015). The ethnoprimatology of the howler monkeys (*Alouatta* spp.): From past to present. In M. M. Kowalewski, P. A. Garber, L. Cortés-Ortiz, B. Urbani, & D. Youlatos, eds., *Howler Monkeys: Behavior, Ecology, and Conservation*. New York: Springer, 259–280.

Vienne, D. M. de, Refrégier, G., López-Villavicencio, M., Tellier, A., Hood, M. E., & Giraud, T. (2013). Cospeciation vs host-shift speciation: methods for testing, evidence from natural associations and relation to coevolution. *New Phytologist*, 198(2), 347–385.

Volf, P. (1994). Localization of the major immunogen and other glycoproteins of the louse *Polyplax spinulosa*. *International Journal for Parasitology*, 24(7), 1005–1010.

Wall, R., & Shearer, D. (1997). Lice (Phthiraptera). In R. Wall, & D. Shearer, eds., *Veterinary Entomology: Arthropod Ectoparasites of Veterinary Importance*. Dordrecht: Springer, 284–312.

Wall, R., & Shearer, D. (2001). *Veterinary Ectoparasites: Biology, Pathology and Control*, 2nd ed. Oxford: Blackwell Science.

Waniek, P. J. (2009). The digestive system of human lice: current advances and potential applications. *Physiological Entomology*, 34(3), 203–210.

Werneck, F. (1950). *Os malófagos de mamíferos. Parte II: Ischnocera (continuacao Thichodectidae) e Rhyncophthirina*. Instituto Oswaldo Cruz.

Whiteman, N. K., & Parker, P. G. (2005). Using parasites to infer host population history: a new rationale for parasite conservation. *Animal Conservation*, 8(2), 175–181.

Zunino, G. E., Gonzalez, V., Kowalewski, M., & Bravo, S. P. (2001). *Alouatta caraya*: Relations among habitat, density and social organization. *Primate Report*, 61, 37–46.

Zuo, X.-H., Guo, X.-G., Zhan, Y.-Z., et al. (2011). Host selection and niche differentiation in sucking lice (Insecta: Anoplura) among small mammals in southwestern China. *Parasitology Research*, 108(5), 1243–1251.

Part II

Europe

9 The Place of Nonhuman Primates in Ancient Roman Culture

Narratives and Practices

Marco Vespa

Il posto dei primati non umani nella cultura romana antica: racconti e pratiche

Riassunto

L'apprensione del mondo naturale, degli ecosistemi e delle specie che li vivono risulta quasi sempre da un combinato disposto di (1) pratiche relazionali interspecifiche, (2) modalità e forme della conoscenza naturalistica e (3) pratiche istituzionalizzate di incontro con gli animali non umani. L'elaborazione di una particolare rappresentazione culturale dei primati non umani non fa eccezione e dipende così largamente da variabili di tipo culturale. La divulgazione scientifica su larga scala, l'industria cinematografica, le occasioni di svago e istruzione borghesi occidentali dallo zoo al circo hanno contribuito a elaborare una parte importante dell'immagine culturale che noi moderni abbiamo ricevuto dei primati, in special modo delle scimmie antropomorfe. Il mondo romano antico tra il I millennio a. C. e il I millennio d. C. è stato caratterizzato da pratiche relazionali, categorie culturali e forme di conoscenza scientifica dei primati non umani molto diverse da quelle che sono (state) operanti nel nostro immaginario occidentale, a partire proprio dagli esemplari con cui più comunemente i Romani hanno avuto occasione di interagire, macachi e babbuini invece di gorilla e scimpanzè. Concentrando l'attenzione su come i primati non umani sono stati integrati nell'enciclopedia culturale romana, questo articolo si soffermerà non sui saperi zoologici e 'primatologici' per se, ma sulla matrice culturale all'interno della quale i primati non umani sono stati percepiti, il loro comportamento è stato interpretato e il loro rapporto con gli esseri umani è stato compreso.

Parole chiave

Antica Roma – imitazione – relazione uomo-animale – primati non umani – zoologia antica

Abstract

One's apprehension of the natural world, of ecosystems, and the species living therein, almost always takes shape in the contexts of (1) interspecific relational practices, (2) modalities and forms of naturalistic knowledge, and (3) institutionalized practices of encounter with nonhuman animals. The elaboration of particular cultural representations of nonhuman primates is no exception: it too largely depends on cultural variables. Scientific thought as disseminated for popular consumption, blockbuster films, and bourgeois entertainments, such as zoos and circuses, have contributed substantially to modern humans' conceptions of primates, especially anthropomorphic apes. The ancient Roman world between the end of the first millennium BCE and the beginning of first millennium CE, however, was characterized by relational practices, cultural categories, and forms of scientific knowledge of nonhuman primates very different from those now operating in the Western imaginary. It is significant, for example, that the Romans most commonly interacted not with gorillas and chimpanzees, but with macaques and baboons. By investigating how nonhuman primates were integrated into Roman cultural encyclopedia, this article will center not on ape lore *per se* but instead upon the distinct cultural matrix within which primates were perceived, their behavior interpreted, and their relationship to humans understood.

Keywords: Ancient Rome, Imitation, Animal–human relation, Nonhuman primates, Ancient zoological knowledge

9.1   Introduction

The study of the cultural representation of nonhuman primates in the Roman world must start from the consideration of a fundamental ecological issue that affects both the possible conceptual and experiential relationships between human beings and primates in the Western Roman world – that is, the condition of captivity, where these animals were subjected to human observation. The presence of monkeys in Italy was questioned even by ancient Roman authors, at least according to some testimonies transmitted through Strabo, Virgil, and then Pliny, who discussed the presence of nonhuman primates on the islands in the Gulf of Naples (see Polara and De Vivo, 2011 and citations therein).

As part of the discussion on an ancient Homeric site where the giant Typhon was supposed to have been crushed and buried (Homer *Iliad*, 2.783), Latin intellectuals wondered about the real presence of monkeys in the past that gave rise to the name of the island of Ischia, in Greek *Pithekoussai*, literally 'Monkey Islands' (Servius *Commentary on Virgil's Aeneid*, 9.712). To be precise, the islands known as *Pithekoussai* were considered the most likely location of the Arimoi of which Homer had spoken. While some authors, such as Strabo (*Geography*, 13.4.6), had associated the Homeric name of Inarime, also used by Virgil (*Aeneid*, 9.716), with an ancient Etruscan term meaning "monkey" (*arimos*), Pliny was very skeptical, denying any link between monkeys and the island of Ischia and preferring to see, at the base of the etymology of *Pithekoussai*, the most banal Greek name for "barrel", *pithos*, whose earlier trade on the island would explain the toponym (Pliny *Natural History*, 3.6.8; Gras, 1994; on the Phoenician etymology of *Inarime / Aenaria*, see Poccetti, 1995). Although the presence of nonhuman primates is not attested in Ischia by archaeozoological findings, ancient discussions about their presence remains of primary importance for a cultural analysis of the monkey in the Roman world and the western sphere of the Mediterranean world.

This chapter will try to account for the presence of nonhuman primates in the Roman world through two different but complementary perspectives. First, by drawing upon encyclopedic texts, it will reconstruct a taxonomy of the species of monkeys actually known by Latin authors. After establishing a profile of the most important zoological specimens at the disposal of ancient authors, we will focus

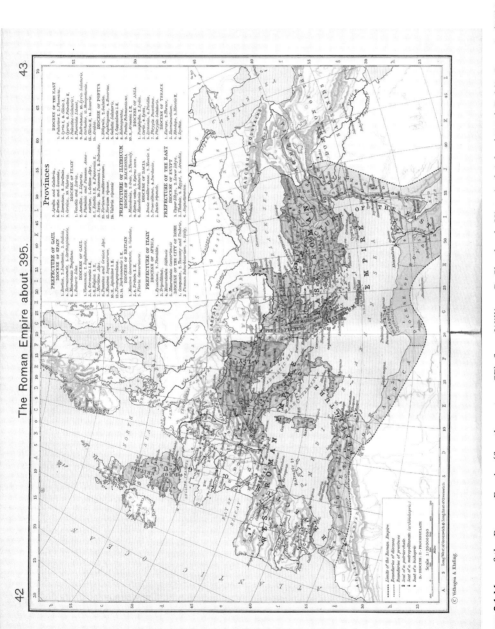

Figure 9.1 Map of the Roman Empire (fourth century CE), from William R. Shepherd, *Historical Atlas* (1911)–Public Domain (Wikimedia Commons–CC BY; Benowar, 2004).

upon the conceptions of interspecific relations that were transmitted by way of the literary texts of the Latin world. While detailing the scarce evidence of human/simian interactions that has emerged from excavations, this essay seeks above all to reconstruct from written texts the elaborate symbolic representations that emerged from the presence of monkeys in Ancient Rome.

9.2   Monkey Species in the Ancient Latin World: Towards a Roman Folk Taxonomy of Nonhuman Primates

While Aristotle provides a synthesis of zoological knowledge about nonhuman primates in the classical Greek world (*History of Animals*, 2. 8–9), for ancient Rome an essential starting point is to be found in two paragraphs of the *Natural History* by Pliny the Elder (8.215–216). Pliny provides with general but important information concerning what a well-read Roman citizen could know about monkeys in ancient Rome in the first century CE:

Simiarum quoque genera hominis figurae proxima caudis inter se distinguntur. mira sollertia: visco inungui, laqueisque calciari imitatione venantium tradunt, Mucianus et latrunculis lusisse, fictas cera nuces visu distinguere, luna cava tristes esse quibus in eo genere cauda sit, novam exultatione adorari: nam defectum siderum et ceterae pavent quadripedes. simiarum generi praecipua erga fetum adfectio. Gestant catulos quae mansuefactae intra domos peperere. omnibus demonstrant tractarique gaudent, gratulationem intellegentibus similes; itaque magna ex parte conplectendo necant. efferatior cynocephalis natura sicut mitissima satyris. Callitriches toto paene aspectu differunt: barba est in facie, cauda late fusa primori parte. hoc animal negatur vivere in alio quam Aethiopiae quo gignitur caelo.

[The species of monkeys, which are the animals closest to the human shape, are distinguished from each other by the tails. They are marvellously cunning: people say that they use bird-lime as ointment, and that they put on the nooses set to snare them as if they were shoes, in imitation of the hunters; according to Mucianus the tailed species have even been known to play at draughts, are able to distinguish at a glance sham nuts made of wax, and are depressed by the moon waning and worship the new moon with delight: and it is a fact that the other four-footed animals also are frightened by eclipses. The genus ape has a remarkable affection for its young. Tame monkeys kept in the house who bear young ones carry them about and show them to everybody, and delight in having them stroked, looking as if they understood that they are being congratulated; and as a consequence in a considerable number of cases they kill their babies by hugging them. The baboon is of a fiercer nature, just as the satyrus is extremely gentle. The pretty-haired ape is almost entirely different in appearance: it has a bearded face and a tail flattened out wide at the base. This animal is said to be unable to live in any other climate but that of its native country, Ethiopia]. (Translation by H. Rackham slightly modified).

In Pliny's presentation, *simiae* (the Latin word for monkeys), although subdivided into different typologies distinguished by shape and ethology, are still the animals that have the greatest similarities with respect to the human morphotype. The term used by Pliny to express this morphotypical similarity between primates, human and nonhuman ones, is *figura*, a noun that indicates the outer shape of the silhouette of an object: the cognitively essential elements for its bodily definition (arms, legs, hips). Significantly, the terms *vultus* and *os*, with which Latin culture traditionally designated the visual identity given to a person by his own face, do not appear in this passage. This matters because the two words define in various ways the uniqueness of human face and, as a consequence, a human's identity in relation with and in opposition to other animals (Cicero *On the Laws*, 1.27; Bettini, 2000: 313–356). In this sense, therefore, the marked similarity that is recognized between the monkeys and human beings is purely morphotypical and limited to the body shape, and does not guarantee these animals any privilege or special status in the entire world of living beings.

Pliny immediately gives us at the beginning of the paragraph the fundamental criterion that organized the distribution of primates in the eyes of a Roman intellectual, the presence or absence of a tail, *caudis inter se distinguntur*. Considering this criterion as important information that comes directly to us from an informant of the culture we are considering, one may essay a more precise description of the species known and named by the Romans. In the above passage Pliny mentions other zoonyms associated with other monkey species for which it is very difficult to look for a precise identikit; apart from the term *simia* he evokes three other zoonyms, in particular the *cynocephalus*, the *satyrus*, and the *callithrix*. The possibility of associating these zoonyms with descriptions that have a greater explanatory richness can come from crossing Pliny's text with other zoological reports from the Latin texts.

A particularly important source is represented by the writings of Julius Solinus, an author from the end of the third century CE who wrote an important treatise, *Collections of Curiosities*, in which mythographic traditions, geographical knowledge, and wonderful stories were intertwined in a *summa* of paradoxographical knowledge (Brodersen, 2014). In the section of the work that focuses on stories and anecdotes coming from Egypt and Africa (whose traditional name in the Greco-Roman world was *Libya*, see Belanger, 2014), Solinus confirms the criterion of the distinction of nonhuman primates on the basis of the possession or lack of the tail. Solinus' text (27.55–60), which is largely dependent on the information provided by Pliny (although the latter is never mentioned in the work; Apps, 2014), mentions six zoonyms related to different species of primates: (1) *simiae*, (2) *cercopitheci*, (3) *cynocephali*, (4) *sphinges*, (5) *satyri*, and finally (6) *callithrices*. If all the other zoonyms refer to one and only one species of monkey, the term *simia* has a wider reference spectrum because it functions both as generic zoonym for the whole group of nonhuman primates and as a more specific zoonym identifying only one variety. Generally speaking, we could say that the zoonym *simia* indicates a superordinate taxon that includes, as a hyperonymic term, all the individual species of nonhuman primates known to the Romans. In the same way, this zoonym would seem to refer specifically also to one of these species, most probably the one with a greater cultural salience than the other species. Paying attention to the texts mentioned above, it is easy to observe such a hyperonymic use of the term in the following expressions: *simiarum genera plura*, which can be translated as the "many families of monkeys", and the *plebes simiarum*, that is the "monkey populations".

A few centuries after Solinus, in the decades around 600 CE, Isidore of Seville wrote a work fundamental for the transmission of knowledge from antiquity to the medieval period, the *Etymologies*. Isidore devotes the twelfth of its 20 books entirely to the animal world (12.2.30–33; André, 1986: 114–116 for a thorough commentary on this section). Here, he reports the names of six zoonyms, confirming those already present in Pliny and Solinus, (1) *simia*, (2) *cercopithecus*, (3) *sphinga*, (4) *cynocephalus*, (5) *satyrus*, and (6) *callithrix*. It may at first appear problematic that the author also speaks of five zoonyms for the world of primates. But this apparent inconsistency can be partly explained by looking at the original text:

Horum (scil. *simiorum*) *genera quinque sunt, ex quibus cercopitheci caudas habent; simia enim cum cauda est, quam quidam cluram vocant.*
There are five kinds of apes. Of these the *cercopitheci* have tails, for it is the ape with a tail, which some people call the *clura*. (Translation by Barney, Lewis, Beach, Berghof).

How to explain this apparent inconsistency in the tradition of zoological knowledge of the educated classes? A possible explanation is that Isidore treats the term *cercopithecus* as a superordinate *taxon* with the meaning of "tailed monkeys", as opposed to the term *simia* (that is, in contrast to every monkey lacking a tail). In other words, Isidore considers the zoonym *cercopithecus* as a general and overarching taxon that comprises all the kinds of monkeys endowed with a tail. The zoonym *cercopithecus*, therefore, would include all the tailed species such as *cynocephaloi*, *satyroi*, *sphingae*, and *callithrices*.

In addition to the substantial confirmation of the zoonyms that had already been listed by Pliny and Solinus, Isidore introduces a rather rare term, which is also found in a quite isolated passage in the Latin comedy by Plautus, that is, the zoonym *clura*. Perhaps because the ancient Plautine text had not given any indication of the type of primates in question, Isidore considers *clura* to be a synonym for *cercopithecus* (Paulus-Festus 48.11 Lindsay; Plautus *Truculentus*, 269 for the *clurinum pecus*, litt. "a herd of monkeys").

Let us now turn from zoonomastic matters, that is, the linguistic labels that Latin authors could use to talk about nonhuman primates, to a more detailed investigation of the particular traits that distinguish each zoonym. This in turn will prepare the way for proposing some identifications with modern species.

We can start with the zoonym that always appears last in the lists of primates mentioned by previous sources: the *callithrix*. The name of the animal must have sounded descriptive, at least for an audience of learned people, since it was a Greek compound composed of the adjective root *kall-* and the noun *thrix* with the meaning of "nice fur". Although ancient sources do not provide many descriptions of the animal, it can be said that this primate was associated with the African sub-Saharan area, particularly the region that ancient geographers called Aethiopia (Isidorus *Etymologies*, 12.2.33; Pliny *Natural History*, 8.216; Solinus 27.60). The ancient texts, even if in a small number, recall how this species of primate rarely survived outside its original ecosystem, a very important ecological note that the ancient descriptions make only for this type of monkey. In the list of morphotypical descriptions trans-mitted, the identikit of the *callithrix* is quite distinct from those of the rest of the primates, both in terms of its anatomical features and its ethology. The two main features which allow us to isolate the *callithrix* from the rest of the primates, at least according to the scarce reports we have, are the possession of a wide tail, *lata cauda*, and the presence of hair strands around the chin and the cheeks, almost giving the illusion of a beard, *producta barba* (e.g. Pliny *Natural History*, 8.216).

Modern scholars have offered two hypotheses regarding the identity of this primate: one considers the *callithrix* to be a *Colobus guereza* of the *Cercopithecidae* family, above all because this species of primate is characterized by a wide white tail (André, 1986: 117); the other identifies the *callithrix* with the *Chlorocebus aethiops*, more commonly known as "grivet" (Masseti & Bruner, 2009: 59–63), in consideration of the fact that this species has hair around the ears and face, and inhabits the Horn of Africa. Certainly we are in no position to offer a decisive judgment about the identity of the *callithrix*. Nonetheless, we would do well to note that ancient sources focus on peculiarities of its appearance (*aspectus*) that would make it very distant from the morphotype and the chromatic and anatomical traits of the other known monkeys. For this reason, it is perhaps preferable to credit the thesis that attempts to match a *callithrix* to the *Colobus guereza*. Moreover, one can add an ecological consideration in favor of an identification with the *Colobus*, namely, that these arboreal primates feed only on tender leaves and have a low-calorie diet, which makes them rather sedentary, not very active, and constantly engaged in the search for food. The folivore diet of this primate taxon would also make it more difficult to keep in captivity. Such a consideration could well explain the ancient indication of the scarce survival of *callithrices* outside their "Aethiopian" ecosystem.

If we turn our attention to the zoonym *satyrus*, the difficulties linked to the identification and definition of the taxon are many, starting with the linguistic label that associates the zoonym with a figure coming from ancient myth, that of *Satyrs*, that is, the feral creatures linked to the Dionysian world (Lissarrague, 2013: 97–130). Very often it is not a simple homonymy, but sometimes there seems to be a possible relationship of co-reference between the two nouns when, for example, several (ancient and modern) texts have tried to naturalize the myth, by seeking in the world of animals the origins of fabulous creatures of traditional tales (Louchart, 2017: 17–53).

If Pliny's "primatological" passage describes the *satyri* as particularly ferocious monkeys which are difficult to tame, on another occasion (*Natural History*, 7.24) he provides a precise geoecological indication of their distribution by mentioning the territories of eastern India, *subsolanis Indorum montibus* (Schneider, 2004: 150–151). In the same excursus in the seventh book (dedicated to the human being), Pliny also confirms the ferocity of the *satyrus* and the difficulty that human hunters have in capturing it, given its extraordinary agility (see also Solinus 27.60). Pliny offers a telling detail about this type of monkey when he recalls how, in addition to having extraordinary speed, the *satyrus* is able to transition from quadruped to biped, running perfectly in a vertical position. Pliny's words, *iam recte currentes humana effigie*, seem to suggest that the human aspect, the human features of this primate, his *humana effigies*, derives from his ability to hold himself on two feet in the manner of a human being (see also Mela 1.48 for the *humana effigies* of the *satyri*.). In this way, therefore, its human or humanoid "identity" would derive primarily from a certain capacity for movement and displacement that it would share with humans (on the manner of walking as an element of identity, see Bettini, 2000: 319–322).

Nevertheless, Isidore's brief note (*Etymologies*, 12.2.33) about the *satyrus*' face, or more generally its aesthetically pleasing aspect (*grata facies*) is not enough for a reconstruction of this animal's morphotype. More precise information is contained in Aelian's treatise *On Animals* (16.10; 15; 21). This Latin rhetorician – who wrote his works in ancient Greek – not only states that such monkeys are part of the fauna of the central-eastern Indian area, but also explicitly claims that the name *satyroi* derives from a certain similarity with those creatures of the Greek folk heritage, the *Satyroi*, by virtue of their being extremely hairy, *lasia*, and with a tail similar to that of horses, *hippouris*. Aelian completes his identikit of such Indian monkeys by talking about their color: specifically, these monkeys have a white-grey body and a face characterized by dark colors ranging from very dark red to black (cf. Strabo *Geography*, 15.1.37; Megasthenes 715 F 21a FGrH; see also Philostorgius *Church History*, 3.11). In view of this information, one may reasonably suggest that these monkeys were some species of *Semnopithecus*, a genus of primates which would correspond very well both to the morphotypical indications provided by the sources and to their geographic information. This may be asserted even if in the past other, perhaps more seductive, hypotheses have tried to identify these monkeys with the great apes, such as the gibbon or the chimpanzee (Jennison, 1937: 21; Keller, 1909: 10; McDermott, 1938: 77).

Continuing in the list of zoonyms recorded by the Latin sources, it is possible to isolate some primates that are placed by the authors in the African area, and in particular the region of the Upper Nile. Without doubt, for a Roman public the most representative monkey of the African world in general, and the Egyptian world in particular, was the one called *cynocephalus* (Cyprian *To Demetrius*, 12). Already in the Hellenistic age, sources placed the habitat of the *cynocephali* in the region south of Egypt, in the area that the Romans called Nubia (see, e.g., Agatarchides *On the Red Sea*, 73–74 Müller). In reporting the testimony of some military explorers stationed in *Targedum*, Pliny confirms (*Natural History*, 6.184) that this Nubian area was important for the capture of these monkeys, and that this was of particular interest to the troops and border legions, who very often had to organize or facilitate commercial trades and product transfers in the northern areas and in Egypt (see Barbara, 2012 on the link between zoological knowledge and troop movements).

This Nubian area can be identified reasonably closely with present-day Sudan, and several of its populations, such as the *Nomads*, would have placed at the center of their diet the products that could be obtained from this species of nonhuman primate, such as their milk (Pliny *Natural History*, 6.190; 7.31). Through its name, this monkey is associated with the morphotype of the dog, with which it shares, in particular, the features of the snout and the tail (Aelian *On Animals*, 6.10; 7.19; 10.30). Secondly, numerous testimonies associate it with the Egyptian environment and make it an animal almost prototypical of the zoomorphism characterizing ancient Egyptian polytheism, at least in the eyes of Roman authors, with a constant association of the *cynocephalus* to the god Thoth and the cult of the goddess Isis. In this sense, the information reported above in the so-called primatological section of Pliny's work should be interpreted as referring to the *cynocephali* when the author specifies that caudate monkeys are particularly sensitive to the periods of the waning and new moon, producing real adulatory dances for every new lunar cycle (Bull, 2017). The diffusion of this kind of knowledge, related to ethological notions firmly embedded in a religious and cultic context, may also have taken place through the intercultural exchanges that some Egyptian temples had with Imperial Rome (Naas, 2002: 137–170). One need only think of the construction of the *Iseum Campense*, a center of worship where ritual traditions, including those relating to the cult of animals and, for example, the link between Thoth and the baboons, could reach a wider public in such a cosmopolitan city as Rome in the first century CE (Quack, 2003; Scheid, 2004).

The combination of these elements leads us to believe that the zoonym *cynocephalus* may indicate some species of the genus *Papio*: in particular, the olive baboon, or *Papio anubis*, and the sacred baboon, or *Papio hamadryas* (Kitchell, 2014: 42–43; Masseti et al., 2009).

According to Pliny (*Natural History*, 6.184), along the southern course of the Nile river in the direction of Napata, in the current region of Sudan, Nero's explorers spoke of a monkey named *sphingion* that could be sighted from the Nilotic island of *Articula*, which may correspond to the current Sai, between the river's second and third cataracts (Monneret de Villard, 1932). It seems that the zoonym *sphingion* may derive from the mythical *Sphinx*, since the sources also describe the animal's colorful nature and some morphological traits that give the impression of a sort of zoomorphic figure similar to the *Sphinx* (Agatharcides *On the Red Sea*, 73 Müller; Diodorus Siculus *The Library of History*, 3.35.4; Strabo *Geography*, 16.4.16; Meyboom, 1995: 227 footnote 19).

While most sources provide only cursory information about this monkey, recalling its predisposition to be tamed (Agatarchides *On the Red Sea*, 73 Müller; Solinus 27.59; Isidore *Etymologies*, 12.2.32), it is once again Pliny the Elder who conveys crucial information (*Natural History*, 8.72; 10.199). In the first passage, Pliny mentions the color of the animal's fleece using the adjective *fuscus*, while in the second he alludes to a particularly salient anatomical feature consisting in two cheek pouches designed to store food (...*condit in thesauros maxillarum cibum*). On the basis of Pliny's chromatic indication, several interpreters (Meyboom, 1995: 40 footnote 19) have identified the *sphingia* with specimens of the so-called red monkey or patas monkey (*Erythrocebus patas*), especially given the additional iconographic evidence provided by the famous Nile mosaic of Palestrina, where the plural form *sphingia* is attested and is associated with a tailed animal similar to a lion (Trinquier, 2007: 232–233). It is not possible to exclude, however, a different interpretation given a century earlier (Keller, 1909: 10), which instead associated Pliny's monkey with the "diana monkey" (*Cercopithecus diana*). This kind of interpretation is plausible when we consider the reference field to which the adjective *fuscus* could refer in

Figure 9.2 Relief with a crouching monkey and an inscription, II c. BCE – Copenhagen, Thorvaldsensmuseum, Inv. H 1477. Public Domain.

the Latin world, indicating not just a tawny red, but instead a range of dark colors (Propertius, *Elegies*, 4.6.78; Cicero *Prognostics*, fr. 4.8–9 Soubiran; André, 1949: 123–125).

On the other hand, there are several clues that could lead us to believe that the ancient world did encounter specimens of "red monkey". In reporting a work attributed to Pythagoras, who was a prefect and explorer during the reign of Ptolemy II (Diodorus Siculus *The Library of History*, 3.35.6; Strabo *Geography*, 16.4.16; Masseti et al., 2009), Aelian describes an African monkey (*On Animals*, 17.8). The monkey in question was characterized by a marked dichromy, red hair on its back and white hair on its ventral region. Perhaps because of this combination Aelian, like other authors before him, indicates it with the term *kēpos*, which in Greek means "garden". *Kēpoi* are also mentioned by Pliny when speaking about animals which appeared for the first time at the public celebrations of *ludi* offered by Pompey the Great in 55 BCE (Pliny *Natural History*, 8.70). In Pliny, as too in Solinus' text, this monkey is described as coming from the southern regions of Egypt and Libya, an area that the ancient geography of the age of Pliny, and earlier writers too, called *Aethiopia* (Solinus 30.20). Considering the shape of the face, the uniform nature of the hair, and the length of the tail, we cannot exclude from consideration the possibility that a specimen of *Patas monkey* could be identified on a second-century AD marble relief from Rome (Fig. 9.2).

Compared to the zoonyms previously considered, the last two taxa of nonhuman primates (i.e., *simia* and *cercopithecus*), seem paradoxically to have a smaller number of morphotypic or ecoethological descriptions associated with them, although they enjoyed a greater diffusion in the preserved texts of the Latin literature. Apart from a brief mention in Pliny where *cercopitheci*, coming from the "Aethiopian" region are described as having black heads and emitting different calls than other kinds of monkeys, this kind of zoonym seems to be used as a superordinate taxon. Such a name would indicate clearly all those primates endowed with a tail, as its etymology would suggest, as opposed to tailless primates, which are normally called by the etymologically less transparent term *simia* or *simius* (Solinus 27.58; Isidore's *Etymologies*, 1.2.2.31). Moreover, it is worth noting that the name *cercopithecus* does not appear in the brief "primatological" outline with which we began our survey in this chapter. In book eight Pliny does not use the word, probably because this designation was used as a sort of higher rank label, so as to include all the species of tailed monkey that Pliny (*Natural History*, 8.216) would mention one by one in the course of digression (*satyrus, cynocephalus, callithrix, sphingion*). On the other hand, the only possible species that the zoonym *simia* could refer to is the *Macaca sylvanus*, that is, the Barbary macaque, which is the only nonhuman primate without a tail in the Mediterranean area (Greenlaw, 2011).

9.3   Interactions between Primates: Relations, Places, and Imagery

Although the limits represented by temporal distance and the scarcity of information do not allow a truly anthropological investigation of the relationship between humans and monkeys in the Roman world in the perspective of a relational primatology (Leblan, 2017: 29–36), some considerations can still be advanced from the standpoint of historical anthropozoology, here having as its objective the reconstruction of the place of nonhuman primates in the cultural encyclopedia of the ancient Roman world (Franco, 2014: 178–184): a role of primary importance is played by the study of relational practices (conflict, cooperation, synanthropy, etc.) that the Roman world chose to negotiate with monkeys. It is precisely the taking into account of such interspecific interactions, whether in urban, domestic, or wild and exotic contexts, that can provide some affordance for more complex symbolic elaborations, such as those found in the literary texts that constitute our primary sources for Greco-Roman antiquity.

A first consideration is ecological and concerns the condition of captivity in which individual specimens of monkeys were transported and placed in anthropized environments as a result of hunting and trade practices that occurred far from Rome, mainly on the coast of North Africa (Ptolemy VIII 234 F 8 FGrH). This foreign animal, coming from another region of the Mediterranean and the object of a real and expensive trade, is described for the first time in a fragment of the Latin poet Ennius (III-II s. BCE). In his *Satires* discussing the nature of human beings, Ennius introduces a comparison with the nature of the monkey (Ennius *Satires*, 69 V^2; cf. Puelma Piwonka, 1949: 189 for a commentary):

> Simia quam similis turpissuma bestia nobis
>
> [How like us is that ugly brute, the ape!]. (Translation by H. Rackham).

The Latin in this brief hexameter neatly encapsulates the essential coordinates for understanding the cultural representation that part of the Roman world could have of the *simia*. First of all, it highlights the paretymological link between the zoonym *simia* and the Latin adjective *similis*, "resembling", and then the neutral term *bestia*, which indicates a living being, is characterized negatively by the adjective *turpis*, which has a broad semantic spectrum whose meanings unravel from "lower" to "awful". Though its nature is not specified, the link surely includes physical appearance, but also may involve nature and character (Cossarini, 1983; Traina, 1984). Finally, there is the preferential link between human nature and that of the monkeys. Anthropozoological research aims to reconstruct, first of all, the ecological conditions of the interspecific relationship. For the ancient Roman world the operation is very complex because the privileged access routes to this culture are mainly literary, and are therefore conceived and built through multiple interpretative filters, from the author's intention to the logic of the literary genre, passing through the representations and cultural expectations in which each text is inserted and in respect of which it constructs deviations of meaning.

Written around the time of Ennius, the Latin comedy *Miles gloriosus* by Plautus is played out in the enclosed space of two houses. The first is inhabited by a swaggering soldier called Pyrgoplynices who lives with Philocomasium, a girl, and his servant Sceledrus, while the second one is inhabited by the old Periplectomenus, who hosts the young Pleusicles (Plautus *Miles Gloriosus*, 162–179). A monkey, which will never appear on the stage, is the real driving force of the entire plot, because it is by chasing the *simia* onto the roof of the neighbor's house that Sceledrus will be able to look inside the backyard (the *impluvium*) and discover the secret love affair between the slave girl and Pleusicles (*quod ille gallinam aut columbam se sectari aut simiam / dicat*) – a scene constantly evoked during the drama as one of great importance (Cleary, 1972; Connors, 2004). When asked by Palaestrio, a former slave of Pleusicles, about what he had seen when he looked in the courtyard of the house, Sceledrus prefers not to answer, contenting himself with saying that the only thing that worried him was the capture of the house monkey, *simia nostra*. The expression *simia nostra* clearly indicates, at least in the communicative intentions of the slave, that the animal was part of the patrimony of the braggart soldier, and, if we can believe it, as a domestic animal. Furthermore, considering the narrative structure and dramatic aspects of the *pièce* that characterize the mercenary soldier as a boaster, it cannot be excluded that the monkey represents the exotic and extravagant companion animal of a soldier who tells of amazing conquests in distant and unknown lands. One of the most interesting narrative elements of the first scenes of the play consists in the progressive identification that seems to be drawn between the slave Sceledrus and the domesticated monkey. According to Palaestrio (Plautus *Miles gloriosus*, 285), only Sceledrus could have run after a monkey, only he could have been the worthy hunter of it, since only someone who is worth nothing, *homo nihili*, like a domestic slave, could have hoped to get his hands on an animal so worthless as well as harmful to others, *nequam bestia*. The *fil rouge* that in the first part of the play unites the slave and the monkey on the basis of their similarity of nature is also explicitly expressed by the elderly Periplectomenus (Plautus *Miles gloriosus*, 505 ff.). While blaming the slave for causing him economic damage by destroying part of the roof in running after the monkey, the old man considers the monkey a worthy prey for the slave (*ibi dum condignam te sectaris simiam*), most likely alluding to the harmful and dangerous character that they could both have towards their master, on whom they depended but whom were ready to betray, perhaps by fleeing, at any time.

For what reasons would Roman culture associate the figure of a domestic slave with that of a monkey? Let us look more closely at the comedy. A possible answer may lie in the nature of the relationship that ancient Romans imagined existing between a free man – a *paterfamilias* or simply a *dominus* – and living beings of a subordinate position, without freedom or independent agency. This inferiority, though, both concerning the legal status of the slave and his prestige in the society, could have triggered in the master a great number of suspicions and concerns. From the master's point of view the slave embodied the constant risk of betrayal ready to emerge at the first opportunity. Several studies have shown that one of the most important traits characterizing slaves in ancient Roman comedy is the lack of *fides*, or the risk of its loss: slaves are normally unfair, *perfidi*, with no obligation of loyalty simply because they are not deemed able to enter the relationship of mutual benefit that is only valid for free people (Plautus *Pseudolus*, 125–128; *Asinaria*, 561–562; for *perfidia* see Freyburger 1977; cf. Raccanelli, 1998: 155–160). In this sense it would not be unreasonable to look at the monkey as the animal counterpart of the slave in the imagery of the ancient *palliatae*, where monkeys can be thought of as runaways or disloyal animals, always ready to betray the owner.

This hypothesis receives clear confirmation from another comedy by Plautus, the well-known *Pseudolus*, where a slave (here, a minor character) is known as the "Monkey", Simia. Despite the secondary role that the slave Simia plays in the comedy, one of the fundamental scenes consists in the deception that he weaves to the harm of a fishmonger, Ballion, by pretending to be another person (Connors, 2004: 190; McDermott, 1938: 152). The name Simia might well depend on his ability to deceive. Furthermore, the lack of trust he inspires could also be among the associations triggered by such a telling name. It does not sound like a coincidence that Pseudolus tries to flatter Simia, in order to convince him to play the role of the trickster, with the following words (Plautus *Pseudolus*, 944):

Pseud. *Vt ego ob tuam, Simia, perfidiam te amo et metuo et magni facio.*
   [as I love you for your perfidy, Simia, and respect and honor you"] (Translation by de Melo, 2012)

Simia is such a malicious slave that he deserves admiration even from Pseudolus, the prototype of the *servus callidus*.

In another play by Plautus, the exotic setting, the interspecific relationship of cohabitation with humans, and the risk of the animal's sudden turnaround are at the center of a recognition scene (*agnitio*). In *Poenulus* ("The Little Punic"), a young boy, Agorastocles, is recognized by his uncle Hanno on account of the scar from a monkey bite that he had received as a child while playing with the animal (*ludenti puero*) in his rich father's house in Carthage, before being kidnapped by pirates (Plautus *Poenulus*,1074; Maurach, 1988).

While the episode certainly stages a parodic comparison to the epic model of heroic recognition in Ulysses' wound from the wild boar (cf. Homer *Odyssey*, 19.382–466), it could also hint at important aspects of the animal–human relationship: in particular, the role that monkeys could play as animal partners of (rich) Roman children. Here, too, the threat of violence and insubordination seems to appear as the dark side of a relationship that is ambiguously characterized by the ancient Roman texts examined above. Plautus is not the only ancient author to mention the risk of being bitten by a *simia*; somehow conflicting and potentially dangerous relationships seem to be the background of some medical prescriptions. Discussing the remedies of traditional Roman medicine, Quintus Serenus Sammonicus (second/third century CE) lists some preparations provided by the ancient pharmacopoeia to treat the bite of the monkey (*Liber medicinalis*, 819–823 Vollmer; on monkeys used for public medical shows in Rome, see Vespa, 2017).

Already some centuries before, under the emperor Tiberius, Cornelius Celsus, in his books on medicine (*De medicina*) indicated the possibility of being bitten by human beings or monkeys, although this was certainly less likely than the possibility of being bitten by a dog (*On Medicine*, 5, 27, 1a). In the presentation of the species that could be dangerous for the bite they could inflict, the reader's attention is struck by the fact that the monkeys are not included in the group of wild and ferocious animals, the *fera* (cf. Seneca, *On Anger*, 2.31, as for the *fera animalia*). Although in Western society today nonhuman primates are routinely viewed as exotic and potentially dangerous animals, the situation was not that simple in ancient Rome (Bodson, 1998). According to Celsus, monkeys seem to have a particular status, inasmuch as they are not listed among the *fera*, a term that normally indicates wild animals, which very often come from abroad (Africa or India), and which could be (even if they were not always) characterized by murderous savagery (cf. Isidore *Differences*, 1.248, on the distinction between *bestiae* and *ferae*). On the one hand, nonhuman primates could not be considered entirely as wild animals: the objects of intense trade between the African coasts and Italy, they could share anthropic spaces under the domus of wealthy Roman citizens (Ptolemy VIII 234F 8 FrGrHist, *apud* Athen. 518 E-F). On the other hand, as we have seen, monkeys could always call their submission to human beings into question by running away or by biting the human master. After all, Solinus (27.59) talked about *sphingia* as the only monkey species that was easy to tame, since it was the only one that could forget its original wildness (*dociles ad feritatis oblivionem*). The logical referent of the statement is the highly complex practice of monkey domestication, which was difficult to achieve in a complete manner, especially in ecological conditions such as those in which the human–monkey relationship in Rome was articulated, where the animals were often isolated and in captivity, came from far-away places, and were only rarely born in captivity in the anthropic space where they would live (Fuentes, 2007). The conditions of the interspecific relationship between humans and monkeys in the Roman world cannot, however, be limited to a simple "domestic" – "wild" dichotomy, which is also problematic with regard to ancient legal distinctions in respect of other nonhuman animals (Onida, 2012: 137–154).

As Pliny reminds us in a passage already discussed (*Natural History*, 8.216), it could happen that monkeys gave birth to their offspring within a domestic framework (*intra domos peperere*), where humans and *simiae* could live together in the same environment. Discussing the parental care that these animals could give through caresses and attention to their offspring, for example cradling and carrying around their progeny in a Roman *domus*, Pliny calls them *mansuefactae*, an interesting term that could shed some light on the interspecific relation ancient Romans could conceive having with monkeys.

While the term *mansuefactus* is often translated and conceived as if it indicates a condition of domesticity, the composition of its parts allows us to reconstruct a more articulated meaning. The adjective form corresponds to a participle of the verb *mansuefacio* which is composed of the verb *facere* – "to make" – and of an adverb coming from the adjective *mansues*. And, *mansues* is itself fabricated from the noun *manus* – the "hand" – and another verb, *suesco* – "to get accustomed" (Bodson, 2000; Ernout-Meillet, 1979: 384; Oniga, 2014: 166–167). As an ancient Latin lexicographer clearly shows, an animal referred to as *mansuetus* or *mansuefactus* had undertaken a critical process of dealing with a human being, through which it would lose a defined set of habits and learn other ones; a *mansues* was a living being able to get close to the hands of a human as the result of a partial change in its nature (Paulus-Festus s.v. *mansuetum*, p. 117 L.).

It is perhaps not by chance that Pliny (*Natural History*, 8.217–218) chose to talk about monkeys just before another animal species that presents some similar traits in relating with humans, the hare – *lepus*. After having described the most important characteristics of hares, such as fecundity, Pliny adds that it is difficult to define them when it comes to their domesticity: although they cannot be referred to as wild animals (*cum feri dici iure non possint*), still it is very hard to make them *mansuetes* (*hi mansuescunt raro*). According to Pliny (*Natural History*, 8.220), there would be a huge number of animals that, like the hare, possess a double nature, being neither a completely friendly nor a wild animal vis-à-vis the human being (*nec placida nec fera, sed mediae inter utrumque naturae*). No immediate, somehow mechanical link exists, of course, between the wild and feral condition of certain species, their being tamed and inserted in Roman anthropic environments, and their possibly being regarded as malevolent or unreliable. The cases of elephants and camels, whose condition as wild and exotic species (see Digest, 9.2.2.2, Gaius 7 *ad edictum provinciale*) in human Roman environments is very similar to that of the monkey, do not seem to have given rise to representations of treacherous wickedness. In contrast, elaborations of this kind are generated by Roman culture for the dog, an animal nonetheless considered completely domestic (Tutrone, 2019).

The cultural representations that make the monkey a treacherous, malicious, and rarely trustworthy animal find a fertile background in the peculiar ecological conditions of their interspecific relationship with humans. Monkeys represent one of the few species of wild and potentially aggressive or dangerous animals (e.g. Seneca *On Anger*, 2.31.5; Cassius Dio 78.7.2) that were introduced into anthropic environments, and shared spaces of social life with humans. As attested by the treatise on the interpretation of dreams by Artemidorus Daldianus (2.12; Monbrun, 2015), a Greek author of the Roman age (second century CE), monkeys could be considered wild animals (*agria*) coming from distant lands, such as African forests or Indian mountains. Unlike other wild and dangerous animals, however, some monkeys could find themselves living together with humans in totally anthropized places of Roman cities, as archaeological sources seem to confirm, even if on the basis of limited data. In the excavations of Pompeii, the bones of a juvenile monkey were found: a Barbary macaque (*Macaca sylvanus*). Strikingly, the skeleton was found in the Sarno baths, a public thermal construction made up of four floors; although the context of the discovery is not clear, it is likely that the monkey's skeletal remains were found not too far from the human ones, and probably come from the period of the volcanic eruption in 79 CE (King, 2002: 433–434; Bailey et al., 1999). Not only frequenting thermal baths, but also attending banquets and symposia in the houses of rich Romans could provide an opportunity to admire and interact with monkeys, as a rarely cited passage by Pliny suggests (*Natural History*, 23.44). In a section dedicated to the therapeutic and zootechnical uses of wine, he reports the opinion of anonymous experts that monkeys should not be given pure wine, because this would compromise the process of their growth. Already Aristotle had declared in a fragment of his lost work *On Drunkenness* that one of the infallible techniques for trapping monkeys was to offer them wine (fr. 107 Rose). Such anecdotes may have originated from the participation of tamed primates in occasions of human conviviality, such as banquets or shows in the *domus* of wealthy patricians. In such circumstances, the practice of administering wine or other food from the banquet to animals that were allowed to take part, even if from a different position than the diners, seems at least conceivable. Some iconographic evidence seems to refer to this privileged relationship between wine and monkeys: notably, a lamp from the Roman period in which a tailed monkey is preparing to pick bunches of grapes from a lush vine.

Figure 9.3 Vessberg Type 10, Roman mold-made lamp, first century. BCE Monkey at left facing right reaching up to grapes hanging from a tall vine to right – New York, Metropolitan Museum, 74.51.1915. Public Domain.

By virtue of their *mansuetudo*, monkeys, just like the most appreciated among the pet animals in Roman antiquity (dogs and horses), could earn highly regarded honors. This was the case in the western part of *Gallia*, not far from the ancient city of *Lemonum* (close to modern-day Poitiers). Here a monkey belonging to the *Cercopithecidae* was buried in a necropolis that probably belonged to a rich family of the Gallo-Roman élite and that dates to the end of the third century CE (Gerber and Baudry-Dautry, 2012). And this case is not unique: a Barbary macaque was discovered to have been interred in another grave, in a Gallo-Roman necropolis near Cutry that dates back to the end of the second century CE (Liéger et al., 1997). In the Gallo-Roman cultural context of the imperial age, moreover, the presence of nonhuman primates, mainly macaques, is also confirmed by the production of a few vases modeled in the shape of a monkey where these animals wear the typical leather travel cloak with overhanging cap, the *bardocucullus*, produced in Gaul and then exported (Martial, *Epigrams*, 1.53.4-5; 14. 128.1). A somewhat controversial epigram written by Martial (*Epigrams*, 14.128. 2) even seems to allude to the possibility that this kind of cloak could be made of monkey fur (Salanitro, 1992).

A very important vector for the circulation of exotic animals, and in particular for the diffusion of some specimens of monkeys in captivity, is represented by the movements of the armies in the most peripheral territories of the Empire (Hornig,

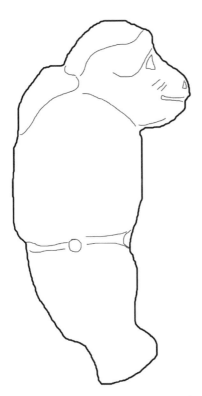

Figure 9.4 Saint-Pourçain-sur-Besbre (Allier), now at the Musée Archéologique National, France. Illustration by A. Pace.

Figure 9.5 Ancient Roman city of *Iulia Libica*, macaque's skeleton, LL LC 01, UE 74 – Fossa del Mono. Archaeological Museum of Llivia, photograph by Oriol Mercadal.

2000). The late antique burial of a sub-adult macaque at the settlement of *Iulia Libyca*, the site of a Roman military garrison near the Pyrenees, must surely be framed in such a military context. The individual was buried with a minimal set of objects, consisting of fragments of the fabric typical of a military tunic, a belt, and a chain, which would suggest a link with the world of legionary soldiers, although it remains difficult to establish whether the animal was a luxury companion of a high general or instead one of the animals taking a part in the animal shows that were organized in the camps (Olesti et al., 2013).

From Greco-Roman sources (e.g. Philo of Alexandria *On Animals*, 23; 90; Lucian *The Fisherman*, 36; cf. Martial *Epigrams*, 14.202), we know that the staging of street circus shows often included plays with monkeys (on the mimetic nature of monkey exploited for shows, see Vespa and Zucker, 2020). An iconographic motif on some lamps from the Roman era clearly shows a performer during a period of rest, surrounded by his fellow animals, including a leashed monkey.

A similar iconographic testimony also comes from Pompeii and dates back to the middle of the first century CE. In the sumptuous house of the Dioscuri in *Regio* VI of Pompeii, a painting, now completely destroyed, depicted a young man dressed in a green chlamys who held by a leash a monkey in a bipedal position, dressed in a white cape (Richardson, 1955: 61). From what we can reconstruct from drawings done immediately after the excavations in the nineteenth century, the young man appears to be using a whip to spur the animal to march on both feet (Fig. 9.7).

This was also the case in military camps, where the organization of entertainment spectacles was an integral part of the soldiers' life (Libanius *Orations*, 46.14). After all, the massive introduction of exotic specimens, including primates, for urban contests in the city of Rome dates from the first century BCE, in a context of military triumph during the games instituted by Pompey the Great during his second consulate in

Figure 9.6 Roman mold-made pottery lamp, first century CE discovered in Sernhac (Gard). The discus is decorated with an emaciated entertainer seated with his props: a monkey, a cat or a dog climbing a ladder and two juggling rings – Nîmes, Centre de Documentation Archéologique, photograph by Yves Manniez.

Figure 9.7 Watercolor drawing by G. Marsigli (1828) after a wall painting located in the peristyle of the Pompeian house 'La casa dei Dioscuri' (VI, 9, 6) – Napoli, Museo Archeologico Nazionale, Archivio dei Disegni, Inv. 00572859. Public Domain.

55 BCE (cf. Pliny the Elder, *Natural History*, 8.70). Although the references are few, it seems very likely that at some point in these games, tamed and trained monkeys could be put on show for the Roman audience, either as skilled jugglers and acrobats (cf. Martial *Epigrams*, 14.202) or as jockeys of large dogs, as is suggested by some bone or ivory handles of Italian production found in specimens in Gaul at Morienval (Oise).

Figure 9.8 Handle of ivory knife dating back to the Roman Imperial Age and found at Carrière-du-Roi, Morienval (Oise), now on display at the National Archaeological Museum, France. Illustration by A. Pace.

While testimonies at our disposal are quite limited, archaeozoological studies at the least do not invalidate the presence of nonhuman primates in human contexts, such as houses or other public spaces in the city. Moreover, the cultural plausibility of human–monkey interactions in the households of the Roman élite is consistent with some written sources of the Roman imperial period. In particular, a kind of horror story seems to have circulated in ancient Rome, at least from the time of the emperor Claudius onward: according to the testimony of Phlegon of Tralles (*Mir.*, 22), a handmaiden of Marcus Raecius Taurus' wife gave birth to a monkey, which resulted in a great scandal offending public decency, above all for the reputation of Raecius Taurus, a *vir praetorius* (*PIR*[2] R 11).

As unlikely as it seems, this kind of tale was not that strange in Greco-Roman antiquity when we consider certain traditions concerning the so-called maternal impression, which applies to women being affected by intense experiences, such as the sight of a statue or an animal, during intercourse. The intense perceptual experience of the woman would affect somatic traits of the unborn child (Bettini, 1992: 167–178; Deonna, 1965). The very act of gazing at an object or a living being could result in the transmission of certain of the object's visible traits to the foetus, as happened to some women who gave birth to simian babies, according to the sober account by the physician Soranus (*Gynaecology*, 1.12.101–104, Burguière, Gourevitch, Malinas) in the second century CE. Exactly the same kind of situation is described by Isidore (*Etymologies*, 12.1.60) a few centuries later, confirming the likelihood of encounters between nonhuman primates and women, probably in the environs of élite Roman families.

Moreover, it is important to note that sexual intercourse with animals on the part of women could be the subject of erotic popular mimes, a kind of street performance, where real animals could play the role of actors and become the key characters of amusing sketches. The witnessing of such scenes, when combined with bizarre fancies of Roman male citizens concerning their wives' behavior when alone, could certainly make pertinent the depiction of bestialities on those common, widespread objects, that were the ancient lamps (Franco, 2017: 46–53). Along with donkeys and horses, which are also mentioned as erotic partners in ancient tales (Iuvenal *Satires*,

Figure 9.9 Roman Mould-made pottery lamp, second to third century, CE The discus has an air-hole pierced near the edge, and is decorated with a woman in intercourse with a monkey – London, British Museum, 1814,0704.53. © The Trustees of the British Museum.

6.629–634; Apuleius *Metamorphoses*, 10.20–21), the most widely represented animals in the bestiality scenes depicted on the lamps are undoubtedly monkeys. In the British Museum's collection of ancient Roman lamps coming from Italy during the second century CE, for example, all the lamps displaying bestiality depict tailed monkeys in the act of penetrating a woman (Fig. 9.9). Furthermore, in three cases the animals are leashed, a detail perhaps hinting at their having been at least somewhat tamed (Bailey, 1980: 70–71; 353–354; 370–371).

9.4 Conclusion

Following our brief excursus on the testimonies that the ancient Roman world has left of human interactions with nonhuman primates, let us turn to one of the most famous and authoritative stories about monkeys in all Latin literature. This is a mythical tale contained in the epic poem of the *Metamorphoses* written by the Latin poet Ovid at the beginning of the first century CE. In retelling a traditional story dating back at least to archaic Greece, that of the punishment of the Kerkopes, who were brigands and impostors, Ovid shapes it in ways that appear to reflect contemporary Roman discourse on primates (on this myth see Vespa, 2021). He tells us (Ovid *Metamorphoses*, 14.90–100) that it was Jupiter, the father of the gods, who transformed the Kerkopes into monkeys, that is, misshapen humans (*in deforme viros animal mutavit*), following their attempt to deceive him. Jupiter then relegated them to punishment far from the rest of humanity, on some islands (above all, Ischia) which from that moment on would be inhabited by monkeys. It was precisely those same places that under the name of Inarime were at the centre of the debate among scholars by which this chapter was introduced. The two pertinent traits that have been the common thread of our discussion – on the one hand, the morphotypal similarity between monkeys and humans, and on the other, the perfidious and devious character attributed to monkeys – find a synthesis in the punishment decided by the father of the gods. The Kerkopes, devious bandits, are transformed into those animals whose very physical appearance, similar to yet different from that of humans, manifests their moral ambiguity (*dissimiles homini possent similesque videri*). Thus in the Roman cultural tradition, many centuries before Buffon or Darwin, we find a link posited between simians and humans, but one in which the direction of descent was reversed. Effected by supernatural rather than natural selection, this transformation diminished their outward appearance to match inner disposition, producing a hideous harmony that could only have thwarted any further effort to make monkeys of others.

Acknowledgments

I am indebted to Caroline Belanger and Jean Trinquier for their valuable comments and help on previous drafts of this paper. It is my pleasure to thank Kenneth Gouwens, who revised the English version of this text for the final publication. Many thanks are due to Alessandro Pace for helping me with the drawings of the pictures.

References

Apps, A. (2014). Source citation and authority in Solinus. In K. Brodersen, ed., *Solinus. New Studies*. Heidelberg: Antike Verlag, 32–42.

Bailey, J. F., Henneberg, M., Colson, I. B., et al. (1999). Monkey business in Pompeii. Unique find of a juvenile Barbary macaque skeleton in Pompeii identified using osteology and ancient DNA techniques. *Molecular Biology and Evolution*, **16**, 1410–1414

Barbara, S. (2012). Armées en marche et découvertes herpétologiques dans l'Antiquité. *Anthropozoologica*, **47**(1), 15–49.

Belanger, C. (2014). Solinus' Macrobians: A Roman literary account of the Axumite Empire. In K. Brodersen, ed., *Solinus. New Studies*. Heidelberg: Antike Verlag, 96–118.

Bettini, M. (1992). *Il ritratto dell'amante*. Torino: Einaudi.

Bettini, M. (2000). *Le orecchie di Hermes*. Torino: Einaudi.

Bodson, L. (1998). Ancient Greek views on the exotic animal. *Arctos*, **32**, 61–85.

Bodson, L. (2000). Motivations for pet-keeping in ancient Greece and Rome: A preliminary survey. In A. L. Podberscek, E. S. Paul, & J. A. Serpell, eds., *Companion Animals and Us: Exploring the Relationship between People and Pets*. Cambridge: Cambridge University Press, 27–41.

Brodersen, K. (ed.) (2014) *Solinus. New Studies*. Heidelberg: Antike Verlag.

Bull, C. H. (2017). Monkey business. Magic vowels and cosmic levels in the *Discourse on the Eight and Ninth* (NHC VI, 6). *Studi e materiali di storia delle religioni*, **83**, 75–94.

Cleary, V. J. (1972). *Se sectari simiam*: Monkey Business in the Miles Gloriosus. *The Classical Journal*, **67** (4), 209–305.

Connors, C. (2004). Monkey business: Imitation, authenticity, and identity from Pithekoussai to Plautus. *Classical Antiquity*, **23** (2), 179–207.

Deonna, W. (1965). *Le symbolisme de l'œil*. Paris: de Boccard.

Franco, C. (2014). *Shameless. The Canine and the Feminine in Ancient Greece*. Oakland: University of California Press.

Franco, C. (2017). Greek and Latin words for human–animal bonds: Metaphors and taboos. In T. Foegen, & E. Thomas, eds., *Interactions between Animals and Humans in Graeco-Roman Antiquity*. Berlin-Boston: De Gruyter, 39–60.

Fuentes, A. (2007). Monkey and human interconnections: The wild, the captive, and the in-between. In R. Cassidy, & M. Mullin, eds., *Where the Wild Things Are Now: Domestication Reconsidered*. Oxford: Berg.

Gerber, F., & Baudry-Dautry, A. (2012). La mode de l'animal exotique dans la haute société gallo-romaine. Sépolture d'un singe dans la nécropole de la rue des Caillons à Poitiers. *Archéopages*, **35**, 42–47.

Gras, M. (1994). Pithécusses : de l'étymologie à l'histoire. *Annali di Archeologia e Storia Antica, n.s.* **1**, 127–131.

Greenlaw, C. (2011). *The Represenation of Monkeys in the Art and Thought of Mediterranean Cultures. A New Perspective on Ancient Primates*. Oxford: BAR Publishing.

Hornig, K. (2000). Großtiertransporte nach und innerhalb Europas in der Antike – methodische Probleme, Fallbeispiele und kulturelle Rezeption. In H.von Schmettow, ed., *Schutz des Kulturerbes unter Wasser: Veränderungen europäischer Lebenskultur durch Fluß- und Seehandel: Beiträge zum Internationalen Kongreß für Unterwasserarchäologie (IKUWA '99), 18.-21.* Lübstorf: Archäologisches Landesmuseum Mecklenburg-Vorpommern, 177–185

Jennison, G. (1937). *Animals for Show and Pleasure in Ancient Rome*. Manchester: Manchester University Press.

Keller, O. (1909). *Die Antike Tierwelt*. Vol. I. Leipzig: Engelmann.

King, A. (2002). Mammals. Evidence from wall paintings, sculpture, mosaics, faunal remains, and ancient literary sources. In J. W. Feemster, & F. G. Meyer, eds., *The Natural History of Pompeii*. Cambridge: Cambridge University Press, 401–450.

Leblan, V. (2017). *Aux frontières du singe. Relations entre hommes et chimpanzés au Kakandé, Guinée (XIXᵉ-XXIᵉ siècle)*. Paris: Éditions EHESS.

Lissarrague, F. (2013). *La cité des satyres. Une anthropologie ludique*. Paris: Éditions EHESS.

Louchart, F. (2017). *Que faire de l'orang-outan ? Reconstruire la nature à Nyaru Menteng (Indonésie)*. Paris: L'Harmattan.

Masseti, M., & Bruner, E. (2009). The primates of the western Palaearctic: A biogeographical, historical, and archaeozoological review. *Journal of Anthropological Science*, **87**, 33-91.

Maurach, G. (1988). *Der Poenulus des Plautus*. Heidelberg: Carl Winter Verlag.

McDermott, W. C. (1938). *The Ape in Antiquity*. Baltimore: John Hopkins University Press.

Meyboom, P. G. P. (1995). *The Nile Mosaic of Palestrina. Early Evidence of Egyptian Religion in Italy*. Leiden, Brill.

Monbrun, Ph. (2015). Quand on rêve d'animaux: place de l'animal et bestiaire du rêve dans les *Oneirokritika* d'Artémidore. In G. Weber, ed., *Artemidor von Daldis und die Antike Traumdeutung. Texte, Kontexte, Lektüren*. Berlin-Boston: De Gruyter, 127–160.

Monneret de Villard, U. (1932). Note Nubiane. *Aegyptus*, **12** (4), 305–316.

Naas, V. (2002). *Le projet encyclopédique de Pline l'Ancien*. Roma: École française de Rome.

Olesti, O., Guàrdia, J., Maragall, M., et al. (2013). Controlling the Pyrenees: A macaque's burial from Late Antique *Iulia Libica* (Llívia, La Cerdanya, Spain). In A. Sarantis & N. Christie, eds., *War and Warfare in Late Antiquity*. Leiden: Brill, 703–731.

Onida, P. P. (2012). *Studi sulla condizione degli animali non umani nel sistema giuridico romano*. 2nd ed. Torino: G. Giappichelli.

Oniga, R. (2014). *Latin. A Linguistic Introduction*. Oxford: Oxford University Press.

Poccetti, P. (1995). Sui nomi antichi dell'isola di Ischia: una traccia di remoti contatti tra vicino Oriente e Italia, *Incontri linguistici*, **18**, 79–103.

Polara, G., & De Vivo, A. (2011). Aenaria – Pithecusa – Inarime. *Bollettino di Studi Latini*, **41** (2), 495–521.

Quack, J. F. (2003). Zum ägyptischen Ritual im Iseum Campense in Rom. In C. Metzner-Nebelsick, ed., *Rituale in der Vorgeschichte, Antike und Gegenwart: Studien zur Vorderasiatischen, Prähistorischen und Klassischen Archäologie, Ägyptologie, Alten Geschichte, Theologie und Religionswissenschaft*. Rahden: Leidorf, 57–66.

Richardson, L. (1955). *Pompeii: The Casa dei Dioscuri and its Painters. Memoirs of the American Academy in Rome* vol. XXIII. Rome: American Academy in Rome.

Salanitro, M. (1992). Il bardocucullo e i cuculli liburnici. Mart. XIV 128 e 140 (139). *Atene e Roma*, **37** (1), 10–15.

Scheid, J. (2004). Quand fut construit l'Iseum Campense? In L. C. Ruscu, ed., *Orbis antiquus: studia in honorem Ioannis Pisonis*. Cluj-Napoca: Nereamia Napocae, 308–311.

Schneider, P. (2004). *L'Éthiopie et l'Inde. Interférences et confusions aux extrémités du monde antique (VIIIe siècle avant J.-C. – VIe siècle après J.-C.)*. Rome: École française de Rome.

Traina, A. (1984). *Belva* e *bestia* come metafora di 'uomo'. *Rivista di Filologia e Istruzione Classica*, **112**, 115–119.

Trinquier, J. (2007). L'Éthiopie vue de Grèce et de Rome aux époques hellénistique et romaine. In *Pharaons noirs. Sur la Piste des Quarante Jours*. Mariemont: Musée Royal de Mariemont, 217–244.

Tutrone, F. (2019). Barking at the threshold. Cicero, Lucretius, and the ambiguous status of dogs in Roman culture. In T. Schmidt, & J. Pahlitzsch, eds., *Impious Dogs, Haughty Foxes and Exquisite Fish*. Berlin-Boston: de Gruyter, 73–102.

Vespa, M. (2017). Why avoid a monkey: The refusal of interaction in Galen's *epideixis*. In T. Fögen, & E. Thomas, eds., *Interactions between Animals and Humans in Graeco-Roman Antiquity*. Berlin: de Gruyter, 409–434.

Vespa, M. (2021). *Geloion mimēma. Studi sulla rappresentazione culturale della scimmia nei testi greci e greco-romani*. Turnhout: Brepols.

Vespa, M., & Zucker, A. (2020). Imiter ou communiquer : l'intention du singe dans la littérature gréco-romaine. *Mètis. Anthropologie des mondes grecs anciens*, **18**, 233–250.

10 Minoan Monkeys

Re-examining the Archaeoprimatological Evidence

Bernardo Urbani & Dionisios Youlatos

Μινωικοί πίθηκοι: Επανεξέταση των Αρχαιοπρωτευοντολογικών στοιχείων

Περίληψη

Το παρόν κεφάλαιο παρέχει μια λεπτομερή ανασκόπηση του διαθέσιμου υλικού σχετικά με την αναπαράσταση πρωτευόντων και του περιβάλλοντός τους στον Μινωικό κόσμο. Πιο συγκεκριμένα, αναλύσαμε τις απεικονίσεις πρωτευόντων σε δύο τοιχογραφίες από την Κνωσό της Κρήτης και τέσσερις τοιχογραφίες από το Ακρωτήρι της Θήρας. Επιπλέον, μελετήσαμε αναπαραστάσεις πρωτευόντων σε μεταφερόμενα αντικείμενα από την Κρήτη. Το υλικό αποτελείτο από δύο ειδώλια, δύο περίαπτα, δύο κοσμήματα, δώδεκα σφραγίδες με πρωτευοντόμορφες λαβές και δεκαεπτά σφραγίδες με πρωτευοντόμορφες επιφάνειες. Σε όλα αυτά τα αντικείμενα, εντοπίσαμε δύο είδη πιθήκων, τους κερκοπίθηκους (*Chlorocebus* spp.) και τους μπαμπουίνους (*Papio* spp.). Οι αναλύσεις μας συμφωνούν με προηγούμενες αναφορές και υποστηρίζουν τους ισχυρισμούς ότι (α) υπήρξε εκτεταμένη πολιτιστική ανταλλαγή μεταξύ Μινωιτών και Αιγυπτίων, (β) οι Μινωίτες υπήρξαν είτε άμεσοι παρατηρητές πρωτευόντων σε αιχμαλωσία είτε ήταν ζωγράφοι λεπτομερών αφηγήσεων, (γ) μερικοί πίθηκοι (κερκοπίθηκοι) σχετίζονται με τον ελεύθερο χρόνο, αλλά σε ένα φυσιοκρατικό πλαίσιο, ενώ μερικοί άλλοι (μπαμπουίνοι, οι οποίο είχαν ήδη θεοποιηθεί στην Αίγυπτο) ενεργούν ως διαμεσολαβητές μεταξύ θεών και ανθρώπων σε τελετουργικά πλαίσια, (δ) τα πρωτεύοντα φτάνουν ως εικόνες στους Μινωίτες σε δύο διαφορετικές περιόδους και (ε) η αναπαράσταση των πρωτευόντων μεταξύ των Μινωιτών είναι ένα παράδειγμα της αρχαιότερης μετάδοσης «εξωτικών» στην Ευρώπη.

Λέξεις κλειδιά

Αίγυπτος – Ακρωτήρι – αρχαιοπρωτευοντολογία – κερκοπίθηκοι – Κνωσός μπαμπουίνοι – *Chlorocebus* spp. – *Papio* spp.

Abstract

The present chapter provides a detailed review of the available material evidence concerning the representation of primates and their context in the Minoan civilization. More specifically, we analyzed the depictions of primates in two frescos from Knossos, Crete, and four frescos from Akrotiri, Thera/Santorini. Furthermore, we studied primate representations in portable objects from Crete. The material consisted of 2 figurines, 2 pendants, 2 pieces of jewelry, 12 seals with primatomorphic handles, and 17 seals/sealings with primatomorphic printing surfaces. In these pieces, we identified two kinds of monkeys, vervets (*Chlorocebus* spp.) and baboons (*Papio* spp.). Our analyses concur with previous reports and support the contentions that: (a) there was an extensive cultural exchange between Minoans and Egyptians, (b) Minoans were either first-hand observers of primates or were painters of detailed narratives, (c) some monkeys (vervets) are related to a leisure –yet naturalistic– context and some others (baboons –by then deified in Egypt) act as mediators in ritual contexts,

(d) primates reach Minoan imageries in two time periods, and (e) the representation of primates among Minoans is an example of the earliest transmission of exotica into Europe.

Keywords: Akrotiri, Archaeoprimatology, Baboons, *Chlorocebus* spp., Egypt, Knossos, *Papio* spp., Vervets

10.1   Introduction

The Minoan civilization constitutes one of the earliest European civilizations and flourished in the islands of the Aegean Sea during the Bronze Age, between 3000 and 1100 BCE (Renfrew, 2011). Their territory occupied the Aegean Sea around the island of Thera (present-day Santorini) and Crete Melos as well as a presence in northern Africa and the Levant (Fig. 10.1). Minoans are well-known for their rich material culture evidenced by the development of writing (Cretan Hieroglyphic and Linear A, both undeciphered) and the variety and quality of their art (Betancourt, 2007; Renfrew, 2011). In effect, the art of the Minoan civilization demonstrates a fondness for animal and plant life which appeared in frescos, pottery, jewellery, vessels, and sculpture (Betancourt, 2007). Considering that Minoans were a seafaring culture with an extended trading network across the Mediterranean, Minoan artists were constantly exposed to diverse stimuli that promoted a unique artistic combination. It is thus of no surprise, that these artistic manifestations included representations of both native and exotic species. Among them, primates (monkeys) attracted scientific investigations ever since their discovery. Primates (except humans) are not, and have never been, native to the Aegean. It was thus always tempting to identify, understand, and provide functional interpretations for their depictions in frescos, jewellery, seals, and sealings (e.g. Betancourt, 2007; Canciani, 1973; Evans, 1921; Greenlaw, 2005, 2006, 2011; Komninos, 2009; Marinatos, 1987b; Masseti, 1980; Papageorgiou and Birtacha, 2008; Pareja, 2015, 2017, 2020a; Phillips, 2008a, b; Platon, 1947). The objectives of this chapter are to provide an extended review of the published information on primate representations by Minoans, to re-analyze this evidence, build a new dataset based on the actual identification of the represented primates, and elucidate the acquisition and potential functions of primates and/or their imageries among Minoans.

10.2   Monkeys and Minoan Frescos

In the Bronze Age Aegean, there was an intimate relationship between Minoans and nature, as the latter appeared to be central to their culture (Herva, 2006). Animals posited a special role in religion for Minoans, as they were not only ideally located in geographical terms, but also for the circulation of animal imageries within the Aegean (Castleden, 1990). Actually, in the representation of fauna, they showed an interest in nature by providing evidence of iconographic originality

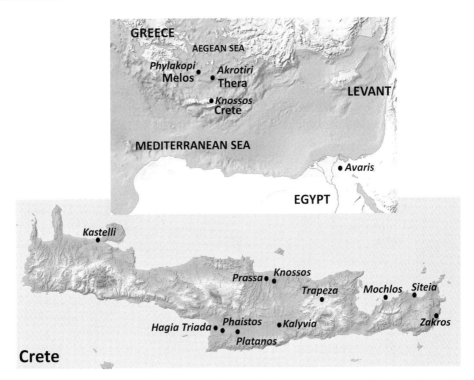

Figure 10.1 Location maps of Minoan sites discussed in this chapter. (above) Main localities with Minoan frescos. (below) Minoan locations in Crete with portable objects referred in the text and tables (based on data from Hogarth, 1901; Mountjoy, 2004; Müller and Pini, 2007a; Siebenmorgen, 2000; Tyree, 2001. Map by D. Youlatos).

(Vanschoonwikel, 1990), as exemplified by the cases discussed in this chapter. In addition, Marinatos (1984) suggested that the Cretan and Theran scenes have similar compositions, particularly using the same colors, that might suggest that those from Thera actually have Cretan origin. Moreover, the frescos show landscapes that are mostly symbolic and transcendental for these peoples (Komninos, 2009). In this sense, Walberg (1992) suggested that the prolific use of flowers, including palms, lilies, and crocuses, as iconographic elements in the Minoan frescos have a clear religious purpose in many contexts. But perhaps, the symbolic, ritual, and religious elements were part of everyday life in Aegean society and may all construct their conception of nature as part of their existence (Komninos, 2009). It is difficult, however, to elucidate whether the relation between Minoans and nature is ideological, ritualistic, religious, or ecological (Komninos, 2009). The frescos show that there was a special relationship that determined their existence and marked their identity by providing them with a special cultural place among the peoples of the eastern Mediterranean during the Bronze Age (Komninos, 2009). As indicated by this author, the monkeys with their human-like behavior most likely depict go-betweens gods and humans and are rarely depicted along with humans. In effect, monkeys with their human-like characters were considered as creatures with specific powers and may have already been adopted as cultic images by the Minoans by Protopalatial times (Phillips, 2008a). Spiros Marinatos (1971a, b, 1972b) was the first to observe that frescos in both Knossos, Crete, and Akrotiri, Thera/Santorini, have similar natural elements such as reeds, crocuses, and, of course, blue monkeys (hereafter, unless otherwise indicated, when referring to Marinatos from the 1980s, we refer to his daughther, Nanno Marinatos). Marinatos (1987b: 420) stated that "it might offend to our modern sensibilities that for the Minoans and Therans an animal was deemed worthy of such much attention. But, in fact, monkeys are the perfect intermediaries between nature and culture and tread on the subtle threshold between reality and fantasy." In terms of the internal locations of the frescos of Akrotiri and Knossos, Cameron (1978: 580) indicated that at "convenient standing eye-level below lintel-level of the room's doorways; [where] three of the restored Knossian monkeys' postures and the compositionally" could be easily observed.

Warren (1995) pointed out that the variety of poses and anatomical details suggested that the Knossian and Theran painters had observed live animals in the Aegean (regarding accurate animal depiction and its role for classification by Minoans, see Legendart 2020). This is supported by Evely (1999), Greenlaw (2011), Pareja (2017), Parker (1997), Phillips (2008a, b), Shaw (1997), and Strasser (1997). In contrast, Morgan and Cameron (2007: 377) indicated that "there appears to have been no standardisation in the representation of [them]. . . On the contrary, each artist had a particular method of depiction. Not only was the animal probably not well known to the artist, but its depiction was restricted to a few centres during a relatively short span of time." Nevertheless, Massetti (2003) and Masseti and Bruner (2009) believed that these monkeys were depicted so naturally and in a great degree of detail because (a) Egyptian observers had transmitted this first-hand knowledge to Minoan painters or (b) real animals might have been imported from Egypt and were held in special places like menageries or large enclosures because of the exoticism, value, and rarity, where painters could observe the depicted behaviors. Masseti (2006) even suggested that primate ethological studies started with the Minoans while representing behavioral features of these monkeys. Castleden (1993) indicated that the monkeys represented in blue seem to be similar to the "convention" of painting monkeys by the Egyptians of that time. He also argued that monkeys might not only have had a sacred meaning but also that they might have been obtained for meat. In both, the realism of the depictions as well as the use of bright colors is common in Akrotiri and Knossos (Immerwahr, 2000). The presence of vivid and realistic representation in the Minoan frescos differs between the islands, as in Knossos it is more standardized while in Thera it is more naturalistic and with a "sense" of individuality (Greenlaw, 2011; Höckmann, 1978; Pareja, 2017). Also, it is worth mentioning that in the paintings from the House of the Frescoes at Knossos and from Sector Alpha at Akrotiri there are blue birds (rock doves) in addition to the monkeys; doves are very rarely depicted in Egyptian art, so this combination seems to be an Aegean invention (J. Binnberg, pers. comm.). In Cretan and Theran frescos, the use of the so-called Egyptian blue was the rule (Filippakis et al., 1976), and it also possibly indicated the origin of this pigment in the Aegean –referring to Egypt, not the lapis azuli quarries of central Asia (Asimenos, 1978; Concoran, 2016).

The primates of the Minoan frescos had been the subject of multiple interpretations and debates since they were discovered. Conferring proper taxonomic identifications has evaded a final resolution for decades until recently (Table 10.1). This was, in part, because the phenotypic and behavioral characterization of such primates were not properly explained (Table 10.2), due to, likely, lack of communication between scholars of multiple disciplines who explored these primatomorphic representations (see Pareja et al., 2020a, b; Urbani and Youlatos, 2012, 2020a, b). Baboons, especially, had been the subject of particular misidentification when dealing with the study of Minoan primates (Table 10.1). Today, two primate genera have been identified in the Minoan frescos of Knossos and Akrotiri by using morphological and behavioral attributes: vervet monkeys, *Chlorocebus* spp. (*C.* cf. *aethiops* or *C.* cf. *tantalus*) and baboons, *Papio* spp, (*P.* cf. *anubis* or *P.* cf. *hamadryas*) (Table 10.2). Five out of six primate panels represent baboons, while the remaining one depicts vervets (Table 10.3). Baboons are associated with ritual contexts while vervets are related to a leisure context (Urbani and Youlatos, 2012, 2020a).

10.2.1 Baboons in the Frescos of Knossos, Crete

McDermott (1938: 23–24) sugestted that "the most beautiful representation of apes in ancient art are blue monkeys in two Late Minoan paintings from the House of Frescos at Cnossus [that likely] some wealthy man had imported monkeys or received them as gifts from Egypt." Monkeys might have been imported to Crete for serving as divinities after inspiration from Egypt (Marinatos, 1993). Evans (1921, 1935) suggested that some of the objects brought to the island seemed to come from far away – from the Nile Delta, particularly the region of Nubia. Bietak (1995, 2000c) suggested that the natural scenery in Knossian frescos represents putative maps of areas that resemble Nilotic landspaces. However, in Minoan frescos, there is evidence of possible local biotic elements such as Aegean plants . Representations in which saffron is also a common denominator seem to be particularly important among the Minoans (Morgan, 1990). Cretan monkeys also might have provided libations, while practicing a "peaceful activity" such as crocus gathering (Marinatos, 1993). Parker (1997: 348) suggested that the monkeys were transported to Crete as gifts to the rulers, and as such "the monkeys' role as exotic holding intrinsic power by virtue of their foreign origin." In terms of the fresco technique, during the Old Palace period in Phaistos and Knossos, it improves not only by having better plaster but also by adding the so-called "Egyptian blue" in the paintings where blue monkeys are included (Immerwahr, 1990). Earlier, Nilsson (1927) indicated that even though the monkeys are not native animals to Crete, they might have come from other lands, where they were probably a "monster," combining animal and human parts.

10.2.1.1 Baboons, Papyri, and Lilies
In 1923, the British archaeologist Arthur Evans (1851–1941) and his collaborator, the Swiss painter and amateur archaeologist Émile Gilliéron (1850–1924), reconstructed a large panel with monkeys (Cameron, 1968) (Fig. 10.2). The location of these

Table 10.1. Historical identifications (and misidentifications) of the Minoan 'blue' monkeys

Primate taxa (after Urbani and Youlatos, 2012, 2020a, b, this study)	Previous species identification	References
	Cercopithecus callitrichus	Marinatos (1970, 1971)
	Green monkey (*Cercopithecus* [*Chlorocebus*] *aethiops*)	Masseti (1980, 2000, 2003, 2006, 2019, 2021)
	Cercopithecus aethiops	Parker (1997)
	Vervet monkey	Strasser (1997)
	Cercopithecus aethiops	Schmitz-Pillmann (2006)
	Chlorocebus sabaeus, C. aethiops, C. tantalus (most likely)	Groves (2008)[a]
Vervet monkeys, *Chlorocebus* spp.	*Cercopithecus aethiops*	Papageorgiou and Birtacha (2008)
(= *C.* cf. *aethiops* or C. cf. *tantalus*)	*Cercopithecus*	Phillips (2008a,b)
	Cercopithecus aethiops	Masseti and Bruner (2009)
	Vervet monkey	Greenlaw (2011)
	Vervet monkey	Pareja (2015, 2017)
	Hanuman or gray langur (*Semnopithecus* spp.) [b]	Pareja et al. (2020a, b)
	Possibly *Cercopithecus diana Allochrocebus lhoesti*, or *Chlorocebus sabaeus*	Pruetz and Greenlaw (2021) [c]
	Cercopithecus callitrichus sabbaeus	Evans (1928b)
	Greenish guenon (*Lasiopyga tantalus*)	McDermott (1938)
	Cercopithecus aethiops, C. aethiops tantalus	Cameron (1968)
	Green monkey (*Cercopithecus* [*Chlorocebus*] *aethiops*)	Masseti (1980, 2000, 2003, 2006, 2019, 2021)
	Baboon-like monkey	Vanschoonwinkel (1990)
	Cercopithecus aethiops	Parker (1997)
	Vervet monkey	Strasser (1997)
Baboons, *Papio* spp.	*Cercopithecus aethiops aethiops*	Rehak (1999)
(= *P.* cf. *anubis* or P. cf. *hamadryas*)	Vervet monkey	Porter (2000)
	Baboon-like primate	Schmitz-Pillmann (2006)
	Olive baboon (*Papio anubis*), vervet monkey (House of Frescos, Knossos) *Cercopithecus* (seals)	Phillips (2008a,b)
	Cercopithecus aethiops	Masseti and Bruner (2009)
	Baboon (*Papio anubis*), hamadryas baboon, patas monkey (Xeste 3), vervet monkey (Sector Alpha), rhesus macaque (saffron gatherer)	Greenlaw (2011)
	Baboon	Wolfson (2018)

[a] Groves (2008: 18) actually wrote that "everything else about them is accurate... the black stripe from eye to ear and fan-shaped cheek whiskers suggest that they are *C. tantalus*." Grove's text is the first description of the Minoan monkeys with a fully primatological perspective. It is not clear if he reviewed the primates rendered in sites other than Room 6 of Building Complex Beta at Akrotiri; [b]For a discussion on this species misidentification, see Pareja et al. (2020a, b), Urbani and Youlatos (2020b), and Binnberg et al. (2021) as well as Masseti (2021) and Pruetz and Greenlaw (2021). Pareja et al. (2020a) also indicated other primates as the ones that had been suggested for Minoan frescos: *Chlorocebus pygerythrus*, *C. aethiops*, *Papio anubis*, and *P. hamaydras*. Chapin and Pareja (2021) also suggested that they identified langurs as part of a group of "Wild Animals from Indirect Exchange Networks;" [c]Pruetz and Greenlaw (2021) did not exclude vervets (*Chlorocebus aethiops* or *C. tantalus*) as suggested by Urbani and Youlatos (2020a, b). Although, in a comment article to Pruetz and Greenlaw (2021), Urbani et al. (2021) provided further evidence that the depiction of vervets is still more parsimonious in Room 6 of Complex/Building Beta.

Comment: When referring to primatomorphic frescos and portable objects, Langdon (1990: 417) anticipated that "whether the Minoans made an iconographic distinction between smaller monkeys of various genera and the sacred hamadryas baboon is uncertain; their representations vary in precision and apparently in species."

Knossian monkeys was a small villa about 100 m west of the location where Evans excavated in 1923 (Immerwahr, 1990). Evans (1928b) realized that humans were excluded from the scene that depicted only monkeys and birds in natural landscapes with rocky areas and flowers, with papyrus and ivies. This is suggestive that these monkeys represent wild animals with no traces of domestication (Greenlaw, 2011) and behave as wild animals do in nature (Pareja, 2017). In the papyrus scene, Evans (1928b) suggested that the panel shows a more ochreous background with animals of lighter blue that, according to him, are clearly in a Nilotic environment with Minoan adaptations, but with connection to Egypt. Evans (1928b) considered it similar to what was found in the Tomb of Ken-Amun where monkeys are along with palms while picking fruits. The arrival of ostrich eggs, ivory, gold, as well as monkeys might have used the Nile route, or other northern African routes.

In 1966, A. Caravella and T. Phanourakis expanded this panel significantly by including new fragments depicting monkeys (Cameron, 1968). These fragments were two representations of monkey heads with a black iris, pinky ear, white band and muzzle, and blue forehead (Cameron, 1968). The third piece of a tail surrounded by red crocuses and two more fragments appeared to represent the ventral area of blue monkeys likely in a "hunched position" (Cameron, 1968). Cameron (1968: 3–4), actually stated that "there is now evidence for six monkeys, their heads all in right profile, the similar coloring of which suggest animals of the same species: *Cercopithecus callitrichus* (a synonyn for *C. sabaeus*) according to Evans; but the representation of a white band on the forehead and indication of side-whiskers, absent in *C. sabaeus*, point either to *C. aethiops* (Ethiopia) or to *C. aethiops tantalus* (south of the Sahara to Chad and central West Africa) as the animal depicted on our frescos." According to Phillips (2008b), the variability of body shapes indicates that the living models may have been different species. In fact, the monkeys depicted in this fresco appear to differ

Table 10.2. Minoan 'blue' monkeys phenotypic and behavioral characteristics (based on data from Urbani & Youlatos, 2012, 2020a, b, this study)

Vervet monkeys, *Chlorocebus* spp. (= *C.* cf. *aethiops* or *C.* cf. *tantalus*)	Baboons, *Papio* spp. (= *P.* cf. *anubis* or *P.* cf. *hamadryas*)
Phenotypic characteristics	
Elongated limbs and arms	Elevated limb configuration
Extended/longer tail	Dorsal position of the tail base
White ventral part	Expanded thorax in relation to the whole torso
Dark grayish[a]/blackish masks, snouts/noses	Hairless nasal dorsum
Occurrence of capillary mustaches	Long snout and prognathic face
White chin, jawline, cheeks, and band forehead	Narrow waist
Very short fringes	Shortened hair in the inguinal part
Rounded heads	Elliptically shaped eyes
Orange and reddish-orange rounded eyes	'Blue' color
'Blue' color	Conspicuous cheek whiskers[c]
Long thumbs[b]	
Behavioral characteristics[d]	
a. Leap	Foraging behavior (omnivorous/granivorous) as
b. Clamber or hop	observed in the wild
c. Climb	Quadrupedal walk
d. Quadrupedal crouch	Seating/squatting posture
e. Clamber	Tripod posture (biped behavior assisted with the tail)
f. Assisted bipedal	
g. Hop or bridge	
h. Arm suspension	

[a] Some faces look as having dark greyish snout rather than black likely because of color decay/fading process after centuries; [b]D. Gommery (pers. comm.) pointed out that the developed thumbs of the monkeys of Room B of Complex Building Beta (Fig. 10.8) are characteristic of vervets. In contrast, langurs, and colobines in general, possess very short thumbs; [c]The cheek whiskers in the primates of Sector Alpha (Fig. 10.7b, c) are very similar to those found in baboons, and more likely in the hamadryas baboon (*Papio hamadryas*). The images were published by Vlachopoulos (2007) and went unnoticed by Papageorgiou and Birtacha (2008), Phillips (2008a, b), Greenlaw (2005, 2006, 2011), Pareja (2015, 2017), and Urbani and Youlatos (2020a); [d]See Hunt et al. (1996) for the definitions of locomotion and postural modes inferred for the vervets (Fig. 10.8). The letters refer to labels in Fig. 10.8.

Comments: (a) Morgan and Cameron (2007) already noted that in Knossos, monkeys possess pink ears, black pupils within a yellow eye, and white lines between the blue color of the head and the nasal/eye area. In contrast, the monkeys from Thera (Complex Beta) have "shorter snouts" than the blue monkeys of Xeste 3 and Knossos (Morgan and Cameron, 2007). Vanschoonwikel (1990) also described the blue monkeys of Knossos as having a white throat and ventral area, a face delineated in black with yellow-orange color, small heads with pointed black ears, and oranged and rounded eyes. He suggested that the monkeys of Thera and Knossos have a similar pattern, such as a blue body, white belly, white cheeks with black dots in Thera and black lines in Knossos. In Thera, the eyes are generally rounded, red with black iris, while are white and with red iris in Knossos. The face is yellowish in Knossos while white with black nose in Thera as well as the ears are relatively pointed. He also indicated that "besides the features mentioned, the more pointed head, elongated snout and kind of mane clearly indicate another species, in which it is perhaps possible to identify a baboon" (Vanschoonwikel, 1990: 336). Strasser (1997: 348) further indicated that "the only monkeys that naturally exist on the Mediterranean shores are the Barbary macaques. Since the Barbary macaque is tailless, it is not the species in the fresco." (b) As mentioned in the text, Binnberg et al. (2021) proposed that the white ventrum in depicted vervets and baboons might be an iconographic amalgamation in Minoan primatomorphic representations that can be better explained by folk taxonomical clumping. Recently, Pruetz and Greenlaw (2021) suggested that, previously, the white inner thighs were not considered for identifying cercopithecines by Pareja et al. (2020a, b) and Urbani and Youlatos (2020a). This is certainly true, and as in the case of the white bellies in Minoan primate frescos, this depicted feature is also shared by both baboons and vervets (even if it is naturally present in the latter). Nevertheless, it is not as widely found in Akrotirian and Knossian locations. Thus, it is not feasible to suggest that it is an iconographic canon shared in all Minoan primate frescoes but in some, that also can likely be explained as a pictorial amalgamation and part of a common Minoan (folk) taxonomy grouping.

Saffron Gatherer fresco (see Section 10.2.1.2) and from the Theran frescos, by their ears, squarish muzzle, robust necks, sturdier body and forelimbs, and shorter tails (Phillips, 2008a,b). Phillips (2008a,b) further suggests that these body and facial characters and coloration are indicative of olive baboons (*Papio anubis*) and not vervets. We agree with this interpretation, although the features of these baboons do not aid to identification at the species level.

Cameron (1968: 19) described the primate scene as that "the natural daily life of monkeys in general may be broadly divided into two parts: sleeping and hunting for food. Two of our monkeys are undoubtedly actively engaged: one is clambering among papyrus stems [...]; the other, with paw raised, is peering through the undergrowth [...] To judge from the positions of the limbs, [another] monkey... may well have been represented in an active posture, and the positions of the monkeys' tails on two other fragments suggest the animals denoted by those pieces were at least portrayed in upright postures. Our monkeys then may reasonably be considered as hunting for food. Monkeys are usually vegetarian, but given the right opportunity they can be predators, too, with an appetite for young animals and bird's eggs." A reconstruction of the "Monkeys and Bird Frieze" of the House of Frescos in Knossos is presented in a folded illustration by Cameron (1968), reprinted by Chapin (2004) and colored in Morgan (2005). Marinatos (1987a) suggested that these primates, surrounded by birds, gathered around the papyri, and moving around rocks, may represent a sort of idealized scenery with probable symbolic functions. Cameron (1968) also suggested that the panel seems to represent early summer or spring because of the presence of flowering irises and crocuses that occurs from February and March until early summer. He also indicated that this group of monkeys were also after birds or bird eggs, as in Egyptian depictions of primates, and this was also earlier observed by Arthur Evans. These eggs may have been either of waterfowl or doves (Cameron, 1968; Masseti, 2003; Masseti and Bruner, 2009). This egg-consumption scene was used to identify these primates as vervets (e.g. Masseti, 1980, 2003), but baboons are omnivorous and prey on eggs. In any case, a closer

Table 10.3. The Minoan 'blue' monkeys of Knossos (Crete) and Akrotiri (Thera)

Fig. no.	Primate taxa	Number of individuals	Common name of the fresco/ pictorial context	Date[a]	Location
10.2	Baboons	4[b] (6?)[c]	"Monkeys and Bird Frieze" (Monkeys within a landscape of papyri and lilies)	LM-IB/ MM IIIB (1540 BCE; 1450–1600 BCE)	House of Frescos, Knossos, Crete
10.3	Baboons	2	"The Saffron Gatherer's Fresco" (Monkeys searching within and gathering saffron plants)	LM-IB/ MM-IIIB (1550 BCE; 1450–1650 BCE)	Early Keep, Knossos, Crete
10.4	Baboon	1	"Mistress of Animals (*Potnia Theron*) and Safroon Gatherers" or the "The Offering to the Seated Goddess" (Monkey worshipping a goddess)	LM IA (1540 BCE; 1550–1500 BCE)	Xeste 3, north wall of Room 3a, Upper Store/first floor, Akrotiri, Thera
10.5	Baboons	4	"Frieze of Monkeys" (Monkeys playing lyre-like instrument and using swords)	LM IA (1540 BCE; 1550–1500 BCE)	Xeste 3, Room 4, ground floor, Akrotiri[d], Thera
10.6, 10.7	Unknown primate species + baboons	2 or 3[e] +2[6]	"Monkeys at a Shrine" (Monkeys squatting in front of a pillar and/or shrine)	LM IA (1600–1540 BCE)	Sector Alpha ("Altar"/*Thyroreion*; "Porter's Lodge"), Akrotiri, Thera
10.8	Vervets	8	"Wall painting of the monkeys" (Monkeys moving along an open landscape)	LM IA (1540 BCE; 1550–1500 BCE)	Complex/Building Beta, north and west walls of upper floor, Room 6 or Room Beta 6, Akrotiri, Thera

[a]Dates based on Evans (1928b), Cameron (1978), Doumas (1992), Immerwahr (1990), Masseti (2003), and Hood (2005); [b]Only four monkeys were observed by the authors. Also these four primates appeared in the published photographic records (see Fig. 10.2); [c]According to the illustrative reconstruction reproduced in Cameron (1968), Chapin (2004), and Morgan (2005); [d]In the same location there is a fresco fragment with a couple of quadrupeds, likely ungulates and a swallow above (Museum of Prehistoric Thera, Inv. #346). Below these mammals, there are blue paintings that slightly resemble the body of the like one represented in Fig. 10.6; however, with the current visual evidence, it cannot be determined if they are monkeys (B. Urbani, pers. obs.;

Doumas, 1992: 125, plate 91, labeled as the "Cows"); [5]"Two monkeys around the pillar based on the presence of two independent tails; one of them likely associated with a primate body (Fig. 10.6) plus an additional possible knee and torso part of a monkey reported by Vlachopoulos (2007, plate 15.11 [Fig. 10.7a). Vlachopoulos (2007, plate 15.4) suggests that the tail at the right of the pillar (Fig. 10.6) is part of the same monkey he reported in his plate 15.11; [6]Based on two papionins identified in this study from a pair of baboon-like cheek whiskers (Fig. 10.7b, c), two baboon snouts (Fig. 10.7d, e), and a couple of torsos (Fig. 10.7f, g). Thus, in this fresco, the number of depicted monkeys may correspond to at least four individuals.

Comment: A painted plaster (SF 1175) was found at a site known as the Pillar Crypt (IIS) in Phylakopi, island of Milos. On it, dark grey and grayish-blue silhouette lines were painted around a white area with a red-iris eye of larger size compared to the size of the head (Morgan and Cameron, 2007). They described it as an "enormous eye, narrow head, and lack of ear [that] make this a curious creature" (Morgan and Cameron, 2007: 376) that, when compared with painted monkey heads from Knossos, Morgan and Cameron (2007: 377) identified it as a *Cercopithecus aethiops aethiops* or *C. a. tantalus* (for a color photograph of this "monkey fragment," see Renfrew, 2007: n.p., color plate). Morgan and Cameron (2007: 377) suggested that " [a]lthough occasional thin black lines were used to delineate the blue on the Theran monkeys, the thick outlines of the Philakopi head are a local variant... . The context of the Phylakopi monkey is slightly later than those from Thera, and most, if not all, of those from Knossos. [This monkey] is an idiosyncratic rendering as though the model were only half remembered." These authors also suggested that a series of fragments of greyish-blue/blue, grey/black outlines and white contour lines might eventually be part of a monkey aggregation. Looking at the published pictorial and textual information, we found no substantial morphological evidence for listing the painted living being of this fragment as a primate. Alternatively, considering the external contour of the head, it might possibly be a bird (for ornithological comparisons, see Masseti, 1997; Birnberg, 2019) or, more specifically, a falconid (Morgan and Cameron, 2007). Morgan (1988) suggested that the "monkey" of Phylakopi might be part of a ceremony while considering the offering frescos of the adjacent rooms that might be associated with an offering to the goodess (Morgan, 1990). Houlihan and Hood (1990) indicated that there is evidence, not only architectural but also from pottery, that Cretan settlers might have been in Akrotiri and Phylakopi. Minoans in Phylakopi are dated to 1500 BCE (LM IB) (Mountjoy, 2004). Minoan Akrotiri was known for having a close relationship with the Cyclades and Crete, and during the Middle Bronze age with Philakopi and its Milos thalassocracy around the time the Theran settlement was destroyed (Thorpe-Scholes, 1978). Finally, neither Coleman (1973) nor Abramovitz (1980) cataloged evidence of primate depictions in Minoan-related frescos from the Aegean sites of Afia, Keos, and Irino as there are none in the African site of Avaris –Tell El-Dab'a– (Bietak, 2000a, b, c; Bietak and Marinatos, 1995) and the Levantine locations of Alalakh, Tel Kabri, and Qatna (Niemeier and Niemeier, 2000; Pfälzner, 2008, Cline et al., 2011).

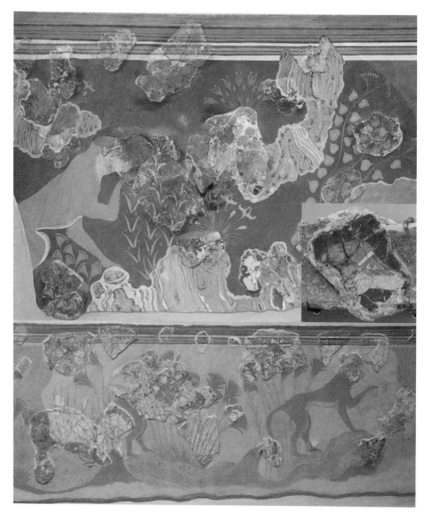

Figure 10.2 Large Cretan fresco with papionins, Herakleion Archaeological Museum. Width: 5.5 m, height: 0.8 m (Immerwahr, 2000: 475). (above) Baboon and the lilies (Wikimedia Commons-CC BY. Author: Zde, 2014). Detail (inset): baboon face (Wikimedia Commons-CC BY. Author: ArchaiOptix, 2019). (below) Baboons and the papyri (Wikimedia Commons-CC BY. Author: Zde, 2014). According to Cameron (1968) and Morgan (2005), the baboon with the reddish background (image above) was located in the right section of the fresco panel, while the rest in the central and left sections of the fresco (image below).

look at the reconstructed fresco fragments shows no open mouth, nor egg. From this part of the fresco, there is limited photographic evidence (see Fig. 10.2, detail right); thus, the original reconstruction by Cameron (1968) must be re-evaluated.

Immerwahr (1990) suggested that the blue monkeys from Knossos may be either a predatory allegory or have a possible religious meaning because they are aesthetically associated with the gathering of saffron as observed in other Cretan frescos. In fact, Marinatos (1993: 200) found that "monkeys [are] element[s] of lightness in a realm where power and predation are the main qualifications to high status. The Minoan perception of nature thus allows many facets to surface: dominance and killing juxtaposed with nurture and play are all interwoven in a cycle of life and death." In fact, Pareja (2017) argued that although the divine figure is not depicted in the wall painting, the presence of a nature deity can be inferred from the context in which the animals move (a fertile, abundant landscape) and from the inclusion of the monkeys behaving in a natural way (for a constested view on the notion of deities in Minoan religion, see Thomas and Wedde, 2001). Shaw (1993) proposed three possible scenarios for this fresco, either the natural environment inhabited by the monkeys, a natural sanctuary, or a garden. According to Marinatos (1986), Minoans had a very ritual character that included sacrifices. Once more, it was underlined that the landscape appeared similar to that found in Egypt (Marinatos, 1987a). Vanschoonwikel (1990) indicated that the landscape in Knossos is more "luxuriant" than in Akrotiri, with more tranquil monkeys than the vivid Theran ones from Complex Beta 6 (see Section 10.2.2.4). Marinatos (1987a) also specified that conical cups were excavated in the room of the Cretan fresco, implying ritual functions. In fact, Niemeier (1992) advocated that because of the multiple "portable ritual objects" found in the room, this fresco was probably used for communal cults under a temporary regime, but also at a rather domestic scale.

The Knossos frescos were reconstructed by Gilliéron after fragments of murals with papyrus flowers and a water fountain (Chapin, 2004). Chapin (2004) also pointed out that in 1966, N. Marinatos incorporated new fragments in to this primate fresco deposited in the Archaeological Museum of Herakleion. These fragments had been described by Cameron (1968). Chapin (2004), citing N. Marinatos, found a religious significance to this representation since lilies, as well as birds and monkeys, seem to be related to the goddess of nature. Marinatos (1984) also diagnosed spring scenery, based on the blooming of crocuses and lilies, and underlined the connection between these animals and the ways nature is ideally and symbolically represented. Chapin (2004) argued that in Knossos, Minoans appeared to be divided between "participants and spectators" with a ceremonial person directing the rituals to the nature goddess, while others observed. These landscape frescos might imply social stratification by showing the dominant class in contact with the goddess, and consequently using these images to support their status (see also Crooks et al., 2016).

The papyrus in this fresco is likely *Cyperus papyrus* and is similar to that in the sacralized Minoan 'Fresco of the Ladies' (Rackham, 1978; Warren, 2000). Rackham (1978) indicated that this plant is of African origin and it would have hardly grown wild in the Aegean, because of lack of wetlands. In contrast, Sarpaki (2000) suggested that *C. papyrus* might have been cultivated in Crete and the Cycladic islands but suggested that sea lilies (*Pancratium maritimum*) were possibly found in the House of the Ladies. Looking at both plants in context, Porter (2000) suggested that the papypi of Knossos are actually *P. maritimum* as in the column of Sector A. He indicated that sea lilies are aromatic flowers of late summer and are indicative of a local environment and a seasonal event. Rackham (1978) also indicated that the Minoan representation of lilies seems to indicate their interest in gardens. Lilies (*Lilium candium* [white] x *Lilium chalcedinicum* [red]) blossom from May to July, supporting the spring-early summer scenery (Chapin, 2004). Ivies might possibly be *Hedera helix* which is wild in Crete (Porter, 2000). Furthermore, Vlachopoulos (2000) suggested that the reeds represented in the Minoan frescos are either *Arundo donax* or *Phragmites communis*, while Sarpaki (2000) indicated that reeds are *A. donax* and *Phragmites australis*. Regardless of the origin of these plants, the location of the depicted scenery remains difficult to interpret. Many landscapes may refer to sub-tropical habitats (Komninos, 2009; Doumas, 2013), for which Aegean painters may have had a first-hand experience. On the other hand, some others are clearly Aegean. The question is if monkeys were projected on such exotic landscapes or they were actually kept as pets in large enclosures, as suggested by Massetti (2003).

In general, this scenery is very fragmentary and only partially reconstructed posing a serious problem for thorough evaluation. For the time being, those panels are only known from a reconstructed illustration (Cameron, 1968; Chapin, 2004; Morgan, 2005; see foodnotes 2 and 3 of Table 10.3). Althought the whole pictorial narrative provided by Cameron (1968) is highly plausible, for instance, the alleged scene of the primate eating an egg, was only presented, and reconstructed as an illustration, and to our knowledge, there are no available photographs for further examination (except Fig. 10.2, detail right). It is interesting though, that this baboon-depicting fresco is located in a room connected with sacred activities supporting the relationship between these papionins and ritual contexts (Urbani and Youlatos, 2020a, see also Section 10.4). However, as suggested by Chapin (2004) and Chapin and Shaw (2006), further studies are required to properly investigate the representations on this fresco. We concur, paradoxically, even that it appears to be the largest primatomorphic iconographic narrative in any Minoan site, possibly depicting six monkeys –including the one supposedly eating an egg, and still deserves additional detailed examination.

10.2.1.2 Baboons Gathering Saffron

Marinatos (1984) indicated that Arthur Evans first erroneously reconstructed the Saffron Gatherer fresco as a blue boy (Fig. 10.3). This fresco was exhibited in Herakleion Museum Gallery XVI (Immerwahr, 1990), and was reconstructed again by Nikolaos Platon in 1947 who confirmed that the depicted beings were actually monkeys (Marinatos, 1987b), as it was later confirmed with similar discoveries in Thera (Marinatos, 1993). Platon made the early suggestion "that the monkey had ritual associations and that he collected flowers in a royal garden" (Marinatos, 1987b: 417). The monkeys have specific roles as adorants as well as collectors of flowers for the goddess (Marinatos, 1993; Pareja, 2017). Both authors suggested that, contrary to Thera (see Fig. 10.4), in Knossos, the context of crocus gathering is a controlled space like a garden where the monkeys collected flowers and place them in a basket. In fact, Platon (1947) argued in favor of royal gardens, hosting all these exotic animals and plants, most likely gifts from the Egyptians, for the pleasure and amusement of kings and royal officials. Platon (1947) commented on the adornment of these animals supporting their tamed nature, while Kontorli-Papadopoulou (1996: 123) indicated that the monkeys at

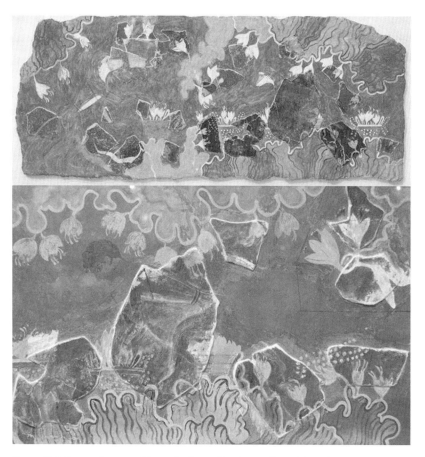

Figure 10.3 Cretan frescos with papionins collecting saffron. (above) Baboons and the saffron crocuses. Text in the label at the Herakleion Archaeological Museum as in 2010: "The Saffron-Gatherer's Fresco. Depiction of monkeys gathering crocus flowers in a rocky landscape. Knossos. New Palace period (1600 BC)" (Wikimedia Commons-CC BY. Author: ArchaiOptix, 2019). (below) Early anthropomorphic reconstruction of a baboon gathering saffrons in the same Cretan fresco. This representation was credited to É. Gilliéron. (Wikimedia Commons-CC BY. Author: Zde, 2014).

Knossos wear "the jewelry (red bracelets, anklets and circlets) worn around the waist and chest of the animal, which indicated a tamed monkey, participating in ritual acts." Similarly, Marinatos (1984) indicated that probably the monkeys of Knossos are collecting crocuses for ritual purposes in the context of goddess offerings and are therefore related to ceremonial contexts (see also Pareja, 2017).

Even further, Platon (1947) said that Knossos might have served as a royal park, particularly in the case of the saffron gatherer scene (Matz, 1962). Greenlaw (2011) argued that these monkeys, although anthropomorphized, display "simian" proportions. Moreover, she suggests that the surviving fragment of the monkey facing the saffron gatherer shows a more rounded muzzle with peachy flesh color, slender body, and relatively smaller size indicating that they are likely rhesus macaques (*Macaca mulatta*),

Figure 10.4 Theran fresco of "The Offering to the Seated Goddess", Museum of Prehistoric Thera. Width 3.22 m, height 2.3 m (Doumas, 1992: 158–159, plate 122). (Wikimedia Commons-CC BY. Author: Klearchos Kapoutsis, 2011).

an Asian species, with a western-most distribution to western Afghanistan. On the other hand, Phillips (2008b) assumes that their characters are suggestive of *Cercopithecus* (= *Chlorocebus* spp.), but of a different subspecies considering the coloration and the thinner and more elongated body. We disagree with those interpretations. The visible narrow waist, the distal end of the tail that suggests a tuft, the elevated limb configuration, the expanded thorax in relation to the torso, and the relatively long dorsally hairless muzzle, actually suggest papionins (baboons) with no further possible specific identification.

Regarding this monkey scene, Marinatos (1993: 63) also added that it seems to be represented as a "dreamy landscape where large crocuses and projecting rocks predominate." Douskos (1980) suggested that crocus gathering should appear in multiple contexts; however, they seem to be real events of Minoan life. The depiction of crocus gathering can be seen as both a celebrating ritual event and also as a collective work. Crocuses (*Crocus cartwrightianus*) blossom in late October to December (Chapin, 2004). Crocuses flower in October once the rain returns (Porter, 2000). This plant has multiple attributes: it serves as medicine and perfume, and it is also useful for flavoring food (Porter, 2000). According to Day (2011), the reconstruction of this fresco and the botanical configuration is rather "challenging."

In general, the monkeys on this fresco appear different from those depicted elsewhere in Minoan art and probably the scene indicates dominance of humans over monkeys (animals) and over the surrounding landscape (Pareja, 2017). When this fresco is closely observed, even if the crocus gathering is performed by a baboon, it appears very human-like. This is also evident by the very human-like hand that holds the basket. According to Platon (1947) connecting human hands with monkeys was common, as these animals were considered as human mimes. Overall, the scene bears similarities to the scene in the tomb of Khnemhotep of the 12th Egyptian Dynasty (1991–1785 BCE) at Beni Hassa as recorded by Wikinson (1878). In this Egyptian scene, baboons collect fruit directed by a person handling a basket. In the Cretan scene, the baboon with cords is also collecting plant parts. Furthermore, the relationship of the baboons with the gathering of saffron might be associated with a narrative related to the concept of fecundity. In addition, the environment has some coastal features that might imply that the monkeys were part of Cretan or Egyptian contexts, a common representational pattern (Platon, 1947). These monkeys appear to belong to the greater visual account that emerges about monkeys, crocuses, and the supernatural (Pareja, 2017). We concur with this scene interpretation.

10.2.2   Baboons and Vervets in the Frescos of Akrotiri, Thera (Santorini)

Vanschoonwinkel (1990) recorded 76 animal representations in Theran frescos. Only a small fraction (5%: 4/76) of these frescos depict primates. Certainly, this number is quantitatively low, but they are qualitatively among the most conspicuous and frequently discussed by scholars. As suggested by Doumas (1983) and Laffineur (1990), the wall-paintings of Akrotiri are part of a space shared by the majority of Minoan society, so it is more likely that they represent moments of everyday life or moments experienced by common people, rather than the elitistic royal space of the depictions at Knossos. Thus, in contrast to the Palatial context of Knossos, Akrotiri is a house complex (Morgan, 1990). The interpretations of the Theran frescos are divergent. Kontorli-Papadopoulou (1996) suggested that overall wall-paintings from Santorini have a religious meaning, albeit stating that a final interpretation of the fragmentary frescos requires further studies. Strasser (1997) advocated that the monkeys depicted in such a detailed fashion implied that they were most likely closely observed (see also Papageorgiou and Birtacha, 2008), and traded from sub-Saharan Africa under special care (see Section 10.4). Apart from monkeys, Minoans might have also brought or closely observed Grant's or Soemmering's gazelles (*Nanger granti, N. soemmeringi*) and African felids (Bury, 1967; Chaix, 1994; Kleinsgütl, 2000, Masseti, 2003). In Thera, Strasser (1997) also suggested that the monkeys would have been kept in captivity to avoid crop-raiding and the unfavorable winter conditions. In general, Theran wall-paintings appear to have domestic-private purposes giving the "impression of the total environment" and do not reflect a relationship with the Levant/Near East (Winter, 2000). Recently, Binnberg et al. (2021) suggested that amalgamations of physical attributes in Minoan monkeys, such as, the white underbelly, naturally visible only in vervets, but depicted in Aegean baboons also, may be suggestive of folk taxonomical grouping among the Minoans. Regarding Akrotirian primatomorphic frescos, multiple options and interpretations are open. Below we present detailed information on the primates depicted on the Theran frescos.

10.2.2.1 A Baboon Standing and a Seated Goddess

Xeste 3 is a two-floor complex of frescos, where girls are gathering saffron, and a girl and a monkey are offering it to the goddess (Immerwahr, 1990) (Fig. 10.4). This building that might have served for rites of passage (Immerwahr, 1990). The depicted monkey has been identified by Greenlaw (2011) as a hamadryas baboon based on the elongated muzzle. We cannot agree with this identification. The monkey features, such as the narrow waist, the short inguinal hair, the dorsal position of the tail base, the elevated limb configuration, the expanded thorax in relation to the torso, and the long dorsally hairless muzzle are indeed suggestive of a baboon, but without any further possible specific identification. Moreover, this baboon has the rounded hips and back of humans and those curves are similar to those of the female figure, sometimes following the lines of the skirts (Greenlaw, 2011). Marinatos (1976) suggested that the receiver of the saffron was the "Mistress of Animals" with goats and monkeys as the most associated fauna. The fresco appears as a ritual context of offering to a goddess (Angelopoulou, 2000; Vanschoonwikel, 1990). In Xeste 3, the monkey serves as adorant of the goddess while offering crocuses (Marinatos, 1984), actually "the monkey was elevated to the status of divine servant probably because [it has] animal and human characteristics. Indeed, on the Thera fresco, he is true intermediary between the goddess and the crocuses gathering girls. He stands on a higher level than the girls on the platform, but he is below the goddess. It is he, and not the girls who is doing the offering" (Marinatos, 1993: 200). In fact, the anthropomorphization of the monkey enables the animal to perform the ceremonial action that is central to the scene and serves as the liminal being that bridges the gap between the human and supernatural realms (Pareja, 2017). When inspected closely, the unusual fully stylized and bipedal stance places this baboon into a human pose. This apparently shortens the liminality between the two stages. Marinatos (1987a) additionally suggested that the wall-painting in Xeste 3, Room 3 has a woman handling a basket with crocuses associated with a griffin and a blue monkey. The latter is acting as a ritual servant which stays close to the throne while picking the flower from the basket to offer to the goddess in a ritual association. The heraldic element of this scene is reminiscent of many Cretan seals (e.g. seal no. 359 from the Giamalakis collection), where the seated position of the woman indicates her divine status and monkeys flank an object of importance (Greenlaw, 2011). Marinatos (1987a) further suggests that the monkeys appeared to have a "ministrant" function to god entities but also "adorants" as alleged for the squatting monkey that looks at a column in an Akrotiri fresco (referring to fig. 6 of Marinatos [1987a]). Additional information indicates that these monkeys might have served for ritual purposes, and according to the notes on the diaries of Sp. Marinatos, they were possibly associated with the fragment of a female who was also probably a goddess (Marinatos, 1987a). According to her, at Xeste 3, blue monkeys might have served as servant gathering flowers, and participanting in "playful activities, and entertaining games" (Marinatos, 1987a: 130). The use of monkeys as adorants to the gods might was probably "borrowed" from the Egyptians since they had baboons that served in god worship (Greenlaw 2011; Marinatos, 1984). Porter (2000: 621) stated that:

the exotic African vervet monkeys, standing bipedally, are acting, in presenting the stigmas to the goddess... Whether such vervet monkeys actually assisted in crocus gathering, as depicted in the Knossos mural (something they are capable of doing with their human-like hands and their agility to climbing rocks), or whether it is imagined, remains an open question. That the vervets were real, rather than mythical animals (unlike the griffin), associated with priestesses and cult, and appears assured. Animals, birds, and humans adored and paid homage to the goddess – animals more closely associated than humans with the supernatural world because of their wildness.

Regarding those monkeys, "a mythic content is apparent in the inclusion of monkeys involved in human activities and their association in this capacity with a presentation scene intimates the presence of the divine. The focal point of the cycle – the presentation scene – reflects a ritual, perhaps undertaken in an enactment of a mythic event, hence the inclusion iconographically of the monkey" (Morgan, 1990: 261). This is a clear example, of what Morgan (1990) coined as the juxtaposition of the natural sphere with the ritual life of the Minoans. The deity that received the saffron from the standing blue monkeys in Xeste 3 probably is a healing goddess related to a phytotherapy saffron ritual event (Ferrence and Bendersky, 2004).

Cameron (1978) indicated the relation of certain attributes such as crocuses, blue monkeys, and flower offerings to the goddess. In Thera, all these were represented in private spaces, while in Knossos, they were painted in a space controlled by the ruling class, which might have ordered the form of the composition. Platon (1947) suggested that in the Thera fresco the crocus gathering was not in a confined space like in the royal gardens of the Knossos fresco. Here "we find a fully bipedal (anthropomorphic) monkey placed in a liminal zone halfway up a tripartite shrine, handing an offering of saffron to a goddess" (Parker, 1997: 348). In fact, in Knossos, the monkeys are depicted collecting crocuses but not offering them to the deities (Marinatos, 1984). Patrianakou-Iliaki (1983) suggested that the Therans might have seen the wall-paintings of Knossos and represented them superficially in Thera. Morgan (1988) indicated that in Thera and Knossos, the monkeys present high degrees of anthropomorphism where, the monkey –not the girls– of Xeste 3 is the one who offers the crocuses to the goddess with the crocus flowers in her dress. Similarly, Parker (1997) proposed that the detailed representation of monkeys suggests that the artist must have had contact with the animals, and the anthropomorphic depiction (e.g. bipedal posture offering saffron to the goddess) provided an "exotic status." The monkeys are part of the cosmological cycle in Thera, or, in association with the crocuses and the adored women, of a Minoan myth (Morgan, 1988).

Douskos (1980) suggested that the crocuses of Xeste 3 are *Crocus sativus*. This species is cultivated in the Greek mainland and Aegean islands, has pharmaceutical uses, and also serves as pigment and perfume. In the Theran fresco, the collection of crocus stigmas, which have coloring properties, indicates a difficult productive task (Douskos, 1980). As further noted by Dewan (2015: 50), the "laborious stigma-separation and drying processes are not shown, but the significance of the final product, saffron is emphasized by the presentation of red crocus stigmas to the goddess by a blue monkey, commonly seen as a divine attendant in Minoan art."

Cameron (1978), following Marinatos (1976), suggested that this might have been an initiation rite among girls, as saffron has medical sedative properties and is normally used during menstruation. Alternatively, the use of saffron may represent regeneration, as in Egypt (Wesołowska, 2017). Finally, the reddish "flying" flowers are probably the pink rock rose *Cistus creticus* (Warren, 2000).

Marinatos (1987a) pointed out that a similar saffron-gathering-offering scene is also present in a ring (Fig. 10.9e [CMS II.3 103]) and seal/sealing (Fig. 10.11b [CMS III 358], 10.11c [CMS III 357]; the latter is the only one with floating plants as in the referred fresco, see Day, 2011) from Crete. She further suggested that in these seals, females seem to serve as adorants to monkeys, and their large size indicates a significant social position. Thus, it was not unusual that monkeys were receivers of worship, as they seemed to be more important than humans in Xeste 3. This might actually indicate that the "monkey was an intermediary between humans and the divinity. Thus, it is natural that it would be worshipped. The importance of the monkey explains its frequent appearance on seals and sealings where no narrative scene is depicted and the animal is shown for its own sake" (Marinatos, 1987a: 127–128). Apart from being in between the human and divine world, the monkey had a double role of being adored and being an adorant (Marinatos, 1987a). Its position and actions designate its intermediary role between Minoans (humans), their natural products (saffron), and a female deity (see also Pareja, 2017). In sum, in this Theran fresco, the baboon is anthropomorphically depicted in terms of its postural behavior and the interconnection with the saffron appears to be possibly related to a pictorial event linked to a notion of fecundity.

10.2.2.2 Baboons, the Lyre, and the Swords

This fresco from Room 4 of Xeste 3 of Akrotiri was found as fragments of anthropomorphic monkeys holding swords and a lyre in a context associated with human-like activities and gesticulations that seemed to represent a ritual context (Doumas, 1992; Morgan, 1988; Parker, 1997; Vanschoonwikel, 1990) (Fig. 10.5). Marinatos (1976, 1984) indicated that the monkeys with a lyre and swords were found close to probably one of the most important cult areas in Akrotiri. This area is relatively large (Angelopoulou, 2000). Monkeys playing a lyre or handling a sword might have served as ritual worship (Angelopoulou, 2000; Pareja, 2017). An extended hand of a monkey was interpreted as hand-clapping (Vlachopoulos, 2008).

This depiction is showily known as the "Frieze of Monkeys" (Rehak, 1999). Greenlaw (2011: 48) suggests that although the long snout of these monkeys is a papionine feature, "... it is the dark stripe running along their muzzles, terminating in a black/brown spot." that is reminiscent of patas monkeys (*Erythrocebus patas*). However, patas monkeys, apart from being red/orange, bear a very characteristic black facial mask, hairy-tipped ears and a conspicuous whitish mustache above the mouth. In contrast, the long, pointed snout, the relatively low front, the hairy cheeks, the arched back, the relatively expanded thorax, and the visibly narrow waist are suggestive of baboons, probably the yellow (*P. cynocephalus*) or olive (*P. anubis*) baboon. However, such a distinction cannot be supported by the depicted features.

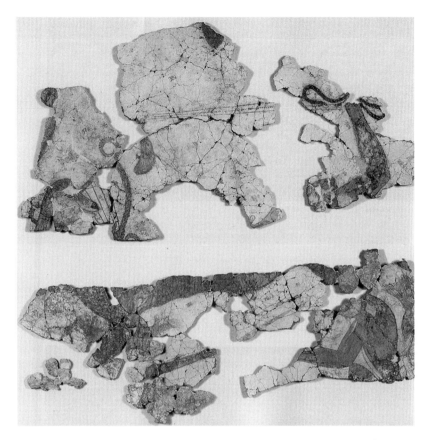

Figure 10.5 Baboons and the lyre and swords in a Theran fresco, Museum of Prehistoric Thera (Doumas, 1992: 134, plates 95, 96). (Courtesy of Christos G. Doumas, Excavations at Akrotiri, Thera).

Once more, baboons play lyre-like instruments and use swords that might have a ritual purpose of possible Egyptian origin (Rehak, 1999). Looking for the origin of this scene, Doumas (1985) indicated that the monkey with the lyre from Akrotiri is similar to images found in Egypt and the Near East, reflecting an aesthetic continuity through time and space among the peoples of the pan-Mediterranean region and its periphery (Doumas, 1985; Marinatos, 1993; see also Vanschoonwikel, 1990). The association of baboons with lyres can be further and extensively observed in Egypt (e.g. Vandier d'Abbadie, 1966; Younger, 1998).

   The scene represented in this fresco is very particular as it clearly depicts anthropomorphized animals in terms of both morphology and behavior. Despite the absence of any obviously divine figure, the actions in the fresco indicate the unearthly nature of the animals and their actions (Pareja, 2017). Herein, the baboons are explicitly assuming human ludic activities. The actions appear to be related to specific ritual or sacred contexts. Unfortunately, the frieze is so fragmentary that no further interpretation can be provided yet.

Figure 10.6 Partial monkey in a Theran fresco. Text in the label at the Museum of Prehistoric Thera as in 2010: "Wall-painting with adorant monkeys. Akrotiri. Mature Late Cycladic I period (17th c. BCE). Inv. no. 332." A larger label stated that this fresco is entitled "Rural shrine with adorant monkeys" and continued: "Preserved is the left part of a shrine with yellow columns decorated with blue papyri and topped by steps with horns of consecration, one of the chief symbols of Minoan religion. In front of the shrine squat blue monkeys with their hands raised in a gesture of prayer." (Photograph by B. Urbani).

10.2.2.3 The Vanished Monkey(s), the Pillar, and the Other Baboons

Marinatos (1987b) indicated that the monkey is located in front of an "altar" and in an Egyptian-like column (Fig. 10.6). An illustrative reconstruction of this frieze is published by Marinatos (1987b), who also suggested that the frescos of Sector A ("the African fragment") are part of a ritual context since it is an association of a pilar with a papyrus-like ending column, that is similar to those of Egyptian "shrines." The representation of a column of these characteristics is unique for a Minoan fresco (Marinatos, 1987b). Morgan (2005, plate 4) referred to this fresco as "Monkeys at a shrine, from the '*Thyroreion*,' Akrotiri". These columns are clearly religious, and the arms of the monkey indicate a worship posture (Marinatos, 1987a). Greenlaw (2011) pinpointed the fact that the arms of the monkey are strangely deformed terminating in club-like wrists. The monkey might be a servant under a papyrus pillar (Marinatos, 1984). She found parallelism of this behavior with similar representations of worshipping primates of ancient Egypt. Considering that this fresco is in a room close to Room 3, Marinatos (1984) also suggested that they might be part of a similar ritual context, in which the monkey extends the arm as an adorant facing the column (Marinatos, 1987b). Marinatos (1987a) pointed out that the squatting monkeys appear in Prepalatial Crete and continue in Palatial times, and that a man adoring a column is also depicted in the Knossian Palanquin Fresco. She pointed out the presence of a second tail on the right-hand side of the fresco, which might depict a second monkey engaged in a worshipping behavior at another pillar. However, Kontorli-Papadopoulou (1996) indicated that this evidence needs to be considered with caution.

This fragment is not well preserved. Pareja (2017) highlighted the different scales of the depicted monkeys, which indicate either a physical relationship in size, a hierarchical relationship, or (most unlikely) the inclusion of perspective. The abraded surface impedes a clear conclusion, but Pareja (2017) assumed that there are two species of monkeys of different size in this fresco, the larger ones considered as vervets. We found no elements for scaling the images. The contours of the body of the first animal and the second tail, on the right, are suggestive of a primatomorphic representation, but a more detailed identification is impossible. However, Greenlaw (2011) assumes that the slender arms and wrists and the relatively short muzzle probable indicate a vervet–human composite. Phillips (2005) indicated that these monkeys are assimilated from Egypt in front of a Minoan altar. The author pointed out her interpretation that the pillars represent papyrus in blossom and candidly stated that:

[E]very time I see this particular image I can almost hear a seaman/trader relating tales of his travels to his friend the artist, describing what he had seen in far-away land of Egypt, with its marshy delta and wide river full of water-plants, and its cities with their large mud-brick palaces and huge stone temples, their roofs supported by pillars having papyriform capitals – and then the artist developing the image formed in his mind when he painted this fresco (Phillips, 2005: 45).

We concur, similarly might have occurred with the accurate depictions of vervets and baboons in Akrotiri.

The presence of a possible hilly environment is interesting, as it might have served as a sanctuary, further supported by the pillar with leafy capitals of possible sacred significance, such as the tree of life (Rutkowski, 1978). Morgan (2005) recalled this representation as a papyrus pillar, while Rackham (1978) claimed it as a Cretan palm (*Phoenix theophrasti*). Sarpaki (2000) identified either a papyrus (*C. papyrus*) or an African palm *(Phoenix dactylifera)*, which has religious connotation among Egyptians, and possibly also among Minoans.

Finishing this section, it is extremely relevant to highlight a publication by Vlachopoulos (2007) that has been overlooked in previous reviews on Aegean primates (Greenlaw, 2005, 2006, 2011; Pareja, 2015, 2017; Papageorgiou and Birtacha, 2008; Phillips, 2008a, b; Urbani and Youlatos, 2020a). At Porter's Lodge of Sector Alpha, apart from the main scene reported above, Vlachopoulos (2007)

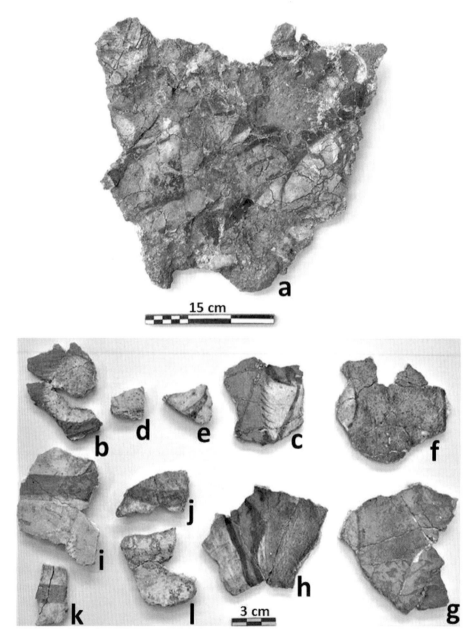

Figure 10.7 Monkey fragments from Porter's Lodge of Sector Alpha, Akrotiri (Vlachopoulos, 2007, plates 15.4, 15.11, and 15.12. Courtesy of Andreas Vlachopoulos, Akrotiri Excavations, Thera. Photographs by D. Sakatzis (above) and M. Hamaoui (below). For a better appreciation of the described details refer to the color plates in Vlachopoulos (2007).

identified a third monkey, possibly represented by a knee and torso part (plate 15.11 [Fig. 10.7a]), equally fragmented as in Fig. 10.6. This purported monkey is reconstructed as standing in front of a reassembled female figure in a way similar to the scene of the "The Offering to the Seated Goddess" (see Fig. 10.4). According to Vlachopoulos (2007, fig. 15.4), the tail of this reconstructed primate (Fig. 10.7a) is the one located at the right of the pillar of this fresco (Fig. 10.6). Vlachopoulos (2007: 134) further indicated that "there may have been up to three [blue] monkeys in the composition" depicted in other smaller trace (plate 15.12 [Fig. 10.7b(l)]). We fully agree with this identification. When closely observed some pieces seem to depict primate-like cheek whiskers (Fig. 10.7b, c, reminiscent of the cheek whiskers of baboons, and more likely, of hamadryas baboons (*Papio hamadryas*). These whiskers are very similar to those of papionins depicted in Egyptian ostraca (B. Urbani, pers. obs.) and Egyptian frescos (e.g. New Kingdon baboons: Pio, 2018). Additionaly, there are two fragments with snouts (Fig. 10.7d, e) that are strikingly similar to the ones depicted in the papionins of Xeste 3 (Figs. 10.4 and 10.5), to a point that they could have been produced by the same painter(s) or different painters with common aesthetic canons. Two more fragments seem to depict monkey torsos (Fig. 10.7f, g). In fact, the torso of Fig. 10.7f has the white underbelly used in Minoan depictions of primates. One fragment (Fig. 10.7h), when observed after turning it 90° to the left, looks like two extended arms, similar to those of the baboon, painted in front of a sword in Room 4 of Xeste 3 (Fig. 10.5, lower right corner), or the ones in front of the pillar of Sector Alpha (when turned 180° to the left; Fig. 10.6). The remaining pieces of this set of fragments are four tail parts (Fig. 10.7i–l). One of them seems to show the base of the tail dorsally located (Fig. 10.7i). When considering the dorsal tail base, the prognathic snout, the white underbelly and the position of the arms, these remains appear to represent two papionin individuals, while the conspicuous cheek whiskers may further tentatively lead to hamadryas baboons.

10.2.2.4 Vervets in a Theran Landscape

The 'Room of the Monkeys' is considered the most impressive group of wall-paintings in Thera (Sp. Marinatos, 1970) (Fig. 10.8). Plasters from Room B were excavated in 1967 and 1968 (Sp. Marinatos, 1971a). On August 7, 1968, a fragment with a monkey was found (Sp. Marinatos, 1969). Later in 1968, the head of a monkey was also found on the upper level of the room. During 1969, many other fragments with primatomorphic motifs were recovered, as pieces showed the monkeys moving in different directions (Sp. Marinatos, 1970). By 1970, the Greek painter and curator of the National Archaeological Museum of Greece, Kostas Iliakis, together with the students of Sp. Marinatos started to assemble the pieces of this fresco. By 1971, the fresco fragments of the monkeys were under *in situ* restoration (Sp. Marinatos, 1971b). On August 3, 1972, this fresco was inaugurated in the National Archaeological Museum in Athens (Marinatos, 1972a).

The fragments were found under poor conditions in the northwestern part of the room, covered by rock debris and ashes. Sector B was among the most destroyed parts of Akrotiri, coincidentally with the area where Beta 1, with the antelopes, and Beta 6, with the monkeys, are located (Televantou, 2009). Sp. Marinatos (1970) suggested that the red substrate contacting the monkey plasters may be the abundant red lava of Thera. Marinatos (1987a) also indicated that in the fresco from Room 6 of

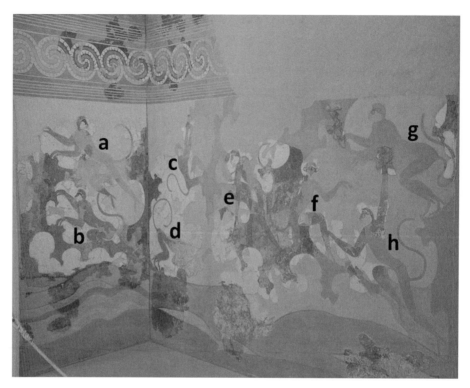

Figure 10.8 Vervets in a Theran fresco. Text in the label at the Museum of Prehistoric Thera as in 2010: "Wall-painting of the Monkeys. Akrotiri. Mature Late Cycladic I period (17th c. BCE). Inv. no. 344-345." A larger label stated that this fresco is titled "D7.2 The wall-painting of the Blue monkeys" and continued: "The Wall-painting of the monkeys decorated the north and west walls of room Beta 6. From broad wavy bands of unequal width, extending across the lower part of the paintings and perhaps denoting water, rise rocks which fill the main field up to its decorative crowning zone and recall the Theran landscape in shape and colors. Blue monkeys, a species foreign to the Aegean fauna, clamber on the rocks, moving freely in all directions. All are depicted in profile except one, which is shown in frontal view, a bold rendering in Aegean wall-painting. The wall-painting of the monkeys, a masterpiece by an avant-garde painter, combines a certain restraint in color and drawing (natural landscape) with freedom of composition, intense movement, varied poses and a registering of the momentary, thus creating an atmosphere that realistically conveys the character of the simians. The felicitous result perhaps indicates that the painter had a direct image of these animals, which will have been imported to the Aegean from the Eastern Mediterranean. The fragmentary wall-painting of the quadrupeds in a rocky landscape with crocuses, by the same painter, adorned room Beta 6. Late Cycladic I period, 17th c. BCE. Inv. nos 344-346." West wall, width1.13 m, height 2.7 m; North wall, width 2.76 m, height 2.7 m (Doumas, 1992: 120–123, plates 85–89). For the interpretation of locomotion and postural modes, see letters in Table 10.2. (Photograph by B. Urbani).

Building Complex Beta, there are fragments, including large swallows, reeds, and hooved animals, which were not used in the reconstruction. Their inclusion would have probably suggested a different scenario.

Considering the depicted monkeys, they are:

especially realistic [...] animals in the Monkey fresco from Thera. Here the variety of poses suggests actual observation from nature; especially effective are the monkey near the top who swings from a rock and braces his legs against another rock or the one who peers out frontally with projecting pink ears and mischievous expression... Unfortunately, this fresco was found so badly preserved, its fragments having collapsed into a small basement room (B6), and consequently, its reconstruction in the National Museum in Athens has undergone several changes. Wavy sinuous bands of blue, yellow, and red, undoubtedly representing a river, occupy the bottom of the frieze, and at the top is an elaborated blue and white spiral band against a red background enclosed by horizontal stripes. The middle section, comprising about half the total height off the wall, is given over to the monkeys, who against a white background clamber over russet cellular rock formations, apparently searching for food. Although no nests or fruit appear in the restoration, the gestures of the monkeys suggest their predatory intentions. (Immerwahr, 1990: 42).

This description shows the disagreements on the interpretation of this panel as reviewed below. Nevertheless, this fresco stands out in that the monkey depictions are so detailed and individualized that, at least one Minoan artist must have observed several live vervets and created preliminary sketches (Pareja, 2017). It is the only wall painting with primates engaging in natural behaviors, interacting in between them, within a purely natural landscape (Pareja, 2017).

The first interpretation of the monkey scene came from K. Iliakis who posited that they were likely chased by hounds (Sp. Marinatos, 1971a, b). In Thera, these animals are fully realistic with great anatomical details and life-like movements (Iliakis, 1978). Lurz (1994) indicated that these primates are found within a more naturalistic landscape while having different positions of their limbs. The monkeys move freely in different directions and all but one are shown in profile, and were probably executed by a so-called *avant-garde* painter of the time, according to Televantou (2009). Televantou (1992: 153) also suggested that "The 'Painter of the monkeys' [is]... another good exponent of the Free Style, has the ability to catch and render the instantaneous and to transmit very realistically the psychology and character of wild animals." This fresco "combines a certain restraint in color and drawing (natural landscape) with freedom of composition, intense movement, varied poses and a registering of the momentary, thus creating an atmosphere that realistically conveys the character of the simians" (Televantou, 2009: 72).

Marinatos (1984) indicated that in Room 6 of Building Complex Beta, the monkeys are part of a spring scenery that might be associated with a space related to the deities, regardless of whether they are adorants or members of a local group of primates. In Knossos, the spirals represent octopus tetancles, and this may suggest a relationship between a venerated sea animal and a venerated land animal. Marine life is the other recurrent representation in Minoan frescos (Morgan, 1990). Similarly,

Sp. Marinatos (1971a) suggested that the continuity of spirals, the monkeys moving in two directions, the wavy lines (described as "water currents"), as well as the red soil, appear to indicate a Theran environment. However, the lack of flowers is noteworthy (Höckmann, 1978). Kontorli-Papadopoulou (1996) suggested that it is still premature to present a final interpretation of a religious context because the primates appear in a rocky landscape, but without the crocuses, as in the case of the monkeys in Knossos.

Morgan (1988) argued that these primates were possibly in controlled places such as park-like areas rather than in the wild. According to Morgan (1990), the presentation of the monkeys in Thera is more abstract than in Crete. Televantou (2009) found that the presence of a watercourse and a landscape with features that resemble Theran sceneries, in both color and shape, seem to indicate that the fresco refers to island scenery. The landscape presents a series of common elements, that Schiering (1992) listed as "straight and wavy bands" that eventually represent creeks or roots, the existence of pasture, and a hilly environment with rocks. Morgan (1988, p 172) termed that as "Theran exoticism [as the] aspects in the Akrotiri paintings which express a Theran predilection for exotic tastes are: palm trees; blue hairlock; earrings; blue monkeys; antelopes; The Priestess." Betancourt (2000) actually indicated that the representation of rocks associated with the Theran blue monkeys is used as a background rather than the actual main elements of the scene. The Theran painters used images of flora and fauna to define exotic landscapes (Doumas, 2013). Thus, he argued that the Theran painter seems to be able to manage freedom in the design of elements that is not necessarily advocated with strict Theran conventionalism. In this sense, Birtacha and Zacharioudakis (2000) argued that the curvature of the lines of the monkeys in Thera seems to emphasize the movement characteristics of these animals, as they are similarly represented in different individuals. In addition, Guralnick (2000) posited that the use of grids for representing proportionally human bodies, as in Egypt, was possibly adopted here as the monkeys might have been depicted using similar techniques (we suggest observing the lines over the pillar in Fig. 10.6). In fact, it is very likely that the artists of this fresco were relatively independent of the other fresco compositions (Angelopoulou, 2000; Pareja, 2015, 2017). In Thera, the degree of detail was so high that even accurate dragonflies and butterflies are depicted (Coutsis, 2000). Considering the extraordinary detail of primate depictions, the painter probably observed them from a very close distance, as they might have been imported to the island (Televantou, 2009). According to Televantou (2009), all monkeys were likely executed by the same painter. This was also asserted by Sp. Marinatos (1971b), who noticed the painter's astonishing knowledge of monkey behavior, indicating that the monkeys probably lived on the island. Similarly, Doumas (1992) argued that the painter knew the animals as they are climbing the rock and using their tails. According to Bury (1967) and Chaix (1994), the detailed representation of an African oryx and the monkeys in Thera support the contention that these animals were probably brought to the island as pets. Finally, Trantalidou (2000) also argued that Africa imageries were brought to Thera, with the depiction of an African landscape on the island.

Concerning the generic or specific attribution of the depicted primates, opinions seem to diverge, despite the fact that it is generally accepted that the animal phenotypic characters are depicted in detail. According to Greenlaw (2011), the faces of the monkeys along with their long agile tails are suggestive of vervets. However, she does not consider that as an exact match based on the difficulty of correctly rendering the face and the depiction of graceful, anthropomorphized limbs. In previous work, Urbani and Youlatos (2020a), based on a detailed description of characters, concluded that these animals represent vervets (*Chlorocebus* spp.) (see Table 10.2). Nevertheless, other researchers, although initially described those monkeys as vervets (Pareja, 2017), changed their opinion towards a more exotic option. In a recent couple of articles, Pareja et al. (2020a, b) argued that these animals depict Indian langurs (*Semnopithecus* spp.) (see also Chapin and Pareja, 2020). We strongly disagree with this diagnosis and we have further elaborated on the facial descriptions of the monkeys as well as on the virtual lack of primatomorphic representation in the Bronze Age Indus River Valley (Binnberg et al., 2021; Urbani and Youlatos, 2020b). Masseti (2021) and Pruetz and Greenlaw (2021) also differ with this recent identification proposed by Pareja and collaborators.

Regarding this fresco, Urbani and Youlatos (2020a) pointed out that this frieze might represent a leisure context or a place for the enjoyment of the depiction itself. No factual elements point to a ritual context, as in frescos related to baboons. If closely observed, the background is composed of a rocky environment of reddish, orange, and ochre tones. These colors and *topos* are similar to those observed in present-day Santorini (B. Urbani & D. Youlatos, pers. obs.). This probably suggests that the monkeys in Room 6 of Building Complex Beta were very likely transported to and then depicted roaming on the island or that the imageries of vervets were placed within a Theran landscape.

10.3   Monkeys and Minoan Portable Objects in Crete

Most of the representations of primates in portable objects correspond to the Prepalatial period, as they seem to have Egyptian influence and might have been created after direct observation of monkeys (Vanschoonwinkel, 1996). Apart from monkeys, other exotic animals were particularly appreciated among the Minoans. For example, lions were also represented in seals, as these animals seem to have a very strong symbolism among Minoans (Bloedow, 1992). This suggests that animals had a potent sense for this Bronze Age society. All Minoan portable objects with primatolomorphic motifs were found in Crete; none of them has been recovered in Thera.

10.3.1   Minoan Primatomorphic Figurines, Pendants, and Jewelry

In Crete, there are a couple of figurines with primatomorphic motifs held in the Herakleion Museum of Archaeology. The first one is made of clay and is from Phaistos, dating from MMII, 1700–1800 BCE (Fig. 10.9a). At the Herakleion

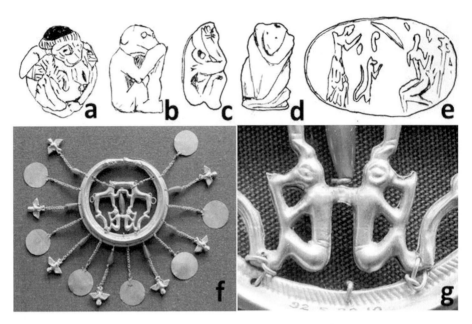

Figure 10.9 Cretan primatomorphic figurines, pendants, and jewelry (Above: made by B. Urbani based on images cited in the text. Below: Wikimedia Commons CC BY. Author: Einsamer Schütze, 2011).

Museum it is exhibited as a primate. However, most authors consider it as a crouching woman with long hair or a cap, lacking a tail (e.g. Phillips, 2008b, ill. 452). We agree with this interpretation. The second figure is made of yellow steatite and dates from EMII (2300 BCE), comes from Crete, and represents a monkey in a squatting posture (Buchholz and Karageorghis, 1973, fig. 1184) (Fig. 10.9b). Considering the flat shape of the head, the forward set eyes, the visible ears at the level of the eyes, and the prognathic snout, it most likely represents a papionin.

Two pendants have been identified as possibly primatomorphic. A crystal pendant that probably depicts a monkey was recovered in Knossos and dates from MMIB-II period, 1900–1800 BCE (Langdon, 1990, fig. 3; Coldstream, 1973, plate 95.258) (Fig. 10.9c). The animal looks like a squatting monkey with both forelimbs and hindlimbs extremely flexed. The stout body, the short tail, low front, and prognathic snout are suggestive of a papionin. Phillips (2008b) even considers it as a hamadryas baboon. However, the pendant is highly stylized and cannot be identified with certainty (Greenlaw, 2011). The second piece is a bone pendant that was discovered in Funerary Building 9 of Archanes, Phoumi dating from MMIA-B, 2100–1800 BCE (Fig. 10.9d). It also represents a crouching monkey-like animal, probably similar to a baboon (Phillips, 2008b, ill. 55), but a clearer identification is yet impossible (Sakellarakis and Sapouna-Sakellaraki, 1991, fig. 97).

There are two pieces of Minoan jewelry that potentially represent monkeys. The first is a ring made of an alloy of gold and copper (Fig. 10.9e [CMS II.3 103]). This piece comes from the Noble Tomb 2 of the Kalyvia Necropolis in Phaistos possibly dated at LM IIIA1, 1400–1350 BCE (Evans 1928a, fig. 492c; Papageorgiou and Birtacha, 2008, fig. 8ζ; Phillips, 2008b, ill. 84; Platon and Pini, 1984, Nr. 103; Savignoni, 1904, fig. 51). On the bezel, there is a representation of a baboon-like animal with the tail placed dorsally, and a head with pointed ears and prognathic face. It bears a certain resemblance to the baboon of the scene of the 'The Offering to the Seated Goddess' (Fig. 10.4) (see also Pareja, 2015, 2017). However, Phillips (2008b: 53) suggests it resembles the *Cercopithecus* (=*Chlorocebus*) monkey. The depicted ritual context, along with the posture and the relatively long muzzle of the monkey probably suggest a papionin. The second piece of jewelry is found in the British Museum, is made of gold and is part of the so-called Aegina Treasure, dating from MMIB [?] to MM III period, 1900–1600 BCE (Buchholz and Karageorghis, 1973, fig. 1304; Philips 2008b, ills. 578, 581; Platon and Pini, 1984, Nr. 103; Sargnon, 1987, fig. 179). The golden pieces are a set of penannular hoops that depict squatting primates, dogs (or jackals: see Greenlaw [2011]), snakes, and owls (Fig. 10.9f). The whole set of four baboon-like primates have elongated snouts, round heads, and enlarged lateral ear tufts reminiscent of similar baboon tufts in Egyptian representations (Greenlaw, 2011). We agree that the depicted primates are most likely baboons (Fig. 10.9g). However, Phillips (2008b) posited similarities to vervets based on the long tails and relatively short muzzles. As indicated by Langdon (1990) "addorsed baboons squatting with hands to faces, apparently eating, and point toward the motif's ultimate origin. . . the ultimately Egyptian inspiration for the piece as seen in a similar pendant composition of the 13th Dynasty from Dahshur." In fact, these penannular hoops are possibly Minoan and were collected by the late Bronze Age Mycenaeans (Greenlaw, 2011; Phillips, 2008a, b; Spier et al., 2018; Wolfson, 2018).

10.3.2 Minoan Primatomorphic Seals and Sealings

Table 10.4 summarizes the Minoan seals with primatomorphic motifs in their handling parts (Fig. 10.10). After an extensive literature review, we identified a total of 12 of these seals. Based on their phenotypic features (third column in Table 10.4), they were identified as baboons or baboon-like primates. Most of them represent single individuals (83%, 10/12 seals); the remaining two show addorsed pairs. In 11 of 12 seals (92%), the primates are shown seated or squatting. This posture, along with upraised arms and particularly flexed legs suggests an abstracted monkey type (Pareja, 2017). In fact, the postural repertoire is highly reminiscent of similar images from Egypt, including, for example, baboons with hands on knees (i.e. Figs. 10.10b [CMS XI:78 69], 10.10d [CMS II.1 435], 10.10e [CMS II.1 20], 10.10j [CMS X:26 31]). Although wild monkeys readily flex their hindlimbs when sitting and squatting, forelimbs are rarely stretched upwards, except when reaching for food, located above the animals. Most of these seals are carved in ivory (83%, 10/12); one is carved in amethyst, and another one in black steatite. All dated seals fall at the beginning of the third millennium BCE (Phillips, 2008b). Moreover, those from known locations were found in central Crete, south of Knossos, with one exception that originates from Mochlos Island (northeastern Crete).

Table 10.4. Primatomorphic motifs in Minoan seals (handling parts) from Crete

Fig. no.	Primate species (no. of individuals), CMS code	Posture	Phenotypic feature(s)	Measurement	Material	Date	Location	References
10a	Baboon (1) -CMS VIII: 109	Squatting	Short tail, flat head, hair tufts around the head	-	Amethyst	EM III-MM I or MM II (2200–2000 BCE)	Crete	Kenna (1966, Nr. 109, Robert Erskine Coll.), Greenlaw (2011, fig. 66), Phillips (2008b, ill. 562)
10b	Baboon (1) -CMS XI:78 69	Squatting	Long snout, flat head, robust body	Ht. = 1.89 cm	Ivory	EM III- MM IA (2200–2000 BCE)	Crete	Pini (1988, Nr 69, E. Grumach Coll.), Vandervondelen (1994, fig. 4), Papageorgiou and Birtacha (2008, fig. 26), Phillips (2008a,b, ill. 569)
10c	Baboon (1) ("ape" [Evans, 1912, 1935], "barbary macaque" [Evans 1921], *Cynocephalus* [Phillips, 2008b]) -CMS II.1 249	Squatting	Long pointed snout, hair tufts, evident mane on shoulders	Ht. = 3.38 cm	Ivory	MM IA–(B?) (2200–2000 BCE)]	Platanos, Messara	Platon (1969, Nr. 249), Xanthoudides (1924, 114, Nr. 1040, Pl. XIII, Zervos (1956, fig. 205), Evans (1921a: 486, Evans (1935, fig. 411), Vandervondelen (1994, fig. 2), Dimopoulou-Rethemiotaki (2005: 64), Papageorgiou and Birtacha (2008, fig. 2ε), Phillips (2008b, ill. 469), Greenlaw (2011, fig. 65)
10d	Baboon (1) (young individual *Cercopithecus* [Phillips, 2008a,b]) -CMS II.1 435	Tripod	Young individual, reltively short snout, slender limbs and body, long tail (?)	Ht. = 4.4 cm	Ivory	EM III-MM I (2200–2000 BCE)	Trapeza Cave, Lasithi	Platon (1969, Nr. 43], Zervos (1956, fig. 208), Buchholz-Karageorghis (1973, fig. 1185), Dimopoulou-Rethemiotaki (2005: 412), Papageorgiou and Birtacha (2008, fig. 2στ], Phillips (2008b, ill. 509), Greenlaw (2011, fig. 64), Pareja (2015, fig. 4.1)

ID	Identification	Posture	Features	Dimensions	Material	Period	Location	References
10e	Baboon-like monkey (1) ("cynocephalus" [Platon, 1969], Cynocephalus [Phillips, 2008b]) -CMS II.1 20	Seating	Hair tufts, long pointed snout, robust body, mane on shoulders	Ht. = 1.8 cm	Ivory	EM III – MM I (2200–2000 BCE)	Hagia Triada	Platon (1969, Nr. 20, Inv. Nr. 447), Vandervondelen (1994, fig. 1), Papageorgiou and Birtacha (2008, fig. 2γ), Phillips (2008b, ill. 30)
10f	Baboon (1) (Cercopithecus [Phillips, 2008b]) -CMS II.1 416	Squatting	Hair tufts, long pointed snout, hunched back, robust built, presence of mane (?)	Ht. = 1.65 cm	Black steatite	MM I[B]-II (1900–1800 BCE)	Malia (?)	Vandervondelen (1994, fig. 7a, 7b), Phillips (2008b, ill. 386)
10g	Baboons (2) (Cercopithecus [Phillips, 2008b])	Squatting	Short snout, slender configuration	Ht. = 3.7 cm	Ivory	MM IA-B (2200 BCE)	Platanos, Messara	Xanthoudides (1924, Pl. XV, Zervos 1956, fig. 199), Phillips (2008b, ill. 459), Pareja (2015, fig. 4.2)
10h	Baboon (1) (Cynocephalus [Phillips, 2008b])	Squatting	Long pointed snout, hunched back, robust build, lack of mane	Ht. = 3.2 cm, Diam. = 0.23–0.28 cm	Ivory	EM III- MM IA (2200–2000 BCE)	Crete	Xenaki-Sakellariou (1958, Pl 15, Nr. 300), Marinatos (1973, PL.12, Giamalakis Coll.), Vandervondelen (1994, fig. 3a, 3b), Greenlaw (2011, fig. 65), Phillips (2008b, ill. 563)
10i	Baboon-like primates (2) (Cercopithecus [Phillips, 2008b]) -CMS II.1: 436	Seating (?)	The long pointed snout seems to indicate baboon-like primates (probably young considering body slenderness)	Ht. = 2.5 cm	Ivory	EM III-MM IA (2200–2000 BCE)	Trapeza Cave, Lasithi	Platon (1969, Nr. 43), Zervos (1956, fig. 208), Buchholz-Karageorghis (1973, fig. 1185), Dimopoulou-Rethemiotaki (2005: 412), Papageorgiou & Birtacha (2008, fig. 2στ), Phillips (2008b, ill. 509), Greenlaw (2011, fig. 64), Pareja (2015, fig. 4.1)
10j	Baboon (1) ("ape" [Betts, 1980], Cynocephalus [Phillips, 2008b]) -CMS X.:26 31	Squatting	Hair tufts, long pointed snout, hunched back	Ht. = 2.75 cm	Ivory-Bone	MM IA-[B?] (2200–2000 BCE)	Crete	Betts (1980, fig. 31, Erlenmeyer Coll.)[b], Vandervondelen (1994, fig. 5, Papageorgiou and Birtacha (2008, fig. 2β), Phillips (2008b, ill. 565)

Table 10.4. (cont.)

Primate species Fig. no. (no. of individuals), CMS code	Posture	Phenotypic feature(s)	Measurement	Material	Date	Location	References
10k	Baboon (1) (*Cynocephalus* [Phillips, 2008b]) -CMS II.1 416	Squatting	Hair tufts, long pointed snout, hunched back, robust built	Ht. = 1.77 cm	Glazed ivory (?)	MM IA [B?] (2000–1900 BCE)	Crete	Mitsotakis collection (KM Σ4), Phillips (2008b, ill. 567)
10l	Baboons (1 in handling part, 2 in surface part) ("cynocephalus" [Seager, 1912], "cynocephali" [Evans A., 1921], hamadryas baboon [Phillips, 2008b]) -CMS II.1.473	Handling part: squatting (?). Print surface: seating	Handle: hair tufts, robust built, presence of mane, long snout, relatively short tail. Printing surface: long snout, pointed ears, short tail, waisted torso	Ht. = 1.8 cm, Diam. 1.2 cm	Ivory	EM II-III (~2200 BCE)	Mochlos (tomb chamber)	Seagler (1912, fig.11.II.42a, b?), Platos (1969, Nr. 473), Papageorgiou and Birtacha (2008, fig. 2α), Phillips (2008a,b, ill. 402), Greenlaw (2011, fig. 71), Crowley (2021, fig. XII.2)

[a] Found by Dr. Xanthoudides (Evans, 1921) and related to "proto-dynastic Egyptian models" (Evans, 1935: 486); [b] This piece likely is the same one registed as part of the J. Paul Getty Museum (Accession No. 2001.14.37); [c] Seager (1912: 34) indicated that "the design has an Egyptian look."

Comments: (1) CMS refers to the codes in the *Corpus der minoischen und mykenischen Siegel* [Corpus of the Minoan and Mycenaean Seals]; (2) Vandervondelen (1994, fig. 6) presented a photograph of a statuette in white faience depicting an animal that looks like a baboon (Metaxas Collection inv. 1216); however, the extended back part of the body and the separated front limbs (that differ from the papionin depictions in this chapter, i.e. Figs. 10.10b [CMS XI:78 69], 10.10c [CMS II.1 249], 10.10g, 10.10h, 10.10k [CMS II.1 416], 10.10l [CMS II.1.473]), as well as a very flat and pointed muzzle and the expanded and rounded face appear to probably indicate a lion-like mammal; (3) Ferrence (2011: 603, fig. 3a) presented a highly reconstructed image of a carved primate-like animal from a severely damaged figurine found at the cave of Hagios Charalambos in Lasithi (Crete, HN 13,907). It seems more of pictorial interpretation rather than a reconstruction based on remaining traits. For this reason, this seal is not listed in this table.

Monkeys are also depicted on the printing parts of the seals or in sealings with primatomorphic depictions (Table 10.5). Most of the depicted primates are baboons (76%, 13/17). The remaining four seals and sealings most likely represent vervet-like monkeys (Fig. 10.11k [CMS II.6 282], 10.11o [CMS VS1A 159], 10.11p [CMS II.3 115], 10.11q [CMS II.7 217]). In most pieces (70%, 12/17) primates are single individuals. There is one sealing that depicts six vervet-like faces (Fig. 10.11q [CMS II.7 217]). In most of the seals, the primates are shown in profile seated or squatting (65%, 11/17). The squatting posture, combined with the presence of a tail, upraised arms, and particularly folded legs may be indicative of an abstracted prototype of Egyptian influence (Pareja, 2015, 2017). In four seals, primates are depicted in a bipedal position. In 11 of 17 seals (65%), the primates have raised arms, either towards the sky or close to the muzzle. In the remaining seals, the arms are put straight downwards in a more natural position. Finally, one seal and one sealing depict the faces of vervet-like monkeys in frontal view (Fig. 10.11p [CMS II.3 115], 10.11q [CMS II.7 217]). In six sealings, single primates are found squatting in front of humans (Figs. 10.11a [CMS II.8.1 262], 10.11b [CMS III 358], 10.11c [CMS III 357, 10.11d [CMS II.7 24], 10.11e [CMS II.6 73]). Of these primatomorphic items, 65% (11/17) are sealings on clay; the rest are seals made of stone, agate, and carnelian. Dated seals are chronologically located at mid-second millennium and are geographically spread, mostly in central and eastern Crete (Fig. 10.1).

When referring to the Minoan seals, Evans (1928b) suggested that the ivory monkey from Platanos (see Fig. 10.10c [CMS II.1 249]) resembles the monkeys from Knossos, with clear Egyptian influence and related to a natural environment. Evans (1928b) also indicated that Egyptian designs appeared earlier than the ones from the House of the Frescos, at the time when Amenhotep II ruled (around 1450 BCE). Referring to the sealing in Fig. 10.11a (CMS II.8.1 262), Evans (1928b: 763) wrote that this "young minotaur" seems to be offering to the goddess as "we may venture to trace the influence of Egyptian figures of the Cynocephalus ape, the companion of the lunar god Thoth, as represented worshipping the rising sun. There is clear evidence that the dog-faced ape of the Soudan, who was credited by the Egyptians with wisdom beyond that of mankind, had been early impressed into the service of Minoan religious imaginary." Moreover, when referring to the sealings of Figs. 10.11d (CMS II.7 24), 10.11e (CMS II.6 73), and particularly the ring from Phaistos (Fig. 10.9e [CMS II.3 103]), Evans (1928b: 764) wrote that it "carries the scene a step farther. Here a female votary with raised hands is seen beside the Cynocephalus, and the adoration of both is directed to a seated figure of the Minoan Goddess behind whom rises a column indicative of her pillar-shrine. We may, in this case, detect a further allusion to this chapter of Egyptian beliefs concerning the Cynocephalus ape in the plume-like object seen in the field above him." While comparing frieze and glyptic representations of primates, Vanschoonwikel (1990) indicated that the erected position of the Theran frescos is rare in the glyptic representations (seals, sealings, and ring), where the monkeys appear in banding position, as adorants, and are lacking other "narrative elements" that might have accompanied the monkeys in the ring (Fig. 10.9e [CMS II.3 103]).

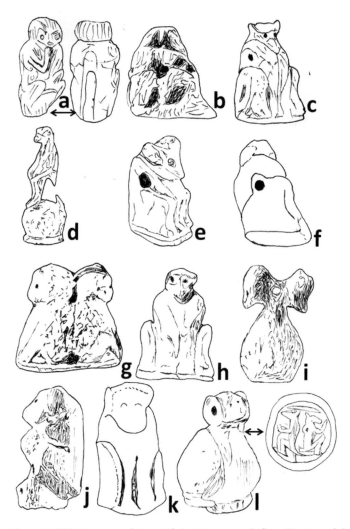

Figure 10.10 Primatomorphic motifs in Minoan seals (handling parts) from Crete (illustrations not to scale; prepared by B. Urbani based on images from sources indicated in Table 10.4).

Regarding an Egyptian connection between Minoans and Egypt, Langdon (1990: 416–417) indicated that "Minoan craftsmen were imitating popular Egyptian baboon amulets… A 12th Dynasty Egyptian scarab found with a Minoan seated ivory monkey from the Trapeza Cave supports this picture, as does, conversely, a Minoan vessel in Abydos Tomb 416, which also contained a faience baboon amulet. The renewal of Egyptian contact in the 18th Dynasty coincided with an apparent second wave of popularity for the simian motif in Crete."

   The seals of Crete come from as early as the Prepalatial Period, and they clearly are the earliest representation of primates among the Minoans (see also Philips, 2008a). In fact, Castleden (1993) specified that some seals with monkeys in the handling parts date from the early and middle Minoan civilization. The depiction of primates in the

Table 10.5. Primatomorphic motifs in Minoan sealings and seals (printing parts) from Crete

Fig. no.	Primate species (no. of individuals), CMS code	Posture	Phenotypic feature(s)	Measurement	Material	Date	Location	References
11a	Baboon (1) -CMS II.8.1 262	Seating	Robust built, mane, hair tufts	-	Clay (sealing)	LM I[B?]-III (1600–1400 BCE)	Crete	Evans (1901, fig. 7a), Evans (1928b, fig. 491), Papageorgiou and Birtacha (2008, fig. 8ε), Phillips (2008b: ill. 142), Pareja (2015, fig. 5.4), Crowley (2021, fig. XLI.14)
11b	Baboon (1) ["cynocephalo" [Xénaki-Sakellariou, 1958]] -CMS III 358	Squatting with both hands raised in front of a person	Waisted torso, long snout, bent tail	-	Clay (sealing)	MM III-LM II (1600–1400 BCE)	Siteia	Xénaki-Sakellariou (1958, XII.359, Nr. 3054), Müller and Pini (2007b, fig. 358, HM. Giam 3054), Pareja (2015, fig. 5.8), Crowley (2021, fig. XLI.10)
11c	Baboon (1) ["cynocephale" [Xénaki-Sakellariou, 1958], Cercopithecus [Phillips, 2008b]] -CMS III 357	Squatting with both hands raised in front of a person	Waisted body, absence of mane, bent tail	Diam. 0.8cm	Carnelian	LMI (1600–1400 BCE)	Prassa	Xénaki-Sakellariou (1958, XIII.372 Nr. Inv. 3438), Müller and Pini (2007b fig. 357, HM. Giam 3438), Papageorgiou and Birtacha (2008, fig. 8η), Phillips (2008b: ill. 495), Pareja (2015, fig. 5.7), Crowley (2021, fig. XLI.11)
11d	Baboon (1) ["dog-ape" [Hogarth, 1902], "cynocephalus" [Evans 1928], baboon and Cercopithecus [Phillips, 2008b]] -CMS II.7 24	Squatting with both hands raised in front of a person	Long snout, waisted torso, bent tail	Diam. 1.4–1.5 cm	Clay (sealing)	LM IA-B (1600–1400 BCE)	Zakros (House A, Room VII)	Evans (1928, fig. 492aᵃ), Hogarth (1902: 77), Platon et al. (1998, fig. 24 HMs. 83), Papageorgiou and Birtacha (2008, fig. 8στ), Phillips (2008a,b, ill. 111), Greenlaw (2011, fig. 72), Pareja (2015, fig. 5.9), Crowley (2021, fig. XLI.8)
11e	Baboon (1) ("cynocephalus" [Evans 1928], female Cercopithecus [Phillips, 2008b]) -CMS II.6 73	Squatting with both hands raised in front of a person (?)	Short tail, mane	-	Clay (sealing)	LM IB (1600–1400 BCE)	Hagia Triada	Evans (1928, fig. 492b), Halbher (1903, fig. 32), Papageorgiou and Birtacha (2008, fig. 8α), Phillips (2008b, ill. 11), Pareja (2015, fig. 5.6), Crowley (2021, fig. XLI.9)

Table 10.5. (cont.)

Fig. no.	Primate species (no. of individuals), CMS code	Posture	Phenotypic feature(s)	Measurement	Material	Date	Location	References
11f	Baboons (2) -CMS X 50	Biped	Long snout, absence of mane, bent tail, waisted torso	Diam. 1.25 × 1.13 cm	Agate	MM II–III (2200–2000 BCE)	Crete	Betts (1980, Nr. 50, Basel H. M. L. Erlenmeyer Coll.), Phillips (2008b, ill. 564)
1 g	Baboons (2) (*Cynocephalus* and *Cercopithecus* [Phillips, 2008b]) -CMS II6 74	Biped	Long snout, absence of mane, bent shaped short tail	Diam. 1.35–1.4 cm	Clay (sealing)	LM IB (1600–1400 BCE)	Hagia Triada	Levi (1929a, fig. 70), Platon et al. (1999, fig. 74, HMs. 577), Greenlaw (2011, fig. 73), Papageorgiou and Birtacha (2008, fig. 8y), Phillips (2008a,b, ill. 10), Crowley (2021, fig. XLI.16)
11h	Baboon-like monkeys (3) [probably *Cercopithecus* [Phillips, 2008b]] -CMS V 233	Biped	Left: Hair tufts, robust body, mane present, short snout Right: robust, presence of mane, long snout	Diam. 3.4–3.8 cm	Clay (sealing)	LM IB (1600–1400 BCE)	Chania-Kastelli	Pini (1975, Nr. 233, Inv. GSE 71 T43), Phillips (2008a,b, ill. 128), Greenlaw (2011: fig. 63), Crowley (2021, fig. XLI.6)
11i	Baboon-like monkeys (2) ("cynocephalus" [Pini, 1992]) (*Cercopithecus* [Phillips, 2008b]) -CMS V S1A:131 128-137	Seating	Bent tail, waisted body, no mane, prominent ears, long snout	Diam. 1.1 cm	Clay (sealing)	LM IB (1600–1400 BCE)	Chania-Kastelli	Pini (1992, fig. 131, Inv. Nr. 1559D), Phillips (2008a,b, ill. 127D), Pareja (2015, fig. 5.11)
11j	Baboon(1)-CMS III 236c	Seating	Presence of mane, hair tufts, robustly built	–	Carnelian	MM II (1800–1700 BCE)	Mallia (?)	Müller and Pini (2007a, fig. 236)
11k	Vervet-like monkey (1) (*Cercopithecus* [Phillips, 2008b]) -CMS II.6 282	Seating	Short snout, very long tail, slim body	Diam.2.33 cm	Clay (sealing)	LM I [?] (1600–1400 BCE)	Hagia Triada (?)	Platon et al. (1999, fig. 282. HMs. 1695), Phillips (2008b, ill. 566), Pareja (2015, fig. 5.12), Crowley (2021, fig. XLI.7)
111	Baboon (1) [*Cynocephalus* (Papapostolou, 1977)]	Squatting	Presence of mane, waisted torso	Diam. 2.2 cm	Clay (sealing)	Palatial	Chania	Papapostolou (1977, Pl. 18.7)[b]
11m	Baboon (1) -CMS I 377	Biped	Long snout, waisted body, relatively short tail with tuft at the end	Diam. 1.66–1.68cm	Stone	LM I–II (1600–1400 BCE)	Phaistos or Pylos[c]	Tamvaki (1985), Younger (1989), Krzyszkowska (2005), Phillips (2008a, footnote 952), Pareja (2015, fig. 5.10), Crowley (2021, fig. XLI.12)

11n	Baboon (1) ("scimmiottino" = little monkey [Levi, 1958]) -CMS II.5 297	Seating	Clay (sealing)	MM II[B?] (1700 BCE)	–	Long snout, rounded head, waisted torso, absence of mane	Phaistos	Pini (1970, Nr. 297. Inv. Nr. 696, 945 D), Levi (1958, fig. 307), Papageorgiou and Birtacha (2008, fig. 7), Phillips (2008b, ill. 447), Pareja (2015, fig. 5.2), Crowley (2021, fig. XLL.4)
11o	Vervet-like monkey (1) (Cercopithecus [Phillips, 2008b]) -CMS VS1A 159	Squatting	Clay (sealing)	LM I[B?] (1600–1400 BCE)	Diam. 1.12 cm	Short snout, rounded head, slender body and limbs, long tail (tuft at the end?)	Chania-Kastelli	Pini (1992, fig. 159, Inv. Nr. 2065), Phillips (2008b, ill. 126), Pareja (2015, fig. 5.11)
11p	Vervet-like monkey (1) -CMS II.3 115	Facial representation[d]	Agate	LM IIIA (1300–1400 BCE)	Diam. 1.7 cm	Short snout, nose closer and in-between the eyes, nostrils above end of snout, wide line above the eyes (brows), ears visible above the line of eyes, flat top of head, broad lips	Necropolis of Kalyvia	Platon and Pini (1984, fig. 115. Inv. Nr. 175)
11q	Vervet-like monkeys (6) -CMS II.7 217	Facial representation	Clay (sealing)	LM I (1500 BCE)	–	Short snout, rounded top head, expanded whiskers, ears visible, narrow line above eyes, eyes set at the level of ears	Zakros	Levi (1929b, fig. 186, Platon, et al. (1998: Nr. 217, HMs 93/1,2)

[a] Evans (1928: 764) indicated that this "Minoan seal-type [is] showing [an] adorant cynocephalus," while Hogarth (1902: 77) stated that this "monster is nearly related to the adoring dog-apes of Egypt;"

[b] Considering the criterium of Simandiraki-Grimshaw (2010), possibly this monkey shows hybrid elements, e-g., the multipointed tail (for frescos, Greenlaw [2011] and Chapin and Pareja [2021] presented their suggestions of hybrid elements between humans and monkeys); "Seal from Phaistos (Pareja 2015) or Pylos on the Greek mainland (Tamvaki, 1985, Phillips, 2008a). CMS reported that its origin is unknown;

[d] Krzyszkowska (2016) considers that this seal represents an apotropaic image.

Comments: (1) CMS refers to the codes in the *Corpus der minoischen und mykenischen Siegel* [Corpus of the Minoan and Mycenaean Seals]; (2) Platon (1969, fig. 3497. Inv. Nr. 1266) presented an image that resembles a baboon-like animal; however, because of the body aspect, quadruped behavior, curly tail, and pointy ear, we classify it as a lion-like animal as in Platon (1969, fig. 312. Inv. Nr. 1104; see also Blakolmer, 2020), (3) Müller and Pini (2007a, fig. 237) presents a human face that resembles fig. 10.11m of this study, (4) Xénaki-Sakellariou (1958, fig. 10.355, Nr. 33111, "cynocephalo"), Müller and Pini (2007b, fig. 377, HM Giam 3311), Marinatos (1987b, fig. 5), and Papageorgiou and Birtacha (2008, fig. 8β), and Crowley (2021, fig. XLL15) suggested that two biped dog- or monkey-like animals from Phaistos (Palatial) flanking an amphora are two baboons (CMS III 377). Cautionary, we prefer not to assign a primatomorphic label to it as the body complex does not properly resemble as primate as in other Cretan seals, and the tails are too curvy. (5) According to Crowley (2021, fig. XLL5), monkeys in seals/sealings are associated with so-called Very Important Persons (VIP). Crowley (2021) also suggested that two tailess crouched animals in CMS II.8 286 might be a couple of monkeys. Even though they may appear similar to primates, the image does not provide further diagnostic elements for a final identification.

early Minoan world is most probably related to the typological and iconographic similarities to the Old Kingdom Egyptian monkey representations (Greenlaw, 2011; Pareja, 2015, 2017; Philips, 2008a, b; Vandervondelen, 1994; Vandier d'Abbadie, 1964). Primates were still represented during the Middle and New Egyptian Kingdoms and they were probably venerated as representations of the god of wisdom, Thoth, and also as fruit-pickers (Vanschoonwikel, 1990). Vanschoonwinkel (1990) and Phillips (2008a) also suggested that Cretan seals, the earliest representations of primates in the Aegean, must have originally been subject to Egyptian influence. This influence is also supported by the raised arms of most monkeys indicating that the artists were most likely working from art and not from nature (Greenlaw, 2011). Subsequently, primate representations might have been based on real monkeys, brought to Crete and Thera as gifts from northern Africa (Vanschoonwinkel, 1990). The earliest representations of monkeys in Cretan seals were most likely earlier than the arrival of Anatolian and Syrian influences on this island (Vanschoonwinkel, 1990). Marinatos (1987a) also suggested striking Egyptian influence in the Minoan monkey representations, implying an early contact between Crete, Africa, and the Near East by 2000 BCE. In fact, monkeys were probably known to Crete, and this knowledge most likely originated from Egypt, where baboons were represented seated in relation for Thoth (Marinatos, 1993). This stylistic representation is evident in the anthropomorphic figures on the seals from Knossos and Hagia Triada (Marinatos and Hägg, 1983). Marinatos (1987a) suggested that, apart from being intermediaries between the human and divine world, being adored, and being adorants while serving the deities, the monkey glyptic representations from Hagia Triada may also serve as guardians (possibly referring to Fig. 10.11g [CMS II6 74]). The monkey in the seal of Prassas is accompanied with crocus-like flowers as in the fresco likely related to a divine milieu (Day, 2011; see also Pareja, 2016) (Fig. 10.11c [CMS III 357]). Despite the large variety of primate depictions in Minoan seals, Pareja (2015, 2017) managed to identify certain common patterns, related to outdoor activities or interaction with human-made objects, being solitary or enjoying the company of other monkeys or humans, and body proportions and postures. All these features appear to emphasize the plurality of monkey glyptic representations of the Minoans. In this context, Minoan seals with monkey motifs appear to represent a multitude of configurations with representational counterparts in Egypt: monkeys that worship divinities, monkeys that are worshipped, and monkeys engaged in ritual activities (Marinatos, 1987b).

10.4   Conclusion

In previous work, Urbani and Youlatos (2012, 2020a) proposed that Minoans painted two primate taxa in their frescos on Thera and Crete (baboons *Papio* spp. and vervets *Chlorocebus* spp.) by identifying and describing their diagnostic morphological features (see Table 10.2). Additionally, we found that baboons were involved in sacred/ritual contexts and vervets in leisure/naturalistic ones. Finally, we suggested

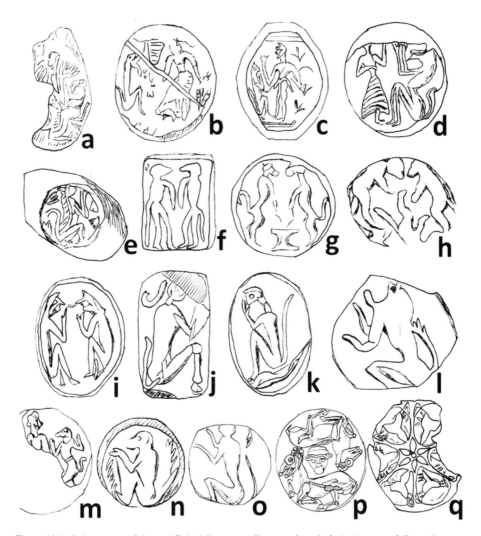

Figure 10.11 Primatomorphic motifs in Minoan sealings and seals (printing parts) from Crete (Illustrations not to scale; made by B. Urbani based on images from sources indicated in Table 10.5).

that Minoans eventually lacked the color "blue" and the grayish/greenish chromatic scale of their pelage was depicted in actual blue for both monkeys. This is relatively common as in the ethnographies of different societies worldwide (e.g. Bright 1992; Fortescue, 2016; McLaughlin 2013; Roberson et al. 2005). It is also very likely, that this color was also culturally lacking among the Minoans, based on the fact the "blue," as we currently understand it, was missing in later post-Minoan Greek ancient peoples and their contemporary societies of adjacent regions (Deutscher, 2010; Gladstone, 1858) as well as adjacent societies such as Egyptians, Akkadians, and Sumerians (Warburton 2014).

After observing the dates and locations of the primatomorphic handling parts of the Cretan seals, and later the primate motifs on printing surfaces of Cretan seals and sealings and the frescos from Thera and Crete, we confirm two "waves" of interest by Minoans in primates, as already noticed by Langdon (1990). Going into further detail, it can be found that the first wave of interest for primates paralles the rise of the 12th Egyptian Dynasty (1991–1783 BCE) (Langdon, 1990). However, this interest in primates might have actually occurred even earlier when the dates of the seals with primatomorphic handling parts are taken into account (c. 2200–2000 BCE, see Table 10.4). This period covers mainly the 11th Egyptian Dynasty (c. 2130–1991 BCE), when Mentuhotep I mostly ruled. During that period, at Deir el-Bahri (Upper Egypt), as part of the royal treasure of Khety that belonged to Mentuhotep II (c. 2051–2000 BCE), it was particularly common to observe baboons on board Egyptian ships (i.e. MetMuseum, 2020) (Fig. 10.12, above). In central and east Crete, baboons were present among Minoan artifacts, especially seals, long before they were represented in ritual contexts in the palatial areas of Knossos.

Later, during the second "wave" of interest in primates (*sensu* Langdon, 1990), it was also found that the dates of the Minoan monkey frescos (~1540 BCE) fit within the 18th Egyptian Dynasty (1550–1295 BCE) of the New Kingdom, in part when Ahmose I ruled. From that period, for instance, there is a well-preserved tomb in El Kab that belongs to Ahmose, son of Ibama, one of his naval military chiefs (Davies, 2009). In this tomb, there is a baboon represented in the north wall under the chair of the so-called Upper register (Davis, 2009). Monkeys were popular at El Kab (Davis, 2009), and baboons were commonly represented during the New Kingdom (Pio, 2018). The monkey is seated in front of a recipient or bowl (Davis, 2009: 167–168) that is strikingly similar in shape and size proportion to that of baboons collecting and offering saffron (Knossos: Fig. 10.3, and Thera: Fig. 10.4, respectively). The lateral representation of monkeys, originally executed in Egypt, was also common for the Minoan monkeys (Bietak, 1995, 2000c). Many other analogous scenes depicting baboons under seats or thrones of Egyptian rulers have been recorded in different locations and periods by Vandier D'Abbadie (1964, 1965, 1966; see also El-Kilany and Mahran, 2015). Vandier D'Abbadie (1964, 1965, 1966) further reported multiple scenes of baboons and vervet-like monkeys on board Egyptian ships. In addition, what seems remarkable – from a current primatological perspective – is that Minoan depictions of primates are, in general, equally or even more detailed in term of phenotypic attributes than their contemporary representations of monkeys in the Egyptian New Kingdom (e.g. images in sites listed by Pio, 2018).

A recent isotopic study by Dominy et al. (2020) found that hamadryas baboons were traded during the second millennium BCE from the Horn of Africa ("Punt") or the southwestern part of the Arabian Peninsula to New Kingdom Egypt, through exchange networks in the Red Sea. Shells from this maritime region have been reported in the Minoan zooarchaeological record for Crete (Reese, 2006; Reese and Betancourt, 2008). A similar route might have been followed in the trade of monkeys or exchange of their imageries. Hamadryas baboon mummies were found in the New Kingdom tombs of Thutmose III and Amenhotep II as well as Horemheb (Dominy et al., 2020). A panel from the New Kingdom 18th Dynasty tomb of Rekhmine (TT100), a high officer of

Figure 10.12 (above) Scene with baboons (*) on a ship. *c.* 2051–2000 BCE. Middle Kingdom. (MetMuseum, 2020; Accession Number: 26.3.354-4-related. The Metropolitan Museum of Art of New York, Public Domain-CC BY). (below) "Grand procession" of Minoans (*Keftiu*), Puntians, and Nubians with a vervet (+) and baboons (*) represented in the fresco of the tomb of Rekhmire (TT100). *c.* 1479-1425 BCE. New Kingdom (The New York Public Library, Public Domain-CC BY). The symbols (+, *) are located above the monkeys.

Thutmose III (*c.* 1479–1425 BCE), shows Minoans from Crete (*Keftiu*), Puntians, and Nubians paying tribute, that also involves a vervet and hamadryas baboons (Dominy, 2020; Güell i Rous, 2018; Hoskins, 1835; Panagiotopoulos, 2001; see also, the scene of a 'blue' tamed vervet and a 'blue' tied baboon brought to Egypt by Nubians as depicted in the tomb fresco of Sobekhotep, Thutmosis IV's treasurer [TT63, c. 1400 BCE]) (Fig. 10.12). It is very likely, that during such events, Minoans might have contacted peoples from African lands with native baboon and vervet populations. Moreover, Bietak (2000a) confirmed the existence of Minoan frescos at Avaris (Tell El-Dab'a) on the eastern side of the Nile Delta during the period of the Egyptian 18th Dynasty. Avaris was a multiethnic port village inhabited by Levantines, Minoans, Nubians, and Egyptians (Bietak, 2018). It was a citadel dating from the Hyksos period, retaken by Ahmose I, during the 18th Dynasty, from Khamudi, the last ruler of the Hyksos, around the time the Theran frescos were made. Earlier, the Hyksos, people of Levantine origin, also had maritime contacts with Crete. The presence of Minoanizing pottery appeared to have permeated different Egyptian socioeconomic levels, weakening the idea of elite-only exchange (Barret, 2009). Regarding the Cretan primatomorphic seals and sealings, both baboons and vervets can be primatologically confirmed during this second "wave" of primate depictions (Table 10.2).

The frescos of Avaris were part of the palatial site of the Hyskos during the time of Tuthmosis of the 18th Dynasty between 1500 and 1450 BCE (Bietak, 2005). It also was during the reigns of Tuthmosis I and II, when Egyptians initiated contact with Minoan Crete and Egypt (Bietak, 2005), or vice versa. However, archaeological evidence, and more particularly Tell el-Dab'a (Avaris), indicates sea links between Crete and Egypt through delta ports (Warren, 1995). Sakellarakis and Sakellarakis (1984) and Niemeier (2004) specified that Aegean peoples were known in Egypt and traded in northern Africa during the Minoan thalassocracy. Egyptian frescos, such as the ones in the tomb of Rekhmire, seem to represent such encounters; Minoans brought objects from the islands to Egypt during the Palatial period, and Egyptian scarab seals were found in the royal tombs of Knossos (Davis, 2006; Platon et al., 1977). Similar indications for Aegean–Egyptian contact have been also found in the tomb of Amenmose (Pinch-Brock, 2000). The evidence (frescos and portable objects) compiled in this chapter appears to reaffirm the contention that the Minoans traded or exchanged imageries about monkeys at least during two time periods and provides further evidence on the peoples from Egypt with whom the Minoans had these contacts. Centuries later, during the late Aegean Late Bronze Age (14–13th centuries BCE), the presence of two imported monkey figurines at the sites of Tiryns and Mycenae reflect contact with the Egypt of Amenhotep II (Cline, 1991, 1995; Kilian 1979; McDermott, 1938).

Despite the pictorial primatomorphic evidence in the Aegean, there are no primate remains that have ever been recovered in any Minoan sites. Certainly, we pass over the doubtful and outrageous "finding" of the petrified skull of an alleged primate described by Poulianos (1972), which turned out to be nothing else than a shapely portion of lava (Doumas, 2000; Sp. Marinatos, 1971b). After reviewing multiple sources (e.g. Bedwin, 1984; Gamble, 1978), Trantalidou (1990) found that during the late Bronze age, sheep/goats (*Capra ovis*) were the most ubiquitious animals in Minoan sites, followed by pigs (*Sus* spp.) and cattle (*Bos* spp.). Sheep and goats formed over 90% of their diet (Knossos: 96.2%, Akrotiri: 96.4%, Phylakopi: 99.8%). In Akrotiri, Trantalidou (1990) and Gamble (1978) found that there were also other species available, such as dogs, birds, rabbits, hares, fishes, horses, and cervids, while in Knossos, Bedwin (1984) reported dogs and other wild animals. As many cercopithecid fragments and bones can be very similar to those of other mammals, we would recommend a thorough reevaluation of the archaeofaunal remains from Minoan locations. In fact, already excavated skeletal remains of mammalian groups, such as ungulates and carnivores could have been easily misidentified. Furthermore, exhaustive and detailed analyses of newly discovered material should also be considered. We do not claim that primate remains would be found, but primate comparative material should be involved in further Minoan zooarchaeological studies.

After a thorough review of the available material evidence concerning the representation of primates among Minoans, we affirm that (a) there was an extensive cultural exchange between Minoans and Egyptians; (b) Minoans were either first-hand observers of captive primates or were painters of detailed narratives; (c) some monkeys (vervets, *Chlorocebus* spp.) are related to a leisure – yet naturalistic – context and some others (baboons *Papio* spp., then deified in Egypt) act as intermediaries between gods and humans in sacred contexts; (d) primates reach Minoan imageries in two time periods (*sensu* Langdon, 1990; specific moments and rulers indicated in this chapter); and (e) the representation of primates among Minoans is an example of the earliest transmission of exotica into Europe. In fact, as suggested by Urbani and Youlatos (2020a: 3) "this Aegean Bronze Age society was the first European civilisation to perceive, represent, socially construct, and, eventually, have physical interaction with nonhuman primates."

Acknowledgments

Vielen Dank goes to Julia Binnberg whose insightful remarks and suggestions greatly serve for improving an earlier draft of this chapter. Julia also suggested the overlooked reference of A. Vlachopoulos (2007) to us. *Merci* to Dominique Gommery who provided valuable information on a monkey feature that further supports the evidence that Theran β monkeys are vervets. *Efharisto* to Christos G. Doumas (Excavations at Akrotiri, Thera) and Andreas Vlachopoulos (University of Ioannina/Akrotiri Excavations) for kindly providing the photographs for Figs. 10.5 and 10.7, respectively. Also, the constructive comments of Andrzej T. Antczak and the external reviewers served to significantly improve early drafts of this chapter. B. Urbani was funded by an I.K.Y. (Greek State Scholarship Foundation, Ministry of Education of the Hellenic Republic) Post-doctoral Fellowship. The School of Biology, Aristotle University of Thessaloniki also provided research travel support to Crete (B.U.). B. Urbani and D. Youlatos thank the Venezuelan Institute for Scientific Research (IVIC) and the Aristotle University of Thessaloniki, respectively, for research support. In Crete, Ioannis Maniakas provided important logistical care. We would like to thank the personnel at the National Archaeological Museum (Athens), the Herakleion Archaeological Museum (Iraklio, Crete), the Museum of Prehistoric Thera (Fira, Santorini), and the archaeological sites of Knossos (Crete) and Akrotiri (Santorini) for their collaboration. We express our gratitude to Aristotelis Mentzos and the librarians of the Historical-Archaeological Library of the Aristotle University of Thessaloniki, to Stefano Garbin at the Biblioteca della Scuola Archaeologica Italiana di Atene as well as to the personnel at the Blegen Library of the American School of Classical Studies at Athens. Thanks to the library of the University of Illinois at Urbana-Champaign. Davis S. Reese shared significant Minoan zooarchaeological references, and Nathaniel J. Dominy provided us with the interesting paper on Egyptian baboon mummies right after its publication. We appreciate the effort of the people at the Metropolitan Museum of Art of New York and the New York Public Library and anonymous photographers who share their images under Creative Commons licenses for open access use by scholars and the general public.

References

Abramovitz, K. (1980). Frescoes from Ayia Irini, Keos. Parts II–IV. *Hesperia*, **49**, 57–85

Angelopoulou, N. (2000). Nature scenes: An approach to a symbolic art. In S. Sherratt, ed., *The Wall Paintings of Thera, Vol. II: Proceedings of the First International Symposium, August 30–4 September 1997*. Athens: Petros M. Nomikos Centre-Thera Foundation, 545–554.

Asimenos, K. (1978). Technological observations on the Thera wall-paintings. In C. Doumas, ed., *Thera and the Aegean world I*. London: The Thera Foundation, 571–578.

Barrett, C. E. (2009). The perceived value of Minoan and Minoanizing pottery in Egypt. *Journal of Mediterranean Archaeology*, **22**, 211–234.

Bedwin, O. W. (1984). The animal bones. In J. Popham, ed., *The Minoan Unexplored Mansions at Knossos*. British Society at Athens, Suppl. 17, 307–308.

Betancourt, P. (2000). The concept of space in Theran compositional systemics. In S. Sherratt, ed., *The Wall Paintings of Thera, Vol. I: Proceedings of the First International Symposium, August 30–4 September 1997*. Athens: Petros M. Nomikos Centre-Thera Foundation, 359–363.

Betancourt, P. P. (2007). *Introduction to Aegean Art*. Philadelphia: INSTAP Academic Press.

Betts, J. H. (1980). *Die Schweizer Sammlungen. Corpus der minoischen und mykenischen Siegel X*. Berlin: Gebrüder. Mann Verlag

Bietak, M. (1995). Connections between Egypt and the Minoan world: New results from Tell el-Dab'a/Avaris. In W. V. Davies, & L. Schofield, eds., *Egypt, the Aegean and the Levant: Interconnections in the Second Millennium BC*. London: Trustees of the British Museum, 19–28.

Bietak, M. (2000a). Minoan paintings in Avaris, Egypt. In S. Sherratt, ed., *The Wall Paintings of Thera, Vol. I: Proceedings of the First International Symposium, August 30–4 September 1997*. Athens: Petros M. Nomikos Centre-Thera Foundation, 33–42.

Bietak, M. (2000b). The tableau from Tell el-Dab'a. In S. Sherratt, ed., *The Wall Paintings of Thera, Vol. I: Proceedings of the First International Symposium, August 30–4 September 1997*. Athens: Petros M. Nomikos Centre-Thera Foundation, 77–88.

Bietak, M (2000c). The mode of representation in Egyptian art in comparison to Aegean Bronze age art. In S. Sherratt, ed., *The Wall Paintings of Thera, Vol. I: Proceedings of the First International Symposium, August 30–4 September 1997*. Athens:

Petros M. Nomikos Centre-Thera Foundation, 209–246.

Bietak, M. (2005). The setting of the Minoan wall paintings at Avaris. In L. Morgan, ed., *Aegean Wall Painting. A Tribute to Mark Cameron*. Athens: British School at Athens Studies 13, 83–90.

Bietak, M. (2018). The many ethnicities of Avaris: Evidence from the northern borderland of Egypt. In J. Budka, & J. Auenmüller, eds., *From Microcosm to Macrocosm: Individual Households and Cities in Ancient Egypt and Nubia*. Leiden: Sidestone Press. 73–92.

Bietak, M., & Marinatos, N. (1995). The Minoan wall paintings from Avaris. *Ägypten und Levante/Egypt and the Levant*, **5**, 49–62.

Binnberg, J. (2019). Like a duck to water – Birds and liquids in the Aegean Bronze Age. *The Annual of the British School at Athens*, **114**, 41–78.

Binnberg, J., Urbani, B., & Youlatos, D. (2021). Langurs in the Aegean Bronze Age? A review of a recent debate on archaeoprimatology and animal identification in ancient iconography. *Journal of Greek Archaeology*, **6**, 100–127.

Birtacha, K., & Zacharioudakis, M. (2000). Stereotypes in Theran wall paintings: Modules and patterns in the procedure of painting. In S. Sherratt, ed., *The Wall Paintings of Thera, Vol. I: Proceedings of the First International Symposium, August 30–4 September 1997*. Athens: Petros M. Nomikos Centre-Thera Foundation, 159–171.

Blakolmer, F. (2020). Gab es Löwen und Affen im minoischen Kreta? Ein ikonographisches Problem. In L. Berger, L. Huber, F. Lang, & J. Weilhartner, eds., *Akten des 17. Österreichischen Archäologentages am Fachbereich Altertumswissenschaften, Klassische und Frühägäische Archäologie der Universität Salzburg vom 26. bis 28. Februar 2018*. Salzburg: Universität Salzburg, 39–49.

Bloedow, E. (1992). On lions in Mycenaean and Minoan culture. In R. Laffineur, & J. L. Crowley, eds., *Aegean Bronze Age Iconography: Shaping a meThodology*. Liège: Aegeum 8 (Annales d'archéologie égéenne de l Université de Liège), 295–306.

Bright, W. (ed.) (1992). *Southern Paiute and Ute Linguistics and Ethnography. The Collected works of Edward Sapir*. New York: De Gruyter Mouton.

Buchholz, H. G. (1980). Some obervations concerning Theras's contacts overseas during the Bronze Age. In C. Doumas, ed., *Thera and the Aegean World II. Papers and Proceedings of the Second International*

Scientific Congress. Santorini Greece August 1979. London: Thera and the Aegean World, 227–240.

Buchholz, H. G., & Karageorghis, V. (1973). Prehistoric Greece and Cyprus. An Archaeological Handbook. London: Phaidon.

Bury, H. P. R. (1967). Analysis of mammalian bones at Hagfet. In C. B. M. McBurney, ed., The Haua Fteah (Cyrenaica) and the Stone Age of the Southeast Mediterranean. New York: Cambridge University Press, 354–357.

Cadogan, G. (2004). The Minoan distance: The impact of Knossos upon the twentieth century. In G. Cadogan, E. Hatzaki, & A. Vasilakis, eds., Knossos: Palace, City, State. Nottingham: British School at Athens Studies 12, 437–545.

Cameron, M. A. S. (1968). Unpublished paintings from the 'House of Frescoes' at Knossos. The Annual of the British School at Athens, 63, 1–31.

Cameron M. A. S. (1978). Theoretical interpretations among Theran, Cretan and mainland frescoes. In C. Doumas, ed., Thera and the Aegean world I. London: The Thera Foundation, 579–592.

Canciani, F. (1973). Scimmie a Creta. Chronache di Archeologia, Rivista annuale dell'Università di Catania, 12, 107–110.

Castleden, R. (1990) The Knossos Labyrinth. A New View of the 'Palace of Minos' at Knossos. London: Routledge.

Castleden, R. (1993) Minoan Life in Bronze Age Crete. London: Routledge.

Chaix, L. (1994). Nouvelles données de l'archéozoologie du nord du Soudan. In : C. Berger, G. Clerc, & N. Grimal, eds., Hommages a Jean Leclant. Vol. 2. Nubie, Soudan, Ethiopie, Cairo, Paris: Institut français d'archeologie orientale,105–110.

Chapin, A. P. (2004). Power, privilege, and landscape in Minoan art. Hesperia (Charis: Essays in Honor Sara A. Immerwahr) Suppl., 33, 47–64.

Chapin, A. P. & Shaw, M. C. (2006). The frescoes from the House of the Frescoes at Knossos: A reconsideration of their architectural context and a new reconstruction of the Crocus Panel. The Annual of the British School at Athens, 101, 57–88.

Chapin, A. & Pareja, M. N. (2020). Peacock or poppycock? Investigations into exotic animal imagery in Minoan and Cycladic art. In B. Davis and R. Laffineur, eds., ΝΕΩΤΕΡΟΣ – Studies in Bronze Age Aegean art and archaeology in honor of Professor John G. Younger on the occasion of his retirement. Aegaeum, 44, 215–226.

Chapin, A. & M. N. Pareja (2021). Betwixt and beyond the boundaries: an ecosocial model of animal human

relations in Minoan and Cycladic animal art. In R. Laffineur and T. Palaima, eds., Zoia – Animal-human interactions in the Aegean Middle and Late Bronze Age. Aegaeum, 45, 125–134.

Cline, E. H. (1991). Monkey business in the Bronze Age Aegean: The Amenhotep II faience figurines at Mycenae and Tiryns. The Annual of the British School at Athens, 86, 29–42.

Cline, E. H. (1995). Egyptian and Near Eastern imports at late Bronze Age Mycenae. In W. V. Davies, & L. Schofield, eds., Egypt, the Aegean and the Levant: Interconnections in the Second Millennium BC. London: British Museum Press, 91–115.

Cline E. H., Yasur-Landau A., & Goshen, N. (2011) New fragments of Aegean-style painted plaster from Tel Kabri, Israel. American Journal of Archaeology, 115, 245–261

Coldstream, J. N. (1973). Knossos. The Sanctuary of Demeter. British School at Athens Suppl. 8 London.

Coleman, K. (1973). Frescoes from Ayia, Irini, Keos. Parts II-IV. Hesperia, 42, 284–296.

Concoran, N. L. H. (2016). The color blue as an 'animator' in Ancient Egyptian art. In R. B. Goldman, ed., Essays in Global Color History, Interpreting the Ancient Spectrum. Piscataway, NJ: Gorgias Press, 59–82.

Coutsis, J. G. (2000). The insects depicted on the wall paintings of Thera: An attempt at identification. In S. Sherratt, ed., The Wall Paintings of Thera, Vol. II: Proceedings of the First International Symposium, August 30-4 September 1997. Athens: Petros M. Nomikos Centre-Thera Foundation, 580–584.

Crooks, S., Tully, C. J., & Hitchcock, L. A. (2016). Numinous tree and stone: Re-animating the Minoan landscape. Metaphysis: ritual, myth and symbolism in the Aegean Bronze Age. Aegaeum, 39, 157–164.

Crowley, J. L. (2021). The fabulous five: monkey, lion, griffin, dragon, genius. In R. Laffineur, & T. Palaima, eds., Zoia – Animal-human interactions in the Aegean Middle and Late Bronze Age. Aegaeum, 45: 199–214.

Davis, B. E. (2006). Trade in goods between Crete and Egypt in the Minoan Palace Period (ca.1950 – ca.1490 BCE). Postgraduate thesis. University of Melbourne.

Davis, W. V. (2009). The tomb of Ahmose Son-of-Ibana at Elkab. Documenting the family and other observations. In W. Claes, H. Meulenaere, & S. de Hendrick, eds., Elkab and Beyond. Studies in Honour of Luc Limme (Orientalisa Lovaniensa Analecta 191). Leuven: Uitgeverij Peeters, 139–175.

Day, J. (2011). Crocuses in context: A diachronic survey of the crocus motif in the Aegean Bronze Age. *Hesperia* 80, 337–379.

Dimopoulou-Rethemiotaki, N. (2005). *The Archaeological Museum of Herakleion*. Athens: The John S. Latsis Foundation.

Deutscher, G. (2010). *Through the Language Glass: Why the World Looks Different in Other Languages*. New York: Metropolitan Books.

Dewan, R. (2015). Bronze Age flower power: The Minoan use and social significance of saffron and crocus flowers. *Chronika*, 5, 42–55.

Dominy, N. J., Ikram, S., Moritz, G. L., et al. (2020). Mummified baboons reveal the far reach of early Egyptian mariners. *eLife*, 9, e60860.

Doumas, C. (1983). *Thera: Pompeii of the Ancient Aegean: Excavations at Akrotiri 1967–1979*. London: Thames & Hudson.

Doumas, C. (1985). Conventions artisitiques à Théra et dans la Mediterranée orientale à l'époque préhistorique. In P. Darcque, & J.-C. Poursat, eds., *L'Iconographie Minoenne*. Athens: *Bulletin de correspondence hellénique*, Suppl. XI, 29–34.

Doumas, C. (1992). *The Wall-Paintings of Thera*. Athens: The Thera Foundation-Petros M. Nomikos.

Doumas, C. (2000). Discussion comment of Trantalidou, K (2000). In S. Sherratt, ed., *The Wall Paintings of Thera, Vol. II: Proceedings of the First International Symposium, August 30–4 September 1997*. Athens: Petros M. Nomikos Centre-Thera Foundation, 735.

Doumas, C. (2013). Akrotiri, Thera: Reflections from the East. In J. Aruz, S. B. Graff, & Y. Rakic, eds., *Cultures in Contact*. New Haven: Yale University Press, 180–186.

Douskos, I. (1980). The crocuses of Santorini. In C. Doumas, ed., *Thera and the Aegean world II. Papers and Proceedings of the Second International Scientific Congress. Santorini Greece August 1979*. Athens: Thera and the Aegean World Publisher, 141–145.

El-Kilany, E., & Mahran, H. (2015). What lies under the chair! A study in Ancient Egyptian private tomb scenes, Part I: Animals. *Journal of the American Research Center in Egypt* 51, 243–264.

Evans, A. (1901). The Palace of Knossos. *The Annual of the British School at Athens* VII, 1–120.

Evans, A. (1921). *The Palace of Minos. A Comparative Account of the Successive Stages of the early Cretan Civilization as Illustrated by the Discoveries of Knossos. Volume I: Part I*. London: Macmillan and Co.

Evans, A. (1928a). *The Palace of Minos. A Comparative Account of the Successive Stages of the early Cretan Civilization as Illustrated by the Discoveries of Knossos Volume II: Part I*. London: Macmillan and Co.

Evans A. 1928b. *The Palace of Minos. A Comparative Account of the Successive Stages of the early Cretan Civilization as Illustrated by the Discoveries of Knossos Volume II: Part II*. London: Macmillan and Co.

Evans, A. (1935). *The Palace of Minos. Volume IV, Part II*. London: MacMillan and Co.

Evely, D. (1999). *Fresco: A Passport into the Past. Minoan Crete through the Eyes of Mark Cameron*. Athens: British School at Athens.

Ferrence, S. C. (2011). Variety is the spice of life: Figurines from the Cave of Hagios Charalambos in: M. Andreadaki-Vlazaki, & E. Papadopoulou, eds. *Πεπραγμένα του Διεθνούς Κρητολογικού Συνεδρίου (Χανιⱥ, 1-8 ⱥκρωβρίου 2006). Τόμος Α3 Προϊστορικοί Χρόνοι*. Chania: Philological Association "O Chrysosomos", 597–611.

Ferrence, S. C., & Bendersky, G. (2004). Therapy with saffron and the goddess at Thera. *Perspectives in Biology and Medicine*, 47, 199–226.

Filippakis, S., Perdikatsis, V., & Paradellis, T. (1976). Analysis of blue pigment from the Greek Bronze Age. *Studies in Conservation*, 21, 143–153

Fortescue, M. (2016). The colours of the Artic. *Amerindia*, 38, 25–46

Gamble, C. S. (1978). The Bronze Age animal economy from Akrotiri: A preliminary analysis. In C. Doumas, ed., *Thera and the Aegean World I*. London: The Thera Foundation, 745–753.

Gladstone, W. E. (1858). *Studies on Homer and the Homeric Age*. Oxford: Oxford University Press.

Greenlaw, C. (2005). How monkeys evolved in Egyptian and Minoan art and culture. In C. Briault, J. Green, A. Kaldelis, & A. Stellatou, eds., *SOMA 2003-Symposium on Mediterranean archaeology*. Oxford: Archaeopress. 71–73.

Greenlaw, C. (2006). Monkeying around the Mediterranean: A fresh perspective on ancient primates. In J. Day, C. Greenlaw, H. Hall, et al., eds., *SOMA 2004-Symposium on Mediterranean archaeology*. Oxford: Archaeopress. 63–67.

Greenlaw, C. (2011). *The Representation of Monkeys in the Art and Thought of Mediterranean cultures: A New Perspective on Ancient Primates*. Oxford: British Archaeological Reports.

Groves, C. (2008). *Extended Family, Long Lost Cousins: A Personal Look at the History of Primatology*. Arlington: Conservation International.

Güell i Rous, J. M. (2018). *The Tomb of Vizier Rekhmire (TT100): A Textual and Iconographic Study*.

Rekhmire Receiving Foreign Tribute. Volume 1. Barcelona: Editorial La Vocal de Lis.

Guralnick, E. (2000). Proportions of painted figures from Thera. In S. Sherratt, ed., *The Wall Paintings of Thera, Vol. I: Proceedings of the First International Symposium, August 30–4 September 1997.* Athens: Petros M. Nomikos Centre-Thera Foundation, 173–188.

Halbher, F. (1903). Resti dell'età micenea scoperti ad Haghia Triada presso Phaestos. Raporto sulle ricerche del 1902. *Monumenti Antichi*, **XIII**, 7–74.

Herva, V.-P. (2006). Flower lovers, after all? Rethinking religion and human-environment relations in Minoan Crete. *World Archaeology*, **38**, 586–598.

Höckmann, O. (1978). Theran floral style in relation to that of Crete. In C. Doumas, ed., *Thera and the Aegean World I.* London: The Thera Foundation, 604–616.

Hogarth, D. G. (1901). Excavations at Zakro, Crete. *The Annual of the British School at Athens*, **VII**, 121–149.

Hogarth, D. G. (1902). The Zakro Sealings. *Journal of Hellenic Studies*, **22**, 76–93.

Hood, S. (2005). Dating the Knossos frescoes. In L. Morgan, ed., *Aegean Wall Painting. A Tribute to Mark Cameron.* Athens: British School at Athens Studies 13, 45–81.

Hoskins, G. A. (1835). *Travels in Ethiopia, Above the Second Cataract of the Nile.* London: Longman, Rees, Orme, Brown, Green & Longman.

Houlihan PF. Hood, S. (1990). The Cretan elements on Thera in Late Minoan IA. In D. A. Hardy, C. G. Doumas, J. A. Sakellarakis, &. P. M. Warren, eds., *Thera and the Aegean World III. Vol. One: Archaeology.* London: The Thera Foundation, 118–123.

Hunt, K. D., Cant, J. G. H., Gebo, D. L., Rose, M. D., Walker, S. E., & Youlatos, D. (1996). Standarized descriptions of primate locomotor and postural modes. *Primates*, **37**, 363–387.

Iliakis, K. (1978). Theran floral style in relation to that of Crete. In C. Doumas, ed., *Thera and the Aegean world I.* London: The Thera Foundation, 617–628.

Immerwahr, S. (1985). A possible influence of Egyptian art in the creation of Minoan wall paintings. In P. Darcque and J.-C. Poursat., eds., *L'Iconographie Minoenne.* Athens: Bulletin de correspondence hellénique Suppl. XI, 40–50.

Immerwahr, S. (1990). *Aegean Painting in the Bronze Age.* Philadelphia: Pennsylvania State University Press.

Immerwahr, S. (2000). Thera and Knossos: Relation of the paintings to their architectural space. In S. Sherratt, ed., *The Wall Paintings of Thera, Vol. I: Proceedings of the First International Symposium, August 30–4 September 1997.* Athens: Petros M. Nomikos Centre-Thera Foundation, 467–490.

Kenna, V. E. G. (1966). *Die englischen Privatsammlungen. Corpus der Minoischen und Mykenischen Siegel VIII.* Berlin: Gebrüder. Mann Verlag.

Kilian, K. (1979). Ausgrabungen in Tiryns 1977. *Archäologisher Anzeiger* **27**, 379–411.

Kleinsgütl, D. 2000. Some remarks on the felids of Thera. In S. Sherratt, ed., *The Wall Paintings of Thera, Vol. I: Proceedings of the First International Symposium, August 30–4 September 1997.* Athens: Petros M. Nomikos Centre-Thera Foundation, 699–708.

Komninos, P. (2009). To Topio stis Toihografikes Parastaseis tou Aegeakou Chorou kata tin Ysteri Epohi tou Chalkou. PhD dissertation, Aristotle University of Thessaloniki (in Greek).

Kontorli-Papadopoulou, L. (1996). *Aegean Frescoes of Religious Character.* Götenborg: Paul Åströms Förlag.

Krzyszkowska, O. (2005). *Aegean Seals: An Introduction.* Oxford: Oxford University Press.

Krzyszkowska, O. (2016). Warding off evil: Apotropaic practice and imagery in Minoan Crete. In E. Alram-Stern, F. Blakolmer, S. Deger-Jalkotzy, R. Laffineur, & J. Weilhartner, eds., *Metaphysis. Ritual, Myth and Symbolism in the Aegean Bronze Age. Proceedings of the 15th International Aegean Conference. Aegaeum 39.* 115–121.

Laffineur, R. (1990). Composition and perspective in Theran wall-paintings. In D. A. Hardy, C. G. Doumas, J. A. Sakellarakis, & P. M. Warren, eds., *Thera and the Aegean World III. Vol. One: Archaeology.* London: The Thera Foundation, 246–251.

Langdon, S. (1990). From monkeys to man: The evolution of a geometric sculptural type. *American Journal of Archaeology*, **94**, 407–424.

Legendart A. (2020). Une classification animale crétoise à l'âge du bronze? Le point de vue des Minoens par le prisme de l'iconographie. *Anthropozoologica*, **55**, 247–255.

Levi, D. (1929a). Le cretule di Hagia Triada. *Annuario della Scuola Archeologica di Atene e delle Missione Italiane in Oriente*, **VIII–IX** (1925-1926), 71–156.

Levi, D. (1929b). Le cretule di Zakro. *Annuario della Scuola Archeologica di Atene e delle Missione Italiane in Oriente*, **VIII–IX** (1925-1926), 157–201.

Levi, D. (1958). L'archivio di cretule a Festòs. *Annuario della Scuola Archeologica di Atenes e dell Missione Italiane in Oriente*, XXXV–XXXVI, 7–192.

Lurz, N. (1994). *Der Einfluß Ägyptens, Vorderasiens und Kretas auf die Mykenischen Fresken. Studien zum Ursprung der Frühgriechischen Wandmalerei. Europäische Hochschulschriften Archäologie 38(48)*. Frankfurt: Perter Lang.

Marinatos, N. (1984). *Art and Religion in Thera: Reconstructing a Bronze Age Society*. Athens: Mathioulakis.

Marinatos, N. (1986). *Minoan Sacrificial Ritual. Cult Practice and Symbolism*. Götenborg: Skrifter Utgivna av Svenska Intitutet I Athen, 8°, IX. Paul Åströms Förlag.

Marinatos, N. (1987a). Offering of saffron to the Minoan goddess of nature. The role of the monkey and the importance of the saffron In T. Linders, & G. Nordquist, eds., *Gifts to the gOds. Proceedings of the Uppsala Symposium 1985*. Uppsala: Acta Universitatis Upsaliensis Boreas. Uppsala Studies in Ancient Mediterranean and Near Eastern Civilization, 123–132.

Marinatos, N. (1987b). The monkey in the shrine: A fresco fragment from Thera. In L. Kastranaki, G. Orphanou, & N. Giannadakis, eds., *Eilapini. Tomos Timitikos gia ton Kathigiti Nikolao Platona*. Irakleion: Ekdotiki Frontida Vikelaia Demotiki Vivliothiki, 417–421.

Marinatos, N. (1993). *Minoan Religion. Ritual, Image, and Symbol*. Columbia, SC: University of South California Press.

Marinatos, N., & Hägg, R. (1983). Anthropomorphic cult images in Minoan Crete? In O. Krzyszkowska, & L. Nixon, eds., *Minoan Society. Proceedings of the Cambridge Colloquium 1981*. Bristol: Bristol Classical Press, 185–201.

Marinatos, Sp. (1969). *Excavations at Thera II (1968 Season)*. Athens: Bibliothiki tis en Athinais Archaiologikis Etaireias.

Marinatos, Sp (1970). *Excavations at Thera III (1969 Season)*. Athens: Bibliothiki tis en Athinais Archaiologikis Etaireias.

Marinatos, Sp. (1971a). *Excavations at Thera IV (1970 Season)*. Athens: Bibliothiki tis en Athinais Archaiologikis Etaireias.

Marinatos, Sp. (1971b). *A Brief Guide to the Temporary Exhibition of the Antiquities of Thera*. Athens: General Direction of Antiquities and Restoration.

Marinatos, Sp. (1972a). *Excavations at Thera V (1971 Season)*. Athens: Bibliothiki tis en Athinais Archaiologikis Etaireias.

Marinatos, Sp. (1972b). *Treasures of Thera*. Athens: Commercial Bank of Greece.

Marinatos, Sp. (1973). *Kreta, Thera und das mykenische Hellas*. Munich: Hirmer Verlag.

Marinatos, Sp. (1974). *Excavations at Thera VI (1972 Season)*. Athens: Bibliothiki tis en Athinais Archaiologikis Etaireias.

Marinatos, Sp. (1976), *Excavations at Thera, VII (1973 Season)*. Athens: Bibliothiki tis en Athinais Archaiologikis Etaireias.

Masseti, M. (1980). Le scimmie azzurre. La fauna etiopica degli aff reschi minoici di Santorino (Thera). *Mondo archeologico*, 51, 32–37.

Masseti, M. (1997). Representation of birds in Minoan art. *International Journal of Osteoarchaeology*, 7, 354–363.

Masseti, M. (2000). Did the study of ethology begin in Crete 4000 years ago? *Ethology Ecology & Evolution*, 12, 89–96.

Masseti M. (2003). Taxonomic and behavioural aspects of the representation of mammals in Aegean Bronze Age art. In E. Kotjabopoulou, Y. Hamilakis, P. Halstead, C. Gamble, & P. Elefanti, eds., *Zooarchaeology in Greece. Recent Advances*. Athens: British School at Athens Studies 9, 273–281.

Masseti, M. (2006). Did the study of primatology begin on the Island of Crete (Greece) 4000 years ago? *Folia Primatologica*, 77, 296–297.

Masseti, M. (2019). Monkeys in the Ancient Greek World (2000–500 B.C.). In C. C. N. Casanova, F. M. C. Scalfari, & C. Veracini, eds., *History of Primatology: Yesterday and Today. The Western–Mediterranean Tradition*. Canterano: Aracne, 21–51.

Masseti, M. (2021). An analysis of recent literature regarding the Minoan "blue monkeys" represented in Aegean Bronze Age art. *Journal of Anthropological Sciences*, 99, 1–4.

Masseti, M., & Bruner, E. (2009). The primates of the western Palaearctic: A biogeographical, historical, and archaeozoological review. *Journal of Anthropological Sciences*, 87, 33–91.

Matz, F. (1962). *Crete and Early Greece: The Prelude to Greek Art*. London: Methuen.

McDermott, W. C. (1938). *The Ape in Antiquity*. Baltimore: The John Hopkins University Press.

McLaughlin, C. (2013). *A Lakota War Book from the Little Bighorn: The Pictographic "Autobiography of*

Half Moon". Harvard/Peabody Museum Press, Cambridge.

Medleson, C. (1983). More monkey business. *Anatolian Studies*, **33**, 81–83.

MetMuseum (2020). Scene with monkeys and baboons ca. 2051–2000 B.C. Middle Kingdom Dynasty 11, Reign of Mentuhotep II Rogers Fund, 1926 Accession Number: 26.3.354-4-related. New York, Metropolitan Museun of Art. Available at: www .metmuseum.org/art/collection/search/590882

Morgan, L. (1988). *Miniature Wall Paintings of Thera. A Study in Aegean Culture and Iconography.* Cambridge: Cambridge University Press.

Morgan, L. (1990) Island iconography: Thera, Kea, Milos. In D. A. Hardy, C. G Doumas, J. A. Sakellarakis, & P. M. Warren, eds. *Thera and the Aegean World III. Volume One: Archaeology.* London: The Thera Foundation, 252–266.

Morgan, L. (ed.) (2005). *Aegean Wall Painting. A Tribute to Mark Cameron.* Athens: British School at Athens Studies 13.

Morgan, L., & Cameron, M. A. S. (2007). The painted plasters and their relation to the wall painting of the Pillar Crypt. In C. Renfrew, ed., *Excavations at Phylakopi in Melos 1974-77. Suppl. Vol. 42.* Athens: British School at Athens, 371–399.

Mountjoy, P. A. (2004). Knossos and the Cyclades in Late Minoan IB. In G. Cadogan, E. Hatzaki, & A. Vasilakis, eds., *Knossos: Palace, City, State.* Nottingham: British School at Athens Studies 12, 399–404.

Müller, W., & Pini, I. (2007a). *Iraklion Archäologisches Museum. Teil 1. Sammlung Giamalakis. Corpus der minoischen und mykenischen Siegel III (I).* Berlin: Gebrüder. Mann Verlag.

Müller, W., & Pini, I. (2007b). *Iraklion Archäologisches Museum. Teil 2. Sammlung Giamalakis. Corpus der minoischen und mykenischen Siegel III (II).* Berlin: Gebrüder. Mann Verlag.

Niemeier, W.-D. (1992). Iconography and context: The Thera frescoes. In R. Laffiner, & J. L. Crowley, eds., *Aegean Bronze Age Iconography: Shaping a Methodology.* Liège: Aegeum 8 (Annales d'archéologie égéenne de l'Université de Liège), 97–104.

Niemeier, W.-D. (2004). When Minoans ruled the waves: Knossian power overseas. In G. Cadogan, E. Hatzaki, & A. Vasilakis, eds., *Knossos: Palace, City, State.* Nottingham: British School at Athens Studies 12, 393–398.

Niemeier, B., & Niemeier, W.-D. (2000). Aegean frescoes in Syria-Palestine: Alalakh and Tel Kabri. In S.

Sherratt, ed., *The Wall Paintings of Thera, Vol. II: Proceedings of the First International Symposium, August 30-4 September 1997.* Athens: Petros M. Nomikos Centre-Thera Foundation, 763–802.

Nilsson, M. P. (1927) *Minoan Mycenaean Religion and its Survival in Greek Religion.* London: Lund C. W. K Gleerup.

Panagiotopoulos, D. (2001). *Keftiu* in context: Theban tomb-paintings as a historical source. *Oxford Journal of Archaeology*, **20**, 263–283.

Papageorgiou, I., & Birtacha, K. 2008. Η εικονογραφία του πιθ⊠κου στην Εποχ⊠ του Χαλκού. Η περίπτωση των τοιχογραφιών από το Ακρωτ⊠ρι Θήρας, in: Doumas, C., ed., *Ακρωτ⊠ρι Θ⊠ρας: Τρι⊠ντα χρόνια έρευνας 1967-1997. Επιστημονικ⊠ συν⊠ντηση 19-20 Δεκεμβρίου 1997.* Athens: The Archaeological Society at Athens, 287–316 (in Greek)

Papapostolou, I .A. (1977). Τα Σφραγίσματα των Χανίων. Συμβολ⊠ στη Μελέτη της Μινωικ⊠ς Σφραγιδογλυφίας. N. 87. Athens: Archaeological Society of Athens (in Greek)

Pareja, M. N. (2015). Monkey and ape iconography in Aegean Art. PhD dissertation. Temple University.

Pareja, M. N. (2016). Reconstructing cult practices from secondary sources in Minoan Crete. *Proceedings of the 12th International Congress of Cretan Studies*, 1–8

Pareja, M. N. (2017). *Monkey and Ape Iconography in Aegean Art.* Uppsala: Astrom Editions.

Pareja, M. N., McKinney, T., Mayhew J. A., Setchell, J. M., Nash, S. D., & Heaton, R. (2020a). A new identification of the monkeys depicted in a Bronze Age wall painting from Akrotiri, Thera. *Primates*, **61**, 159–168.

Pareja, M. N., McKinney, T., & Setchell, J. M. (2020b). Aegean monkeys and the importance of cross-disciplinary collaboration in archaeoprimatology: a reply to Urbani and Youlatos. *Primates*, **61**, 767–774.

Parker, P. (1997). African vervets on Crete and Thera during MM IIIBLM IA. *American Journal of Archaeology*, **101**, 348

Patrianakou-Iliaki, A. (1983). Wall-painting and painters in Minoan society. Anthropomorphic cult images in Minoan Crete? In O. Krzyszkowska, & L. Nixon, eds., *Minoan Society. Proceedings of the Cambridge Colloquium 1981.* Bristol: Bristol Classical Press, 245–249.

Pendlebury, H. W., Pendelbury, J. D. S., & Money-Coutts, M. B. (1939). Excavation in the Plain of Lasithi. I. The Cave of Trapeza. *The Annual of the British School at Athens*, **XXXVI**, 5–131.

Pfälzner, P. (2008). Between the Aegean and Syria: The wall paintings from the royal palace of Qatna. In D. Bonatz, R. M. Czichon, & F. G. Kreppner, eds., *Fundstellen: Gesammelte Schriften zur Archäologie und Geschichte Altvorderasiens ad Honorem Hartmut Kühne*. Wiesbaden: Harrassowitz Verlag, 95–118

Phillips, J. P. (2005). A question of reception. In J. Clarke, ed., *Archaeological Perspectives on the Transmission and Transformation of Culture in the Eastern Mediterranean*. Barnsley: Oxbow Books, 39–47.

Phillips, J. P. (2008a). *Aegyptiaca on the Island of Crete in their Chronological Context: A Critical Review, Vol. 1*. Vienna: Verlag der Österreichischen Akademie der Wissenschaften.

Phillips, J. P. (2008b). *Aegyptiaca on the Island of Crete in their Chronological Context: A Critical Review, Vol. 2*. Vienna: Verlag der Österreichischen Akademie der Wissenschaften.

Pinch Brock, L. (2000). Art, industry and the Aegeans in the tomb of Amenmose. *Ägypten und Levante / Egypt and the Levant*, **10**, 129–137.

Pini, I. (1970). *Iraklion Archäologisches Museum. Teil 5. Corpus der minoischen und mykenischen Siegel II (5)*. Berlin: Gebrüder Mann Verlag.

Pini, I. (1975). *Kleinere Griechische Sammlungen. Die Siegel der Vorpalastzeit. Corpus der minoischen und mykenischen Siegel V (1)*. Berlin: Gebrüder. Mann Verlag.

Pini, I. (1988). *Kleinere europäische Sammlungen. Corpus der minoischen und mykenischen Siegel XI*. Berlin: Gebrüder Mann Verlag.

Pini, I. (1992). *Kleinere Griechische Sammlungen. Agina - Korinth. Corpus der minoischen und mykenischen Siegel V (Suppl. I A)*. Berlin: Gebrüder Mann Verlag.

Pio, H. (2018). The significance of the baboon motif in the funerary art of the New Kingdom. Master's thesis. Stellenbosch University.

Platon, N. (1947). Συμβολ⬜ εις την σπουδ⬜ν της μινωικ⬜ς τοιχογραφίας. ⬜ κροκοσυλλέκτης πίθηκος. *Κρητικ⬜ Χρονικ⬜* 1, 505–524 (in Greek).

Platon, N. (1969). *Iraklion Archäologisches Museum. Teil 1. Corpus der minoischen und mykenischen Siegel II (1)*. Berlin: Gebrüder Mann Verlag.

Platon, N., & Pini, I. (1984). *Iraklion Archäologisches Museum. Teil 3. Die Siegel der Neupalastzeit. Corpus der minoischen und mykenischen Siegel II (3)*. Berlin: Gebrüder. Mann Verlag.

Platon, N., Pini, I., & Salies, G. (1977). *Iraklion Archäologisches Museum. Teil 2. Die Siegel der Altpalastzeit. Corpus der minoischen und mykenischen Siegel II (2)*. Berlin: Gebrüder Mann Verlag.

Platon, N., Müller, W., & Pini, I. (1998). *Iraklion Archäologisches Museum. Teil 7. Die Siegelabdrücke von Kato Zakros. Corpus der minoischen und mykenischen Siegel II (7)*. Berlin: Gebrüder. Mann Verlag.

Platon, N., Müller, W., & Pini, I. (1999). *Iraklion Archäologisches Museum. Teil 6. Die Siegelabdrücke von Ajia Triada und anderen Zentral- und Ostkretischen Fundorten. Corpus der minoischen und mykenischen Siegel II (6)*. Berlin: Gebrüder Mann Verlag.

Porter, R. (2000). The flora of the Theran wall paintings: Living plants and motifs – Sea lily, crocus, iris and ivy. In S. Sherratt, ed., *The Wall Paintings of Thera, Vol. II: Proceedings of the First International Symposium, August 30–4 September 1997*. Athens: Petros M. Nomikos Centre-Thera Foundation, 603–630.

Poulianos, A. (1972). The discovery of the first known victim of Thera's Bronze Age eruption. *Archaeology*, 25(3), 229–230.

Pruetz, J., & Greenlaw, C. (2021). Occam's razor revisited: Overlooked guenon species provide equally robust evidence for an African influence in Bronze Age Aegean fresco primate iconography from Akrotiri, Thera. *Primates* **62**, 703–707.

Rackham, O. (1978). The flora and vegetation of Thera and Crete before and after the great eruption. In C. Doumas, ed., *Thera and the Aegean World I*. London: The Thera Foundation, 755–764.

Rehak, P. (1999). The Monkey Frieze from Xeste 3, Room 4: Reconstruction and interpretation. In P. P. Betancourt, V. Karageorghis, R. Laffineur, & W. D. Niemeier, eds., *Meletemata. Studies in Aegean Archaeology Presented to Malcolm H. Wiener as He Enters his 65th Year, (Aegaeum) 20*. Liège: Peeters Publishers, 705–708.

Reese, D. S. 2006. The invertebrates, in E. Hallager, & B. P. Hallager, eds., *The Greek-Swedish Excavations at the Agia Aikaterini Square Kastelli, Khania 1970-1987, 2001, 2005 and 2008*: 396–417. Stockholm: Svenska Institutet i Athen.

Reese, D. S. & Betancourt, P. P. 2008. The neritid shells. *Hesperia* **77**, 576.

Renfrew, C. (2007). *Excavations at Phylakopi in Melos 1974–77*. Athens: British School at Athens, Supplementary volume 42.

Renfrew, C. (2011). *The Emergence of Civilisation. The Cyclades and the Aegean in the Third Millenium BC*. Oxford: Oxbow Books.

Roberson, D., Davinoff, J., Davies, I. R. L., & Shapiro L. R. (2005). Color categories: Confirmation of the relativity hypothesis. *Cognitive Psychology*, **50**, 378–411.

Rutkowski, B. (1978). Religious elements in the Thera frescoes. In C. Doumas, ed., *Thera and the Aegean World I*. London: The Thera Foundation, pp. 661–664.

Sakellarakis, E., & Sakellarakis, J. A. (1984). The Keftiu and the Minoan an. In R. Hägg, & N. Marinatos, eds., *The Minoan Thalassocracy. Myth and Reality. Proceedings of the Third International Symposium at the Swedish Institut in Athens. 31 May–5 June 1982*. Stockholm: Svenska institutet i Athen, 197–202.

Sakellarakis, J. A., & Sapouna-Sakellaraki, E. (1991). *Archanes*. Athens: Ekdotike Athenon S. A.

Sargnon, O. (1987). *Les Bijoux Préhelléniques*. Paris: Institut francais d'archeologie du Proche-Orient - Librairie orientaliste P. Geuthner.

Sarpaki, A. (2000). Plants chosen to be depicted on Theran wall paintngs: Tentative interpretations. In S. Sherratt, ed., *The Wall Paintings of Thera, Vol. II: Proceedings of the First International Symposium, August 30–4 September 1997*. Athens: Petros M. Nomikos Centre-Thera Foundation, 657–680.

Savignoni, L. (1904). Scavi e scoperte nella necropoli di Phaestos. *Monumenti Antichi*, **XIV**, 503–675.

Schiering, W. (1992) Elements of landscape in Minoan and Mycenaeean art. In R. Laffineur, & J. L. Crowley, eds., *Aegean Bronze Age Iconography: Shaping a Methodology. Aegeum 8*. Liège: Annales d'archéologie égéenne de l'Université de Liège, 317–324.

Schmitz-Pillmann, P. (2006). *Landschaftselemente in der minoisch-mykenischen Wandmalerei*. Berlin: Willmuth Arenhövel Verlag.

Seager, R. B. (1912). *Explorations in the Island of Mochlos*. New York: American School of Classical Studies at Athens.

Shaw, M. C. (1993). The Aegean Garden. *American Journal of Arhcaeology*, **97**, 661–685.

Shaw, M. C. (1997). Aegean sponsors and artists: Reflections on their roles in the patterns of distribution of themes and representational conventions in the murals. In R. Laffineur, & P. P. Betancourt. eds., *Texnh. Craftsmen, Craftswomen and Craftsmanship in the Aegean Bronze Age. Aegaeum 16*. 481–504.

Sherratt, S. (ed.) (2000). *The Wall Paintings of Thera, Vol. II: Proceedings of the First International Symposium, August 30–4 September 1997*. Athens: Petros M. Nomikos Centre-Thera Foundation.

Siebenmorgen, H. (ed) (2000). *Im Labyrinth des Minos. Kreta – Die erste europäische Hochkultur*. München: Biering & Brinkmann.

Simandiraki-Grimshaw, A. (2010). Minoan animal-human hybridity. In D. B. Counts, & B. Arnold, eds., *The Master of Animals in Old World Iconography*. Budapest: Archaeolingua Foundation, 93–106

Spier, J., Potts, T., & Cole, S. E. (2018). *Beyond the Nile: Egypt and the Classical World*. Los Angeles: J. Paul Getty Museum.

Strasser, T. (1997). The blue monkeys of the Aegean and their implications for Bronze Age trade. *American Journal of Archaeology*, **101**, 348.

Tamvaki, A. (1985). Minoan and Mycenaean elements in the iconography of the Pylos sealings. In P. Darcque, & J.-C. Poursat, eds., *L'Iconographie Minoenne. Actes de la Table Ronde d'Athènes, 21–22 avril 1983*. Athens, BCH Suppl. 11, 267–292.

Televantou C. (1992). Theran wall-painting: Artistic tendencies and painters. In R. Laffineur, & J. L. Crowley, eds., *Aegean Bronze Age Iconography: Shaping a Methodology. Aegeum 8*. Liège: Annales d'archéologie égéenne de l Université de Liège, 145–161.

Televantou, C. (2009). The wall-painting of the monkeys. In C. Doumas, M. Marthari, & C. Televantou, eds., *Museum of Prehistoric Thera. Brief Guide*. Athens: Hellenic Ministry of Culture-Archaeological Society of Athens, 72–75.

Thomas, C., & Wedde, M. (2001). Desperately seeking Potnia. In R. Laffineur, & R. Hägg, eds., *Potnia: Deities and Religion in the Aegean Bronze Age. Aegeum 2*. Liège: Annales d archéologie égéenne de l Université de Liège, 3–14.

Thorpe-Scholes, K. (1978). Akrotiri: Genesis, life and death. In C. Doumas, ed., *Thera and the Aegean World I*. London: The Thera Foundation, 437–447.

Trantalidou, K. (1990) Animals and human diet in the prehistoric Aegean. In D. A. Hardy, J. Keller, V. P. Galanopoulos, N. C. Flemming, & T. H. Druitt, eds., *Thera and the Aegean World III. Volume Two: Earth Sciences*. London: The Thera Foundation, 285–308.

Trantalidou K. (2000). Animal bones and animal representations at Late Bronze Age Akrotiri. In S. Sherratt, ed., *The Wall Paintings of Thera, Vol. II: Proceedings of the First International Symposium, August 30–4 September 1997*. Athens: Petros M. Nomikos Centre-Thera Foundation, 709–735.

True, M. (2000). The role of formal decorative patterns in the wall paintings of Thera. In S. Sherratt, ed., *The*

Wall Paintings of Thera, Vol. II: Proceedings of the First International Symposium, August 30–4 September 1997. Athens: Petros M. Nomikos Centre-Thera Foundation, 345–358.

Tyree, L. (2001). Diachronic changes in Minoan cave cult. In R. Laffineur, & R. Hägg, eds., *Potnia: Deities and Religion in the Aegean Bronze Age. Aegeum 2*. Liège: Annales d'archéologie égéenne de l'Université de Liège, 39–50.

Urbani, B., & Youlatos, D. (2012). Aegean monkeys: From a comprehensive view to a re-interpretation. *Proceedings of the 12th International Congress on the Zoogeography and Ecology of Greece and Adjacent Regions*, 160.

Urbani B., & Youlatos D. (2020a). A new look at the Minoan 'blue' monkeys. *Antiquity*, **94**(374), e9.

Urbani B., & Youlatos D. (2020b). Occam's razor, archeoprimatology, and the 'blue' monkeys of Thera: A reply to Pareja et al. (2020). *Primates*, **61**, 757–765.

Urbani, B., Youlatos, D., & Binnberg, J. (2021). Galilei's mutter, archeoprimatology, and the 'blue' monkeys of Thera: a comment on Pruetz and Greenlaw. *Primates*, **62**, 879–886.

Vandervondelen, M. (1994). Singes accroupis: étude de quelques statuettes de la période prépalatiale crétoise. *Studia varia Bruxellensia*, **3**, 175–183.

Vandier d'Abbadie, J. (1964). Les singes familiers dans l'ancienne Egypte (Peintures et bas reliefs) I. L'ancien empire. *Revue d'Egyptologie*, **16**, 147–177.

Vandier d'Abbadie, J. (1965) Les singes familiers dans l'ancienne Egypte (Peintures et bas reliefs) II. Le Moyen empire. *Revue d'Egyptologie*, **17**, 177–188.

Vandier d'Abbadie, J. (1966) Les singes familiers dans l'ancienne Egypte (Peintures et bas reliefs) III. Le nouvel empire. *Revue d'Egyptologie*, **18**, 143–201.

Vanschoonwinkel, J. (1990) Animal representations in Theran and other Aegean arts. In D. A. Hardy, C. G. Doumas, J. A. Sakellarakis, & P. M. Warren, eds., *Thera and the Aegean World III. Volume One: Archaeology*. London: The Thera Foundation, 327–347.

Vanschoonwinkel, J. (1996). Les Animaux dans l'art minoen. In D. S. Reese, ed., *The Pleistocene and Holocene fauna of Crete and its Settlers*. Madison: Prehistory Press, 351–412.

Vlachopoulos, A. (2000). The red motif in the Thera wall paintings and its association with Aegean pictorial art. In S. Sherratt, ed., *The Wall Paintings of Thera, Vol. II: Proceedings of the First International Symposium, August 30–4 September 1997*. Athens:

Petros M. Nomikos Centre-Thera Foundation, 631–656.

Vlachopoulos, A. (2007). *Disiecta Membra*: The wall paintings from the 'Porter's Lodge' at Akrotiri. In P. P. Betancourt, M. C. Nelson, & H. Williams, eds., *Krinoi kai Limenes: Studies in Honor of Joseph and Maria Shaw*. Philadelphia: NSTAP Academic Press, 131–138.

Vlachopoulos, A. (2008). The wall paintings from the Xeste 3 building at Akrotiri, Thera. Towards an interpretation of its iconographic programme. In N. Brodie, J. Doole, G. Gavalas, & C. Renfrew, eds., *Horizon. A Colloquium on the Prehistory of the Cyclades*. Cambridge: McDonald Institute for Achaeological Research, 451–461.

Vlachopoulos, A., & Sotiropoulou, S. (2012). The blue colour on the Akrotiri wall-paintings: from the palette of the Theran painter to the laboratory analysis. *Talanta*, **44**, 245–272.

Walberg, G. (1992). Minoan floral iconography. In R. Laffineur, & J. L. Crowley, eds., *Aegean Bronze Age Iconography: Shaping a Methodology. Aegeum 8*. Liège: Annales d'archéologie égéenne de l'Université de Liège, 241–246.

Warburton, D. (2014). Ancient color categories. In L. Ronnier, ed., *Encyclopedia of Color Science and Technology*. New York: Springer.

Warren, P. M. (1995). Minoan Crete and Pharaonic Egypt. In W. V. Davies, & L. Schofield, eds., *Egypt, the Aegean and the Levant: Interconnections in the Second Millennium BC*. London: British Museum Press, 1–18.

Warren, P. M. (2000). From naturalism to essentialism in Theran and Minoan art. In S. Sherratt, ed., *The Wall Paintings of Thera, Vol. II: Proceedings of the First International Symposium, August 30–4 September 1997*. Athens: Petros M. Nomikos Centre-Thera Foundation, 364–380.

Wesołowska, M. (2017). Human life hidden in the symbol of a flower. Between the Minoan world and Egypt. *Papers in Aegean Archaeology (Sympozjum Egejskie)*, **1**, 79–83.

Wikinson, J. G. (1878). *Manners and Customs of the Ancient Egyptians. Vol. I*. New York: Dodd, Mead and Company.

Winter, I. J. (2000). Thera painting and the ancient Near East: the private and public domains of wall decoration. In S. Sherratt, ed., *The Wall Paintings of Thera, Vol. II: Proceedings of the First International Symposium, August 30–4 September 1997*. Athens: Petros M. Nomikos Centre-Thera Foundation, 745–761.

Wolfson, E. G. (2018). Pictorial representations of monkeys and simianesque creatures in Greek Art. PhD dissertation, University of Missouri.

Xanthoudides, S. (1924). *The Vaulted Tombs of Mesara. An Account of Some Early Cementeries of Southern Greece.* London: University Press of Liverpool and Hodder & Stoughton.

Xénaki-Sakellariou, A. (1958). *Les cachets minoens de la collection Giamalakis. École francaise d'Athènes.*

Études Crétoises Tome X. Paris: Librairie orientaliste P. Geuthner.

Younger, J. (1989). *Aegean Seals of the Late Bronze Age: Stylistic Groups. VII.* Concordance. *Kadmos*, XXVIII, 101–136.

Younger, J. G. (1998). *Music in the Aegean Bronze Age.* Uppsala: Astrom Editions.

Zervos, C. (1956). *L'art de la Crète néolithique et mino-enne.* Paris : Édition Cahier d'art.

Part III

Africa

11 Primate Behavior in Ancient Egypt

The Iconography of Baboons and Other Monkeys in the Old Kingdom

Lydia Bashford

سلوك الرئيسيات في العصور القديمة في مصر: أيقونية البابون والقرود التانية في المملكة القديمة

نبذه

في الوقت الي كانت القرود بتتفسح في الطبيعة الجذابة الي كانت في العصور القديمة في مصر، لما دخلنا في العصر الدولة القديمة، مبقتش قرود البابون وغيرها تيجي مصر. الطريقة الوحيدة الي تيجي بيها كانت عن طريق الاستيراد من الجنوب البعيد. بس مع كده برضو، فضلت القرود ايقونة متكررة في الفترة دي والفترة الي بعدها. الناس كانت بتجيب القرود من دوافع دينية. بس الطبيعة العلمانية كانت برضو موجودة ودي قدرنا نشوفها في المقابر الملكية والعادية عن طريق انهم دخلوها في المشاهد البشرية العادية وحاولوا يبينوا سلوكهم الطبيعي أو تقليد حتى سلوك البشر. الدراسة دي بتوضح سلوك القرود الي لاحظها المصريين وقدروا يكتبوها علي حيطان المقابر الي فضلت لحد دلوقتي موجودة

الكلمات الدالة

مصر القديمة ـ الدولة القديمة ـ البابون ـ القرد ـ سلوك الرئيسيات ـ الايقونية

Abstract

While various primates may have originally roamed in the formally lush prehistoric landscape of Egypt, by the Old Kingdom period, baboons and other monkeys were not native to Egypt proper and only available through foreign import from further south. Yet monkeys remained a recurrent feature in the iconography of this and later periods. A motivation of great religious significance was likely behind the baboon's continual importation. Of a more secular nature, however, are reliefs from both royal and non-royal tombs where they are inserted into traditionally human scenes, exhibiting their own natural behavior, or imitating human actions, often rather humorously. This study examines the type of primate behaviors observed by the Egyptians and recorded on the walls of their tombs for eternity.

Key words: Ancient Egypt, Old Kingdom, Baboon, Monkey, Primate behavior, Iconography

11.1 Introduction

In general, animal behavior may be defined as an "animal's active response to its environment, to members of its own or other species, and to its personal requirements" (Evans, 2010: 13). The study of animal behavior in Egyptian art is a relatively new and growing field (see especially Evans, 2010). This work aims to review some of the specifically primate behaviors depicted in Egyptian art during the Old Kingdom from Dynasties IV (*c.* 2613–2494 BCE), V (*c.* 2494–2345 BCE), and VI (*c.* 2345–2181 BCE). Based on the iconographic repertoire and zoological observations, the behavioral categories selected were locomotion, aggression, imitation, ingestion, and parental care. This is by no means an exhaustive investigation, thus, for further discussion of the depiction of monkeys in Egyptian art, see Kilany (2013), Greenlaw (2011: 7–34), and Osborn and Osbornová (1998: 32–42). Most notably, excluding recently discovered evidence, occurrences of monkeys in Egyptian art from the Old, Middle, and New Kingdoms periods are recorded and discussed across a series of three articles, grouped by time period, by Vandier d'Abbadie (1964, 1965, 1966).

The primate species predominantly depicted during the Old Kingdom, and for most of Egyptian history, were the hamadryas baboon (*Papio hamadryas*), the olive baboon (*Papio anubis*), and long-tailed monkeys, such as the grivet monkey (*Chlorocebus aethiops*), the closely related vervet monkey (*Chlorocebus pygerythrus*), and the larger patas monkey (*Erythrocebus patas*) (Bashford, 2016: 27–32; Osborn and Osbornová, 1998: 32–42).

Distinguishing between these species in Egyptian art is sometimes made possible through an evaluation of the typical rendering of certain phenotypic characteristics. One artistic distinction between baboons and long-tailed monkeys seems to have been made by the position of the tail. The baboon tail is shown curving downward, while other species are usually illustrated with tails curving upwards. This is best exemplified through the rendering of the animals in the hieroglyphic script: 🐒 (baboon) and 🐒 (long-tailed monkey) (Bashford, 2016: 31). Furthermore, while baboons in general were often marked by their emphasized buttocks (females in particular), the male hamadryas's depictions are made clear by their prominent penis and distinguishing cape. Despite such features, specific species frequently remain indistinguishable in Egyptian art.

It is likely that by the beginning of Dynastic Egypt (*c.* 3100 BCE), monkeys were long-since absent from the Nile Valley as native species and were continually imported from regions south of Egypt as part of foreign trade (Bashford, 2016: 14ff), from areas which still today roughly correspond to their natural dispersal (Fig. 11.10). During the Old Kingdom, this importation is recorded on the walls of the king Sahure's mortuary temple, where seagoing ships full of foreign peoples are accompanied by baboons, long-tailed monkeys, and dogs (Table 11.1 no. 4). This rarity, as well as the nature and behavior of the monkey itself, led to their status as a valuable exotic and prestigious item, and afforded them many roles in both religious and daily life (Bashford, 2016: 33–52). Thus, the aims of this chapter are to evaluate the types of interactions the ancient Egyptians had with primates and how this was expressed in the artistic evidence using a zoological approach.

Table 11.1 Current extant representations of baboons in Old Kingdom Egypt

No.	Tomb owner	Date	Cemetery	Theme	Description	References
Dynasty IV						
1	Nefermaat	IV.1	Meidum	'Pet'	A leashed baboon tugs on the rope around its neck being held by a boy. Another boy follows, holding the leash to a long-tailed monkey, which stands bipedally and rests a hand on the boy's shoulder.	Harpur (2001: 61–62, fig. 74)
2	Atet	IV.1	Meidum	'Pet'	A female baboon holds the hand of a young boy, the boy touches the rump of a long-tailed monkey, and the monkey pulls on the tail feather of a crane.	Harpur (2001: 86–87, fig. 86)
3	Nebemakht	IV.6–V.1	Giza	'Pet'	A male hamadryas walks quadrupedally with visible cape and penis, but ears incorrectly erect and pointed.	Hassan (1943: 141, fig. 81)
Dynasty V						
4	King Sahure	V.2	Abusir	Aboard ships	Eight leashed baboons in various lively movements of walking, squatting, and clambering, are illustrated upon on the lowered tripod masts of two seagoing ships returning from Punt.	El Awady (2009: 155–157, pl. V)
5	Iymer	V.E	Saqqara	Animal-husbandry(?)	A baboon leads an oryx.	Unpublished, see Harpur and Scremin (2015: 456 fn. 203)
6	Iymer	V.E	Saqqara	Steering a boat	A baboon works the rudder-oar of a boat.	Unpublished, see Harpur and Scremin (2015: 456 fn. 203)
7	Iymer	V.E	Saqqara	Unknown	A baboon stands (on all fours) beside a monkey which is on top of a pile of grain and appears to be helping an agricultural worker to stack the sheaves.	Unpublished, see Harpur and Scremin (2015: 456 fn. 203)

Table 11.1 (cont.)

No.	Tomb owner	Date	Cemetery	Theme	Description	References
8	Kaikhent	V.E	el-Hammamiya	Aboard a boat	A baboon walks along the stern of a boat on the Nile, while a long-tailed monkey walks on the prow.	El-Khouli and Kanawati (1990: 42, pls. 11, 44)
9	Kaikhent	V.E	el-Hammamiya	Aboard a boat	A baboon clambers down the stays of the mast, aboard a boat sailing the Nile.	El-Khouli and Kanawati (1990: 35, pls. 35, 37)
10	Hetepet	V.E-M	Giza	Orchard	A female baboon, with an emphasized buttock, and an infant clinging to her back, harvest fruit from a tree in an orchard.	Ministry of Antiquities (2018)
11	Hetepet	V.E-M	Giza	Orchestra	A baboon, kneels(?) behind an Egyptian musician, and appears to accompany him, imitating the actions of a human singer.	Ministry of Antiquities (2018)
12	Nefer/Kahay	V.6	Saqqara	Boatbuilding	A large hamadryas male, with penile display, steals the role of the overseer and stands upon the stern of the boat wielding a large baton above his head.	Moussa and Altenmüller (1971: 27, pls. 19, 23), Lashien (2013: 36, pls. 32b–33a, 83)
13	Nefer/Kahay	V.7	Saqqara	Winemaking	Four men wring a sack filled with grape pulp, collecting the must beneath. The conventional fifth worker above the sack is replaced with a large male hamadryas with penile display.	Moussa and Altenmüller (1971: 24, pls. 8, 12), Lashien (2013: 31–32, pls. 19a, 81)
14	Tepemankh [II]	V.6	Saqqara	Marketplace	A pair of leashed baboons walk quadrupedally through a marketplace. A female clutches an infant to her chest, and a male, with penile display, labelled *rnr*, attacks a naked youth.	Cairo, CG 1556; Smith (1942: 516–518, fig. 5), Manuelian (1999: 404–407[150a–d])
15	Niankhkhmum/ Khnumhotep	V.6L–7	Saqqara	Marketplace	In a marketplace, a leashed male hamadryas with penile display steals food from a basket while further along	Moussa and Altenmüller (1977: 81–82, fig. 10, pls. 24, 27)

No.	Name	Date	Location	Category	Description	Reference
					the register a leashed female bites the leg of a naked youth.	
16	Itisen	V.6–8	Giza	'Pet'	A leashed male hamadryas with penile display walks quadrupedally in a chair-carrying scene with two dogs, a long-tailed monkey, and a dwarf.	Hassan (1944: 266–267, fig. 122)
17	Weirmi	V.8–9E	Sheikh Saïd	'Pet'	Fragmentary baboon with a collar and an inscription above identifying it as *mr*, 'baboon'. The long-tailed monkey in the register above is named *gf*, 'monkey'.	Davies (1901: 19, pl. 15)
18	Khuwnes	V.8–9	Zawyet el-Maiyitin	'Pet'	A male hamadryas, with an oddly shaped head and distinctive cape, is being led on a leash by an attendant in a subregister behind Khuwnes.	Varille (1938: 23, fig. 9)
19	King Unis	V.9	Saqqara	Marketplace	A pair of leashed hamadryas baboons, a male and female, are led by a keeper and his attendant in a marketplace.	Labrousse and Moussa (2002: 33, fig. 36, Doc. 22)
20	Anon.	V–VI?	Unknown	Steering a boat	A baboon accompanied by a dwarf stands at the stern of a boat, holding the rudder, reminiscent of a modern-day coxswain steering and coordinating the rowers.	Kestner-Museum, Hannover, 1935.200.201 Houlihan (2001: 20, fig. 11)
21	Anon.	V–VI?	Saqqara	'Pet'	A leashed male hamadryas, with possible penile display, has 'cause to come' inscribed above its head and is led by an attendant labelled 'keeper of baboon'.	Hassan (1975: pl. XIV[c]).
Dynasty VI						
22	Niankhpepi	VI.2–7	Zawyet el-Maiyitin	Carrying a yoke	A baboon walks bipedally, carrying a load on either end of a yoke.	Varille (1938: 20, pls. X, XI)
23	Pepi II	VI.4	Saqqara	Religious	Two seated baboons behind an Upper Egyptian shrine.	Jéquier (1938: pls. 50, 52)

11.2   Locomotor Behavior

11.2.1 On a Leash

The largest group of representations of baboons and other monkeys during the Old Kingdom exhibit no apparent behavior other than walking quadrupedally while being led on a leash by a handler, who is often an achondroplastic dwarf (Fig. 11.1a–c; Table 11.1 nos. 1–3, 16–18, 21; see Vandier d'Abbadie, 1964: 151–163). This pose is one standard for four-legged animals in Egyptian art, regardless of size and species (Evans, 2010: 33–35). This consists of both the forelimbs and hindlimbs being parted, with the forward being the more distant limb of each pair, regardless of the direction the animal is facing. The limbs are held rigidly, with all four feet shown in contact with the ground at one time. Monkeys are typically specialized for quadrupedal locomotion, their natural gait has the diagonal footfall sequence of right hindlimb, left forelimb, left hindlimb, right forelimb (Vilensky and Larson, 1989: 18). This allows for at least three feet to be in contact with the ground at one time, for support while walking. When a limb is advanced, it is bent and lifted off the ground before being swung forwards (Evans, 2010: 34).

In modern times monkeys are generally avoided as pets since they are excitable animals (Kingdon, 1971: 215), and the males are particularly prone to lashing out (Evans, 2000: 75). Modern reports describe the baboon especially as highly intelligent, but extremely dangerous and difficult to handle as a pet. The hamadryas baboon is feared by animal trainers and importers more so than the "great cats" and is known to have injured or killed humans (Macdonald, 1965: 3). Despite these tendencies, both species could be portrayed as accompanying and interacting with the ancient Egyptian tomb owner. It is perhaps significant that baboons are, with few exceptions (e.g. Fig. 11.1a), always leashed in these scenes. Depicting an animal seated under a chair (see Kilany and Mahran, 2015) or walking tamely on a leash showed the dominance and control of the tomb owner, and thus their social standing. The monkey is unmistakably meant to appear as an animal under the power of the tomb owner, one not only notorious for its inability to be controlled, but one that had to be imported, increasing its prestige (see also Sweeney, 2015: 807–808).

11.2.2 Climbing

Another recurrent theme depicts monkeys scaling and sitting aboard boats travelling along the Nile (see Vandier d'Abbadie, 1964: 171–177). Most scenes show long-tailed monkeys freely climbing ropes and along the masts of Nile boats (see also Kilany, 2013: 29). For example, in the Dynasty VI tomb of Hemre: Isi at Deir el Gebrawi, a monkey 'sailor' climbs the forestay as if copying the actions of the nearby Egyptian sailor scaling the boat's mast (Davies, 1902b: pl. XIX; Harpur and Scremin, 2015: 456 fn. 203). Baboons are much rarer in this type of scene but appear on at least three occasions (Table 11.1 nos. 4, 8, 9). As adept and curious climbers, perhaps such amusing escapades and liveliness by monkeys was observed aboard ships and boats when transporting the animals to and around Egypt and were recreated in tomb scenes.

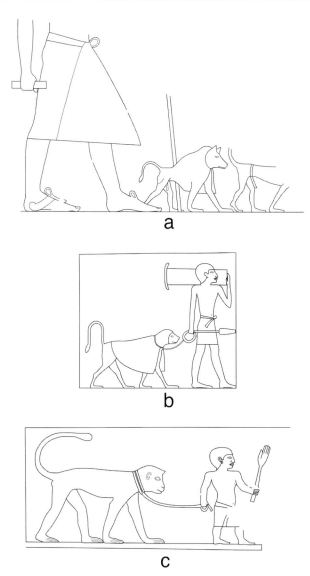

Figure 11.1 (a) Relief from the tomb of Nebemakht (Table 11.1 no. 3) depicting a male hamadryas with visible cape and penis, and oddly pointed ears, walking quadrupedally in front of the tomb owner and behind a long-tailed monkey. Based on images from Lepsius (1897–1913: pl. 13) and Hassan (1943, fig. 81); (b) Relief from the tomb of Khuwnes (Table 11.1 no. 18) depicting a male hamadryas with a rounded head being led on a leash by an attendant to the tomb owner. Based on image from Lepsius (1897–1913: 107); (c) Relief from the tomb of Ti (Dynasty V, Saqqara) depicting an achondroplastic dwarf leading a leashed long-tailed monkey in a procession of goods for the tomb owner. Based on image from Wild (1953: pls. XCIV, CXXVI).

11.3   Aggressive Behavior

Baboon aggression was well-known to the Egyptians, a fact which is immediately highlighted through its metaphorical use as a hieroglyphic classifier for the word 'to be angry' ⸺𓃀𓈖 *qnd* (Wilson, 1997: 1064–1065).

11.3.1   Attacking

Two examples from the Old Kingdom corpus depict baboons exhibiting attacking behavior. Both belong to the thematic category of so-called market-scenes found in the reliefs of two high-ranking officials. The inclusion of baboons in this type of scene is relatively rare, and only one further example is known, in a royal relief, but no aggression is shown directly from the baboon (Table 11.1 no. 19).

From the mastaba of Tepemankh II (Fig. 11.3a; Table 11.1 no. 14), come fragments of relief with the most well-known version of this scene. Occupying its right portion is the famous vignette of the "keeper of baboons, Hemu". As their handler, Hemu is shown controlling two leashed baboons, and holds a short policing stick, not uncommon for those tending to monkeys (Fischer, 1978: 19).

The baboon to the right is clearly male, evident from its visible penis, which was omitted in some facsimiles (Smith, 1942, fig. 5), but apparent on the original fragment (Manuelian, 1999: 405). The species, however, is somewhat ambiguous. It lacks the defined cape of a male hamadryas, but possesses an emphasized buttock, downward curving but not sharply angular tail, and fur covering the ears. Thus, it may instead represent the more rarely depicted olive baboon (Evans, 2010: 186).

The male grapples with the outstretched leg of a naked youth whose hand is apparently in the middle of plucking fruits/vegetables from a basket. This has led some scholars to interpret this scene as one of 'police baboons' (e.g. Janssen and Janssen, 1989: 25), employed in the marketplace with their handlers as watch-dogs against thievery. It is unclear whether the boy is an assistant or a common thief, but the image and accompanying inscription (see Bashford, 2016: 45) does seem to imply humor was also intended (Houlihan, 2001: 18; Manuelian, 1999: 405–406). Beyond this, natural baboon behavior is also exhibited. The animal attacks the young man as it would a perceived subordinate – rearing up on its hind legs, it strains against its leash to launch itself forward and grasp the boy by the thigh. The youth appears to have been caught while running as his body is inclined to the right, his legs are wide apart, and his left knee is bent (Evans, 2010: 145).

In the slightly later tomb of Niankhkhnum and Khnumhotep, a leashed baboon also attacks a young man (Fig. 11.3b; Table 11.1 no. 15), while a hamadryas male depicted further along in the same register attempts to help itself to some food as its handler holds it back with a leash (Fig. 11.8). This time however, the primate attacker succeeds in biting the boy on the leg. Again, the victim has his right heel lifted, as though trying to escape (Evans, 2010: 145). Previously, this animal has been identified as a long-tailed monkey, rather than a baboon (Moussa and Altenmüller, 1977: 82). Indeed, it is certainly distinguished from the male hamadryas in the same register, whose large cape and discernible penis make for an easy identification. However, the tail of the attacker curves downward, and most significantly, the rump of the animal is extremely pronounced, a trait not illustrated in Old Kingdom depictions of long-tailed monkeys (Evans, 2010: 145, fn. 91). In addition, while the luminous red backside of the hamadryas baboon is a conspicuous characteristic in both sexes, during estrous the female develops a large perineal swelling, certainly a memorable detail of the animal (Wickler, 1967: pl. 1). This would seem to indicate that the intended species depicted here was undoubtedly a baboon. It therefore seems likely it could in fact be a female mate to the male shown in the same scene since, unlike other baboon species, the hamadryas family is formed by one or more unique one-sided "marriage bonds" between the male and female (Kummer, 1997: 99–100). It should be noted however, a study on the effect of sexual phase on aggression in baboons does suggest that, during the swollen phase, there is a substantial reduction in the performance of threat and attack behaviors by females (Noll et al., 1982: 70–71). Nevertheless, the swollen perineum may simply be an attempt by the Egyptian artist to identify its gender through a characteristic feature.

In both tomb scenes, the young victims try to fend off their attacker. As mentioned, some scholars have argued that it may be plausible that the youths have been 'caught' in an act of thievery and based on the accompanying inscriptions they were instructed to do so by their keepers holding the leash. Well-known to be irritable and aggressive, they are also highly intelligent animals, who in theory could have been trained to chase and bite on command (Evans, 2010: 146). A hamadryas troop comprises smaller one-male units consisting of a dominant male and his 'marriage-bonded' female and their young. Each alpha male must both protect and control his group within the troop, asserting his dominance via a variety of threat displays, and will chase and attack both subordinates and females, including biting them. The males have long canine teeth, capable of inflicting considerable damage (Evans, 2010: 138, 145; Kummer, 1968: 47–52). In *Papio hamadryas* an expression of attack-threat may start with the baboon immediately launching himself after his objective (Hall and DeVore, 1965: 99). If he catches his victim, he grapples with it and seizes it in his jaw. Such attacks are usually of a short duration and even though they appear very vicious do not often result in physical injury to the victim (Hall and DeVore, 1965: 99). While the canine teeth of female hamadryas are smaller and less dangerous, they are also known to bite and attack, more often in play (Kummer, 1968: 46–47; Kummer, 1997: 166). An inscription behind the attacking female, spoken by her handler, excites the female against the young boy ('Catch! Catch!').

Evans (2010: 146) suggests it is more likely that the animals in these scenes have "acted spontaneously in response to sudden movement" of the boys, possibly in the act of thieving or simply holding food, which could have "triggered the natural tendency" of the baboon to chase. Furthermore, in modern day Africa, loss of natural habitat for the animals has led to closer proximity to humans, and an increased number of aggressive interactions has been reported. Often venturing into settlements in search of food, children especially are frequently attacked (Evans, 2010: 146; Kingdon, 1971: 182).

Additionally, there is one possible instance of aggression shown by a long-tailed monkey in Egyptian art. Heralding from the Dynasty VI tomb of Pepyankh the Middle at Meir, a man leads three dogs and a monkey on leashes. The monkey however, rather than falling in line beside the obedient dogs, clambers up the arm of its handler and appears to be reaching out and attacking his face or nose (Fig. 11.3c; Kanawati, 2012: 41, pls. 25, 81). While somewhat ambiguous, this same grasp can be found in scenes of fighting boatmen (e.g. Lashien, 2013: pl. 82), and thus lends itself to this interpretation (Kanawati, 2012: 41).

11.3.2 Penile Display

A notable feature during the Old Kingdom, occurring in at least seven examples of male baboons, is the illustration of their prominent genitalia, despite none of the scenes having any sexual context (Figs. 11.1a, 11.3a, 11.4a–b, 11.8; Table 11.1, nos. 3, 12–16, 21). Evans (2010: 138) notes that this detail is apparently exclusive to baboons since it is omitted in depictions of long-tailed monkeys, suggesting a significance beyond indicating their sex. When their groups are eating and vulnerable, dominant

Figure 11.2 Relief from the tomb of Hemre: Isi depicting a monkey scaling the forestay of a ship in a similar fashion to the nearby human sailor. Based on image from Davies (1902b: pl. XIX).

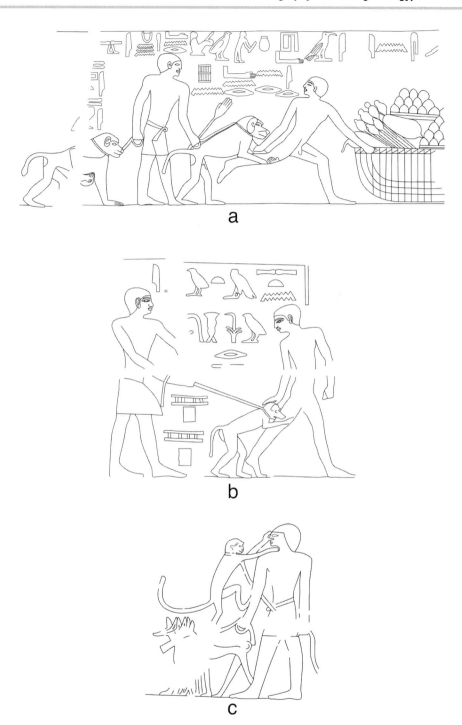

Figure 11.3 (a) Relief fragments from the tomb of Tepemankh [II] (Table 11.1 no. 14), depicting a marketplace scene which includes two baboons. Based on images from Manuelian (1999: 405) and Smith (1942, fig. 5); (b) Relief fragments from the tomb of Niankhkhnum and Khnumhotep

male baboons usually sit in a conspicuous place nearby, such as on a tree stump or mound of earth and scan their surroundings. It has been observed that, while 'guarding' their group in this manner, males often squat with their thighs parted, hands resting on their knees, and their penis extended out, showing up bright pink against their fur. This display acts not only as an optical marker of their presence in the troop, but an indirect warning of their aggressive potential (Evans, 2010: 138; Wickler, 1967: 116–119). Referred to as a 'guardian pose', this image is found throughout Egyptian history (Gordon and Schwabe, 2004: 131–132). Evans (2010: 139), suggests the depiction of these behavioral features may also have a magicoreligious function, associated with potency and power (see Bashford, 2016: 50–52).

11.4   Imitation Behavior

11.4.1   Can Monkeys Ape?

The phenomenon of true imitation behavior in nonhuman primates, and its definition, remains a fiercely debated topic (Subiaul, 2007: 35). It is generally accepted that monkeys do not perform rational imitation but rather goal emulation, meaning they are capable of novel cognitive imitation and are able to copy familiar motor rules, but they cannot perform novel motor imitation (Subiaul, 2007: 56–57). Nevertheless, they are portrayed in Egyptian art as apparently performing spontaneous imitation of commonly depicted actions and behaviors of Egyptian figures, with whom the main human actor of the traditional scene has been replaced instead with monkeys. Whether a realistic image, or more likely a humorous twist based on observed aping behaviors, it clearly captured the imagination of the Egyptians, so much so it was preserved for eternity on the walls of their tombs.

11.4.2   Work

A lively category of scenes features the direct copying of usually human work activities, such as carrying a yoke (Table 11.1 no. 22), sailing a boat (Table 11.1 nos. 6, 20), or leading an oryx (Table 11.1 no. 5), by baboons and occasionally long-tailed monkeys. Two of the most enigmatic images from this category are found in tomb of Nefer and Kahay.

11.4.2.1 Twisting the Must-Sack (Table 11.1 no. 13)

Amongst the limestone reliefs, the final stage of winemaking, the pressing of grapes through a must-sack is illustrated (Fig. 11.4a). Here, four men are depicted engaged

---

Figure 11.3 (*cont.*) (Table 11.1 no. 15), depicting a marketplace scene which includes a female baboon. Based on images from Harpur and Scremin (2010: 155 [165]) and Moussa and Altenmüller (1977, fig. 10); (c) Relief from the tomb of Pepyankh the Middle, depicting a long-tailed monkey climbing the arm of its handler and grabbing his face. Based on image from Kanawati (2012: pls. 25, 81).

in wringing a long narrow sack filled with grape pulp, in order to collect the juice beneath. Conventionally, an additional worker would be shown performing an acrobatic act in between the twisting poles, assisting in this process. Delightfully, the center figure in this tomb is replaced by a large male hamadryas baboon. While such a feat of strength and flexibility would certainly be within the baboon's capabilities, it is doubtful the baboon would purposefully do so with the intention of assisting, let alone take direction from his 'colleagues'.

11.4.2.2 Directing the Boatbuilding (Table 11.1 no. 12)

In the same tomb, a large hamadryas male steals the role of overseer in the later stages of a boatbuilding scene (Fig. 11.4b). He stands bipedally and imposingly upon the stern of the boat, wielding the large baton of a director above his head (Fischer, 1978: 16), giving the impression that he is commanding the nearby human workmen (Greenlaw, 2011: 14). The baboon perhaps even takes a threatening stance, since baboons rearing onto their hind legs can preface an aggressive action (Hall and DeVore, 1965: 92; Evans, 2010: 138). In this scene the baboon may be paired with a long-tailed monkey (identified by the upward curl of its tail, although it has an emphasized rear), which walks quadrupedally across a rope. The planked ship is being lashed using a hogging truss to maintain tension while being launched. One worker tightens a rope, while another uses a bar to twist the cord, creating tension (Moussa and Altenmüller, 1971: 27).

   Although it has been suggested (Lashien, 2013: 36), it is impossible to know whether it is the same baboon intended in both representations in this tomb. In both, the virility of the male is captured with the rendering of his large phallus (Greenlaw, 2011: 14) but the purpose of inserting the baboon into these scenes is elusive. As Moussa and Altenmüller (1971: 24, 27) point out, both scenes depict the action of 'twisting' the sack and ropes, respectively. They propose that a visual *paronomasia* is exhibited (i.e. the ancient conceptual counterpart to a pun) playing on the word ⟐ *iꜥn* 'baboon', and ⟐ *ꜥn* 'to turn'. This interpretation is questioned by Hein (2006: 5), who argues that in the boat scene, the baboon has no direct involvement in the twisting action. In fact, the baboon faces in the opposite direction, his arm outstretched to an overseer who stands beside the boat. She instead interprets this scene as a parody of the position of overseer, with the baboon having stolen his baton. The scenes were perhaps simply meant to commemorate a similar humorous incident which had occurred in reality (Lashien, 2013: 32), eternalizing the antics of a tame monkey, kept as a prestige pet by the high-ranking family. The theme is further elaborated on a Dynasty V or VI fragment of relief of unknown provenance, which illustrates a baboon standing at the stern of a boat in transit along the Nile (Houlihan, 2001: 20, 22, fig. 11; Kestner-Museum, Hannover, 1935.200.201). This time, the monkey holds the rudder, while a dwarf stands atop a beam wielding a baton. The Egyptian men aboard are rowing while being overseen by the baboon, reminiscent of a modern-day coxswain steering and coordinating the rowers (Fig. 11.4c; see Bashford, 2016: 48–49).

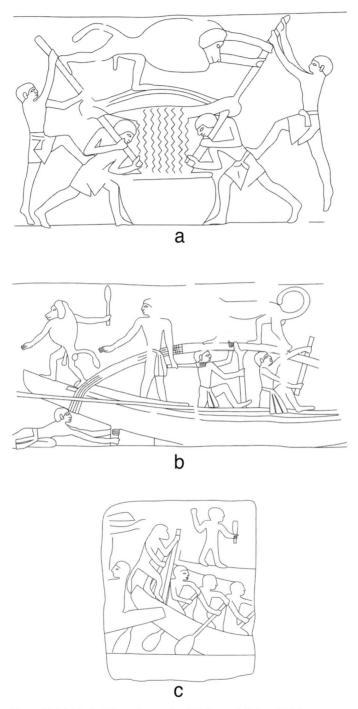

Figure 11.4 (a) Relief from the tomb of Nefer and Kahay (Table 11.1 no. 13), depicting a large male hamadryas baboon 'assisting' with the pressing of grapes. Based on images from Harpur and Scremin (2015: 76–77 [100–101]) and Lashien (2013: pls. 19a, 81); (b) Relief from the tomb

11.4.3 Musical Monkeys

The role of a dancer or musician was apparently a favored one for the monkey in Egypt, which began during the Old Kingdom, and was expanded on greatly in the later periods (see Flores, 2004: 246).

11.4.3.1 Musician

During the Old Kingdom, the motif of animals playing instruments was restricted to the depiction of flute-playing monkeys on cylinder seals (Fischer, 1959: 252, fig. 20). But by the Middle Kingdom musical monkeys reappeared in limestone figurines and later also on the ostraca and papyrus of the New Kingdom. These later images belong to the thematic category of the animal orchestra, which diversifies the repertoire to include a variety of animals playing many instruments, and far from an attempt to represent reality (Flores, 2004: 244–248).

11.4.3.2 Singer

In the Dynasty V tomb at Saqqara of Kaaper, in a subregister beside the tomb owner and his wife is a long-tailed monkey, who faces a human harpist (Fig. 11.5a; Fischer, 1959: 18, fig. 8). The pose of the monkey, left hand raised to mouth and right hand raised in front with the index finger and thumb touching, are both standard gestures of human singers directing their musicians, and is certainly meant as an imitation of these actions (Barta, 2001: 156–158; Dominicus, 1994: 167–173).

Most recently the rediscovery of the Giza tomb of a high-ranking female official of Dynasty V, named Hetepet, adds to this small corpus (Table 11.1 no. 11). This time, however, it is a baboon who accompanies a human orchestra. The tomb is currently unpublished, and the scene has been initially described as a dancing baboon, but with a preliminary examination based on the photos released by the Ministry of Antiquities (2018), it seems more likely the baboon is intended to be accompanying the musicians who sit before it (see also Maître, 2018: 44–45, fig. 1). The images show a distinctly baboon-like red-brown face and a body covered in white-grey fur. The baboon is possibly kneeling, and holds out its right arm, palm facing upwards and flat, in a gesture well known to an Egyptian minstrel (Dominicus, 1994: 167ff). It sits directly behind three kneeling Egyptian males who plays instruments and sing. In the register below are four female musicians, and it is in the register above that female dancers move to the music.

11.4.3.3 Dancer

From the Dynasty V tomb of Serfka at Sheikh Saïd, comes the vibrant image of dancers, with the addition of a monkey to the traditional scene (Fig. 11.5b; Davies,

---

Figure 11.4 (*cont.*) of Nefer and Kahay (Table 11.1 no. 12), depicting a large male hamadryas baboon stealing the role of overseer in a boatbuilding scene. Based on images from Harpur and Scremin (2015: 103–131 [169]) and Lashien (2013: pls. 32b–33a, 83); (c) Fragment of relief of unknown provenance (Table 11.1 no. 20), depicting a baboon steering the rudder-oar of a boat, accompanied by a dwarf. Based on image from Houlihan (2001, fig. 11).

1901: 13, pl. iv). The monkey, with conical breasts and a tail, seems to be imitating their movements.

Both ancient and modern authors alike tell tales of dancing and music-making monkeys and other animals trained to perform for the amusement of humans. The ancient Roman author Aelian (born *c.* 165–170 CE), known for his curious collection *De Natura Animalium* (On the Nature of Animals) wrote:

> Here is more proof that animals are capable of learning. Under the Ptolemies the Egyptians taught baboons how to read, how to dance, how to play the harp and flute. One of the baboons would go around after a performance with a bag demanding money, just as human beggars do. *Book VI, line 10* (McNamee, 2011: 61).

The validity or reality of monkeys being performers in Egyptian art is questionable. Certainly, monkeys could be trained to move alongside dancers to music or pluck the strings of a harp, but this would by no means be easy listening. While historically the practice of training busking monkeys in Egypt was not limited to ancient times (Houlihan, 1997: 32), it is a far cry from the complex associations required in flute playing or singing to the accompaniment of an orchestra (see Sweeney, 2015: 804–805).

11.5   Ingestive Behavior

Ingestion refers to any intake of foods and fluids, and in this discussion will also include the acquisition of food.

11.5.1   Eating

In Old Kingdom iconography, leashed or collared long-tailed monkeys are occasionally depicted squatting, usually on the head of a caretaker or under a chair, with food available nearby (see Evans, 2010: 94–95; Vandier d'Abbadie, 1964: 165–169). These monkeys all have one hand reaching to their mouth, in which an object could be depicted. The other hand might be placed on their handler's head (presumably for support) or reaching into a basket or bowl of fruit (Fig. 11.6b). In the Dynasty VI tomb of Ibi at Deir el-Gebrawi, a strikingly human-like female long-tailed monkey, made clear by her conical breasts, and adorned with a collar as well as bracelets and anklets, squats under a chair (Fig. 11.6a). Her right arm reaches to a bowl full to the brim with fruit, her left is held to her mouth, as though feeding on a juicy morsel (Kanawati, 2007: 60, pl. 75a).

Omnivorous monkeys mainly consume fruits, seeds, leaves, flowers, grass, and invertebrates (Evans, 2010: 94). In Egyptian iconography, it is not always possible to determine exactly which rounded fruit is being depicted, but generally they would be illustrated dining on the economically important crops of the time (Houlihan, 1997: 32): figs (*Ficus sycomorus*), dates (*Phoenix dactylifera*), and doum palm nuts (*Hyphaene thebaica*), a diet not unfamiliar to the species. Further south in Kenya, vervets have been observed feeding predominantly on the doum palm (Whitten, 1983: 140). In Ethiopia, a likely source location for hamadryas baboons imported

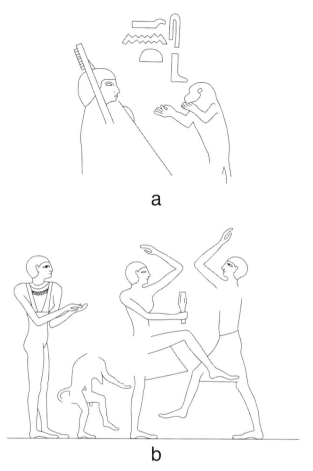

Figure 11.5 (a) Relief from the tomb of Kaaper illustrating an Egyptian musician playing the harp, accompanied by a long-tailed monkey, who makes a classic gesture of a singer. Based on image from Fischer (1959, fig. 8); (b) Relief from the tomb of Serfka depicting a monkey alongside human dancers. Based on images from Houlihan (2001, fig. 10) and Davies (1901: 13, pl. iv).

into Egypt (see Fig. 11.10), they chiefly feed on the nuts of the doum palm trees, which were richly distributed in the northern Rift Valley (Swedell, 2002: 99). No doubt their ancient equivalents would be just as willingly to feed on the nutritious fruit, which given its high fat content, would satisfy much of the daily caloric intake needs (Duke, 2001: 174), particularly when presented before them picked and ready to eat in a bowl or basket.

11.5.2   Food Acquisition: Harvester or Thief?

Egyptian iconography encompassed not only hungry monkeys eating, but also documented the gathering of fruit by monkeys themselves. Much like scenes of work,

Figure 11.6 (a) Relief from the tomb of Ibi where a long-tailed monkey seated under the chair of the tomb owner, feeds on a bowl full of juicy fruit. Based on images from Fischer (1959, fig. 17c) and Davies (1902a: pl. XIX); (b) Relief from the tomb of Ankhmahor: Sesi (Dynasty VI, Saqqara) where a long-tailed monkey holds its hand to its mouth as though eating, and squats on the shoulders of its caretaker, an achondroplastic dwarf who holds a basket of fruit. Based on images from Fischer (1959, fig. 18c) and Kanawati and Hassan (1997: pl. 42).

many have interpreted these images to represent trained monkeys, who were utilized by the Egyptians to help workers with harvesting fruit from cultivated orchards and gardens (for examples, see Houlihan, 1997: 32 fn. 10). These monkeys could be depicted either alone, as a group, in trees, or alongside human harvesters. Furthering this theory is the interpretation that the occasional images of monkeys sat atop the heads of achondroplastic dwarfs, who sometimes carry a basket of fruit (Fig. 11.6b), or the monkey hold a handful themselves (see Evans, 2010: 94–95), are workers returning from the fields with their trained harvester monkeys. This is questioned by Houlihan (1997: 34) who rightly notes they are never shown in any context relating to orchards or harvesting and are more likely carrying a supply of treats for their charge. Additionally, baboons are by no means out of place sitting or resting in trees, and in some areas hamadryas baboons may even use stands of doum palm trees full of the fruit as sleeping sites (Schrier and Swedell, 2008).

Certainly, primates possess the agility, arboreality, and dexterity, combined with intelligence, allowing them to clamber up high to the branches and bunches out of reach to human hands, taking fruit and leaves from trees, by twisting and pulling the chosen item (Whitten, 1983: 146). But recent examinations have called into question the claims of trained monkey harvesters ever existing in ancient Egypt (Houlihan, 1997).

In southern Thailand, pig-tail macaques (*Macaca nemestrina*) have long (and controversially still today) been employed by humans to assist with the demanding task of harvesting coconut crops. The monkeys are captured from free-ranging populations at a young age, and on average it takes only two to three weeks to train them. Through punishment and reward, they can learn to respond to verbal commands, choose various phases of ripeness, and twist the coconut at the stem to remove from the tree. The leashed monkey is then set to climb high in the trees, dropping the heavy picked fruits to the ground below to be collected by workers. Usually, a bond develops between the monkey and one male handler, reducing the risks associated with monkey aggression by utilizing the macaque dominance hierarchy (Houlihan, 1997: 33–34; Sponsel et al., 2002: 291). Whether the monkeys brought into Egypt had this capacity too is nevertheless questionable.

A fascinating image from the recently discovered tomb of Hetepet is the newest and earliest example in a series of representations that show a monkey harvesting fruit in an orchard (Table 11.1 no. 10). The initial press release photographs (Ministry of Antiquities, 2018) reveal a monkey with an emphasized rump and offspring which clings to its back, indicating a female baboon is intended (see also Maître, 2018: 44–45, figs. 2, 4a). She stands upright, and with her front arms reaches out to a fruit-laden tree. Depicted in an unusual crossed over fashion, her left arm appears to reach out to the tree, in the process of plucking a piece of fruit from it. The right hand reaches up to her open mouth, about to take a bite of the juicy fruit, while a basket looped around her arm was presumably to be filled with more fruit. She stands to the left of the first of a row of three trees, and up in the tree itself squats another baboon, holding its hand to its mouth. Various types of baskets hang from the trees and between the second and third tree a male figure squats, with his hand to his head. His position is reminiscent of an earlier scene which represents the only other monkey in a tree from the Old Kingdom. In the Dynasty IV tomb of the prince Nefermaat at Meidum, a long-tailed monkey, far from acting as a fruit-picking assistant, playfully climbs the trunk of the tree, swinging from a branch (Fig. 11.7a). Squatting beneath the shade of the tree is a male figure, with knees under chin, staff leaning against his shoulder his arm is curved over his head as if to shield eyes from the light, in much the same manner as the Hetepet worker (Egyptian Museum JE 43809; Harpur, 2001: 63, pl. 6, fig. 75). Neither monkey in the Old Kingdom scenes appears to be taking direction from an Egyptian handler, although admittedly the current sources for the tomb of Hetepet are limited.

In a continuation of this tradition, a painting at Beni Hassan shows three baboons, with red faces and buttocks, and green coats, in a tree "helping" men harvest the ripe fruits. But more so than handing fruit to any workers, the baboons are busy taking their fill from the tree, and even out of the hand of a worker (Kanawati and Evans, 2014: 39 and pls. 19b–20b, 118, 122c). In fact, it could be said far from helping the harvest process, they are hindering it (Houlihan, 1997: 34).

It is really with the later iconographic corpus from the New Kingdom that the theory of monkey-harvesters is cemented. Several variations on ostraca, and one stele (Fig. 11.7b), show monkeys in connection with trees and dining on their fruit (Houlihan, 1997: 37–42; Vandier d'Abbadie, 1966: 193–198). However, Houlihan (1997: 42) concludes that these scenes are misunderstood, since the monkeys are never portrayed delivering fruits to Egyptian keepers and rather, being a highly

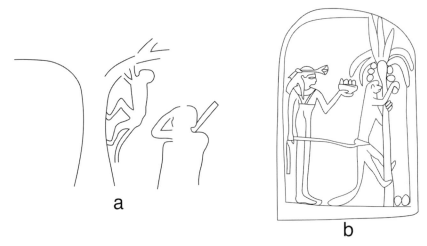

Figure 11.7 (a) Relief from the tomb of Nefermaat where a monkey swings from the branch of a fruit tree while a human figure sits below. Based on image from Harpur (2001: pl.6); (b) Painted wood stele (now in Egyptian Museum, Cairo JE 46982) depicting an oversized leashed long-tailed monkey climbing up a palm tree and grabbing its fruit. A woman holds the leash in one hand, and in the other, a bowl full of fruit. Based on image from Vandier d'Abbadie (1966, fig. 57).

valued exotic commodity, are simply being allowed to do what monkeys do, and the Egyptian delight in their antics was recorded on ostraca and preserved in the tombs of their owners for eternity. On the other hand, being allowed to dine on some of the fruit whilst picking it, could no doubt have been an incentive to work (Sweeney, 2015: 805–806).

In modern times the sticky-fingered nature of baboons, entering urban areas to steal food, is well documented (Fehlmann et al., 2017). Furthermore, the Egyptians seemed to be more than aware of the mischievous nature of monkeys, recording it in both word and image. In the tomb of Niankhkhnum and Khnumhotep, a leashed hamadryas male attempts to help itself to food from a basket of vegetables for sale in the marketplace, as his handler holds him back (Table 11.1 no. 15; Fig. 11.8). Additionally, a spell from the Old Kingdom *Pyramid Texts* reproaches the baboon's thievery when he steals an offering, "You have taken the thigh-joint of your goddess to your mouth" (PT 549 § 1349b, see Allen, 2015: 177 [549]).

11.6   Parental Behavior

In Egyptian art, mating, birth, and care of offspring is portrayed by many species (see Evans, 2010: 151–187), but such behavior being exhibited by monkeys is rare. Indeed, there are no examples of primate copulation at any time in Egyptian history. A unique birthing scene from the Middle Kingdom tomb of Wekhhotep I at Meir exists as the only extant instance of monkey birth portrayed in Egyptian art (Kanawati and Evans, 2017: 45 and pls. 46c, 85).

Figure 11.8 Relief fragments from the tomb of Niankhkhnum and Khnumhotep (Table 11.1 no. 15), depicting a marketplace scene which include a male hamadryas baboon. Based on images from Harpur and Scremin (2010: 155 [164]) and Moussa and Altenmüller (1977, fig. 10).

11.6.1   Infant-Carrying

Infant-carrying is one of the most widely observed parental behaviors in primates and is apparently crucial for the survival of infants (Estes, 1991: 518). The reconstructed fragments depicting the activities in a market from the tomb of Tepemankh II (Fig. 11.3a; Table 11.1 no. 14) offer a unique display of primate maternal care. A leashed female baboon walks forward quadrupedally, and in her left forelimb she clutches an infant, whom she presses to her breast (Evans, 2010: 186, fn. 98). The head of the young baboon is visible under her chest. New-born baboons are not completely mobile until at least one month old, so up until then, their mothers transport them by holding them against their torso, often supporting their bodies with one hand as the infant holds onto her chest fur (Anvari et al., 2014: 393; Estes, 1991: 518). Similarly, in this scene, the baboon evidently has only three limbs. While it cannot be said for certain whether her missing forelimb was originally drawn beneath the infant due to a break in the relief, it was likely with the artist's intention to show the female supporting an infant as she walks (Evans, 2010: 186). Certainly, the artist has ignored convention and shows the animal with the forelimb closest to the viewer advancing first, which Evans (2010: 186) suggests was chosen as an "alternative arrangement to ensure that the infant remained visible while simultaneous implying the presence of the mother's supporting arm."

At around two months or more, the now more mobile infants usually transition to climbing onto their mothers back and riding or clinging to her as she goes throughout her day (Anvari et al., 2014: 393; Estes, 1991: 518). This stage is depicted once during the Old Kingdom (but appears later during the Middle Kingdom with long-tailed monkeys, e.g. Kanawati and Evans, 2018: pls. 44b–45a, 79–80), in the tomb of Hetepet (Table 11.1 no. 10). In this instance, the mother baboon is actually in the act of picking and eating fruit from a tree while standing bipedally and has the charming addition of a young baboon clinging to her back while she 'works'. Accordingly, most primates carry their young during foraging rather than leaving them unattended (Young and Shapiro, 2018: 38).

11.6.2 Tail-Grabbing

The Dynasty IV tomb of Atet at Meidum, tells the story of a young boy playing with assumedly, his pets (Table 11.1 no. 2). From the right, an unleashed baboon grasps the hand of a young boy, who in turn touches the back of a long-tailed monkey, perhaps in an effort to restrain him since the mischievous monkey looks to be pulling the tail feathers of a crane (Fig. 11.9a; Harpur, 2001: 87, fig. 86, pl. 6). The fact that the baboon lacks any morphological features of a male baboon, and possesses an emphasized rump, could indicate it is a female and thus apparently exhibits a humorous twist on the natural behavior of monkeys. When a baboon is very young its mother never lets her infant out of her sight and will prevent it from wandering away by holding on to its tail (Kummer, 1997: 205). Indeed, this behavior is portrayed in the later Theban Tomb (TT100) of the Dynasty XVIII Vizier, Rekhmire. Amongst the illustrations of the collection of various goods as taxes from southern cities (e.g. south of Thebes) are two subregisters of monkeys (Davies, 1943: pl. XXIX[2]; Vandier d'Abbadie, 1966: 155, fig. 15). The upper subregister depicts four monkeys feasting on fruit, while the lower subregister shows a seated female monkey holding onto the tail of her smaller offspring, who stands bipedally before her (Fig. 11.9b).

11.7 Conclusions

Through an examination of primate behavior, it is evident that in the art of the Egyptian Old Kingdom (Fig. 11.10), many of the action's monkeys are portrayed engaging in are in fact well within their natural capacities. The Egyptians undoubtedly categorized nonhuman animals as fundamentally different from themselves (Evans, 2010: 195). The insertion of monkeys into traditionally human positions is therefore significant, and perhaps emphasizes the perceived 'humanness' of their actions. The antics of baboons in particular, seemed to capture the imagination of the ancient Egyptian tomb owner. Additionally, the sexual dimorphism between male and female baboons is especially emphasized.

Several temporal and spatial observations can also be made. The bulk of the depictions are found in the Lower Egyptian (i.e. Northern) cemeteries of Giza, Saqqara, Meidum, and Abusir. This is unsurprising since this was the location for the central government of the Egyptian king and his officials during the Old Kingdom, and thus the site of most tomb burials at this time. Of note, however, are

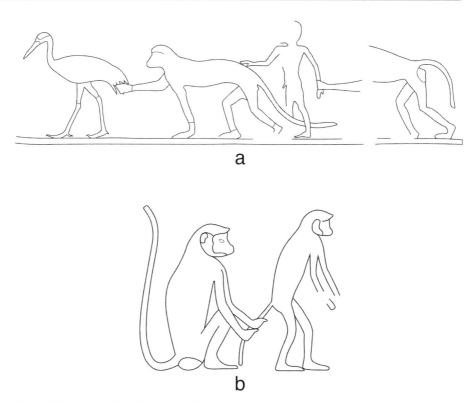

Figure 11.9 (a) Relief from the tomb of Atet (Table 11.1 no. 2), where a female baboon holds the hand of a young boy, the boy touches the rump of a long-tailed monkey, and the monkey pulls on the tail feather of a crane. Based on image from Jørgensen (1996: 39 [ÆIN 1133]); (b) Relief from the tomb of Rekhmire, where a squatting female monkey grabs the tail of her small standing offspring. Based on image from Davies (1943: pl. XXIX[2]).

the 'baboons in the marketplace' scenes of Saqqara from late Dynasty V that occur only here, including one royal example (Table 11.1 no. 19) appearing slightly later than the private examples of Tepemankh [II], and Niankhkhnum and Khnumhotep. Thus, according to Smith (1942: 516–518), this may indicate the existence of another earlier now lost example, from which these scenes could have been copied. Furthermore, the 'imitation of work' scenes of Giza and Saqqara from Dynasty V, for which only one regional example currently exists and dates to Dynasty VI (Table 11.1 no. 22), again indicates an iconographic trend confined to this region, one where baboons and other monkeys may have been more readily available. The baboons depicted in the tombs of Middle Egypt, found at el-Hammamiya, Sheikh Saïd, and Zawyet el-Maiyitin, are either found walking on a leash or aboard a boat sailing the Nile, possibly representing their transport to elsewhere in Egypt where they were kept as a valuable symbol of social standing by the regional rulers.

The exotic nature of monkeys gave them a rarity, and while their depiction is relatively infrequent, the images often exhibit knowledge that could only have come

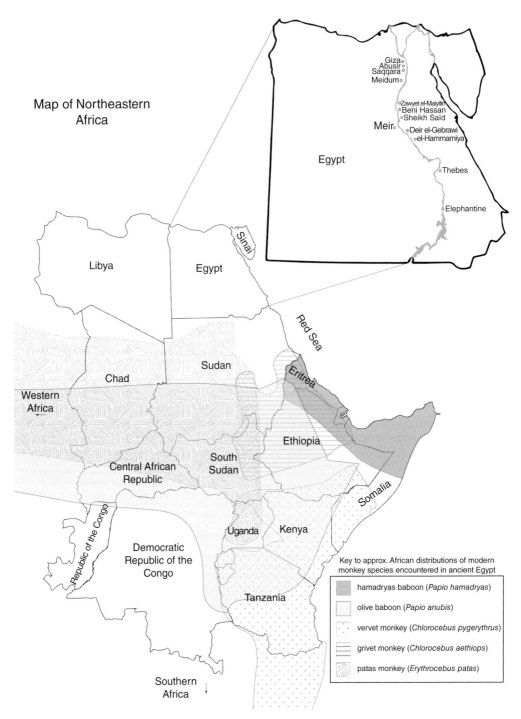

Figure 11.10 Map of ancient sites in Egypt and Northeastern Africa showing distributions of monkey species which inhabit the regions closest to Egypt.

from observations of natural behavior, indicating regular interaction with several primate species. Despite some small inaccuracies, such as rounded heads or pointed ears (Fig. 11.1a, b), the tomb owners and artists must have derived much of their knowledge about monkeys from imported captive animals, used in life and death as a symbol of prestige and Egyptian foreign domination.

Acknowledgments

I would like to thank Joyce Bashford, Dr Anna Chilcott, and Associate Professor Linda Evans for their comments on earlier versions of this manuscript. I also thank the editors (B. Urbani, D. Youlatos, and A. T. Antczak) for inviting me to contribute to this volume.

References

Allen, J. P. (2015). *The Ancient Egyptian Pyramid Texts*. Atlanta: SBL Press.

Anvari, Z., Berillon, G., & Asgari Khaneghah, A., et al. (2014). Kinematics and spatiotemporal parameters of infant-carrying in olive baboons. *American Journal of Physical Anthropolology*, **155**(3), 392–404.

Bárta, M., (2001) *Abusir V: The Cemeteries at Abusir South I*. Praha: Set Out.

Bashford, L. (2016) The iconography of exotic animals and other exotica: Interconnections during the Old Kingdom. MA thesis. University of Auckland.

Davies, N. de G. (1901). *The Rock Tombs of Sheikh Saïd*. London: Egypt Exploration Fund.

Davies, N. de G. (1902a). *The Rock Tombs of Deir el Gebrâwi I*. London: Egypt Exploration Fund.

Davies, N de G. (1902b). *The Rock Tombs of Deir el Gebrâwi II*. London: Egypt Exploration Fund.

Davies, N. de G. (1943). *The Tomb of Rekh-mi-rē' at Thebes II*. New York: The Plantin Press.

Dominicus, B. (1994). *Gesten und Gebärden in Darstellungen des Alten und Mittleren Reiches*. Heidelberg: Heidelberger Orientverlag.

Duke, J. (2001). *Handbook of Nuts*. Boca Raton: CRC Press.

El Awady, T. (2009). *Abusir XVI: Sahure – The Pyramid Causeway: History and Decoration Program in the Old Kingdom*. Prague: Charles University in Prague.

El-Khouli, A., & Kanawati. N. (1990). *The Old Kingdom Tombs of el-Hammamiya*. Sydney: Australian Centre for Egyptology.

Estes, R. D. (1991). *The Behavior Guide to African Mammals*. Berkeley: University of California Press.

Evans, L. (2000). Animals in the domestic environment. In L. Donovan, & K. McCorquodale. eds., *Egyptian Art Principles and Themes in Wall Scenes*. Guizeh: Foreign Cultural Relations, 73–82.

Evans, L. (2010). *Animal Behaviour in Egyptian Art: Representations of the Natural World in Memphite Tomb Scenes*. Oxford: Aris and Phillips.

Fehlmann, G., O'Riain, M. J., & Kerr-Smith, C., et al. (2017). Extreme behavioural shifts by baboons exploiting risky, resource-rich, human-modified environments. *Scientific Report*, **7**, 1–8.

Fischer, H. G. (1959). A scribe of the army in a Saqqara mastaba of the early Fifth Dynasty. *Journal of Near Eastern Studies* **18**, 233–272.

Fischer, H. G. (1978). Notes on sticks and staves in Ancient Egypt. *Metropolitan Museum Journal*, **13**, 5–32.

Flores, D. (2004). The topsy-turvy world. In G. N. Knoppers, & A. Hirsch, eds., *Egypt, Israel, and the Ancient Mediterranean World: Studies in Honor of Donald B. Redford*. Leiden; Boston: Brill, 233–255.

Greenlaw, C. (2011). *The Representation of Monkeys in the Art and Thought of Mediterranean Cultures: A New Perspective on Ancient Primates*. Oxford: Archaeopress.

Gordon, A. H., & Schwabe, C. W. (2004). *The Quick and the Dead: Biomedical Theory in Ancient Egypt, Leiden*. Boston: Brill; Styx.

Harpur, Y. (2001). *The Tombs of Nefermaat and Rahotep at Maidum: Discovery, Destruction and Reconstruction*. Cheltenham: Oxford Expedition to Egypt.

Harpur, Y., & Scremin, P. (2010). *The Chapel of Niankhkhnum and Khnumhotep: Scene Details*. Oxford: Oxford Expedition to Egypt.

Harpur, Y., & Scremin, P. (2015). *The Chapel of Nefer and Kahay: Scene Details*. Oxford: Oxford Expedition to Egypt.

Hall, K. R. L. & DeVore, I. (1965). Baboon social behaviour. In I. DeVore, eds., *Primate Behaviour: Field Studies of Monkeys and Apes*. New York: Holt, Rinehart, and Winston.

Hassan, S. (1943). *Excavations at Gîza IV (1932–1933)*. Cairo: Government Press.

Hassan, S. (1944). *Excavations at Gîza V (1933–1934)*. Cairo: Government Press.

Hassan, S. (1975). *Mastabas of Princess Ḥemet-R' and Others*. Cairo: General Organisation for Government Printing Offices.

Hein, K. (2006). Der Pavian im Boot: ein Deutungsversuch. *Göttinger Miszellen*, **210**, 5–6.

Houlihan, P. F. (1997). Harvester or monkey business? *Göttinger Miszellen*, **157**, 31–47.

Houlihan, P. F. (2001). *Wit and Humour in Ancient Egypt*. London: Rubicon Press.

Janssen, R., & Janssen, J. (1989). *Egyptian Household Animals*. Princes Risborough: Shire Publications.

Jéquier, G. (1938). *Le monument funéraire de Pepi II. Vol. II*. Cairo: Institut français d'archéologie orientale.

Jørgensen, M. (1996). *Catalogue Egypt I (3000–1550 BC) Ny Carlsberg Glyptotek*. Copenhagen: Ny Carlsberg Glyptotek.

Kanawati, N. (2012). *The Cemetery of Meir I: The Tomb of Pepyankh the Middle*. Oxford: Aris and Phillips.

Kanawati, N. (2007). *Deir el-Gebrawi II: The Southern Cliff. The Tombs of Ibi and Others*. Oxford: Aris and Phillips.

Kanawati N. & Evans, L. (2014). *Beni Hassan I: The Tomb of Khnumhotep II*. Oxford: Aris and Phillips.

Kanawati N., & Evans, L. (2017). *The Cemetery of Meir IV: The Tombs of Senbi I and Wekhhotep I*. Oxford: Aris and Phillips.

Kanawati N., & Evans, L. (2018). *Beni Hassan IV: The Tomb of Baqet III*. Oxford: Aris and Phillips.

Kanawati, N., & Hassan, A. (1997). *The Teti Cemetery at Saqqara. Volume II: The Tomb of Ankhmahor*. Warminster: Aris and Phillips.

Kilany, E. El-. (2013). Monkeys in the daily life scenes of Ancient Egypt. *Göttinger Miszellen*, **238**, 25–39.

Kilany, E. El-., & Mahran, H. (2015). What lies under the chair! A study in ancient Egyptian private tomb scenes, Part I: Animals. *Journal of the American Research Center in Egypt*, **51**, 243–264.

Kingdon J. (1988). *East African Mammals: An Atlas of Evolution in Africa Vol. I*. London; New York: Academic Press.

Kummer, H. (1968). *Social Organization of Hamadryas Baboons: A Field Study*. Basel: Karger.

Kummer, H. (1997). *In Quest of the Sacred Baboon: A Scientist's Journey*. Princeton: Princeton University Press.

Labrousse, A., & Moussa, A. (2002). *La chaussée du complexe funéraire du roi Ounas*. Cairo: Institut français d'archéologie orientaleIF.

Lashien, M. (2013). *The Chapel of Kahai and his Family*. Oxford: Aris and Phillips.

Lepsius, C. R. (1897–1913). *Denkmaeler aus Ägypten und Aethiopien*. Vol. II (pts. 3-4). Leipzig: J.C. Hinrichs.

Macdonald, J. (1965). *Almost Human. The Baboon: Wild and Tame – In Fact and in Legend*. Philadelphia: Chilton Books.

Maître, J. (2018). Malin comme un babouin" Le rôle des singeries comme faire-valoir de l'idéal de vie à l'égyptienne dans la chapelle du mastaba d'Hétepet à Gîza. *Egypte, Afrique and Orient*, **89**, 43–52.

Manuelian, P. D. (1999). Market scene from the Tomb of Tep-em-ankh. In Anonymous, ed., *Egyptian Art in the Age of the Pyramids*. New York: Metropolitan Museum of Art, 404–407.

McNamec, G. (2011). {*Aelian's*} *On the Nature of Animals*. San Antonio: Trinity University Press.

Ministry of Antiquities. (2018). *The Discovery of an Old Kingdom Tomb of a Lady who was a Top Official in the Royal Palace*. Cairo, Egypt: Available at: www.egyptologyforum.org/bbs/Hetpet_tomb.pdf

Moussa, A. M., & Altenmüller, H. (1971). *The Tomb of Nefer and Ka-hay: Old Kingdom Tombs at the Causeway of King Unas at Saqqara*. Mainz: Zabern.

Moussa, A. M., & Altenmüller, H. (1977). *Das Grab des Nianchchnum und Chnumhotep*. Mainz: Zabern.

Noll, P. E., Coelho, A. M., & Bramblett, C .A. (1982). The effects of sexual status on threat, attack, and subordinate behaviors of *Papio* monkeys. *Archive of Sexual Behavior*, **11**, 65–72.

Osborn, D. J., & Osbornová, J. (1998). *The Mammals of Ancient Egypt*. Warminster: Aris and Phillips.

Schrier, A., & Swedell, L. (2008). Use of palm trees as a sleeping site for hamadryas baboons (*Papio hamadryas hamadryas*) in Ethiopia. *American Journal of Primatology*, **70**, 107–113.

Smith, W. S. (1942). The origin of some unidentified Old Kingdom reliefs. *American Journal of Archaeology*, **46**, 509–531.

Sponsel, L. E., Ruttanadakul, N., & Natadecha-Sponsel, P. (2002). Monkey business? The conservation implications of macaque ethnoprimatology in southern Thailand. In: A. Fuentes, & L. D. Wolfe, eds., *Primates Face to Face: Conservation Implications of Human-Nonhuman Primate Interconnections.* Cambridge: Cambridge University Press, 288–309.

Subiaul, F. (2007). The imitation faculty in monkeys: evaluating its features, distribution and evolution. *Journal of Anthropological Science*, **85**, 35–62.

Swedell, L. (2002). Ranging behavior, group size, and behavioral flexibility in Ethiopian hamadryas baboons (*Papio hamadryas hamadryas*). *Folia Primatologica*, **73**, 95–103.

Sweeney, D. (2015). Monkey business at Deir el-Medina. In H. Amstutz, A. Dorn, M. Müller, M. Ronsdorf, & S. Uljas, eds., *Fuzzy Boundaries: Feitschrift für Antonio Loprieno.* Vol. II. Hamburg: Widmaier Verlag, 801–813.

Vandier d'Abbadie, J. (1964). Les singes familiers dans l'ancienne Égypte (Peintures et Bas-reliefs): I. L'Ancien Empire. *Revue d'égyptologie*, **16**, 147–177.

Vandier d'Abbadie, J. (1965). Les singes familiers dans l'ancienne Égypte (Peintures et Bas-reliefs): II. le Moyen Empire. *Revue d'égyptologie*, **17**, 177–188.

Vandier d'Abbadie, J. (1966). Les singes familiers dans l'ancienne Égypte (Peintures et Bas-reliefs): III: le Nouvel Empire. *Revue d'égyptologie*, **18**, 143–201.

Varille, A. (1938). *La tombe de Ni-Ankh-Pepi à Zâouyet el-Mayetîn.* Cairo: Institut français d'archéologie orientale.

Vilensky, J., & Larson, S. (1989). Primate locomotion: Utilization and control of symmetrical gaits. *Annual Review of Anthropology*, **18**, 17–35.

Wickler, W. (1967). Socio-sexual signals and their intra-specific imitation among primates. In D. Morris, ed., *Primate Ethology.* London: Weidenfeld and Nicolson, pp. 69–147.

Wild, H. (1953). *Le Tombeau de Ti II: La Chapelle* (pt. 1). Cairo: Institut français d'archéologie orientale.

Whitten P. L. (1983). Diet and dominance among female vervet monkeys (*Cercopithecus aethiops*). *American Journal of Primatology*, **5**, 139–145.

Wilson, P. (1997). *A Ptolemaic Lexikon: A Lexicographical Study of the Texts in the Temple of Edfu.* Leuven: Peeters.

Young, J. W., & Shapiro, L. J. (2018). Developments in development: what have we learned from primate locomotor ontogeny? *American Journal of Physical Anthropology*, **165**, 37–71.

12 The Nonhuman Primate Remains from the Baboon Catacomb at Saqqara in Egypt

Douglas Brandon-Jones & Jaap Goudsmit

البقايا الغير بشرية الرئيسية التي تم العثور عليها في جبانه القرود بسقارة في مصر

نبذه

بعد مسح سريع لمحتويات جبانة القرود بسقارة في مصر، تمت إزالة معظم بقايا والتي تقدر بنحو 180 فردًا من القرود (حوالي 40 في المئة من الناجين) مؤقتًا لمزيد من الدراسة. بالنسبة للأنواع فيلاحظ أن النوع السائد هو الـPapio anubis، كما تم العثور أيضا علي أنواعا أخري مثل الـMacaca sylvanus وعددها 21، و اثنان من الـChlorocebus aethiops. استخدم المصريون القدماء في العهد المتأخر من الأسرات طريقة فريدة لتغليف موميأوات القرود المغلفة بالكتان، حيث غلفوها في الجبس في سراديب الموتى، ولكن من المحتمل أن تكون معظم جثث القرود قد نقعت قبل الدفن. تظهر معظم الجماجم أعراض النقص الغذائي أو الحرمان من أشعة الشمس، بينما ظهر على البعض الأخر علامات عنف. من الملحوظ أنه من حيث الجنس يشير فإن أعداد الذكور هي الطاغية وهذا يدل على حدوث القليل من التكاثر. من المرجح أن سبب تفضيل الذكور يرجع إلى تقديس الإنسان لوضعية الجلوس المميزة، والتي كانت غالبًا مع قضيب منتصب، التي تتخذها القرود عند الإعلان سيادتها على أرضا ما. ومن الجدير بالذكر أن البشر كانوا يتبعون نفس الطريقة، مستعملين فيما بعد الدمى كقوائم احتياطية، ولكن مع تطور الحضارة، تم قمع هذه الطريقة في إظهار السيادة ال

الكلمات الدالة

شلل بالقفص الصدري – هيرودوت – إمحوتب-لين العظام – عبادة الشمس – تحوت

Abstract

After a rapid survey of the contents of the Baboon Catacomb at Saqqara in Egypt, most of the remains of an estimated 180 monkey individuals (the surviving 40%) were temporarily removed for further study. The predominant species is *Papio anubis*, but 21 *Macaca sylvanus* and 2 *Chlorocebus aethiops* were present. Late Dynastic Egyptians employed a unique method of encasing linen-wrapped baboon mummies in plaster at the catacomb, but most of the monkey corpses were probably macerated before interment. Most of the skulls show symptoms of dietary deficiency or sunlight deprivation; some show signs of violence. The disproportionate male representation indicates that little breeding occurred. Males were probably preferred because of human reverence for the characteristic sitting posture, often with penis erect, that monkeys adopt when advertising land occupancy. Humans once displayed in a similar manner, later using effigies as stand-ins, but as civilization developed, this territorial behavior was suppressed.

Keywords: Cage paralysis, Herodotus, Imhotep, Osteomalacia, Sun worship, Thoth

12.1 Introduction

In about 3000 BCE (Bard, 2015: 117), the Early Dynastic pharaohs consolidated their spreading influence from Upper (southern) to Lower (northern) Egypt by transferring

Figure 12.1 Map of Northeast Africa, showing Saqqara and some other places mentioned in the text. Modified from Hel-hama / River Nile map.svg / CC-BY-SA-3.0.

their capital from Abydos to Memphis (Fig. 12.1) on the west bank at the conjunction of the Nile delta. Nearby Saqqara probably became its main necropolis (major cemetery) because its situation on an escarpment above the annual Nile inundation reduced the risk of flooding and made it conspicuous and less desirable for cultivation. The river course is now farther from both sites than it was in pharaonic times (Bard, 2015: 55, pl. 3.2).

Saqqara is best known as the site of the first ever pyramid, the Step Pyramid built in *c.* 2650 BCE as a tomb for the first king of the Third Dynasty, Netjerikhet, the 'Djoser' of later texts (Baud, 2014: 63). Its designer, his vizier Imhotep was deified in the Late Period (664–332 BCE). Pilgrimages to Imhotep's possibly nearby tomb (yet to be firmly identified, see below) or to his architectural masterpiece can explain the origin of the two extensive ibis catacombs at Saqqara, the ibis being sacred to Thoth, the god of wisdom linked with Imhotep (Bard, 2015: 140, 328; Emery, 1965: 8; Wilson, 1999: 40). The first inscription clearly associating Imhotep with the ibis and falcon cults at Saqqara was the demotic ink writing, securely datable to 89 BCE (Emery, 1971: 6), below figures of an ibis facing a falcon on the limestone stela that sealed a small niche containing a mummified falcon in a wooden box in the main Falcon Catacomb passageway. A gallery opposite had a small ink drawing of the ibis and baboon forms of Thoth and Imhotep, respectively (Emery, 1971: 5–6, pl. 5). From the seventeenth to the nineteenth century CE, the North Ibis Catacomb was a tourist attraction, but its location was then lost until Emery rediscovered it in 1964 (Emery, 1965: 6; Nicholson, 1996).

The second most impressive monument at Saqqara is probably the Serapeum, a subterranean gallery built to house in massive granite sarcophagi the mummified remains of the Apis bulls, regarded as reincarnations of the creator-god Ptah (Szpakowska, 2014: 510; Wilson, 1999: 28). When the bull died, its successor was taken to the temple of Imhotep to be consecrated by the god's touch (Emery, 1967: 145). The bull cult may have existed at Memphis since the Early Dynastic Period, but the earliest discovered bull burials at Saqqara date from the reign of Amenhotep III (c. 1390–1352 BCE). The Lesser Vaults, begun in the reign of Rameses II (c. 1279–1213 BCE), remained in use until the Greater Vaults were begun under Psamtek I (664–610 BCE). Vast resources invested in this and other animal cults during the Saite Dynasty continued through to Ptolemaic times (332–330 BCE) (Bard, 2015: 302). The Greeks disapproved of animal worship, but the Ptolemaic kings, as foreign conquerors, sought cultural and religious ties between Egyptians and the Greek newcomers. The resulting cult of Serapis with its associated Serapeum in Alexandria paralleled the older one at Saqqara, but with a more anthropomorphic approach to the Osiris–Apis cult (Cruz-Uribe, 2014: 492). Much of the evidence is Ptolemaic for pilgrim multitudes, large communities of priests, other temple personnel, astrologers, dream diviners, and scribe-drafted petitions, but Saqqara was not the only Late Dynastic Egyptian animal cemetery. Pilgrims left the mummified remains (some comprising substitute species) as offerings perhaps associated with the Osirian cycle of life, death, and rebirth, involving concepts of fertility and procreation (Bard, 2015: 305–306). After consecration, animal mummies remained in a 'house of waiting' until final interment at a festival occurring at least once a year (Ray, 2011).

The presence of Ptolemaic–Roman pottery convinced Emery (1965) that the valley of mainly Early Dynastic monuments at the extreme west of North Saqqara was a place of pilgrimage. Third Dynasty brickwork, two bull burials, ibis mummies in lidded pottery jars, and Ptolemaic votive pottery exposed by two test pits sunk in 1956, raised his hopes of finding the long-lost Asklepieion (a healing temple, sacred to the god Asklepios) and Imhotep's tomb. The debris in the Baboon Catacomb included plaster casts of various human anatomical parts, such as complete heads, the upper halves of faces, hair, torsos, hands, legs, feet, and other unidentifiable pieces. They were probably medical votive offerings, either seeking cures or in gratitude for health restored. A further cache of such objects outside the entrance to Tomb 3518 whose shaft penetrated the upper gallery, the unusual design and magnitude of this tomb, and unlike other great Third Dynasty burials, its matching orientation with the Step Pyramid, evidently left Emery (1970) optimistic that this was Imhotep's tomb. The two caches of Ptolemaic anatomical *donaria* puzzled Emery (1971), as the shaft of Tomb 3518 continued down to the burial chamber breached by the Lower Baboon Gallery, and the still-present original filling would have prevented through communication to the ground surface above. The bottom of the shaft yielded fine quality, broken stone vessels, but no evidence of ownership. Streets of smaller

Archaic Period mastabas (flat-roofed tombs) surrounded the tomb superstructure, with no pottery fragments beyond the Third Dynasty. Emery (1971) conceded that the Catacomb and tomb association may be fortuitous, but noted that the tunnellers ignored nearby fallow sites to excavate in an area riddled with Archaic Period burial shafts.

Smith (in Emery, 1970: 8) dated the hundred or so graffiti in the Baboon Catacomb, one in Carian, but most in hieroglyphic and demotic, from the fourth century BCE to the Roman period. Outside the Catacomb, Emery (1971) found the remains of a series of rough-stone huts, probably accommodation for the tunnellers. Pottery dated them to not earlier than the Thirtieth Dynasty (380–343 BCE) (Emery, 1971: 4), after over a century of Persian rule, as Egypt reasserted its independence. An agricultural boom prompted Nectanebo II (360–343 BCE) to widespread temple embellishment. He also favored animal cults, especially the bull cult, perhaps to distance himself from the heavy temple taxes imposed by his predecessor to fund an expedition against the Persians (Perdu, 2014: 155–156). Textual evidence convinced Ray (2011: 72) that the baboon cult at Saqqara died out before the Roman era, but in Greco-Roman times other animal cults thrived as never before. The sacred bulls and lions in bullrings and menageries could substitute as 'living images' for the great gods (Clarysse, 2014: 278) deep within the temple from which the public were excluded beyond the first forecourt (Szpakowska, 2014: 512, 523). The wrapping of one ibis mummy has an embroidered or appliqué design of a seated baboon in a wheeled shrine (Emery, 1965: 4, pl. 5). The conveyance is little larger than its occupant, and it is unclear whether the monkey is alive (and compliant), mummified, or an effigy. Ibises by the thousand were raised for sacrifice and supply as votives (Szpakowska, 2014: 510), although (c. 450 BCE) according to Herodotus (II: 65), the penalty was death for deliberately or accidentally killing an ibis or a hawk. The hawk cemeteries at Saqqara were only loosely associated with the main temples. Both priests and tourists could feed crocodiles, and ibises were ubiquitous in villages. Being selected to carry a crocodile mummy to a necropolis was apparently prestigious. Ancillary to the official temple cult were the cult guilds or religious associations known mainly from their extensive regulations. Paying regular dues, members drank wine or beer at monthly meetings where the gods and kings received offerings. Many members belonged to the lower priestly class, participating in processions, festivals, and the burial of sacred animals (Clarysse, 2014: 278–279). These guilds existed from the sixth century BCE onwards, but are known primarily from Ptolemaic documents (Spencer, 2014: 260).

Organized Egyptian religion flourished until the first half of the third century CE, but then seems to have abruptly collapsed. Dedicatory inscriptions in the temples disappeared, as did priestly activities in the papyrus documentation. The grand old gods became pantheistic, virtually monotheistic, or newcomers replaced them. Traditional personal names became less diverse and in the fourth century yielded to moralistic and Biblical ones. The Roman government is often blamed, but the probable cause was irrelevance to its adherents, leaving a vacuum exploited by Christianity. Most of the violent clashes between Christians and pagans are probably later inventions (Clarysse, 2014: 289–290). The Roman emperor Constantine accepted Christianity in 312 CE (Bard, 2015: 312). In 391 CE a decree by the emperor Theodosius forbad entry into Egyptian sanctuaries and temples, enabling them to be considered 'abandoned'. Defenders of the Serapeum in Alexandria barricaded themselves inside with Christian hostages, some of whom they forced to make sacrifices; others they tortured and killed. Theodosius pardoned the offenders, but had the temple images destroyed in an early example of state-sponsored Christian iconoclasm (Thomas, 2014: 1045). The bishop of Alexandria, Theophilus preserved a baboon statue as an example of the objects of pagan reverence. Among the fugitive pagans was the grammarian, Ammonius, a priest of Thoth (McDermott, 1938: 37).

Christians who destroyed Pharaonic monuments at North Saqqara to make way for a monastic settlement, deliberately obliterated a small temple of Nectanebo II, but some of its small rooms, barely altered, were incorporated into the development. The discovery of a cache of over 100 bronze, wood, and stone statuettes of deities, three wooden shrines, and a human-sized wooden statue of Osiris in a pit below the monastic settlement indicates that the Christians were not obsessed with erasing their pagan heritage. It is improbable that they would have missed this hoard when preparing the foundations for their settlement. Some who preferred to hedge their religious options may even have amassed it, but Emery (1970: 6) thought the deposit contemporary with the construction of the temple. Amongst the monkey remains, smashed blocks of encasing cement, and burial chest fragments in the Upper Baboon Gallery, he most prized the many limestone false-door stelae inscribed with brief Carian texts, evidently brought from an adjacent burial ground as building material, like those supporting the walls of the pit holding the hoard.

The Baboon Catacomb entrance was discovered behind the temple enclosure on December 7, 1968. Plunderers had bypassed the stone-sealed, stone-built doorway behind its cavetto cornice and also just below the architrave. Like the ibis catacombs, the galleries are cut into a soft rock bluff, but unlike them they are lined with fine limestone masonry, much still in perfect condition. The workmanship of the lower gallery reached by a stairway exceeds that of the upper, but its design suggests it was added later. What at first was assumed to be an Ibis Catacomb gallery (Emery, 1970: 9, pl. 13), but later proved to be a Falcon (or Hawk) Catacomb gallery (Emery, 1971: 5), has breached the wall near the bottom of this stairway. A shaft in the floor of the southeast corner of the vestibule descends to an underground complex with more wall-niches for baboon burials, two of which contained the mausoleum's only undisturbed burials (Emery, 1970: 7, pl. 13). A Third Dynasty (c. 2686–2613 BCE) ravaged stone sarcophagus indicated that this was a burial chamber of that period. Also present was a possibly unique, three-quarter life-size limestone statue of Isis nursing the infant Horus. Its natural nursing pose in a squatting position attests a Greek influence. At the bottom of the stairway were two life-size limestone baboon statues (Emery, 1970: 8, pl. 14). Although damaged, their presence and the undisturbed burials further question that the Catacomb was wrecked for religious reasons.

A similar picture emerged from the Falcon Catacomb whose entrance stairway descends to a vestibule with ransacked side rooms still containing mummified falcons in small stone coffins, a limestone Canopic jar, and hundreds of fine quality

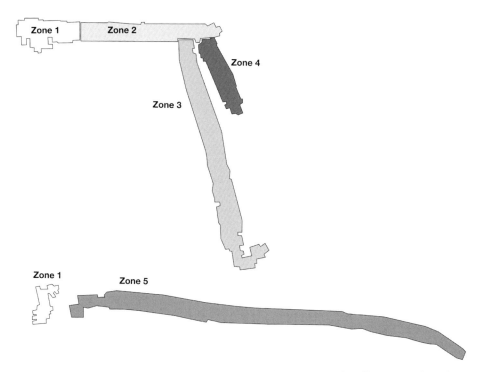

Figure 12.2 Zone divisions in the Upper and Lower Baboon Catacomb galleries. Based on data from Goudsmit and Brandon-Jones (2000, fig. 1).

statuettes of faience, bronze, limestone, steatite, and wood, although many broken and blackened by fire. The jar was inscribed to Hapy, usually represented by a baboon, but had a falcon-headed lid and contained a resinous substance, presumably enclosing mummified remains that were not examined. If made for this purpose, the jar would date the Falcon Catacomb to the late seventh to early sixth century BCE, predating the other known catacombs, a conclusion Emery (1971: 5) considered discordant with other evidence. When stacked mummy pots were cleared from a gallery chosen at random, it proved to contain a large collection of copper and bronze temple furniture, provisionally dated to the last centuries BCE. Their donors dedicated several of the objects to the great god Thoth, Osiris the Ibis, and Horus the Falcon.

Between March 24 and May 9, 1996, with permission from the Supreme Council for Antiquities (SCA), a joint expedition of the Egypt Exploration Society and the University of Amsterdam investigated the contents of the Baboon Catacomb. Harry S. Smith and Rutger Perizonius divided the catacomb into five zones numbered from 1 to 5 (Fig. 12.2), with the niches separately numbered 1 to 437. Zone 1 (the Pre-Gallery Stage) includes niches 1–31 and 431–436; zone 2 (the Upper Gallery) includes niches 32–76 and 426–429; zone 3 (Side Gallery West) includes niches 101–188 and 437; zone 4 (Side Gallery East) includes niches 77–100 and 430; and zone 5 (the Lower Gallery) includes niches 189–425. Niche numbers run from the entrance to the end of each gallery and, apart from areas where side lobbies complicate the catacomb architecture, alternate with even numbers on one wall and odd numbers opposite them. Adjacent niches therefore seldom have consecutive numbers. Four-figure composite numbers in this chapter, such as 1.005, refer to zone 1 and the included niche 5. A subordinate number suffixed to the zone and niche number, such as 1.005.01, uniquely identifies each item of nonhuman primate material or associated primate material from the same niche. Petrie Museum (University College London) specimens without zone and niche provenance are prefixed 0.000. The term 'skull' here implies the whole of the cephalic part of the skeleton, including the mandible (the lower jaw). The term 'calvarium' (plural: calvaria) is used to denote a skull without a mandible. Where relevant, the front and rear components of the calvarium are distinguished as rostrum (muzzle or facial region) and cranium (braincase). The underside of the cranium is termed the basicranium. Taphonomy is the study of the processes that alter the condition and location of animal remains after death and deposition.

The two intact monkey interments found in 1968 each held one monkey, indicating that the 437 detected niches originally housed approximately 437 monkeys. Including the 16 monkey calvaria removed to the Petrie Museum in about 1969 (accessioned as U.C.30792-30807), we identified 169 monkey individuals from cephalic remains (Goudsmit and Brandon-Jones, 1999: 47). Regrettably, no record exists of the Baboon Catacomb zone or niche provenance of the Petrie Museum monkeys, but from its distinctive stain pattern, one of us (D. Brandon-Jones) identified U.C.30797 as the baboon second from the left of four calvaria in a photograph by Bryan Emery of niche 321 in zone 5. The two other featured baboons and one macaque are unaccounted for (possibly now in the South Ibis Catacomb), indicating that more than 16 were removed from the Baboon Catacomb. During our expedition, four calvaria (three baboons and one macaque) were photographed in the Falcon Catacomb. This potentially adds at least 7 surviving cephalic-based individuals to the 169 estimated in this analysis. A couple of intact monkey mummies, monkey cranial material noticed in the South Ibis Catacomb, but not fully examined; and possibly some postcranial remains would probably bring the total to about 180 individuals. This indicates that partial remains of only about 40% of the originally interred monkeys now survive. Nevertheless, this reasonably represents the original contents, allowing probably valid inferences about the missing 60%. The remains provide evidence of their taxonomic identity, age, sex, physical condition, pre- and post-mortal treatment, and arrangement in the catacomb, allowing speculation on their geographic origin, live treatment, and the motives for their veneration. Since the final official sealing of the catacomb in antiquity, humans have severely damaged and disrupted its contents perhaps for mischief, curiosity, plunder, shelter, or utility rather than for religious reasons, but even if it had remained pristine and undisturbed, the catacomb would not have fully explained the monkey cult. In its heyday, cult practitioners probably only hazily understood its fascination, much of the attraction being subconscious, as we shall discuss.

12.2   Methods

12.2.1   Preparation of a Niche Inventory

Commencing on March 29, 1996, a niche survey and provisional contents inventory were undertaken to assist in orientation and to determine priorities for further research. It was a lightning survey with little guidance and prior knowledge of the site. Its compilation proved fortuitous as, apart from thorough sorting of some Pre-Gallery niches and full examination of the nonhuman primate material removed from the catacomb, limited subsequent access to the catacomb precluded a methodical follow-up.

12.2.2   Removal to the Laboratory and Re-association

All the postcranial material from zones 3 and 4 and a small proportion of the postcranial material from zones 1 and 2, and all apparently cephalic primate osteological material were collected niche-by-niche in brown paper bags and cardboard boxes and removed from the catacomb on March 31, 1996. At the end of the study, they were returned to the catacomb but not to the niches. Only a cursory examination was possible of the zone 5 postcranial material, which was brought to the front of each niche, but not removed. To prevent later confusion, each item was annotated in indelible ink with its niche number before removal.

The material was laid out in approximate niche order in the laboratory at the excavation headquarters at the SCA rest-house. Attempts were made to identify individual monkeys whose remains had been spread between niches. When sufficient teeth are present and positioned correctly in their sockets, a monkey calvarium and mandible occlude almost as reliably as reassembling a fragmented skull. Where possible, fragmented material was reconstructed with acetone-soluble adhesive. This improved the taxonomic, age, and sex diagnosis, and reduced the risk of associated fragments being interpreted as separate individuals. Further such individuals may have been overlooked. If the intermediate nasal and orbital regions are missing, crania and rostra cannot be reliably associated. When two such complementary cranial components from the same niche had apparently identical age, sex, and (taphonomic) color, they were treated as one individual to avoid inflating the number of identified individuals. Ageing and sexing of monkey crania (as opposed to rostra) is unreliable, so this also lessens this potential error. Reducing such inaccuracies outweighs the disadvantage of possibly underestimating the number of individuals.

Only the zone 4 postcrania could be extensively examined. This was fortuitous as further investigation indicated that zone 4 retains the best representation of the original deposition of the material (see Section 12.3.1). Skeletons were re-associated where possible, so that an estimate of the number of individuals present and their scatter could be determined. The pairing of long bones, pelves, and (to a lesser extent owing to frequent extensive damage) scapulae can be quite confidently accomplished, as can the association of fibula with tibia. Elbow articulation, and the articulation of the femur with the pelvis are surprisingly individual-specific, but less reliable than bone-pairing associations. Further association is still less reliable and is primarily based on size and color. Leg bones were associated by condylar width and morphology. In a couple of re-associated individuals, apparent similar pathology influenced the association. As a last resort bone color was used, but the unreliability of this method was demonstrated by cases where reassembled bone fragments were (taphonomically) disparately colored, presumably because the fragments had experienced different environmental conditions since their separation. Bone color was used sparingly to clear up loose ends when all else failed. Its only undue influence may have been in skull and postcranial association, the least confident association. Some false associations may have resulted, but the number of recognized individuals is probably fairly reliable. Shortage of time and resources left no other option.

10.2.3   Distinguishing Primates from Other Animals

Osteological material from niches near the entrance to the catacomb, which included large amounts of ibis material, was temporarily removed from the catacomb on trays, so that the primate material could be isolated, and the ibis material roughly sorted anatomically, packed in cardboard boxes and re-deposited in the source niche. Where present, cat material was simultaneously extracted and bagged separately. Niches 15, 23–24, 27, 29–30, 32, 34, 36, 47, 48, 50–53, 60, 62, 68, 119, 122, 189, 199, and 202 require further work.

Bird remains were confirmed as ibis by the presence of several crania, and a smaller number of upper mandibles. Although comprehensive bird identification was beyond the scope of this study, the apparent lack of discernible anatomical variation indicates that only one mummified bird genus was present. Their denser bone mass and, where present, generally marked anatomical differences distinguish mammal osteological remains from bird remains. In most cases where the relevant anatomical component is present, the presence of teeth or tooth sockets readily distinguishes mammal skulls from those of birds. The presence of an orbital bar distinguishes primate skulls from those of other mammals. Their characteristic bilophodont molar cusp pattern distinguishes cercopithecid primate teeth from most other mammal teeth. This is most evident in the first and second molars which have four cusps, one at each end of two parallel bucco-lingual ridges.

10.2.4   Primate Generic Determination

Baboon teeth (genus *Papio*) are (without metric confirmation) discernibly larger than macaque teeth (genus *Macaca*), and their molar crown bases are more swollen. These larger teeth are accommodated in a longer rostrum whose expansion is dramatic in large-skulled adult male baboons, but less marked in immature specimens and adult females. Baboons and macaques are almost indistinct in orbital size and in anterior nasal aperture size, accentuating the increased distance with rostral elongation (or prognathism) between the lower orbital margin and the inferior edge of the nasal bones forming the upper rim of the nasal aperture. This usually allows instant generic diagnosis from the facial aspect of the skull. The guenon skull (genus *Chlorocebus*) is essentially a petite version of the macaque skull, especially in its dentition. The guenon mandibular third molar lacks the fifth cusp or hypoconulid present in baboons and macaques.

12.2.5 Cercopithecid Age Class Definition

The nonhuman primate remains were divided into the following age categories:

Infant: Incomplete or complete deciduous dentition only. Less than 21 months of age.

Juvenile: Permanent first molar crown apex above the level of the alveolar rim, to all permanent first molars in occlusal position. Aged about 15–33 months.

Adolescent: Any permanent tooth erupting after the permanent first molar with crown apex above the level of the alveolar rim, to one permanent tooth still below this level. Aged about 2.5–7.5 years in males, 2.5–6.5 years in females. Puberty is reached at 3.5–4 years in females, and at 4–6 years in males (Napier, 1981).

Subadult: Crown apices of all permanent dentition above the level of the alveolar rim, but final occlusal position unattained in at least one tooth. Aged about 5.5–7.5 years in males, 5.8–6.5 years in females.

An adult age classification (Brandon-Jones, 1997) devised for the Colobinae would have required modification in order to accommodate the larger molar size in baboons, but might have suited the macaques. Even if modifications had been made, time would have precluded its application. Instead, experience gained in recording dentine exposure in the Colobinae was generalized to produce an equivalent, but more subjective age assessment. Assessment was restricted to the maxillary first and second molars, and dentine exposure was quantified by gauging the maximum mesio-distal or the maximum bucco-lingual width of exposure, whichever distance was shorter. In the colobine analysis, the smallest dimple to 1 mm scored 1; >1 mm to <2 mm scored 2; and >2 mm scored 3. The aggregate score from the 16 relevant cusps yields the following classification.

Adult minimal: Complete permanent dentition. Dentine exposure score <16. The 'subadult' and 'adult minimal' age categories discriminate only males with incomplete eruption and females. The dentine exposure is indistinguishable. The fusion of the basal suture approximately marks the end of both age categories. The high incidence in the catacomb of 'subadults' with basal suture closed, and one with moderate dentine exposure, indicates retarded dental eruption. Aged about 6.5–10 years. This and the following age estimates should be considered tentative. They were extrapolated from the dentine exposure scores of juvenile and adolescent colobines whose age could be accurately assessed from their state of dental eruption.

Adult little: Dentine exposure score 16–20. Aged about 9–13 years.
Adult moderate: Dentine exposure score 21–30. Aged about 11–20 years.
Adult extensive: Dentine exposure score >30. Aged about 16 years or over.

If the captive diet abraded the dentition less than the natural diet, then these age estimates may be conservative. This potential inaccuracy is partly mitigated by the derivation of the dental eruption data from laboratory specimens, whose diets were perhaps more balanced, but probably of comparable hardness to those in antiquity.

When the basal suture and relevant dentition are missing, cranial material without evidence of immaturity is identified as 'indeterminate, probably adult'. Rare in immature specimens, an occipital crest indicates adulthood. If such material is uncertainly associated with the anatomical part verifying adulthood, then the assessment is as reliable as the association. Unless it has considerable tooth wear, a mandible without a maxilla cannot be confirmed as adult because the maxillary third molar is the last tooth to erupt.

A specimen is described as 'indeterminate, probably subadult' if the basicranium is missing, but with a clean break along the suture line, indicating that the sutures were unfused or incompletely fused. The alveolus contracts around the root after the crown has emerged, so a broad socket indicates that a missing tooth was incompletely erupted. If the matching maxilla or mandible is absent, the precise state of maturity of an animal with erupting third molars cannot be confirmed. If the basal suture is open or dental eruption apparently incomplete, adolescent specimens cannot be discriminated from subadults. Small size in an apparently male animal may indicate immaturity, but only as reliably as the sexing of the specimen.

Some specimens have a subnumerary dentition, indicating a lack of maturity contradicted by their closed basal sutures and dentine exposure. These animals are probably adults with defective dental eruption. The closure of the basal suture is more reliable than dental eruption as an indicator of adulthood. Similarly, unerupted third molars where the basal suture is incompletely closed may indicate the animal is subadult, rather than adolescent.

The only unequivocal age indicators in postcranial material are detached or incompletely fused epiphyses indicating immaturity, perhaps unreliably, owing to captive and post-mortal conditions. In some cases, size or absence of evidence of immaturity are the only age indicators.

12.2.6 Cercopithecid Sex Determination

Adult baboon skulls and, with less reliability, adult macaque and guenon skulls can be sexed on size, but an almost infallible indication of sex is the permanent canine and mandibular third permanent premolar morphology. (The first of the two Old World monkey permanent premolars is referred to as the third premolar because their ancestors are thought to have lost two anterior premolars during their evolution.) Sexual dimorphism of the permanent canine is marked in most Old World monkeys, especially in baboons. The male maxillary permanent canine has a sabre-like curve on both the crown and the root, with a characteristic furrow along the leading surface. Apart from the furrow which presumably serves to strengthen the tooth by corrugating its enamel, the tooth is roughly oval in cross-section, including its long tapering root. The root and crown of the female permanent canine is more triangular in cross-section; the furrow is disrupted at the crown–root interface; and the crown has distinct buccal and lingual surfaces, more closely resembling the hastate deciduous canine than does the male permanent canine. The sex of a skull with missing permanent canines can usually be decided by the cross-section of the canine socket and sexual dimorphism in socket depth. If the canine is approaching eruption and sufficient is visible, examining the canine tip or, if part of the surrounding maxilla is damaged, its side, can usually determine the sex. Old World monkeys, especially the cercopithecines, have a further adaptation assisting sex determination. The anterior sectorial cusp of the mandibular third premolar is elongated to form a honing complex which produces a sharp disto-lingual edge on the maxillary canine. The premolar cusp is more elongated in the male than in the female, and so verifies or, if the canine sockets are absent, independently determines the sex of the skull.

If the dental part of the skull is missing, but the upper part of the cranium is present, occipital and sagittal ridges can indicate the sex. A sagittal crest is a fairly reliable masculine indicator, but temporal or occipital ridges are more equivocal, and sex determination must be based on their degree of development. Sexing of post-crania is based on size or, if based on associated cranial material, the sex determination is as reliable as the association.

12.3 Results

12.3.1 Niche Inventory

The results of the niche survey and provisional contents inventory are presented in Table 12.1. The classification of the mineral and vegetable contents is tentative. Some of the contents are probably modern materials discarded by workers involved in reinforcing parts of the catacomb for safe investigation.

12.3.2 The Distribution of Animal Remains in the Baboon Catacomb

Remains of pigeons, presumably entering the catacomb through tomb shafts or other openings, had previously been detected. The desert fox whose intact skeleton was on the gallery floor opposite niche 3.107 between niches 3.110 and 3.112, evidently died *in situ*, presumably since 1968. Other fox bones, and fox and rodent dung occurred elsewhere. The coarse, apparently greenish hair of the skin fragment found on the gallery floor next to niche 5.226 and another on the floor near niche 5.258 indicate that they were from baboons, but their scarcity and presence on a well-trod surface suggests that they detached from recently moved specimens.

Ibis skeletal material and a smaller quantity of cat bones and claws were unexpectedly found in the niches near the catacomb entrance. Two ibis leg bones had

Table 12.1. Niche inventory

Baboon (*Papio anubis*) cephalic material	(Zone 1) 5, 8, 13–14, 16, 18, 22, 31, (Zone 2) 37, 40–42, 44, 54, 57, 61, 70–72, 75, 427, (Zone 3) 114, 117–118, 132, 134, 137, 139–140, 146, 149–150, 156, 159, 167, 169, 171, 175–176, (Zone 4) 81, 83, 89, 91–92, 95, 97–98, 100, 430, (Zone 5) 189, 194, 220, 242, 246, 257, 259, 262, 279, 291, 293, 304, 308, 313, 317, 321 (no longer holds the three calvaria Emery photographed here; one is at the Petrie Museum, see Introduction), 335, 337, 340, 343, 345, 347, 349, 355, 378, 385–386, 388–390, 392, 394, 398, and 400.
Baboon mummy	(Zone 2) 58 (incomplete) and (Zone 3) 134 (fragment).
Baboon (*Papio anubis*) postcranial material	(Zone 1) 5, 14, 16, 24, 31, (Zone 2) 37, 41, 44, 54–55, 61, 72, 74, (Zone 3) 117, 137, 143, 146, (Zone 4) 81, 83, 88, 93, 97–98, 100, 430, (Zone 5) 191, 264, 317, 369, 377, 385, 390, 392, 394, 398, and 400.
Beam support	(Zone 4) 77.
Bird skeletal material, possibly ibis	(Zone 1) 15, 21, 26, (Zone 2) 66, (Zone 3) 112, (Zone 4) 430, (Zone 5) 196 (possibly cat), 203, and 209.
Carnivore mandible (cat or fox)	(Zone 1) 8.
? Carnivore post-crania	(Zone 1) 9–10.
Cat (probably domestic) skeletal material	(Zone 1) 25, (Zone 2) 33, 40, (Zone 3) 104, 106, 108, 114, and (Zone 5) 220.
Debris, mineral (mainly material inventoried as 'rocks', 'spoil' and 'stone')	(Zone 1) 17, 20, (Zone 2) 34–36, 53–57, 59, 65, 68–69, 75, (Zone 3) 105, 120, (Zone 5) 204, 206, 208, 230, 238, 242, 248, 255–256, 258, 266, 269–270, 272, 274–293, 295–318, 320, 322, 324, 326–327, 329–342, 344, 346, 348, 350–365, 368, 370, 372–374, 377, 379–382, 384–385, 390, 393, 395, 399, and 402–425.
Dog mandible	(Zone 5) 220.
Earthenware	(Zone 3) 179 (reconstructed pot containing plaster), (Zone 4) 79 (cubic) and 85.
Empty (see also, no data)	(Zone 1) 2, (Zone 2) 43, 76, (Zone 3) 109–111, 115, 126, 142, 144, 163, 181–183, 186, 188, 437, (Zone 4) 80, (Zone 5) 190, 192, 211, 213–214, 219, 221, 223–225, 227–229, 231, 233, 235–237, 239–241, 243, 245, 247, 249, 251–254, 260–261, 263, 265, 319, 325, and 370.
Fox faeces	(Zone 2) 428 and (Zone 3) 105.
Guenon (*Chlorocebus aethiops*) post-cranium	(Zone 3) 177, 178, and 180.
Gypsum fragment(s)	(Zone 1) 4, 5, 11–12, 17, 19, 21–22, 26, 29, 31, (Zone 2) 34, 36–42, 47–62, 64–65, 67, 71–74, 427, (Zone 3) 101, 103, 107, 113–114, 116–117, 119, 122–125, 127–131, 136, 138,

Table 12.1. (cont.)

	140–141, 143, 146–162, 164–173, 174 (almost intact block), 175 (unusual fragments), 177, 179, 185 (basket impression), 186A (high niche with resin fragments lining inside of block), (Zone 4) 84, 86–88, 90 (one with stave impression), 92, 94, 96, 99, (Zone 5) 376 (? surplus plaster knocked from bucket), and 400 (surplus knocked from bucket).
Human bones	(Zone 1) 3 and 7.
Ibis skeletal material	(Zone 1) 13–15, 23–25, 27, 29–30, (Zone 2) 32–34, 38, 40, 42, 44 and 72, (Zone 5) 203 (? ibis foot), and 209.
Macaque (*Macaca sylvanus*) skeletal material	(Zone 1) 24, 30, 32, (Zone 2) 74, (Zone 3) 119, 130, 137, 165, 169, 177–178, (Zone 4) 81, 83–85, 88, 91, (Zone 5) 193, 216, 220, 246, 248, 264, 273, 278, 282–283, 286 and 321 (no longer holds the calvarium Emery photographed here, see Introduction).
Monkey postcranial material (probably baboon, but possibly macaque)	(Zone 1) 7, 12–13, 17, 27, 29–30, (Zone 2) 33, 39, 49, 61, 64, 427, (Zone 3) 119, 139, 152, 158, 164–165, 168–169, 180, (Zone 4) 84–85, 90, 94–95, (Zone 5) 189, 193, 194–195, 197, 199–201, 218, 220, 244, 250, 262, 268, 273, 278, 283, 295–296, 298, 301, 308, 311, 313, 317, 321, 323–324, 326, 329, 334–335, 337, 341, 343, 345, 349, 351–353, 355, 368, 373, 375–376, 380, 385, 390, 392, 398, 412, and 421.
Mummy material	(Zone 3) 172–173, 177, (Zone 4) 93, 100, (Zone 5) 193, 218, 324, 331, and 351.
No data (probably empty niches unclearly numbered when the inventory was compiled)	(Zone 1) 1 and 431–436.
Pigeon bones	(Zone 2) 48, 428, (Zone 3) 127, 131, (Zone 5) 412, 414, 418, 422, and 424.
Plugs (possibly detached packing material from monkey eye sockets, as in 4.430.1, or perhaps part of falcon pot seal)	(Zone 3) 138, tomb chamber at end of Side Gallery West, (Zone 5) 202, 212, 215, and 267.
Potsherds	(Zone 2) 34, 55, 426, (Zone 3) tomb chamber at end of Side Gallery West, (Zone 4) 78, 99, (Zone 5) 199, 201–202, 210, 212, 215, 217–218, and 264.
Receptacle of unspecified material facetiously likened to a small 'font' (perhaps merely set plaster discarded from a container)	(Zone 2) 37.
Resin fragment(s)	(Zone 1) 28–31, (Zone 2) 32, 37, 40–42, 55, (Zone 3) 103, 147, 154, 178, (Zone 5) 264, 323, 353, 367, 380, 411, and 416.

Table 12.1. (cont.)

Rodent faeces	(Zone 3) 187.
Skin fragment	(Zone 5) 226 and 258.
Stela	(Zone 1) 6, (Zone 2) 53 (attached to half a gypsum block), and 429 (sealed niche).
Stones, see Debris.	
? Vegetable matter, glossy brown	(Zone 5) 234.
Wood dust	(Zone 2) 64, 75, (Zone 3) 125, (Zone 5) 205, 209, 216, 222, 271, 277–278, 280, 282, 285, 290–291, 294, 297, 299–300, 304, 306–307, 309–311, 314, 316–318, 320, 322, 326, 328, 330–331, 333–334, 336, 339, 342, 345–347, 349, 359–362A, 364, 366–367, 369, 372, 376–379, 381, 383, 387, 391, 393, 395, 397, 399, 401–402, 405–407, 421, and 423.
Wood fragment(s) (probably from plaster rendering bucket, possibly from mummy case)	(Zone 1) 3, 19, 31, (Zone 2) 41, 61, 63, 67, 72, 74, (Zone 3) 102, 106, 114, 116–117, 121–123, 127–128, 132–135, 137–140, 143, 145–147, 154–155, 158–160, 165–167, 169–171, 173, 175, 179–180, 184 (bucket parts), (Zone 4) 77, 88, 93, 98, 100, 430, (Zone 5) 200, 207, 218 (bucket parts), 250 (half bucket base), 275, 281 (half bucket base), 287, 296 (half casket base), 332 (half bucket base), 350, 373, 375, 396 (cache of bucket components), 404, 408, 410, 412 (bucket), 416, 417 (half bucket base), 419 (bucket fragments), and 424–425.
Wooden stave(s) (probably from plaster rendering bucket)	(Zone 1) 8, 10, 22, (Zone 2) 42, 47 (probably modern), 49–50, 55, 57, 64, 69, 75, (Zone 3) 185, (Zone 4) 82, (Zone 5) 198, 210, 212, 232, 262, 272–273, 279, 283–284, 289, 293, 301, 305, 313, 315, 324, 327, 329, 341, 343, 351–352, 368, 370, 374, 380, and 394.

transverse fractures healed with the two broken ends side by side, instead of head-on, indicating that injured ibises were artificially fed, possibly with some remedial care, although humans might well have been involved in inflicting the fracture. Definite ibis material was virtually restricted to the upper gallery from niche 1.013 in the southwest to niche 2.042 in the northeast. The 5 ibis crania in niche 1.013, 13 in niche 1.014 (effectively subsections of one large niche) and at least 25 in niche 1.025 illustrate the quantity. Cat material was found in the second, third, and fourth niches on the west wall of zone 3, and in niche 3.114 (three niches further along that wall). Niche 5.220 had part of the left side of a dog mandibular corpus, about 110 mm long (its shortness indicating domestic origin, D. M. Hills, pers. comm.). All ibis, cat, and dog material showed traces of mummification. The isolated ibis material in niche 2.072 was probably transferred there from nearer the entrance. Its six baboon calvaria confirm that niche 2.072 was a repository for animal material of possibly diverse catacomb origins. Niches 3.118, 3.159, 4.098, 5.189, and 5.392, each with 3 cephalic individuals; niche 5.398 with 5 such individuals; niches 3.140 and 4.430, both with 6; and niche 5.220 with approximately 11, further confirm that monkey remains have been aggregated, as has wood, such as in niche 5.396. These accumulations were probably mostly made by archeologists sorting debris from the gallery floor.

The abundant but localized ibis material is informative. Bringing ibis mummies from the Ibis Catacombs some distance away would be pointless, as plunderers could have unwrapped them closer to their source. The possible interment of ibises in the pregallery stage before it was extended into a Baboon Catacomb is countered by the probability that unless they had already decayed before the extension occurred, they would have been transferred to an Ibis Catacomb, once it was constructed. The most likely explanation, corroborated by the presence of potsherds, is that these mummies were brought from the Falcon Catacomb for dismantling in the daylight upstairs. If so, this implies that most mummies in this part of the Falcon Catacomb are imposters. No definite raptor cranium was detected. The apparently less prestigious ibises were probably more readily available. Niches 1.027, 1.029, and 1.030, directly over the stairs to the lower level, are not easily accessible to plunderers or to excavators instructed to stash displaced animal material in the nearest niche. This might suggest that the ibises here remain where they were originally deposited, but more probably they ended up there as plunderers discarded unwanted remains. Apart from a bird sternum, possibly not ibis, in niche 1.021, no evidence of ibis was found in the recessed niches 1.015–1.020 and 1.431–1.436, and none in Vault E.

Macaques were also concentrated along the north wall of the 'ibis area' (the bones in some of the south wall niches were not fully sorted), and in the second and fourth quarters of zone 3, perhaps indicating that their mummies were especially attractive to plunderers. Only postcranial remains, not unequivocally distinguishable from female baboons, attest their presence in the first half of zone 4. The incomplete macaque mandible in niche 5.193 is likely to have fallen there down the stairway. Zone 5 macaques are otherwise confined to niches 5.216 to 5.286, mainly from 5.246 onwards.

12.3.3 The Attrition of Animal Remains in the Baboon Catacomb

Assessing the disarray in the catacomb is essential to understanding its original arrangement but is severely handicapped by the destruction of most of the contents. Multiple factors contribute towards the durability of mummified material. These include the age of the bones at death, their degree of mineralization, variations in the original preparation of the material, elemental destructive forces, human destructive forces, and nonhuman animal destructive forces. Linen-wrapped primate remains encased in plaster are likely to outlast those subjected to secondary bone preparation after soft tissue removal (see Section 12.3.6). Damp, fungus, and mineral contamination primarily determine survival. The recent structural necessity to block some of the tomb shafts exploited by the catacomb excavators for ventilation has exacerbated these adverse factors. The resulting drop in air circulation has raised the humidity in

Table 12.2. Cephalic material and associations

	Papio	*Macaca*	*Chlorocebus*
Crania	110	19	2
Rostra	91	17	2
Mandibles	61	5	–
Associated crania and rostra	71	12	2
Associated rostra and mandibles	3	–	–
Associated crania, rostra, and mandibles	23	3	–
Equivocal crania and rostra	12	2	–
Equivocal rostrum and mandible	1	–	–
Equivocal crania, rostra, and mandibles	5	–	–

the catacomb, especially during human ingress, threatening the preservation of the organic material both directly and indirectly by encouraging mold.

More material survives at the ends of the catacomb galleries than in the main thoroughfares, indicating that the ransacking was not methodical, but sufficient to obscure evidence of changing species availability, species selection, and/or mummification practices. All but two niches on the west side of the lower gallery from 211 to 253 were empty; both exceptions, niches 215 and 217, contained bird pot fragments. The niche partitions in this stretch have undergone modern reconstruction, and access through niche 211 to the Falcon Catacomb has probably caused further disruption.

In two cases, interconnecting fragments of one cranium were found in different niches. Their unequivocal association confirms that such scatter has occurred. The greatest detected separation of parts from one individual was a baboon mandible from niche 5.293, which occluded with a calvarium from niche 5.317. The degrees of association in cephalic material (Table 12.2), and in postcranial material (Table 12.3) are given separately to avoid prejudicing the results by the unreliable association of skull and postcrania. This breakdown treats each body element as an individual component, even when re-associated or found combined. It illustrates that a conservative estimate, based on one selected body component, would indicate a maximum of 131 individuals (from crania alone), while that based on all body components would grossly exaggerate the number of individuals present.

With only 25, Zone 4 has the fewest niches, but more than two thirds contain monkey cephalic material, and proportionately the most individuals (18), indicating that partial remains of 72% of the monkeys interred here may survive. Zone 4 was partially blocked off, has a lower ceiling than most of the rest of catacomb, and is the most remote of the upper level galleries. This relative inaccessibility may have deterred pillagers, but may also have encouraged other catacomb users to clear material into there from other zones. Zone 5 has the smallest proportion (one third) of niches with monkey cephalic remains, and the greatest discrepancy between this and the number of individuals (Table 12.4), indicating that it has suffered the greatest loss of monkeys.

Table 12.3. Post-cranial material and associations

	Papio	*Macaca*	*Chlorocebus*
No. of individuals (from cephalic material)	146	21	2
Clavicles	2	–	–
Scapulae, left	10	–	–
Scapulae, right	8	1	1
Scapulae, associated pairs	3	–	–
Humeri, left	18	1	1
Humeri, right	16	1	1
Humeri, associated pairs	5	–	1
Radii, left	14	–	1
Radii, right	10	1	–
Radii, associated pairs	4	–	–
Ulnae, left	13	–	–
Ulnae, right	15	–	1
Ulnae, associated pairs	1	–	–
Sacra	5	–	–
Pelves, left	20	2	–
Pelves, right	19	–	1
Pelves, associated pairs	10	–	–
Femora, left	18	2	1
Femora, right	16	1	1
Femora, associated pairs	8	–	1
Fibulae, left	4	–	–
Fibulae, right	7	–	–
Fibulae, associated pairs	3	–	–
Tibiae, left	17	1	1
Tibiae, right	15	–	1
Tibiae, associated pairs	6	–	1

12.3.4 Age Breakdown of the Baboon Catacomb Monkeys

Of the total of 143 baboons, 79 (55%) died as adults, 28 (20%) as subadults, and 29 (20%) as adolescents; only five (4%) as juveniles and two (1%) as infants. Of the 21 macaques, 14 (67%) and both guenons died as adults (for specimens with niche provenance, see Table 12.5). At least 140 (83%) of the 169 monkeys died at an age estimated at less than 13 years. The potential longevity is about 30–45 years in baboons and about 20 years in macaques (Goudsmit and Brandon-Jones, 2000: 115).

Table 12.4. Number of individuals identified from cephalic material per zone, compared with the number of monkey niches

Zone	Niches per zone	Niches with monkey bones	Male	Female	Adult	Subadult	Adolescent	Juvenile	Infant	Total of individuals
1	37	15 (41%)	9	4 (31%)	7 (44%)	5 (31%)	2 (13%)	1(6%)	1 (6%)	16
2	49	20 (41%)	13	6 (32%)	14 (70%)	3 (15%)	3 (15%)	–	–	20
3	89	30 (34%)	18	12 (40%)	19 (63%)	8 (27%)	3 (10%)	–	–	30
4	25	17 (68%)	16	2 (11%)	13 (72%)	1 (6%)	4 (22%)	–	–	18
5	237	78 (33%)	42	19 (31%)	34 (51%)	13 (19%)	16 (24%)	3 (4%)	1(1%)	67
Total	437	160	98	43	87	30	28	4	2	151

Table 12.5. Age and sex breakdown by zone of *Papio* and *Macaca*

		Male	Female	Adult	Subadult	Adolescent	Juvenile	Infant	Total of individuals
Papio	Zone 1	8	3	6	4	2	1	1	14
	Zone 2	12	6	13	3	3	–	–	19
	Zone 3	16	12	18	7	3	–	–	28
	Zone 4	16	2	13	1	4	–	–	18
	Zone 5	31	16	24	12	13	3	1	56
	Totals	83	39	74	27	25	4	2	135
Macaca	Zone 1	1	1	1	1	–	–	–	2
	Zone 2	1	–	1	–	–	–	–	1
	Zone 3	2	–	1	1	–	–	–	2
	Zone 4	–	–	–	–	–	–	–	–
	Zone 5	11	3	10	1	3	–	–	14
	Totals	15	4	13	3	3	0	0	19

12.3.5 The Zonal Arrangement by Age and Sex of the Baboon Catacomb Monkeys

The sample sizes are too small to demonstrate significant zonal variation in the age of monkey cephalic material. Zone 5 presents the most normal distribution, but zone 1 probably has a subadult bias. Infants and juveniles are absent in the other zones, which show an adult bias and in zone 3, a subadult bias. Greater vulnerability to damage may contribute to this absence of young, but although exaggerated by retarded dental eruption, the subadult bias indicates poor health and longevity.

Three females occur in niche 3.167 and in 3.169, and two in niche 5.337. Five females seem to cluster in niches 3.137, 3.139, and 3.140, but niche 3.140 also has three males. Similarly, a male in 5.390 mitigates the cluster of three females in niches 5.390 and 5.392. The three females in niches 5.378, 5.385, and 5.386 barely qualify as a cluster. Other females seem randomly distributed among the males, making it improbable that interments were sexually segregated.

12.3.6 Mummification Differences in the Baboon Catacomb Monkeys

Available evidence indicates that no monkeys were kept alive in or near the catacomb. They were held in Memphis at the temple of Ptah-under-his-Moringa-Tree (Goudsmit and Brandon-Jones, 2000: 116) or perhaps occasionally in homes at nearby Babylon (McDermott, 1938: 37). Monkeys were mummified in the Nile valley, before transport to the catacomb. In Emery's (1970: 7) experience, a unique method of entombment was employed in the vestibule. One incomplete cloth-wrapped mummy from niche 1.014 with some of the skeleton *in situ* indicates that after processing for preservation, the baboon cadaver was posed in a sitting posture with the tail enfolding the ankles, and a hand resting on each flexed knee. After conventional bandaging with narrow rolls of linen, the wrapped mummy was placed upright in a rectangular wooden crate. The 1968–1969 expedition discovered an intact crate in niche 1.006. The gap between the mummy and the crate lid, base and sides was filled with rock aggregate and gypsum plaster or cement, which hardened to encase the mummy in a rectangular cube. The crate was then sealed in a niche with a stone blocking on which a demotic inscription was written in ink. Smith (in Emery, 1970: 7) reported that these texts give the date of interment and a short prayer for the baboon's eternal welfare, sometimes adding its name, its source, and its date of installation in the temple of Ptah. An earthenware pot in niche 3.179, clearly used for bailing liquid plaster, and the plaster impression of a basket base in both niches 1.011 and 3.185 are probably relics of niche-sealing or wall-rendering, rather than the plaster encasement of mummies.

In the vestibule, niche 1.433 opens into the adjacent, previously unexplored Old Kingdom tomb chamber designated Vault E. Blocking access was half a gypsum block retaining a good impression of the monkey mummy it once encased, and beneath it, one of the most intact skulls in the catacomb: an inverted baboon calvarium with its mandible in occlusal position. Precarious overhanging rock made it judicious to enter Vault E by its front entrance. After removal of a large conical pile of sand emanating from the shaft at its rear, it transpired that the chamber had served as a dump for catacomb despoilers, presumably ejecting mummies and their casings from vestibule niches. The intact plaster block found in Vault E seems to discount a religious motive. That any intact block should survive is surprising, as an impression on a broken block shows that an amulet was hung from the baboon's neck, providing an incentive for plunder. The remains of the appropriate side of its wooden casket, *in situ* beneath at least one of the other plaster blocks found in Vault E, indicates that the blocks were jettisoned there in their crates, possibly only being damaged by the fall or by others landing on top of them. The vestibule therefore may have been cleared purely for habitation, temporary shelter, or as a workplace, perhaps for processing mummies from the Falcon Catacomb.

A second (probably later) mummification procedure, more resembling Herodotus' (II: 87–88) medium-priced and economy versions, appears to have involved secondary preparation of the primate material after the bones had been cleared of most or all soft tissue. The most convincing evidence of such treatment is rostrum 4.999.01, found in the tomb chamber at the end of Side Gallery East, but occluding with mandible 4.430.05, and probably originating from niche 4.095, the source of most of its associated postcrania. It was separated from its missing cranium before a black viscous substance (probably resin) was applied. The break runs from just above the apex of the premaxillae, to the rear of the internal nares, with the left pterygoid fossa almost intact, and the solidified substance covering some of the fractured edge of the bone. The jagged break would have required some force, either with a blunt instrument or by dashing the cranium against a hard surface, and would have been difficult or impossible to achieve while soft tissue was present, or even while the bones were still moist, fatty, and pliable. The monkey (probably baboon) scapula found as part of the plaster block aggregate in Vault E provides further evidence for the processing of monkey cadavers before interment. Most of the material so treated seems associated with a polygonal-based multistaved wooden container, as opposed to the rectangular wooden crates holding the more conventional mummies. Increasing demand perhaps necessitated this cruder but probably swifter method of mummification, or it might reflect the changing status of the devotees.

Dark gray mummy material coats the rostrum of skull 3.169.01. Similar material extensively encrusts calvarium 2.072.05 (Fig. 12.3), the unstriated deposit replacing temporal muscle attachment on its cranium indicating that soft tissue was removed before mummification. Calvarium 3.178.01 is similar, with material penetrating the canine sockets, the left first incisor socket, and the probably post-mortal fracture surface of the left second incisor, indicating post-mortem tooth loss before mummification. A macerated skull is far more likely to suffer such loss than one that retains dried tissue. Grey material covers the mesio-lingual right third molar cusp fracture surface, but this fracture is uncertainly post-mortem. Grey material also encrusts the frontal, central facial region and left parietal, near inion of calvarium 3.140.04, occluding with mandible 3.137.01, and surmounts calvarium 5.220.07, with a thick black solidified viscous substance on its underside. Mummy material encrusts mandible 5.313.02, especially on its symphysial region. A concretion of mummy material covers the anterior of mandible 5.349.03, and a brown concretion cover s the anterior teeth of mandible 5.392.02.

Figure 12.3 Adult female baboon 2.072.05, showing gray mummy material. Photograph by and courtesy of Wim van Est.

Black material encrusts calvaria 2.072.06 and 4.098.03, especially on the basicranium in 2.072.06. A solidified black viscous substance coats skull 3.159.01, and smears the left side of the cranium of 3.149.01. A similar substance is poured over rostrum 4.092.01 and its occluding mandible 4.430.02; and coats the underside and mandible (the latter seems to have soft tissue adhering) of skull 4.093.01, with apparent mummy wrapping adhering. Calvarium 4.095.01 is similarly coated, with a plug of mummy material in its right eye socket. Calvarium, 4.430.06 has mummy material in its braincase, eye sockets, and nose. A vomer is present in calvarium 5.220.06, preventing the removal of brain tissue through its nose. No specimen was detected with mechanical damage to the anterior nares, indicating that brain tissue was either flushed or scooped out through the foramen magnum. A puzzling aspect, however, is that no trace of hair was found in the more substantially surviving mummified remains, although the *in situ* survival of hand and tail bones indicates that the cadaver was intact when wrapped. Perhaps the monkeys were skinned before mummification. If not caused by later disturbance, a medial incision on the occipital condyle of 1.433.07 and transverse incisions on the mesial edge of that of 1.433.11 may result from this process.

Mummification techniques vary sufficiently to indicate the catacomb origin of some of the Petrie Museum calvaria. Calvarium 0.000.02 has a greyish encrustation, with a dark solidified viscous substance on the basicranium, including a fairly thick fragment between the second molar cusps, a substantial amount in the right canine socket and right maxillary fovea (concavity), and some on the right parietal. This resemblance to 5.220.07 suggests that it too was from the Lower Gallery. Most Lower Gallery bones seem devoid of gypsum, so the gypsum encrustation on calvarium 0.000.07 indicates an Upper Gallery origin. Calvarium 0.000.11 has a T-shaped (resin) stain along the supraorbital torus and interorbital region to the nasal aperture, and a similar stain in the choana with traces on the cranium. Calvarium 0.000.12 has a (resin) stain around the foramen magnum, and fragments of possible resin-covered scalp on the cranium, with similar lifting tissue on the palate. This treatment links both calvaria with specimens from Side Gallery East.

12.3.7 Species Determination of the Baboon Catacomb Macaques

Glans penis shape splits extant macaque species into four subgroups: bluntly bilobed and narrow in the *fascicularis* group; bluntly bilobed and broad in the *silenus-sylvanus* group; apically acute and broad (sagittate in dorsal view) in the *sinica* group; and apically acute and elongate (lanceolate in dorsal view) in the *arctoides* group. The uterine cervix and cervical colliculi are moderately large in the two groups with a bilobed glans penis, but greatly hypertrophied in the *sinica* group. In the *arctoides* group, a unique vestibular collicle replaces the cervical colliculi (Fooden, 1980). Corresponding cranial variation has not been detected. On average the adult male skull in species such as *Macaca nemestrina* is larger than in some other species, and the muzzle is more inflated. The only macaque species confidently identifiable from cranial characters alone is the Sulawesi species, *Macaca nigra* whose mandrill-like muzzle ridges were once thought to merit monotypic generic status.

The only macaque species conceivably accessible to ancient Egyptian trade routes are *Macaca mulatta* whose range includes coastal India between Ahmadabad and Mumbai, and extends along the Himalayan foothills to eastern Afghanistan; *M. radiata* of southern India; *M. silenus* of southwest India; *M. sinica* of Sri Lanka; and *M. sylvanus* of northwest Africa. These represent three of the four macaque subgroups: *M. mulatta* pertaining to the *fascicularis* group, and *M. radiata* to the *sinica* group. The diminutive skull size in the latter group, especially *M. sinica*, probably eliminates it. *M. sylvanus* appears to have the broadest interorbital region of any accessible macaque species, and is therefore almost certainly the catacomb species. Of the catacomb macaque skulls, only 1.024.01, 3.177.01, 5.264.01, and possibly 5.246.02 compare in relatively gracile inter-orbital region with *M. sylvanus* skulls at the Natural History Museum, London (NHM). It is abnormally robust in the others, especially in 5.248.01, 5.278.01 (Fig. 12.4), and 5.278.02. This character generally diagnoses a colobine, but that the catacomb monkeys are cercopithecines is confirmed by the nasal aperture not protruding between the orbits (the colobine exception is *Nasalis larvatus*); the lacrimal fossa being entirely formed by the enlarged lacrimal bone; the molar bases being relatively swollen; and in 5.278.02 the mandibular incisors having thick buccal enamel and thin lingual enamel. The NHM *M. sylvanus* collection is too small to establish whether this interorbital robustness is partly pathological, but 5.278.01 has no other marked signs of gross pathology, possibly indicating a distinct (presumably eastern, see section 12.4.2) population.

The high incidence of a bregmatic ossicle, present in 4 (0.000.14, 2.283.01, 3.177.01, and 5.282.01) of 19 macaque crania, corroborates the catacomb macaques as *M. sylvanus*. In another (5.286.01) probably without one, there was an indentation in the relevant area. A bregmatic ossicle occurred in 5 of the 15 NHM *M. sylvanus* skulls retaining that part of the cranium. Another, ZD.1975.569 had an incompletely fused suture with the frontal bone. Only 4 of 125 NHM *M. mulatta* specimens had a bregmatic ossicle. The sixth cusp on both mandibular third molars in 5.278.02, and

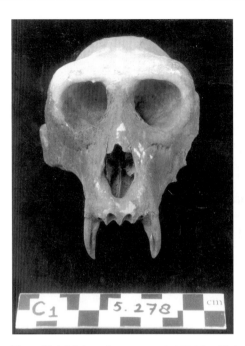

Figure 12.4 Adult male macaque 5.278.01 with broad interorbital region. Photograph by and courtesy of Wim van Est.

on the left and only surviving one in 5.193.01 is little smaller than the hypoconulid. It is incipient in 3.177.01, the only other macaque mandible with third molars. Three NHM *M. sylvanus* mandibles had six cusps on their mandibular third molars, four had an incipient sixth cusp, while only two had five cusps. Such extra cusps are rare in *M. mulatta*, mainly confined to specimens from Burma eastwards.

12.3.8 Species Determination of the Baboon Catacomb Baboons

Baboon classification has swung from that of Simpson (1945) who accepted the hamadryas baboon as a monotypic genus, to that of Groves (1993) who regarded it and the savanna baboons as subspecies of a single species. On external features, the savanna baboons are readily divisible into four main populations although, except for the contact zone between the Guinea and the olive baboon, all show evidence of intergradation where their ranges meet (Napier, 1981). Brandon-Jones (1995, 1996) and Brandon-Jones et al. (2004) noted that excessive reliance on intergradation as negating specific distinction can produce the unacceptable phenomenon of granting a species sympatric subspecies. The four savanna baboon populations are equivalent in morphological divergence to most recognized cercopithecid species and are here so treated, as did Groves (2001). Nevertheless, consistent species level cranial characters in baboons seem as elusive as they are in macaques.

No *Papio hamadryas* skull (from the Gulf of Aden to the south Red Sea coast) Groves (1972) measured exceeded 204 mm in total length. The 12 Petrie Museum

Figure 12.5 Adult male baboon 2.071.01, displaying classic *Papio anubis* traits. Photograph by and courtesy of Wim van Est.

Saqqara baboon calvaria surpass this and also outgrow *P. papio* (from Senegal to Guinea). Groves (1972) further distinguished the Saqqara calvaria on other unspecified features. *P. ursinus* (of southern Africa) resembles them in size but its muzzle dips sharply on the braincase. *P. cynocephalus* (from south Somalia along coastal Africa to central Mozambique and westward to central Angola) has a broad postorbital constriction (averaging 58 mm), a long narrow face, and distinct suborbital fossae. *P. anubis* (from Sierra Leone to western Ethiopia, and southward to northern Tanzania) is larger (total skull length 203–219 mm, versus 199.7 mm in *P. cynocephalus*); the postorbital constriction averages somewhat less than in *P. cynocephalus*; the maxillary fossae are less evident; the upper facial region is shallower and broader; and the orbits and teeth are relatively smaller. The Saqqara adult male baboon calvarium Groves (1972) examined (U.C.30792, here designated 0.000.01) conforms to the *P. anubis* range of metric variation, as do females, and there is no sign that juveniles differ. *P. anubis* subspecies are poorly differentiated, but metrically, some populations significantly differ. Calvarium 0.000.01 metrically conforms to the subSaharan 'Sudan grasslands' group, extending from Mauritania to the west bank of the Nile, and including the Lake Chad region. Female *P. anubis* are less geographically differentiated (Groves, 1972).

The other catacomb baboons all seem referable to *Papio anubis*, but more than one distinct cranial morphology is discernible, most evident in the adult male, but detectable in a few adult females. In the more common morphotype, exemplified by 2.071.01 (Fig. 12.5), the orbital part of the skull is set more obtusely to the plane of the rostrum with the dual effect of more prominently projecting forward the rostrum, and diminishing the horizontal distance between the frontozygomatic suture and the posterior of the zygomatic arch. These specimens tend to have a more curved central sagittal ridge along the maxillary bone with a more marked involution immediately below it. In the other type, exemplified by 5.259.01 (Fig. 12.6), the orbital part of the

Figure 12.6 Adult male baboon 5.259.01, possibly referable to *Papio cynocephalus*. Photograph by and courtesy of Wim van Est.

skull is more or less perpendicular to the plane of the rostrum producing effects opposite to those of the first type on the relationship of the rostrum and cranium to an axis approximately passing through the frontozygomatic sutures and the interorbital region. The overall skull length is accordingly shorter. In this morphotype the maxilla is more rectangularly folded along its approximate midline with less involution below the fold. The greatest length of skull 5.259.01 is 196 mm, within Groves' (1972) upper limit for *P. hamadryas*, but *P. hamadryas* skulls at the NHM, London, invariably display a sharper fold along the maxilla, and the distance between the folds is narrower. A series of Kenyan skulls at the NHM, however, does resemble 5.259.01, raising the possibility that it and similar catacomb skulls may be attributable to *P. cynocephalus*, although *P. anubis* might have two distinct morphologies. This requires further investigation.

12.3.9   Species Determination of the Baboon Catacomb Guenons

Using Verheyen's (1962) cranial diagnosis, Groves (1972) identified the two Saqqara guenons at the Petrie Museum as *Chlorocebus aethiops*: the external auditory meatus is inferiorly V-shaped; the orbits are strongly angular; the free ends of the nasal bones are pointed; the pyriform anterior nares are medially angular; and anteriorly the temporal lines in the male diverge from the posterior borders of the supraorbital torus. The skull dimensions of male 0.000.16 (U.C.30807) most closely resemble those of the West African green monkey, *C. a. sabaeus*. Groves (1972) found such measurements unreliable in determining the subspecies of skulls at the NHM, but in palate length, the best discriminator, he noted that 0.000.16 fell two beyond the standard deviation limit for other subspecies. Skull 0.000.16 also resembles *C. a. sabaeus* in its steeply sloping forehead, narrowing the angle between the facial and the cranial vault axes. Groves (1972) had only "a single specimen of *C. a. tantalus*, the race from between the Volta and Nile rivers." It cranially resembles *C. a. sabaeus*, but in biorbital breadth his sole specimen is much shorter than is 0.000.16.

Twelve baboons in 16 Petrie Museum calvaria (75%) approximate their 87.6% representation in the Baboon Catacomb, the two (12.5%) macaques match their 12.4%, but the two guenons grossly exaggerate their presence. Postcranial remains from one *Chlorocebus* were recovered, but no further cephalic material. The team surveyor, Kenneth J. Frazer, a participant in the 1968–1969 investigation, assured DB-J that the Petrie Museum calvaria were selected without zoological expertise. Pure chance seems to have secured the only guenon calvaria, perhaps aided by an eye for the exceptional.

12.3.10 Congenital Abnormalities of the Baboon Catacomb Monkeys

One *Macaca* (3.177.01) retained a complete metopic suture, and three *Papio* (1.433.09, 2.061.01, 5.386.01) retained a partial metopic suture. Specimen 5.386.01, however, shows several pathological symptoms (see below) indicating retarded physical development. Four *Macaca* had a bregmatic ossicle, and another had remnants of one (see section 12.3.7). A supernumerary left fourth premolar is erupting through the mandibular corpus of *Papio* 3.118.02; and *Papio* 5.392.01 has a possible supernumerary maxillary left third premolar.

12.3.11 The Pathology of the Baboon Catacomb Monkeys

Advances in nutrition and veterinary care now protect primates from most of their former diseases in captivity, but Sutton (1883) autopsied 93 of the 110 primate deaths at London Zoo in the 16 months to March 30, 1883. Twenty-two died of bronchitis, 10 of pneumonia, 4 of typhoid fever, 2 of empyema, and single individuals of a ruptured lung abscess, lung oedema, jejunal intussusception, of leukocytosis. Vitamin C deficiency may have killed a young chimpanzee with an alveolar abscess. Sutton (1883) attributed only three deaths to tuberculosis, but it could have caused the three from scrofula, one from 'a cascating lymphatic gland' (Sutton 1883: 582), and some of the lung conditions. Perhaps unaware of the counteracting effect of the partly open-air Carnivora Terrace constructed at London Zoo in 1843, he derided the public and medical perception that monkeys in England usually died of tuberculosis. Formerly fatal, phthisis and catarrh virtually disappeared from the monkey house when the carnivores' marked improvement led to the open-fire hot-water system being abandoned (Scherren, 1905: 83). Phthisis is the progressive debilitation and weight loss caused by tuberculosis and other lung diseases. Sutton (1883) noted that this afflicted only one of the up to 17 captive monkeys that Percy (1844) kept simultaneously, but Percy (1844: 81) knew that 'artificial heat … is at all times … injurious'. Although probably not artificially heated, monkey enclosures at Memphis were perhaps small, poorly ventilated and without direct sunlight.

Little soft tissue is preserved in the Baboon Catacomb, so clues as to the captive conditions experienced by the monkeys rely on osteology. Many diseases leave no trace on bones; others, including tuberculosis, can leave none. Wild-caught primates in museum collections seldom show pathological symptoms. When present, they are usually physical injuries. Symptoms of malnutrition therefore indicate a period in captivity. All examined monkeys appear to have died well short of their potential life span, but none provides a definite cause of death. Eight *Papio*, two males (3.159.01 and 5.345.01), four females (1.433.09, 3.156.01, 4.089.01, and 5.337.01), one probable female (4.083.02), and one of indeterminate sex (0.000.12), and three *Macaca*, one male (5.220.06), one probable male (5.220.07), and one female (5.264.01) suffered *in vivo* skull damage. (As it bears on the geographic origins of the macaques, the apparent crossbow injury to 5.264.01 is described in Section 12.4.2.)

Sutton (1883) reported that 'rickets' (evidently osteomalacia) was second only to bronchitis in primate deaths at London Zoo. The disease was prevalent, but fatalities hard to quantify as mild cases were often overlooked. During the summer of 1882 he observed that affected monkeys stay on the floor, reducing activity as paralysis envelops the legs. Eventually paraplegia sets in, bladder and rectal control is lost, and occasionally priapism occurs. Overstrained in use as crutches for hauling the body, the arm bones bend. The ribs and sternum soften, and muscle wasting and agony from fractured ribs (rather than Sutton's [1883] unscientific explanation of atmospheric compression on the chest wall), probably causes the ensuing breathing difficulty. Bronchitis develops and the animal soon dies. Such victims have enlarged bones, as sliceable as a potato. In severe cases, bones including the hyoid are in a poorer condition than those of a young child with rickets. In most monkeys the softened cranial bones become partially thinned, the skull sometimes even perforated, occasionally through its roof, but more often through the cerebellar fossae and roof of the orbit. In other monkeys, especially baboons, the skull bones thicken, the cranial roof sometimes 13 mm thick. Sutton (1883) found that the vertebrae also soften and overgrow, constricting the spinal cord by narrowing the spinal canal, explaining the incontinence and priapism. An upright posture worsens the pain by compressing the vertebrae, spinal cord, and nerves emerging from the intervertebral foramina. Brooks and Blair (1904: 147) found that monkeys "ordinarily evince little or no pain on pressure of the bone, even to the point of crushing it, for in a large proportion of cases the femurs, for instance, may readily be broken with the fingers." Brooks and Blair (1904: 142, 149) believed victims especially prone to tuberculosis and, in the terminal stages, to leukocytosis.

Known as "cage paralysis" (Brooks and Blair, 1904), osteomalacia is caused by calcium or phosphorus deficiency, not necessarily in the diet, but when inadequate sunlight or compensating vitamin D in the diet prevents the animal from absorbing these elements. Percy (1844: 83) diagnosed leg dragging in a capuchin monkey as the first symptom. Several bones were broken, and canine tooth development continued after skull growth ceased, forming a tubercle below each eye. This male's "habit of masturbation" during its terminal illness, obliging Percy (1844) to castrate it, may have been to relieve the discomfort of priapism. Percy (1844) was more enlightened in providing environmental enrichment for his monkeys by scattering rice or wheat amongst the sawdust, but he supplied an inadequate diet of "bread and milk, potatoes roasted and occasionally raw, onions roasted as well as raw, lettuce, carrots, and any scraps of food which the house may furnish" (Percy, 1844: 82).

Osteomalacia probably explains the Egyptian belief that baboons, being able to predict the conjunction of the sun and moon, become apathetic, lose their appetite, and double up in misery at the temporary loss of the moon. The female simultaneously menstruates (McDermott, 1938: 42). The bright red sexual swellings of adult female baboons, recurring at approximately lunar-cycle intervals, probably contributed to the deification of Thoth as a moon-god. In baboons these swellings appear monstrous to the uninitiated human observer. This intimates that osteomalacia ran its course in 30 days, but in Percy's (1844) experience, it lasted several months and Sutton (1883) saw an apparently healthy monkey die, severely deformed, in four months. Brooks and Blair (1904: 153) reported that acute cases average three to four months, but milder cases can survive several years. In ancient times the monkeys had probably suffered a long journey on a poor diet before reaching their destination.

"These animals, nourished and carefully tended in the temples, do not die in a single day as the rest of the animals do, but part of them dying each day, is buried by the priests, the rest of the body remains in its natural state, until the seventy-two days are completed, then they die completely" (*Hieroglyphica* of *c.* 400 CE, translated by McDermott, 1938: 43). Thoth was the god of astronomy and the Egyptians divided the heavens into 72 parts: the embalming process took 70 days, but priests considered the monkey truly dead only after its two-day funeral. This explanation McDermott (1938: 44–45) gave for the myth seems inadequate, as the baboon was the only animal thought to die piecemeal. Presumably because of its control in humans, leprosy is absent or rare in nonhuman primates, but Fiennes (1967: 85, 89) found evidence of a bacilli-fungal symbiosis, which may produce skin ulceration. In ancient times temple monkeys may have contracted leprosy. Another possibility is that this is yet another symptom of osteomalacia. Brooks and Blair (1904: 141) reported that paraplegia causes abscesses and "sloughs are common over the bony prominences of the pelvis and at the base of the tail. These ulcerations [tend] to spread, forming irregular and sometimes deep sloughing excavations, with no tendency to heal." A less plausible prognosis is scurvy.

Adult 4.089.01 (Fig. 12.7) has a sagittal fissure from inion almost to the supra-orbital torus over the left orbit. It resembles a miniature canyon of varying width with two lakes at the rear surrounded by fairly level, but uneven shore land at a lower depth than the canyon rim. In reality, the lakes are areas where the brain has no bony cover. The rift looks as if made by a flexible lash, such as a hunting crop, but such a blow would have fairly cleanly fractured the skull without the accompanying bony erosion. The rightward distortion of the rostrum, making the left suborbital region much more broadly dished than the right one, seems to have caused the diversion from the midline. In adolescent 5.345.01 a Y-shaped fissure resembles a miniature, flooded gorge centered on the junction between the sagittal and lambdoid sutures, but with a tributary running directly from the stem of the Y across the right parietal to continue slightly anteriorly along the temporal ridge. Bone resorption caused by osteomalacia thus apparently commences at the thin bone of the sagittal suture. It

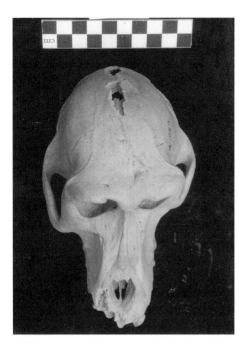

Figure 12.7 Adult female baboon 4.089.01, severely afflicted with osteomalacia. Photograph by and courtesy of Wim van Est.

was probably the indirect cause of death, both animals perhaps finally succumbing to bronchitis or bronchopneumonia (Brooks and Blair, 1904: 149).

Specimen 5.337.01 has a small bony outgrowth at the junction of the coronal and sagittal suture and irregularities at the posterior of the cranium. On the right parietal, it seems as if a blade held almost horizontal to the surface has slit the bone from left to right to finish under a thin layer of bone that crosses the slit. This may indicate some recovery from osteomalacia.

Groves (1972) suspected that adolescent 0.000.12 had received "a heavy blow", as the muzzle swells out on either side of a dent along the inner corner of the left orbit, including the glabella. He noted osteoporosis on the vault and muzzle, but the calvarium shows other signs of malnutrition: osteoporosis creases the occipital condyles and mandibular articulation; the maxilla abruptly recedes behind the roots of the deciduous second molars; the cranium has two pin-prick perforations behind glabella and one darning needle-sized one anterior to bregma; and bregma and the sagittal suture region are thin. The interorbital region is distorted to the right and the left supraorbital torus is deformed. The left side of the frontal bone in adolescent 4.083.02 looks as if the end of a rod has struck it obliquely from the outer corner of the orbit. This injury could only have been made without fracture if the bone was soft when hit. The injury to adolescent 5.220.07 is similar, but runs obliquely across the top of the right parietal. In all three cases, the blow may have been inadvertently self-inflicted after osteomalacia had softened the cranial bones.

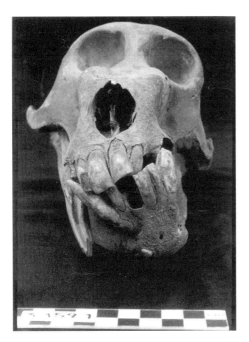

Figure 12.8 Adult male baboon 3.159.01, probable recipient of a heavy blow to the left side of the head. Photograph by and courtesy of Wim van Est.

In 1.433.09 the supraorbital torus, zygomatic arches and mandibular ascending rami show osteoporosis, and the premaxillae are slightly distorted to the left. Otherwise the skull is in fairly good condition except that the right temporal ridge juts out laterally behind the postorbital constriction, indicating a healed injury to the temporal muscle. The maxillary first incisors are somewhat dimpled with hypoplasia, so perhaps this adult female suffered rough treatment earlier in life.

In 3.156.01, the premaxillae and nasion are distorted to the left, and the choana distorted to the right, producing a bowed palatal suture. There are supernumerary foramina below the right orbit and a slight tuberosity laterally below them. This may indicate that this adult female has recovered from a blow to the right cheek received before bone growth ceased. Skull 3.159.01 (Fig. 12.8) has a severely deformed mandible, with the left ascending ramus being markedly narrower than the right one, and the rightward rotation of the symphysial part being especially noticeable in occlusion when the maxillary left first incisor occludes with the mandibular right first incisor, and the maxillary right first incisor partially occludes with the mandibular right canine. The left zygomatic arch is compressed and contorted, indicating that this adult male has recovered from a major blow to the left side of its head, again probably received before bone growth ceased. Skull 5.220.06 has recovered from a similar injury which fractured its right zygomatic arch, probably after bone growth had ceased. The bone has set over the glenoid fossa, so the injury presumably dislocated the missing mandible. Both canines were broken off at the root in life, probably in an attempt to subdue this young adult macaque.

Two *Papio* calvaria, 1.433.10 and 5.343.1 are laterally distorted (both to the left), but such distortions occur in wild-caught primates and may be congenital rather than traumatic. Only one post-cranial specimen shows evidence of trauma: *Papio* 4.430.08 has an apparently healed left humeral fracture with considerable bony overgrowth.

Three *Papio* (1.433.10, 2.072.02, and 4.093.01) and four *Macaca* (3.178.01, 5.220.06, 5.248.01, and 5.278.02) with thickened cranial bone, and five *Papio* (1.433.11, 5.257.01, 5.317.02, 5.378.01, and 5.392.01) with a sagging orbital region (the interorbital region and orbital sides evidently losing the strength to adequately support the more robust supraorbital torus) probably suffered from osteomalacia. Compressed orbits presumably affect the vision, adding headaches to the other experienced discomforts. These animals had probably reached the terminal stage of the condition. Some animals mentioned below may have been at an earlier stage.

Infection or nutritional deficiency during tooth development causes the enamel hypoplasia in seven *Papio* (0.000.04, 1.433.11, 3.140.04, 5.321.01, 5.392.01, 5.398.01, and 5.398.03) and two *Macaca* (5.220.06 and 5.278.02). Four *Papio* (1.018.01, 3.118.02, 4.430.04, and 5.386.01) exhibit ectopic dental eruption (tooth eruption in an abnormal position, such as through the palate), caused by bone softening allowing erupting teeth to stray from their proper channel. This may also have disorientated teeth in the following three baboons, although such abnormalities occasionally occur in wild-caught primates. In 5.242.01 the right second incisor is abnormally lingual, possibly obstructing the eruption of the right canine. In 5.321.01 the right fourth premolar and first molar are buccally inclined, possibly with the lingual surface in occlusion. In 5.343.01 the right fourth premolar is slightly inclined buccally, the right third molar more so. Two *Papio*, 1.433.07 and 5.388.01, have malocclusion.

Retarded dental eruption probably accounts for the absent maxillary third molars in three *Papio*: 5.389.01, 5.189.01 (right side only), and 5.392.01 (left side only). In *Papio* 5.355.02 the left third molar is incompletely erupted, and there is an anomalous vacant socket between the right fourth premolar and first molar. In *Papio* 5.398.03 no fourth premolar replaces either deciduous second molar. In *Papio* 5.386.01 the basal suture is almost closed, but the third molars are unerupted; its zygomaxillary suture remains open; and closure of the parietal suture is delayed. Only the left end of the basal suture is open in *Papio* 5.392.01, but the left third molar is absent, and the right third molar is incompletely erupted. A right possible deciduous second molar is retained between the right third and fourth premolar. In *Papio* 1.433.10, the basal suture is centrally fused, but the maxillary right deciduous second molar (now missing) and the mandibular left deciduous second molar are unshed; the canines and the maxillary right fourth premolar are incompletely erupted; and there are precursory alveolar apertures where the third molars should be. Instead of the mandibular left fourth premolar replacing the left deciduous second molar, there is a single aperture between the latter and the third premolar. In *Papio* 5.388.01 the basal suture is closed; the maxillary left first molar is incompletely erupted; the mandibular left third molar is erupting; a large aperture surrounds the unerupted maxillary left third molar whose crown is well below the alveolar margin; and the maxillary right third molar is unerupted with only a small aperture. *Papio* 1.433.04 with basal suture closed, has an aperture where the maxillary left third molar should be. The other third molars and maxillary left fourth premolar are incompletely erupted. In *Papio* 5.242.01 with basal suture closed and third molars incompletely erupted, the right second incisor is abnormally lingual, possibly obstructing the eruption of the right canine. The unerupted left fourth premolar is visible through an aperture in the centre of the left maxilla. *Papio* 5.385.01, with basal suture open and third molars unerupted, shows seemingly retarded eruption of the right canine as in 5.242.01, and apparently retains the (missing) deciduous canine. The third molars are unerupted in *Papio* 5.355.01, which not only has a closed basal suture, but also a pronounced sagittal crest.

Fourteen *Papio* (0.000.07, 0.000.08, 1.433.09, 1.433.10, 3.140.06, 3.150.01, 4.081.01, 4.091.01, 5.189.01, 5.259.01, 5.337.02, 5.343.01, 5.355.01, and 5.388.01) and one *Macaca* (1.030.01) have dental caries. Alveolar abscesses, a complication of untreated dental caries, occur in seven *Papio* (0.000.05, 2.072.02, 4.091.01, 4.430.02, 5.242.01, 5.308.01 and 5.355.01) and three *Macaca* (0.000.13, 5.248.01, and 5.273.01). The potentially fatal transmission of this condition to the lungs would leave no skeletal symptoms. A further ten *Papio* (1.433.09, 1.433.11, 3.139.01, 3.171.01, 3.178.04, 4.083.01, 4.430.02, 5.189.01, 5.317.02, and 5.343.01) and one *Macaca* (0.000.14) show alveolar defects possibly indicating periodontitis. Sixteen *Papio* specimens (0.000.05, 0.000.07, 1.018.01, 1.433.09, 3.134.01, 4.081.01, 4.083.01, 4.091.01, 4.092.01, 5.220.01.1, 5.257.01, 5.317.02, 5.321.01, 5.337.02, 5.343.01, 5.389.01, and 5.398.01) and seven *Macaca* (0.000.13, 3.178.01, 5.220.06, 5.220.08, 5.264.01, 5.273.01, and 5.278.01) had *in vivo* tooth fractures. Six *Papio* (4.091.01, 4.092.01, 5.337.02, 5.388.01, 5.390.01, and 5.398.01) and two *Macaca* (0.000.13 and 5.220.08) had *in vivo* tooth loss. An abscess can precede or follow the fracture of a tooth, and caries can make a tooth more susceptible to breakage, so it is unclear whether the cause was trauma or dental disease.

Most *Papio* and *Macaca* individuals (80%), regardless of age, and both *Chlorocebus* displayed porotic or pitted bone. However, this was surprisingly prevalent in NHM wild-caught baboons, especially those from the Sudan area. Chemicals sometimes used to macerate skulls may have contributed. The manifestation and degree of surface pitting or porosity varies: in some cases it is extensive but superficial, in others localized but deeper. Some pitting was undoubtedly vascularization caused by local infection, and in several cases disease or parasites had left small channels or pits in limited areas, but the porosity is probably mainly attributable to metabolic bone disease. Environmental deficiency possibly caused the following conditions: abnormalities in the temperomandibular joint in six *Papio* (1.018.01, 1.433.07, 1.433.12, 3.140.06, 3.178.04, and 5.220.04.2) and two *Macaca* (0.000.14 and 5.278.02); inflammation of the surviving coronoid process in a baboon (1.031.01); and an abnormal mandibular symphysis in another (2.41.01). Other possible indications of environmental deficiency include supernumerary foramina (1.018.01 and 3.156.01) and poor formation of ectotympanic foramina (1.433.12). Dense porous bone surrounds the mental foramen in 5.388.01. One *Papio*, 5.343.01 has temporal ridges laterally overgrown to the extent that they almost impede post-orbital measurement.

Several postcranial specimens (2.427.2, 3.140.07, 3.158.01, 3.164.01, and 4.081.01) with (partial) fusion of the spine are tentatively diagnosed with spondyloarthropathy. It is a complex condition apparently not directly linked to nutritional deficiency (B. Rothschild, pers. comm.) and occurring in wild populations (Rothschild and Woods, 1992). Alternative possibilities are osteomalacia and/or tuberculosis.

Incidences of apparently healed injuries, and the relatively low frequency of dental disease indicate that the Saqqara primates usually received adequate levels of vitamin C and other nutrients, but sunlight deprivation caused vitamin D deficiency. Conditions such as anaemia and renal or liver disease can cause metabolic bone disorders, but osteological material cannot confirm or exclude these conditions. The etiology of the noncongenital and nontraumatic pathology requires more thorough examination than time allowed, ideally employing forensic procedures, such as X-ray and bone mineral analysis.

12.4   Discussion

12.4.1   Nonhuman Primate Burials at Other Egyptian Sites

The second largest Egyptian animal cemetery after Saqqara is the Ptolemaic one at Tuna el-Gebel, 5 km west of Hermopolis in Middle Egypt. Although fire destroyed most of the contents, von den Driesch (1993a, 1993b) recorded 34 male *Papio anubis* (one possibly *P. hamadryas*), 28 females, and 20 indeterminate *P. anubis*. Fifty-three were adult or subadult baboons. Juveniles occurred, but infants only as postcrania. Thirty-eight individuals displayed pathological symptoms, mostly postcranial, but two had dental caries and one had paradontosis. Crooked long bones diagnosed 15 with rickets. An adult male victim had a healed fracture of the deformed arm bones. A case of chondrosarcoma was found in the pelvis of an adult male. The young baboon from Thebes whose 'monstrously' thickened skull bones von den Driesch (1993a, 1993b) could not diagnose, clearly suffered from osteomalacia. Von den Driesch (1993a) commended the aftercare given to a young adult female baboon, but the severe injury to its left mandibular condyle was probably not accidental and indicates assault with a blunt instrument by a right-handed person, perhaps only once. At Hierakonpolis, Van Neer et al. (2015) found pathologies, mainly healed fractures, in 15 of 16 *P. anubis* skeletons, most of them adult, seven with mandibles, two with calvaria. Of a total of 47 fractures, 45 affected the hands and feet, but a left ulna showed a parry fracture consistent with warding off a blow to the head. Despite this evidence of mistreatment, the dental wear on mandibles 3 and 5 (Van Neer et al., 2015, figs. 5 & 7) indicates that in c. 3800–3700 BCE these two individuals lived to a good age, but this might be misleading as a microwear study revealed that their diet was abrasive. The gut contents of herbivores from Hierakonpolis implicated chaff from cereal processing, mainly of emmer, as a major dietary component. The wear in mandible 3 is abnormally asymmetric.

Although vastly outnumbered by the over a million bird mummies deposited during the Saite-Ptolemaic era, the 247 nonhuman primates specimens reported by von den Driesch et al. (2004), are the predominant mammal at Tuna el-Gebel. *Papio anubis* remained the principal species, followed by *Chlorocebus aethiops* and *P. hamadryas*. Two *Macaca sylvanus* and one patas monkey (*Erythrocebus patas*) were detected, but some monkeys may have been misidentified (note the hypoconulids in their fig. 14 and the rounded muzzle in their fig. 16). Metabolic disorder, the commonest pathology, rose from 15% of individuals in the oldest Saite period gallery to 46% in the youngest Late Ptolemaic gallery. Von den Driesch et al. (2004: 258, 262) suggested that inbreeding may have contributed, but as monkey breeding was apparently negligible (see Section 12.4.2), deteriorating captive conditions are probably to blame. Healed fractures were rare, and some of these may be misdiagnosed cases of osteomalacia. Female baboons predominate in the oldest gallery, but most died while sexually immature. Males greatly outnumber females in the larger, mostly sexually mature sample from the Persian to Early Ptolemaic period gallery. The sex ratio is more balanced in the Late Ptolemaic gallery, but many are sexually immature. Among adults, males predominate in these younger galleries. Von den Driesch et al. (2004: 261) speculated that a small, rectangular construction of limestone slabs in the corner of the temple of Osiris-Baboon may have served to isolate exceptionally aggressive baboons, but perhaps this was the sole monkey enclosure, housing one at a time, which like the Apis bull, was replaced when it died.

12.4.2   The Geographic Origins of the Baboon Catacomb Monkeys

The usual baboon species in ancient Egyptian art is *Papio hamadryas* (McDermott, 1938: 6), probably because of the impressive mane and pseudosexual swelling (Wickler, 1967, pl. 1) in the adult male. The mane exaggerates the body size, which like the weight actually averages lower than in its less glamorous cousin, the olive baboon (*P. anubis*). Both species have long and similar captive maintenance success, so unsuitability for captivity cannot explain the absence of *P. hamadryas*. Nevertheless, none of the Saqqara baboons is confidently referable to *P. hamadryas*. This indicates that trading contacts between Memphis and *P. hamadryas* range in Eritrea, Ethiopia, north Somalia, western Yemen, and adjacent Saudi Arabia, were negligible or non-existent during the operation of the Baboon Catacomb. It also strongly suggests that monkeys were seldom captive bred because if they were, *P. hamadryas* would surely have been the selected breeding stock.

The modern distribution of the three confirmed species approaches Egypt no closer than northern Algeria and Chad. Explorers in Nero's time (54–68 CE) found *Papio anubis* as far north as the Nile–Atbara confluence in Sudan (McDermott, 1938: 66). Based on place names and classical sources, McDermott (1938: 3, 56) suspected that the distribution of *Macaca sylvanus* once reached western Libya. One of his sources, Lucian may have merely parodied Herodotus in saying that the Garamantes (the modern Fezzan) "in the Libyan desert ate apes" (McDermott, 1938: 57), but perhaps the troglodytes (cave-dwellers) screeching like bats when the Garamantes hunted them in four-horse chariots (Herodotus, IV: 183), were macaques. Without exactly locating the Gyzantians, Herodotus (IV: 194) claimed that they eat monkeys,

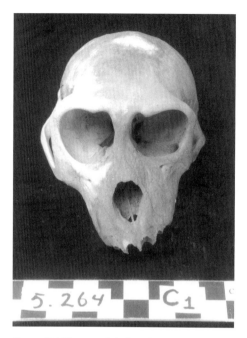

Figure 12.9 Young adult female macaque 5.264.01 with perforated left orbit. Photograph by and courtesy of Wim van Est.

"inexhaustibly" obtainable in the hills. The Gyzantians, Zavecians, Maxyans, and Auseans in turn, bordered one another. The Triton River, draining Lake Tritonis, separated the Auseans to the west from the Machlyans. Lake Tritonis is apparently Chott Djerid, so the Gyzantians probably lived in the Kairouan vicinity, indicating that in Herodotus' time (c. 450 BCE), *M. sylvanus* was plentiful in the Tunisian section of the Atlas Mountains. Juvenal associated Thabraca (now Tabarqah) with apes. McDermott (1938: 58) inferred that this was one of the three ape-cities Diodorus described. The inhabitants shared their food and lodging with these abundant honored guests, naming their children after them. Killing an ape was a capital offence. During Agathocles' expedition against the Carthaginians, Eumachus captured one of these cities in 310 BCE. The differences between Saqqara and Tuna el-Gebel in primate species representation indicate that macaques arrived from the north, while other species came from the south. The Ptolemaic Egyptian trading network must therefore have extended at least as far as Sudan and, presumably by sea, to Tunisia or ancient Mauretania (now northern Algeria and northern Morocco).

Pertinent to this is a female *Macaca* calvarium 5.264.01 (Fig. 12.9) with a 3 mm diameter hole in the floor of the left orbit, behind the zygomaxillary suture. Bony wisps emerging posteriorly and slightly laterally from below the hole indicate that the penetrating object entered the orbit almost perpendicularly from above, with a slight medial and anterior inclination. In other words, the assailant was above and to the macaque's right-hand side. Although probably blinded in its left eye by the object, the monkey evidently survived, as bone healing has occurred and the hole now resembles a large foramen. The impact of the object is the probable cause of leftward flexion of the rostrum around the point of entry. The left zygomatic arch is noticeably shorter and more contorted than the right one, and the left orbital height (21 mm) is 2 mm shorter than the right one. This skull distortion may have caused the incomplete eruption of the left third molar. A skull with completed bone growth would be more resistant to such impact, indicating that this young adult macaque with fused basal suture, lived for some years after receiving the injury as a juvenile. The hole is too small and round to have been made by a spear or pole, which would probably have left a more jagged entry wound. If made by an arrow, it would have to be one with a wingless head, so it seems more likely that the projectile responsible was a crossbow bolt. If so, it would confirm (if confirmation were necessary) that the animal was shot after 500 BCE, as crossbows are unknown in Europe before then, although in about 760 BCE, engineers apparently made machines capable of firing arrows for Uzziah, king of Judah (II Chronicles 26: 15). The angle of entry indicates either that the archer was on a higher substrate than the macaque or more probably was in a chariot or on horseback and the macaque on the ground. Unless the aim was to collect young monkeys by killing their mothers and the hunter missed the intended target, this macaque seems to have been hunted for meat or sport. Clearly it was worth more alive as, despite its serious injury, it was allowed to live and at least initially, judging by the otherwise good pathological condition of the calvarium, received adequate living conditions. The above historical evidence suggests that it was probably shot in east Tunisia.

12.4.3 Preferential Male Acquisition of the Baboon Catacomb Monkeys

Of the 154 monkey cephalic specimens whose sex could be determined, 50 are female, but more than twice that number (104) are male. The breakdown for *Papio* is 86 males and 45 females, and for *Macaca*, 17 males and 4 females. If restricted to adult monkey cephalic specimens, the sex ratio is still 60 males to 35 females. The breakdown for adult *Papio* is 48 males and 31 females, and for adult *Macaca*, 11 males and 3 females. Although the adult *Papio* sex ratio is less imbalanced than that for *Macaca* and for monkeys as a whole, it is still incompatible with their regular maintenance in social groups, or even in male–female pairs. Given the likely protracted journey time from their nearest natural distribution in Sudan, the two discovered baboon infants were too young to have been brought alive from the field so, unless they were imported dead, or born *en route*, or from a female who arrived pregnant, they must have been conceived in captivity. At least one baboon was born at the temple of Ptah-under-his-Moringa-Tree in Memphis (Goudsmit and Brandon-Jones, 2000: 118), but the preponderance of males, and scarcity of infants and young juveniles indicate that captive breeding was rare, and solitary confinement customary. Unless extensive space is available, potentially fatal intermale aggression precludes maintaining more than a single adult male per enclosure in captivity. The preponderance of males is unlikely to be the result of differential mortality or taphonomic factors, and indicates preferential acquisition of males.

Sex ratios in the five zones are inconsistent. In zones 1, 2, and 5, 31–32% of individuals sexually diagnosed from cephalic specimens are female, 40% are female in zone 3, but only 11% in zone 4 (Table 12.4). Zone 4 apparently retains the best representation of its original contents (see Section 12.3.3), so the whole catacomb might originally have had a female complement of about 11%. After zone 5 at 33%, zone 3 at 34% has the smallest proportion of niches with monkey cephalic remains. If all 89 niches in zone 3 received a monkey, the percentage of individuals is the same (34%). Its larger proportion of females could therefore indicate that zone 3 subsequently lost fewer females than did zone 4. The 29% discrepancy between them, however, seems too large to be discounted in this way, especially as female specimens, being smaller, are probably more vulnerable to damage which was greater in zone 3 than in zone 4. Proportionately more females were therefore probably interred in zone 3. Both zone 3 macaques are male. If these are excluded, the female representation in zone 3 baboons rises to 43%. This indicates that the preference for males abated while zone 3 was operational, possibly with more breeding attempts, perhaps owing to a problem of supply from the wild. Conversely, the guenon postcranium came from zone 3, suggesting that trading networks expanded during this period. The sex ratio is still too male-biased to suggest a major change in husbandry practices.

Some museum collections of monkey species, such as the Indian hooded leaf monkey, *Semnopithecus johnii*, show a preponderance of males (Brandon-Jones, 1995: tables 3 and 4), probably not through collectors' bias, but because adult male monkeys are more active than females in troop or home range defense, and are therefore more likely to be the first to approach and the last to retreat from the range of weapons. Adult male baboons and macaques may match or exceed male leaf monkeys in this respect, but collecting live individuals poses a greater challenge, as wild adult male baboons and macaques are potentially dangerous and, even if successfully captured, would be virtually unmanageable unless broken teeth or mineral deficiency subsequently debilitated them. Monkeys caught for captivity, especially those intended as pets or at least for situations of close human proximity, are usually captured when immature and tractable. If accustomed to human presence and physically restrained in some way (such as with a leash or enclosure), they can remain relatively tame, but unpredictable into adulthood. The *Hieroglyphica* conceded that baboons are the most bad-tempered of animals (McDermott, 1938: 43). Adult female monkeys have smaller canines, tend to be more docile than males, and may be easier to catch if carrying an infant, and are therefore more suited to captivity. The preponderance of males thus seems a case of demand rather than one of supply.

So why did the ancient Egyptians forego practical considerations in their predilection for male monkeys? Circumcision originated in Egypt, but in classical times was probably practiced only by priests. Seemingly already circumcised, male baboons were born priests and like them, (reputedly) spurned fish and fish-bread, regarded as unclean through association with Typhon (McDermott, 1938: 43, 45). Typhon was the Greek mythical monster identified with Seth, indicating that the fish taboo was a

Figure 12.10 Red quartzite sculpture of a hamadryas baboon in characteristic sitting posture (c. 1370 BCE). British Museum EA38. Steven G. Johnson / CC-BY-SA-3.0.

late import. According to Plutarch, Seth tricked Osiris into lying in a magnificent chest which with the help of 72 co-conspirators, Seth then secured and dumped in the Nile. Isis eventually recovered Osiris' body, but a fish (a phallic symbol) had swallowed his penis, hence the taboo (Warner, 1975: 96). Priestly attributes may have contributed towards baboon veneration, but can scarcely account for it. Circumcision could have been devised to make the human prepuce more like that of a baboon. That monkeys were Thoth incarnate, not only questions why Thoth was male, but why his penis is frequently shown tumescent or erect, its prominence accentuated by the most commonly depicted body posture (McDermott, 1938: 9–10, 82–83), seated with legs apart (Fig. 12.10). This is presumably a comfortable resting posture for baboons, which have ischial callosities (or sitting pads) on their haunches, but its symmetry and stereotyped representation indicates an underlying resonance with humans perhaps consciously appreciated by few, if any of the artists. This significance is evinced by the fact that, although subsequently concealed in a plaster-filled casket behind a limestone slab, monkey mummies were meticulously set in this same characteristic posture with hands on knees, before bandaging. Baboons at Thebes and elsewhere were also usually mummified in this posture (McDermott, 1938: 10).

Wickler (1967: 72, 116) saw this thighs-apart sitting posture in captive *Papio hamadryas* and on three trips to East Africa in 1964–1966. In the African bush, often with their backs to the rest of the troop who behave as normal, *P. anubis* troop males conspicuously station themselves on tree-stumps, earth mounds, and in branch forks, gazing about. Contrasting with the dark olive-grey fur, the bright pink penis hangs extended but usually not fully erect. Semi-tame or tame male *Chlorocebus aethiops* relaxing quietly in familiar territory usually sit with thighs spread, but the penis retracted. Wild males watching beside the two troops Wickler (1967: 89–90, 117–118) observed in the Serengeti National Park, Tanzania, adopted this same posture, facing away from the troop members, but with the penis usually erect and spasmodically struck against the stomach. These distinctive movements, sometimes coinciding with high arousal (approach of a human observer; approach of other long-tailed monkeys), emphasize the already conspicuous male genital color. In *C. aethiops*, the penis is scarlet and the scrotum powder blue. Baboons and vervets never warned of Wickler's (1967) approach, but silently withdrew when he came too close. Hall (1960) rejected as misleading terms such as sentinel, guard, or leader for these males sitting apart from the troop. His observations of *Papio ursinus* indicate that these supposed sentinels infrequently warn of predators or approaching human beings, but instantly warn of another *P. ursinus* troop. Adult male patas monkeys also keep watch for the approach of conspecific troops (Hall et al., 1965). These 'look-out posts' or optical markers inform a rival troop that a site is already occupied (Wickler, 1967).

Poirier's (1972) observations of feral *Chlorocebus aethiops* on St Kitts Island in the West Indies, can explain how Thoth became associated with sun worship:

The male exposes his chest by sitting rigidly upright with his arms extended at the side. The hindlimbs are laterally rotated, exposing the lightly pigmented medial surfaces of the thighs, plus, in many cases, an erected pigmented penis. The animal leans back, lifting his head slightly. Thus, the chest and thigh surfaces receive maximal exposure. While the behavioral pattern is common usually of the leader male, occasionally two males of the same group simultaneously expose their chests.

Exposing of the white chest also serves as a means of intertroop avoidance. Early in the morning one male ascends to the open tree tops and exposes his chest, usually towards the sun. Males of adjacent troops do likewise. This signal acts as an individual and thus group-locating mechanism, perhaps analogous to the early morning vocalizations of gibbons, howlers, and langurs. Occasionally during a territorial vocal exchange, the male exposing his chest moves from view, whereupon another takes its place and continues the visual display. During territorial encounters males occasionally stand on their hind limbs, stretching to their full height. This increases the amount of white chest hair visible. (Poirier, 1972: 47).

Home range defense is fundamental to the survival of most animals, as it controls population density, preventing the over-exploitation of food, water, and other resources, such as defensive, nesting, or bivouac sites. As climate cooling during the Pleistocene contracted closed-canopy forest distribution, forcing primates into more open habitats, territorial urine-marking useful to prosimians in a nocturnal or gloomy environment, gave way to the visual genital display of many higher pri-mates. The mandrill, for example, has the brightest genital skin and mimicking facial color of any mammal (Wickler, 1967: 120), but the Asian doucs, snub-nosed monkeys, and some New World monkeys are almost as ornate, and the nose of the proboscis monkey is more physically modified to mimic the penis. Facial signals are more visible than genital signals. Monkeys have no alternative to themselves as totems at the troop frontier, but humans can create substitute effigies. Some grotesques (such as sheela na gigs), baubos, and prehistoric and tribal art indicate that in humans, at any rate, females once shared this marker duty. Pubic hair and enlarged labia minora (Wickler, 1967: 125) may be intersexual mimicry, enhancing the female display. Once territorial effigies become grotesques, gargoyles, or ithyphallic hermes, they are euphemistically said to promote fertility or to ward off evil spirits, but the primate studies reveal their true function. Conscious awareness of this purpose may have faded even in the late pre-dynastic period, *c.* 3500–4000 BCE when McDermott (1938: 10) suspected that the earliest squatting baboon figurines were made at Abydos and Hierakonpolis.

As the development of agriculture inflated food reserves, allowing and necessitating a less nomadic human life-style, territorial effigies would have become more practical because the group would seldom have to transport them to new venues or create replacements at each stop. Effigies previously made of wood could now be made of stone. With the development of civilization and a truly settled existence, these effigies would increasingly become counterproductive, as they would urge separation in an artificially dense population trying to coalesce and overcome its natural inclination to disperse. To promote cohesion, the nonverbal sociosexual signals inherited from our primate ancestors prompting flight or fight required suppression. God idols may have originally been territorial effigies that were later secluded by enclosure in temples: the inner sanctum of temples in India, for example, often contains a lingam (giant phallus). Such effigies were too precious to discard, but too divisive to prominently display. Presumably only the priests and rulers were considered tough, objective, or educated enough to be able to handle the emitted subliminal message. Eventually there was a backlash in the Middle East and all idols were condemned, but their abiding hold on us is demonstrated by their reappearance as gargoyles, and statues of luminaries and religious figures.

Acknowledgments

We thank Harry S. Smith of the Egypt Exploration Society (EES) for directing the site work on the 1996 expedition, Rutger Perizonius for his archaeological contributions, Wim van Est for the invaluable photographic record of the catacomb monkeys, the late Colin Groves for unpublished information, Christine Brandon-Jones for early drafts of some of the text, much of the data organization and text and image formatting, Theya M. Molleson and Bruce Rothschild for their generous assistance with the diagnosis of cranial and postcranial abnormalities respectively. We thank a reviewer for constructive comments and for guiding us to relevant literature. Salima

Ikram kindly supplied copies of hard-to-access literature, and her student, Mohamed Wael Taha translated the title, abstract and keywords into Arabic. S. Karger AG, Basel, permitted the quote from Poirier (1972). The gracious cooperation of the Supreme Council for Antiquities in Egypt, the EES and the Netherlands Institute for Archaeology and Arabic Studies was essential to the success of this study, which was part funded by the EES and the University of Amsterdam.

References

Bard, K. A. (2015). *An Introduction to the Archaeology of Ancient Egypt*, 2nd edn, Chichester: Wiley Blackwell.

Baud, M. (2014). The Old Kingdom. In A. B. Lloyd, ed. *A Companion to Ancient Egypt*. Chichester: Wiley Blackwell 63–80.

Brandon-Jones, D. (1995). A revision of the Asian pied leaf monkeys (Mammalia: Cercopithecidae: superspecies *Semnopithecus auratus*), with a description of a new subspecies. *Raffles Bulletin of Zoology*, 43, 3–43.

Brandon-Jones, D. (1996). *Presbytis* species sympatry in Borneo versus allopatry in Sumatra: an interpretation. In D. S. Edwards, W. E. Booth, & S. C. Choy, eds., *Tropical Rainforest Research – Current issues*, Dordrecht: Kluwer Academic, *Monographiae Biologicae*, 74, 71–76.

Brandon-Jones, D. (1997). The zoogeography of sexual dichromatism in the Bornean grizzled sureli, *Presbytis comata* (Desmarest, 1822). *Sarawak Museum Journal*, 50(71), 177–200.

Brandon-Jones, D., Eudey, A. A., Geissmann, T., et al. (2004). Asian primate classification. *International Journal of Primatology*, 25, 97–164.

Brooks, H., & Blair, W. R. (1904). Osteomalacia of primates in captivity. A clinical and pathological study of "cage paralysis". *Annual Report of the New York Zoological Society*, 9, 135–175.

Clarysse, W. (2014). Egyptian temples and priests: Graeco-Roman. In A. B. Lloyd, ed., *A Companion to Ancient Egypt*. Chichester: Wiley Blackwell 274–290.

Cruz-Uribe, E. (2014). Social structure and daily life: Graeco-Roman. In A. B. Lloyd, ed., *A Companion to Ancient Egypt*. Chichester: Wiley Blackwell, 491–506.

Driesch, A. von den (1993a). The keeping and worshipping of baboons during the later phase in Ancient Egypt. *Sartoniana*, 6, 15–36.

Driesch, A. von den (1993b). Affenhaltung und Affenverehrung in der Spätzeit des Alten Ägypten. *Tierärztliche Praxis*, 21, 95–101.

Driesch, A. von den, Kessler, D., & Peters, J. (2004). Mummified baboons and other primates from the Saitic-Ptolemaic animal necropolis of Tuna el-Gebel, Middle Egypt. In G. Grupe, & J. Peters, eds., *Conservation Policy and Current Research*, Rahden/Westf.: Leidorf, *Documenta Archaeobiologiae*, 2, 231–278.

Emery, W. B. (1965). Preliminary report on the excavations at North Saqqâra 1964–5. *Journal of Egyptian Archaeology*, 51, 3–8.

Emery, W. B. (1967). Preliminary report on the excavations at North Saqqâra 1966–7. *Journal of Egyptian Archaeology*, 53, 141–145.

Emery, W. B. (1970). Preliminary report on the excavations at North Saqqâra, 1968–9. *Journal of Egyptian Archaeology*, 56, 5–11.

Emery, W. B. (1971). Preliminary report on the excavations at North Saqqâra, 1969–70. *Journal of Egyptian Archaeology*, 57, 3–13.

Fiennes, R. (1967). *Zoonoses of Primates*. London: Weidenfeld & Nicholson.

Fooden, J. (1980). Classification and distribution of living macaques (*Macaca* Lacépède, 1799). In D. G. Lindburg, ed., *The Macaques: Studies in Ecology, Behavior and Evolution*. New York: Van Nostrand Reinhold, 1–9.

Goudsmit, J., & Brandon-Jones, D. (1999). Mummies of olive baboons and Barbary macaques in the Baboon Catacomb of the sacred animal necropolis at North Saqqara. *Journal of Egyptian Archaeology*, 85, 45–53.

Goudsmit, J., & Brandon-Jones, D. (2000). Evidence from the Baboon Catacomb in North Saqqara for a west Mediterranean monkey trade route to Ptolemaic Alexandria. *Journal of Egyptian Archaeology*, 86, 111–119.

Groves, C. P. (1972). Primate remains from Saqqara. Unpublished report.

Groves, C. P. (1993). Order Primates. In D. E. Wilson, & D. M. Reeder, eds., *Mammal Species of the World: A*

Taxonomic and Geographic Reference. Washington, DC: Smithsonian Institution Press, 243–277.

Groves, C. P. (2001). *Primate Taxonomy*. Washington, DC: Smithsonian Institution Press.

Hall, K. R. L. (1960). Social vigilance behaviour of the chacma baboon (*Papio ursinus*). *Behaviour*, **16**, 261–294.

Hall, K. R. L., Boelkins, R. C., & Goswell, M. J. (1965). Behaviour of patas monkeys (*Erythrocebus patas*) in captivity, with notes on the natural habitat. *Folia Primatologica*, **3**, 22–49.

Herodotus. (1996). *Histories* (Translated with notes by George Rawlinson, first published in 1858). Wordsworth Editions.

Lloyd, A. B. (ed.) (2014). *A Companion to Ancient Egypt*. Chichester: Wiley Blackwell.

McDermott, W. C. (1938). *The Ape in Antiquity*. Baltimore: Johns Hopkins Press.

Napier, P. H. (1981). *Catalogue of Primates in the British Museum (Natural History) and Elsewhere in the British Isles. Part II: Family Cercopithecidae, subfamily Cercopithecinae*. London: British Museum (Natural History).

Nicholson, P. (1996). The North Ibis Catacomb at North Saqqara. *Egyptian Archaeology*, **9**, 16–17.

Percy, Professor [John]. (1844). On the management of various species of monkeys in confinement. *Proceedings of the Zoological Society of London*, **1844**, 81–84.

Perdu, O. (2014). Saites and Persians (664–332). In A. B. Lloyd, ed., *A Companion to Ancient Egypt*. Chichester: Wiley Blackwell, 140–158.

Poirier, F. E. (1972). The St. Kitts green monkey (*Cercopithecus aethiops sabaeus*): ecology, population dynamics, and selected behavioral traits. *Folia Primatologica*, **17**, 20–55.

Ray, J. D. (2011). *Texts from the Baboon and Falcon Galleries: Demotic, Hieroglyphic and Greek Inscriptions from the Sacred Animal Necropolis, North Saqqara*, edited and updated by C. J. Martin (2008). London: Egypt Exploration Society.

Rothschild, B. M., & Woods, R. J. (1992). Spondyloarthropathy as an Old World phenomenon. *Seminars in Arthritis and Rheumatism*, **21**, 306–316.

Scherren, H. (1905). *The Zoological Society of London: A Sketch of its Foundation and Development and the Story of its Farm, Museum, Gardens, Menagerie and Library*. London: Cassell and Co.

Simpson, G. G. (1945). The principles of classification and a classification of mammals. *Bulletin of the American Museum of Natural History*, **85**, 1–350.

Spencer, N. (2014). Priests and temples: Pharaonic. In A. B. Lloyd, ed., *A Companion to Ancient Egypt*. Chichester: Wiley Blackwell, 255–273.

Sutton, J. B. (1883). On the diseases of monkeys in the Society's Gardens. *Proceedings of the Zoological Society of London*, **1883**, 581–586.

Szpakowska, K. (2014). Religion in society: Pharaonic. In A. B. Lloyd, ed., *A Companion to Ancient Egypt*. Chichester: Wiley Blackwell, 507–525.

Thomas, T. K. (2014). Egyptian art of Late Antiquity. In A. B. Lloyd, ed., *A Companion to Ancient Egypt*. Chichester: Wiley Blackwell, 1032–1063.

Van Neer, W., Udrescu, M., Linseele, V., De Cupere, B., & Friedman, R. (2015). Traumatism in the wild animals kept and offered at Predynastic Hierakonpolis, Upper Egypt. *International Journal of Osteoarchaeology*, **27**, 86–105.

Verheyen, W. N. (1962). Contribution à la craniologie comparée des primates. *Annales du Musée Royal de l'Afrique Centrale. Série in Octavo, Science Zoologique*, **105**, 1–255.

Wickler, W. (1967). Socio-sexual signals and their intra-specific imitation among primates. In D. Morris, ed., *Primate Ethology*. London: Weidenfeld and Nicholson, 69–147.

Wilson, H. (1999). *People of the Pharaohs: from Peasant to Courtier*. London: Brockhampton Press.

13 Primates in South African Rock Art

The Interconnections between Humans and Baboons

Ndukuyakhe Ndlovu

Imidwebo eqotshwe ematsheni eNingizimu neAfrica: Ukuxhumana phakathi kwabantu nezimfene

Okufinqiwe

Izwe laseNingizimu neAfrica libusisiwe ngemidwebo eqotshwe ematsheni. Zintantu izinhlobo zalemidwebo kulelizwe. Ngizoxoxa kabanzi ngowodwa walemidwebo, nokuyileyo eyaqoshwa ngaBathwa. Ziningi izinto ababezidweba abaThwa, kusukela ezilwaneni ezihlukahlukene, kuya ezithombeni zaBantu, kanye nezinye izithombe okucatshwanga ukuthi bezibonwa ngabalaphi ngesikhathi semigidi. Kulesisigatshana sencwadi ngikhombisa ngokusobala ukuthi abantu yibona ababedwetshwa kakhulu kanti futhi nemidwebo yezimfene ayandile nokho. Nalapho ithe ukuba mningana imidwebo yezimfene, ngasosonke isikhathi kutholakala ukuthi ayidluli eyezinye izilwane eziqoshwe kuwona lawomatshe. Ngaphezulu kwalokho, zintathu ezinye izihloko engizicubungulayo kulesisigatshana. Okokuqala, nginikezela ngolwazi olucacisa kabanzi ukuthi kunemidwebo ehlanganisa izitho zabantu kanye nezimfene ukwakha inhlanganyela. Okwesibili, ngithi qaphu qaphu ngolwazi oluqoqelwe ngocwepheshe abahlukahlukene mayelana nokubaluleka kwezimfene ezinkolweni zaBathwa. Okwesithathu, ngicwaninga ulwazi olumayelana nokuthi ikuphi kahle-hle lapho kunemidwebo yezimfene.

Amagama agqamile

Ama-primates – izimfene – ama-therianthropes – ubuciko bokudweba ematsheni – abalaphi – aBaThwa

Abstract

South Africa is richly endowed with rock art, with three specific rock art traditions having been identified. This chapter is based on one of those rock art traditions, most specifically, the Bushmen rock art. There are many motifs made by Bushmen, ranging from animals, human figures, to schematic images. For the purpose of this chapter, I focus on the representation of primates in the rock art made by these peoples. Chacma baboons (*Papio ursinus*), as the other primates represented in the rock art, are not found in large quantities. Even in locations where they are relatively well represented, their numbers are still much lower than other animals that were incorporated into rock art imagery. Furthermore, I address three other aspects. First, to provide evidence that shows that some of the baboon features were incorporated into human figures to produce what are known as therianthropic images, that is, half-human and half-animal images. Second, to explore how the representation and significance of baboons have been understood by scholars over the years. Third, to examine their geographical distribution in southern African rock art.

Keywords: Primates, Baboons, Therianthropes, Rock Art Traditions, Shaman, Bushmen

13.1   Introduction

As stated by Anati (2004), human beings hold a very unique position in that they are the only primate species that has produced art over centuries. Rock art was produced by various communities throughout the world. This art, which has attracted much interest from scholars, was made in different styles. Some of the rock art was painted, while in other instances, engravings were the preferred technique. Other less common techniques have been used too. Among these are bas-relief, finger fluting on soft surfaces, and scraping (Bednarik, 2020; Karimi, 2020). These styles are generally found apart, even though there are exceptions where these have been found together either at the same site or within a similar geographic locality. There are some instances where these techniques have also been used together in producing one single motif (Aujoulat et al., 1993: 247–254). Earlier, it was even suggested that different styles indicated rock art was made by different groups (Stow, 1905). This has since been proven to be an inappropriate view of rock art representations. My focus in this chapter is on South African rock art. In particular, I identify the primates that were represented in this rock art, with the aim of understanding how they have been understood by the various scholars over the years. Most specifically, South African rock art has been largely dominated by a nonhuman primate: chacma baboons (*Papio ursinus*, Fig. 13.1). In some instances, baboon features were incorporated into humans to produce therianthropic images, that is, half-human, half-animal representations.

13.2   Brief Background to Southern African Rock Art Studies

Interest in southern African rock art dates back over three centuries (Cooke, 1969; Harding, 1951; Lewis-Williams 1990; Mguni 2016; Renaud, 2019; Schönland, 1905; Vinnicombe 1972). Such interest has varied widely. Some rock art enthusiasts were interested in simply collecting examples of rock art, others in recording the paintings and engravings they came across, while some had an interest in understanding the origins and meaning of this rock art (Henry, 2007; Hollmann and Msimanga, 2008; Loubser, 1990, 1994; Morris 1989; Vinnicombe, 1966; Ward, 1997). While the interest in collecting examples of rock art may have waned along the way probably instigated by heritage legislation of various African countries (Deacon, 2019; Ndlovu, 2011a, 2011b), recording of rock art has been incorporated into much more vigorous investigation into the origins and meaning behind rock art. Discussion on rock art interpretation still attracts a growing interest even in the twenty-first century, well over hundred years since the interest began in the 1900s (Witelson, 2019).

Figure 13.1 An image of a chacma baboon (Creator: Bernard Dupont, 2013. Wiki Commons Images-CY BY).

In studying these painted and engraved images, researchers were aiming to improve their understanding of the origins of the art and develop insights into the people and environments whose art they study. In addition, the aim had, in general, been to reconstruct palaeoclimates (Clottes, 1989; Layton, 1992), ecosystems (Gonzalez-Echegaray, 1974), belief systems (Lewis-Williams, 1981; Lewis-Williams and Dowson, 1988), seasonal mobility (Mazel, 1983), to develop models about ritual practices from the imagery; and to provide chronologies for the art, for example, to identify the migration of people (Breuil, 1948, 1949a, 1949b) by assuming the more complex art represents a later date (Solomon, 2011). During this rock art research period lasting many decades, many potential interpretations have been offered. At the beginning, these were largely informed by outsider's viewpoints to what was represented by the art. It is mainly through the insider's viewpoints increasingly applied from the 1970s that our view of rock art changed considerably (Lewis-Williams, 1981; Vinnicombe, 1976). Since then, a complex spiritual meaning has been confidently attached to southern African rock art.

While noting the ethnographic significance in the study of rock art, one of the strategies of studying southern African rock art has also been to categorize the art into predefined categories. Categorization of art is done with the intention of attempting to identify its meaning. Among these categories are human representations (also generally called anthropomorphs), animals, and geometric signs, which are not always as distinct as one may think (see Abadia and Morales, 2004). There are not a lot of plants in southern African rock art. Plants are not seen to have the same "intelligence" nor the ability to help humans in the same way animals are able to (Kent, 1989). This might explain, unlike animal representations in rock art, the near absence of plants in southern African rock art (see Mguni, 2009). Beyond these categories, a further distinction has generally been made of sex and age in animals, and sex and economic activity in the case of human figures. As it can be expected, some motifs do not fit any

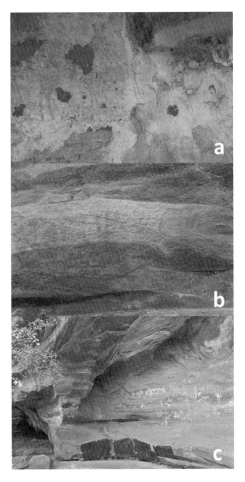

Figure 13.2 Three rock art traditions in southern Africa: (a) Bushmen rock art; (b) Khoekhoe rock art (c) 'Late Whites' rock art. (Courtesy/permission from SARADA).

of these categories. As a result, they are therefore considered either to be indeterminable or therianthropic (half animal and half human). Thus once again, the aim of this chapter is to focus on animals in southern African rock art. Most specifically, it is the nonhuman primates that are of central interest.

It is commonly agreed that there are three main rock art traditions south of the Zambezi (Fig. 13.2 b, c). One of these has been demonstrated to be associated with the hunter-gatherer communities of Bushmen, a second with Khoi Khoi pastoralists, and the third with Bantu-speaking pastoralist communities. I prefer not to use the word San, which is commonly used in rock art studies. I will use the word Bushmen, because of my familiarity with it. I attach none of the negative connotations in my use of the terminology. Stylistic differences have generally been used as a differentiating tool with the Bushmen rock art, which is quantitatively much more dominant over the two other rock art traditions, being generally composed of fine line paintings and engravings of various styles. Of the three, Bushmen rock art is considerably older and has attracted the greatest interest in terms of research (Mallen, 2008). We have certainly come to know far more about this rock art tradition than the other two recognized rock art traditions in Southern Africa. The Bushmen rock art was made in rock shelters from mountainous areas and open boulders in the interior of the region (Fock, 1979). Engravings are mainly found on open boulders, and very rarely in rock shelters, and the opposite is true of paintings. Twyfelfontein in Namibia, however, provides one of the few exceptions. In this area, there are instances where both engravings and paintings have been made in the same shelter. The content of Bushmen rock art is mainly defined by human figures which are quantitatively dominant. Other motifs include animals, therianthropes, and geometric designs.

Khoi Khoi rock art was generally made of finger paintings, including handprints (Smith and Ouzman, 2004: 512). The greater majority of rock art produced by the Khoi Khoi was defined by geometric designs, finger dots, and handprints that set it apart from the other two rock art traditions. Nevertheless, and like Bushmen rock art, Khoi Khoi produced both engraved and painted images. As already indicated, their painted images were mainly produced through the use of fingers, thus providing a significant contrast with the Bushmen rock art defined by fine-line images made through the use of brush. Unlike the widely distributed Bushmen rock art, Khoi Khoi rock art is comparatively very rare. This is because the occupation of the South African landscape by the Khoi Khoi was not as extensive. Not enough is known of this rock art tradition, compared to the two other rock art traditions in South Africa: it is not discussed further in this chapter because of its general lack of humans, geometric, and animal motifs.

The third tradition, rock art made by Bantu-speaking pastoralist communities, is among the least known in South Africa (Eastwood et al., 1999; Eastwood and Eastwood, 2006; Maggs, 1998; Moodley, 2008; Prins and Hall, 1994; Smith and van Schalkwyk, 2002). It is commonly called the 'Late Whites.' This is largely because most of the art was made using thick layers of white pigment made from clay, with most of it also finger-painted (Smith and Ouzman, 2004). There are limited instances where other colors, such as red and black, were used. The description of this tradition as 'late' is because it is the most recent of the rock art traditions. Bantu rock art was painted and engraved, but the majority was painted. The exception is found in the provinces of KwaZulu-Natal and Mpumalanga. In these two provinces, Bantu rock art is represented by engravings depicting settlement layouts. In contrast, the Bantu rock art from the Limpopo Province was always painted, with no engravings ever recorded. In general, the subject matter is highly varied. However, besides this high level of variability, the content of the 'Late Whites' can largely be grouped into three motifs: humans, animals, and settlement patterns.

The main argument that has been made about South African rock art over the years is that there is no direct correlation between what is painted and the surrounding environment. With specific reference to animals, it has been argued that rock art was not indicative of menu options nor preferences that were made by the authors of the art. Furthermore, an argument has been made to express the view that animals in rock art do not completely match with those found in the surrounding environments where these images are found (see Wilcox 1956, 1963, 1983; Lewis-Williams and Hollmann, 2006). These arguments have been used to argue that rock art is thus not representative of the food usage by Bushmen or the environments they occupied during their seasonal migration patterns. These arguments have been further entrenched by the use of ethnographic records that have not confirmed such a literal interpretation of South African rock art. Instead, we have learnt of the complex set of beliefs represented in South African rock art instead of representations of day to day lifeways by the various Bushmen groups.

While the argument that rock art is not representative of food consumed by Bushmen and what they would have seen around them, has gained a lot of support, there are instances where correlations between rock art and the surrounding environment exists. Taking this into consideration, it would seem that animals have been seen as a source of spiritual potency, and thus their representation in the art, instead of them as sources of food. Based on faunal analysis, it has been argued by various researchers that the choices of animals in rock art relate more closely to Bushmen social practice and religious beliefs than to subsistence (Deacon and Deacon, 1999; Lewis-Williams, 1981; Mazel, 1989; Vinnicombe, 1976). This is not only the case in southern African rock art, but has been noted in other international contexts as well (Chaloupka, 1984; Flood, 1989; Lenssen-Erz 1994; Rice and Paterson, 1996). Noting this argument, there are clear correlations between the choice of an animal and the geographic location where such animal is represented. This directly challenges the argument that no such correlation exists between the art and prevailing environments (see Ndlovu, 2013). I return to this argument later on in this chapter.

With this brief background to South African rock art studies, I now change my focus specifically to discuss primates depicted in the rock art. My use of the word 'primates' here is not to be confused as meaning this is how Bushmen perceived such motifs in rock art. Bushmen did not necessarily consider themselves as primates. Instead, this is a western taxonomy of human species. The aim of such a discussion on primates is to understand the past relationship between human and nonhuman primates as represented in rock art, thus improving our understanding of South African archaeoprimatology. I begin exploring such relationship by first focusing on the general value of animals to hunter-gathering communities in Southern Africa. Beyond that, I discuss baboons and therianthropic figures that have been recorded in South African rock art. As indicated above, chacma baboons (*Papio ursinus*) are the primates that have been recorded in South African rock art.

13.2.1   The Value of Animals to Hunter-Gatherers in South Africa

Various researchers, in studying world rock art, have previously argued that imagery and ethnographic records seem to indicate that humans and animals had a much closer relationship (Kent, 1989: 12). Some researchers have even argued that earlier societies considered themselves inferior to animals (Kent, 1989). This is because animals were supposedly more intelligent and could help humans in ways they could not do for each other (Kent, 1989). In this latter context, this was considered to be the main reason why animals are depicted in rock art (see Hodgson and Helvenston, 2006). The relationship between humans and animals supposedly changed over time and animals lost their individuality and became part of the physical world, open to human exploitation for their various resources (Drouin, 1989: 355; Lorblanchet, 1989; Molyneaux, 1989). Animals were, therefore, seen to be important to Bushmen hunter-gatherers and this makes them an appropriate motif to analyse in studying rock art (Biesele, 1993; Deacon and Dowson, 1996; Dowson, 1989, 2009; 2009; Guenther, 1999, 2007, 2015, 2017, 2020; Hewitt, 2008; Hollmann, 2005; Lewis-Williams, 1981, 1998, 2001; Lewis-Williams and Biesele, 1978; Low, 2014; McGranaghan, 2012; McGranaghan and Challis, 2016; Mullen, 2018; Skotnes, 2007). The significance of animals among Bushmen is emphasized in the different oral histories that have been recorded over the years (i.e. Bleek, D. F., 1923; Bleek and Lloyd, 1911). Even though animals among the hunter-gathering communities might have been seen to be 'intellectually' similar if not superior to humans, there have been more emphasis on some animals in rock art (see Lewis-Williams, 1981). The 'intellectual' similarity, or even superiority, between animals and humans I am referring to here is informed by indigenous cosmologies as told through the many narratives they have shared with various scholars over the years (Bird-David, 1999). Some animals, therefore, are honored for their intelligence and power. This ensures that their souls can be returned back to life (Ingold, 1986). The same preferences have been noticeable in South African rock art. Some of these animals came to be seen as defining particular societies or groups within those societies. What southern African rock art researchers have continuously emphasized, however, is that there is no direct link between what animals were depicted and the source of meat that was consumed by the authors of the art. In other words, the rock art record was not meant to be directly representative of the animals that were found within specific geographical environments that were accessed by the hunter-gatherers. For instance, some animals were extensively consumed, such as sea birds, fish, and crayfish, but were hardly represented in rock art (Parkington, 2003). Rhebuck occurs in the faunal record of the uKhahlamba Drakensberg Park (uDP) long before they are represented in the rock art from around 2,000 BP. Wildebeest were widely available in the uDP and Barkly East but very few were painted (Pager, 1971; Vinnicombe, 1976). Eagles are known to have been abundantly available in Brandberg/Daureb, yet they do not have any dominance in the rock art of the area (Lenssen-Erz, 1994). These animals have been defined, indirectly so, as less significant on the basis that they have a limited representation in southern African rock art. As argued earlier, their cameo representation in rock art has been interpreted to mean two things. First, that rock art does not represent local ecology. Second, that rock art does not portray the animal species consumed by Bushmen.

Besides this supposed mismatch between what existed in nature and what got painted or engraved by the few examples presented here, there is a correlation between depicted animals and their presence in the surrounding environment. My previous research has established that there is a link between the animals that are dominantly depicted in various geographical locations of Southern Africa and their natural existence in those particular areas (Ndlovu, 2013). This provides a challenge to the notion that ecology had no impact in what got painted or engraved. For example, elephants are known to have existed in great numbers along the mouth of the Orange River on South Africa and this is reflected in the rock art made in this particular locality (Fock, 1972; Fock and Fock, 1984). Springbok are known to prefer dry areas, and their dominance has been noted in Brandberg/Daureb rock art (Lenssen-Erz, 1994, 1997). Giraffe and kudu were historically widespread in Namibia and Botswana, and once again, this is reflected in the rock art from these two countries where they are significantly represented. Eland, considered the most spiritually significant animal in southern African rock art and naturally found in much diverse environments than they were painted or engraved, were equally well represented in localities where their natural occurrence was widespread (Lewis-Williams, 1981). There are many other instances where the animals that dominate in the different localities are known to have been painted or engraved within their natural occurrence zones. The selection of those animals that were well present in nature and the exclusion of some of those which were equally well represented illustrate the complexity behind the choices made by the authors of rock art. Also, some of these faunal representations are rock art examples that might also reflect current local extinctions of animals in the regions where they were depicted.

Statistical analyses of South African rock art have revealed that there are more human figures depicted than those of animals in the paintings (Pager, 1971; Smits, 1971; Vinnicombe, 1976). In contrast, there are more animals depicted in the engravings, particularly those made by Bushmen. As indicated earlier (see Section 13.2), the Khoi Khoi rock art is not defined by any animals. Furthermore, it has been shown that there are more painted rock art sites than those that have been engraved. Altogether this translates to there having been more human figures than animals in South African rock art. There was once a view that paintings and engravings were made by different communities (see Stow, 1905). This was largely informed by the stylistic differences between the two forms of rock art.

Even though animals are outnumbered by human figures (particularly in rock art paintings), they were clearly significant among the authors of the various rock art traditions represented in South Africa. Understanding this general relationship between hunter-gatherers and animals provides a context under which we could potentially consider the relationship that might have existed between artists and the different animals represented in rock art across southern Africa. As argued earlier, the relationship between people and animals, particularly among hunter-gatherers, is important to consider. This is because animals have been considered significant among the various societal groups of South Africa. However, it is largely with the Bushmen rock art that we find animals represented in greater numbers compared to the art made by the Bantu people.

There have been different arguments put forward regarding this relationship between animals and humans. That noted, the main central argument has been that their representation is indicative of the deeply spiritual relationship between animals and humans. In terms of animal species depicted in the paintings and engravings of

South Africa, these range from large herbivores (such as eland, rhinoceros, elephants, and giraffe), large carnivores (such as lions), domestic animals, and other smaller and medium-sized animals like baboons, tortoises, aardvarks, and different reptiles. Rock art researchers have argued that the choice of large herbivores in South African rock art, both paintings and engravings, was based on their large body size which provided large quantities of fat. This part of the animal plays an important role in the performance of various rituals because of its supernatural potency. For instance, fat from large herbivores was used "to heal and to control the movements and behavior of game animals" (Holmann and Lewis-Williams 2006: 511; see also Ouzman, 1996). In addition, large herbivores, specifically giraffe, elephant, and rhinoceros, have been associated with rain and rain-making (Garlake, 1989). A number of Bushmen groups identify rain as an animal.

Other than large herbivores, South African rock art has also been characterized by large carnivores. Lewis-Williams and Challis (2010) have argued that there was cordial respect between Bushmen and lions, which were believed to have supernatural abilities and were much more than a dangerous predator (see also Biesele, 1993:149; Hollmann, 2004: 33–36; Lewis-Williams, 1981: 95–97; Vinnicombe, 1976: 218, 332). Being both nocturnal and diurnal, lions were able to bridge the opposition of day and night, this in the same way shamans were able to travel between this and the spiritual worlds during a trance dance (Lewis-Williams and Challis, 2010). It must be noted though, however, that depictions of lions are extremely rare in South African rock art. For example, Pager (1971: 321) found only 45 depictions of lions among the 12,762 images in the uKhahlamba Drakensberg Park (for comparative statistical results, see also Smits, 1971; Vinnicombe, 1976;). The rarity with which lions were depicted in South African rock art could be indicative of the reluctance by the Bushmen communities to depict images of threatening and feared animals.

Lions and human beings had a closely linked relationship, with the latter leaving meat for the lions after a kill to ensure that they are not pursued by the former (see Biesele, 1993; Bleek, 1932; Heinz, 1975; Katz et al., 1997; Guenther, 1999). The relationship between lions and human beings is best captured by what Vinnicombe (1976: 218) once said (see also Biesele, 1978):

These records of Xam Bushman attitudes towards the larger carnivores suggest that lions and leopards were associated with harm as opposed to benefit, with disease as opposed to health, insecurity not security, malevolence rather than benevolence, with death as opposed to life. The essence symbolized by carnivores – the large biting animals – was the opposite of the essence symbolized by herbivores – the large non-biting animals. Antelope were regarded as a constructive force in Bushman symbolism. Lions and leopards were destructive.

South African rock art has also been defined by the presence of domestic animals. It has sometimes been difficult, however, to confidently distinguish between domestic animals and wild species. Nevertheless, there are more paintings of domestic animals than there are engravings (Fock, and Fock 1984; Huffman, 1983). The motifs representing domestic animals in South African rock art include the fat-tailed sheep, cattle, and horses. According to Manhire et al. (1986), domestic animals in South African rock art must be seen in shamanistic context because of their associations with trancing figures.

Among the primates, baboons are represented in South African rock art. They are particularly found among the Bushmen rock art rather than the paintings and engravings made by Bantu speakers. Primates are not well represented in South African rock art, and this may largely be as a result of the limited natural distribution of these animals.

13.2.2 Baboons in South African Rock Art

One of the elements that defined early studies of South African rock art was the political dimension applied by early scholars of the rock art. In particular, they did not consider Bushmen as having human values. As a result, Bushmen were described as different "things" to different people. All these discriminatory descriptions indicated their low status in life. According to Lagden (1909), Bushmen had intelligence too low for development. Ergates (1905: 113) further described Bushmen as ". . . lazy, cunning, treacherous, suspicious, and thieving, and unless captured in infancy they were wholly untameable." Some of these early scholars did not only see Bushmen as humans of a lower class, but even compared them to baboons. They "bear a striking physical resemblance to baboons" (Harrison, 1903: 215). Bushmen were further described as the thieving "pigmies" who were not human enough (Ergates, 1905; Harrison, 1903; see also Bleek and Lloyd, 1911).

Noting earlier views of Bushmen, baboons, which were earlier considered to have close resemblance to Bushmen, are depicted in southern African rock art. According to Dornan (1925), baboons, springbok, and snakes were people depicted in another state of existence (see Lewis-Williams and Dowson 1989). It has also been further argued that baboons represent spirits-of-the-dead instead of physically transformed shamans (Turner, 2006). Turner (2006) also indicated that baboons, which are part of a favorite wedding dish for the Hadzabe people in Tanzania (Bwasiri, 2014), were incorporated into Bushmen mythology (Vinnicombe, 1976; see also Leakey, 1983). They were believed to provide protection and could not be affected by evil and sickness. Their potency could be used by ritual specialists among the Bushmen to provide protection during raids or heal those in need. Baboons were considered to be the "symbolic point of contact within this multiethnic mix" (Smith 2010: 354; see Challis, 2009) and they became a source of protective medicine. For the raiding AmaTola (Challis, 2009) the baboon was associated with root medicines which thus enabled them to raid livestock of their enemies without getting harmed. The baboon potency, therefore, became important for these raiders, and was thus incorporated into their rock art (Smith 2010). Another view, besides the one linked to raiding activities, is that baboons and shamans had similar spiritual powers, in the same way lions had similar abilities. The incorporation of baboon elements to produce therianthropic figures is a confirmation of the closeness of baboons to people. Interestingly, baboons also feature more prominently in the myth and folklore as told by Bushmen themselves.

Table 13.1. The quantitative distribution of selected animal species at various locations around South Africa showing that baboon is not numerically dominant (Courtesy/permission of SARADA)

Animal species	uThukela-uMzinyathi district	The Cape regions	uKhahlamba Drakensberg Park
Baboon	5	40	189
Eland	30	263	3,570
Elephant	4	96	28
Rhebuck	5	–	671

As summarized in Table 13.1, the distribution of baboons in South African rock art is not extensive, and even in instances where they have been depicted, these animals rarely take the dominant role. For example, there are 189 representations of baboons in the uKhahlamba Drakensberg Park (Fig. 13.3). These represents about 11% of the total number of images recorded in this locality. The greatest concentration of baboon images within uKhahlamba Drakensberg Park is at Didima Gorge where there are 51 baboons that were painted, representing 6.4% of rock art images from this area (Pager, 1971; Vinnicombe, 1976). Of the images recorded at the Magaliesberg, only three (3.7%) were found to be representing baboons out of a total of 81 images discovered in this area. Quantitative analyses of rock art from other locations in South Africa provide the same findings, whereby baboons are not well represented in the rock art. For example, there were only five baboons discovered in the uThukela-uMzinyathi district (eland were the most painted animals, with 30 images represented) and about 40 were found in the Cape regions (eland were equally dominating, with 263 images). The very limited representation of baboons is not unique to South Africa, but is further applicable in other regions with rock art, such as Zimbabwe, Botswana, and Namibia. There are only five baboon motifs (0.3%) recorded by Pager (1971) in the Brandberg/Daureb in Namibia out of 3,821 images recorded, while only six baboon paintings (0.7%) were discovered at the Tsediso Hills out of 907 images recorded (Campbell et al. 1994). Garlake (1987) recorded only six baboons (1.7%) out of 350 images while Nhamo (2005) found 11 (4.8%) similar images at Zimunya out of 228 other images.

South African rock art depicting primates are concentrated in the uKhahlamba Drakensberg Park (Fig. 13.4). All the instances where baboons have been recorded are within Bushmen rock art. The only potential link to Bantu speakers is through the creolized group that used baboon as the source of their protective medicine which enabled them to conduct raiding activities (Challis, 2009). Bushmen, therefore, were authors of baboon images depicted in South African rock art. There are extremely limited instances where either baboons or some of their features were represented in the rock art. Among these few instances are the four baboon handprints that were recorded in Riverslee and Basinghall, in Botswana.

Judging from the baboons represented in South African rock art, some were painted in groups (Fig. 13.5) showing the whole troop with males, females, and the young ones. There were also baboons painted in isolation (Fig. 13.6). Most of these

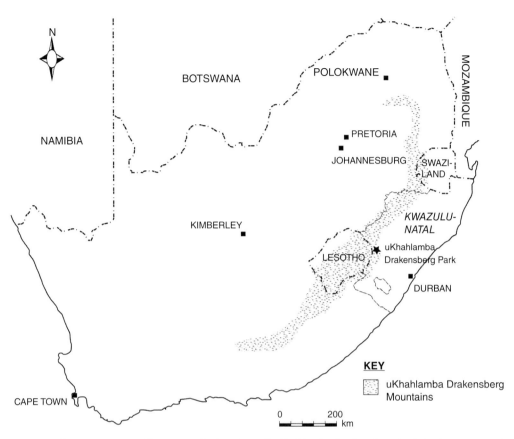

Figure 13.3 A map illustrating the location of uKhahlamba Drakensberg Park in the context of South Africa (map supplied by and courtesy of Catherine Namono).

images were painted in rock shelters. This correlates with how baboons are generally experienced in the wild, which would seem to indicate that Bushmen paid close attention to the behavior of these animals. Such would not be different from how other animals were observed by Bushmen, which determined how they were represented in the rock art (Ndlovu, 2013). Some researchers have argued that animals were chosen based on their behavior, which mirrored Bushmen lifeways (Eastwood, 1999; Eastwood et al., 1999). However, there are exceptions to this rule. For example, springboks are territorial, but Bushmen were not. Giraffe are not territorial, but they do not have family units. Kudu and eland are not territorial and are known to live in family units. There does not seem to be a constant reasoning that can apply across the southern African sub-region regarding the relationship between Bushmen and the main animals represented in rock art.

The dominant color used in South African rock art made by Bushmen is red. The same is applicable to baboons, a majority of which were painted using the same red color. All of the colors used in Bushmen rock art came from naturally occurring pigments that were mined in the vicinity of painted landscapes. The red color came

Figure 13.4 Two baboons from the uKhahlamba Drakensberg Park. (Courtesy/permission from SARADA).

Figure 13.5 A troop of baboons from the uKhahlamba Drakensberg Park. (Courtesy/permission from SARADA).

Figure 13.6 A single baboon motif from the uKhahlamba Drakensberg Park. (Courtesy/permission from SARADA).

from red ochre which was grounded into powder, then mixed with binders such as animal blood, fat, beeswax, egg white, water, and plant sap (see Lewis-Williams, 1990; Pager, 1971). For example, out of a total of 332 eland paintings at Didima Gorge, 177 (53.3%) are shaded as opposed to only 12 (48%) for Harteebeest, 4 (100%) for Reedbuck, 1 (2%) for baboon, and 9 (63.3%) for feline (Mazel, 2011).

13.2.3 Baboon-Human Therianthropes in Southern African Rock Art

Besides baboons depicted in South African rock art, these animals were also incorporated into the therianthropic images (Fig. 13.7). Therianthropes are motifs that combine human and animal features. In such instances, human representations were depicted merged with baboon features defined by baboon snouts and tails (Ndlovu, 2013). Often, the head and feet would be that of baboon while the general body is that of a human. The pelvic area can also be very descriptive of baboons (Fig. 13.8). In most therianthropic representations, feet are generally of the animal featured in the motif, but in the instances where baboon features have been incorporated, feet are not indicated. Besides baboons, there is a wide range of animals that were also incorporated into therianthropic depictions. These ranged from large herbivores (rhinoceros, elephants, and giraffe), large carnivores (such as lions), birds (ostrich), snakes, to primates such as baboons (Butler, 1993; Dawson, 1990; Fordred, 2011; Forssman and Gutteridge, 2012; Hollmann, 2005a; Jolly, 2002; Lewis-Williams, 1981; Loubser, 1993; Ouzman, 2001; Parkington, 2003; Vinnicombe, 1967, 1976).

Figure 13.7 Baboon therianthropes from the uKhahlamba Drakensberg Park. (Courtesy / permission of SARADA).

Figure 13.8 A baboon therianthrope from the uKhahlamba Drakensberg Park. The pelvic area is very descriptive of a baboon. (Courtesy /permission of SARADA).

Their incorporation represented a spiritually significant aspect in the belief system of Bushmen. While noting their special features, therianthropes are quantitatively not well represented in Bushmen rock art (Jolly, 2002). For instance, these images represented a very small number of the total images recorded by Pager (1971) at Didima and Lewis-Williams (1981) in Barkly East. Baboon therianthropes are even rarer in southern African hunter-gatherer rock art. According to Jolly (2002), this could be because of what he defines as rare 'possession' relationships that existed among few shamans and baboons.

The relationship between people and animals was not only limited to the instances where the latter were depicted in the art. Instead, this relationship is also evident in terms of how human figures were represented in the art. Among the motifs that have been represented in South African rock art are therianthropes, which occur in various parts of South Africa (Deacon, 2002). These images were particularly limited to the Bushmen rock art, and they are thus absent from both the Khoi Khoi and Bantu rock art. Rock art scholars have argued that therianthropic motifs are depictions of human beings that have become physically transformed during states of altered consciousness commonly associated with trance dance (Jolly, 2002). In other words, shamans were becoming one with the animal. In such trance-defined instances, shamans travel to the spirit world (Forssman and Gatteridge, 2012; Jolly, 2002; Parkington, 2003). The transformation is part of a belief that certain animals contained supernatural potency. This potency could then be used to heal people, make rain, control movements of animals, and ensure the general well-being of Bushmen society. Bushmen communities believe that when an animal is killed, it releases a supernatural potency, creating a dense spiritual atmosphere (Lewis-Williams, 1981).

13.3   Discussion

There can be no argument against the significant role animals had, and continue to have, in the lives of Bushmen, Khoi Khoi, and Bantu speakers. This view is informed by the extent onto which animals are represented in the three South African rock art traditions (Fig. 13.2). Baboons are among the least represented animals. On the contrary, human figures are by far the most represented living being in the South African rock art. This does not necessarily mean that animal representation had a much lesser value than their human counterparts.

Baboon depiction in rock art is also regionally varied, meaning that the motifs are not as well represented in some other geographical areas. As indicated in Table 13.1 when comparing their representation in the Cape regions and the uKhahlamba Drakensberg Park, there are far more baboons in the latter than they are in the former. Even within the uKhahlamba Drakensberg Park where they are reasonably well represented compared to their presence in other geographical locations, baboon representation is still uneven. There are more baboons at the Didima Gorge in the uKhahlamba Drakensberg Park. I must highlight, however, that where these baboons are quantitatively well represented, they are still much less than the paintings of eland. Within the same locality of uKhahlamba Drakensberg Park, there are 336 eland against 51 baboons. Similarly, there are five baboon images in uThukela-uMzinyathi district in KwaZulu-Natal. The quantitative representation of baboon here is second to eland. However, they only account for 9.6% (five images) against eland representation which comes to 57.7% (30 images). This is an area without a lot of rock art images, even though there are many potential rock shelters that could have been painted (Ndlovu, 2013).

I earlier mentioned that South African rock art researchers have mostly argued that the representation of animals in the art was not representative of the surrounding environments, nor were they selected on the basis of their appearance as preferred food sources. Evidence, however, will suggest otherwise. I have, based on data from excavated sites, established correlation between animals represented in the rock art and their presence in the landscape (Ndlovu, 2013). Similarly, a match between the presence of primates in nature and their incorporation into rock art could be positively identified on the basis of baboon representation and behavior. Chacma baboons seem to indicate a greater representation in the rock art of shelters found in mountainous locations as opposed to flatter surfaces. This is illustrated in their dominance in the rock art of uKhahlamba Drakensberg Park. Such a discovery is a further confirmation of a correlation between motifs represented in rock art and their presence in the surrounding environments (Parkington et al. 1994; Smith and Blundell 2004), thus confirming what Hollmann (2005b: 84) emphasized when he argued that "... species choice varies according to the geographic area." The notion that there is no direct link between rock art and surrounding environments is directly challenged (Garlake, 1987; Eastwood, 1999; Lewis-Williams, 1981; Parkington, 2003). This correlation could be the main reason why there are limited depictions of primates in South African rock art, particularly in nonmountainous locations.

Baboons also featured in the narratives that were told by different Bushmen to the scholars they encountered (Bleek, 1931; Bleek and Lloyd, 1911; Orpen, 1874). Their representation in these narratives is personified, meaning that they are able to converse and perform activities that are directly linked to humans, for example, killing a child (Bleek and Lloyd, 1911: 32).

In summary, human beings are the only primate species, under a Linnaean taxonomy, that have produced rock art over the years (Anati, 2004), and they are depicted in various contexts. Other than the quantitatively dominant human figures, animals are well depicted particularly across Bushmen rock art. Of these animals, only the baboons represent the nonhuman primate motifs that were depicted in the rock art. These animals were further incorporated into therianthropic figures, signifying their spiritual relevance in the religious beliefs of Bushmen in whose rock art they are represented. South African rock art, therefore, has been largely dominated by a significant nonhuman primate, namely, chacma baboons (*Papio ursinus*).

Acknowledgments

My research into southern African rock art was funded by the National Research Foundation (grant no: N0083). Thanks to Dr. Catherine Namono for providing the map and Mr. Azizo da Fonseca from the Rock Art Research Institute for granting the permission for using some of the rock art photographs sourced from the African Rock Art Digital Archive (SARADA). I would also like to thank Bernardo Urbani, Dionisios Youlatos, and Andrzej T. Antczak for inviting me to contribute to this book and the necessary assistance offered. I am also highly appreciative of the reviewers who provided valuable comments that improved the quality of the chapter. However, I take responsibility for the ideas and conclusions presented in this chapter. They cannot be attributed to my funder, editors, nor the reviewers.

References

Abadía, O. M. & Morales, G. M. R. (2004). Towards a genealogy of the concept of "Paleolithic Mobiliary Art." *Journal of Anthropological Research*, **60**(3), 321–339.

Anati, E. (2004). Introducing the World Archives of Rock Art (WARA): 50,000 years of visual arts. In *Prehistoric and Tribal Art: New Discoveries, New Interpretations and New Methods of Research. XXI Valcamonica Symposium, Capo di Ponti, Italy*.

Aujoulat, N., Sur l'Art, G. D. R., & Paléolithique, P. (1993). *L'art pariétal paléolithique: techniques et méthodes d'étude*. Éd. du Comité des Travaux Historiques et Scientifiques.

Bednarik, R. G. (2020). Petroglyphs of Victoria. *Proceedings of the Royal Society of Victoria*, **132**(1), 7–11.

Biesele, M. (1978). Religion and folklore. In P. Tobias ed., *The Bushmen*. Cape Town: Human and Rousseau, 162–172.

Biesele, M. (1993). *Women Like Meat: The Foklore and Foraging Ideology of the Kalahari Ju/'hoan*. Johannesburg: Witwatersrand University Press.

Bird-David, N. (1999) "Animism" revisited: personhood, environment, and relational epistemology. *Current Anthropology*, **40**(1), 67–91.

Bleek, D. F. (1923). *The Mantis and his Friends*. Cape Town: Maskew Miller.

Bleek, D. F. (1931). Customs and beliefs of the /Xam Bushmen 1: Baboons. *Bantu Studies*, 5, 167–179.

Bleek, D. F. (1932). Customs and beliefs of the /Xam Bushmen. Part IV: Omens, wind-making, clouds. *Bantu Studies*, 6, 321–342.

Bleek, W. H. I., & Lloyd, L. (1911). *Specimens of Bushmen Folklore*. London: G. Allen, Limited.

Breuil, H. (1948). The White Lady of the Brandberg, South-West Africa, her companions and her guards. *South African Archaeological Bulletin*, 3(9), 2–11.

Breuil, H. (1949a). The age and the authors of the painted rocks of Austral Africa. *South African Archaeological Bulletin*, 4(13), 19–27.

Breuil, H. (1949b) Some foreigners in the frescoes on rocks in Southern Africa. *South African Archaeological Bulletin*, 4(14), 39–50.

Bwasiri, E. J. (2014). Kondoa rock paintings: traditional use. *Encyclopedia of Global Archaeology*, 1, 4301–4307.

Challis, W. (2009). Taking the Reins: The Introduction of the hOrse in the 19th Century Maloti-Drakensberg and the Protective Medicine of Baboons. In P. Mitchell, & B. W. Smith, eds., *The Eland's People: New Perspectives in the Rock Art of the Maloti-Drakensberg* Bushmen. Johannesburg: Wits University Press, 104–107.

Chaloupka, G. (1984). *From Paleoart to Casual Paintings*. Darwin: Northern Territory Museum of Arts and Sciences (Monograph Series 1).

Clottes, J. (1989). The identification of human and animal figures in European Palaeolithic art., H. Morphy, ed., *Animals into Art*. London: Unwin Hyman, 21–52.

Cooke, C. K. (1969). *Rock Art of Southern Africa*. Cape Town: Books of Africa.

Deacon, J. (2002). Southern African Rock-Art Sites. International Council on Monuments and Sites (ICOMOS). Available at: www.icomos.org/studies/sarockart.htm (Accessed 03 December 2019)

Deacon, J. (2019). The legal and political framework for archaeology and the protection of archaeological resources in South Africa. In *Oxford Research Encyclopedia of African History*.

Deacon, H. J., & Deacon, J. (1999). *Human Beginnings in South Africa: Uncovering the Secrets of the Stone Age*. Johannesburg and Cape Town: David Philip Publishers.

Dornan, S. S. (1925). *Pygmies and Bushmen of the Kalahari*. London: Seely, Service and Co.

Dowson, T. A. (2009). Re-animating hunter-gatherer rock-art research. *Cambridge Archaeological Journal*, 19(3), 378–387.

Drouin, J. (1989). The bestiary of rupestrian and literary origin of the Sahara and the Sahel: an essay in the investigation of contradictions. In H. Morphy, ed., *Animals into Art*. London: Unwin Hyman Ltd, 343–356.

Eastwood, E. B. (1999). Red lines and arrows: attributes of supernatural potency in San rock art of the Northern Province, South Africa and south-western Zimbabwe. *South African Archaeological Bulletin*, 54(169), 16–27.

Eastwood, E. B., & Eastwood, C. (2006). *Capturing the Spoor: An Exploration of Southern African Rock Art*. Claremont: New Africa Books.

Eastwood, E. B., Bristow, C., & Van Schalkwyk, J. A. (1999). Animal behaviour and interpretation in San rock-art: a study in the Makgabeng plateau and Limpopo-Shashi confluence area, Southern Africa. *South African Field Archaeology*, 8, 60–75.

Ergates (1905). Bushmen's stock raids in Natal. *Natal Agricultural Journal* 8(2), 113–123.

Fock, G. J. (1972). Domestic cattle on rock engravings. *South African Journal of Science*, 68, 243–245.

Fock, G. J. (1979). *Felsbilder in Sudafrika, Teil 1: Die Gravierungen auf Klipfontein, Kapprovinz*. Koin: Bohlau Verlag.

Fock, G. J. & Fock, D. (1984). *Felsbilder in Südafrika. Teil II. Kinderdam und Kalahari*. Böhlau Verlag, Cologne.

Forssman, T. & Gutteridge, L. (2012). *Bushman Rock Art: An Interpretive Guide*. Pinetown: Southbound, South Publishers.

Flood, J. (1989). Animals and zoomorphs in rock art of the Koolburra region, north Queensland. In H. Morphy, eds., *Animals into Art*. London: Unwin Hyman Ltd, 287–300.

Garlake, P. (1989). The power of the elephants: scenes of hunting and death in the rock paintings of Zimbabwe. *Heritage of Zimbabwe*, 8, 9–33.

Génin, F., Yokwana, A., Kom, N., et al. (2016). A new galago species for South Africa (Primates: Strepsirhini: Galagidae), *African Zoology* 51(3), 135–143.

Gonzalez-Echegaray, J. (1974). Arte paleolitico 2: Pinturas y grabados de la Cueva de Las Chimeneas, Puente Viesgo, Santander. *Monografias de Arte rupestre*. Barcelona: Instituto de Prehistoria y Arqueologia and New York (NY): Wenner Gren Foundation for Anthropological Research.

Guenther, M. (1999). *Tricksters and Trancers: Bushman Religion and Society*. Bloomington: Indiana University Press.

Guenther, M. G. (2007). "The return of myth and symbolism" articulation of foraging, trance curing and storytelling among San of the Old Way and today. *Before Farming*, 3, 1–10.

Guenther, M. G. (2015). Therefore their parts resemble humans, for they feel that they are people: Ontological flux in San myth, cosmology and belief. *Before Farming*, 1(3), 277–315.

Guenther, M. G. (2017). The eyes are no longer wild. You have taken the kudu in your mind: The supererogatory aspect of San hunting. *The South African Archaeological Bulletin*, 72 (205), 3–16.

Guenther, M. G. (2020). Therianthropes and transformation in San art. In *Human-Animal Relationships in San and Hunter-Gatherer Cosmology*. Cham, Palgrave Macmillan, 95–160.

Harding, J. R. (1951). Painted rock-shelters near Bethlehem, O.F.S: I. Saulspoort. *South African Archaeological Bulletin*, 6(21), 14–29.

Harrison, C. W. F. (1903). *Natal: An Illustrated Official Railway Guide and Handbook of General Information*. London: Payne Jennings.

Henry, L. (2007). A history of removing rock art in South Africa. *South African Archaeological Bulletin*, 62 (185), 44–48.

Hewitt, R. (2008). *Structure, Meaning and Ritual in the Narratives of the Southern San*. Johannesburg: Wits University Press.

Hodgson, D. & Helvenston, P. A. (2006). The emergence of the representation of animals in palaeoart: Insights from evolution and the cognitive, limbic and visual systems of the human brain. *Rock Art Research*, 23(1), 3–40.

Hollmann, J. C. (ed.) (2004) *Customs and Beliefs of the/Xam Bushmen*. Johannesburg: Witwatersrand University Press.

Hollmann, J. C. (2005). Using behavioural postures and morphology to identify hunter-gatherer rock paintings of therianthropes in the Western and Eastern Cape Provinces, South Africa. 60 (182) *South African Archaeological Bulletin*, 84.

Hollmann, J. C., & Msimanga, L. (2008). "An extreme case": the removal of rock art from uMhwabane (eBusingatha) rock art shelter, Bergville, KwaZulu-Natal. *Southern African Humanities*, 20(2), 285–315.

Huffman, T. N. (1983). The trance hypothesis and the rock art of Zimbabwe. *South African Archaeological Society Goodwin Series*, 4, 49–53.

Ingold, T. (1986). Territoriality and tenure: the appropriation of space in hunting and gathering societies. *The Appropriation Of Nature*, Manchester: Manchester University Press, 130–164.

Jolly, P. (2002). Therianthropes in San rock art. *South African Archaeological Bulletin*, 57(176), 85–103.

Karimi, E. (2020). Abstract markings in the rock art of Iran: relative dating and possible function of the markings. *Time and Mind*, 13 (2), 141–163.

Kent, S. (ed.) (1989) *Farmers as Hunters: the Implications of Sedentism*. Cambridge, UK: Cambridge University Press.

Lagden, G. (1909). *The Basutos*. London: Hutchinson and Co.

Layton, R. (1992). *Australian Rock Art*. Cambridge: Cambridge University Press.

Leakey, M. (1983). *Africa's Vanishing Art: the Rock Paintings of Tanzania*. London: Hamish Hamilton.

Lenssen-Erz, T. (1994). Jumping about: springbok in the Brandberg rock paintings and in the Bleek and Lloyd Collection. An attempt at a correlation. In T. A. Dowson, & J. D. Lewis-Williams, eds., *Contested Images. Diversity in Southern African Rock-art Research*. Johannesburg: Witwatersrand University Press, 275–291.

Lenssen-Erz, T. (1997). Metaphors of intactness of environment in Namibian rock paintings. In P. Faulstich, ed., *IRAC Proceedings*. Tucson (AZ): American Rock Art Research Association, 43–54.

Lewis-Williams, J. D. (1981). *Believing and Seeing: Symbolic Meanings in Southern San Rock-Paintings*. London: Academic Press.

Lewis-Williams, J. D., & Challis, S. (2010). Truth in error: an enigmatic 19th century San comment on southern African rock paintings of "lions" and "shields". *Before Farming*, 1(2), 1–13.

Lewis-Williams, J. D., & T. A. Dowson, (1988). The signs of all times: entoptic phenomena in Upper Palaeolithic art. *Current Anthropology*, 29(2), 201–245.

Lewis-Williams, J. D., & Hollmann, J. C. (2006). Species and supernatural potency: an unusual rock painting from the Motheo District, Free State province, South Africa. *South African Journal of Science*, 102(11), 509–512.

Loubser, J. H. N. (1990). Removals and in situ conservation: strategies and problem in rock art conservation at the National Museum, Bloemfontein. *Pictogram*, 3(3), 2–5.

Loubser, J. H. N. (1994). The conservation of rock engravings and rock paintings: removals to museums or selected exhibitions in the field? *South African Journal of Science*, 90(8-9), 454–456.

Lorblanchet, M. (1989). From man to animal and sign in Palaeolithic art. In H. Morphy, ed., *Animals into Art*. London: Unwin Hyman Ltd, 109–143.

Low, C. (2014). Khoe-San ethnography, 'new animism' and the interpretation of southern African rock art, 2014. *The South African Archaeological Bulletin*, 164–172.

Maggs, T. (1998). Cartographic content of rock art in Southern Africa. *The History of Cartography Volume Two, Book Three: Cartography in the Traditional African, American, Arctic, Australian, and Pacific Societies*, Chicago: University of Chicago Press, 13–23.

Mallen, L. (2008). Rock art and identity in the north Eastern Cape Province. MA dissertation, University of the Witwatersrand.

Manhire, A. H., Parkington, J. E., & Mazel, A. D. (1986). Cattle, sheep and horses: a review of domestic animals in the rock art of southern Africa. *South African Archaeological Bulletin: Goodwin Series*, 5, 22–30.

McGranaghan, M. & Challis, S. (2016). Reconfiguring hunting magic: Southern Bushman (San) perspectives on taming and their implications for understanding rock art. *Cambridge Archaeological Journal*, 26(4), 579–599.

Mguni, S. (2009). Natural and supernatural convergences: Trees in Southern African Rock Art. *Current Anthropology*, 50(1), 139–148.

Mguni, S. (2016). *Archival Theory, Chronology and Interpretation of Rock Art in the Western Cape, South Africa*. Oxford: Archaeopress.

Mazel, A. D. (1983). Eland, rhebuck and cranes: Identifying seasonality in the paintings of the Drakensberg, Natal. *Goodwin Series: New Approaches to Southern African Rock Art*, 4, 34–37.

Mazel, A. D. (1989). People making history: the last ten thousands years of hunter-gatherer communities in the Thukela Basin. *Natal Museum Journal of Humanities*, 1, 1–168.

Molyneaux, B. (1989). Concepts of humans and animals in post-contact Micmac rock art. In H. Morphy, ed., *Animals into Art*. London: Unwin Hyman Ltd, 193–214.

Moodley, S. (2008). Koma: The crocodile motif in the rock art of the Northern Sotho. *South African Archaeological Bulletin*, 63(118), 116–124.

Ndlovu, N. (2011a). Legislation as an instrument in heritage management – is it effective?. *Conservation and Management of Archaeological Sites*, 13, 31–57.

Ndlovu, N. (2011b). Management versus preservation: archaeological heritage management in a transforming South Africa. *Conservation and Management of Archaeological Sites*, 12(2–3), 123–133.

Ndlovu, N. (2013). A comparative analysis of rock art in Southern Africa: Animals and cosmological models,. Unpublished PhD thesis, Newcastle University, .

Pager, H. (1971). *Ndedema: a Documentation of the Rock Paintings of the Ndedema Gorge*. Graz: Akademische Druck.

Parkington, J. (2003). *Cederberg Rock Paintings*. Cape Town: Krakadouw Trust.

Prins, F. E. & Hall, S. (1994). Expressions of fertility in the rock art of Bantu-speaking agriculturists. *African Archaeological Review*, 12(1), 171–203.

Ouzman, S. (1996). Thaba Sione: place of rhinoceroses and rain-making. *African Studies*, 55(1), 31–59.

Renaud, E. (2019). *Visionary Animal: Rock Art from Southern Africa*. Johannesburg: Wits University Press.

Rice, P. C. & Paterson, A. L. (1996). Bone art in the Upper Paleolithic: regional, temporal, and art class comparisons. *Cross-Cultural Research*, 30(3), 211–242.

Schönland, S. (1905). Arts and crafts of the natives of South Africa. *South African Journal of Science*, 3(1), 130–146.

Skotnes, P. (ed.) (2007) *Claim to the Country: The Archive of Lucy Lloyd and Wilhelm Bleek*. Johannesburg: Jacana.

Smith, B. W., & Ouzman, S. (2004). Taking stock: Identifying Khoekhoen herder rock art in Southern Africa. *Current Anthropology*, 45 (4), 499–526.

Smith, B. W., & Van Schalkwyk, J. A. (2002). The white camel of the Makgabeng. *The Journal of African History*, 43(2), 235–254.

Smits, L. G. A. (1971). The rock paintings of Lesotho, their content and characteristics. *South African Journal of Science, Special Publication*, 2, 14–19.

Solomon, A. (2011). Towards visual histories: Style interdisciplinarity and southern African rock art research, 2011. *South African Archaeological Bulletin*, 66 (193), 51–83.

Stow, G. W. (1905). *The Native Races of South Africa*. London. Swan Sonnenschein and Co. Ltd.

Turner, C. V. (2006). An interpretation of baboon, hartebeest and significantly differentiated figures at RSA-TYN2 Rock Art Site, Maclear District, Eastern Cape Province. Unpublished Honours dissertation, University of the Witwatersrand.

Vinnicombe, P. (1966). The early recording and preservation of rock paintings in South Africa. *Studies in Speleology*, 1(4), 153–162.

Vinnicombe, P. (1967). Rock painting analysis. *South African Archaeological Bulletin*, 22(88), 129–141.

Vinnicombe, P. (1972). Myth, motive, and selection in southern African rock art. *Africa: Journal of the International African Institute*, 42(3) 192–204.

Vinnicombe, P. (1976). *People of the Eland: Rock paintings of the Drakensberg Bushmen as a Reflection of their Life and Thought*. Pietermaritzburg: University of Natal Press.

Ward, V. (1997). A century of change: Rock deterioration in the Natal Drakensberg. *South African Natal Museum Journal of Humanities*, 9, 75–97.

Witelson, D. (2019). *A Painted Ridge: Rock art and performance in the Maclear District, Eastern Cape Province, South Africa*. Oxford: Archaeopress.

14 Citizens of the Savanna

An Account of Three Million Years of Interaction between Baboons and Hominins in South Africa

Shaw Badenhorst

Izakhamizi ze-Savanna: I-akhawunti Yeminyaka Eyizigidi Ezintathu Yokuxhumana phakathi kwezimfene namaHominins eNingizimu Afrika

Okungabonakali

INingizimu Afrika isingathwe ngaphansi kwezinhlobo eziyisikhombisa zama-primates wakudala, futhi inomlando omude wokutholwa kwezinsalela zasekhaya. Izinhlobonhlobo zezilwaneezinjengemfene namakhaya ziye zahlangana futhi zaxhumana iminyaka engaba yizigidi ezintathu esifundeni. Lokhu kube khona kokubumbana kwashintsha kakhulu phakathi kweminyaka eyikhulu. Ngesikhathi sePlio-Pleistocene, izimfene namakhaya kwakudla izinyamazane ezinjengezingwe namakati wamazinyo amade, kanti futhi zazivame ukulala emihumeni ebusuku ukuze zibalekele izinyamazane. NgeNkathi ye-Stone Age yakamuva, izinsalela zemfene zilungisiwe ngokwe-anthropology, futhi ukuqondana okusha komphakathi kungenzeka kuhlobene nezimo zesiko. Indima ethile yesiko lezinkawu yashintsha ngokufika kwabalimi be-Iron Age, lapho izimfene zakhangwa amasimu atshaliwe. Ngokwe-Ethnoprimatology, izimfene zaziwa ngokuthi zinobudlelwane nabathakathi, okubonisa isithombe esingesihle salezi zilwane. AbaseYurophu baletha izibhamu eNingizimu Afrika, futhi lobu buchwepheshe obusha basiza ekuqothulweni kwezinyamazane ezingxenyeni eziningi zaseNingizimu Afrika. Namuhla, izimfene zigcinwe ezindaweni zemvelo nasezindaweni zasemakhaya.

Amagama agqamile

Hominin – Primate – imfene – *Papio ursinus* – *Homo* – *Australopithecus*

Abstract

South Africa is host to no less than seven extant primate species and also boasts a long history of findings of hominin fossils. Large primates, such as baboons and hominins, have coexisted and interacted for some three million years in the region. This coexistence changed radically over the millennia. During the Plio-Pleistocene, baboons and hominins were both prey to predators, such as leopards and saber-toothed cats, and they often slept in caves at night to escape predation. By the Later Stone Age, baboon remains are anthropologically modified, and the new social connotations are likely associated with ritual contexts. The potential ritual role of baboons changed with the arrival of the Iron Age farmers, when baboons were attracted to cultivated fields. Ethnoprimatologically, baboons became known as familiars of evil persons, reflecting largely a negative image of these primates. Europeans introduced rifles to South Africa, and this new technology assisted in the extermination of baboons in many parts of South Africa. Today, baboons are confined to nature reserves and rural areas.

Keywords: Hominin, Primate, Baboon, *Papio ursinus*, *Homo*, *Australopithecus*

14.1   Introduction

Charles Darwin (1871) was correct that the origins of *Homo sapiens* were to be found in Africa, a point corroborated in the following 150 years with the discovery of numerous species of human ancestors in eastern and southern Africa (e.g. Mitchell, 2002). It is known today that various species of primates and hominins (including earlier forms of *Homo*, *Australopithecus*, and *Paranthropus*) coexisted and interacted with one another for more than three million years in South Africa. The relationship between primates and hominins are challenging to elucidate during large parts of the Plio-Pleistocene as evidence is often lacking or ambiguous. However, it has long been realized that the behavior of large-bodied, extant chacma baboons (*Papio ursinus*) provide some clues about life and behavior of hominins on the dry, open African savannas in the distant past (Pfeiffer, 1969). By the Late Pleistocene, archaeological evidence, albeit scanty, helps to elucidate this interaction between primates and hominins. In more recent centuries, ethnohistorical sources further contribute to an understanding and extrapolation of these relationships and interactions to deeper time periods in human history. In this chapter, I trace the relationship between hominins and the main primate in South Africa, baboons, drawing on paleoanthropological, archaeological, ethnohistorical, and zoological information (Fig. 14.1).

South Africa has been at the forefront of primate and hominin research over the course of the last century. The South African poet, journalist, and amateur naturalist, Eugène Marias (1871–1936), made an early contribution to ethology with his study of baboons in the Waterberg region of South Africa. These studies were originally published in the 1920s in a series of articles written in Afrikaans. The collected information was published subsequently (Marais, 1938, 1974). Marais was interested in the evolutionary origins of the subconscious mind of humans (Ardrey, 1974) and he postulated that in lower animals such as insects, birds, and fish, instinctive behavior dominates life (Marais, 1938). However, with higher primates such as baboons, apes, and humans, behavior is determined by instinct shortly after birth, and subsequently replaced by social learning, mostly transferred from parents to children. The implication of this finding is that lower animals can easily become extinct when they cannot adapt to changing environments, whereas higher animals can overcome this obstacle (Ryke, 1984). At the same time, a remarkable discovery shook the world. In 1924, Raymond Dart, then at the University of the Witwatersrand in Johannesburg, South Africa, discovered *Australopithecus africanus*, a direct ancestor of *Homo*, at Taung (Dart, 1925). This discovery let to a plethora of hominin and primate species being found and described in subsequent decades. The vast

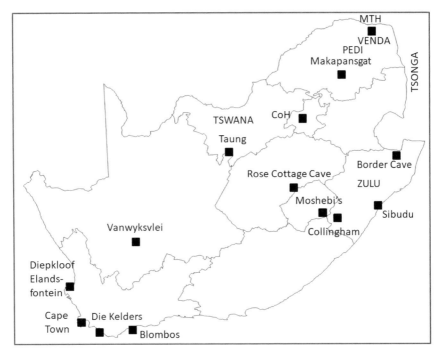

Figure 14.1 Location of sites and groups mentioned in the text. Historic Cave is located at Makapansgat. The Cradle of Humankind (CoH) includes a number of sites, including Sterkfontein, Gladysvale, Kromdraai, Swartkrans, Drimolen, Gondolin, Cooper's Cave, Bolt's Farm, and Plover's Lake. Mutokolwe, Tshitheme, and Ha-Tshirundu (MTH) are all in the same general area. Jagt Pan 7 and Vlermuisgat are located close to Vanwyksvlei.

majority of these discoveries emanated from what is called today, the Cradle of Humankind, a fossil-rich area of dolomite formations located close to Johannesburg.

14.2   Extant Primates of South Africa

Notwithstanding long gone rumors of the presence of large ape-men creatures (Hall and Marsh, 1996; Sanderson, 1860), today, southern Africa is inhabited by seven primate species. These include, from large to small, humans (*Homo sapiens sapiens*), chacma baboons (*Papio ursinus*), vervet monkeys (*Chlorocebus pygerythrus*), samango monkeys (*Cercopithecus mitis* ssp. *labiatus*), greater galagos (*Otolemur crassicauda-tus*), South African lesser galagos (*Galago moholi*), and the Mozambique dwarf galago (*Paragalago granti*) (Skinner and Chimimba, 2005). Of all the extant primates of South Africa, baboons are the "most humanlike" in behavior and intelligence (*cf.* De Vore and Washburn, 1966; Marais 1938, 1974; Stevenson-Hamilton, 1947). Their remains also far exceed that of the other primates in the paleoanthropological and archaeological

Figure 14.2 A female chacma baboon. (Image from Sharp Photography, sharpphotography.co.ukon Wikimedia Commons).

record (e.g. Brain; 1981; Plug and Badenhorst, 2001). Recorded ethnohistorical accounts of hunter-gatherers and farmers also refer to baboons and almost never to other smaller primates (e.g. Krige, 1957). For these reasons, this chapter will focus on the interaction between hominins and baboons (Fig. 14.2).

Baboons are highly social animals, living in troops ranging from 10 to more than 100 individuals consisting of both sexes and all age groups. A few of the strongest adult males control the troop (Rautenbach, 1982). Unlike vervet monkeys (Cheney and Seyfarth, 1983), baboons rarely change troops resulting in a high degree of inbreeding (De Vore and Washburn, 1966). Troops have home ranges, and these often overlap with those of other baboon troops – peaceful coexistence seems to be the norm between them. Females mate with most of the males in the troop. Baboons never sleep on the ground in fear of predators but seek shelter at night in caves, trees, or inaccessible rock ledges (Rautenbach, 1982). Baboons are aggressive animals and fierce opponents with great physical strength, and leopards have little chance of a successful kill by day (Wolhuter, 1967). Leopards are fond of them as part of their diet and usually stalk them at night (O'Connell, 2007). Most of the day is spent searching for food, with some social interaction, such as grooming and courtship, during the early mornings and late afternoons (Wolhuter, 1967). Baboons are omnivores, but plants form the bulk of the diet (Rautenbach, 1982). They rarely scavenge. Troops of baboons have been within close distance of kills made by predators and never formed part of the scavenger group (van Lawick-Goodall and van Lawick-Goodall, 1970).

Baboons are common in southern Africa. They have a wide habitat tolerance, and their range is only limited by the availability of water and suitable sleeping places like caves, trees, and rocky cliffs (Rautenbach, 1982). Baboons feed mostly on the ground, often crossing rivers, and may live in dry areas away from trees. They are aggressive and dominant-oriented, and their troop sizes large. These factors enable baboons to occupy large areas of Africa, and this distribution is compatible with that of early *Homo* (De Vore and Washburn, 1966).

Baboons can learn quickly to manipulate objects (Rautenbach, 1982), and they are easily tamed (Stevenson-Hamilton, 1947): evidence abounds of their ability to perform various learned tasks, such as herding goats (Dart, 1965), working railway signals (Cheney and Seyfarth, 2007), guarding a farmstead (Pike, 1891), and accompanying men to war (Rossouw, 2013). Their behavior is therefore often described as "human-like" in many ways (Stevenson-Hamilton, 1947; Wolhuter, 1967), and the sound of a dying baboon is like that of a human (Pike, 1891; Schoeman, 1973). Accounts of human children that grew up amongst and were adopted by troops of baboons (Foley, 1940) turned out to be false (Zingg, 1940). Instances have been recorded where baboons utilized stones as tools. In the far northern parts of South Africa, baobab trees grow to great heights and size. The trees produce a fruit with an extremely hard outer shell and the size of a small coconut, and the chacma baboon is one of the few animals that can access the edible core of the fruit. A particular troop in the region would travel great distances to reach the baobab trees over sandy and stoneless terrain. The fallen fruit would be picked up, and transported to the foot of hills where the nearest stones are located. Adults usually carried four fruits at a time. This was accomplished by one being held in the teeth by the stalk, one under the right arm (it was never observed that they were carried under the left arm), and one in each hand, with the baboons treading on those held in the hands. When they reached the hills, the fruit was placed on a flat rock, and smashed open with another rock. This behavior was only noted amongst one particular troop, and in other regions with the same trees, baboons did not display this behavior (Marias, 1974). In Lesotho, it is possible that young baboons used sticks to dig out roots (Arbousset and Daumas, 1968).

14.3   Plio-Pleistocene and Early Stone Age

Comparisons of blood and DNA demonstrate that humans and chimpanzees had a common ancestor between six and seven Mya (Steiper et al., 2004). Fossils of various human ancestors, such as species of *Australopithecus* and *Homo*, have been discovered in South Africa. A possible direct human ancestor, *A. africanus*, appeared about 3 Ma and lived until about 2.1 Ma. Evidence for this species has been found at sites in South Africa, such as Taung, Sterkfontein, Gladysvale, and Makapansgat (Herries et al., 2009). Members of the genus *Australopithecus* were bipedal but retained skeletal features showing that climbing of trees was still important. Their brain sizes were small, ranging between 350 and 530 cm², and they had large projecting faces and large cheek teeth (Klein, 1999). They possibly had the ability to make bone tools (Backwell and d'Errico, 2001). The robust australopithecine *Paranthropus robustus* existed between 2 and 1.2 Ma ago, and is found at sites like Kromdraai, Swartkrans, Drimolen, Gondolin, and Cooper's Cave (Steininger et al., 2008).

In East Africa, the earliest current evidence for the genus *Homo* appears between 2.80 to 2.75 Ma (Villmoare et al., 2015), followed by *Homo* aff. *Homo habilis* dating from about 2.33 ± 0.07 Ma (Kimbel et al., 1997). By 1.8 million Ma, *Homo ergaster* also lived in Africa (Klein, 1999). Evidence of *Homo* is present at Sterkfontein and Swartkrans (Mitchell, 2002). Many members of *Homo* had a larger cranial capacity of between 530 and 1500 cm², a larger stature and body weight, a reduction in dentition, jaws, and cranial crest, delayed maturation rates, and more obligatory bipedalism (Klein, 1999), although some species, like *Homo naledi*, are smaller in stature with smaller cranial capacity (Berger et al. 2015). Although the first stone tools from the Oldowan industry may be associated with *Australopithecus*, they flourished with *Homo*, and the earliest lithics are found at Sterkfontein, dating to between 2 and 1.7 Ma. These earliest tools were used for removing meat from carcasses, scraping and sawing wood, cutting grass or reeds, and heavy-duty butchering (Isaac, 1984). Bone tools were used to dig plant roots and excavating termite mounds (Backwell and d'Errico, 2001).

The Pliocene to Middle Pleistocene (from about >3 Ma to 126 Kya) are characterized by a diversity of primate species living in South Africa. The taxonomic status and evolutionary trajectory of many of these species are debated (e.g. Thackeray, 2003). During this time, various species of extant and extinct baboons existed in the area, such as *Parapapio broomi*, *Pa. whitei*, *Pa. jonsi*, *Papio hamadryas*, *P. robinsoni*, *P. angusticeps*, *Theropithecus* sp., *Dinopithecus ingens*, and *Gorgopithecus major* (Brain, 1981; Deacon and Deacon, 1999). Some baboon species, such as *Theropithecus oswaldi* from Elandsfontein, existed into the Middle Pleistocene (Deacon and Deacon, 1999). Interestingly, almost no extant monkeys have been found at Plio-Pleistocene fossil localities in South Africa, except colobine monkeys, *Cercopithecoides williamsi* (Brain, 1981). The classification of extinct and extant baboons has been problematic for decades due to the issue of species recognition. *Papio* seems to have arisen during the Late Pliocene in South Africa and have been found at sites like Sterkfontein (Member 5), Kromdraai A and B, Drimolen, Swartkrans, and Bolt's Farm (Jablonski and Frost, 2010). This likely represents the first indirect evidence of interactions between hominins and nonhuman primates in South Africa as both shared the same space and time and are found in the same deposits. However, it is important to keep sight that a single deposit (or member) likely had multiple depositional episodes in the region.

Very little is known about the interaction between baboons and hominins during large parts of the Plio-Pleistocene. Any compelling evidence like taphonomical indicators, such as butchering marks, is lacking on nonhuman primate remains. Nevertheless, both baboons and hominins likely competed with one another for foods, such as bulbs and fruits. This would have brought them into contact with one another during daytime when feeding. Perhaps such contact was peaceful like in modern baboon troops (*cf.* Rautenbach, 1982). They also competed for shelter at night, which often offered water and protection from predators. It is conceivable that troops of baboons and hominins did not share the same sleeping places at night. Both would have sought shelter in caves and overhangs as they were hunted by carnivores, such as leopards and saber-toothed cats. Raptors such as eagles also preyed upon hominins and baboons (Berger and Clarke, 1995). Baboons today prefer to spend their daytime with impala to avoid predators, and hominins like *Australopithecus* and *Paranthropus* could have done the same (Badenhorst, 2018). Not all primate remains from Plio-Pleistocene deposits are the result of predators and raptors. For example, at Cooper's Cave, the abundance of juvenile and sub-adult primates, the geomorphology of the cave, and the low impact of carnivore damage on the bones, argue in favor of the occupation of the cave by large-bodied cercopithecids followed by the natural death of some individuals (Val et al., 2014). While there is no evidence for hominin occupation of the cave, isolated remains of *Paranthropus robustus* have been discovered at Cooper's Cave (Steininger et al., 2008).

Between two and one million years ago, early *Homo* discovered how to control fire (James, 1989), which enabled our ancestors to defend themselves against predators, especially at night (Brain and Sillent, 1988). Interestingly, an account conveyed to Pike (1891) mentions how baboons were attracted to a fire left by people in recent times, with baboons found resting close to the fires and even continuing to push branches into the fire. Although this behavior of baboons was not witnessed by Pike (1891), considering the intelligence of baboons, this account may be confirmed eventually.

14.4   Middle Stone Age

The Middle Stone Age (MSA) of southern Africa, dating back more than 300,000 years, is a time of major cultural changes for humans. Not only do anatomically modern humans appear, but also archaeological evidence for symbolic behavior, improved flake technology, hafting of stone tools, active hunting, shellfish consumption, and fishing (Deacon and Deacon, 1999; Mitchell 2002). Some of these behaviors had already appeared before the MSA (Ungar and Grine, 2006). Humans established themselves as formidable predators (Pfeiffer, 1969) during the MSA, often taking down large and dangerous prey (Milo, 1998). Nevertheless, a great deal of similarities likely remained between the lifeways of baboons and people. Both groups continue to live in shelters, living mainly on plant remains, hunting vulnerable young animals, and those living at the coast, collecting shellfish (Badenhorst et al., 2014; De Vore and Washburn, 1966; Du Toit, 1929; Hall, 1962; Henshilwood, 2008; Pfeiffer, 1969).

The new way of life that became established during the MSA had a profound impact on the social structure of humans. In baboons, their social structure ensures survival with adult males always close to other troop members. With regular hunting of large game during the MSA, human hunters had to leave the local group, sometimes for days, and then return to their home base. It is therefore possible that hunting with tools caused a great deal of changes in the social structure of human bands, the interrelations of bands, the size and use of a range, and relations with other animals (*cf.* De Vore and Washburn, 1966). What these impacts were remains as yet poorly understood.

Remains of primates, such as baboons, vervet monkeys, and samango monkey, occur in low numbers at MSA sites of South Africa (Table 14.1). In most cases, only

Table 14.1 Examples of primates found at MSA sites and their representation in the samples (% number of identified specimens [NISP] of the total NISP)

Sites	% NISP Baboon	% NISP Vervet Monkey	% Samango Monkey	Reference
Die Kelders	<0.1	–	–	Klein and Cruz-Uribe (2000)
Sibudu Cave	0.2	1	0.6	Clark and Plug (2008)
Diepkloof Shelter	0.1	–	–	Steele and Klein (2013)
Blombos Cave	<0.1	–	–	Badenhorst et al. (2016a); Henshilwood et al. (2001)
Plover's Lake	<0.1	<0.1	–	De Ruiter et al. (2008)

isolated remains are reported, often barely exceeding 1% of the total identified sample (e.g. Cruz-Uribe, 1983; Klein, 1977), with no discussion on the skeletal elements or taphonomy of primates. The low numbers of baboons and other primates in these samples mean that there is often uncertainty as to whether baboons died naturally, or were killed by predators in caves during periods when people did not used these shelters, or whether these primates were actively hunted. The low representations suggest, however, that they were not hunted by people. Since baboons live in caves (e.g. Farini, 1973; Sanderson 1860), it is highly probable that the remains of baboons found at MSA sites represent prey of carnivores such as leopards (Thackeray, 1990). From the few isolated baboon remains, there is no evidence for the consumption of primates by humans during the MSA, although, both shared the same landscape.

14.5   Later Stone Age

The last 40,000 years, often referred to as the Later Stone Age (LSA) in South Africa, are associated for the largest part with the San, who are hunter-gatherers. People during this time made microlithic stone tools, and rock art appears. Some 2,000 years ago, the first sheep arrived in southern Africa, initiating the spread of pastoral people, called the Khoekhoe, to South Africa. Hunter-gatherers continued to live in shelters and open camps, while herders made temporary camps in search of water and pasture (Deacon and Deacon, 1999). The few isolated remains of baboons and, to a lesser extent, vervet monkeys (summary of distribution in Plug and Badenhorst, 2001), suggest possible natural intrusions such as through leopard activity, just as during the MSA. An interesting exception is Collingham Shelter, where the baboon remains appear fresh with attached sinew still present, and many limb bones clearly articulate with one another. This suggests that baboons died in the shelter (Plug, 1992).

Importantly, there are indications that during the LSA, baboons obtain a new cultural significance. A lower canine of a baboon was cut and polished at Rose Cottage Cave, suggesting that these animals obtained social meaning to hunter-gatherers in the region (Plug and Engela, 1992). At Moshebi's Shelter, also in the

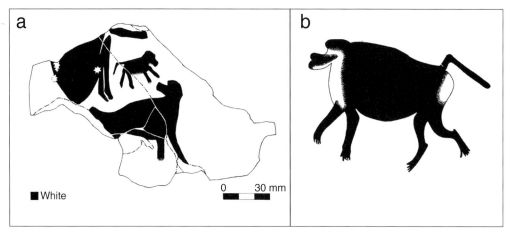

Figure 14.3 (a) Redrawing of a rock painting of baboons collected in 1893 by Louis E. Tyler in South Africa. (RARI 03 7R). (b) Redrawing of a rock painting of a baboon from South Africa. (RARI RSA MEL8 2R). Used with permission from the Rock Art Research Institute, University of the Witwatersrand.

same vicinity but located in bordering Lesotho, a complete polished astragalus of an adult baboon stands out from a heavily fragmented sample, suggesting that baboons had some ritual connotations (Badenhorst et al., 2019). This archaeological evidence pointing to a new social construction for baboons is supported by ethnohistorical accounts which show that baboons feature in San folklore (e.g. Orpen, 1919), where they are often portrayed as strong and intelligent beings (Challis, 2009; Von Wielligh, 1919), fond of trickery and teasing (Silberbauer, 1981). Depictions made by San hunter-gatherers of baboons also appear in rock art (e.g. Challis, 2009; Cooke, 1969; Harding, 1951; Plug et al., 2003; Schönland, 1905; Vinnecombe, 1972), further supporting the novel relevance of these primates (Fig. 14.3).

San ethnoprimatological information serves to contextualize the social significance of the archaeological material found in Cottage Rose Cave and Moshebi's Shelter. The Kalahari San of Botswana consider baboons to be people in another state of existence. For this reason, they are not consumed. For the /Xam San of South Africa, baboons had similar powers than a shaman. Baboons derive their powers from a small stick of a plant called *sho://äõ*, which the baboon keeps in its left cheek. This stick enabled the baboon to tell of approaching danger and to protect itself from illness. When a /Xam shaman killed a baboon, he removed the *sho://äõ* for himself. Baboons also have the ability to fire arrows back at people. If someone kills a baboon, a man must cut fine lines around the points of his bow. Failing to do this will bring about the curse of the baboon that will remain in the bow (Bleek, 1931). Baboons also possessed the ≠*gebbigu*, a song sung at the dance. People acquired theirs when the lion and ostrich fought. Somehow baboons retained theirs. Some rock art depictions of baboons show whole troops with males, females, and young, as well as therianthropic baboons, which reflects the closeness of baboons and people, as well as the closeness between baboons and shamans (Lewis-Williams and Dowson, 1989). The

Baboon Dance of the San imitate the actions of baboons: dancers spring, gambol, run on all four legs, chat, and grin like a troop of baboons (Stow, 1964).

The San living on the plains distinguished themselves from those San living in the mountains in the Vanwyksvlei area of the Northern Cape. It is said that those San living in the mountains eat baboon (Deacon, 1986). However, no other information is available on this supposed practice. The area is not well studied archaeologically (Plug and Badenhorst, 2001), and the only LSA faunas from two sites in the vicinity, Jagt Pan 7 and Vlermuisgat, contains no baboon remains (Badenhorst et al., 2015). It is likely that the supposed consumption of baboons may rather have been an 'othering' by one group of hunter-gatherers towards another. Similarly, in neighboring Namibia, a Herero pastoralist denied the practice of eating baboons and pointed to this practice being found under the Berg Damara (Shortridge, 1934), a group widely considered inferior by them (Stow, 1964). Late Stone Age faunas from the region occupied by the Berg Damara do not suggest any such practice (Badenhorst et al., 2016b).

The San eat most animals as part of their diet, with the universal exception of baboons, on account that they resemble humans (Bleek, 1931; Schapera, 1930). Baboons often competed directly with humans for food. For example, in arid Botswana, baboons feed extensively on tsamma melons, which are also highly important food for hunter-gatherers (Silberbauer, 1965). Baboons may have been a menace to food collectors and may have been killed at times (Cooke, 1969). A lot of rock art featuring baboons occur in the Drakensberg (e.g. Challis, 2009), which is located in South African and Lesotho. Today, baboons still occur in the mountains of Lesotho (e.g. Fairclough, 1905), but they are rare, like in other parts of the Drakensberg. They could have suffered the same fate as baboons in neighboring KwaZulu-Natal and elsewhere, where they were exterminated following crop damage and attacks on livestock (Lynch, 1994; Whiten et al., 1987).

14.6   Iron Age

By about AD 200, the first wave of Bantu-speaking farmers arrived in South Africa. This period is often called the Iron Age. These farmers lived in sedentary villages, cultivated plants, kept domestic animals, and made metal and ceramic objects (Huffman, 2007). The arrival and settlement of farmers in South Africa brought a dramatic and abrupt change to the interaction between baboons and humans. Their raids of crops and destructive nature (e.g. Mönnig, 1967; Stevenson-Hamilton, 1947) meant that farmers regarded them as pests. In recent times, they were eradicated from many areas (Rautenbach, 1982). Farmers often had to camp out in their lands just before reaping to prevent destruction of crops by baboons (Wolhuter, 1967). Old male baboons will only submit to being chased away if a man appears as they are able to distinguish between men and women (Wolhuter, 1967). Vervet monkeys have the same ability (Bryant, 1949). Remains of baboons are not common in faunas from Iron Age sites (Le Roux and Badenhorst, 2016; Plug and Badenhorst, 2001). For example, from more than 53,000 specimens identified from various sites in the Limpopo Valley spanning several centuries of occupation, less than 0.1% of the remains are those of nonhuman primates (Plug, 2000). Those few specimens retrieved may reflect individuals killed in cultivated fields as pests (Badenhorst et al., 2016c; Shortridge, 1934; Van der Waal, 1981). The fact that primate material is often lacking during this period, might be understandable as today's Bantu-speaking farmers in general, like San hunter-gatherers, do not eat baboons or monkeys because they resemble humans (Hammond-Tooke, 1981; Schapera and Goodwin, 1953; Schoeman, 1973).

14.7 Historical Times

By 1652, the Dutch East Indian Company established a supply-station in Table Bay where modern Cape Town is located, marking the first permanent settlement of Europeans in South Africa (Van Jaarsveld, 1971). The extermination of baboons only intensified with the arrival of the new inhabitants, who possessed rifles. Baboons soon learned that when sighting a man with a rifle to keep at a distance (Gunning, 1904; Pike, 1891; Schoeman, 1973). The earliest gardens of the new inhabitants were allegedly frequently raided by baboons, who found the newly introduced sweet potatoes, melons, guavas, and other fruits irresistible (Raven-Hart, 1971). Baboons often resorted to stone-throwing during these raids (Raven-Hart, 1971, also see Holub, 1976; James, 1881; Pike 1891 on baboons throwing stones at people). The killing of poultry and lambs by baboons also caused severe damage for these inhabitants (Burtt-Davy, 1905). The raiding of the newly established gardens in Cape Town was done with great precision by baboons. Some baboons of the troop would enter the gardens, and others remain on the walls, and yet others would wait outside. Those inside the garden then throw apples, melons, gourds, and fruits to those on the wall, who in turn throws it to those waiting below. This raid is done in silence without any fruit dropping to the ground. If the sentinel makes an alarm, the whole troop retreats with their bounty to the mountains (Anonymous 1825, also Pike, 1891). In recent times, baboons frequently feature in folk songs and stories of the descendants of these early Europeans (e.g. Bosman, 2004). As indicated, baboons are generally not consumed by the different people of South Africa. An exception is that of the early days of Dutch settlement at the Cape. Famine was threatening the colonialists in the early days of establishing the settlement, and a dead baboon found in the nearby mountains was consumed on an occasion (Frere, 1885).

Archaeoprimatological remains in the South African historical times are limited. Even more, galagos and other smaller primates are rare in the archaeological record of the country. An interesting exception is Historic Cave in the Makapan Valley, where there is evidence that a galalgo may have been consumed (Le Roux et al., 2013). The cave was home to a siege between Kekana Ndebele farmers and the Boers for 24 days in 1854. The siege was preceded by a number of skirmishes between the two groups, and the Kekana Ndebele, expecting an attack, fortified and stocked the cave with provisions, which included a diverse selection of hunted animals. This included a galago, which had a cut mark on an ulna retrieved from the site. This individual was probably encountered close to the cave in preparation for the siege, and opportunistically killed, taken to the cave and consumed. However, this practice was not widespread, and likely reflects a group under severe pressure to obtain as much food as possible in a short time. This particular faunal assemblage also contained teeth of baboons, but they are clearly fresher than the rest of the faunal assemblage, suggesting later and natural intrusions (Le Roux et al., 2013) sometime after the siege.

According to the Pedi, meat of a baboon is tasty and eaten by men and boys only. When the head of a baboon is eaten though, the face of the animal is turned away from the consumer. Apart from consuming baboons, the Pedi men and boys also consume vervet monkeys and galagos. Moreover, amongst the Pedi, the skins of vervet monkeys are used as ornamental dress, and necklaces of beads are made of bones of vervet monkeys, and worn by children suffering from coughs. Baboon skulls are impaled at the great gate of Pedi villages. Baboon hair is worn as necklaces by traditional healers who also used the skin of a baboon as a cap. The grounded remains of a baboon pelvis serve as an inoculation against rheumatism (Quin, 1959). In this particular case, it is evident that baboon consumption is related to a supernatural aspect.

Apart from a menace to farmers, baboons also, and likely as a result of their reputation as pests as well as their human-like qualities, obtained a more sinister role amongst many farming societies of South Africa. Skeletal parts of baboons feature in divining sets of various farming groups in South Africa (Plug 1987; Plug and Badenhorst 2009; Quin 1959; Stayt 1968). The Tsonga uses three different baboon astragali in divining sets; those of male, female and young baboons, all symbolizing the village. Baboons are said to represent the village as they never move; the ruins of their habitations are never seen, yet each year at spring baboons arrive (Junod, 1913). Various tales are told of baboons amongst the Tsonga, Zulu, and Venda, and all portray baboons in a negative light (Junod 1913; Krige, 1957; Stayt, 1968). Dreams containing baboons amongst the Venda is regarded as a bad omen (Stayt, 1968). Baboons are generally symbolic for treachery, and a saying goes, "tis the foot of the baboons", which is a proverb for unfair dealings (Macdonald, 1892).

Baboons also often take the role of familiars; beings who do the evil work (e.g. Hammond-Tooke, 1981; Marwick, 1966). Amongst the Zulu, the *umthakathi* is a wizard who uses magic for anti-social ends. He injures the health of people, destroys life, prevents rain, make cows go dry, and cause other forms of misfortune. This wizard has familiars who help him in his evil work and obey his commands. One of these, the *umKhovu*, is said to be a cross between a baboon and a human. An *umthakathi* will tame a female baboon and give her dirt to eat, and will then have sexual intercourse with it. The baboon will give birth to a creature half-animal, half-human, which will be taught to speak some phrases, and it will be sent at night to run errands. It hides in the shadows, and throw stones at people. Dogs never bark at them, as they will become dumb at the sight of the *umKhovu*. It moves in the village at night; its noise is like the rustle of a skirt. If it comes to a village where there is a sick person, there is no hope of recovery (Krige, 1957). The Zulu also tell of the *iZingogo*, a fabulous animal, which is a kind of baboon or degenerated human, who can speak but has a tail and walk on all fours and eats human flesh. They also devour their own dead (Krige, 1957).

Amongst the Pedi, *dithongwa* are various animals that evil persons tame and teach to carry out instructions. These animals include baboons, skunks, wild cats, snakes, owls, and bats. They are used during day and night time, when they can be seen stealing crops off the lands. If a man courts a women against the wishes of a person with magic power, they will place a baboon on the footpath leading to his home. He will be frightened so that he will not court the women again (Mönnig, 1967).

The Zulu describe the origins of baboons in the following manner: the people of the Amamfene group (some say the Amathusi group) were habitually idle, and would not cultivate their own food. They decided to leave their homes and live in the wilderness. They collected all types of food, made bread for the journey, took their hoe-handles which they fastened on their behind. These grew and became tails, hair appeared on their bodies, their foreheads became overhanging, and they turned into baboons (Krige, 1957).

Not all associations between baboons and farmers are negative. For the Bahurutshe from the Northwest Province of South Africa, which is part of the larger Tswana-language group, baboons are their totems animals. This meant that they were forbidden to shoot baboons (Bammann, 2016; Stow, 1964). There are different accounts as to how the baboon became the totem animal of this group. One version has it that when the Bahurutshe split from a related group, the Bakuana, baboons ate the pumpkins of the Bahurutshe before the time to begin eating the fruits of the New Year. The Bahurutshe were unwilling to let the pumpkins go to waste, and subsequently ate them, giving rise to the use of the baboon as a totem (Lang et al., 1904; Stow, 1964). In another version, the totem of the Bahurutshe is the eland and wildebeest. However, a section of the group keeps baboons as totems. This came about as a certain chief of the Bahurutshe caught and tamed a baboon. On a certain day, the son of the chief let the baboon get away. As there had always been friction between the chief and his son, this incident was the last straw. The chief gave the son a thrashing, and this led to the son seceding, forming his own tribe with the baboon as totem (Willoughby, 1905). The baboon is also the totem animal of the Bakoni (Quin, 1959). The Vha-ila-Pfene sib of the Venda people also has the baboon as a totem animal. People become baboons when they die and then go to the sacred hill of Lomondo to dwell there. Amongst them is a particularly large old baboon, who is the principle ancestral god. In time of trouble, the old baboon comes from the forest shouting loudly. This baboon also fetches those that died far away from Lomondo (Stayt, 1968).

In another case where baboons are regarded in a positive light, baboons are said to protect women against lions and other animals. A legend tells of a woman lost in a forest, and as night fell, baboons gathered around her to protect her, bringing her to a place of safety where she was given milk and maize. She learned the language of baboons, and often went to talk to them in the forest (Macdonald, 1892). The similarities between baboons and humans have special significance for the Venda. According to records, a medicine man visits new born babies, and makes small incisions all over the baby. Medicine that contains the ground-up skull of a baboon is rubbed into the incisions. A skull of a baboon is used because the Venda are aware of how quickly young baboons become strong and independent (Stayt, 1968). Interestingly, isolated baboon remains have been found at some sites occupied by Venda-speakers, including Mutokolwe (Magoma et al., 2018), Tshitheme (De Wet-Bronner, 1995), and Ha-Tshirundu (Raath Antonites and Kruger, 2012), albeit in low quantities.

14.8   Discussion and Conclusion

The relationship and interaction between baboons and hominins changed over the millennia in South Africa. Baboons occupied several MSA sites, or they were prey of leopards frequenting caves; and this is reflected in the few isolated skeletal finds at these sites. However, it was not until the LSA that baboons, as observed in anthropologically modified remains, acquired novel social configurations, notably the astragalus from Moshebi's Shelter and the canine from Rose Cottage Cave. In the Iron Age, few archaeoprimatological remains are found and reflect other uses by *Homo* as they might be considered crop pests. Therefore, the roles of baboons have historically included ally, shamanistic entity, familiar of evil persons, foe, protector, and companion. It has been suggested previously (Deacon, 1986; Plug and Badenhorst, 2001) that baboons could have been eaten by people in South Africa, but the only evidence is amongst the Pedi, where only men and boys eat the flesh of baboons. In this case, the consumption likely had a supernatural cause. Baboons, resembling humans, were never consumed by hunter-gatherers, most other farmers, or Europeans, except in times of famine. Elsewhere in Africa though, some groups like the Forest People of the Democratic Republic of the Congo regularly consume baboons and other monkeys (e.g. Davenport, 1945; Gatti, 1946).

Baboons and hominins faced predators such as leopards, lions, and saber-toothed cats on the savannas of South Africa during the Early Pleistocene. As possible allies, baboons and hominins had to endure nights in dark caves to escape these predators. From here, *Homo* acquired the ability to make and control fire and keep themselves safe at night. In time, our ancestors made more complex tools and learned to hunt large game. Hunter-gatherers from the LSA recognized baboons as human-like animals, and regarded them as a close ally of shamans. The arrival of farming with Iron Age people and Europeans brought conflict between baboons and humans, and baboons often became associated with persons with magic powers, bringing about their extermination in many areas.

14.9   Postscript

Baboons continue to make headline news in South Africa, but for all the wrong reasons. The word "baboon" is sometimes used as a derogatory name. The conflict between humans and baboons intensifies in urban and rural areas. Sadly, they can correctly be called "the least loved primate" of South Africa (Oosthuizen, 2018).

Acknowledgments

I took part of the title from wording found in the foreword of *The Soul of the Ape* by Robert Ardrey (1974: 43). I thank the editors of this volume for the invitation to write this contribution, as well as the reviewers for their comments and suggestions. N. Vilakazi assisted with the Zulu translation of the abstract.

References

Anonymous. (1825). The naturalist. No. 1. On the food of animals, in connexion with their habits. *The Belfast Magazine and Literary Journal*, 1(2), 97–102.

Arbousset, T., & Daumas, F. (1968). *Narrative of an Exploratory Tour to the North-east of the Colony of the Cape of Good Hope.* Cape Town: C. Struik.

Ardrey, R. (1974). Introduction. In *The Soul of the Ape*, by E. N. Marais, Pretoria: Human & Rousseau, 1–55.

Badenhorst, S. (2018). Possible predator avoidance behaviour of hominins in South Africa. *South African Journal of Science*, 114(7/8), Available at: https://doi.org/10.17159/sajs.2018/a0274

Badenhorst, S., Van Niekerk, K. L., & Henshilwood, C. S. (2014). Rock hyraxes (*Procavia capensis*) from Middle Stone Age levels at Blombos Cave, South Africa. *African Archaeological Review*, 31, 25–43.

Badenhorst, S., Parsons, I., & Voigt, E. A. (2015). Fauna from five Later Stone Age sites in the Bushmanland region of South Africa. *Annals of the Ditsong National Museum of Natural History*, 5, 1–10.

Badenhorst, S., Van Niekerk, K. L., & Henshilwood, C. S. (2016a). Large mammal remains from the 100 ka Middle Stone Age layers of Blombos Cave, South Africa. *South African Archaeological Bulletin*, 71 (203), 46–52.

Badenhorst, S., Veldman, A., & Lombard, M. (2016b). Late Holocene fauna from Kuidas Spring in Namibia. *African Archaeological Review*, 33(1), 29–44.

Badenhorst, S., Ashley, C., & Barkhuizen, W. (2016c). A consideration of garden hunting by Iron Age farmers in the Limpopo Valley and surrounding regions of southern Africa. *Annals of the Ditsong National Museum of Natural History*, 6, 18–25.

Badenhorst, S., Mitchell, P., Arthur, C., & Capelli, C. (2019). Late Holocene fauna from Moshebi's Shelter, a Later Stone Age site in Lesotho. *Southern African Humanities*, 32, 83–107.

Balkwell, L. R. & d'Errico, F. (2001). Evidence of termite foraging by Swartkrans early hominids. *Proceedings of the National Academy of Science of the United States of America*, 98(4), 1358–1363.

Bammann, H. (2016). *The Bahurutshe*. Münster: LIT Verlag.

Berger L. R. & Clarke R. J. (1995). Eagle involvement in accumulation of the Taung child fauna. *Journal of Human Evolution*, 29, 275–299.

Berger, L. R., Hawks, J., De Ruiter, D. J., et al. (2015). *Homo naledi*, a new species of the genus *Homo* from the Dinaledi Chamber, *South Africa. eLife*, 4, e09560.

Bleek, D. F. (1931). Customs and beliefs of the ¡Xam Bushmen. *Bantu Studies*, 5(1), 167–179.

Bosman, M. (2004). Die FAK-fenomeen: populêre Afrikaanse musiek en volksliedjies. *Tydskrif vir Letterkunde*, 41(2), 21–46.

Brain, C. K. (1981). *The Hunters of the Hunted? An Introduction to African Cave Taphonomy.* Chicago: University of Chicago Press.

Brain, C. K. & Sillent, A. (1988). Evidence from the Swartkrans Cave for the earliest use of fire. *Nature*, 336, 464–466.

Bryant, A. T. (1949). *The Zulu People as They Were before the White Man Came.* Pietermaritzburg: Shuter and Shooter.

Burtt-Davy, J. (1905). The climate and life zones of the Transvaal. *South African Journal of Science*, 3(1), 513–541.

Challis, W. (2009). Taking the reins: the introduction of the horse in the 19th century Maloti-Drakensberg and the protective medicine of baboons. In P. Mitchell, & B. W. Smith, eds., *The Eland's People: New Perspectives in the Rock Art of the Maloti-Drakensberg Bushmen.* Johannesburg: Wits University Press, p. 104–107.

Cheney, D. L. & Seyfarth, R. M. (1983). Nonrandom dispersal in free-ranging vervet monkeys: social and genetic consequences. *The American Naturalist*, 122 (3), 392–412.

Cheney, D. L. & Seyfarth, R. M. (2007) *Baboon Metaphysics. The Evolution of a Social Mind.* Chicago: The University of Chicago Press.

Clark, J. L. & Plug, I. (2008). Animal exploitation strategies during the South African Middle Stone Age: Howiesons Poort and Post-Howiesons Poort fauna from Sibudu Cave. *Journal of Human Evolution*, **54**, 886–898.

Cooke, C. K. (1969). *Rock Art of Southern Africa*. Cape Town: Books of Africa.

Cruz-Uribe, K. (1983). The mammalian fauna from Redcliff Cave, Zimbabwe. *South African Archaeological Bulletin*, 38(137), 7–16.

Dart, R. A. (1925). *Australopithecus africanus*: the man-ape of South Africa. *Nature*, 115(2884), 195–199.

Dart, R. A. (1965). Ahla, the female baboon goatherd. *South African Journal of Science*, **61**(9), 319–324.

Darwin, C. (1871). *The Descent of Man, and Selection in Relation to Sex*. London: John Murray.

Davenport, C. B. (1945). The dietaries of primitive peoples. *American Anthropologist New Series*, **47**(1), 60–82.

Deacon, J. (1986). "My place is the Bitterputs": the home territory of Bleek and Lloyd's /Xam San informants. *African Studies*, **45** (2), 135–156.

Deacon, H. J. & Deacon, J. (1999). *Human Beginnings in South Africa: Uncovering the Secrets of the Stone Age*. London: Altamira Press.

De Ruiter, D. J., Brophy, J. K., Lewis, P. J., Churchill, S. E., & Berger, L. R. (2008). Faunal assemblage composition and paleoenvironment of Plovers Lake, a Middle Stone Age locality in Gauteng Province, South Africa. *Journal of Human Evolution*, 55(6), 1102–1117.

De Vore, I. & Washburn, S. L. (1966). Baboon ecology and human evolution. In Howell, F. C., & Bourlière, F., eds. *African Ecology and Human Evolution*. Chicago: Aldine Publishing Company, 335–367.

De Wet-Bronner, E. (1995). The faunal remains from four Late Iron Age sites in the Soutpansberg region: Part II: Tshitheme and Dzata. *Southern African Field Archaeology*, **4**, 18–29.

Du Toit, S. J. (1929). Na die Kaprivi. *Journal of the Medical Association of South Africa*, December, 676–678.

Fairclough, T. L. (1905). Notes on the Basuto, their history, country, etc. *Journal of the Royal African Society*, 4(14), 194–205.

Farini, G. A. (1973). *Through the Kalahari Desert. A Narrative of a Journey with Gun, Camera, and a Note-book to Lake Ngami and Back*. Cape Town: C. Struik.

Foley, J. P. (1940). The 'baboon boy' of South Africa. *American Journal of Psychology*, 53(1), 128–133.

Frere, B. (1885). Historical sketch of South Africa. *Transactions of the Royal Historical Society*, **2**, 1–60.

Gatti, A. (1946). *South of the Sahara*. London: Hodder and Stoughton.

Gunning, J. W. B. (1904). The chacma baboon. *Transvaal Agricultural Journal*, **2** (8), 528–531.

Hall, K. R. L. (1962). Numerical data, maintenance activities and locomotion of the wild chacma baboon, *Papio ursinus*. *Journal of Zoology*, **139**(2), 181–220.

Hall, S., & Marsh, R. (1996). *Kan dit waar wees? Moorde en raaisels van Suider-Afrika*. Cape Town: Struik.

Hammond-Tooke, W. D. (1981). *Boundaries and Belief. The Structure of a Sotho Worldview*. Johannesburg: University of the Witwatersrand Press.

Harding, J. R. (1951). Painted rock-shelters near Bethlehem, O.F.S: I. Saulspoort. *South African Archaeological Bulletin*, 6(21), 14–29.

Henshilwood, C. S. (2008). *Holocene Prehistory of the Southern Cape, South Africa: Excavations at Blombos Cave and the Blombosfontein Nature Reserve*. Oxford: Archaeopress.

Henshilwood, C. S., Sealy, J. C., Yates, R., et al. (2001). Blombos Cave, Southern Cape, South Africa: Preliminary report on the 1992–1999 Excavations of the Middle Stone Age Levels. *Journal of Archaeological Science* 28, 421–448.

Herries, A. I. R., Curnoe, F., & Adams, J. W. (2009). A multi-disciplinary seriation of early *Homo* and *Paranthropus* bearing palaeocaves in southern Africa. *Quaternary International*, **202**, 14–28.

Holub, E. (1976). *Seven Years in South Africa. Travels, Researches, and Hunting Adventures between the Diamond-Fields and the Zambesi, 1872–79*. Volume II. Johannesburg: Africana Book Society.

Huffman, T. N. (2007). *Handbook to the Iron Age: The Archaeology of Pre-Colonial Farming Societies in Southern Africa*. Scottsville: University of KwaZulu-Natal Press.

Isaac, G. L. (1984). The archaeology of human origins: studies of the Lower Pleistocene in East Africa: 1971–1981. *Advances in World Archaeology*, 3, 1–87.

Jablonski, N. G. & Frost, S. (2010). Cercopithecoidea. In L. Werdelin, & W. J. Sanders, eds., *Cenozoic Mammals of Africa*. Berkeley: University of California, 393–428.

James, J. F. (1881). The reasoning facility of animals. *The American Naturalist*, 15(8), 604–615.

James, S. R. (1989). Hominid use of fire in the Lower and Middle Pleistocene: a review of the evidence. *Current Anthropology*, 30(1), 1–26.

Junod, H. A. (1913). *The Life of a South African Tribe. II. The Psychic Life.* Neuchatel: Imprimerie Attinger Freres.

Kimbel, W. H., Johanson, D. C., & Rak, Y. (1997). Systematic assessment of a maxilla of *Homo* from Hadar, Ethiopia. *American Journal of Physical Anthropology*, **103**(2), 235–262.

Klein, R. G. (1977). The mammalian fauna from the Middle and Later Stone Age (Later Pleistocene) levels of Border Cave, Natal Province, South Africa. *South African Archaeological Bulletin*, **32**(125), 14–27.

Klein, R. G. (1999). *The Human Career: Human Biological and Cultural Origins.* Chicago: University of Chicago Press.

Klein, R. G., & Cruz-Uribe, K. (2000). Middle and Later Stone Age larger mammal and tortoise remains from Die Kelders Cave 1, Western Cape Province, South Africa. *Journal of Human Evolution*, **38**, 169–195.

Krige, E. J. (1957). *The Social System of the Zulus.* Pietermaritzburg: Shuter & Shooter.

Lang, A., Thomas, N. W., & Stow, G. W. (1904). Bantu totemism. *Folklore*, **15**(2), 203–205.

Le Roux, A., & Badenhorst, S. (2016). Iron Age fauna from Sibudu Cave in KwaZulu-Natal, South Africa. *Azania: Archaeological Research in Africa*, **51**(3), 307–326.

Le Roux, A., Badenhorst, S., Esterhuysen, A., & Cain, C. (2013). Faunal remains from the 1854 siege of Mugombane, Makapans Valley, South Africa. *Journal of African Archaeology*, **11**(1), 97–110.

Lewis-Williams, D. & Dowson, T. (1989). *Images of Power. Understanding Bushman Rock Art.* Johannesburg: Southern Book Publishers.

Lynch C. D. (1994). The mammals of Lesotho. *Navorsinge van die Nasionale Museum Bloemfontein*, **10**, 177–241.

Macdonald, J. (1892). Bantu customs and legends. *Folklore*, **3**(3), 337–359.

Magoma, M., Badenhorst, S., & Pikirayi, I. (2018). Feasting among Venda-speakers of South Africa: the Late Iron Age fauna from Mutokolwe. *Anthropozoologica*, **53**(17), 195–205.

Marais, E. N. (1938). *Burgers van die berge.* Pretoria: JL van Schaik.

Marais, E. N. (1974). *The Soul of the Ape.* Pretoria: Human & Rousseau.

Marwick, B. A. (1966). *The Swazi. An Ethnographic Account of the Natives of the Swaziland Protectorate.* London: Frank Cass & Co.

Milo, R. G. (1998). Evidence for hominid predation at Klasies River Mouth, South Africa, and its implications for the behaviour of early modern humans. *Journal of Archaeological Science*, **25**(2), 99–133.

Mitchell, P. (2002). *The Archaeology of Southern Africa.* Cape Town: Cambridge University Press.

Mönnig, H. O. (1967). *The Pedi.* Pretoria: J. L. van Schaik.

O'Connell, C. (2007). *The Elephant's Secret Sense. The Hidden Life of the Wild Herds of Africa.* London: Free Press.

Oosthuizen, N. (2018). Baboons: the least loved primates. Available at: https://africageographic.com/blog/baboons-least-loved-primate/. (Accessed 30 May 2019)

Orpen, J. M. (1919). Folklore of the Bushmen. *Folklore*, **30**(2), 139–156.

Pike, N. (1891). The chacma or South African baboon. *Scientific American*, **65**(24), 371–372.

Pfeiffer, J. E. (1969). *The Emergence of Man.* London: Harper & Row, Publishers.

Plug, I. (1987). An analysis of witchdoctor divining sets. *Research by the National Cultural History and Open-Air Museum*, **1**(3), 49–67.

Plug, I. (1992). The macrofaunal remains from Collingham Shelter, a Late Stone Age site in Natal. *Natal Museum Journal of Humanities*, **4**, 53–59.

Plug, I. & Badenhorst, S. (2001). *The Distribution of Macromammals in Southern Africa over the Past 30 000 years as Reflected in Animal Remains from Archaeological Sites.* Transvaal Museum Monograph No. 12. Pretoria: Transvaal Museum.

Plug, I. & Badenhorst, S. (2009). Ethnography and southern African archaeozoology. In G. Grupe, G. McGlynn, & J. Peters, eds., *Tracking Down the Past: Ethnohistory Meets Archaeozoology. Documenta Archaeobiologiae 7.* Rahden/Westf: Verlag Marie Leidorf. 187–201.

Plug I., & Engela, R. (1992). The macrofaunal remains from recent excavations at Rose Cottage Cave, Orange Free State, South Africa. *South African Archaeological Bulletin*, **47**, 16–25.

Plug, I., Mitchell, P., & Bailey, G. (2003). Animal remains from Likoaeng, an open-air river site, and its place in the post-Wilton of Lesotho and eastern Free State, South Africa. *South African Journal of Science*, **99**(3), 143–152.

Quin, P. J. (1959). *Foods and Feeding Habits of the Pedi.* Johannesburg: Witwatersrand University Press.

Raath Antonites, A. & Kruger, N. (2012). A preliminary assessment of animal distribution on a 19th century VhaVenda settlement. *Nyame Akuma*, **77**, 3–10.

Rautenbach, I. L. (1982). *Mammals of the Transvaal*. Pretoria: Ecoplan Monograph No. 1. Ecoplan.

Raven-Hart, R. (1971). *Cape Good Hope 1652-1702. The First Fifty Years of Dutch Colonisation as Seen by Callers*. Cape Town: A. A. Balkema.

Rossouw, S. (2013). Jackie, the baboon mascot of 3 SAI during the Great War, 1914-1918. *Military History Journal*, 16(2), 79-80.

Ryke, P. A. J. (1984). *Dierkunde. 'n Funksionele benadering*. Pretoria: Butterworth.

Sanderson, J. (1860). Memoranda of a trading trip into the Orange River (Sovereignty) Free State, and the country of the Transvaal Boers, 1951-1852. *Journal of the Royal Geographical Society of London*, 30, 233-255.

Schapera, I. (1930). *The Khoisan Peoples of South Africa. Bushmen and Hottentots*. London: George Routledge & Sons.

Schapera, I. & Goodwin, A. J. H. (1953). Work and wealth. In I. Schapera, ed., *The Bantu-Speaking Tribes of South Africa. An Ethnographic Survey*. London: Routledge & Kegan Paul, 131-171.

Schoeman, B. (1973). *Jag-avonture*. Johannesburg: Perskor-Uitgewery.

Schönland, S. (1905). Arts and crafts of the natives of South Africa. *South African Journal of Science*, 3(1), 130-146.

Shortridge, G. C. (1934). *The mammals of South West Africa*. Volume I. London: William Heinemann Ltd.

Silberbauer, G. B. (1965). *Report to the Government of Bechuanaland on the Bushman survey*. Gaberones: Bechuanaland Government.

Silberbauer, G. B. (1981). *Hunter and Habitat in the Central Kalahari Desert*. Cambridge: Cambridge University Press.

Skinner, J. D. & Chimimba, C. T. (2005). *The Mammals of the Southern African Subregion*. Cambridge: Cambridge University Press.

Stayt, H. A. (1968). *The BaVenda*. London: Frank Cass & Co. Ltd.

Steele, T. E. & Klein, R. G. (2013). The Middle and Later Stone Age faunal remains from Diepkloof Rock Shelter, Western Cape, South Africa. *Journal of Archaeological Science*, 40, 3453-3462.

Steininger, C., Berger, L. R., & Kuhn, B. F. (2008). A partial skull of *Paranthropus robustus* from Cooper's Cave, South Africa. *South African Journal of Science*, 104, 143-146.

Steiper, M. E., Young, N. M., & Sukarna, T. Y. (2004). Genomic data support the hominoid slowdown and an Early Oligocene estimate for the hominoid-cercopithecoid divergence. *Proceedings of the National Academy of Sciences of the United States of America*, 101(49), 17021-17026.

Stevenson-Hamilton, J. (1947). *Wild Life in South Africa*. London: Cassell and Company.

Stow, G. W. (1964). *The Native Races of South Africa*. Cape Town: C. Struik.

Thackeray, J. F. (1990). Carnivore activity at Klasies River Mouth: a response to Binford. *Palaeontologia Africana*, 27, 101-109.

Thackeray, J. F. (2003). Comparison of hominid fossils attributed to *Australopithecus* and *Homo*. *South African Journal of Science*, 99, 241-242.

Ungar, P. S., & Grine, F. E. (2006). Diet in early *Homo*: A review of the evidence and a new model of adaptive versatility. *Annual Review of Anthropology*, 35, 208-228.

Val, A., Taru, P., & Steininger, C. (2014). New taphonomic analysis of large-bodied primate assemblage from Cooper's D, Bloubank Valley, South Africa. *South African Archaeological Bulletin*, 69(199), 49-58.

Van der Waal, C. S. (1981). Boukonstruksies van die Venda. *South African Journal of Ethnology*, 4, 15-32.

Van Jaarsveld, F. A. (1971). *Van Van Riebeeck to Verwoerd 1651-1966*. Johannesburg: Voortrekkerpers.

van Lawick-Goodall, H. & van Lawick-Goodall, J. (1970). *Innocent Killers*. London: Collins.

Villmoare, B., Kimbel, W. H., Seyoum, C., et al. (2015). Early *Homo* at 2.8 Ma from Ledi-Geraru, Afar, Ethiopia. *Science*, 347(6228), 1352-1355.

Vinnecombe, P. (1972). Myth, motive, and selection in southern African rock art. *Africa: Journal of the International African Institute*, 42(3), 192-204.

Von Wielligh, G. R. (1919). *Boesman-stories. Deel 1, mitologie en legendes*. Kaapstad: De Nationale Pers.

Whiten, A., Byrne, R. W. & S. P. Henzi. (1987). The behavioural ecology of mountain baboons. *International Journal of Primatology*, 8, 367-387.

Willoughby, W. C. (1905). Notes on the totemism of the Becwana. *Journal of the Anthropological Institute of Great Britain and Ireland*, 35, 295-314.

Wolhuter, H. (1967). *Memories of a Game-Ranger*. Johannesburg: Wild Life Protection and Conservation Society of South Africa.

Zingg, R. M. (1940). More about the "baboon boy" of South Africa. *American Journal of Psychology*, 53(3), 455-462.

15 Lemur Hunting in Madagascar's Present and Past

The Case of *Pachylemur*

Natalie Vasey & Laurie R. Godfrey

Fihazana ny gidro tamin'ny fotoana taloha sy ankehitriny ao Madagasikara: Mahakasika manokana ny *Pachylemur*

Famintinana

Pachylemur dia gidro iray efa lany tamingana izay niparitaka be teto Madagasikara ary velona hatramin'ny 500 taona lasa izay. Mbola miteraka adihevitra lehibe momba ny andraikitry ny olombelona amin'ny fanjavonan'ny biby lehibe an'i Madagasikara. Eto izahay dia manombatombana ny fiantraikan'ny olombelona nalaina avy tamin'ny fikarohana momba ny fihazana lemur ankehitriny miaraka amin'ny porofo avy amin'ny tantara am-bava an'i Madagascar ary koa ireo firaketana arkeolojika sy paleontolojika. Ny gidro velona dia hazaina manerana an'i Madagasikara, indrindra eo amin'ny hahazoana fivelomana ary hamidy mba hampidi-bola. Ny fahantrana sy ny tsy fahampiantsakafo no mitarika fihinanana bibidia. Ny sata miaro, ny fady eo amin'ny fihinana ny bibidia, ary ny safidin'ny hena any an-toerana dia toa tsy ampy hanampiana ny fiarovana ny ankamaroan'ny taxa gidro tsy ho lany tamingana nohon'ny taha-mpamokarana misy any amin'ny faritra Makira, raha tsy any an-kafa. Ny fanazavana tokana amin'ny fahalanian-tamingan'ireo biby lehibe, toy ny famonoana haingana na ny fiovan'ny toetrandro, dia tsy ampy. Niara-niaina nandritran'ny fotoana maharitra ny olombelona sy ny *Pachylemur* teto Madagasikara. Tsy nisy haintany nanerana ny Nosy rehefa nanomboka ringana ny biby lehibe tokony ho 1200 taona lasa izay; ny faritra sasany eto madagasikara dia mando ary ny hafa kosa maina. Ny "isotope" maritoeran'ny azota (δ^{15}N) ho an'ny taolan'ny *Pachylemur* nodatina tamin'ny radiocarbon dia tsy mampiseho porofo koa fa ny hain-tany dia nandray anjara tamin'ny fahafatesany. Taolana *Pachylemur* avy any amin'ny toeranm-pikaroana palezaolojika Tsirave dia mitombo isa maherin'ny 1 000 taona lasa izay, maneho ny fitrandrahana maharitra mandritra ny ~ 100 taona. *Pachylemur* dia misy toetra maro hitovizany tamin'ny havany akaiky indrindra, ny gidro miovaova (*Varecia*), anisan'izany ny ireo izay mihinana voankazo. Ny tantaram-bavan'ny biby heverina fa *Pachylemur* dia nonina tao amin'ireo ala misy hazo lehibe indrindra izy ary naneho fihetsika fanoherana mahery setra. Toa an'i *Varecia*, *Pachylemur* dia azo inoana fa niankina tanteraka tamin'ny hazo mamokatra voakazo ary manaparitaka tsara ny voankazo, ary mety hoan'ny fananahana koa (ohatra: mametraka akany ary mitahiry ny biby izay efa tsy mifikitra amin'ny reniny), izay mahatonga azy io ho mora tohina indrindra amin'ny fahasimban'ny toeram-ponenana. Noho izany dia namintina izahay fa ny fahasimban'ny toeram-ponenana sy ny fihazana dia samy nandray anjara tamin'ny famongorana an'i *Pachylemur*.

Teny fanalahidy

Bushmeat – gidro – lany tamingana – *Pachylemur* – *Varecia* – subfossiles

Abstract

Pachylemur is a large extinct lemur once widespread on Madagascar that survived in pockets until at least 500 years ago. The role of humans as agents of megafaunal extinction on Madagascar is heavily debated. Here we evaluate human impacts drawing from research on lemur hunting today combined with evidence from

Madagascar's oral history as well as its archaeological and paleontological records. Living lemurs are hunted throughout Madagascar, primarily for subsistence but also for commercial trade. Wildlife consumption is driven primarily by poverty and resultant food insecurity. Protected status, wildlife consumption taboos, and broad preference for domestic meats appear insufficient to buffer most lemur taxa from extinction at current harvest rates in the Makira region, if not elsewhere. Single-factor explanations for megafaunal extinction, such as rapid overkill or climate change, are not viable. There was long temporal overlap for *Pachylemur* and humans on Madagascar. There was no island-wide drought when the megafauna began to crash around 1,200 years ago; some parts of Madagascar were unusually wet while others were unusually dry. Stable isotope ($\delta^{15}N$) values for radiocarbon-dated *Pachylemur* bones also show no evidence that aridification contributed to its demise. Butchered bones of *Pachylemur* from the paleontological site Tsirave spike in frequency just over 1,000 years ago, indicative of sustained exploitation over a ~100-year period. *Pachylemur* shared many traits with its closest living relative, variegated lemurs (*Varecia*), including frugivory. Oral histories of an animal presumed to be *Pachylemur* indicate it dwelt in the largest trees in the forest, was active at twilight, and exhibited highly aggressive antipredator behavior. Like *Varecia*, *Pachylemur* was likely dependent on large, patchily distributed trees for fruit, and possibly also for reproduction (e.g. to nest and stash non-clinging young), making it especially vulnerable to habitat degradation. We thus conclude that both habitat degradation and hunting played a role in the extinction of *Pachylemur*.

Key words Bushmeat, Lemurs, Extinction, *Pachylemur*, *Varecia*, Subfossils

15.1   Introduction: The Role of Humans as Agents of Megafaunal Extinction

In 2015, Radimilahy and Crossland reviewed the archaeological history of Madagascar, including evidence of early encounters of humans with now-extinct species. Since then, new data have emerged, provoking renewed debate over the time of initial arrival of humans to Madagascar. Some have argued that humans arrived over 10,000 years ago (Godfrey et al., 2019; Hansford et al., 2018), others by at least 2,000 years ago (Douglass et al., 2019a; Pierron et al., 2017; Wang et al., 2019), and still others not until ~1,500 years ago or later (Anderson et al., 2018; Mitchell, 2020). Debate also centers around the role of humans as agents of megafaunal extinction and how this relates to the timing of human arrival. For example, Godfrey et al. (2019) and Hansford et al. (2018) both argue that humans arrived early, but that early human populations had little or no impact on the megafauna: the megafaunal collapse occurred much later.

Some of the most provocative data come not from archaeological sites but from sites that yield paleontological and paleoecological (including paleohydrological) data, but no single record taken alone establishes a major role for humans as agents

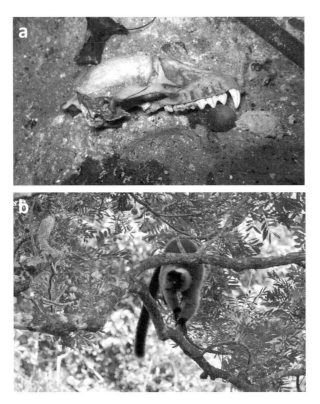

Figure 15.1 (a) *Pachylemur insignis* skull under water at Vintany Cave, Tsimanampesotse National Park, southwest Madagascar, 2016. Photograph by Barry Coleman. (b) *Varecia rubra* photographed from the forest canopy, Andranobe Forest, Masoala National Park, Madagascar, 2009. Photograph by Natalie Vasey.

of megafaunal extinction on Madagascar. Taken together, however, and in the context of understanding wild animal hunting on Madagascar today, an interesting, though complex, picture emerges. Here we focus on one extinct lemur, *Pachylemur* (Fig. 15.1a), an animal that may have survived in pockets on Madagascar until very recently, and for which clear evidence of butchery by humans occurs in the fossil record. *Pachylemur* was widespread across the island, large-bodied, and frugivorous, and presumably an important disperser of large seeds. We begin by reviewing wild animal hunting as part of the broader economy in Madagascar and continue by examining evidence from Madagascar's oral history as well as its archaeological and paleontological records.

15.2   Hunting Wild Animals as an Integral Part of the Human Diet in Madagascar

Irrespective of the debate over whether or not humans played a primary role in the extinction of Madagascar's megafauna and the impact of hunting (as opposed to

Makira

Masoala Peninsula

Figure 15.2 *Pachylemur* subfossil sites on Madagascar. White circles represent individual subfossil sites with *Pachylemur*; white star represents the subfossil site of Tsirave. The Masoala Peninsula and the Makira region are labeled; extensive research on the ecology, behavior, reproduction, and bushmeat hunting of *Varecia* have taken place in these regions.

other human activities) on large-bodied endemic species, it is certain that humans hunt lemurs and other wild animals in Madagascar today. From this standpoint, the debate over whether humans hunted lemurs in the remote past can appear belabored. We therefore begin by providing background on the hunting of lemurs today, particularly those that are the closest extant relatives of *Pachylemur*, that is, the variegated lemurs (*Varecia* spp.) (Fig. 15.1b). Variegated lemurs occur in the Makira region and on the Masoala Peninsula (Fig. 15.2) as well as in other rain forests in eastern Madagascar, although the subfossil record reveals they were previously much more widespread (Burney et al., 2020). They likely shared a host of ecological, behavioral, and reproductive characteristics with *Pachylemur*.

Madagascar today has an economy dominated by agropastoralism, but where hunting of wild animals is also routine. The vast majority of its people are rural; they grow rice and raise livestock, supplementing these with wild and other domesticated or cultivated foods. During the French colonial period, Decary (1939), administrative head of colonies, wrote at length about hunting and trapping of wild animals among native Malagasy, echoing the observations of Flacourt (1661) before him. Decary enumerated the wild animal species that were hunted, described and illustrated snares and other implements used for hunting, and even summarized motives: "The Malagasy do not take up hunting for pleasure or sport; above all they view this work as utilitarian which they carry out moreover to get rid of animals that are a nuisance (wild boar, crocodiles) as well as to obtain needed meaty nourishment (tenrecs, birds, bats) or to increase their herds (wild cattle)" (p. 3). The first section of Decary's article describes methods used to hunt lemurs, prefaced by an acknowledgment of how easy it is to extirpate them. After the colonial era, the hunting of wild animals in Madagascar became governed by a legal framework which classifies species as protected, game, or nuisance (Rakotoarivelo et al., 2011). "Protected" species cannot be killed or collected; "game" species can be hunted during a defined season for subsistence as long as certain methods are avoided; and "pest" species can be killed at any time by anyone.

From the late 1980s onward the Malagasy government began allowing wildlife researchers into the country after nearly two decades of limited interchange with the West following independence. Behavioral, ecological, and phylogenetic studies of lemurs and other wildlife flourished, much of it in the service of conservation. As a by-product, a considerable number of records concerning hunting and consumption of wild animals were published. Table 15.1 summarizes many of these early records for lemurs, documenting that they were being hunted throughout Madagascar despite being classified as protected. These records relied on interviews or bodily remains and spurred development of more systematic study, which began with the work of Golden (2009). Recent research on bushmeat hunting in Madagascar draws on a wide range of methodological approaches and incorporates conservation objectives as well as human livelihoods. Some of the current methods used to study wildlife hunting in Madagascar include structured household interviews, daily diet diaries, human health monitoring, interviews and observation of hunters, and direct recording by local monitors of bushmeat passing through villages and towns (e.g. Borgerson, 2015, 2016; Borgerson et al., 2016, 2018; Golden, 2009; Golden et al., 2011, 2013; Jenkins et al, 2011; Randrianandrianina et al., 2010; Razafimanahaka et al., 2012; Reuter et al., 2016a, 2016b).

Wild animals are hunted for two reasons, first for subsistence, to be consumed primarily by the hunters' households, and second for commercial trade. A prominent example of subsistence hunting comes from the Makira region in northeastern Madagascar where 98% of consumed wildlife was collected by the hunter and his family and the remaining 2% was purchased (Golden et al., 2014). In a village on the Masoala Peninsula (also in northeastern Madagascar), lemur trappers consumed all of the lemurs they had trapped; none were sold (Borgerson et al., 2016). A focal hunter did sell 24% (by biomass) of bush pig during the study year as this is the largest forest mammal, too large for his family alone to consume (Borgerson, 2016). The village lacked electricity and refrigeration, as do many villages throughout Madagascar. In contrast to these prominent examples of subsistence hunting, Reuter et al. (2016a) document that transport and trade of wild meats in

Table 15.1 Records of lemur hunting (1995–2008) prior to systematic bushmeat research

Species	Location	Type of record	Reference
Daubentonia madagascariensis	Near Marojejy National Park (NE)	Bodily remains	Glaw et al. (2008)
Daubentonia madagascariensis	Near Ambanja village (N)	Bodily remains	Koenig and Zavasoa (2008)
Hapalemur occidentalis	Near Masoala National Park (NE)	Interviews	Martinez (2008)
Eulemur albifrons	Makira Natural Park (NE)	Interviews	Patel and Andrianandrasana (2008)
Varecia rubra *Varecia variegata subcincta*	Makira Natural Park (NE)	Interviews	Hekkala et al. (2007)
Lemur catta	Andohahela National Park (SE)	Bodily remains	Moniac and Heitman (2007)
Propithecus edwardsi *Varecia variegata variegata*	Fandriana Marolambo corridor (SE)	Interviews	Lehman et al. (2006)
Daubentonia madagascariensis	Near Betomendry village (NW)	Bodily remains	Koenig (2005)
Eulemur albifrons *Eulemur rubriventer* *Propithecus candidus*	Marojejy National Park (NE)	Interviews Bodily remains	Patel et al. (2005)
Eulemur rufifrons *Lemur catta* *Lepilemur ruficaudatus* *Propithecus verreauxi*	Kirindy-Mite National Park (SW)	Interviews Skeletal remains	Goodman and Raselimanana (2003)
Avahi occidentalis *Eulemur fulvus* *Lepilemur edwardsi* *Propithecus coquereli*	Ankarafantsika National Park (NW)	Skeletal remains	Garcia and Goodman (2003)
Lepilemur mustelinus *Propithecus edwardsi* *Varecia variegata variegata*	Fandriana Marolambo corridor (SE)	Interviews	Lehman and Ratsimabazafy (2001)
Daubentonia madagascariensis	Anjimangirana (NW - eaten); Various other sites – killed, not eaten	Interviews	Simons and Meyers (1991)
Eulemur coronatus *Eulemur sanfordi* *Lepilemur ankaranensis*	Daraina Forest fragments (N)	Interviews	Randrianarisoa et al. (1999)
Eulemur albifrons	Marojejy National Park (NE)	Interviews	Duckworth et al. (1995)

Madagascar is often formalized (i.e., commercial), though hunting usually is not. Across a multitude of study locations between Antananarivo (central Madagascar) and Antsiranana (far north), both urban and rural people purchased a substantial proportion of the wild meat they consumed through third parties, though the majority was obtained for free by hunting or as gifts. Furthermore, a significant proportion of these wild animals were moved long distances using the intercity transit system and then sold at wild meat selling establishments, including market stalls and restaurants (Reuter et al., 2016a).

In some rural areas hunting is carried out primarily opportunistically during the course of other activities based around forest use. For example, in Ranobe in southwestern Madagascar, most villagers are farmers who have little time or reason to enter the forest regularly, but when they do they take a slingshot and a knife, and are thus prepared to capture animals to supplement their diet. Only a few individuals in Ranobe hunt regularly to generate an income; all of them have little land and are therefore unable to derive a livelihood through farming (Gardner & Davies, 2014). Similarly, at Ankarafantsika National Park in northwestern Madagascar, villagers feed on forest animals while collecting raffia palm (*Raffia farinara*). Raffia (used for weaving, building, and food) is harvested seasonally from forest-based camps. Rice is the only food brought to the forest and additional sustenance is obtained from hunting forest animals. At one such camp, butchered lemur skeletal remains were the most abundant based upon estimated minimum number of individuals (Garcia & Goodman, 2003).

In other rural areas, targeted hunting of wild animals is much more common. This is so in regions occupied by *Pachylemur*'s smaller-bodied relatives, *Varecia rubra* on the Masoala Peninsula and *Varecia variegata* in Makira. Here hunting may be targeted (e.g. using snares), opportunistic (e.g. using sling shots, rocks, or sticks), or incidental (i.e. by-catch). In one particular village on Masoala, 75% of households had hunted forest mammals and 22% had intentionally trapped lemurs in the year prior to the study. Thirty three percent of households reported having caught a lemur in the prior year and 26% of village men trapped lemurs (Borgerson et al., 2016). In a study involving over 600 households bordering Masoala National Park (13 villages) and Makira Natural Park (26 villages), 16% of households hunted bats, 23% hunted bush pigs, 40% hunted carnivores, 49% hunted lemurs, and 91% hunted tenrecids (Golden et al., 2014).

The methods used to trap lemurs in Decary's day, such as snare traps set within *laly*, are still in use today (Borgerson, 2015; Decary, 1939; Golden, 2009). A *laly* is a swath of cleared forest, either linear or circular, which lemurs cross via horizontally-placed "bridges" made of saplings on which snares are built. Unlike trapping sites for other forest mammals, *laly* are owned by the hunters who clear the land. Surrounding one small village on Masoala containing 36 households, there were 73 *laly* (Borgerson, 2015). One hunter owned 14 of these but used only three in the study year. Hunters rotate use of *laly* from year to year, pausing use when lemurs are depleted and the *laly* goes "fallow". They select *laly* to re establish the next year based on number of years since previous use and number of lemurs observed in the area. Hunters know their wild prey well and this knowledge dictates when and how they hunt particular types of prey in order to maximize catch. For example, on the Masoala Peninsula *Varecia rubra* and *Eulemur albifrons* are hunted primarily in the austral winter (Mar–Aug) when they are fatter and when their primary food trees are especially large. These trees can be isolated within circular *laly* laden with snare traps (Borgerson, 2016).

Although the number of households that hunt and consume wild animals can be considerable in any given rural area, terrestrial wild animals typically contribute a relatively small proportion of animal protein to the overall diet. For example, in the Aloatra-Mangoro region of eastern Madagascar, most meals (74.5%) contained no meat, 11.8% contained protein from domestic animals, and 13.7% contained protein from wild-caught animals (Jenkins et al., 2011). Most of the latter consisted of fish and invertebrates. Just 1.3% of meals were from terrestrial wild animals and just 0.5% included meat from legally protected species. During a year-long study in one village on the Masoala Peninsula, villagers ate just over one meal containing meat (wild or domestic) per day ($1.29 \pm$ SD 0.19) (Borgerson, 2016). During the austral summer more animal protein was consumed with 89% of meals containing fish, 9% domestic animals, and 2% forest mammals. The two most commonly eaten forest mammals in terms of number of individuals were tenrecs (36%) and lemurs (26%), and in terms of biomass, bushpigs (65%) and lemurs (13%). In the austral winter proportionally more bushpigs, tenrecs, and lemurs were consumed as they are targeted at this time of year.

Even though wild terrestrial animals contribute a relatively small proportion of animal protein to the overall diet, these animals are broadly consumed; that is, many people eat them. Golden and colleagues working in the Makira region found hunting of lemurs to be unsustainable while acknowledging that removing this source of animal protein, whether through wildlife depletion via overhunting or through legal intervention, would diminish health and livelihoods of the local population (Golden, 2009; Golden et al., 2011). Jenkins et al. (2011), working in the Aloatra-Mangoro region, found that 95% of individuals reported having eaten protected species at some point in their lives and 44.5% had eaten 10 or more legally protected species over their lifetime. Likewise, in a village on the Masoala Peninsula 89% of households had consumed lemurs during their lifetime and 36% had eaten them during the prior year (Borgerson et al., 2016). Local extirpation of lemur species has been documented in recent decades in connection with this broad, shallow pattern of consumption (e.g. Gardner & Davies, 2014).

From the various bushmeat studies cited above, it is clear that wild animals are hunted throughout Madagascar irrespective of protected status. Endangered taxa are sometimes sheltered from exploitation by taboos, known as *fady* in Malagasy (referring to a system of ritualized regulation obeyed by individuals or families for moral or spiritual reasons). However, some have suggested that traditional taboos against hunting certain wild species (e.g. *Indri*) may be breaking down due to rapid social change, such as migration associated with artisanal goldmining (Jenkins et al., 2011; Jones et al., 2008). But as Golden and Comaroff (2015) note, "Madagascar is no stranger to massive religious, economic, and social transformation," and based on protracted study near Makira Natural Park, they find erosion of wildlife consumption taboos to be more complex and to occur at low rates, if at all, mediated differentially by migration, modernization, and the spread of Western religion. Whether taboos buffer wildlife extinctions or not, domestic meats are preferred over wild meats in many parts of Madagascar (Gardner & Davies, 2014; Jenkins et al., 2011; Merson et al., 2019; Randrianandrianina et al., 2010; Reuter et al., 2016b).

In light of the above factors we are impelled to ask why lemurs and other endangered species are hunted, both in the present and the past. Taking the remote Masoala Peninsula in northeastern Madagascar as an example once again, factors that appear primarily responsible for lemur hunting today are poverty, poor health, and child malnutrition. Knowledge of laws prohibiting lemur hunting has no appreciable impact, nor does level of education, involvement in ecotourism, traditional cultural values, taste preferences, opportunism, or human–wildlife conflict (Borgerson et al., 2016). In other regions of Madagascar poverty and resultant food insecurity also drive consumption of protected species (Borgerson et al., 2018; Golden et al., 2011, 2014; Jenkins et al., 2011; Merson et al., 2019; Reuter et al., 2016b). Population viability analysis incorporating hunting rates of lemurs in Makira Natural Park show that harvest rates are unsustainable (Brook et al., 2019). While we lack the information required to conduct population viability analyses for extinct lemurs, oral histories and the archaeological and paleontological record provide evidence concerning when and why *Pachylemur* went extinct.

15.3 Extinct Animals, including *Pachylemur*, Appear in the Oral History of Madagascar

There are numerous stories of hippopotamuses in ethnohistoric records and folklore of Madagascar (e.g. Burney & Ramilisonina, 1998; Dandouau, 1922; Godfrey, 1986), some of which involve killing. Stories of giant lemurs are less common, but they occur. Etienne de Flacourt (1661) recorded the existence of a large lemur called the *tretretretre* that purportedly still lived in the late 1600s in the region of Fort Dauphin (Tolognaro). This animal appears to match the sloth-like *Palaeopropithecus* (Mahé & Sourdat, 1972; Godfrey & Jungers, 2003). Other tales of giant lemurs describe different taxa, probably *Archaeolemur* (Burney & Ramilisonina, 1998) and *Pachylemur*. The latter is connected with tales of the *kisoala*, which translates literally to "knife of the forest." Descriptions of this animal were recorded by C. Borgerson (pers. comm.) on the Masoala Peninsula in northeastern Madagascar in 2011 and 2012.

On August 1, 2011, Borgerson interviewed eight male trappers each of whom was over the age of 60 at the time. Each had heard of the *kisoala*, but none had seen it. They said that it dwells in the largest of trees, and is too big to use the small peripheral branches. It climbs to the top, where it sleeps until foraging begins at dusk. Its claws are sharp and its call as loud as thunder; this is why the animal is called *kisoala* (*kiso* = knife, *ala* = forest). One of the trappers made a sound like a long continual "kiiiiiiiiiiiing" while everyone else nodded and affirmed "like a knife." They knew three men from the next village to the north, now deceased, who had long ago seen the animal in the interior of the forest when they were collecting *bilahy* bark. These men had encountered the animal in the dark; they were frightened so they ran and hid. The next day they searched for the *kisoala*, at first unsuccessfully, so they put a hat on a spear, sharp end up, to mark the place of their sighting. When they returned later that evening, they found the *kisoala* skewered on the weapon. It had mistaken the hat for a person, and had impaled itself by jumping onto the hat. The trappers claimed that the animal was much larger than *Varecia rubra* and had larger, more pointy ears. Most said it was greyish-black, and some noted that its fur reddened toward the hands and tail. Its arms and legs were roughly equal in length. They added that there was, still living, an old man who had seen the *kisoala*. His hamlet was about a week's walk from the trappers' village.

On January 31, 2012, Borgerson visited the old man, who affirmed that he had indeed seen a *kisoala*. Pointing to some mountains above his hamlet, he said the big lemur used to live there. It had red eyes and a call so loud that it hurts your ears (like a machete hitting metal). It would sleep high in the canopy during the day and forage at dusk. The old man said he had seen the animal around 10 years earlier, maybe more (his family suspected that it had been at least 40 years). One morning, when he went to the forest to check his *laly*, he was surprised to see that it had snared a big quadrupedal lemur, much bigger than *Varecia* – approximately the size of a fosa (*Cryptoprocta ferox*) or slightly larger (ca. 9 kg). The animal's fur was *maintikintina* (blackish with light specks). He suspected the animal had only just been caught, as it was actively trying to escape. Terrified and amazed that a trap so small could snare the leg of an animal this big, the man ran away. When he returned, the animal was gone and the area around the trap was torn up. He never saw the *kisoala* again and stated that he never again wanted to.

15.4   Parallels between *Pachylemur* and Its Close Phylogenetic Relative *Varecia*

Pachylemur was the largest member of the family Lemuridae (11.5–13.4 kg, Jungers et al., 2008) and is widely recognized by paleoanthropologists as having been an arboreal frugivore (Federman et al., 2016; Godfrey et al., 2008, 2012). It was probably the most important disperser of large seeds on Madagascar (Richard & Dewar, 1991). It would have been less destructive to seeds than *Archaeolemur* spp. or *Daubentonia robusta*, frugivorous extinct lemurs with clear morphological specializations for seed predation (e.g. Godfrey et al., 2004, 2008, 2012). In contrast to extant indriids (e.g. sifakas), extant lemurids such as *Varecia* and *Eulemur* tend to swallow medium or large seeds whole or with minimal damage, and seeds passing through their guts have high germination success (Dew & Wright, 1998). These two lemur genera are Madagascar's most effective extant dispersers of medium or large seeds. At three times the body mass of *V. rubra* (2.1–3.6 kg, Dutton et al., 2008; Vasey, 2003) and *V. variegata* (2.5–4.8 kg, Baden et al., 2008), *Pachylemur* would have been able to disperse even larger seeds.

Pachylemur traits relayed in the above oral histories suggest that this animal resembled *Varecia* in its pelage coloration and aspects of its ecology, behavior, and reproduction. *Pachylemur* evidently shared *Varecia*'s tri-color pelage (red, black, and grey in *Pachylemur*/white in *Varecia*) and dwelled high in the canopy in the largest trees, as do *Varecia* who spend the majority of their time in mid-to-upper forest strata of (Vasey, Baden & Ratsimbazafy, 2022 and refs. therein). *Varecia* has an unusual suite of reproductive traits given its relatively large size and predominantly diurnal activity pattern, including the bearing of litters, nesting of altricial young, and an absentee parenting system (i.e. oral transport of young combined with infant stashing) (Vasey, 2007). On Masoala, trees selected for nesting and stashing young (x = 40 per litter) are the largest in the forest, even larger than those used for feeding (Vasey et al., 2018).

A prominent feature of the oral histories relayed above is the description of *Pachylemur*'s loud calls, which likewise distinguish variegated lemurs. *Varecia*'s "roar-shriek" chorus is a group advertisement call that likely facilitates dispersed intracommunity communication within large home ranges amid a fission–fusion social system (Vasey, 2000, 2007). Their highly aggressive antipredator behavior consists of mobbing accompanied by alarm calls that continue long after the stimulus (i.e., predator) has departed. Ground predators evoke "pulsed squawks" and aerial predators evoke "abrupt roars." In captive observations that included experiments employing live raptors, live mammals, and decoys, *Varecia* routinely approached, lunged at, and at times even pounced upon or struck these perceived threats during antipredator displays (Macedonia, 1993). These confrontational antipredator tactics are reflected in the trappers' tale of the *kisoala* dropping onto a spear covered by a hat. If *Pachylemur* shared *Varecia*'s suite of reproductive traits and if any of its loud calls were part of an antipredator display, then these confrontational tactics could be interpreted not only as an effect of large body size, but also as a consequence of bearing sessile young bound to nest and stash sites, which would prevent caregivers from fleeing predators without risking reproductive loss, as proposed for *Varecia* (Macedonia, 1993).

Pachylemur and *Varecia* shared a daily rhythm involving foraging at dusk. In the morning and late in the day *V. rubra* shows bimodal peaks in time spent feeding and traveling with rest predominating midday. For reproductive females these peaks grow significant during the four-month lactation period (Vasey, 2005). Aside from sharing a daily feeding rhythm near dusk, *Pachylemur* and *Varecia* appear, at first, to have had different activity patterns. The trappers' stories suggest *Pachylemur* was cathemeral (or nocturnal), whereas *Varecia* are primarily diurnal (e.g. Vasey, 2000, 2003 and refs. therein). In cathemeral species daily routines are performed under all light conditions, throughout the 24h light/dark cycle (Halle, 2006). Among arboreal mammals, small and large body sizes are closely associated with nocturnality and diurnality, respectively (Charles-Dominique, 1975). Therefore a fully nocturnal active-period would be unlikely in a large-bodied arboreal primate such as *Pachylemur*, especially when contrasted with the predominantly diurnal niche of its smaller-bodied relative *Varecia*. However, one of us (N.V.) has observed sporadic nocturnal activity in *V. rubra* over the course of many field seasons on Masoala (loud calls and travel). Low levels of night-time activity also characterize captive *Varecia*

(Bray et al., 2017; Rea et al., 2014). Thus, cathemerality may very well be facultative in *Varecia*. And presumably the shared common ancestor of *Varecia* and *Pachylemur* would also have been facultatively cathemeral, in common with most extant lemurids (Curtis & Rasmussen, 2006; Tattersall, 2008).

Anatomical inference adds further insight concerning activity pattern reconstruction. As in other large subfossil lemurs, *Pachylemur*'s small orbital diameter signals diurnal activity, whether scaled relative to body size (Jungers et al. 2002) or its proxy – skull length (Martin 1990; Walker 1967). However, in contrast to similarly sized diurnal anthropoids (e.g. African apes), the subfossil lemurs appear to have had small optic canals, indicating comparatively low visual acuity under well-lit (i.e. diurnal) conditions (Jungers et al., 2002). An expanded interpretation, prompted by the twilight activity reported by the trappers, is that small optic canals underlie an adaptation among the large subfossil lemurs to *retain* visual sensitivity for activity in dim light. Small optic canals (a proxy for optic nerve size) indicate high retinal summation, an adaptation to low light levels. In retinas with high summation, there is typically a higher proportion of rod photoreceptor cells (linked to nighttime vision) versus cone photoreceptor cells (linked to daytime/color vision). Whereas each individual cone typically connects with a single nerve ganglion cell, several rods normally connect to one nerve ganglion (i.e., they undergo summation), which narrows the width of the fibers that form the optic nerve. This visual system configuration, a compromise, would have served *Pachylemur* well during both daytime and nighttime activity. We therefore conclude, based on both behavior and anatomy, that *Pachylemur*, like *Varecia*, was facultatively cathemeral.

15.5   When Did *Pachylemur* Go Extinct?

Pachylemur is known from virtually every part of Madagascar where extinct lemurs have been found, including, most recently, the northwest (Beanka) (Burney et al., 2020). We know from radiocarbon records compiled by Crowley (2010) that *Pachylemur* was geographically widespread and that it survived until at least ~1,000 years ago across most of Madagascar. It was present on the west coast at Andolonomby (1295 cal yr BP [calibrated years before present]) and in central Madagascar at Ampasambazimba (1178 cal yr BP). At Tsirave in south central Madagascar, it lived for several hundred years into the last millennium (Fig. 15.2). Indeed, there is indirect evidence of its survival, in pockets, until at least 500 years ago (Muldoon, 2010). Radiocarbon dates on *Megaladapis* and *Palaeopropithecus* from Ankilitelo Cave in southwest Madagascar cluster around this time, and Muldoon (2010) infers that the entire community of extinct lemurs whose bones were found in this cave may date to this period. That community included *Pachylemur*. On the basis of the small mammals also found there, Muldoon (2010) reconstructed the region as semiarid 500 years ago, not very different from today. *Pachylemur* was among the last survivors of the megafauna. Thus, even if humans arrived as recently as 1,500 years ago, and certainly if they arrived earlier, we can infer long temporal overlap for *Pachylemur* and humans on Madagascar.

15.6   Why Did *Pachylemur* Disappear?

Various mechanisms have been posited for the demise of the megafauna of Madagascar. At one extreme lies the notion that the megafauna were hunted to extinction shortly after humans arrived (the blitzkrieg overkill hypothesis; Walker, 1967); at the other lies the notion that the megafauna succumbed to an island-wide drought that peaked ~1,000 to 950 years ago (Virah-Sawmy et al., 2010). The megafaunal crash peaked several hundred years earlier than this (Godfrey et al., 2019), thus *before* the proposed peak drought and *after* the arrival of humans – perhaps up to 9,000 years later (Hansford et al., 2018, 2020). Many species survived in small pockets for centuries following this initial, precipitous decline. If the megafaunal populations collapsed well after humans arrived, then any blitzkrieg model of rapid overkill is not viable.

But climate change is also a weak explanation of megafaunal decline and extinction on Madagascar. Recent paleoclimatological research has clarified two things: first, there have been major changes in hydroclimate since the Last Glacial Maximum (LGM) ~21,000 years ago (e.g. Scroxton et al., 2019) without negative consequences for megafauna; and second, that there was no island-wide drought ~1,000 years ago (Faina et al., 2021). Megafauna disappeared in regions that were both wet and dry, regardless of the local rainfall amount.

We are beginning to understand regional differences in hydroclimate during the Holocene. In northwestern Madagascar there is evidence of an early Holocene wet event (~8,200 years ago), coinciding with a wet period on the African mainland, and an extended mid-Holocene dry event (Voarintsoa et al., 2017; Wang et al., 2019). There was little exceptional about the rest of the record in the northwest, although there were wet/dry fluctuations and several small wet peaks at the time of the Little Ice Age of the northern hemisphere (Scroxton et al., 2017).

Other parts of Madagascar are less well-studied than the northwest, although the record for the southwest from the LGM onward is currently being analyzed in great detail (Dawson et al., 2020). This is the driest part of Madagascar, and the region most likely to suffer in the event of a severe drought. We know that as temperatures rose during the deglaciation period (post LGM) in the southwest, there were fluctuating wet and dry periods prior to the beginning of the Holocene (Scroxton et al., 2019). We also know that there was a prolonged drought during the late Holocene, beginning between 1,500 and 1,600 years ago and lasting 700 years. This drought appears to have impacted local plants and animals. However, it primarily affected the biota of the coastal region, some of which survived the drought by moving elsewhere (Faina et al., 2021).

Stalagmites from the northwest provide no evidence of a simultaneous late Holocene drought. A dramatic shift in regional vegetation from C3 woodland to C4 savannah did occur in northwest Madagascar at ~ 1,100 years ago, but this was during the wettest interval of the past 1,700 years in that region (Burns et al., 2016; Scroxton et al., 2017) and it occurred at around the time of the megafaunal collapse. The mid-Holocene drought ~4,000 years ago does not appear to have had any important negative impact on the megafauna, and the significant drought beginning ~1,600 years ago in the southwest appears to have had only local effects on the large-bodied animals (Faina et al., 2021), without ultimately causing their extinction.

Stable isotope (δ^{15}N) values for radiocarbon-dated subfossil lemur bones also cast doubt on a major role for climate change in giant lemur extinction. Controlling for diet and salinity, δ^{15}N values in bone are correlated with habitat moisture; higher values occur in drier habitats. If increasing aridity were responsible for megafaunal decline, we would expect an island-wide increase in δ^{15}N values culminating in the highest values at the time of proposed maximum drought at ~1,000 years ago. Nitrogen isotope data are available for different taxa, so that each can be tracked independently, assuring that differences in diet do not confound the habitat moisture signal. Trends over time were tested for *Pachylemur* between 7,730 cal yr BP and 1,175 cal yr BP in the Central Highlands, and between 3,800 cal yr BP and 1,010 cal yr BP in the southwest (Crowley et al., 2017). Crowley et al. (2017) found no change in subfossil nitrogen isotope values in the more arid parts of Madagascar and a significant change (p = 0.004) in nitrogen values in the Central Highlands (but getting wetter over time!). Hixon et al. (2018) went one step further, examining δ^{15}N for specific amino acids rather than bulk collagen δ^{15}N values at a single site in south central Madagascar, Tsirave, from ~3,800 cal yr BP to ~800 cal yr BP. Specific amino acids provide better proxies for habitat aridity than bulk values, given the possible influence of variation in diet on the latter. These data also demonstrated no evidence that aridification contributed to the demise of *Pachylemur*. In summary, we cannot rule out climate as a factor impacting the megafauna of Madagascar, but it is unlikely to have had a major effect.

If climate change did not trigger the decline of megafaunal populations, then humans must have, even if blitzkrieg can be ruled out. Hints concerning what must have happened come from both archaeological and paleontological sites (Table 15.2). The earliest archaeological sites suggest that diverse economies existed, some of which (such as coastal fishing) depended minimally or not at all on exploitation of megafauna (Douglass et al., 2018). Elephant bird eggshells have been found in archaeological context at Tony, Velondiake on the coast of western Madagascar (Douglass et al., 2019a) but the middens contain no bones of megafauna. The earliest archaeological site where megafaunal bones have been found in clear archaeological context is Anja Cave in northern Madagascar (Douglass et al., 2019a; Table 15.2). The archaeological record also suggests that by 1,000 years ago, introduced domesticated animals had become primary sources of animal protein at sedentary sites. Megafaunal remains have not been found at large settlement sites such as Mahilaka in northwestern Madagascar, where urbanization grew as a product of an expanding Indian Ocean trade economy (Radimilahy, 1998).

No *Pachylemur* bones have been reported at archaeological sites. In contrast, as stated above, butchered bones of *Pachylemur* have been reported at a paleontological site, Tsirave (Fig. 15.3; Godfrey et al., 2019; Perez et al., 2005). Sustained exploitation over a period of ~100 years can be demonstrated at this site (Godfrey et al., 2019), but no artifacts were collected there and there is no direct evidence of human occupation

Table 15.2 Direct evidence of early human interaction with megafauna, in archaeological context where indicated

What	When	Where	Source
Butchery of elephant bird, *Aepyornis maximus*	>10,000 years ago	Christmas River, south central Madagascar	Hansford et al. (2018)
Butchery of elephant bird, *Mullerornis modestus*	~6,000 years ago	Lamboharana, southwest Madagascar	Hansford et al. (2018)
Butchery of hippopotami	~4,000 years ago	Anjohibe, northwest Madagascar	Gommery et al. (2011)
Butchery of *Palaeopropithecus*	Beginning ~2,300 years ago	Taolambiby, south central Madagascar	Perez et al. (2005)
Aepyornis eggshell in archaeological context	Beginning just under 2,000 years ago	Tony, Velondiake, western Madagascar	Douglass et al. (2019a)
Butchery of hippopotami	Between 2,000 and 1,500 years ago	Ambolisatra and Lamboharana, southwestern Madagascar	MacPhee and Burney (1991)
Extinct lemur, *Palaeopropithecus* sp., in archaeological context	Beginning ~1,500 years ago	Anja Cave, archaeological site, northern Madagascar	Douglass et al. (2019a)
Butchery of *Archaeolemur*	~1,300 years ago	Manombo Toliara, southwestern Madagascar	Godfrey et al. (2019)
Butchery of *Pachylemur*	Beginning ~1,200 years ago	Tsirave, south central Madagascar	Godfrey et al. (2019)
Aepyornis eggshell in archaeological context	Beginning ~1,200 years ago	Talaky	Battistini et al. (1963)
Butchery of *Aepyornis*	Over 1,000 years ago	Ambolisatra, southwestern Madagascar	Hansford et al. (2018)
Remains of giant tortoise and megafauna in archaeological context	Beginning in the 10th century	Andranosoa	Rasamuel (1984)
Remains of giant tortoise and extinct lemurs in archaeological context	Late 11th century	Andavakoera Gorge	Dewar and Rakotovololona (1992)
Remains of extinct animals and *Aepyornis* eggshell in archaeological context	13th century	Lakaton'ny akanga	Dewar and Rakotovololona (1992)

Figure 15.3 Left femur of an adult *Pachylemur insignis* from Tsirave (UA3059, Lamberton Collection), showing chop and cut marks made during disarticulation. Note the alignment of the cut marks on the medial and lateral condyles (modified from Perez et al., 2005).

at this site. We know nothing about the economy of the people at Tsirave just over 1,000 years ago, apart from the fact that they hunted *Pachylemur*.

This is typical of megafaunal butchery records at paleontological sites on Madagascar; that is, there is no record of archaeological context. Indeed, the lack of archaeological context has been used as a reason to question the butchery records themselves (e.g. Mitchell, 2020). In part, the absence of archaeological context at paleontological sites may reflect the fact that few paleontological sites were excavated by archaeologists. The butchered bones of *Pachylemur* at Tsirave were collected by paleontologist Charles Lamberton in the early 1930s. Radiocarbon dating of 41 subfossil *Pachylemur* at this site reveals a span of dates between 3,800 and 800 years, with a spike for a short period just before 1,000 years ago (Fig. 15.4). It is within this spike that all of the dated butchered *Pachylemur* bones fall. This suggests that Lamberton dug through a human occupation zone, without recognizing it as such (Godfrey et al., 2019). All dated butchered bones of megafauna are older than 1,000 years and most are from paleontological sites (Table 15.2).

We would argue that populations of *Pachylemur* and other megafauna did decline because of humans, but the story of their demise is not a simple one. Human economies are not monolithic, and it was not until the population of humans on Madagascar increased with the expansion of the Indian Ocean trade network (bringing more settlers, increased sedentarism, urbanization, and the introduction of an increasing number of domesticated plants and animals) that rapid megafaunal

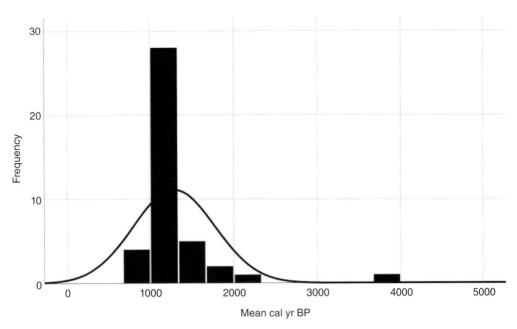

Figure 15.4 Distribution of 41 radiocarbon-dated bones of *Pachylemur* at Tsirave in south central Madagascar. All butchered bones fall in the spike in frequency just over 1,000 years ago, likely representing a human occupation zone.

decline occurred (Godfrey et al., 2019). It may seem counterintuitive that the megafauna would have declined as alternative sources of animal protein such as cattle were introduced to Madagascar, but domesticated animals support a larger human population than do wild animals, and human population size is a critical factor. Reflected globally in biomass distribution today, the biomass of humans at ≈0.06 gigatons of carbon (Gt C) and the biomass of livestock at ≈0.1 Gt C (dominated by cattle and pigs) far surpass that of wild mammals (≈0.007 Gt C) (Bar-On et al., 2018). Comparison of these values with estimates prior to the advent of humans indicate that while the total biomass of wild mammals (both marine and terrestrial) decreased by a factor of ≈6, the total biomass of mammals increased approximately fourfold (from ≈0.04 Gt C to ≈0.17 Gt C) due to vast increase of the biomass of humanity and its associated livestock (Bar-On et al., 2018).

Communities in the past, like communities in the present, were "not blanket consumers of all resources" (Douglass et al., 2019b). Researchers who model the persistence or decline of modern species around the world understand this complexity (Levi et al., 2011; Lu et al., 2010, 2011; Winterhalder & Goland, 1993; Winterhalder & Lu, 1997). Part of that complexity involves variation in the ways in which different species respond to humans and to habitat fragmentation, and variation in reproductive resilience and other aspects of species' life histories (Rahantaharivao et al., 2021). Wild animals vary in their tolerance of humans and human commensals. For some species, the mere presence of humans can elicit a costly predator-avoidance

Figure 15.5 A reconstruction of *Pachylemur* by artist Joel Borgerson. Used by permission.

response, causing animals to flee even when fleeing reduces their access to resources and results in changes in foraging, ranging, and activity patterns (Frid & Dill, 2002). A recent meta-analysis of 76 studies has identified a systematic increase in nocturnality as a response of wild mammals to the rapid global expansion of human activity (Gaynor et al., 2018). This phenomenon may account for *Pachylemur*'s cathemeral (or possibly nocturnal) activity as reported by Masoala trappers.

While gaps remain concerning our knowledge of *Pachylemur*'s demise, we do know that it was a target of human predation and that its confrontational antipredator tactics (involving loud calls and possibly mobbing) made it highly conspicuous, and in turn more vulnerable to human weaponry. We also know that *Pachylemur* lived in regions that, because of habitat degradation, can no longer support a large-bodied, arboreal, frugivorous quadruped (Fig. 15.5). Likewise, degraded forest seems unable to support its highly frugivorous extant relative *Varecia* whose densities are greatly diminished or absent in such areas (Vasey et al., 2022). Cathemerality may have provided *Pachylemur* some protection from human predation, but frugivory, on the other hand, would have made this species more vulnerable to habitat fragmentation due to the spatial distribution and patchiness of fruit, as Janson (1992) has argued for primates generally. Habitat fragmentation has had a strongly negative effect on the occurrence of *V. variegata* in particular (Eppley et al., 2020) and this factor poses the most significant barrier to dispersal for the genus (Baden et al., 2014; Holmes et al., 2013). Habitat degradation and logging of large trees in Madagascar's eastern rain forests are considered major factors resulting in local extinctions of *Varecia*, not only because they rely heavily upon large, patchily distributed trees for fruit (Balko & Underwood, 2005; Borgerson, 2015; Herrera et al., 2011; Vasey, 2000, 2006), but more poignantly because they rely upon them for reproduction. *Varecia* are the only extant primates that build nests exclusively to care for young and the trees they select for nesting and stashing their non-clinging litters are the largest in the forest (Vasey et al., 2018). *Pachylemur*'s highly aggressive antipredator behavior suggests it may have possessed *Varecia*'s unusual suite of reproductive traits, demanding that they confront rather than flee from predators, tactics that would be selectively advantageous in protecting non-clinging, nested young. If so, *Pachylemur* would have shared the same grave vulnerabilities to local extinction as *Varecia*. On the basis of information currently available, we cannot know which human activities contributed the most to the demise of *Pachylemur*, but it is highly likely that both habitat degradation and hunting played a role.

Acknowledgments

We graciously thank Cortni Borgerson for sharing two of her unpublished interviews with Masoala Peninsula hunters and for granting us permission to publish the hunters' descriptions of the *kisoala*. We also thank Cortni Borgerson and Tim Eppley for advice that improved earlier versions of this manuscript, Peterson Faina for translating the abstract into Malagasy, and Joel Borgerson for allowing us to include his artistic rendition of *Pachylemur*. Some of the research on *Pachylemur* reported here was supported by a grant from the National Science Foundation (NSF BCS 1750598) to LRG. We thank cave diver Barry Coleman for permission to publish his underwater photo of a skull of *Pachylemur insignis* at Vintany Cave, Tsimanampesotse National Park, 2015. Paleontological field research was conducted under a collaborative accord with colleagues at the Université d'Antananarivo and a collaborative convention with Madagascar National Parks.

References

Anderson, A., Clark, G., Haberle, S., et al. (2018). New evidence of megafaunal bone damage indicates late colonization of Madagascar. *PLoS ONE*, **13**(10), e0204368.

Baden, A. L., Brenneman, R. A., & Louis, E. E., Jr. (2008). Morphometrics of wild black-and-white ruffed lemurs [*Varecia variegata*, Kerr 1972]. *American Journal of Primatology*, **70**, 913–926.

Baden, A. L., Holmes, S. M., Johnson, S. E., Engberg, S. E., Louis, E. E. Jr., & Bradley, B. J. (2014). Species-level view of population structure and gene flow for a Critically Endangered primate (*Varecia variegata*). *Ecology and Evolution*, **4**, 2675–2692.

Balko, E. A. & Underwood, H. B. (2005). Effects of forest structure and composition on food availability for *Varecia variegata* at Ranomafana National Park,

Madagascar. *American Journal of Primatology*, 66, 45–70.

Bar-On, Y. M., Phillips, R., & Milo, R. (2018). The biomass distribution on earth. *Proceedings of the National Academy of Sciences of the United States of America*, 115 (25), 6506–6511.

Battistini, R., Vérin, P., & Rason, R. (1963). Le site archéologique de Talaky. *Annales Malgaches*, 1, 111–142.

Borgerson, C. (2015). The effects of illegal hunting and habitat on two sympatric endangered primates. *International Journal of Primatology*, 36, 74–93.

Borgerson, C. (2016). Optimizing conservation policy: The importance of seasonal variation in hunting and meat consumption on the Masoala Peninsula Madagascar. *Oryx*, 50(3), 405–418.

Borgerson, C., McKean, M. A. Sutherland, M. R., & Godfrey, L. R. (2016). Who hunts lemurs and why they hunt them. *Biological Conservation*, 197, 124–130.

Borgerson, C., Vonona, M. A., Vonona, T., et al. (2018). An evaluation of the interactions among household economies, human health, and wildlife hunting in the Lac Alaotra wetland complex of Madagascar. *Madagascar Conservation & Development*, 13(1), 25–36.

Bray, J., Samson, D. R., & Nunn, C. L. (2017). Activity patterns in seven captive lemur species: Evidence of cathemerality in *Varecia* and *Lemur catta*? *American Journal of Primatology*, 79, e22648.

Brook C. E., Herrera, J., Borgerson, C., et al. (2019). Population viability and bushmeat harvest sustainability for Madagascar lemurs. *Conservation Biology*, 33(1), 99–111.

Burney, D. A., & Ramilisonina. (1998). The kilopilopitsofy, kidoky, and bokyboky: Accounts of strange animals from Belo-sur-mer, Madagascar, and the megafaunal "extinction window". *American Anthropologist*, 100(4), 957–966.

Burney, D. A., Andriamialison, H., Andrianaivoarivelo R. A., et al. (2020). Subfossil lemur discoveries from the Beanka Protected Area in western Madagascar. *Quaternary Research*, 93, 187–203.

Burns, S. J., Godfrey, L. R, Faina, P., et al. (2016). Rapid human-induced landscape transformation in Madagascar at the end of the first millennium of the Common Era. *Quaternary Science Reviews*, 134, 92–99.

Charles-Dominique, P. (1975). *Ecology and Behavior of Nocturnal Prosimians*. New York: Columbia University Press.

Crowley, B. E. (2010). A refined chronology of prehistoric Madagascar and the demise of the megafauna. *Quaternary Science Reviews*, 29, 2591–2603.

Crowley, B. E., Godfrey, L. R., Bankoff, R. J., et al. (2017). Island-wide aridity did not trigger recent megafaunal extinctions in Madagascar. *Ecography*, 40, 901–912.

Curtis, D. J., & Rasmussen, M. A. (2006). The evolution of cathemerality in primates and other mammals: A comparative and chronoecological approach. *Folia Primatologica*, 77, 178–193.

Dandouau, A. (1922). *Contes Populaires des Sakalava et des Tsimihety de la Région d'Analava*. Alger: Jules Carbonel, 299–301.

Dawson, R. R., Burns, S. J., McGee, D., et al. (2020). Using speleothem fluid inclusion isotopic composition to reconstruct the temperature and hydrologic record of the last 60,000 years in southwestern Madagascar. *Geological Society of America Abstracts with Programs*, 52(6), 355941.

Decary, R. (1939). La chasse et le piégage chez les indigènes de Madagascar. *Journal des Africanistes*, IX, 3–41.

Dew, J. L., & Wright, P. C. (1998). Frugivory and seed dispersal by primates in Madagascar's eastern rainforest. *Biotropica*, 30, 425–437.

Dewar, R. E., & Rakotovololona, S. (1992). La chasse aux subfossiles: les preuves de XIème siècle. *Taloha*, 11, 4–15.

Douglass, K., Antonites, A. R., Quintana Morales, et al.. (2018). Multi-analytical approach to zooarchaeological assemblages elucidates Late Holocene coastal lifeways in southwest Madagascar. *Quaternary International*, 471, 111–131.

Douglass, K., Hixon, S., Wright, H. T., et al. (2019a). A critical review of radiocarbon dates clarifies the human settlement of Madagascar. *Quaternary Science Reviews*, 221, 105878. https://doi.org/10.1016/j.quascirev.2019.105878

Douglass, K., Quintana Morales, E., Manahira, G., et al. (2019b). Toward a just and inclusive environmental archaeology of southwest Madagascar. *Journal of Social Archaeology*, 19, 307–332.

Duckworth, J. W., Evans, M. I., Hawkins, A. F. A., Safford, R. J., & Wilkinson, R. J. (1995). The lemurs of Marojejy Strict Nature Reserve, Madagascar: A status overview with notes on ecology and threats. *International Journal of Primatology*, 16, 545–559.

Dutton, C. J., Junge, R. E., & Louis, E. E. Jr. (2008). Biomedical evaluation of free-ranging red ruffed lemurs (*Varecia rubra*) within the Masoala National

Park, Madagascar. *Journal of Zoo and Wildlife Medicine*, 39, 76–85.

Eppley, T. M., Santini, L., Tinsman J. C., & Donati, G. (2020). Do functional traits offset the effects of fragmentation? The case of large-bodied diurnal lemur species. *American Journal of Primatology*, 82, e23104.

Faina, P., Burns, S. J., Godfrey, L. R., et al. (2021). Comparing the paleoclimates of northwestern and southwestern Madagascar during the late Holocene: implications for the role of climate in megafaunal extinction. *Malagasy Nature*. 15, 108–127.

Federman, S., Dornburg, A., Daly, D. C., et al. (2016). Implications of lemuriform extinctions for the Malagasy flora. *Proceedings of the National Academy of Sciences of the United States of America*, 113(18), 5041–5046.

Flacourt, É. de. (1661). Chapter XXXIII. *De la chasse et de la pêche. Histoire de la Grande Isle Madagascar*. Paris: G. de Lvyne, 106–108.

Frid, A., & Dill, L. (2002). Human-caused disturbance stimuli as a form of predation risk. *Conservation Ecology*, 6(1), 11.

Garcia G., & Goodman S. M. (2003). Hunting of protected animals in the Parc National d'Ankarafantsika, north-western Madagascar. *Oryx*, 37, 115–118.

Gardner, C. J., & Davies, Z. G. (2014). Rural bushmeat consumption within multiple-use protected areas: qualitative evidence from southwest Madagascar. *Human Ecology*, 42(1), 21–34.

Gaynor, K. M., Hojnowski, C. E., Carter, N. H., & Brashares, J. S. (2018). The influence of human disturbance on wildlife nocturnality. *Science*, 360, 1232–1235.

Glaw, F., Vences, M., & Randrianiaina. (2008). Killed aye-aye (*Daubentonia madagascariensis*) exposed on the gallows in northeastern Madagascar. *Lemur News*, 13, 6–7.

Godfrey, L. R. (1986). The tale of the tsy-aomby-aomby, in which a legendary creature is revealed to be real. *The Sciences*, 26, 48–51.

Godfrey, L. R., & Jungers, W. L. (2003). The extinct sloth lemurs of Madagascar. *Evolutionary Anthropology*, 12, 252–263.

Godfrey, L. R., Semprebon, G. M., Jungers, W. L., Sutherland, M. R., Simons, E. L., & Solounias, N. (2004). Dental use wear in extinct lemurs: Evidence of diet and niche differentiation. *Journal of Human Evolution*, 47, 145–169.

Godfrey, L. R., Jungers, W. L., Schwartz, G. T., & Irwin, M. T. (2008). Ghosts and orphans: Madagascar's vanishing ecosystems. In J. G. Fleagle and C. C. Gilbert, eds., *Elwyn Simons: A Search for Origins*. New York: Springer, pp. 361–395.

Godfrey, L. R., Winchester, J. M., King, S. J., Boyer, D. M., & Jernvall, J. (2012). Dental topography indicates ecological contraction of lemur communities. *American Journal of Physical Anthropology*, 148(2), 215–227.

Godfrey, L. R., Scroxton, N., Crowley, B. E., et al. (2019). A new interpretation of Madagascar's megafaunal decline: The "Subsistence Shift Hypothesis." *Journal of Human Evolution*, 130, 126–140.

Gommery, D., Ramanivosoa, B., Faure, M., et al. (2011). Les plus anciennes traces d'activités anthropiques de Madagascar sur des ossements d'hippopotames subfossils d'Anjohibe (Province de Mahajanga). *Comptes Rendus Palevol*, 10, 271–278.

Golden, C. D. (2009). Bushmeat hunting and use in the Makira Forest north-eastern Madagascar: a conservation and livelihoods issue. *Oryx*, 43(3), 386–392.

Golden, C. D., & Comaroff, J. (2015). Effects of social change on wildlife consumption taboos in northeastern Madagascar. *Ecology and Society*, 20(2), 41.

Golden, C. D., Fernald, L. C. H., Brashares, J. S., Rasolofoniaina, B. J. R., & Kremen, C. (2011). Benefits of wildlife consumption to child nutrition in a biodiversity hotspot. *Proceedings of the National Academy of Sciences of the United States of America*, 108, 19653–19656.

Golden, C. D., Wrangham, R. W., & Brashares, J. S. (2013). Assessing the accuracy of interviewed recall for rare, highly seasonal events: the case of wildlife consumption in Madagascar. *Animal Conservation*, 16(6), 597–603.

Golden, C. D., Bonds, M. H., Brashares, J. S., Rasolofoniaina, B. J. R., & Kremen, C. (2014). Economic valuation of subsistence harvest of wildlife in Madagascar. *Conservation Biology*, 28, 234–243.

Goodman, S. M., & Raselimanana, A. P. (2003). Hunting of wild animals by Sakalava of the Menabe region: a field report from Kirindy-Mite. *Lemur News*, 8, 4–6.

Halle, S. (2006). Polyphasic activity patterns in small mammals. *Folia Primatologica*, 77, 15–26.

Hansford, J., Wright, P. C., Rasoamiaramanana, A., et al. (2018). Early Holocene human presence in Madagascar evidenced by exploitation of avian megafauna. *Science Advances*, 4, eaat6925.

Hansford, J. P, Wright, P. C., Pérez, V. R., Muldoon, K. M., Turvey, S. T., & Godfrey, L. R. (2020). Evidence for early human arrival in Madagascar is robust: A response to Mitchell. *Journal of Island and Coastal Archaeology*, 15, 596–602.

Hekkala, E. R., Rakotondratsima, M., & Vasey, N. (2007). Habitat and distribution of the ruffed lemur, *Varecia*, north of the Bay of Antongil in northeastern Madagascar. *Primate Conservation*, 22, 89–95.

Herrera, J. P., Wright, P. C., Lauterbur, E., Ratavonjanahary, L., & Taylor, L. L. (2011). The effects of habitat disturbance on lemurs at Ranomafana National Park. *International Journal of Primatology*, 32, 1091–1108.

Hixon, S. W., Smith, E. A. E., Crowley, B. E., et al. (2018). Nitrogen isotope (δ^{15}N) patterns for amino acids in lemur bones are inconsistent with aridity driving megafaunal extinction in southwestern Madagascar. *Journal of Quaternary Science*, 33(8), 958–968. https://doi/10.1002/jqs.3073.

Holmes, S. M., Baden, A. L., Brenneman, R. A., Engberg, S. E., Louis, E. E. Jr., & Johnson, S. E. (2013). Patch size and isolation influence genetic patterns in black-and-white ruffed lemur (*Varecia variegata*) populations. *Conservation Genetics*, 14, 615–624.

Janson, C. H. (1992). Evolutionary ecology of primate social structure. In E. A. Smith & B. Winterhalder, eds., *Evolutionary Ecology and Human Behavior*. New York: Aldine de Gruyter, pp. 95–130.

Jenkins, R. K. B., & Racey, P. A. (2008). Bats as bushmeat in Madagascar. *Madagascar Conservation & Development*, 3(1), 22–32.

Jenkins, R. K. B., Keane, A., Rakotoarivelo, A. R., et al. (2011). Analysis of patterns of bushmeat consumption reveals extensive exploitation of protected species in eastern Madagascar. *PLoS One*, 6(12), 12.

Jungers, W. L., Godfrey, L. R., Simons, E. L., Wunderlich, R. E., Richmond, B. G., & Chatrath, P. S. (2002). Ecomorphology and behavior of giant extinct lemurs from Madagascar. In J. M. Plavcan, R. F. Kay, W. L. Jungers & C. P. van Schaik, eds., *Reconstructing Behavior in the Primate Fossil Record*. New York: Kluwer Academic/Plenum Publishers, 371–411.

Jungers, W. L., Demes, B., & Godfrey, L. R. (2008). How big were the "giant" extinct lemurs of Madagascar? In J. G. Fleagle, & C. C. Gilbert, eds., *Elwyn Simons: A Search for Origins*. New York: Springer, 343–360.

Koenig P. (2005). Découverte d'une dépouille de Aye-aye (*Daubentonia madagascariensis*) dans le nord-ouest de Madagascar. *Lemur News*, 10, 6–7.

Koenig P., & Zavasoa A. (2008). Et le massacre continue... Nouvelle découverte d'une dépouille d'Aye-aye (*Daubentonia madagascariensis*) dans le nord de Madagascar. *Lemur News*, 13, 6

Lamberton, C. (1932). Verbal report on excavations at Tsirave, presented to the Académie Malgache on Jan 15, 1931. *Bulletin de l'Academie Malgache*, 14, 21–22.

Lehman S. M., & Ratsimazafy J. H. (2001). Biological assessment of the Fandriana Marolambo Corridor. *Lemur News*, 6, 8–9.

Lehman S. M., Ratsimbazafy J., Rajaonson A., & Day S. (2006). Decline of *Propithecus diadema edwardsi* and *Varecia variegata variegata* (Primates: Lemuridae) in south-east Madagascar. *Oryx*, 40, 108–111.

Levi, T., Lu, F., Yu, D. W., & Mangel, M. (2011). The behavior and diet breadth of central-place foragers: An application to human hunters and neotropical game management. *Evolutionary Ecology Research*, 13, 1–15.

Lu, F. (2011). Patterns of indigenous resilience in the Amazon: A case study of Huaorani hunting in Ecuador. *Journal of Ecological Anthropology*, 14(1), 5–21.

Lu, F., Gray, C., Bilsborrow, R. E., et al. (2010). Contrasting colonist and indigenous impacts on Amazonian forests. *Conservation Biology*, 24(3), 881–885.

Macedonia, J. M. (1993). Adaptation and phylogenetic constraints in the antipredator behavior of ringtailed and ruffed lemurs. In P. M. Kappeler and J. U. Ganzhorn, eds., *Lemur Social Systems and Their Ecological Basis*. New York: Plenum Press, 67–84.

MacPhee, R. D. E., & Burney, D. A. (1991). Dating of modified femora of extinct dwarf hippopotamus from southern Madagascar: Implications for constraining human colonization and vertebrate extinction events. *Journal of Archaeological Science*, 18, 695–706.

Mahé, J., & Sourdat, M. (1972). Sur l'extinction des vertébrés subfossiles et l'aridification du climat dans le Sud-Ouest de Madagascar. *Bulletin de la Société Géologique de France*, 1, 295–309.

Martin, R. D. (1990). *Primate Origins and Evolution: A Phylogenetic Reconstruction*. Princeton: Princeton University Press.

Martinez, B. (2008). Occurrence of bamboo lemurs (*Hapalemur griseus occidentalis*) in an agricultural landscape on the Masoala Peninsula. *Lemur News*, 13, 11–14.

Merson, S. D., Dollar, L. J., Johnson, P. J., & Macdonald, D. W. (2019). Poverty not taste drives the consumption of protected species in Madagascar. *Biodiversity and Conservation*, 28, 3669–3689.

Mitchell, P. (2020). Settling Madagascar: When did people first colonize the world's largest island? *The Journal of Island and Coastal Archaeology*, 15, 576–595.

Muldoon, K. M. (2010). Paleoenvironment of Ankilitelo Cave (late Holocene, southwestern Madagascar): Implications for the extinction of giant lemurs. *Journal of Human Evolution*, 58(4), 338–352.

Moniac N.,& Heitman A. (2007). *Lemur catta* and hunting around Andohahela. *Lemur News*, 12, 11.

Patel E. R., & Andrianandrasana, L. H. (2008). Low elevation silky sifakas (*Propithecus candidus*) in the Makira Conservation site at Andaparaty-Rabeson: Ranging, demography, and possible sympatry with red ruffed lemurs (*Varecia rubra*). *Lemur News*, 13, 18–22.

Patel, E. R., Marshall, J. J., & Parathian, H. (2005). Silky sifaka (*Propithecus candidus*) conservation education in northeastern Madagascar. *Laboratory Primate Newsletter*, 44, 8–11.

Perez, V. R., Godfrey, L. R., Nowak-Kemp, M., Burney, D. A., Ratsimbazafy, J., & Vasey, N. (2005). Evidence of early butchery of giant lemurs in Madagascar. *Journal of Human Evolution*, 49(6), 722–742.

Pierron, D., Hieske, M., Razindrazaka, H., et al. (2017). Genomic landscape of human diversity across Madagascar. *Proceedings of the National Academy of Sciences of the United States of America*, 114(32), E6498–E6506.

Radimilahy, C. M. (1998). *Mahilaka: An Archaeological Investigation of an Early Town in Northwestern Madagascar*. Uppsala: Uppsala University.

Radimilahy, C. M., & Crossland, Z. (2015). Situating Madagascar: Indian Ocean dynamics and archaeological histories. *Azania – Archaeological Research in Africa*, 5(4) SI, 495–518.

Rahantaharivao, N.J., Godfrey, L.R., Schwartz, G.T., et al. 2021. The growth and development of *Pachylemur*, a large-bodied lemurid. *Malagasy Nature*, 15, 141–158.

Rakotoarivelo, A. R., Razafimanahaka, J. H., Rabesihanaka, S., Jones, J. P. G., & Jenkins, R. K. B. (2011). Lois et réglements sur la faune sauvage à Madagascar: Progrès accomplis et besoins du futur. *Madagascar Conservation and Development*, 6, 37–44.

Randriamanalina, M. H., Rafararano, L., Babary, L., & Laha. R. (2000). Rapport des enquêtes sur les chasses dans les Fokontany d'Ivondro, d'Erara et d'Etsilesy. *Lemur News*, 5, 11–14.

Randrianandrianina, F. H., Racey, P. A., & Jenkins, R. K. B. (2010). Hunting and consumption of mammals and birds by people in urban areas of western Madagascar. *Oryx*, 44(3), 411–415.

Randrianarisoa, P. M., Rasamison, A. A., & Rakotozafy, L. (1999). Les lémuriens de la région de Daraina: Forêt d'Analamazava, forêt de Bekaraoka et forêt de Sahaka. *Lemur News*, 4, 19–21.

Rasamuel, D. (1984). Alimentation et techniques anciennes dans le sud malgache à travers une fosse à ordures du XIe siècle. *Etudes Océan Indien*, 4(4), 81–109.

Razafimanahaka, J. H., Jenkins, R. K. B., Andriafidison, D., et al. (2012). Novel approach for quantifying illegal bushmeat consumption reveals high consumption of protected species in Madagascar. *Oryx*, 46(4), 584–592.

Rea, M. S., Figueiro, M. G., Jones, G. E., & Glander, K. E. (2014). Daily activity and light exposure levels for five species of lemurs at the Duke Lemur Center. *American Journal of Physical Anthropology*, 153, 68–77.

Reuter, K. E., Randell, H., Wills, A. R., Janvier, T. E., Belalahy, T. R., & Sewall, B. J. (2016a). Capture, movement, trade, and consumption of mammals in Madagascar. *PLoS ONE*, 11(2), e0150305.

Reuter, K. E., Randell, H. R., Wills, A. R., & Sewall, B. J. (2016b). The consumption of wild meat in Madagascar: drivers, popularity and food security. *Environmental Conservation*, 1(3), 1–11.

Richard, A. F., & Dewar, R. E. (1991). Lemur ecology. *Annual Review of Ecology and Systematics*, 22, 145–175.

Scroxton, N., Burns, S. J., McGee, D., et al. (2017). Hemispherically in-phase precipitation variability over the last 1700 years in a Madagascar speleothem record. *Quaternary Science Reviews*, 164, 25–36.

Scroxton, N., Burns, S. J., McGee, D., et al. (2019). Competing temperature and atmospheric circulation effects on southwest Madagascan rainfall during the last deglaciation. *Paleoceanography and Paleoclimatology*, 34(2), 275–286.

Simons, E. L., & Meyers, D. M. (1991). Folklore and beliefs about the Aye aye (*Daubentonia madagascariensis*). *Lemur News*, 6, 11–16.

Tattersall. I. (2008). Avoiding commitment: cathemerality among primates. *Biological Rhythm Research*, 39 (3), 213–228.

Vasey, N. (2000). Niche separation in *Varecia variegata rubra* and *Eulemur fulvus albifrons*: I. Interspecific patterns. *American Journal of Physical Anthropology*, **112**, 411–431.

Vasey, N. (2003). *Varecia*, ruffed lemurs. In S. M. Goodman and J. Benstead, eds., *Natural History of Madagascar*. Chicago: University of Chicago Press, pp. 1332–1336.

Vasey, N. (2005). Activity budgets and activity rhythms in red ruffed lemurs (*Varecia rubra*) on the Masoala Peninsula, Madagascar: Seasonality and reproductive energetics. *American Journal of Primatology*, **66**, 23–44.

Vasey, N. (2006). Impact of seasonality and reproduction on social structure, ranging patterns, and fission-fusion social organization in red ruffed lemurs. In L. Gould & M. Sauther eds., *Lemurs: Ecology and Adaptation*. New York: Springer/Kluwer, 275–304.

Vasey, N. (2007). The breeding system of wild red ruffed lemurs (*Varecia rubra*): A preliminary report. *Primates*, **48**, 41–54.

Vasey, N., Mogilewsky, M., & Schatz, G. E. (2018). Infant nest and stash sites of variegated lemurs (*Varecia rubra*): The extended phenotype. *American Journal of Primatology*, **80**(9), e22911.

Vasey, N., Baden, A. L., & Ratsimbazafy, J. (2022). *Varecia*, Ruffed or Variegated Lemurs. In S. M. Goodman, ed., *The New Natural History of Madagascar*. Princeton: Princeton University Press.

Virah-Sawmy, M., Willis, K. J., & Gillson, L. (2010). Evidence for drought and forest declines during the recent megafaunal extinctions in Madagascar. *Journal of Biogeography*, **37**, 506–519.

Voarintsoa, N. R. G., Matero, I. S. O., Railsback, L. B., et al. (2019). Investigating the 8.2 event in northwestern Madagascar: insight from data-model comparisons. *Quaternary Science Reviews*, **204**, 172–186.

Walker, A. C. (1967). Patterns of extinction among the subfossil Madagascan lemuroids. In P. S. Martin & H. E. Wright, eds., *Pleistocene Extinctions*. New Haven: Yale Univ. Press, pp. 425–432.

Wang, L., Brook, G. A., Burney, D. A., et al. (2019). The African Humid Period, rapid climate change events, the timing of human colonization, and megafaunal extinctions in Madagascar during the Holocene: Evidence from a 2m Anjohibe Cave stalagmite. *Quaternary Science Reviews*, **210**, 136–153.

Winterhalder, B., & Goland, C. (1993). On population, foraging efficiency, and plant domestication. *Current Anthropology*, **34**, 710–715.

Winterhalder, B., & Lu, F. (1997). A forager resource population ecology model and implications for indigenous conservation. *Conservation Biology*, **11**(6), 1354–1364.

Part IV

Asia

16 The Monkey in Mesopotamia during the Third Millennium BCE

Marcos Such-Gutiérrez

القرد في بلاد ما بين النهرين خلال الألفية الثالثة ق.ح.ع

نبذه

ترجع ندرة الأدلة على وجود القردة في بلاد ما بين النهرين بشكل عام ، وخلال الألفية الثالثة ق.ح.ع على وجه الخصوص ، إلى حقيقة أنها لم تكن موطنًا لبلاد ما بين النهرين ولكن تم جلبها من وادي السند (ثقافة هارابان) أو غرب وسط آسيا. تم التعرف على هذه القرود على أنها ريسوس المكاك في شمال الهند أو غرب آسيا الوسطى ، على الرغم من أن القرود الأخرى من الهند قد تكون معروفة خلال الألفية الثالثة ق.ح.ع. تم العثور على المراجع الأولى للقرود في بلاد ما بين النهرين خلال الألفية الثالثة ق.ح.ع في التمثيلات الفنية من فترة الأسرات المبكرة (٢٩٠٠-٢٣٤٠ ق.ح.ع تقريبا) بينما تم توثيق أقدم الإشارات في المصادر المكتوبة في فترة أور الثالثة (٢١٠٠-٢٠٠٠ ق.ح.ع تقريبا). في كلا المصدرين ، الفن والنصوص ، تُصوَّر القرود على أنها ذات طابع مضحك وتم الاحتفاظ بها بشكل أساسي كحيوانات أليفة للترفيه. لذلك تم استخدام القرد في المصادر المكتوبة للسخرية من الأعداء الذين هاجموا سومر ، والذين جاءوا بشكل أساسي من الجبال الشرقية (زاغروس) في الألفية الثالثة ق.ح.ع، حيث بدأ تقليدًا طويلًا لكلمة "قرد" كمصطلح فكاهي أو انتقاص في التاريخ الذي نجا حتى الوقت الحاضر.

الكلمات الدالة

الرئيسيات – بلاد ما بين النهرين – الألفية الثالثة ق.ح.ع – السومرية – الأكادية – "الحيوانات الغريبة"

Abstract

The scarcity of attestations to the presence of monkeys in Mesopotamia in general, and during the third millennium BCE in particular, is due to the fact that they were not native to Mesopotamia but brought from the Indus Valley (Harappan culture) or western-central Asia. These monkeys have been identified as the rhesus macaque of northern India or western-central Asia, although other monkeys from the India subcontient might have been known during the third millennium BCE. The first references to monkeys in Mesopotamia during the third millennium BCE are found in artistic representations from the Early Dynastic period (*c.* 2900–2340 BCE) while the earliest mentions in the written sources are documented in the Ur III period (*c.* 2100–2000 BCE). In both sources, art and texts, monkeys are depicted as having a ludic character and were kept mainly as pets for entertainment. The monkey was therefore used in the written sources to ridicule the enemies that attacked Sumer, who in the third millennium BCE came fundamentally from the eastern mountains (Zagros), initiating a long tradition of the word "monkey" as a humorous or derogative qualification in the history that has survived to the present day.

Key words Primates, Mesopotamia, 3rd millennium BCE, Sumerian, Akkadian, Exotic animals

16.1   Introduction

References to monkeys in cuneiform sources are scarce, as monkeys were not native to Mesopotamia (Fig. 16.1). Indeed, monkeys were grouped under "exotic animals"[1] and were one of the less attested animals because, contrary to other "exotic animals," such as bears, gazelles, or red deer, they were never captured directly by the Mesopotamians. They were brought to Mesopotamia as tribute or gifts, as shown in the royal inscriptions from the second half of the second millennium BCE onwards, when kings established permanent relations with Egypt. Therefore, the comprehensive survey of monkeys in Mesopotamia by Dunham (1985) is nowadays still current in many respects. This chapter aims to add some new data concerning the third millennium BCE and to compare this information with the data on the second and first millennia BCE assembled by S. Dunham.

16.2   The Sumerian and Akkadian Words for Monkey

The Sumerian term for monkey was probably pronounced /ugubi/ and written in different ways, basically $^{ugu(2)}$ugu$_4$-bi or ^{ugu}u-gu$_5$-bi,[2] whose chronological distribution is the following: the word is documented for the first time as ^{ugu2}ugu$_4$-bi in the year name IS 23 (see Table 16.1: 1.1). At the beginning of the second millennium BCE it was substituted by ^{ugu}ugu$_4$-bi, which became the predominant form, documented principally in literary texts, sometimes replaced by the older form ^{ugu2}ugu$_4$-bi. The unique form documented in the first millennium BCE is ^{ugu}u-gu$_5$-bi, which is attested in omens and medical texts.[3] The Akkadian terms for monkey are pagû(m) and uqūpu. The former, according to the lexical lists, is the equivalent of ^{ugu}ugu$_4$-bi / ^{ugu}u-gu$_5$-bi[4] and is documented from the Ur III period (c. 2100–2000 BCE) onwards,[5]

---

[1] Note that the lexical lists from the second millennium BCE, such as ḪAR-ra = ḫubullu, mention the monkey within the wild animals (in the sense of non-domesticated), alongside with some non-indigenous or "exotic animals": it appears before other foreign animals such as lu-lim, "red deer", udu-TIL, "wild sheep (planet)", maš-da$_3$, "gazelle", and amar-maš-da$_3$, "young gazelle", see CDLI P228700 r. III 24-IV 3, P229423 r. II ⌜10⌝-15, P229518 r. I 19-II 1 – here the order is udu-TIL, lu-⌜lim⌝, and maš-da$_3$ is omitted –, P235805 r. II 1'-5', P461397 305-310, cp. ePSD (http://oracc.org/epsd2/o0041200 sub Old Babylonian), or between ⌜ab$_2$⌝-[za-za], "water buffalo", and [az], "bear", see CDLI P228065: II 1'-4' – Middle Babylonian period –.

[2] For the reading and the different writings of the Sumerian word for monkey see Klein (1979: 149 ff).

[3] See Klein (1979: 153 ff.) and the attestations of monkey in the written sources in Dunham (1985: 236 ff. II) and in CAD P p. 17 ff. pagû A "monkey".

[4] See AHw II p. 809 pagû(m) I "'Affe'", Klein (1979: 156) and CAD P p. 17 ff. pagû A "monkey".

[5] The first attestations are PN from the Ur III period: Pa$_2$-gu$_5$-a, "my little monkey", JCSSS 5 65: 7 (AS 5 / -), 47: 7 (ŠS 1 / -) – both texts from "Ir$_{11}$-gu$_{10}$ archive" –, Nisaba 1 11: 12 (ŠS 4 / i 18) – Umma –; Pa$_2$-gu$_5$-ti, "my female monkey", CDLI P107425: 8 (IS 3 / vi -) – Sippar –; Pa$_2$-gu$_5$-tum, "female monkey", CUSAS 3 308: I 4 (ŠS 6 / v -), 316: I 7 (ŠS 6 / vii -) and 324: I 7 (ŠS [6] / ⌜vii⌝ -) – all three texts from GARšana –, cp. Kleinerman and Owen (2009: 613) pá-gu$_5$-tum and for the PN Pa$_2$-gu$_5$-tum Heimpel (2009: 356) Pá-gu$_5$-tum; Pa$_2$-gu$_5$-um, "monkey", Nisaba 15/2 953 r. VII 258 (IS 3 / iti-kir$_{11}$-si-AK -), CUSAS 40/2 499 r. 2 (- / -) – both texts from Urusagrig – and Pa$_2$-gum, "monkey", CUSAS 40/2 955: 3 (ŠS [] / [iti-ni]g$_2$-^{d}En-lil$_2$-la$_2$ -) – Urusagrig –, CUSAS 22 p. 183 TEXT 57 r. 6 (IS 1 / -) – "SI.A-a Archive" – Nisaba 15/2 910 r. 38 (IS 2 / -) – Urusagrig –. Note that the word pagû(m) is according to CAD P p. 17 ff. pagû A "monkey" attested from the Old Akkadian period onwards. However, the oldest attestation mentioned in CAD is the supposed PN from

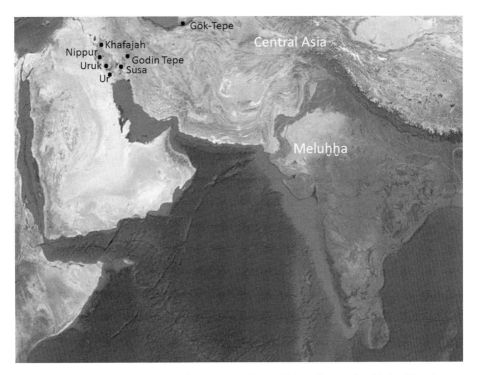

Figure 16.1 Map of Mesopotamia and western and central Asia during the third millennium, including the locations indicated in the text (Base map Google Earth).

whereas the latter is presumably only documented in the first millennium BCE.[6] However, the PN from the Ur III period (c. 2100–2000 BCE) U_2-KU.BI[7] and I_3-KU.BI[8], which with the addition of the first-person singular possessive pronominal suffix seem to correspond to the PN from the first millennium BCE U_2-qu-pu and I-qu-pu,[9] could be interpreted as U_2-qu$_2$-pi$_2$ / I_3-qu$_2$-pi$_2$, "my uqūpu-monkey". If this assumption should turn out to be right, these two PN would be the first attestations of uqūpu

the Ur III period Pa-gu-u$_2$ in TCL 5 6041: II 17 (AS 2 / -) – Umma – (CAD P p. 18 g}) that should actually be interpreted as ugula(PA) Gu-u$_2$, "overseer: Guu", cp. Goetze (1963: 1, 3) and Steinkeller (2013: 375). A PN from the Ur III period that could represent another written form for pagû(m) is BA.GU.UM, documented in the PN of a fowler (mušen-du$_3$) in Drehem texts between Š 41 / viii 17 (SAT 2 294: 2) and Š 47 / x 28 (PDT 1 139: 2), that has been traditionally read Ba-qu$_3$-um, "(small) fly", see Gelb (1957: 99) BQQ and Sallaberger (1999: 255 a). Text 28 [2.]. If this assumption were correct, BA.GU.TUM, attested in the Ur III texts from Lagaš SAT 1 71: 6 (- / xi -) and AuOr 16 p. 227 56 r. 13 ([?] / [] 21), that could be the feminine form of pagû (m), should be interpreted as Ba-qu$_3$-tum, with the tenderness diminutive suffix -ūtum. For -ūtum as tenderness diminutive suffix see e.g. Stamm (1939: 113) and GAG[3] § 56 S 40. Note, however, that neither AHw I p. 105 baqqu(m) "'(kleine) Mücke'" nor CAD B p. 101 baqqu "gnat" mention the PN BA.GU.UM as an attestation of baqqu(m).

[6] See AHw III p. 1427 uqūpu "ein Affe", Klein (1979: 156 f.) and CAD U-W p. 204 uqūpu "(a kind of monkey)".
[7] CUSAS 3 1509: 23 (- / -) –unknown provenance– .
[8] AuOr 17–18 p. 224 No. 26 r. 3 (- / -) –Lagaš– .
[9] For these PN see Stamm (1939: 254), AHw III p. 1427 uqūpu "ein Affe" and CAD U-W p. 204 uqūpu "(a kind of monkey)" c).

Table 16.1. Attestations of [ugu(2)]ugu4-bi in the thrid millennium BCE BCE

1. Administrative Texts from Ur III

1.1. Year name IS 23 in administrative texts from Ur

Passage	Texts
mu ^{d}I-bi$_2$-^{d}Suen lugal-Uri$_5$^{ki}-ma-ra ^{ugu2}ugu$_4$-bi-dugud kur-bi mu-na-e-ra-a "In the year when the heavy monkeys (from) their mountain came to Ibbi-Suen, king of Ur"	Nisaba 5 p. 16 Nr. 16 (IS 23 / ii 5$^?$), UET 3 863 r. 8-⌈9⌉ (IS 23 / -) – abbreviated year without ^{d}I-bi$_2$-^{d}Suen lugal-Uri$_5$^{ki}-ma-ra –, CDLI P375908 (IS 23 / v -) – unpublished text –, UET 9 410 r. ⌈9⌉ (IS 23 / ⌈viii⌉ [?]), UET 3 712 r. 3-6 (IS 23 / xii 5), UET 3 711 r. 3-6 (IS 23 / xii 22), Nisaba 5 p. 16 Nr. 14 (IS 23 / [])

2   Literary Texts (Ur III–Old Babylonian)

2.1. "Curse of Akkad"

a)	^{ugu}ugu$_4$-bi am-si-maḫ ab$_2$-za-za u$_2$-ma-am ki-ba$_9$-ra$_2$, ša$_3$-sila-dagal-la-ke$_4$ teš$_2$-bi tag-tag-ge-de$_3$, ur-gi$_7$ ur-NIM {daraḫ-kur-ra} {(*some mss. have instead:*) kušu-kur-ra} {(*some mss. have instead:*) anše-kur-ra} udu-A.LUM suluḫu si "that monkeys, mighty elephants, water buffalo, exotic animals as thoroughbred dogs, lions, {mountain ibexes} {(*some mss. have instead:*) mountain beasts (?)} {(*some mss. have instead:*) horses}, and *alum* sheep with long wool would jostle each other in the public squares."[1]	ETCSLtransliteration : c.2.1.5 21-23
	.	
	.	
b)	ug$_3$-ga$_2$ nu-si$_3$-ga kalam-ma nu-šid-da, Gu-ti-um^{ki} ug$_3$ keš$_2$-da nu-zu, dim$_2$-ma lu$_2$-u$_{18}$-lu {galga} {(*some mss. have instead:*) arḫuš} ur-ra ulutim$_2$ ^{ugu}ugu$_4$-bi, ^{d}En-lil$_2$-le kur-ta nam-ta-an-e$_3$ "Enlil brought out of the mountains those who do not resemble other people, who are not reckoned as part of the Land, the Gutians, an unbridled people, with human intelligence but canine {instincts} {(*some mss. have instead:*) feelings} and monkeys' features."[2]	ETCSL transliteration: c.2.1.5 154-157

2.2. Ibbi-Suen's letter to Puzur-Numušda/Puzur-Šulgi

u$_4$-na-me ^{d}En-lil$_2$-le ki-en-gi ḫul mu- un-gi$_4$, ^{ugu2}ugu-bi kur-bi-ta e$_3$-de$_3$ nam-sipa-kalam-ma-še$_3$ mu-un-il$_2$ "At some time in the past, Enlil had already come to hate Sumer, and had elevated a monkey descending his mountain (home) to the stewardship of the homeland."[3]	MC 15 p. 463 f. 13-14

[1] Translation according to ETCSL translation: t.2.1.5 21-23.

[2] Translation according to ETCSL translation: t.2.1.5 154-157.

[3] Translation according to Michalowski (2011: 464) *Translation (A)* 13-14.

and would contribute to solving some of the problems pointed out by Jacob Klein in the phonetic relation between Sumerian ugubi and Akkadian *uqūpu*: Klein (1979) reminds us that both of these are also related to other words for monkey in Hamito-Semitic and Indoeuropean languages, which, however, do not have the initial vowel /u/ or /i/, and points to the problems with *uqūpu* as a loanword from ugubi because, among other reasons, *uqūpu* is documented very much later and was also used as PN.[10] However, if the two above-mentioned PN from the Ur III period contained the word *uqūpu*, the Akkadian word had probably already been borrowed in the third millennium BCE from Sumerian or, more likely, from a third language, since monkeys as imported animals were originally unknown to Sumerians and Akkadians who may have taken the term from the language of the place monkeys came from in the third millennium BCE, that is, the Indus Valley (Harappan culture) or western-central Asia. Subsequently, over time and through trading contacts, this word could have been borrowed by other languages.[11]

16.3   Monkeys in the Third Millennium BCE

The first evidences of monkeys in the Near East are found in artistic depictions. Aside from representations found in Iran dating from the fourth and the third millennium BCE[12] and monkey amulets from archaic levels at Uruk (end of the fourth millennium BCE),[13] the first representations of monkeys during the third millennium BCE in Mesopotamia are documented in Khafajah, that is, two pendants representing squatting monkeys dating in the Early Dynastic period (*c.* 2900–2340 BCE),[14] and in the Royal Cemetery at Ur (*c.* 2500 BCE), namely a copper pin topped with a gold monkey

---

[10] See Klein (1979: 156 ff).

[11] J. Klein (1979: 156 ff.) assumes that ugubi was probably not a Sumerian word, but rather a word of unknown origin (p. 156), whereas *uqūpu* could be borrowed from Egyptian (p. 159 f.), and that both of these words, because of the assonance, could have developed from a common origin (p. 160). Furthermore, compare Michalowski (2010: 219 2) who states that the word "monkey" in Sumerian and Akkadian is an independent loan from a third language.

[12] Representations of monkeys in Iran during the fourth and third millennia BCE are frequent; see, for example, a numero-ideographic tablet from Godin Tepe (*c.* 3300 BCE), where the seal impressions show animals without snouts sitting on their buttocks and with a long erect tail that must be identified with monkeys (see Fig. 16.2b), a stone cylinder from Gök-Tepe dating in the Early Dynastic period (*c.* 2900–2340 BCE) where a squatting monkey appears behind a bull-man attendant that holds up a gate post, see Barnett (1973: 3), a cylinder seal from Susa (*c.* 2500 BCE) where a monkey plays a flute, see Spycket (1998: 4 fig. 8, 5), a lapis lazuli monkey forming the head of a pin from Susa, see van Buren (1936–1937: 19), and some figurines from Susa, see, for example, Harper et al. (1992: 64 33, 97 61), that represent a *Papio hamadryas* (*c.* 3300 BCE) and a rhesus macaque (probably late third millennium BCE), according to the authors. Note, however, that identification with *Papio hamadryas* (see Fig. 16.3b) is problematic since it is native to the Horn of Africa and southwestern portion of the Arabian Peninsula, regions with which commercial contacts in the fourth and third millennia BCE are unknown. Although it is difficult to identify a concrete species on the basis of a representation, cp., for example, Dunham (1985: 236 I, 261 note 110), Pruzsinszky (2016: 24 f.) and Pruzsinszky (2018: 43 note 17), might represent langurs (see Fig. 16.3c), a species that is well documented in India, where commercial relations with the Harappan culture during the fourth and third millennia BCE are well documented.

[13] See Barnett (1973: 3).

[14] See van Buren (1936–1937: 19).

a

b

Figure 16.2 (a) Impression of the cylinder seal from the tomb PG 1054 (Ur) (Made by M. S.-G. based on image from Spycket (1998): 4 fig. 9); (b) Numero-ideographic tablet from Godin Tepe (Iran). (Made by M. S.-G. based on image from Englund (1998): 54, fig. 16).

figure[15] and a cylinder seal from the tomb PG 1054 that shows a monkey playing a flute (see Fig. 16.2a).[16] The next artistic attestations are monkey amulets from Ur dating to the Old Akkadian period (c. 2340–2159 BCE).[17] There are three seal impressions on tablets of the Ur III period (c. 2100–2000 BCE) from Nippur that have each been suggested to contain a (squatting) monkey.[18] The problematic interpretation of these three representations as monkeys shows the difficulty in identifying monkeys in artistic representations. In most cases, basically documented in seals impressions, the depiction is so schematic that it is difficult to ascertain whether it is really a monkey. Scholars have usually proposed that these representations are mongooses.[19] However, some of them could be monkeys.

As in the case of artistic depictions, monkeys are very rarely documented in the written sources, since, as stated above, they were not directly captured by the Mesopotamians. Aside from the Akkadian PN from the Ur III period (see Section

---

[15] See van Buren (1936–1937: 19) and Barnett (1973: 3).

[16] See van Buren (1936–1937: 19), Dunham (1985: 248 III) and Spycket (1998: 4 fig. 9, 5).

[17] See van Buren (1936–1937: 19).

[18] Hattori (2002: 82 Monkey, 310 274) – PBS 14 nos. 275–276 = NATN 498 = FAOS 17 p. 40 f. 41 (IS 2 / xi -) –; Hattori (2002: 265) SI#445 – UM 29-16-403 = NATN 722 ([?] / [?] 13⁷) – and Hattori (2002: 326) SI#140 – CBS 86884 = NATN 190 (AS 8 / xii 21) –.

[19] Cp. Dunham (1985: 246), Pruzsinszky (2016: 25) and see, for example, the following proposals of mongoose in seal impressions on tablets of the Ur III period (c. 2100–2000 BCE): Buchanan 1981: 238 629 – "seated mongoose (?)" –; Buchanan (1981: 238 630) – "mongoose (?) on pole" –, cp. Hattori (2002: 82 note 258); Mayr (1996: 370 818) – "'mongoose' in an the third case of the inscription, behind the primary figure" –; Hattori (2002: 282 SI#320) – "Mongoose or something with a long tail" –; Hattori (2002: 326 SI#140) – "An unidentifiable animal (monkey or mongoose?) faces right in front of the lion" – and Hattori (2002: 334 SI#107) – "Perhaps a mongoose because of hanging tail-like lower line but not certain"   .

16.2), the first direct reference to monkeys in the third millennium BCE is the year name of IS 23 (see Table 16.1. 1.1), according to which the [ugu2]ugu$_4$-bi-dugud, "heavy monkeys", came to Ibbi-Suen. It has been pointed out that these "heavy monkeys" may refer to the Elamites who attacked and captured Ibbi-Suen, the last king of the third dynasty of Ur, even though some scholars have translated [ugu2]ugu$_4$-bi-dugud as singular and connected it with Išbi-Erra.[20] This derogative use of [ugu2]ugu$_4$-bi for foreigners coming from the eastern mountains is found in the other two attestations of the same word in the third millennium BCE. Despite the final form of these two texts having appeared in the Ur III (c. 2100–2000 BCE) or Old Babylonian period (c. 1950–1530 BCE), both refer to historical facts that occurred in the third millennium BCE: the first is the "Curse of Akkad" (see Table 16.1. 2.1 b), in which the Gutians, a mountain folk from Zagros, are qualified as "monkeys"[21] and the second is Ibbi-Suen's letter to Puzur-Numušda/Puzur-Šulgi (see Table 16.1. 2.2), where someone, whose identity is difficult to ascertain, is called a "monkey".[22] These passages show a general use of [ugu(2)]ugu$_4$-bi as "monkey" without referring to any particular species, indicating the beginning of a long tradition that is still standing, according to which monkeys, human's closest relatives, did not reach our standing but remained on a lower laughable level, and were therefore used to ridicule people, in the present case in the Sumerians' satire of foreign invaders who came, during the third millennium BCE, principally from the eastern mountains (Zagros). In this regard, the connection between monkeys, humor, and music has been documented at least since c. 2500 (cylinder seal from tomb PG 1054 in the Royal Cemetery at Ur depicting a monkey playing a flute).[23] This connection has a long tradition, documented, for example, in the Sasanian period (224–651 AD) and the Middle Ages during which, probably through cylinder seals brought to Europe by the crusaders,

---

[20] For the identity of the enemy (Elamites or Išbi-Erra), who defeats Ibbi-Suen, according to the year name IS 23 see lately Fink (2016: 117 note 32). For the year name and the reasons for a translation of [ugu2]ugu$_4$-bi-dugud as plural ("heavy/stupid monkeys") see Dunham (1985: 242 f. 10), cp. Such-Gutiérrez (2020: 15 note 28).

[21] Cp. e.g. Dunham (1985: 242 III 8), Michalowski (2011: 476 A13–15 = B18–20, 481 A31 = B51), Beckman (2013: 204), Fink (2016: 117 note 32), and Heeßel (2017: 17).

[22] The identity of the person referred as "monkey" is problematic: e.g. Dunham (1985: 242 III 8) identifies it with the Gutians, even though she translates [ugu2]ugu$_4$-bi as singular (III 9) and it does not fit the historical context, since a Gutian incursion at the end of the III Dynasty of Ur is not documented. Frayne (1997: 365) (23) assumes that "monkey" refers to Išbi-Erra, while Michalowski (2011: 476 A13–15 = B18–20) assumes that it may refer to the Elamites, even though he translates [ugu2]ugu$_4$-bi as singular (see note 36) as well. Whoever was given the epithet "monkey" must have been a person and not a folk, since Enlil elevated him to the shepherdship of Sumer. For other foreigners qualified as "monkeys" see the Amorites according to the literary text "Marriage of MAR.TU" in Michalowski (2011: 476 A13–15 = B18–20), Beckman (2013: 204) and Fink (2016: 117 note 32). For this tradition of monkey as ridiculous animal in literary texts of the second millennium BCE as the "school satires" see Dunham (1985: 243 ff.).

[23] For the monkey as a ludic animal and its connection with the music and entertainment on the basis of literary texts and art in Mesopotamia see Dunham (1985: 243 ff.), Pruzsinszky (2016: 24 ff.), and Pruzsinszky (2018: 42 ff). Note that Pruzsinszky assumes that the monkey represented the "popular" musical culture in the literature and in the art while the nar-musician represented the high-status court musician.

Figure 16.3 (a) Rhesus macaque of northern India. (Photograph by Mieciu K2. Wiki-Commons-Open access); (b) Hamadrayas baboon (Photograph by Sebastian Bergmann. Wiki-Commons-Open access), (c) Gray langur. (Photograph by Thomas Schoch. Wiki-Commons-Open access).

monkeys playing musical instruments were represented on the Romanesque capitals of Catholic churches and cathedrals.[24]

An indirect reference to a specific species is found in the first passage of the "Curse of Akkad" (see Table 16.1. 2.1 a) where monkeys, together with other "exotic animals," such as mighty elephants and water buffalos, would jostle each other in the public squares.[25] It has been convincingly suggested on the basis of this passage that the monkeys mentioned in the third millennium BCE, contrary to those from the middle of the second Millennium BCE onwards, stemmed from Meluḫḫa, that is, the Indus Valley (Harappan culture), and could be identified on the basis of Old Babylonian terracottas with the rhesus macaque of northern India or western-central Asia (see Fig. 16.3a).[26] However, it must be assumed that other species of monkeys would have been known in Mesopotamia during the third millennium BCE since figurines found at Susa (Iran) might represent other monkeys as well as the rhesus macaque (see note 12).

16.4   Recapitulation: Comparison of Data from the Third Millennium BCE with the Second and First Millennia BCE

The few data mentioned in the foregoing paragraph show that monkeys were "exotic animals" brought to Sumer during the third millennium BCE from Meluḫḫa, i.e. the Indus Valley (Harappan Culture) or western-central Asia. This kind of monkey has been identified as the rhesus macaque of northern India or western-central Asia, even though other species might have been known to Mesopotamians during the third

---

[24] For monkeys playing different musical instruments in silver bowls of the Sasanian period (224–651 AD) and on the Romanesque capitals see Spycket (1998: 8 f.). with previous bibliography.

[25] See Cooper (1983: 51 21-22) and cp. Dunham (1985: 236 II 1).

[26] See Dunham (1985: 240, 261 note 110), cp. Potts (1997: 259 *Monkeys*), Spycket (1998: 2), Pruzsinszky (2016: 25) and Pruzsinszky (2018: 46). However, note Ratnagar *apud* Pruzsinszky (2016: 25, note 3) who argues that during the third millennium BCE monkeys were imported from Egypt, whereas in the early 2nd millennium BCE they were primarily imported from India, while in later times, imports from Egypt (via the Levant) increased.

millennium BCE (see note 12). The monkey was recognized from the outset as human's closest cognate and viewed as a comical animal that had remained at a lower stage and was probably kept as a pet for entertainment, as the depiction of a monkey playing a flute on a cylinder seal from tomb PG 1054 in the Royal Cemetery at Ur (c. 2500 BCE) (see Fig. 16.2a and note 16) allows us to assume. This amusing character gave rise to the use of the Sumerian term [ugu(2)]ugu$_4$-bi, "monkey", to mock Sumer's attacking enemies who, in the third millennium BCE, came fundamentally from the eastern mountains (Zagros). This initiated a long tradition in the history of the word "monkey" as a humorous or derogatory epithet that has continued to the present day (see Section 16.3). Outstanding, in this sense, are representations of monkeys playing different musical instruments on the Romanesque capitals of Catholic churches. This derisive nature of [ugu(2)]ugu$_4$-bi is attested mainly in the written sources from the third millennium BCE. In these cuneiform sources, the Akkadian words pagû(m) and the more questionable uqūpu in PN from the Ur III period (c. 2100–2000 BCE) are documented for the first time (see Section 16.2). The use of a term for monkey in PN is another example of the comical character of the word "monkey" in the third millennium BCE, denoting that people thus named acted or looked like monkeys.

In comparing these data with those assembled by Dunham (1985: 236 ff. II) for the second and first millennia BCE, it is evident that the available sources are richer and some of these are being documented for the first time. Literary texts ("school satires", the so-called "Monkey Letter", a proverb, and a new fragment of the Gilgameš epic)[27] and artistic representations (principally representations on terracottas and cylinder seals)[28] show that references to monkeys as amusing animals in a derogatory sense, in connection with entertainment and music, continued. By contrast, the new texts, royal inscriptions, omens, and medical prescriptions introduce novel aspects. Royal inscriptions from the second half of the second millennium BCE onwards show that monkeys no longer originated from the Indus Valley (Harappan culture) or western-central Asia, but from Egypt,[29] and were of different species given that pagû and uqūpu could appear in the same inscription,[30] and that kings such as Ashurnasirpal II

---

[27] For the the so-called "Monkey Letter" and the proverb see lately Kleinerman (2011: 34 note 65, 158 ff.), cp. Pruzsinszky (2016: 26 f.) and Pruzsinszky (2018: 45). Furthermore, see Dunham (1985: 242 ff.). For the new fragment of the Gilgameš epic see Al-Rawi and George (2014: 69 ff.). For the passage of the Gilgameš epic mentioning monkeys see Pruzsinszky (2016: 26, lines 17–26), and Pruzsinszky (2018: 44, lines 24–26).

[28] Dunham (1985: 240 f., 245 ff.) and see also Pruzsinszky (2016: 27 ff.) and Pruzsinszky (2018: 46 ff., 50 f.). For references to monkeys as art objects in three texts from the second and first millennium BCE see Dunham (1985: 257 ff. V).

[29] Dunham (1985: 239).

[30] Dunham (1985: 238 f. 7) and cp., for example, AHw III p. 1427 uqūpu "ein Affe" and CAD U-W p. 204 uqūpu "(a kind of monkey)" a). Note that Dunham (1985: 238 6, 239 7) also considers bazītu, besides pagû and uqūpu, to be a term for another sort of monkey. However, it is very doubtful, see AHw I p. 117 bazītu "'Meerkatze'? (Fauna 88¹: Fehler für ↗ pagītu?)" and CAD B p. 185 bazītu "(a foreign animal)". Note also the identification of bazītu and uqūpu, which are mentioned in the black obelisk of

(c. 883–859 BCE) and Nebuchanedzzar II (c. 605–561 BCE) bred them.[31] Moreover, the omens and medical inscriptions from the first millennium BCE indicate, respectively, that monkeys did not bring good luck (perhaps because of their derogatory nature when applied to enemies), and that "monkey hair" and "monkey bone", if these were not plant names, had curative powers.[32] Monkeys' apotropaic nature can also be found in figurines from tombs (from the second half of the second millennium BCE onwards) and terracottas from the temple of the god Ninurta in Babylon (first millennium BCE).[33]

Acknowledgments

The author would like to express his deepest gratitude to Omar Al Belbeis for providing the abstract in Arabic and B. Urbani for formatting the text and preparing the map (Fig. 16.1) for the chapter. I thank A. T. Antczak, B. Urbani, and the external reviewer for the comments on an early draft of this text.

Author's note

The abbreviations used in this chapter can be found on this website: http://cdli.ox.ac .uk/wiki/abbreviations_for_assyriology. Further abbreviations are the following: AS = Amar-Suen; IS = Ibbi-Suen; PN = personal name; Š = Šulgi; ŠS = Šū-Suen.

Editors' note

This philological chapter uses footnotes in order to facilitate fluent reading of ancient texts.

References

Al-Rawi, F. N. H., & George, A. R. (2014). Back to the Cedar Forest: The beginning and end of Tablet V of the standard Babylonian Epic of Gilgameš. *Journal of Cuneiform Studies, 66*, 69–90.

Barnett, R. D. (1973). Monkey business. *Journal of the Ancient Near Eastern Society, 5*, 1–10.

Battini, L. (2020). L'animal en collection au Proche-Orient ancien (IVe-Ier millénaire av. J.-C.). In J. Förstel & M. Plouvier, eds., *L'animal: un object*

d'étude, Paris: Éditions du Comité des travaux historiques et scientifiques, 1–13.

Beckman, G. (2013). Foreigners in the ancient Near East. *Journal of the American Oriental Society, 133*, 203–215.

Buchanan, B. (1981). *Early Near Eastern Seals in the Yale Babylonian Collection*. New Haven and London: Yale University Press.

Cooper, J. S. (1983). *The Curse of Agade*. Baltimore and London: The Johns Hopkins University Press.

Salmanasar III (c. 858-824 BCE), respectively, with the genera *Cercopithecus* (*Meerkatze*) and *Papio* (*Pavian*) in the outdated work by Hilzheimer 1932: 41 f.

[31] Dunham (1985: 240) and cp. Spycket (1998: 3), Pruzsinszky (2016: 25) and Pruzsinszky (2018: 44). For the passage in the royal inscriptions of Ashurnasirpal II mentioning monkeys as a precedent for the first documented zoo in Sennacherib's reign (c. 705–681 BCE) see Battini (2020: 1 f. 2, 3).

[32] Dunham (1985: 248 ff. IV, 262).

[33] Dunham (1985: 256 f).

Dunham, S. (1985). The monkey in the middle. *Zeitschrift für Assyriologie und Vorderasiatische Archäologie*, **75**, 234–264.

Englund, R. K. (1998). Texts from the Late Uruk Period. In P. Attinger, & M. Wäfler, eds., *Mesopotamien. Späturuk-Zeit und Frühdynastische Zeit (Orbis Biblicus et Orientalis 160/1)*, 15–233. Freiburg and Göttingen: Universitätsverlag Freiburg Schweiz. Vandenhoeck & Ruprecht Göttingen.

Fink, S. (2016). Battle and war in the royal self-representation of the Ur III Period. In Th.R. Kämmerer, M. Köiv, & V. Sazonov, eds., *Kings, Gods and People. Establishing Monarchies in the Ancient World (Alter Orient und Altes Testament 390/4)*, 109–134. Münster: Ugarit-Verlag.

Frayne, D. R. (1997). *Ur III Period (2112-2004 BCE). Vol. 3/2 of The Royal Inscriptions of Mesopotamia. Early Periods*. Toronto, Buffalo and London: University of Toronto Press.

Gelb, I.J. (1957). *Glossary of Old Akkadian. Vol. 3 of Materials for the Assyrian Dictionary*. Chicago: The University of Chicago Press.

Heimpel, W. (2009). *Workers and Construction Work at Garšana. Vol. 5 of Cornell University Studies in Assyriology and Sumerology*. Bethesda: CDL Press.

Hilzheimer, F. (1932). Affe. In E. Ebeling, & B. Meissner, eds., *Reallexikon der Assyriologie 1, 41-42*. Berlin and Leipzig: Walter de Gruyter & Co.

Goetze, A. (1963). Šakkanakus of the Ur III Empire. *Journal of Cuneiform Studies*, **17**, 1–31.

Harper, P.O., Aruz, J., & Tallon, F. (eds.) (1992). *The Royal City of Susa. Ancient Near Eastern Treasures in the Louvre*. New York: The Metropolitan Museum of Art.

Hattori, A. (2002). Texts and impressions: A holistic approach to Ur III Cuneiform tablets from the University of Pennsylvania expeditions to Nippur. PhD thesis, University of Pennsylvania.

Heeßel, N. P (2017). Mesopotamian Demons – Foreign and Yet Native Powers?. In Th. Römer, B. Dufour, F. Pfitzmann, & Chr. Uehlinger, eds., *Entre dieux et hommes: anges, démons et autres figures intermédiaires. Actes du colloque organisé par le Collège de France, Paris, les 19 et 20 mai 2014, (Orbis Biblicus et Orientalis 286)*, 15–29. Fribourg and Göttingen: Academic Press Fribourg. Vandenhoeck & Ruprecht Göttingen.

Klein, J. (1979). The reading and pronunciation of the Sumerian word for "monkey." *Journal of Cuneiform Studies*, **31**, 149–160.

Kleinerman, A. (2011). *Education in Early 2nd Millennium BCE Babylonia. The Sumerian Epistolary Miscellany. Vol. 42 of Cuneiform Monographs*. Boston: Brill.

Kleinerman, A. & Owen, D.I. (2009). *Analytical Concordance to the Garšana Archives. Vol. 4 of Cornell University Studies in Assyriology and Sumerology*. Bethesda: CDL Press.

Mayr, R.H. (1996). Seal impressions on tablets from Umma. PhD thesis, University Leiden.

Michalowski, P. (2010). Learning music: Schooling, apprenticeship, and gender in Early Mesopotamia. In R. Pruzsinszky, & D. Shehata, eds., *Musiker und Tradierung. Studien zur Rolle von Musikern bei der Verschriftlichung und Tradierung von literarischen Werken, (Wiener Offene Orientalistik 8)*, 199–239. Wien and Berlin: LIT Verlag.

Michalowski, P. (2011). *The Correspondence of the Kings of Ur. An Epistolary History of an Ancient Mesopotamian Kingdom. Vol. 15 of Mesopotamian Civilizations*. Winona Lake: Eisenbrauns.

Potts, D. T. (1997). *Mesopotamian Civilization*. Ithaca: Cornell University Press.

Pruzsinszky, R. (2016). Musicians and monkeys: Ancient Near Eastern clay plaques displaying musicians and their socio-cultural role. In A. Bellia, & Cl. Marconi, eds., *Musicians in Ancient Coroplastic Art. Iconography, Ritual Contexts, and Functions, (Telestes. Studi e Ricerche di Archeologia Musicale nel Mediterraneo 2)*, Pisa and Roma: Istituti editoriali e poligrafici internazionali, 23–34.

Pruzsinszky, R. (2018). "The Poor Musician" in Ancient Near Eastern texts and images. In A. García-Ventura, Cl. Tavolieri, & L. Verderame, eds., *The Study of Musical Performance in Antiquity: Archaeology and Written Sources*. Newcastle upon Tyne: Cambridge Scholars Publishing, 39–58.

Sallaberger, W. (1999). Ur III-Zeit. In P. Attinger, & M. Wäfler, eds., *Mesopotamien. Akkade-Zeit und Ur III-Zeit, (Orbis Biblicus et Orientalis 160/3)*, Freiburg and Göttingen: Universitätsverlag Freiburg Schweiz. Vandenhoeck & Ruprecht Göttingen, 121–390.

Stamm, J. J. (1939). *Die akkadische Namengebung. Vol. 44 of Mitteilungen der Vorderasiatisch-Ägyptischen Gesellschaft (E. V.)*. Leipzig: J.C. Hinrichs Verlag.

Steinkeller, P. (2013). Corvée labor in Ur III times. In S. Garfinkle, & M.Molina, eds., *From the 21st Century B.C. to the 21st Century A.D. Proceedings of the International Conference on Neo-Sumerian Studies Held in Madrid 22–24 July 2010*, Winona Lake: Eisenbrauns Publishers, 347–424.

Spycket, A. (1998). "Le Carnaval des Animaux": On Some Musician Monkeys from the Ancient Near East. *Iraq*, 60, 1–10.

Such-Gutiérrez, M. (2020). Year names as source for military campaigns in the third millennium BCE. In J. Luggin, & S.Fink, eds., *Battle Descriptions as Literary Texts. A Comparative Approach*, Wiesbaden: Springer VS, 9–29.

van Buren, E. D. (1936–1937). Mesopotamian fauna in the light of the monuments. Archaeological remarks upon Landsberger's "Fauna des alten Mesopotamien." *Archiv für Orientforschung*, 11, 1–37.

17 The Great Monkey King

Carvings of Primates in Indian Religious Architecture

Alexandra A. E. van der Geer

द ग्रेट मंकी किंग: इंडियन धार्मिक वास्तुकला में प्राइमेट्स की नक्काशी

सारांश

धार्मिक वास्तुकला में गैर मानव मनुष्य-सदृश् जानवरों का चित्रण भारतीय उपमहाद्वीप के उत्तरी भाग में मुख्यत: रीसस बन्दरों तथा दक्षिणी भाग में बोनेट मकको और लंगूरों के बारे में है. सिंधु घाटी सभ्यता में (लगभग 2600 ईशा पूर्व से 1900 ईशा पूर्व तक) बन्दरों का सबसे पुराना प्रतिनिधितव मिटटी की छोटी मूर्तियों या खिलौनों के रूप में मिलता है. खासकर बौद्ध और हिन्दू वास्तुकला में मकको की आकृति का चलन विभिन्न कथात्मक भूमिकाओं और उसके विविध रूपों में मिलता है. कथात्मक रिलीफों पर बनी उभरी हुई नक्काशियों में बन्दरों को एक अनुकरणीय दयालु व्यवहार के प्रतीक के रूप में दिखाया गया है, जैसे कि महान् बन्दर राजा की कहानी में (उदहारण के लिए भारहुत, साँची और नागार्जुनकोंडा स्थित बौद्ध मंदिर अवशेषों में). बन्दरों का चित्रण मजाकिया और चालक पात्रों के रूप में भी किया गया है, जैसा कि बन्दर और घड़ियाल की कहानी में (बौद्ध और हिन्दू दोनों), या बिलकुल मुर्ख, जैसा कि माली और बन्दरों की कहानी में (बौद्ध), या सापेक्ष सौंदर्य की प्रतीकात्मक प्रस्तुति, जैसा कि उड़ते हुए बुद्ध की कहानी में (बौद्ध). उनका उपयोग केवल एक जंगलनुमा पतिस्थिति को दर्शाने या सुसज्जित करने में भी किया जा सकता है. बन्दरों का नियमित चित्रण हिन्दू मंदिरों में कामुक मूर्तिकला के निर्माण में भी हुआ है जहाँ वे असीम इच्छाओं के प्रतीक हैं.

धार्मिक वास्तुकला में लंगूरों को उनके लम्बे अंगों, काफी लम्बी पूंछ और विशिष्ट लहरदार भौंहे की वजह से आसानी से पहचाना जा सकता है. लंगूर मूर्तिकला की बहुतायत संख्या हिन्दू वानर देवता हनुमान से सम्बन्धित है, इसलिए इस प्रकार के बंदरों का धार्मिक महत्व है. लंगूरों की ज्यादातर मूर्तियां प्रायद्वीपीय भारत की हिन्दू मंदिरों में कथात्मक बस- रिलीफों पर हैं जो महाकाव्य रामायण के उस उपकथा से सम्बंधित हैं जिसमे हनुमान वानर राजा सुग्रीव के सेनापति हैं और राम की अपहृत पत्नी सीता को बचाने में राजा राम एवं उनके भाई लक्ष्मण की मदद करते हैं. हनुमान की स्वतंत्र मूर्तियों या स्तेलेसों का पुरे भारत में एक मुख्य किरदार के रूप में पाया जाना आम बात है, खासकर दक्षिण भारत में. इस क्षेत्र में हनुमान का चित्रण या तो एक आक्रमण करने को आतुर योद्धा या एक धर्मनिष्ठ, शांत पात्र के रूप में किया जाता है जो कि राम या हिन्दू भगवान् विष्णु के अवतार की आराधना में लीन है.

प्रमुख शब्द

कथात्मक रिलीफों – बौद्ध वास्तुकला – भारतीय नीति कथा – हिन्दू वास्तुकला – *Macaca – Semnopithecus*

Abstract

Depictions of nonhuman primates on religious architecture of the Indian subcontinent concern mainly rhesus monkeys in the northern half, and bonnet macaques and langurs in the southern half of the region. The earliest representations of monkeys are those of the Indus Valley civilization (c. 2600 BCE to 1900 BCE) of Pakistan and northwestern India, in the form of small earthenware figures or toys. Especially macaques figure widely in narratives in various roles and functions, on Buddhist as well as Hindu religious architecture. In narrative stone reliefs, monkeys can be a symbol of exemplary compassionate behavior, as in the Story of the Great Monkey King (e.g. at the Buddhist relic shrines at Bharhut, Sanchi and Nagarjunakonda). Monkeys can also be portrayed as witty or clever, as in the Story of the Monkey and the Crocodile (Buddhist and Hindu), or as extremely foolish, as in the Story of the

Gardener and the Monkeys (Buddhist), or symbolize the relativity of beauty, as in the Story of the Flying Buddha (Buddhist). They can also merely be used for decoration or indicating a forest setting. Monkeys also figure regularly in erotic sculptures on Hindu temples, where they stand for the unbound desires. Langurs are easily recognized in religious architecture by their long limbs, extremely long tail, and prominent and undulating eyebrows. The vast majority of langur sculptures concerns the monkey god Hanuman, hence the sacredness of this monkey in India. Most langur sculptures are narrative bas-reliefs on Hindu temples of peninsular India, depicting an episode of the epic *Ramayana* in which Hanuman leads the monkey army and assists Prince Rama and his brother Lakshmana to rescue Rama's abducted wife Sita. Independent statues or steles of Hanuman as the main character are commonplace throughout India, but especially in the south. Here, Hanuman is generally depicted either as a fierce warrior about to attack, or as a devout, peaceful character in adoration of Rama.

Keywords: Buddhist architecture, Hindu architecture, Indian fables, *Macaca*, Narrative reliefs, *Semnopithecus*

17.1   Introduction

The Indian subcontinent, or South Asia, has always been isolated from the rest of Eurasia by the world's highest mountain range, the Himalayas, and by the Indian Ocean surrounding its vast peninsular part. Today, India is the largest nation on this vast subcontinent; the other nations being Pakistan, Nepal, Bhutan, Bangladesh, and Sri Lanka (Fig. 17.1). This political division is, however, relatively new, and these contemporary borders have little significance for the archaeological study of the region. The region's long-term isolation has resulted in a unique fauna with many endemic elements that are found nowhere else, as well as distinctive human cultures. Two main zoogeographic units roughly divide the subcontinent: the arid Palearctic section in the western part, and the humid Oriental section in the eastern part and the peninsula. It is mainly in the Oriental section that humans and nonhuman primates (macaques, langurs, and gibbons) have coexisted for millennia, interacting with each other in various ways.

Understanding human–nonhuman primate relations, especially topics like the sacredness of animals and cultural taboos, is important in the context of primate conservation. Also, studying the past helps us in understanding how human–monkey relationships may have changed over time, for example, through environmental or cultural changes. A significant part of the interactions between humans and monkeys in South Asia today has a religious component. Many monkey populations reside in Hindu temple spaces, where they are protected and fed, either because they are considered sacred (see Section 17.4) or, alternatively, because of the sacredness of the space they live in (species taboo and habitat taboo, respectively, in the sense of Colding and Folke, 2001). Despite their sacred status, however, the very same monkeys

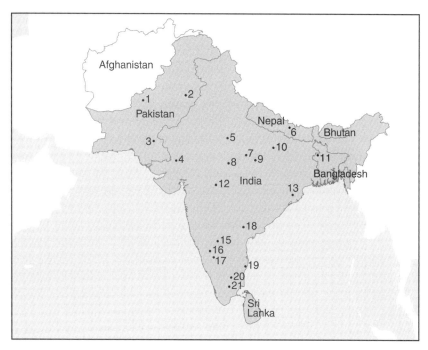

Figure 17.1 Schematic map of the Indian subcontinent with archaeological sites and places mentioned in this chapter. 1 = Sikri; 2 = Harappa; 3 = Chanhu-daro; 4 = Patan; 5 = Gwalior; 6 = Bhaktapur; 7 = Khajuraho; 8 = Sanchi; 9 = Bharhut; 10 = Sarnath; 11 = Ganeshpur; 12 = Nandura; 13 = Hirapur; 14 = Nagarjunakonda; 15 = Hampi; 16 = Balligavi; 17 = Amritapura; 18 = Tirupati; 19 = Mahabalipuram; 20 = Shrirangam; 21 = Madurai. Map based on data from FreeVectorMaps.com, http://freevectormaps.com

are often regarded as a threat to the crops, especially where food is scarce. As a result, they are often chased away or shot. Their special status also does not exempt them from being tamed. Macaques are easily trained as pets, and are employed for street performances in southern India. Another interaction has a more down-to-earth nature: monkeys as a dietary item. Nonhuman primates are eaten by most indigenous peoples in India today. In contrast to its sacred status elsewhere, the common langur serves as a main meat source for the forest-dwelling indigenous peoples (Birhor) of central and eastern India. The Birhor make use of their knowledge of the favorite branches and leaping spots of the langurs along their routes when they set up a trap to capture them (Kirkpatrick, 1955). First, they cut through the underside of the monkeys' take-off branch before a gap until it hangs only by a thread. They then attach a net beneath this severed branch and frighten the monkeys by making noise. When the animals rush to the take-off branch to leap to the safe side and the branch breaks, some of them fall into the nets, and are thus taken to the village as live provision.

Eating monkeys is and likely never was purely nutritional: it is likely that medicinal properties were assigned to monkey meat and organs as well. This is the case today among the Lepchas living in the Himalayas.

Human–nonhuman primate interaction in South Asia is also reflected in literary works and oral tradition. The most important Buddhist tales in which animals play a role are the *Jatakas* (written down *c.* fourth century BCE; Warder, 2000). The *Jatakas* are short stories of the former lives of the Buddha, largely originating as folktales that were woven into episodes from the canonical texts. They are used to illustrate the teachings of the Buddha and praise his virtues. In these *Jatakas*, the future Buddha sometimes appears in animal form. The most important Hindu animal tales are fables from the *Panchatantra* collection (see translation by Olivelle, 1999). These stories, the most frequently translated Indian literature, are among the most widely known fables and figure animals with human virtues and vices. The narratives are part of a collection of five sections or books that bring together Sanskrit short stories and fables by arranging them within a frame story. The tales serve to teach proper conduct, practical wisdom, and ethics. Although the reconstructed original version dates back to *c.* 300 CE or earlier, many of these fables are based on much older, preexisting folktales (Olivelle, 1999) and were adapted to fit the ideas of the Hindu society in which the *Panchatantra* originated. A number of stories is shared with the Buddhist *Jatakas* tales, such as the story of the Monkey and the Crocodile (see Section 17.4.1).

The earliest material evidence for human–nonhuman primate interaction comes from the mature phase of the Indus Valley civilization of northwest India and Pakistan (roughly dating from 2600 BCE to 1750 BCE). The Indus Valley civilization is renowned for its hundreds of steatite seals with animals and short inscriptions in the Indus script. However, seals with an image of a monkey have never been found, nor representations of monkeys in sculptured remains. Instead, terracotta and glazed faience small figurines of pet monkeys have been excavated from the ruins of cities. They invariably represent the short-tailed rhesus macaques (*Macaca mulatta*), and the cord around the neck in many of them indicates a life in captivity (e.g. ceramic monkey figurine or 'toy' from Chanhu-daro, Pakistan, Museum of Fine Arts, Boston, acc. no. 36.2218). A more natural and realistic example is a terracotta 'toy' monkey of just 6 cm high climbing a rope or thin pole (Harappa, Pakistan, *c.* 2500 BCE, National Museum, New Delhi, acc. no. 11625/216). Even the hairs on its body have been depicted in great detail.

After the decline and disappearance of the Indus Valley civilization, it would take about a millennium before the archaeological record of South Asia reveals a new urbanization phase. The first evidence for animal sculptures on religious architecture is provided by the Buddhist structures of king Ashoka (271–232 BCE), the founder of the first large-scale Indian empire, encompassing the entire subcontinent except for its southernmost part. The transition from wood to stone during this period greatly increased the number and quality of archaeological remains. Since then, animals, including monkeys, would regularly figure on Buddhist and Hindu religious architecture. This chapter aims at reviewing this latter material in the context of human–primate interactions in South Asia. Specifically, I will address questions such as what species have been chosen to sculpture, in what context and for what purpose.

17.2   Biology of South Asian Monkeys

South Asia is home to about 20 nonhuman primate species, consisting of 7 macaque species, 1 gibbon and 11 or 12 langur species, as currently listed by the IUCN (2020). Gibbons (*Hylobates hoolock*), the only species of ape of the Indian subcontinent, are not included here, because they have a very restricted distribution and occur only in the deciduous monsoon and evergreen rainforests of the lowlands and hills east of the Brahmaputra river in Assam and Bangladesh. In addition, they do not play a particular role in religion or society, other than serving as food to hill indigenous peoples. More importantly, representations of gibbons seem to be lacking in religious architecture (van der Geer, 2008).

17.2.1   Macaques (*Macaca*)

Macaques have sturdy bodies, strong limbs, and a proportionally long snout, and are up to 71 cm long (excluding the tail) (Nowak, 1999). They are found throughout Asia and North Africa, and are endemic to the Indian subcontinent only on the species level. Easily distinguished by its red hindquarters, the rhesus monkey (*Macaca mulatta*) is the most widely known. The bonnet macaque (*M. radiata*) sports long, dark hairs on top of its head, which radiate in all directions to form a bonnet. Macaques are capable swimmers and may even jump from the trees directly into the stream to swim to the opposite bank. They can temporarily store food in their cheek pouches. Macaques are social, living in large troops of up to several hundred individuals and help and defend each other (Nowak, 1999). The various macaque species have a different distribution (Pocock, 1976; IUCN, 2020). Rhesus monkeys are the most common monkey of northern India and occur from eastern Afghanistan through much of India and Nepal and further eastward. They live in near-desert regions and dense subtropical deciduous forests and mangroves in regions at high altitudes where it snows as well. In some regions, rhesus monkeys mainly live in urban settlements (Singh et al., 2020a). The bonnet macaque is a common monkey of southern India and occurs in peninsular India south of the Godavari and Tapti Rivers, where it lives in most forest types as well as in villages (Singh et al., 2020b). Four other macaques have a very restricted distribution: the stump-tailed macaque (*M. arctoides*) of the eastern hill ranges of the Himalayas, especially near the Brahmaputra River; the Assam macaque (*M. assamensis*) of Assam, Bangladesh, and Nepal; the pig-tailed macaque (*M. nemestrina*) of Nagaland; the lion-tailed macaque (*M. silenus*) of southern India; and the toque macaque (*M. sinica*) of Sri Lanka (Nowak, 1999). Only the stump-tailed macaque lives more on the ground than in the trees. Tail length and tail tip features differ between the species (Prater, 1971), as reflected in their vernacular names. In summary, prominent distinguishing features are a very short tail (stump-tailed macaque, *M. arctoides*), a curled tail (pig-tailed macaque, *M. nemestrina*), a tufted tail (lion-tailed macaque, *M. silenus*), a long tail (bonnet macaque, *M. radiata*; toque macaque, *M. sinica*), or a short tail (rhesus monkey, *M. mulatta*; Assam macaque, *M. assamensis*). Further distinguishing features are the presence of a conspicuous bonnet in the bonnet macaque. Only the Assam macaque and the rhesus monkey cannot be unequivocally distinguished, other than based on their different distribution.

17.2.2   Langurs (*Semnopithecus, Trachypithecus*)

Langurs are larger than macaques, and up to 80 cm long (excluding the tail) (Nowak, 1999). They are all endemic to the Indian subcontinent (IUCN, 2020). With their long limbs and very long tails, they are extremely agile. Like macaques, they locomote quadrupedally on the ground (Nowak, 1999). Langurs typically have prominent brow ridges, which makes them look as if they are permanently raising their eyebrows. They are social and live in large, mixed troops (Nowak, 1999). If possible, they avoid coming to the ground and stay on the high branches. Langurs are frequently reported to raid crops and steal food (Khatun et al., 2013; Chaturvedi and Mishra, 2014). After the rhesus monkey, the gray langurs or Hanuman langurs (genus *Semnopithecus*) are the most common monkeys of the Indian subcontinent, occurring in all countries and states as well as on Sri Lanka, from sea level to 3,500 m high in the Himalayas. The gray langurs have a characteristic blackish face with prominent brow hairs and long, whitish hairs (Nowak, 1999; Prater, 1971). Similar to rhesus monkeys, the gray langurs also live in human settlements and buildings (Kumara et al., 2020). Formerly, all populations of gray langurs were included in a single species, the common langur (*Semnopithecus entellus*), but they are now recognized as separate species, each with its own distribution (e.g. Molur et al., 2003). The different species include (in alphabetical order): the Kashmir gray langur (*S. ajax*) of Kashmir and adjacent states of India; the Southern Plains gray langur (*S. dussumieri*) of western and central India; the Northern Plains gray langur or Hanuman langur (*S. entellus*) of eastern India and since the nineteenth century also in Bangladesh, where it was introduced by Hindu pilgrims (Molur et al., 2003); the Tarai gray langur (*S. hector*) of the Himalayan foothills from Uttaranchal to southwestern Bhutan; the black-footed gray langur (*S. hypoleucos*; perhaps a hybrid between *S. johnii* and *S. dussumieri*; Molur et al., 2003) of southwestern India; the Nilgiri langur (*S. johnii*) of southwestern India (Singh et al., 2020c); the tufted gray langur (*S. priam*) of southern India and Sri Lanka, the Nepal gray langur (*S. schistaceus*) of the high Himalayan elevations of Pakistan, India, Nepal, Tibet and Bhutan; and the purple-faced langur (*S. vetulus*) of Sri Lanka (Rudran et al., 2020). The other species of langur belong to the genus *Trachypithecus* (also known as leaf monkeys) (Osterholz et al., 2008) and have a very limited distribution on the Indian subcontinent. These are the golden langur (*T. geei*) of Bhutan and north-eastern India (Das et al., 2008a); Phayre's langur (*T. phayrei*) of northeastern India and Bangladesh (Bleisch et al., 2020); and the capped langur (*T. pileatus*) of Bangladesh, Bhutan, and northeastern India (Das et al., 2008b).

17.3   Monkeys in Buddhist Religious Architecture

Buddhist religious architecture with figurative reliefs include stupas (solid domes containing relics) with their surrounding railings and terraces and cardinally placed gateways to facilitate circumambulation, monasteries, prayer halls containing a stupa, often rock-cut, and free-standing pillars and votive steles (Dehejia, 1997a; Huntington, 1985).

Macaques figure mainly in narrative bas-reliefs on the generally richly carved stupa railings and gateways of the last centuries BCE and the first millennium CE. The majority of these macaque sculptures are integrated in forest scenes and merely illustrate the woody setting of the depicted narrative, such as that of the Buddha's Sermon to Indra, Pakistan (second to early third century, gray schist with traces of paint, H 39.4 cm; County Museum, Los Angeles M.73.4.6). The monkeys here play no active role, yet are carved with great detail, standing on all fours, and their hairy coats. Another example is a relief from the railing around the stupa at Bharhut (coping stone; *c.* second to first century BCE) with an illustration of the Story of the Lotus Stalk (*Bhisa Jataka*, Pali *Jataka* 488) with a macaque carefully carved as side figure. However, in a few episodes of the Buddha's Life and in a number of *Jatakas* monkeys (list in Lutgendorf, 1997) play an active role, but only few are depicted in stone. Note: Throughout this chapter I use a simplified Romanization of Sanskrit and Pali names, thus without diacritics and with ri and sh substituting for ṛ and ṣ respectively.

17.3.1   The Great Monkey King

The story of The Great Monkey King, known as *Mahakapi Jataka* (Pali *Jataka* 407), narrates the unconditional love of the monkey king for his subjects. The story is as follows (Cowell et al., 1990): Once, a king went on a monkey hunt with his servants. The monkeys escaped, but a river blocked their attempt to get away. The monkey king therefore formed a bridge with his body to allow the safe passage of his subjects. However, a rival wounded the monkey king badly by jumping on his back. Seeing this, the human king was moved, and ordered his servants to fetch the monkey king and take care of him. The monkey king, none else than the future Buddha, then introduced the king to *dharma* or the teachings of the Buddha. In an alternative version (Kawasaki and Kawasaki, 1998), the king only wants to eat the exceptionally juicy mangoes from the tree that is cared for and guarded by the monkeys. Hindered by the monkeys, he orders his servants to shoot them, but the monkeys escape. The rest of this version continues along the above described lines.

The story is nicely illustrated in a medallion on a railing pillar of the stupa at Bharhut (*c.* 100 BCE; Fig. 17.2) and on the western gateway to the Great Stupa at Sanchi (right jamb, upper panel, outside; *c.* 50–25 BCE; Dehejia, 1997b: fig. 39). Judging by the straight and proportionally short tail of the represented monkeys and lack of a bonnet on the head, both panels likely depict rhesus monkeys. The Bharhut

Figure 17.2 Medallion with *Mahakapi Jataka* no. 407 from the railing pillar from the southeast quadrant, Bharhut, Madhya Pradesh (*c.* 100 BCE). India Office List 1900 nr. 1033. Photograph J. D. Beglar. Kern Institute Photography Collections. (owned by the Society of the Kern Institute, Leiden).

relief is livelier with accurately represented monkeys, while the Sanchi relief seems to be lost in details with too many items squeezed into a single panel. Depictions of the story are also known from the south, such as on a frieze of stupa 6 at Nagarjunakonda, Andhra Pradesh (*ayaka* frieze; third to fourth century; van der Geer, 2008: fig. 377). Here, probably a bonnet macaque has been depicted, as can be inferred from the tail that is much longer than that of rhesus monkeys, but still much shorter than that of langurs. The story line has been reduced to a single scene in which the monkey subjects simply sit on their king as if he were a boat instead of walking to the other side of the river. The poor king stretches himself as much as he can, holding on to the opposite bank and bending under the burden of his subjects. The self-sacrifice and obligation of the great monkey king towards his subjects is here magnified and contrasted with the lack of compassion of the human king who commands his servants to kill the monkeys for him.

The king going on a monkey hunt is against expectation, because in the ancient Brahmanical tradition, monkeys are not considered edible (Olivelle, 2002) as they fall in the class of animals with five nails (*panchanakha*) as well as in the class of animals having incisors in both upper and lower jaw (*ubhayatodat*). Later Buddhist texts on the other hand allow for the eating of (any) meat, provided that the animal was not specifically killed for the follower of the faith. The inclusion of the theme of an active hunt for meat might have served the purpose of portraying the human king as in dire need for teaching on dharma.

17.3.2 The Monkey Offering Honey to the Buddha

In Buddhist literature, eight great sacred places (*Ashtamahasthanas*) are mentioned (Deva, 1974). Four of these are connected with the four principal events of Buddha's life: his birth (Lumbini), enlightenment (Gaya, now Bodhgaya), first teaching (Isipatana, now Sarnath), and death (Kushinagar, now Kasia). To these were added four more great places that are otherwise intimately associated with Buddha's life: showing miraculous powers (Sravasti), subduing a drunken elephant (Rajagriha), accepting the offering of a monkey (Vaishali), and the Buddha's descent from heaven after having preached there (Sankasya, now Sankisa). The Vaishali Miracle is important for the purpose of this chapter since a monkey offering honey to the Buddha is at its center. The story, as told in the *Sanghabhedavasti*, the last section of the *Mulasarvastivadivinaya* (Gnoli, 1978), relates how a monkey once grabbed the Buddha's alms bowl and climbed into a tree to fill it with wild honey and subsequently return it to the Buddha. Upon the Buddha's acceptance of this offering, the monkey joyfully jumped in the air, but since it was not careful, it fell in a well and drowned. The tale has a happy ending, however, for his action earns him rebirth in the highest heaven, the Heaven of the Thirty-three (*Trayastrimsha*), ruled by the king of gods, Sakka (Indra). As always, there are textual variations, such as the monkey collecting honey on a leaf instead of in a bowl, and different versions locate the story in different surroundings. However, the key message of the story remains the same: the teachings of the Buddha are directed even towards animals, as evidenced by his acceptance of the gift of a monkey, a creature with an unstable mind. The accidental death of the monkey is a necessary step to allow it to be born to a higher level of existence, closer to enlightenment. There is a second version of this story, found in the first chapter of the *Dhammapada Commentary*, a Pali canonical text by the fifth-century philosopher Buddhaghosha (see translation by Burlingame, 1921). Here, after an unsuccessful attempt to end a monastic quarrel, the Buddha retreated in the Parileyyaka forest. There a solitary elephant took good care of him and even managed to heat water for the Buddha's bath. A monkey offers him food as well, and presents the Buddha a honeycomb on a stick. As in the other version, the Buddha accepted this gift, and while the monkey joyfully leapt from branch to branch, it fell, was impaled on a broken tree and died.

Two rhesus monkeys are part of the depiction of this story on a panel at the east face of the west pillar of the northern gateway to the Great Stupa at Sanchi (east side; *c.* 50–25 BCE) (Fig. 17.3). They can be recognized by their short tails, hairy limbs and rounded muzzles. The same monkey is actually depicted twice, once offering a bowl to the Buddha, represented aniconically here by an empty seat under a bodhi tree, and once raising his arms in adoration. The presentation of various scenes of a single story in one panel or frame is common in ancient India. A similar example is seen on a frieze from the Sikri Stupa, Pakistan (second century, Lahore Museum; Brown, 2009: fig. 2). The main difference with the Sanchi relief is that the "second" monkey is now walking away, while looking backwards. This indicates that its imminent fall in the well and subsequent death was an accident, as specified in the *Mulasarvastivadavinaya* (Brown, 2009). This depicted monkey has relatively long body hair. Centuries later, the story is

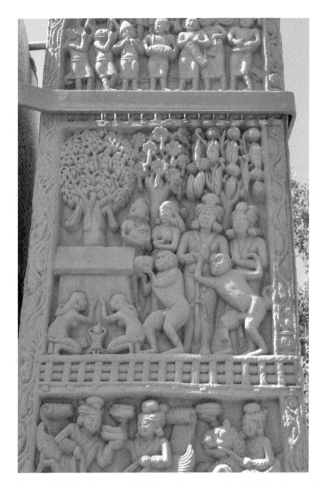

Figure 17.3 The Monkey Offering Honey to the Buddha. Great Stupa, northern gateway, west pillar, east face, at Sanchi, Madhya Pradesh (c. 50–25 BCE). Photograph by Biswarup Ganguly, Creative Commons Attribution 3.0 https://creativecommons.org/licenses/by/3.0/legalcode. Public domain

embedded in representations of the eight sacred places. A stele from Sarnath (seventh century; Sarnath Museum, Uttar Pradesh; Brown, 2009: fig. 3), depicting the Life of the Buddha in eight episodes, figures the monkey's gift as one of these episodes (left column, third episode from top). Here, the "second" monkey has already fallen into the well, as indicated by its protruding legs and feet. Immediately above the well hovers a divine figure (*deva*), likely representing the monkey's ascent to heaven. The exact genus of monkey itself cannot be properly identified, due to heavy damage to its face and lack of a clear tail.

17.3.3 The Flying Buddha

The Story of the Flying Buddha tells the tale of Buddha's disciple and half-brother Nanda's desire to leave the monastic order to reunite with the beautiful wife he had left behind. The story is told in, amongst others (Shulman, 2018), the narrative poem *Saundarananda* by Asvaghosha (first century; see translation by Covill, 2007). Once, the Buddha rose into the air and took the troubled and love-sick Nanda on a journey to heaven to convince him to forget his wife. On their way, the Buddha showed him an ugly female monkey. In heaven, he showed him beautiful nymphs (*apsaras*). He then asked Nanda which he preferred. The longing Nanda then realized that compared to the beauty of the celestial nymphs, his wife was like the monkey. In an alternative version, found in the *Jatakas* (*Nandajataka*, or Pali *Jataka* 39) the monkey is old and scarred with burnt ears and snout, sitting on a charred tree trunk. Nanda then realizes that worldly beauty is transitional, in contrast to the eternal beauty in heaven. In the version as told in the *Khuddaka Nikaya* (*Udana* 3.2, *Nanda Sutta*; see translation by Ireland, 1997), Buddha takes the love-struck Nanda to the Heaven of the Thirty-three (*Trayastrimsha*) in an instant, without showing a monkey on the way. Upon seeing the beautiful celestial nymphs (apsaras), who attend upon Sakka, king of gods, Nanda realized that his beloved one compares to them as a she-monkey with burned skin and with her ears and nose cut off.

In an atypical continuation of the story, Buddha then flew with Nanda over the mountains that surround the world, where the incomparably beautiful monkey-women lived. He then asked Nanda to compare his wife's beauty with theirs. Nanda realizes that they are a thousand times more beautiful, but the celestial nymphs are, in their turn, a thousand times more beautiful than the monkey-women. Perhaps this part of the story represents the heavenly forest Himavanta of the god Indra, where a tree grows that has fruits in the shape of young women, who were confused with the monkey-women of the above story. These trees are known in other Buddhist tales, for example, Indra is told to have planted these particular trees around the grove where the future Buddha Vessantara meditated, as told in the *Vessantara Jataka* (Pali *Jataka* 547).

A rhesus monkey figures in the depiction of this story on a frieze from the *ayaka* platform from Nagarjunakonda, Andhra Pradesh (third to fourth century) (Fig. 17.4). It has a short tail but has neither a bonnet or a tuft of hair on its cheeks. The scene to the left represents heaven, which is full of celestial females, and above it, indicating a remote distance, a tree with two women, either representing the attractive monkey-women, or more likely, Indra's tree in Himavanta. The monkey here is not sitting on a tree trunk, but on a pile of stones, probably symbolizing a rocky landscape, at a river bank, indicated by lotus flowers. Also, the monkey is neither scarred nor mutilated, but simply serves as a contrast with the beauty seen in heaven, as described in Asvaghosha's version of the tale.

17.3.4   The Gardener and the Monkeys

The story of The Gardener and the Monkeys, known as *Aramadusaka Jataka* (Pali *Jataka* 46), portrays monkeys as symbols of foolishness. Once, as the story has it, the king's gardener wished to attend a festival and asked the monkey king, who lived in the king's garden, to water the young trees while he was gone. To avoid any waste of water,

Figure 17.4 Story of the Flying Buddha and Nanda. *Ayaka* platform frieze, panel D2, Nagarjunakonda, second to fourth century. Archaeological Museum, Nagarjunakonda. Archaeological Survey of India, unknown photographer, 1928–1930. Kern Institute Photography Collections (owned by the Society of the Kern Institute, Leiden).

the monkey king ordered his subjects to take the trees out to measure the length of their roots and water them accordingly. The lesson taught being that ignorant people can only do harm, even if they desire to do good. The gardener should have known better.

An illustration of the story, figuring rhesus macaques, is found on a railing around the stupa at Bharhut (coping stone; c. 100 BCE) (Fig. 17.5). The macaques are depicted here in much the same way as in the Story of the Great Monkey King (see Fig. 17.2) on the railing of the same stupa, although here with rounded muzzles instead of more realistic prognathic, angular muzzles, indicating a different sculptor.

17.4   Monkeys in Hindu Religious Architecture

Hindu religious architecture with figurative reliefs and statues includes temples with their sometimes impressive, independent entrance tower and tower-like superstructure, monasteries, hermitages, chariot-shaped shrines, tombs, and pillars (Michell, 1988, 2000; Tadgell, 1990). Solitary memorial or votive steles are also generally decorated with reliefs and are included here.

The majority of sculptures depicting monkeys in these buildings and structures concern fables and episodes of the parts of the ancient Sanskrit epic *Ramayana*, ascribed to the seer Valmiki, that illustrate the adventures of the monkey god Hanuman and his monkey army and their role in the rescue of Rama's abducted wife Sita. Apart from

Figure 17.5 The Gardener and the Monkeys (*Aramadusaka Jataka* 46) on a coping stone from the stupa railing at Bharhut (*c.* 100 BCE). India Office List 1900, nr. 1079. Photograph J. D. Beglar, between 1874 and 1876. Kern Institute Photography Collections (owned by the Society of the Kern Institute, Leiden).

Ramayana episodes, depictions of animal tales can also be found on Hindu religious architecture, generally deriving from the *Panchatantra* tradition of fables.

Especially in the South, however, some Hindu temples bear monkey sculptures that seem not to have a religious meaning but that are entirely decorative. The monkeys in these instances are naturalistically portrayed, often climbing or engaging in natural behavior like grooming. A free-standing statue of a bonnet macaque couple with infant, where the male grooms the female, and the female nurses the infant, is present at Mahabalipuram (seventh to mid eighth century, granite; van der Geer, 2008: fig. 374). It is located close to the monolithic rock-boulder with a bas-relief of a mythic episode encompassing a multitude of naturalistically depicted wild animals, generally referred to as Arjuna's Penance (of the same period) and a number of independent shrines and cave sanctuaries. Another purely decorative example is provided by the Koodal Alagar Kovil (Vishnu Temple) at Madurai (sixteenth century) (Fig. 17.6). Here, a langur, recognized by its prominent undulating eyebrows and very long tail, climbs down a pilaster. To its right, a couple of parrots are eating from a flower. The birds and flower are merely decorative as well, probably to imitate the reality of temples, where animals and plants gradually invade the buildings.

17.4.1 The Monkey and the Crocodile

The Story of the Monkey and the Crocodile (*Panchatantra*, Book 4) illustrates the cleverness of a monkey, and the use of intelligence to master difficult situations. It also underlines that one should never believe a creature as greedy as a crocodile.

Figure 17.6 A langur descends a pilaster of the Koodal Alagar Kovil, Madurai (sixteenth century). Photograph by Anna Ślązcka (2015).

Once, we are told, a crocodile used to rest along the river bank beneath a huge rose-apple tree in which a monkey lived. The monkey regularly threw apples down to the crocodile, and this is how they became friends. The crocodile often delayed going home on time. Jealous, his wife pretended to be mortally ill, and said that only the heart of a monkey could cure her disease. She commanded her husband to kill his friend, but the crocodile refused at first until, at last, he had to give in. And thus he invited the monkey to meet his wife at the opposite bank. He took the monkey on his back and began to swim. Midway, the crocodile told him the truth, upon which the monkey replied that it had forgotten his sweet heart in the rose-apple tree. They returned to get it, but once ashore, the monkey laughed and asked, "Who then has two hearts?", and leaped off into the tree. There are several versions of this story, and the crocodile may be a turtle, a fish, or a river dolphin, as in the Seventy Tales of the Parrot (*Shukhasaptati*, 68th story, ed. Morgenroth, 1969). The story is also found in the Buddhist *Jataka* tales (*Sumsumara Jataka*, or Pali *Jataka* 208), with as main difference that here the crocodile was asked by his wife to get her a monkey heart, and he wasn't the monkey's friend. To obtain the heart, he offers the monkey a ride to the other side of the river, where the fruits were ripe. Halfway, the crocodile submerged, and the monkey almost drowned. The crocodile revealed his plan, upon which the monkey told him that his heart was still in the tree.

The fable is illustrated on a frieze of the Tripurantakeshvara temple at Balligavi (*c.* 1070) (Fig. 17.7). Here, a bonnet monkey figures, judging by the long, thick tail and the lack of the long hairs at the sides of the face. The monkey sits in the tree at the left side, with the crocodile beneath. The monkey and the crocodile are depicted again at the right side, where they swim to the other side. The swimming action is merely a walk through the river, indicated by vertical wavy lines with a turtle in the middle.

Figure 17.7 The Monkey and the Crocodile, a fable from the *Panchatantra*, book 4. Tripurantakeshvara temple, Belgami (*c.* 1070). Photograph Gerard Foekema. Kern Institute Photography Collections (owned by the Society of the Kern Institute, Leiden).

The fable acknowledges the once prevalent use of monkey parts for their medicinal purposes, as is done today by the Lepchas of the Himalayas. Another tale relates about the curative attributes of monkey fat to heal burns (Pali *Jataka* 250), but to my knowledge, no stone relief illustrates this tale.

17.4.2 Hanuman

The common langurs are sacred to the Hindus, as they are the living representatives of the monkey god Hanuman, son of the wind god Vayu, and one of the most popular deities of Hindus present and past, judging by the abundance of Hanuman temples, statues, and reliefs. Especially in South India, Hanuman sculptures in one iconographic form or another abound. Hanuman is the Hindu symbol of loyalty and steadfastness. Like the elephant-headed god Ganesha, Hanuman is considered a remover of obstacles (*samkat-mochan*), but also a warrior-god, the ideal statesman, and, sometimes, an incarnation of Shiva (for the complex and often contradictory theology around Hanuman, see Lutgendorf, 1997; Nagar, 2004; Narula, 2005). As most Hindu deities, Hanuman is referred to with various alternative names or epithets, indicating his descent or role, such as Anjaneya or Anjaniputra (son of Anjana, a celestial nymph or *apsara*), with or without prefix Vira (hero), Vayuputra (son of Vayu, lord of the winds), Pavanaputra (son of Pavana, alternative name for Vayu), Maruti (of or related to the Maruts, a group of storm gods), Kapishvara (Lord of monkeys), or simply Mahavira (Great Hero). The connection with atmospheric deities gives Hanuman his ability to fly.

17.4.2.1 Hanuman in Narrative Reliefs

Hanuman plays a prominent role in the ancient Sanskrit epic *Ramayana*, where he is the leader of a monkey army to assist Rama in finding his wife Sita after she was abducted by the demon-king of Lanka, Ravana (see translation by Griffith, 1870–1874). A major part of *Ramayana* reliefs is devoted to episodes of the fifth book (*Sundara kanda*), where Hanuman and his monkey army are the main characters (Aryan, 1994). A number of temples in South India are richly decorated with *Ramayana* panels illustrating Hanuman's adventures. In all these panels, the monkeys have the very long tail characteristic of langurs.

The Amriteshvara temple at Amritapura (Amruthapura) near Tarikere (*c.* 1196) is such an example. It is decorated with a multitude of *Ramayana* and *Mahabharata* (the other epic of ancient India) panels all around. For example, Rama blesses Hanuman on one panel (south side of the *mandapa*), where Hanuman with his long snout and long, upheld tail kneels in a human way. Elsewhere, six monkey soldiers of Hanuman's army are carrying rounded boulders to the shallow sea to build a causeway to Lanka. The sea strait is indicated by a multitude of sea creatures, including fish, crabs, and turtles.

On another panel at the same temple, Hanuman fights the multiheaded demon Ravana with a few of his monkey soldiers (southern entrance, east side). Here, Hanuman's overly long tail is rolled up for the sake of convenience and functions as a progressively growing throne to sit at a higher level than Ravana. Hanuman is depicted in a way customary for the depiction of higher classes, with elongated earlobes as a result of wearing heavy jewelry, whereas his subjects have shorter ears. One of his soldiers is about to swing a stone using his tail as a sling. A panel on the same column shows Hanuman teaching Ravana after the latter's defeat. Hanuman's exorbitantly long tail is here rolled up to serve as a seat to surpass the level of Ravana's throne. Hanuman sits in a relaxed, human-like posture. This exaggerated tail length is not unique to this panel, but is seen elsewhere too, for example on a pillar of the horse *mandapa* (Sheshagirirayar) of the Ranganatha temple complex on the island of Shrirangam (or Thiruvarangam) in the Kaveri river (late sixteenth century) (Fig. 17.8), where Hanuman ties up the captured Ravana with his extremely long tail. This temple, like the Amriteshvara temple, is richly decorated with *Ramayana* episodes.

His minimal representation in the north is in stark contrast to Hanuman's presence in the south. A typical example of a northern Indian representation can be seen on a statue of Rama from Ganeshpur, Bangladesh (tenth to twelfth century; van der Geer, 2008: fig. 473). It shows Rama flanked by his brother Lakshmana to his right and with his wife Sita to his left. On the pedestal we see the tiny figure of Hanuman, who can be recognized by the long, swinging tail of a langur, carrying the platform on which the trio stands. His role is minor here, and the depiction serves solely as a reference to the epic story and to show Hanuman as the loyal and devoted servant to Rama.

17.4.2.2 Hanuman as Stand-alone

Hanuman is more often portrayed on his own, with at most a hint at an epic scene. At the ruins of Hampi, part of the ancient capital Vijayanagara (sixteenth century), tens of stelcs, stone slabs, and boulders with a Hanuman image, locally referred to as Vira

Figure 17.8 Hanuman captures Ravana. Sheshagirirayar (Horse Mandapa), Rangunatha temple complex, Srirangam, late sixteenth century. Photograph by Anna Ślączka.

Anjaneya, are scattered around. Hanuman is almost invariably depicted as a fierce warrior, striding towards Lanka, ready to fight with his tail upright and above his head and holding a battle mace (*gada*) in one hand (Fig. 17.9). His ornamentation (earrings, necklaces, armband, wristband, waistband, anklets, tiara) indicates a status at least equal to royals. Invariably, he wears a garland of flowers, stretching below his knees, to stress his link with Vishnu, who always wears such a garland. Occasionally, Hanuman tramples a demon, representing the son of Ravana. On some, Hanuman is ready to set fire to the palace of Ravana, judging by his lit tail tip. On others, Hanuman is crossing the causeway of rocks built by the monkeys to reach Lanka. On the more detailed reliefs, large fangs protrude from the corners of his mouth.

On similar steles elsewhere, for example, the one at Gwalior (seventeenth to eighteenth century; Archaeological Museum), Hanuman steps on a subdued opponent, as a symbol of victory, and holds a club in his right hand. The fallen opponent may be Ahiravana, Ravana's brother, ruler of the Netherworld, who had captured Rama and Lakshmana to sacrifice them to his goddess, as told in Tulsi Das' *Ramacaritamanasa*, a vernacular version of the *Ramayana*. Hanuman steles are very common, especially throughout rural peninsular India, and are often rather crude and

Figure 17.9 Boulder with bas-relief of Hanuman among the ruins of ancient Vijayanagara, the capital city of the dynasty of the same name. Hampi, 15th century. Photograph by R. Barry Lewis.

naive. Hanuman frequently functions as a protector of boundaries, and steles depicting Hanuman are typically situated as guardians at the border of a village (Brackett, 2004). Also, shrines dedicated to him in rural Rajasthan were traditionally located outside the village (for a discussion on the liminal character of Hanuman, see Lutgendorf, 1997).

A rare iconography is presented by a stele with Hanuman reading a palm leaf manuscript in one of the nine Hindu shrines (Nava Brindavanam) at Anegundi on a small island in the Tungabhadra river near Hampi (fourteenth to sixteenth century). This holy place is considered to be ancient Kishkinda, the forest where the brothers Rama and Lakshmana first met the monkey king Sugriva and Hanuman. Hanuman is here depicted sitting with his long tail upright and plays his role as a teacher. He can thus be identified as the first avatar or incarnation of the wind god Vayu and this links Hanuman to the philosopher-saint Madhvacharya, who is considered Vayu's third avatar.

Although Hanuman as a warrior is very popular on steles and in bas-reliefs, most Hanuman statues show him in a peaceful posture, standing or sitting with folded hands (*namaskaramudra*, also known as *anjalimudra*) paying respect to Rama or

Figure 17.10 Statue of Hanuman standing peacefully. South India, thirteenth to sixteenth century. British Museum, London. Photograph: Archaeological Survey of India, 1920–1940. Kern Institute Photography Collections. (owned by the Society of the Kern Institute, Leiden).

raising a hand in a reassuring, "fear-not" way (*abhayamudra*) to the spectator. His face often bears the undulating and prominent eyebrows that are typical for gray langurs. A good illustration is a statue from South India (thirteenth to sixteenth century, British Museum, London) (Fig. 17.10) which stands with folded hands, and with its very long tail upright and the tip tightly coiled above its head as a crown, prominent eyebrows, and a rounded monkey muzzle. The majority of Hanuman stone statues follow this iconography, with variations in the posture of the tail.

Stand-alone statues of a peaceful Hanuman have been made since antiquity, and today arise as colossi made out of concrete and fiber glass, vividly painted and up to 32 m high, such as the one at Nandura (raising its right hand in the reassuring pose, and calmly leaning on his club with the left hand), and the one along the trail up to the Hanuman temple on the Tirumala hills of Tirupati (with folded hands). These grotesque statues of Hanuman are evidence of the god's popularity among modern

Hindus (on these ever-larger colossi, see Lutgendorf, 1994). Hanuman became especially popular in the past few centuries, and most Hindus today know his adventures not through the ancient Sanskrit epic *Ramayana*, but the vernacular version *Ramacaritamanasa* in Hindi in the late sixteenth century by the poet-saint Tulsi Das.

Hanuman is sometimes portrayed running swiftly while carrying a mountain in his hands, or opening his chest to show Rama and Sita near his heart. The first iconographic variation relates to the episode where the mortally wounded Lakshmana, brother of Prince Rama, could only be saved with a medicinal herb (*sanjivani*) growing on mount Dronagiri on the slopes of the Himalayas. As told in Tulsi Das' *Ramacaritamanasa* chapter 6 (Hill, 1952), or the vernacular *Ramayana*, Hanuman rushed to the mountain range, but upon arrival, failed to recognize the correct herb. In despair what to do, he decided to bring the whole mountain along. The second variation shows Hanuman's eternal devotion and loyalty to Rama and Sita.

Rarely, Hanuman is portrayed with five heads, in which form he is known as Panchamukhi Hanuman. Each head faces its own cardinal direction: the east for monkey-headed Hanuman, the south for lion-headed Narasimha, north for boar-headed Varaha, west for eagle-headed Garuda, while the horse-headed Hayagriva is watching the sky. This iconography is not mainstream, but mostly restricted to tantric traditions and relatively new, not appearing before the fifteenth century (Lutgendorf, 2001).

17.4.2.3 Hanuman as Macaque

In very rare cases, Hanuman is depicted as a macaque instead of a langur. One example of this can be seen on a stele at the entrance to the Baghbhairava temple at Bhaktapur, Nepal (sixteenth century). Hanuman here swings a hammer-like weapon in his right hand while stepping on a causeway of stones towards the island of Lanka. His tail is as short as the tail of a rhesus monkey and does not resemble the extremely long tail of langurs. Another example is seen on an early panel from the region of Sarnath (fourth to sixth century; Archaeological Museum, Sarnath) where Hanuman meets Rama and his brother Lakshmana, while his army is depicted camping in front of the trio. All monkeys have the short tail that is typical for macaques.

17.4.3 Erotic Scenes

The depiction of erotic scenes is a familiar subject in Hindu religious architecture, as unmistakably exemplified by the famous temple complex at Khajuraho (tenth to eleventh century) with its abundance of voluptuous women and erotic couples (*mithunas*) engaged in all sorts of explicit and often acrobatic sexual acts. Macaques regularly figure in such settings, where they stand symbol for the unbound desires and provide a warning: in Hindu philosophy, attachment to worldly pleasures is the cause of all suffering. In rare cases, the monkeys are actively engaged in a sexual act, such as depicted on a frieze of the Tripurantakeshvara temple at Balligavi (c. 1070) and on a pillar of the Vitthalasvami temple at Hampi (early fourteenth to fifteenth century), both with a copulating pair of macaques.

Figure 17.11 Divine beauty, sandstone, height 94 cm, India, eleventh century, acquired in 1934, inv. no. AK-MAK-185-00. Courtesy Rijksmuseum Amsterdam, the Netherlands.

A fine example of a relief with a more subtle erotic touch is that of a voluptuous nymph (*surasundari*) and a rhesus monkey on a pilaster of unknown provenance (India, eleventh century) (Fig. 17.11). The nymph lowers her garment, showing her private parts, while the monkey climbs up her leg, looking up with desire. Two fellow monkeys are visible in the tree above the nymph. A similar scene is seen at a pilaster haut-relief of the Queen's Step-well (Rani-ki-Vav) at Patan (eleventh century), in between Vishnu as Kalki to the left and Durga slaying the buffalo demon to the right. Here the monkey has already reached a higher part of the nymph's leg. At Khajuraho, a monkey adds a ludic touch to a panel with a love-making couple. The monkey disturbs the amorous couple, and the lover tries to ward it off with a staff (north vestibule, Lakshmana temple, c. 930–950; van der Geer, 2008: fig. 384).

17.4.4 Monkey-Headed Tantric Goddesses

In tantric forms of Hinduism, female goddesses (*yoginis*) may be animal headed. In these traditions, *yoginis* represent the feminine force and are worshipped for their spiritual powers, secret knowledge, and passion, as divine mothers. Paying respect to them is a necessary step for those who seek liberation (*siddhi*) from the eternal cycle of life and death (*samsara*). Often, though, worshippers strive to gain supernatural or magical powers instead of salvation. *Yoginis* are typically enshrined individually in a circular open temple with a narrow entrance, reminiscent of the womb. Their numbers vary up to 64. A famous Chausath Yogini temple is the one at Hirapur (ninth century). The only rectangular version is the Chausath Yogini temple at Khajuraho (*c.* 885 CE). The goddess Vanaramukhi (or Ushtrarudha) here has the head of a monkey and she stands on a dromedary. A rare parallel is seen in tantric forms of *yoginis* in Buddhism, where the goddess Lobha has the head of a monkey. Due to lack of sufficient detail, it is not clear if these heads belong to a macaque or a langur.

17.5 Carvings of Primates in Indian Religious Architecture: Looking at Patterns and Dissimilarities

Religious structures and sites throughout the Indian subcontinent document part of the human–monkey interactions as they played a role in the past. Some of these interactions are doubtlessly of a religious nature (e.g. statues of the monkey god Hanuman), others merely or purely educational (e.g. animal fables with a moralistic twist), and yet others serve merely a decorative purpose or add a playful note, such as the monkey sculptures that decorate temples throughout southern India. Erotic interactions are limited to Hindu religious architecture.

Generally, macaques are depicted in both Buddhist and Hindu architecture, while langurs are restricted to narrative reliefs of the epic Ramayana and the monkey god Hanuman, mostly in a Hindu context.

Common to both Buddhist and Hindu religious architecture is that macaques are a metaphor for the restless and unstable human mind, and the unbound desires. In tales and fables, sculptured both in Buddhist and Hindu contexts, monkeys stand symbol for the undesirable human virtues, ugliness (as compared to heavenly beings), stupidity (uprooting trees to measure root length), incautiousness (stumbling into a well or falling off a branch), and promiscuity (erotic scenes). They are rarely witty and clever (fooling the crocodile). Monkeys thus rather stand for archetypal human behaviors and characters, being 'almost human'. The only important exception is Hanuman, but his amazing powers and qualities (immortality, ability to fly, and to grow as large as a mountain or tiny as a fly in an instant) are inherited not from monkeys but directly from the gods. In Buddhist narrative reliefs, macaques, when used as background figures, often illustrate a forest setting, the wild nature, outside of human society and civilization.

The monkey fables in Buddhist and Hindu literature are often similar or almost identical, and likely derive from an older oral layer. This probably explains the rare reflection of more ancient habits, such as eating monkeys (prohibited in the religious text, yet found in reliefs) and the use of monkey parts for medicine.

In religious architecture, whether Buddhist or Hindu, monkeys are nowhere depicted as auspicious beings, in contrast to elephants, bulls, peacocks, and snakes. This is in agreement with most early Indian literature, which reflects a low estimation of monkeys (Lutgendorf, 1997). Indeed, today monkeys are considered somehow bothersome animals because of their active foraging activities in human places and alleged promiscuous behavior. The status and popularity of the monkey god Hanuman is in this respect paradoxical; on the other hand, he is not just a monkey, but the offspring of various divine powers combined (Siva, Vishnu, Vayu). As Lutgendorf (1997) remarks, langurs around Hanuman temples are venerated because they are part of the tribe of Hanuman, but not vice-versa, and the monkeys of the Ramayana are not comparable with ordinary monkeys. Indeed, apart from Hanuman, there is no evidence in Hindu religious architecture of worship or veneration of monkeys. This veneration of monkeys in and around Hindu temples, though, can perhaps be recognized in the langur and macaque reliefs and statues with a purely decorative purpose on or near temples, mainly in South India. These monkeys, captured in stone, engage in natural behaviors, such as climbing and grooming, as if they inhabit the temple and the grounds around it.

17.6 Concluding Remarks

In general, compared to other animals, monkeys play a relatively minor role in Buddhist and Hindu religious architecture and sculpture, except for depictions of the Hindu monkey god Hanuman. In a Buddhist context, they are restricted to narrative contexts, where they are illustrations for either wittiness or foolishness. They are considered of a lower rank than humans, yet somehow comparable, but with an unstable mind. In a Hindu context, apart from Hanuman, they are in addition considered promiscuous and figure in scenes with an erotic touch. Hanuman dominates Hindu architectural representations of monkeys in South India because of his divine status, which sets Hanuman apart from all other figured monkeys. Hanuman and his companions are almost invariably depicted as langurs, whereas macaques figure in the rest of the sculptures, Buddhist as well as Hindu. Further research must consider why reliefs with langurs are missing from non-*Ramayana* contexts, why only a selection of existing monkey tales adorn religious architecture, and why precisely those.

Acknowledgments

I here take the opportunity to thank the editors Bernardo Urbani, Dionisios Youlatos, and Andrzej T. Antczak for inviting me to contribute to this book. I further thank Dr. Anna Ślączka (Rijksmuseum, Amsterdam, the Netherlands) for discussions on primates in Indian art, and providing me with photographs. I thank George Lyras for drawing the geographic map, and Institute Kern (Leiden), the Rijksmuseum

(Amsterdam), Anna Slączka, and Barry Lewis for permission to use their photographs. I am much indebted to Janet Tiwary Kamphorst and Tamatea McGlinn for editing and correcting the English and the former also for translating the abstract in Hindi. I am grateful to Barry Lewis for his constructive comments and suggestions for improvement of the text.

References

Aryan, K. (1994). *Hanuman in Art and Mythology*, Delhi: Rekha Prakashan.

Bleisch, B., Brockelman, W, Timmins, R. J., et al. (2020). *Trachypithecus phayrei*. The IUCN Red List of Threatened Species 2020: e.T22040A17960739.

Bracket, J. M. (2004). Practically Hindu: contemporary conceptions of Hanuman-Maruti in Maharashtra. PhD thesis, University of Pittsburgh.

Brown, R. L. (2009). Telling the story in art of the monkey's gift of honey to the Buddha. *Bulletin of the Asia Institute, New Series*, 23, 43–52.

Burlingame, E. W. (1921) *Buddhist Legends: Translated from the Original Pali Text of the Dhammapada Commentary, Part 1*, Cambridge, MA: Harvard University Press.

Chaturvedi, S. K., & Mishra, M. K. (2014). Study of man-monkey conflict and its management in Chitrakoot, Madhya Pradesh, India. *International Journal of Global Science Research*, 1(2), 107–110.

Colding, J., & Folke, C. (2001). Social taboos: "invisible" systems of local resource management and bio-logical conservation. *Ecological Applications*, 11(2), 584–600.

Covill, L. (2007). *Handsome Nanda by Ashva-ghosha*, New York: Clay Sanskrit Library.

Cowell, E. B. Francis, H. T., & Neil, R. A. (1990). *The Jātaka (or Stories of the Buddha's Former Births), vols I to VI, First Indian Edition* (reprint of 1897), New Delhi: Munishiram Manoharial Publishers.

Das, J., Medhi, R., & Molur, S. (2008a). *Trachypithecus geei*. The IUCN Red List of Threatened Species 2008: e.T22037A9348940.

Das, J., Molur, S., & Bleisch, W. (2008b). *Trachypithecus pileatus*. The IUCN Red List of Threatened Species 2008: e.T22041A9350087.

Dehejia, V. (1997a). *Discourse in Early Buddhist Art: Visual Narratives of India*, Delhi: Munshiram Manoharlal.

Dehejia, V. (1997b). *Indian Art*, London, New York: Phaidon.

Deva, K. (1974). Buddhist architecture in India. *Bulletin of Tibetology*, 11(3), 12–28

Gnoli, R., & Venkatacharya, T. (1978). *The Gilgit Manuscript of the Sanghabhedavastu: being the 17th and last section of the Vinaya of the Mūlasarvāstivādin. Vol. 49(2) of Serie Orientale*. Roma: Istituto italiano per il medio ed estremo oriente.

Griffith, R. T. H. (1870–1874). *The Rámáyan of Válmiki, Translated into English Verse*, London: Trübner.

Hill, W. D. P. (1952). *The Holy Lake of the Acts of Rama*, Calcutta: Oxford University Press.

Huntington, S. L. (1985). *The Art of Ancient India: Buddhist, Hindu, Jain*, New York and Tokyo: Weatherhill.

Ireland, J. D. (1997). *The Udāna, Inspired Utterances of the Buddha, & The Itivuttaka, The Buddha's Sayings Translated from the Pāli*, Kandy, Sri Lanka. Buddhist Publication Society.

IUCN (2020). The IUCN Red List of Threatened Species. Version 2020-2. Available at: www.iucnredlist.org (Accessed: 12 August 2020)

Kawasaki, K., & Kawasaki, V. (1998). *Jataka Tales of the Buddha, Part III. Vol. 142 of Bodhi Leaves*. Kandy, Sri Lanka: Buddhist Publication Society.

Khatun, U. H., Ahsan, M. F., & Roskaft, M. (2013). Local people's perceptions of crop damage by common langurs (*Semnopithecus entellus*) and human-langur conflict in Keshabpur of Bangladesh . *Environment and Natural Resources Research*, 3(1), 111–126.

Kirkpatrick, K. M. (1955). Aboriginal methods employed in killing and capturing game. *Journal of the Bombay Natural History Society*, 52(2–3), 285–300.

Kumara, H. N., Kumar, A., & Singh, M. (2020). *Semnopithecus entellus*. The IUCN Red List of Threatened Species 2020: e.T39832A17942050.

Lutgendorf, P. (1994). My Hanuman is bigger than yours. *History of Religions*, 33(3), 211–245.

Lutgendorf, P. (1997). Monkey in the middle: the status of Hanuman in popular Hinduism. *Religion*, 27, 311–332.

Lutgendorf, P. (2001). Five heads and no tale: Hanumān and the popularization of Tantra. *International Journal of Hindu Studies*, 5(3), 269–296.

Michell, G. (1988). *The Hindu Temple: An Introduction to Its Meaning and Form*, Chicago: University of Chicago Press.

Michell, G. (2000). *Hindu Art and Architecture*, New York: Thames and Hudson.

Molur, S., Brandon-Jones, D., Dittus, W., et al. (2003). Status of South Asian Primates: Conservation Assessment and Managment Plan Report. Workshop Report, 2003. *Zoo Outreach Organization/CBSG-South Asia*, Coimbatore, India.

Morgenroth, W. (1969). *Shukhasaptati, Das Papageienbuch*, München: Winkler-Verlag

Nagar, S. (2004). *Hanuman: Through the Ages, 3 vols.* Delhi: B.R. Publishing.

Narula, J. (2005). *God and Epic Hero: The Origin and Growth of Hanuman in Indian Literary and Folk Tradition*, New Delhi: Manohar.

Nowak, R. (1999). *Walker's Mammals of the World*, 6th ed., 2 vols. Baltimore and London: The Johns Hopkins University Press.

Olivelle, P. (1999). *Pañchatantra: The Book of India's Folk Wisdom*, Oxford: Oxford University Press.

Olivelle, P. (2002). Food for thought. Dietary rules and social organization in ancient India. *Gonda Lecture 9, Royal Netherlands Academy of Arts and Sciences, Amsterdam*.

Osterholz, M., Walter, L., & Roos, C. (2008). Phylogenetic position of the langur genera *Semnopithecus* and *Trachypithecus* among Asian colobines, and genus affiliations of their species groups. *BMC Evolutionary Biology*, **8**, 58.

Pocock, R. (1976). *The Fauna of British India Including Ceylon and Burma. Mammalia–vol. 1, Primates and Carnivora (in part), Families Felidae and Viverridae*, The Hague: W. Junk (reprint of London: Taylor and Francis, 1939).

Prater, S. (1971). *The Book of Indian Animals*, Bombay: Natural History Society.

Rudran, R., Dittus, W., Gamage, S. N., & Nekaris, K. A. I. (2020). *Semnopithecus vetulus*. The IUCN Red List of Threatened Species 2020: e.T22042A17959452.

Shulman, E. (2018). Aśvaghoṣa's Viśeṣaka: The Saundarananda and Its Pāli "Equivalents." *Journal of Indian Philosophy*, **47**, 235–256.

Singh, M., Kumar, A., & Kumara, H. N. (2020a). *Macaca mulatta*. The IUCN Red List of Threatened Species 2020: e.T12554A17950825.

Singh, M., Kumara, H. N.,& Kumar, A. (2020b). *Macaca radiata*. The IUCN Red List of Threatened Species 2020: e.T12558A17951596.

Singh, M., Kumara, H. N., & Kumar, A. (2020c). *Semnopithecus johnii*. The IUCN Red List of Threatened Species 2020: e.T44694A17958623.

Tadgell, C. (1990). *The History of Architecture in India: From the Dawn of Civilization to the End of the Raj*, London: Architecture, Design, and Technology Press.

van der Geer, A. A. E. (2008). *Animals in Stone. Indian Fauna Sculptured through Time. Vol. 21 of Handbook of Oriental Studies, Section 2 South Asia.* Leiden: Brill.

Warder, A. K. (2000). *Indian Buddhism*, Delhi: Motilal Banarsidass.

18 The Prehistoric Nonhuman Primate Subfossil Remains at Sigiriya Potana Cave, Sri Lanka

Michael A. Huffman, Charmalie A. D. Nahallage, Tharaka Ananda, Nelum Kanthilatha, Nimal Perera, Massimo Bardi, & Gamini Adikari

ලංකාවේ පොතාන ගුහාවෙන් හමු වූ පුාග් ඓතිහාසික මිනිස් නොවන පුාමාටා අවශේෂ

වියුක්ත

ශ්‍රී ලංකාව පුරා විසිරි පැතිර ඇති පුාග් ඓතිහාසික යුගයට අයත් ගුහා ස්ථාන 20ක (කි. පු. 37000-2940 අතර) මිනිස් නොවන පුාමාටා අස්ථි කැණීම් සිදු කර ඇත. මෙම මිනිස් නොවන පුාමාටාවන් එම ගුහාවාසීන්ගේ ආහාර පුභවය විය. මෙකී ගුහා ස්ථානවලින් එකක් වන සිගිරිය පොතාන ගුහා සංකීර්ණය මධ්‍යම පළාතේ අන්තර් දේශගුණික කලාපයක මුහුදු මට්ටමේ සිට මීටර 70ක් උසින් පිහිටා ඇති අතර පරිවාර ගුහා 12කින් සමන්විත ය. වසර 1990න් 1991න් අතර කොළඹ පුරාවිද්‍යා පශ්චාද් උපාධි ආයතනය විසින් මෙම ස්ථානයේ කැණීමක් සිදු කර තිබේ. කාබන් 14 කාල නිර්ණයට අනුව මෙම ගුහා තැන්පතුව ආසන්න වශයෙන් කි. පු. 6000ට අයත් අතර සමුච්චිත සම්භාවිතාවේ (සිග්මා එක) සිට කුමාංකනය කළ කාල පරාසය කි. පු. 3913 - 3727 සහ කි.පු. 3913 - 3709 අතර විය. මිනිස් නොවන පුාමාටා උපපොසිල සහ සම්පූර්ණ මානව සැකිලි ද්විත්වයක් සොයා ගැනුණු අතර පුාමාටා උපපොසිල දිවාචර මිනිස් නොවන පුාමාටා විශේෂ තුන්ත්වයට; එනම් වදුරු විශේෂ දෙකකට (Semnopithecus vetulus, Semnopithecus priam)සහ එක් රිලා විශේෂයකට: (Macaca sinica) අයත් බවට විශ්වාස කෙරේ. සොයාගත් සමස්ත මිනිස් නොවන පුාමාටා උපපොසිල අතර දත් සමග යටි හනු කොටස් 23ක්, දත් සමග උඩු හනු කොටස් 6ක් විය. පශ්චාපාල අස්ථි අර්ථවත් විශ්ලේෂණයක් සිදු කළ නොහැකි ලෙස කැබලිවලට වෙන් වී ඇත. මේ අතරින් සමහර කොටස් පිළිස්සී තිබෙන අතර ගුහාවාසීන් විසින් ගුහාවල වාසය කරන කාලය තුළ මෙම මිනිස් නොවන පුාමාටාවන් ආහාරයට ගන්නට ඇති බවට අනුමාන කළ හැකිය. මෙම උපපොසිල සහ වර්තමාන මිනිස් නොවන පුාමාටා විශේෂ තුන අතර සංසන්දනාත්මක දන්ත රූප විද්‍යාව හා දන්තමීනික අධ්‍යයනයට අනුව මෙම ආදි සහ නුතන සත්ත්ව විශේෂ එකම විශේෂයකට අයත් බව තහවුරුවිය. ශ්‍රී ලංකාවේ සහ දකුණු ආසියාවෙන් ඔබ්බට පිහිටි ස්ථාන වලට අනුරූපව ප්ලයිස්ටොසීන/හොලොසීන පර්යන්ත (කි. පු. ~ 12,000 සිට 3000) කාල වකවානුව තුළ මිනිස් නොවන පුාමාටාවන් වැදගත් ආහාර පුභවයක් වී තිබෙන්නට ඇති බව සැලකිය හැකිය.

පුමුඛ පද

මිනිස් නොවන පුාමාටා උපපොසිල – පුාග් ඓතිහාසික ගුහා ස්ථාන – කි. පු. 6000 – Macaca sinica – Semnopithecus priam thersites – S. vetulus

Abstract

Nonhuman primate subfossils have been excavated from 20 prehistoric (37,000– 2,940 BP) cave sites across Sri Lanka. These nonhuman primates were sources of food for the inhabitants. One of these sites, the Sigiriya Potana cave situated in the intermediate climatic zone in north central Sri Lanka, belongs to a complex of 12 caves located in the Central Province at 70 m above sea level. An excavation was conducted between 1990 and 1991 by the Post Graduate Institute of Archaeology, Colombo. The cave deposits were dated at ca. 6000 BP and the calibrated age ranges from cumulative probability (one sigma) 3913–3727 BCE (UA 5685) and 3913–3709 BCE (UA5686) using carbon-14 dating techniques. These nonhuman primate subfossils were found along with two complete human skeletons. These nonhuman primates are suspected to be the equivalents of the three diurnal species currently present in the area; namely two langur species (*Semnopithecus vetulus, Semnopithecus priam thersites*) and a macaque *(Macaca sinica)*. The total number of nonhuman primate subfossils found were 23 mandible fragments with teeth and 6 maxillary fragments with teeth. The postcranial material was badly fragmented, rendering impossible any meaningful analyses. Some of this material was burnt, and it is presumed that the human inhabitants consumed these nonhuman primates during their occupation of the cave. Odontometrical comparison of the dental morphology of these subfossil samples with those of the three extant nonhuman primate species confirmed that these are the same species. Consistent with other sites in Sri Lanka and elsewhere in South Asia during the Terminal Pleistocene/Holocene (~12,000 to 3000 BP) nonhuman primates are considered to have been an important food resource.

Keywords: Nonhuman primate subfossils, Prehistoric cave site, ca. 6000 BP, *Macaca sinica*, *Semnopithecus priam thersites*, *S. vetulus*

18.1   Introduction

The first hominins in Sri Lanka are thought to have arrived somewhere between 125,000 and 75,000 years ago (Kulatilake, 2016). The earliest archaeological record of modern humans *Homo sapiens* in Sri Lanka is around 45,000 BP (Wedage et al., 2019) and represents the oldest evidence of humans in all of South Asia, along the proposed southern dispersal route out of Africa. The oldest evidence comes from the Fa-Hien Lena cave site, located in the tropical wet zone of southwestern Sri Lanka (Fig. 18.1). These early inhabitants of the island subsisted largely on smaller sized semi-terrestrial and arboreal mammals, such as nonhuman primates, which accounted for over 70% of identified faunal remains excavated from the site. These people appear to have been quite adept hunters, with finely flaked microlithics (stone tools) and other tools modified from macaque long bones and teeth. The earliest evidence for bow and arrow technology outside of Africa has also been found at Fa-Hien Lena cave (Langley et al. 2020). Tools made from the bones and antlers of deer appeared later on, suggesting a strong dependence on nonhuman primates for food and tools for much of their long habitation of the cave (Wedage et al., 2019). Deer and wild boar consumption was limited to the Terminal and Late Pleistocene layers of the cave (Wedage et al., 2019). These trends of foraging on nonhuman primates and other small sized mammals are repeated across the island and elsewhere in tropical south Asia where prehistoric evidence has been unearthed (e.g. Perera et al., 2011; Roberts and Petraglia, 2015; Roberts et al., 2015; 2017).

Thus far, nonhuman primate fossils have been excavated from 20 archaeological sites across Sri Lanka, in the wet zone (n=12), the intermediate zone (*n* = 5) and marginal dry zones (n = 3) (Table 18.1; Fig. 18.1); unfortunately this material remains understudied. The evidence does demonstrate that throughout their cohabitation on the island, humans and nonhuman primates have lived in close proximity to each other. Detailed diagnostic descriptions of these nonhuman primate fossils have not

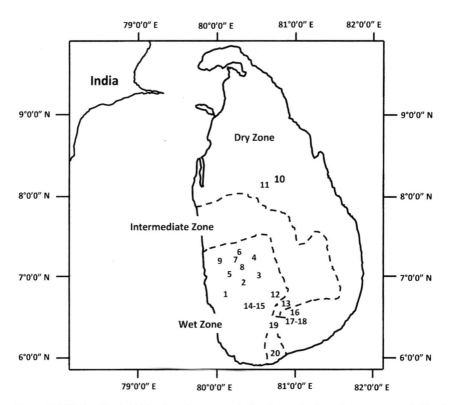

Figure 18.1 Study sites in Sri Lanka where primate fossil remains have been excavated. Numbers correspond with Table 18.1 to their approximate locations. 1: Fa Hien-lena, 2: Batadomba-lena, 3: Beli-lena, 4: Alu-lena, 5: Beli-lena Athula; 6: Dorawaka-lena; 7: Pothgullena, 8: Katarangala; 9: Warana; 10: Sigiriya Potana; 11: Aligala; 12: Kuragala-lena; 13: Bellanbandi-palassa; 14: Alugalge (Level III); 15: Alugalge (Level I); 16: Udupiyangalge, context 3; 17: Lunugalge, context 5, 18: Lunugalge, context 7, 19: Wavulgalge, context 2a, 20: Mini-Athiliya.

been made, rendering a taxonomic designation lacking for the moment, but the sites where they have been found are all within the current distribution of some or all three extant larger bodied nonhuman primate species (Fig. 18.2); namely the toque macaques (*Macaca sinica*), grey langur (*Semnopithecus priam thersites*), and purple-faced langur (*Semnopithecus vetulus*) (Nahallage and Huffman, 2013; Nahallage et al., 2008). In historical times, this connection continued and has become even more multifaceted for humans throughout Asia, where nonhuman primates are viewed not only as a source of food, but also as competitors for food resources, and as a source of religious reverence, medicine, and entertainment (e.g. Campbell-Smith et al., 2010; Nahallage and Huffman, 2013; Riley and Priston, 2010).

One important cave site, Sigiriya Potana cave, is situated in the dry zone in Sri Lanka (Figs. 18.1 and 18.3). This site is a complex of 12 caves located in the Central Province about 5 km from the road to Inamaluwa at 70 m above sea level (Adikari, 1994a, b; 1998; Fig. 18.1). In 1990 a team from the Post Graduate Institute of

Table 18.1. Archaeological sites in Sri Lanka with known fossil primate remains. Site numbers correspond to those locations in Fig. 18.1

Site no.	Name	Location (District, Province)	Chronology (Years Before Present)	Geological Period	References
1	Fa Hien-lena, Rockshelter	Kalutara, Western	c. 38,000 BP	late-Pleistocene to mid-Holocene	Wedage et al. (2019) Deraniyagala (2007) Kourompas et al. (2012) Perera (2010)
2	Batadomba-lena, Rockshelter	Rathnapura, Subaragamuwa	c. 37000–12,000 BP	late-Pleistocene to terminal Pleistocene	Deraniyagala, (2007) Perera 2010, 2011, 2015)
3	Beli-lena, Rockshelter	Kegalle, Subaragamuwa	c. 3778–31.010 BP	late-Pleistocene to mid-Holocene	Wijeyapala (1997) Deraniyagala, (2007) Perera (2010) Kourompas et al. (2009)
4	Alu-lena cave complex	Attanagoda, Subaragamuwa	c. 10,350 BP	terminal Pleistocene or early Holocene	Wijeyapala (1997) Deraniyagala (2007)
5	Beli-lena Athula, cave	Maniyangama, Subaragamuwa	c. 8230 BP	early-Holocene	Gunarathna (1971) Deraniyagala (2007)
6	Dorawaka-lena, rock shelter	Warakapola, Subaragamuwa	c.3700–6300 BP	mid-Holocene	Wijeyapala (1997) Perera (2010)
7	Pothgullena, rock shelter	Attanagala, Gampaha District	c.14,000–7000 BP	terminal Pleistocene or early Holocene	Adikari (2010)
8	Katarangala, cave	Bulathkohupitiya, Subaragamuwa	c. 8000 BP	early-Holocene	Hathurusinghe(2019)
9	Warana, rock shelter	Tihariya, Gampaha District	c. 6000 BP	mid-Holocene	Perera (2010)
10	Potana, rock shelter	Sigiriya, Dambulla	c. 5700–5900 BP	mid-Holocene	Adikari (1994a)
11	Aligala, rock shelter	Sigiriya, Dambulla 1	c. 5500–4300 BP	mid-Holocene	Adikari (1994b)

Table 18.1. (cont.)

Site no.	Name	Location (District, Province)	Chronology (Years Before Present)	Geological Period	References
12	Kuragala-lena, Rockshelter	Balangoda, Subaragamuwa	c. 15,163–2940 BP	late-Pleistocene to mid Holocene	Eregama (2017) Roberts et al. (2015)
13	Bellanbandi-palassa, rock shelter	Rathnapura, Subaragamuwa	c. 12,250 to 11,150 BP	terminal Pleistocene	Deraniyagala (1971) Deraniyagala and Kennedy (1972) Perera (2010)
14	Alugalge Level III), rock shelter	Rathnapura, Subaragamuwa	c. 5455–5375 BP	mid-Holocene	Somadeva et al. (2018)
15	Alugalge Level I), rock shelter	Rathnapura, Subaragamuwa	c. 1550–1405 BP	early-Historic	Somadeva et al. (2018)
16	Udupiyangalge, context 3, rock shelter	Rathnapura, Subaragamuwa	c. 9695–9545 BP	early-Holocene	Derniyagala (1943) Deraniyagala (1958) Somadeva et al. (2018)
17	Lunugalge, context 5, rock shelter	Rathnapura, Subaragamuwa	c. 5905–5730 BP	mid-Holocene	Deraniyagala (1940) Somadeva et al. (2018)
18	Lunugalge, context 7, rock shelter	Rathnapura, Subaragamuwa	c. 5905–9545 cal BP	early Holocene to Mid-Holocene	Somadeva et al. (2018)
19	Wavulgalge, context 2a, rock shelter	Rathnapura, Subaragamuwa	c. 8010–7929 BP	early-Holocene	Somadeva et al. (2018)
20	Mini-Athiliya, shell midden	Kegalle, Subaragamuwa	c. 4400–3800 BP	mid-Holocene	Perera (2010)

(a)   (b)   (c)

Figure 18.2 Nonhuman primates of Sri Lanka. (a) *Macaca sinica*; (b) *Semnopithecus priam thersites;* (c) *Semnopithecus vetulus.* (Photographs by Michael A. Huffman).

Figure 18.3 Sigiriya Potana cave excavation site. (Photograph by Gamini Adikari).

Archaeology (PGIAR) attached to Kelaniya University excavated cave MO14. The Sigiriya Potana cave deposits were dated at c. 6000 BP and the calibrated age ranges from cumulative probability (one sigma) 3913–3727 BCE (UA 5685) and 3913–3709 BCE (UA 5686) using carbon-14 dating techniques (Adikari, 1994a, b).

The remains excavated from the cave represented 34 animal species belonging to 29 genera, including nonhuman primates, and two humans. In addition to the human and animal remains there were tools representing grinding stones, scrapers, cutters, triangulars, chopping tools, core tools, projectile tools, pointed tools, and lunate tools (Ranasinghe and Adikari, 2012). The cave complex was declared a prehistoric site based on this evidence (Adikari, 2008; Nahallage et al., 2010; Chandimal, 2009). The caves were first occupied by *Homo sapiens* in the Mesolithic period, and continuously thereafter in prehistoric, protohistoric, and historic times (Adikari, 1998, 2008).

The aim of this chapter is to provide the first description of nonhuman primate subfossil tooth remains recovered from the Sigiriya Potana cave. Here we compare these remains with dental material from the three relevant extant nonhuman primate species found in the same region today to taxonomically identify them.

18.2   Methods

18.2.1   Materials

Permission was obtained from the Director General of PGIAR prior to conducting the study. Twenty-three subfossil macaque and langur mandible fragments with teeth were available. The nonhuman primate subfossils used for the present study were excavated from context No. 10 and stored at the Osteology Laboratory of PGIAR (Adikari, 1994). Context No. 10 is the stratum that extended over the entire cave floor and contained undisturbed (not mixed) prehistoric data. Large quantities of stone implements, bone remains, and shells were found. Chert, graphite, and some charred seeds were also found here. Soil color when dry was 7.5 YR 5/2 brown and 6/2 light brown. Soil color when wet was 5 YR 3/3 dark reddish brown (Adikari, 1998).

18.2.2   Sampling Procedures

Subfossil mandibular and maxillary parts with teeth intact were stored in numbered bags. Firstly, teeth in different bags were separated into macaque and langur species according to molar occlusal morphological differences related to dietary differences of these two genera. Frugivorous subfossil macaque molars (Fig. 18.4a, b) are high-crowned and low cusped for grinding fruits and seeds, while folivorous subfossil langur molars (Fig. 18.4c, d) are sharp high cusped for crushing, shearing, and grinding leaf fibers (Fig. 18.4). The teeth of the two subfossil langur species were differentiated by clear size differences, reflective of those differences between *S. priam thersites* and *S. vetulus*; the former being distinctively larger.

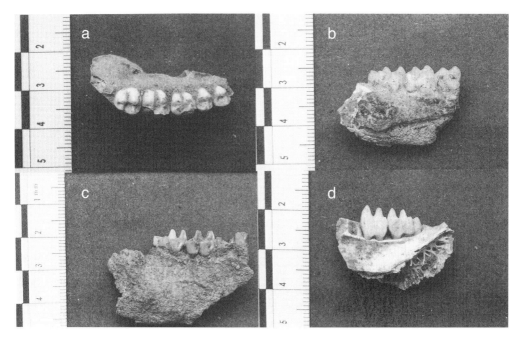

Figure 18.4 Sigiriya Potana nonhuman primate subfossil. (a) Presumed *M. sinica* Left maxilla P3 – M3; (b) Right mandible M1 to M3; (c) Presumed *Semnopithecus priam thersites* Right mandible M1 to M3; (d) Presumed *Semnopithecus vetulus* Right mandible M2 and M3. Scale in cm. (Photograph by Tharaka Ananda).

Subsequently measurements were taken using a sliding caliper. Only complete teeth were measured, so excluding fragmented and broken teeth. Odontometrical measurements were recorded following Swindler (2002: 5–6). Measurements were obtained only from upper and lower premolars and molars, as other subfossil teeth were in fragments.

Premolars
Length: maximum mesiodistal (MD) diameter was obtained between the two contact points. In instances where the mesial point is lacking, the maximum horizontal distance is measured from the distal contact point to the most mesial point on the surface of the premolar.
Breadth: maximum buccolingual (BL) diameter was measured at a right angle to the mesiodistal diameter.

Molars
Length: Maximum mesiodistal diameter taken on the occlusal surface between the mesial and distal contact points.
Breadth: Maximum buccolingual diameter taken at a right angle to the mesiodistal diameter. The breadths of both trigon (TR) and talon (TA) were measured in this manner.

Skulls of extant *Macaca sinica, Semnopithecus vetulus* and *Semnopithecus priam thersites* stored in the Laboratory of Physical Anthropology, Department of Anthropology, University of Sri Jayewardenepura were used to compare tooth measurements of these extent species with the subfossil samples of macaques and langurs excavated from the Sigiriya Potana cave site.

18.2.3 Method of Data Analysis

The measurements were entered into MS Excel. Statistical analyses were performed using SPSS version 16.0. Descriptive statistics; mean and standard deviation (SD) were calculated. All the parametric data were analyzed using the independent sample t-test. Statistical significance was set at $p < 0.05$. To take into account the multi-variate independent association among multiple measures, Euclidean distances among the six species were calculated. An optimally scaled matrix was derived. Disparities greater than 2.0 indicated a significant distance between two species.

18.3   Results

18.3.1 Subfossil Fragments and Extant Primate Material

Table 18.2 presents the detailed odontometrical measurement collected from teeth present in 29 subfossil fragments and 15 individual extent primate samples. The subfossil fragments could be sorted into three groups by their morphological characteristics. From this, 17 *Macaca* (*sinica*) fragments (12 mandible: 6 left and 6 right and 5 maxillary: 4 right, 1 left), four *Semnopithecus* (*vetulus*) fragments (mandible: 3 right and 1 left), and eight *Semnopithecus* (*priam*) fragments (mandible: 4 right and 3 left) were identified.

The 15 individual extant nonhuman primate samples available for comparison included seven *Macaca sinica* (3 mandibles, 6 maxilla), six *Semnopithecus vetulus* (3 mandible, 5 maxilla), and two *Semnopithecus priam thersites* (1 mandible, 2 maxilla). The number of teeth present in each subfossil fragment or nonhuman primate maxillary or mandibular sample varied since none of them had a full set (Table 18.2). For the extant nonhuman primate samples, teeth and sometimes maxillae or mandibles were missing.

Other than a few partial maxillary or mandibular fragments, no complete or partial skulls were excavated. A number of bone fragments were excavated from the site but could not be analyzed for possible use because they were heavily damage. These remains included fragments of eight proximal femora, six distal femora, six distal humeri, three proximal humeri, six proximal ulnae, five proximal radii, one distal radius, one proximal tibia, five calcanei, five tali, and three patellae. The long bones excavated were either smashed into smaller pieces or had been burnt and did not appear to have been modified into tools. These bones were burnt by the humans inhabiting the cave. It is assumed that the bones were burned to harden the bone marrow so it could be pushed out for consumption.

Table 18.2. Descriptive statistics (Mean and SD) of measured tooth parameters of *Macaca sinica*, *Macaca (sinica)* subfossils, *Semnopithecus vetulus*, *Semnopithecus (vetulus)* subfossils, *Semnopithecus priam thersites*, *Semnopithecus (priam)* subfossils

Parameter	Macaca sinica		Macaca (sinica) subfossil		Semnopithecus vetulus		Semnopithecus (vetulus) subfossil		Semnopithecus priam		Semnopithecus (priam) subfossil	
	N	Mean (mm)	N	Mean (mm)	N	Mean (mm)	N	Mean (m)	N	Mean (mm)	N	Mean (mm)
UP3MD	6	4.34 ± 0.30	2	4.54 ± 0.22	8	5.05 ± 0.66	0	-	4	5.00 ± 0.00	-	-
UP3BL	6	4.83 ± 0.22	2	5.22 ± 0.49	8	5.04 ± 0.47	0	-	4	5.03 ± 0.05	-	-
UP4MD	5	4.91 ± 0.26	2	4.53 ± 0.01	8	4.85 ± 0.35	0	-	4	4.90 ± 0.27	-	-
UP4BL	5	5.60 ± 0.11	2	5.94 ± 0.16	8	5.33 ± 0.34	0	-	4	5.78 ± 0.45	-	-
UM1MD	6	6.31 ± 0.30	3	6.30 ± 0.17	8	6.21 ± 0.17	0	-	4	6.63 ± 0.48	-	-
UM1TR	6	6.01 ± 0.12	3	5.90 ± 0.28	8	5.86 ± 0.27	0	-	4	6.00 ± 0.00	-	-
UM1TA	6	5.85 ± 0.22	3	5.92 ± 0.20	8	5.33 ± 0.19	0	-	4	5.78 ± 0.45	-	-
UM2MD	11	7.14 ± 0.36	5	6.85 ± 0.36	10	6.87 ± 0.21	0	-	4	7.03 ± 0.05	1	6.81 ± -
UM2TR	11	6.85 ± 0.20	5	6.51 ± 0.60	10	6.16 ± 0.19	0	-	4	7.00 ± 0.00	1	7.2 ± -
UM2TA	11	6.31 ± 0.18	5	6.18 ± 0.41	10	5.68 ± 0.37	0	-	4	6.23 ± 0.19	1	6.86 ± -
UM3MD	11	6.91 ± 0.37	4	7.23 ± 0.61	8	6.60 ± 0.40	0	-	4	7.15 ± 0.24	1	8.22 ±-
UM3TR	11	6.65 ± 0.16	4	6.45 ± 0.28	8	6.03 ± 0.08	0	-	4	6.88 ± 0.25	1	7.29 ±-
UM3TA	11	5.64 ± 0.33	4	6.12 ± 0.77	8	5.37 ± 0.31	0	-	4	5.68 ± 0.39	1	6.09 ±-
LP3MD	-	-	1	4.96 ± -	8	7.11 ± 0.99	1	3.29 ±	2	9.75 ± 0.35	-	-
LP3BL	-	-	1	4.25 ± -	8	4.08 ± 0.16	1	4.08 ±	2	4.00 ± 0.00	-	-
LP4MD	4	5.03 ± 0.22	2	4.33 ± 0.31	8	4.92 ± 0.23	1	3.92 ±	2	6.00 ± 0.00	-	-
LP4BL	4	4.41 ± 0.10	2	4.35 ± 0.16	8	4.23 ± 0.21	1	4.44 ±	2	4.00 ± 0.00	-	-
LM1MD	3	6.17 ± 0.13	7	6.19 ± 0.33	8	6.57 ± 0.40	2	6.74 ± 0.16	2	7.00 ± 0.00	1	7.32 ±
LM1TR	3	4.77 ± 0.12	7	4.92 ± 0.17	8	4.88 ± 0.19	2	4.96 ± 0.07	2	5.50 ± 0.71	1	6.31 ±
LM1TA	3	4.89 ± 0.18	7	4.87 ± 0.45	8	4.97 ± 0.10	2	5.27 ± 0.06	2	5.00 ± 0.00	1	6.85 ±
LM2MD	6	6.99 ± 0.20	8	6.97 ± 0.42	8	6.95 ± 0.27	3	7.43 ± 0.03	2	7.00 ± 0.00	6	7.92 ± 0.53
LM2TR	6	5.85 ± 0.14	8	5.92 ± 0.37	8	5.38 ± 0.31	3	5.77 ± 0.20	2	5.95 ± 0.07	6	6.45 ± 0.75
LM2TA	6	5.30 ± 0.33	8	5.47 ± 0.44	8	5.44 ± 0.39	3	5.97 ± 0.47	2	6.00 ±0.00	6	6.32 ± 0.66
LM3MD	6	8.31 ± 0.30	7	7.78 ± 0.26	6	8.13 ± 0.20	3	8.77 ± 0.28	2	7.75 ± 0.35	4	9.61 ± 0.89
LM3TR	6	5.51 ± 0.13	7	5.76 ± 0.47	6	5.11 ± 0.15	3	5.64 ± 0.27	2	6.00 ± 0.00	4	6.31 ± 0.20
LM3TA	6	4.96 ± 0.27	7	5.28 ± 0.38	6	5.08 ± 0.06	3	5.53 ± 0.35	2	6.00 ± 0.00	4	6.13 ± 0.07

18.3.2 Comparison of Odontometrical and Morphological Data of Subfossil Nonhuman Primate Bones with Extant Primate Bones

Table 18.3 presents the results of the statistical comparison between tooth parameters. The subfossil teeth closely resembled those of their respective extent nonhuman primate counterparts currently known to inhabit this area of Sri Lanka. Comparison of the odontometrical parameters revealed very few statistically significant differences (Table 18.3). Those differences are not considered to be indicative of species level differences between the subfossil and extant nonhuman primates.

18.3.2.1 Euclidean Distance Model

On the basis of the odontometrical and morphological data, optimal scaled disparities were created among all six species sample sets (Table 18.4). A stimulus configuration map was also created to visually display the difference among species (Fig. 18.5). Among both *Semnopithecus vetulus* and *Macaca sinica* groups, there was no significant difference between the extant and subfossil samples, but the two species groups did differ significantly from each other. In contrast, the data revealed that both subfossil and extant *Semnopithecus priam thersites* samples were significantly different from each other, as well as from all other groups. Given the limited amount of diagnostic samples, however, we cannot conclude whether the extent *Semnopithecus priam thersites* samples and subfossil samples represent different species or is simply due to sample size issues. Given the dating of the subfossils, we assume that they most likely are the same species. More samples from the same time period at other sites are needed for comparison.

18.3.2.2 Post-craniometrical Data and Morphology

No complete or partial cranial bones were excavated other than the partial maxillary and mandibular fragments. Though many small smashed pieces of long bone shafts were excavated, anatomical identification as to the types of bones were not possible due to the size of the bone pieces.

18.4   Discussion

Nonhuman primates have inhabited the island of Sri Lanka for a very long time. Evidence from the faunal remains excavated from Batadombalena (Table 18.1), the rainforest cave site dates the oldest nonhuman primates back to c. 36,000 cal BP. Other wet zone caves where nonhuman primate fossil remains have been found include Fa Hien-lena (cave), Kithulgala Beli-lena, and Bellan-badi Palassa (Deraniyagala, 1992).

The nonhuman primate subfossils excavated from Sigiriya Potana cave date back to about 6000 years BP (Adikari, 1994a, b). Premathilake and Gunatilaka (2013) reconstructed the paleoenvironment of Sri Lanka from around 20,000 years BP to the present and stated that the climatic conditions have been progressing towards semiarid conditions since around 8700 to 3600 years BP. The prevailing climatic

Table 18.3. Statistical comparison between extent and subfossil tooth parameters measured from the Sigiriya Potana cave site

Parameter	t	df	2-tailed
Macaca sinica - Macaca (sinica) subfossils			
UP3MD	−0.858	6	0.424
UP3BL	−1.700	6	0.140
UP4MD	3.341	4.015	0.029*
UP4BL	−3.318	5	0.021*
UM1MD	0.035	7	0.973
UM1TR	0.867	7	0.415
UM1TA	−0.467	7	0.655
UM2MD	1.516	14	0.152
UM2TR	1.247	4.392	0.275
UM2TA	0.669	4.693	0.535
UM3MD	−1.237	13	0.238
UM3TR	1.382	3.700	0.245
UM3TA	−1.726	13	0.108
LP4MD	2.841	1.520	0.142
LP4BL	0.628	4	0.564
LM1MD	−0.120	8	0.908
LM1TR	−1.353	8	0.213
LM1TA	0.099	8	0.923
LM2MD	0.060	12	0.953
LM2MD	0.066	10.481	0.948
LM2TR	−0.392	12	0.702
LM2TA	−0.807	12	0.435
LM3MD	3.447	11	0.005*
LM3TR	−1.272	11	0.230
LM3TA	−1.752	11	0.107
Semnopithecus vetulus - Semnopithecus (vetulus) subfossils			
LP3MD	3.645	7	0.008*
LP3BL	−0.029	7	0.978
LP4MD	4.173	7	0.004*
LP4BL	−0.951	7	0.373
LM1MD	−0.554	8	0.594
LM1TR	−0.555	8	0.594
LM1TA	−3.922	8	0.004*
LM2MD	−2.584	9	0.03*
LM2TR	−1.974	9	0.08
LM2TA	−1.894	9	0.091
LM3MD	−3.995	7	0.005*
LM3TR	−3.849	7	0.006*
LM3TA	−2.137	2.065	0.162

Table 18.3. (cont.)

Parameter	t	df	2-tailed
Semnopithecus priam - Semnopithecus (priam) subfossils			
UM2MD	3.846	3	0.031*
UM2TA	−3	3	0.058
UM3MD	−4.02	3	0.028*
UM3TR	−1.485	3	0.234
UM3TA	−0.94	3	0.416
LM1TR	−0.935	1	0.521
LM2MD	−2.343	6	0.058
LM2TR	−0.904	6	0.401
LM2TA	−0.655	6	0.537
LM3MD	−2.729	4	0.053
LM3TR	−2.075	4	0.107
LM3TA	−2.365	4	0.077

*Statistical significant is $p < 0.05$.

Table 18.4. Optimally scaled data (disparities) among species

	Extant M. s	Fossil M. s	Extant S. v	Fossil S. v	Extant S.p.t	Fossil S. p.t
Extant M. s	.000					
Fossil M. s	.900	.000				
Extant S. v	1.567	1.895	.000			
Fossil S. v	1.021	1.362	.565	.000		
Extant S.p.t	2.686	2.123	2.123	2.123	.000	
Fossil S. p.t	2.341	3.176	2.006	2.123	4.135	.000

M. s.= *Macaca sinica.*; S. v = *Semnopithecus vetulus*; S. p. t; 6 = *Semnopithecus priam thersites*

condition at present too is intermediate to dry. This indicates that there is not much variation in the climate at present compared to that of around 6000 years BP. This was verified from the faunal remains excavated at the site, with most of the species representing dry zone fauna still inhabiting the region to date. Presently the nonhuman primates inhabiting this region are the dry zone toque macaques, grey langurs, the Northern dry zone purple-faced leaf langurs, and the dry zone slender loris (*Loris lydekkerianus nordicus*). No subfossil evidence of slender loris-like was excavated; suggesting that this much smaller sized nonhuman primate was not hunted.

Some of the other common dry zone mammalian fauna excavated from the cave were sambar deer (*Cervus unicolor*), spotted deer (*Axis axis*), barking deer (*Muntiacus muntjak*), spotted chevrotain (*Moschiola* sp.), wild boar (*Sus scrofa*), wild cattle (*Bos* sp.), water buffalo (*Bubalus arnee*), porcupine (*Hystrix indica*), and giant flying squirrel (*Petaurista philippensis*). Reptiles included the flapshell turtle (*Lissemys punctata*), black turtle (*Melanochelys trijuga*), and python (*Python molurus*). In addition, junglefowl (*Gallus lafayetii*) represented the avian fauna (Ranasinghe and

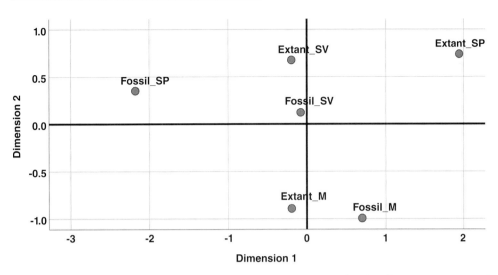

Figure 18.5 Euclidean distance stimulus configuration of subfossil and extant primate species. M. s = *Macaca sinica*, S. p. t. = *Semnopithecus priam thersites*, S. v = *Semnopithecus vetulus*.

Adikari, 2012). All of these species are different from the wet zone species excavated from wet zone cave sites, such as Fa Hien and Batadombalena caves (Fig. 18.1). This indicates that early human dietary adaptations varied across the different environmental conditions they occupied, depending on the availability of wildlife.

The Sri Lankan evidence is mirrored in other sites of similar age across Southeast Asia, suggesting that this region provided its human inhabitants with a variety of important food resources over the last 20,000 years (Roberts et al, 2015b). Evidence for the reliance on whatever was available at the time, including many nonhuman primate species, deer, boar, and several smaller sized mammals such as squirrels and rats is found across Southern Asia throughout the Terminal Pleistocene/Holocene up to 3000 BP (Higham, 2013). With regards to the nonhuman primate species utilized as food in these long-term occupations sites, they are assumed to be the same extant species found in the region today, including orangutans (*Pongo* sp.), gibbons, and macaques. In the Niah cave in Sarawak, Borneo, pig remains accounted for about 30% of the food residuals excavated. Unidentified monkey species accounted for 16%. The remaining species included sambar deer, chevrotain, porcupine, pangolin, and some unidentified birds (Higham, 2013). In the Gua Cha rockshelter site in West Malaysia, the fossil remains included five nonhuman primate species thought to be *Macaca nemestrina*, *M. fascicularis*, *Presbytis melalophos*, *Trachypithecus melalophos*, and *Hylobates lar* that are still found in the region today (Bin Haji Taha, 1981; Southwick and Cadigan, 1972). In the Khao Toh Chong Rockshelter and Moh Khiew Cave in Peninsular Thailand, remains of an unidentified *Macaca* sp. and *Trachypithecus obscurus* have been reported (Van Vlack, 2014). In the Jwalapuram Locality 9 rockshelter of southern India, primate remains were rare, but a langur species (*Presbytis* sp. currently known as *Semnopithecus priam*) was found along with many large and small ungulate species, small and medium carnivores, and hare (Clarkson et al., 2008).

In the current study only nonhuman primate teeth were used, as they were the only measurable parts in the assemblages. No significant differences were found in the overall tooth morphology of the subfossils and the extant nonhuman primate teeth (Nahallage, 2015). The odontometrical data obtained for macaque and langur subfossils excavated from the Sigiriya Potana cave did not differ from that of the teeth of extant macaque and langur species found in the same area today. From this we can conclude that the subfossil nonhuman primate species hunted and eaten by the residents of this cave are most likely the toque monkey and both langur species, the purple-faced langur and the grey langur. This confirms our assumptions and sheds light on the fact that most of the small and medium size mammals including diurnal nonhuman primate in Sri Lanka at the time were being hunted.

From the archaeological evidence, it is assumed that nonhuman primate meat was principally a source of food and material for tools in Sri Lanka (e.g. Wedage et al., 2019). There is evidence that about 70% of the faunal diet of prehistoric people inhabiting wet zone caves c. 36,000 years BP, especially Batadombalena Cave (Fig. 18.1), consisted of nonhuman primates, both macaques and langurs (Perera et al., 2011). In Sigiriya Potana cave as well, the majority of the diet of the people were nonhuman primates, which indicates that these species had a countrywide distribution similar to the present condition. In addition, the crushed long bones and skulls suggest that these people also consumed bone marrow and brain parts. However, at present even though there is evidence of hunting nonhuman primates for food from time to time, people mainly eat the meat, not the marrow or brain. They bury the skeleton after obtaining the meat, to hide the evidence since it is illegal to hunt them (C. A. D. Nahallage, pers. obs.).

Such evidence for osseous technologies was found at four Microlithic sites, Batadombalena (c. 36,000 cal BP), Fa-Hien lena (c. 38,000 cal BP), Kithulgala Beli-lena (c. 13,000 BP), and Bellanbadi Palassa (c. 12,000 cal BP) (Deraniyagala, 1992). From the osseous assemblage and technology of the 21 pointed bone tools excavated from layers 2 to 6 at Batadombalena during the 2005 excavation, 19 were made from the long bones of nonhuman primates and two were from jungle fowl (Perera et al., 2015).

The identified faunal remains of the diet of prehistoric humans largely comprised small- and medium-bodied species of arboreal and mixed terrestrial arboreal habitats. Fluctuating prey population density aside, it is likely that nonhuman primates were a reliable source of food for the inhabitants of the cave for a long period of time. Hunting across the country seems to have persisted well into historical times. Due to the small percentage of terrestrial faunal remains found in the diet it has been argued that the pointed bone tools were used as a part of snare or trapping technology to hunt for arboreal species rather than as projectile tips for hunting terrestrial fauna (Perera et al., 2015). However, no primate bone tools were found from Sigiriya Potana.

In the future, a closer look at the assemblage of nonhuman primate subfossils and fossils excavated from the other sites across the country may shed light onto the dietary habits of these early humans as well as the extent and regional variation of nonhuman primate–human interactions over time. Currently, the majority of primate fossil remains have been found in the wet and intermediate zones. Future work looking closely to the fossil primate fauna is expected to provide more insights into the human-nonhuman primate interface in prehistoric times.

Acknowledgments

We are grateful to the co-members of G. Adikari's excavation team, Professor Senaka Bandaranayake, Professor Mats Mogran, Dr. T. R. Premathilake, and Dr. Arjuna Thanthilage. Also undergraduate students from the University of Kelaniya, University of Peradeniya and University of Sri Jayewardenepura took part in the excavation. Without these people's efforts this chapter would not have been possible. Special thanks also to Dr. Tsuyoshi Itoh for advice on descriptive tooth morphology.

References

Adikari, G. (1994a). Approach to the prehistory of the Sigiriya-Potana region cave complex. In Senake Bandaranayake, & Mats Mogren, eds., *Further Studies in the Settlement Archaeology of the Sigiriya-Dambulla Region*, Colombo: Post-graduate Institute of Archaeological Research, 45–51.

Adikari, G. (1994b). Excavations at the Sigiriya-Potana cave complex: a preliminary account. In Senake Bandaranayake, & Mats Mogren, eds., *Further Studies in the Settlement Archaeology of the Sigiriya-Dambulla Region*, Colombo: Post-graduate Institute of Archaeological Research, 65–68.

Adikari, G. (1998). Aspects of the prehistory of Sigiriya-Dambulla region. Unpublished MPhil thesis, University of Kelaniya.

Adikari, G. (2010). A preliminary excavation report submitted to the Postgraduate Institute of Archaeology Report. Colombo.

Bin Haji Taha. A. (1981). The re-excavation of the rockshelter of Gua Cha, Ulu Kelantan, West Malaysia. Unpublished Master's thesis.The Australian National University.

Campbell-Smith, G., Simanjorang, H. V. P., Leader-Williams, N., & Linkie, M. (2010). Local attitudes and perceptions toward crop-raiding by orangutans (*Pongo abelii*) and other nonhuman NHP in northern Sumatra, Indonesia. *American Journal of Primatology*, 72, 866–876.

Chandimal, K. M., Yasawardene, S. G., & Adikari, G. (2009) *The determination of age, sex and stature of prehistoric human skeletal remains excavated from Sigiriya Potana in Sri Lanka*. Colombo: Sri Lanka Association for the Advancement of Science Proceeding of the 65th Annual Sessions. Part I (Abstract, 416/D).

Clarkson, C., Petraglia, M., Korisettar, R., et al. (2008). The oldest and longest sequence in India: 35,000 years of modern human occupation and change at the Jwalapuram Locality 9 rockshelter. *Antiquity*, 83, 326–348.

Deraniyagala, P. E. P. (1940). The Stone Age and cave men of Ceylon. *Journal of the Royal Asiatic Society (Ceylon)*, 34(92), 351–373.

Deraniyagala, P. E. P. (1943). Some aspect of the prehistory of Ceylon, pt.1. *Spolia Zeylanica*, 23(2), 93–115.

Deraniyagala, P. E. P. (1958). *Administration Report of the Director of National Museums for 1957*, Sri Lanka Government.

Deraniyagala, S. U. (1971). Stone implements from a Balangoda Culture site in Ceylon: Bellan-bandi Palassa. *Ancient Ceylon*, 1, 47–89.

Deraniyagala, S. U., & Kennedy, K. A. (1972). Bellan Bandi Pallassa 1970: A Mesolithic burial site in Ceylon. *Ancient Ceylon*, 2, 18–47.

Deraniyagala, S. U. (1992). *The Prehistory of Sri Lanka: An Ecological Perspective* (2nd ed.). Colombo: Department of Archaeological Survey.

Deraniyagala, S. U. (2007). The prehistory and protohistoric settlement in Sri Lanka. In P. L. Prematilleke, S., Bandaranayake, S. U. Deraniyagala, & R. Siva, eds., *The Art and Archaeology in Sri Lanka*. Colombo: Central Cultural Fund, 1, 1–96.

Eragama, S. (2017). Subsistence pattern of the Prehistoric man from Kuragala Rockshelter in Sri Lanka, Unpublished MA thesis, University of Kelaniya.

Gunarathna H. S. (1971). Beli-lena Athula: another Stone Age habitation in Ceylon. *Spolia Zeylanica* 32 (1), 4.

Hathurusinghe, S. (2019). Archaeology of Kelani River Valley in Sri Lanka. Unpublished PhD Thesis, University of Kelaniya.

Higham, C. (2013). Hunter-gatherers in Southeast Asia: From prehistory to the present, *Human Biology*, 85 (1–3), 21–44.

Kourampas N, Simpson I, Perera H. N., Deraniyagala, S. U., & Wijeyapala W. H. (2009). Rockshelter sedimentation in a dynamic tropical landscape: Late Pleistocene-Early Holocene archaeological deposits in Kitulgala Beli-lena, Southwestern Sri Lanka, *Geoarchaeology*, 24(6), 677–714.

Kourampas, N., Simpson, I., Diaz, A. P., Perera, N., & Deraniyagala, S. (2012). Geoarchaelogical reconnaissance rockshelter and tool bearing sediments of the Iranmadu Formation Rock shelter. *Ancient Ceylon*, 23, 1–25.

Kulatilake, S. (2016). The peopling of Sri Lanka from prehistoric to historic times: Biological and archaeological evidence. In G.Robbins Schug, & S. R. Walimbe (eds.), *A Companion to South Asia in the Past*, Hoboken, NJ: John Wiley & Sons, Inc., 426–436.

Langley MC, Amano N, Wedage O, et al. (2020). Bows and arrows and complex symbolic displays 48,000 years ago in the South Asian tropics. *Science Advances*, 6, eaba3831

Nahallage. C. A. D. (2015). Craniometric analysis of two NHP species from Sri Lanka: *Macaca sinica* and *Thrachypithecus vetulus*. Man and Environment *XL* (1), 27–32.

Nahallage, C. A. D., & Huffman, M. A. (2013). Macaque-human interactions in past and present-day Sri Lanka. In S. Radhakrishna, M. A. Huffman, & A. Sinha *The Macaque Connection: Cooperation and conflict between humans and macaques*. New York: Springer, 135–148.

Nahallage, C. A. D., Huffman, M. A., Kuruppu, N., & Weerasingha, T. (2008). Diurnal primates in Sri Lanka and people's perception of them. *Primate Conservation*, 23(1), 83–87.

Nahallage, C. A. D., Kanthilatha, N., Adikari, G., & Huffman, M. A. (2010) Preliminary Report of non-human primate bones discovered at the prehistoric

Sigiriya Potana cave site in Sri Lanka, *Primate Research*, **96**, 247–248.

Perera, H. N. (2010). *Prehistoric Sri Lanka: Late Pleistocene Rockshelters and an Open Air Site.* Oxford: Archaeopress.

Perera, N., Kaurampas, N., Simpson I. A., et al. (2011). People of the ancient rainforest: Late Pleistocene foragers at the Batadomba-lena rockshelter, Sri Lanka. *Journal of Human Evolution*, **61**(3), 254–269.

Perera, N., Roberts, P., & Petraglia, M. (2015). Bone technology in South Asia from Late Pleistocene rock shelter deposits in Sri Lanka. In M. C. Langley, ed., *Osseous Projectile Weaponry: Towards an Understanding of Pleistocene Cultural Variability.* New York: Springer.

Premathilake, R., & Gunatilaka, A. (2013). Chronological framework of Asian southwest monsoon events and variations over the past 24,000 years in Sri Lanka and regional correlations. *Journal of the National Science Foundation Sri Lanka*, **41**(3), 219–228.

Ranasinghe, R., & Adikari, G. (2012). *Importance of the analysis of animal bones for archaeological interpretation of prehistoric human subsistence patterns.* Proceedings of the 1st International Conference of Humanities and Social Sciences. (November-18⁻19 2012), Nugegoda: University of Sri Jayewardenepura, 100.

Roberts, P., & Petraglia, M. (2015). Pleistocene rainforests: barriers or attractive environments for early human foragers? *World Archaeology*, **47**(5), 718–739.

Roberts, P., Boivin, N., & Petraglia, M. (2015a). The Sri Lanka in "Microlithic" tradition c. 38,000 to 3,000 years ago: Tropical technologies and adaptations of *Homo sapiens* at the southern edge of Asia. *Journal of World Prehistory*, **28**(2), 69–112.

Roberts, P., Perera, N., Oshan Wedage, O., et al. (2015b). Direct evidence for human reliance on rainforest resources in late Pleistocene Sri Lanka. *Science*, **347** (6227), 1246–1249.

Roberts, P., Perera, N., Wedage, O., et al. (2017). Fruits of the forest: Human stable isotope ecology and rainforest adaptations in Late Pleistocene and Holocene (~36 to 3 ka) Sri Lanka. *Journal of Human Evolution*, **106**, 102–118.

Riley, E. P., & Priston, N. E. (2010). Macaques in farms and folklore: Exploring the human-nonhuman primate interface in Sulawesi, Indonesia. *American Journal of Primatology*, *72*, 848–854.

Somadeva, R., Wanninayaka, A., & Devage, D. (2018). Hunters in transition: Advanced hunter-gatherers of the Mid/ Late Holocene, Sri Lanka. *Man and Environment*, *XLIII* (1), 23–38.

Southwick, C., & Cadigan Jr., F. C. (1972). Population studies of Malaysian primates. *Primates*, 13(1), 1–18.

Swindler, D. R. (2002). *Primate Dentition. An Introduction to the Teeth of Non-human Primates.* Cambridge: Cambridge University Press.

Van Vlack, H. G. (2014). Forager subsistence regimes in the Thai-Malay Peninsula: An environmental archaeological case study of Khao Toh Chong rockshelter, Krabi. Unpublished Master's thesis, San José State University.

Wedage, O., Amano, N., Langley, M. C., et al. (2019). Specialized rainforest hunting by *Homo sapiens* ~45,000 years ago. *Nature Communications* 10(739), 1234567890.

Wijeyapala, W. H. (1997). New light on the prehistory of Sri Lanka in the context of recent investigations of cave sites. Unpublished PhD thesis, University of Peradeniya.

19 Monkey Hunting in Early to Mid-Holocene Eastern Java (Indonesia)

Noel Amano, Thomas Ingicco, Anne-Marie Moigne, Anne-Marie Sémah, Truman Simanjuntak, & François Sémah

Memburu monyet selama zaman Holosen Awal dan Tengah di Jawa Timur (Indonesia)

Ringkasan

Dalam tulisan ini kami menelusuri tingkah laku manusia untuk mengeksploitasi sumber daya hewan primata selama zaman Holosen Awal dan Tengah di Jawa Timur, melalui koleksi fosil dari penggalian Goa Braholo. Sisa-sisa Cercopithecidae (monyet) merupakan lebih dari 50% dari semua fosil yang terdapat di situs ini. 90% diantaranya dapat diidentifikasikan sebagai *Trachypithecus auratus* (Langur dari Jawa yang sering disebut monyet daun), dan mengindikasikan tingkah laku berburu manusia terhadap hewan penghuni hutan tersebut. Profil statistik umur individu pada waktu kematian menunjukkan bahwa manusia cenderung mengarah kepada spesimen dewasa muda. Distribusi dari tulang belulang kerangka monyet adalah indikasi bahwa bangkai-bangkai tersebut diproses di situs. Keruntutan posisi dari bekas-bekas proses penyembelihan pada tulang-tulang tertentu mencerminkan ketrampilan dalam pemrosesan bangkai secara rutin, termasuk untuk membuat alat dari tulang. Kami mendiskusikan hasil penelitian ini dalam kerangka ekonomi dan penghidupan manusia pemburu dan peramu di Asia Tenggara.

Kata kunci

Interaksi manusia–monyet – Holosen – Asia Tenggara – Indonesia – Jawa – penghidupan dan ekonomi

Abstract

In this chapter, we explore the patterns of nonhuman primate exploitation in Early to Mid-Holocene East Java by looking at the faunal assemblage recovered from excavations in Braholo Cave. Cercopithecid specimens account for more than 50% of the animal remains recovered from the site. Of these, 90% were identified to represent the Javan langur (*Trachypithecus auratus*), suggesting deliberate hunting of this arboreal species. Age-at-death profiles demonstrate targeting of prime-aged adults and skeletal element representation suggests onsite carcass processing. We observed consistent placement of butchery marks on specific skeletal elements, indicative of routine carcass processing that also involved preparation of skeletal elements for bone tool manufacture. We discuss our findings in the framework of early hunter-gatherer subsistence economies in the region.

Keywords Human–Nonhuman primate interactions, Holocene, Subsistence economy, Southeast Asia, Indonesia, Java

19.1   In Times of Change: Early Holocene in Island Southeast Asia

The end of the Pleistocene in Island Southeast Asia saw pronounced climatic fluctuations, including significant shifts in temperature and precipitation patterns. Evidence from numerous studies, including geomorphology, palynology, and stable isotope analyses, have demonstrated that the onset of the Holocene coincided with a change to more humid climatic conditions and the development of closed rainforests (Dam et al., 2001; Dubois et al., 2014; Kershaw et al., 2001; Maloney and McCormac, 1995, 1996; Newsome and Flenley, 1998; Russell et al., 2014; van der Kaars and Dam, 1995; van der Kaars et al. 2000; Wurster et al. 2010;).

The start of the Holocene witnessed an increase of archaeological evidence in the region, perhaps indicative of an intensification in the occupation of sites or an increase in human population size (Barker, 2005; Barker et al., 2007; Lewis et al., 2008; Pawlik et al., 2014; Rabett, 2012; Sémah et al., 2004; Simanjuntak and Asikin, 2004;). It is also during this period that significant cultural and technological changes occurred, including shifts in subsistence economies and hunting patterns (e.g. Amano et al., 2015); increase manufacture and use of osseous tools (Pasveer, 2004; Rabett, 2005; Rabett and Piper, 2012; Setiagama, 2006); manufacture of shell implements including adzes and fishhooks (Bellwood, 1997; O'Connor, 2007; O'Connor et al., 2011; Pawlik et al., 2015; Szabo et al., 2007); and emergence of a wide range of burial practices including secondary inhumation and cremation (Détroit, 2006; Lloyd-Smith, 2009; Lara et al., 2015; Majid, 2012; Simanjuntak and Asikin, 2004).

Research conducted in past decades have provided important information regarding human behavior during the Pleistocene-Holocene transition, including changes in their subsistence economies, strategies employed to exploit animal and plant resources and how these resources were perceived culturally (e.g. Barker, 2005; Barker and Farr, 2016; Barton et al., 2009; O'Connor, 2007; Morwood et al., 2008; O'Connor et al., 2011; Pawlik et al., 2014; Piper and Rabett, 2009, 2016; Piper et al., 2008). Results of these studies demonstrate how early hunter-gatherer communities employed a complex range of hunting and foraging strategies to take full advantage of specific local conditions. In Java, the Holocene archeological record shows that early communities relied heavily on rainforest resources, including hunting of non-human primates for subsistence.

19.2   The Cave Site

Ingicco et al. (2020) reported the patterns of primate exploitation in Song Terus and Braholo Cave, and discussed in detail the roles that nonhuman primates played in the life of early hunter-gatherer communities in Eastern Java. In this chapter, we expand on this, focusing on the nonhuman primate remains recovered from Braholo Cave.

Braholo Cave is located on the edge of Central Java's Wonosari plateau, around 13 km away from the present-day southern Javanese coast, close to the village of

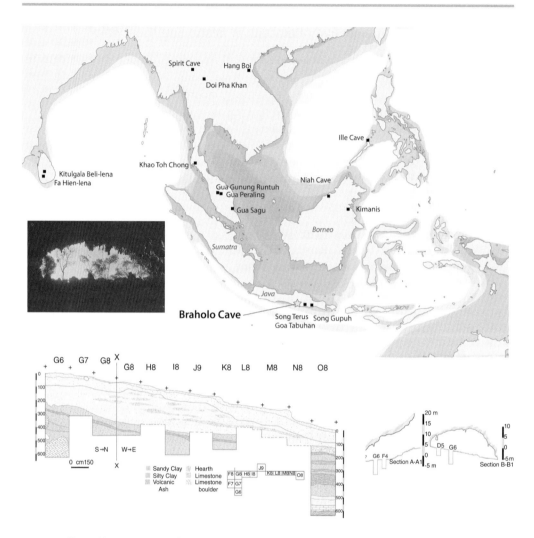

Figure 19.1 Location and stratigraphy of Braholo Cave. The map also shows other archaeological sites in the region where systematic zooarchaeological analyses reveal evidence of Early Holocene nonhuman primate exploitation.

Semugih at 8°4′52.1″S; 110°45′18.5″E (Fig. 19.1). It is on the slope of a c. 45 m high limestone hill and has 15 m high northwest entrance, a domed ceiling reaching c. 12 m and a floor area of c. 600 m². The cave is orientated along a northeast–southwest axis and the eastern and the southern areas of the cave floor are covered with huge boulders and debris from roof falls as well as some stalagmites. Braholo Cave was excavated between 1997 and 2001 by the Indonesian Center for Archaeological Research. A total of 16 excavation squares of 2 × 2 m were excavated, with the deepest squares reaching a maximum depth of 7.3 m. The basal occupation layers were presumed to have not been reached since excavations in most squares were halted due to the presence of huge limestone boulders.

A stalagmitic floor located in the mouth of the cave was sampled for U/Th dating and produced a date of 245 + 69/-40 ka BP (Sémah et al., 2004). The cave has well stratified archaeological deposits dated between 33,100 ± 1,260 and 3,050 ± 100 BP (Fig. 19.1). Excavations yielded numerous archaeological materials including those usually associated with the Neolithic of Southeast Asia such as pottery, shell ornaments, and polished stone adzes (i.e., Bellwood, 1997; 2013), as well as numerous artifacts typical of the pre-Neolithic of Java.

19.3   Targeted Hunting of Leaf Monkeys in Braholo Cave

The Holocene assemblage of Braholo Cave is overwhelmingly dominated by cercopithecid remains, representing 60% (number of identified specimens [NISP] = 5490) of the vertebrate remains identified to taxon in the assemblage analyzed. This is in contrast to the Late Pleistocene layers, which saw a predominance of large-bodied mammals, particularly cervids and bovids (Fig. 19.2).

Dental measurements do not allow for the differentiation of macaques and langurs, and overlap is noted in when archaeological specimens were plotted with comparative *Trachypithecus* and *Macaca* samples (Fig. 19.3). Lucas et al. (1986) observed that the breadth:length ratio of the M_3 is highly correlated to the percentage of leaves in the diet. However, the plot of M_3 length and breadth fails to separate representative colobine and cercopithecine species in Southeast Asia. For instance, there is an extensive overlap in the measurements of female *Macaca fascicularis* and male *Trachypithecus auratus* comparative specimens (Fig. 19.3). The archaeological specimens from Braholo Cave and Song Terus show similar overlap, with most of the values falling within the range of the modern comparative specimens. Slight differentiation is noted when the total toothrow length (M1–M3) is plotted against the length of the M_3 (Fig. 19.3). *Presbytis* (*P. comata* and *P. rubicunda*) specimens can be easily distinguished from *Trachypithecus* and *Macaca* by smaller dental measurements. Overlap in macaque and langur specimens is still observed, albeit not as extensive as in the M_3 breadth–length plot. Two macaque specimens from Braholo Cave are found to be much larger than the museum *M. fascicularis* specimens. The specimens are comparable in length with *M. nemestrina* M_3, but much narrower in breadth. Java is outside the current biogeographic range of *M. nemestrina* (Groves, 2001; Richardson et al., 2008) although it is presumed to have been present in the island during the distant past (Aimi, 1981; Harrison et al., 2006). *M. nemestrina* has not been recorded in any Late Pleistocene faunal assemblage in Java (i.e., van den Bergh et al., 2001; Harrison et al., 2006). Pending higher taxonomic identification, these large macaque specimens are identified as *Macaca* sp. in the current study based on molar morphology (see Section 19.5.1).

Dental morphology is more useful in assigning the archaeological cercopithecid specimens to taxon. Although colobine and cercopithecine monkeys both have bilophodont molars, some characteristics allow for the differentiation between the two groups (see Delson, 1973; Lucas and Teaford, 1994; Swindler, 1976, 2002). The most striking difference between colobine and cercopithecine molars involves the occlusal relief.

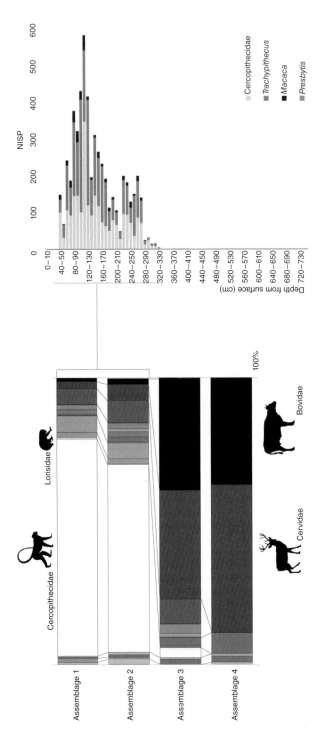

Figure 19.2 Change in the faunal distribution in Braholo Cave through time.

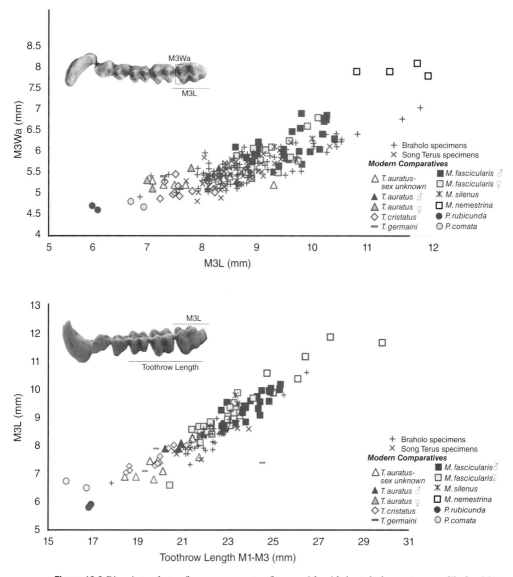

Figure 19.3 Bivariate plots of measurements of cercopithecid dental elements; mandibular M3 mesiodistal length vs buccolingual width (a) mandibular M1-M3 toothrow length vs. M3 mesiodistal length (b).

Compared to cercopithecines, colobine molars are characterized by taller cusps that are set closer to the margins of the tooth. The molars also have a wider intercusp width (Lucas and Teaford, 1994). The longer molar crests of colobines is associated with their more folivorous diet (Kay, 1978; Lucas and Teaford, 1994; Swindler, 2002). Generally, colobines and cercopithecines have a third lower molar with well-individualized fifth cusp (hypoconulid). However, this additional cusp is less individualized in smaller colobines, for instance in *Presbytis* (Delson, 1973; Willis and Swindler, 2004).

Based on morphology, 10.8% of the identified cercopithecid dental remains from the Holocene layers of Braholo Cave were identified as representing *M. fascicularis* whereas *T. auratus* accounts for 89.2%. A right mandible with complete teeth and a maxilla fragment with M^{1-2} from Braholo Cave are identified as representing *P. comata* based on molar length and morphology. Figure 19.4b shows the *P. comata* mandible with the M_3 missing the hypoconulid. Interestingly, remains of the Javan surili have not been recorded from the nearby site of Song Terus.

Differences in the morphology of certain postcranial elements also allow for the identification of specific cercopithecid taxa in the assemblage. Morphological differences between colobines and cercopithecines are well known (Botez, 1926; Delson, 1973; Ji et al., 2020; Jolly, 1965; Knussmann, 1967; Olivier and Caix, 1959; Olivier and Fenart, 1956; Olivier and Fontaine, 1957; Olivier and Piganiol, 1957; Olivier & Soutoul, 1960, 1961; Preuschoft, 1969; Youlatos, 2003; Washburn, 1942). Ingicco et al. (2020) specifically detailed the diagnostic characteristics that would allow for the differentiation of *Trachypithecus* and *Macaca*. They noted for instance, that the femur of *Trachypithecus* is much longer and more slender than that of macaques. In macaques, the greater trochanter overhangs the femoral head, which is not the case for the langurs. The distal condyle of the langur femur is symmetrical, whereas in macaques, the medial condyle is much bigger than the lateral condyle (Ingicco et al., 2020). However, despite clear morphological differences, linear measurements of most postcranial elements in the assemblage fail to differentiate between langurs and macaques. For example, the calcaneus of *Macaca* can easily be differentiated from that of *Trachypithecus* based on the morphology of the calcaneal tubercle and medial articular surfaces (Fig. 19.5). Despite these, a plot of the length and breadth of cercopithecid calcaneus from the Braholo Cave and Song Terus assemblages shows a notable overlap between the taxa (Fig. 19.5).

When it comes to postcranial biometrics, the most useful in differentiating between *T. auratus* and *M. fascicularis* is found to be measurements of the distal humerus (Fig. 19.5). A slight overlap can still be observed in the plot of the measurements of distal humerus breadth and depth, but this is not as extensive as in the plots of the measurements of other postcranial elements. Comparative and archaeological *Macaca* specimens exhibit greater distal humeral depth than *Trachypithecus* specimens (average depth *M. fascicularis* comparative = 14.6 mm; archaeological = 14.09 mm; *T. auratus* comparative = 12.2 mm; archaeological = 12.3 mm). This is brought about by the morphology of the trochlea and the capitulum and the orientation of the medial epicondyle, characteristics that are associated with locomotor habits (Birchette, 1982; Ingicco, 2010; Jenkins, 1973; Jolly, 1967; Rose, 1983, 1988; Senut, 1986; Senturia, 1995).

Specific differences in the morphology of the humerus of Southeast Asian langurs and macaques have been detailed by Ky-Kidd and Piper (2004) and Ingicco et al. (2020). They noted that in addition to the morphological characteristics of the distal humerus, langurs and macaques can also be differentiated by looking at the differences in the shape of the humeral head, shaft curvature, extension of the greater tubercle, definition of muscle attachment regions, and shape of the shaft in cross-

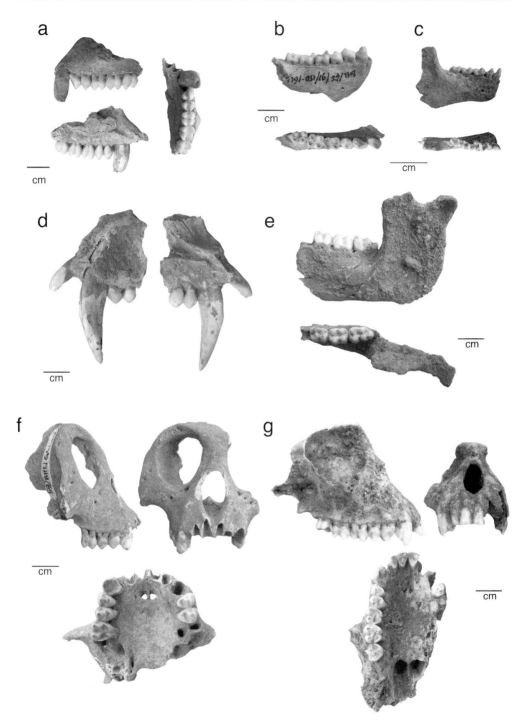

Figure 19.4 Representative nonhuman primate specimens from Braholo Cave (a) *Trachypithecus auratus* left maxilla fragment (Spec no. G6–103); (b) *Presbytis comata* right mandible fragment (Spec no. G6–847); (c) *Nycticebus* cf *javanicus* right mandible fragment (Spec no. G6–5487);

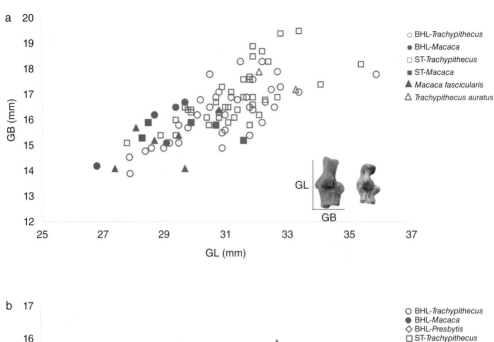

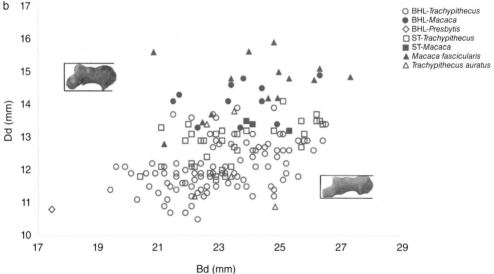

Figure 19.5 Bivariate plot of cercopithecid postcranial elements from Braholo Cave and the nearby cave of Song Terus (a) Calcaneus greatest length (GL) vs greatest breadth (GB) (b) Greatest breadth (Bd) vs. depth (Dd) of the distal end of the humerus.

Figure 19.4 (*cont.*) (d) *Macaca fascicularis* left maxilla fragment (Spec no. G6–100); (e) *M. fascicularis* left mandible (Spec no. G6 –101); (f) *T. auratus* cranium fragment (Spec no. G6-102); (g) *M. fascicularis* cranium fragment (Spec no. G6-209). Scale = 1 cm.

section. These features are associated with quadrupedal locomotion, specifically the differing leverage requirements for the supraspinatus during movement and the degree of shoulder mobility allowed by the close-packed glenoid fossa/humeral head joint (Jolly, 1967; Larson and Stern, 1989). Based on these features, all the distal and proximal humerus fragments recorded in the assemblage were assigned to taxon. *T. auratus* represented 90.5% of the identified cercopithecid humerus fragments, whereas *M. fascicularis* accounted for 9.5%. In other words, there is one *M. fascicularis* for every nine *T. auratus* specimens in the assemblages. This is comparable to the percentage obtained from dental morphology.

T. auratus (Javan langur) and *M. fascicularis* currently exist sympatrically in Java except in monsoon forests where only the latter is present. The Javan langur, endemic to the island, occurs in a wide variety of forest types, from mangrove and freshwater swamp forests; wet lowland and hill forests to dry deciduous forests, in both forest edge and interior. *T. auratus* populations have also been recorded in montane forests up to 3500 masl (Nijman, 2000; Nijman and van Balen, 1998). The Javan langur is highly specialized towards folivory, but is also known to consume unripened fruits and seeds (Nijman, 2000). On the other hand, *M. fascicularis*, with a widespread distribution across mainland and island Southeast Asia, from Bangladesh to Peninsular Malaysia, and the Philippines to Sumatra and Timor, is known to tolerate a wider range of habitats, including disturbed forests and agricultural areas (Groves, 2001). Its diet further covers a broader spectrum of nutrients from plants and fruits to crustaceans.

The large amount of *T. auratus* and *M. fascicularis* remains from the Holocene deposits of Braholo Cave provide evidence for the presence of forests in the region in this period. Furthermore, the dominance of leaf monkeys indicates specialized hunting of arboreal taxa by the hunter-gatherers that utilized Braholo Cave in the Early to Mid-Holocene.

19.4   Other Nonhuman Primates in the Braholo Cave Assemblage

In addition to cercopithecids, the Holocene layers of Braholo Cave also provided evidence for hunting of loris (Fig. 19.4c). A total of 33 loris skeletal elements were identified in Braholo Cave, representing 0.4% of the total identified primate specimens. The specimens were identified as representing *Nycticebus javanicus* based on the current taxonomic scheme and considering this species is the lone slow loris presently found on the island. The Southeast Asian Lorisidae are all assigned to the genus *Nycticebus*, the slow lorises. There are five slow loris species currently present in the region, with the species present in Java assigned to *N. javanicus*. *N. javanicus* was first recognized as a subspecies of the Sunda Slow Loris (*N. coucang*). The subspeciation of *N. coucang* was illustrated by Groves (1971, 1998) with reference to the pattern of the drowned rivers of the Sunda shelf. The elevation of *N. javanicus* as a separate species was first proposed by Supriatna and Hendras (2000) and further supported by studies looking at craniometry (Groves and Maryanto, 2008), morphometry and pelage patterns (Nekaris and Jaffe, 2007) and genetics (Wirdateti et al., 2006).

The identification of the Braholo cave slow loris as representing *N. javanicus* comes with a caveat. The divergence of the Sumatran *N. coucang* and *N. javanicus* is hypothesized to have commenced after the Pliocene (e.g. Pozzi et al., 2020). Whether the Early Holocene *Nycticebus* remains from Braholo Cave represent *N. coucang* or incipient *N. javanicus* populations is still a question. Dental measurements, occlusal tooth patterns, and postcranial morphology do not allow for the discrimination between *N. coucang* and *N. javanicus*. Dental measurements of specimens found in Braholo Cave fall within the range of *N. coucang* and *N. javanicus* museum reference specimens (in contrast to the smaller *N. pygmaeus* which is restricted to Vietnam). Groves and Maryanto (2008) pointed out that of the characters found useful in loris taxonomy, the only one applicable in discriminating the Sundaland taxa is the number of upper incisors. All the *N. javanicus* crania they examined have a single pair of upper incisors (Groves and Maryanto, 2008): 122; Ravosa, 1998 have a bigger sample size and reported that 95% of *N. javanicus* they examined have a single pair of upper incisors). Unfortunately, there are no loris incisive/premaxillae with preserved incisors or alveoli recovered in Braholo Cave.

N. javanicus is a frugivorous, arboreal, nocturnal species that occurs in primary and secondary lowland forests in elevations ranging from sea level to 1600 m (Nekaris et al., 2013; Wirdateti et al., 2011). Nekaris et al. (2013) noted that due to its locomotor behavior, *N. javanicus* needs arboreal connectivity, although it is also known to cross short open spaces on the ground. The *Nycticebus* remains from Braholo Cave show no digestion marks which suggests they were not brought to the cave by any snake, bird, or any other potential predator but by humans. The presence of slow lorises in the assemblage, in addition to the presence of sciurids (*Ratufa*) and colugos (*Galeopterus variegatus*), further support the notion of a specialized hunting strategy focusing on arboreal taxa by people that settled Braholo Cave.

19.5   Food and Implements: Patterns of Primate Exploitation in Braholo Cave

19.5.1   Skeletal Element Representation

All skeletal elements are present in the Braholo Cave assemblage suggesting that complete carcasses were brought to the site (Fig. 19.6). In terms of NISP, 10.8% of the identified remains are cranial fragments, 2.8% are mandible fragments, 6.3% are isolated teeth, 12.6% are ribs and vertebrae, and 67.3% are appendicular skeletal elements. The presence of carpal and tarsal bones (<20 mm), as well as long bone fragments (18.3%) with less than half the shaft circumference, suggests that the assemblage was carefully screened and collected.

At least one *P. comata*, four *M. fascicularis*, and 54 *T. auratus* individuals are represented in the assemblage based on the number of dental elements. A minimum of four *M. fascicularis* individuals is identified based on the number of right M_3 and a single *P. comata* based on a complete right mandible and a maxilla fragment with the M^{1-2}. This minimum number of individuals (MNI) value for *T. auratus* is derived from

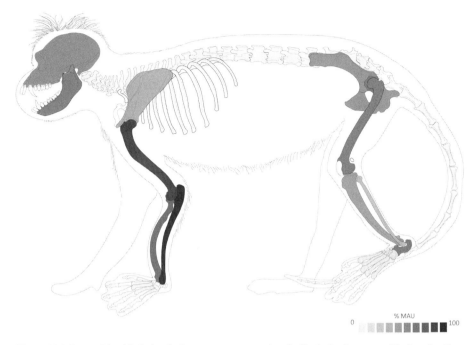

Figure 19.6 Cercopithecid skeletal element representation in Braholo Cave considering the % Minimum Number of Animal Units (%MAU).

the number of left M_2. Teeth are well preserved in archaeological sites and usually provide the highest MNI estimates. But this is not the case for Braholo Cave. At least 114 *T. auratus* individuals are estimated to be present in the assemblage based on the number of the left proximal ulna (see below). This is twice the MNI value estimated from the teeth. This could either be due to processing of the carcasses prior to transport (i.e. removal of the head) or to the selective retention of ulna in the site. The latter appears to be more plausible since MNI estimates based on other long bone fragments correspond to estimates based on dental elements.

A total of 540 skull fragments were recorded in the assemblage, representing a minimum (minimum number of elements, MNE) of 37 crania, as suggested by the presence right zygomatic bone fragments with overlapping features. Parietal and frontal bones are the most common cranial elements but they are mostly fragmented and cannot be used to estimate the MNI/MNE. There is a slight discrepancy in the number of skulls (and maxillary dental elements) compared to the number of mandibles (and lower teeth). The mandibular premolars/molars outnumber their maxillary counterparts by 60.9% (409 vs. 218). The most pronounced difference is observed in the third molar, with a total of 82 M_3 identified as opposed to 37 M^3 (75.6% difference). The lower incisors are also more numerous than the upper incisors (65 vs. 44; 35.8%). The same difference is observed with regards to the number of mandible (NISP = 140) and maxilla (NISP = 73) fragments considering both those with and without dentition (62.9%). Based on these, it appears that mandibles were selectively retained in the site.

With regards to the long bones of the thoracic limb, the ulna is the most common specimen in the assemblage, with a total of 427 recorded fragments representing at least 227 elements from at least 113 individuals. There is an overrepresentation of proximal parts (with the olecranon and/or coronoid process) compared to shaft and distal fragments. Proximal fragments were also recorded in greater number compared to the distal radius. A total of 381 humerus fragments, from at least 107 individuals, are present in the assemblage. In contrast to the radius and ulna, distal humerus fragments are more numerous than the proximal specimens (82.8% difference). The overrepresentation of the distal humerus, proximal ulna and proximal radius indicates that the elbow portion is selectively retained on the site.

A total of 697 cercopithecid leg bone fragments were identified in Braholo Cave. The femur is the most common of the leg bones in the assemblage with a total of 335 identified fragments representing at least 123 elements from at least 66 individuals. The counts for the tibia are comparable. Fibula fragments are not as common as the femur or the tibia, with only 159 specimens recorded (MNE = 61, MNI = 32). Interestingly, 64.1% of the fibula fragments recorded are either finished bone tools or specimens exhibiting modifications suggestive of osseous tool manufacture (see Section 19.5.4).

19.5.2 Age at Death Profile

The mortality profile of *T. auratus* in Braholo Cave is constructed following the dental wear stages described by Ingicco (2010) and Ingicco et al. (2012). The MNI of 54 estimated based on the number of dental elements is reduced to 42 when dental wear stages are taken into consideration. The individuals in the assemblage include: 7 juveniles (stage J1–J4), 6 sub-adults (stage J5–J7, with the eruption of M2); 23 adults (stage A1–A4); and 6 old individuals (A5–A7). The kill-off pattern observed in the assemblage reflects the social structure of wild *Trachypithecus* populations (Kool, 1993; Yeager and Kirkpatrick, 1998). The slight overrepresentation of juveniles relative to the subadults can be explained by the capture of prime adults with weaning juveniles, akin to the observation made by Piper et al. (2008) and Piper and Rabett (2016) in their study of the cercopithecids from Niah Caves. As pointed out by Ingicco et al. (2012), the weaning age in langurs is between 12 and 26 months, depending on group size (Borries et al., 2008), the latter corresponding to stage J4 and sexual maturity takes place between 3 and 5 years which corresponds to stage A1.

19.5.3 Carcass Processing

Butchery marks were recorded in 174 bone fragments (Figs. 19.7 and 19.8), representing 3.2% of the total cercopithecid remains recovered in the site. Figure 19.9 shows the frequency of elements with evidence of butchery as well as the number of cutmarks recorded in specific portions of the cercopithecid skeleton. The most frequent cutmarked element is the humerus, with a total of 39 recorded specimens. This accounts for 10.2% of all the humerus fragments in the assemblage and 22.4%

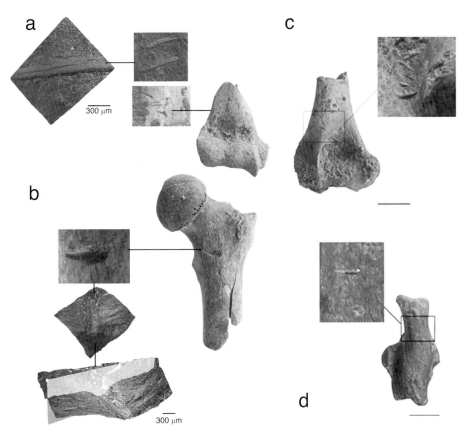

Figure 19.7 Photomicrographs of selected butchery marks in cercopithecid skeletal elements. (a) Cutmarks on *T. auratus* distal humerus (G6–3167); (b) Chopmark on *T. auratus* proximal femur (G6–5655cm); (c) Distal humerus of *T. auratus* (G6–14027) exhibiting cutmarks on the posterior aspect; (d) Cutmarked *T. auratus* calcaneus (G6– 5597). The location of the cutmark is consistent for other calcaneus specimens in the assemblage.

of the fragments with butchery marks. The humerus is the most common cutmarked specimens not only in cercopithecids but also in other intermediate-sized mammals, including the giant tree squirrel, civet cat, and the flying fox (Figure 19.8b-d).

The cutmarks in cercopithecid distal humerus fragments were concentrated on the lateral/medial supracondylar ridge and on the area just above the lateral/medial epicondyle (Figure 19.8). Several cutmarks were also recorded in the radial and coronoid fossae. These indicate that the carcass-processing sequence for cercopithecids involved the cutting of the brachialis muscles during disarticulation. Some distal humerus fragments exhibited large cutmarks on the lateral (NISP = 3) and medial (NISP = 5) epicondyles, suggesting that disarticulation also involved the cutting of common extensor and flexor tendons.

Seven distal humerus fragments exhibited cutmarks on the posterior surface, mostly around the olecranon fossa (e.g. Figs. 19.7 and 19.8). Rabett (2012: 217) noted that the presence of cutmarks in this area indicates that disarticulation took

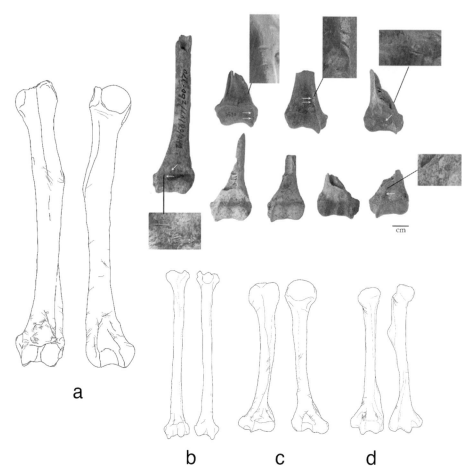

Figure 19.8 Composite butchery marks in the humerus of different intermediate-sized mammal taxa in Braholo Cave. (a) Cercopithecidae; (b) *Pteropus*; (c) Viverridae; (d) Sciuridae. The figure also illustrates the different fracture patterns in cercopithecid humerus fragments, note the presence of cutmarks in some of the specimens.

place with the arm in flexed position possibly when rigor mortis has already set in and therefore reflects processing of the carcass sometime after it has been acquired. The prevalence of cutmarked distal humerus fragments in the assemblage can be explained by the routine disarticulation of the ulna from the humerus as a step in the carcass processing sequence to come up with manageable portions of the carcass and/or selection of the ulna for use in bone tool manufacture. The presence of numerous ulna fragments exhibiting modifications consistent with osseous tool production (e.g. Pasveer, 2004, 2006; Rabett, 2005; Setiagama, 2006; see Section 19.5.4) supports this notion.

Cutmarks on the scapula (NISP = 3) are mostly located on the neck, near the glenoid fossa and most likely represent disarticulation of the joint to separate the thoracic limbs. Two clavicle specimens exhibit cutmarks on the anterior surface and probably resulted from the cutting of the pectoralis muscle. The presence of cutmarks on the occipital bone and the atlas and axis clearly indicates removal of the head. The mandible is separated from the cranium as evidenced by the cutmarks observed in the ascending ramus and notably near the condylar process. Cutmarks on the ribs are mostly located on the ventral surface of the shafts, resulting either from evisceration or meat removal (e.g. Saladie et al., 2015).

The cutmarks recorded in the pelvis (NISP = 6) and proximal femur (NISP = 16) most likely represent the removal of the hind limbs. The majority of the femur fragments (NISP = 12, 75%) exhibit butchery marks in the intertrochanteric area, the anterior aspect of the femoral neck, and posterolateral surface of the greater trochanter. Three fragments have chop marks on the femoral neck (e.g. Fig. 19.7b). These butchery marks suggest a carcass-processing sequence that involved the cutting of the muscles and tendons in the area, including the illiopsoas, vastus medialis, and gluteus muscles as well as the pectioneus tendons (Saladie et al., 2015). Distal femora with evidence of butchery are not as common as the proximal fragments, but several specimens are recorded (NISP = 5). The marks most likely resulted from the cutting of the muscles (e.g. gastrocnemius) to separate the femur from the tibia and fibula. The marks recorded in the fibula, akin to the marks recorded in the ulna, mostly represent modifications resulting from preparation of bone tools, including marks resulting from shaving and grinding.

The calcaneus has the highest frequency of occurrence of butchery traces among posterior limb elements, with a total of 13 (10.2%) cutmarked elements recorded in the assemblage. Notably, all the cutmarks are located in relatively the same position: in the plantar aspect just below the calcaneal tuberosity (e.g. Fig. 19.7d). This most likely resulted from the cutting of the Achilles tendon for the disarticulation of the distal limb extremity (e.g. Saladie et al., 2015) or from skinning of the carcass (Rabett, 2012; Rabett and Piper, 2016).

The placement of the butchery marks suggests that the carcasses were processed in a careful sequence suggestive of intimate knowledge of cercopithecid anatomy. The cutmarks in the mandibles, calcaneus as well as in the medial surface of rib shafts, indicate that the carcass-processing sequence involved skinning and evisceration. The presence of cutmarks in the pelvic and shoulder girdles suggests that the forelimbs and hind limbs were treated as a unit and detached from the carcass. Likewise, the head appears to have been considered as a distinct unit, as evidenced by the cutmarks observed in the first two vertebrae as well as in the occipital bone. The numerous cutmarks observed near the joints indicate further processing of carcass units into smaller portions. Scrape marks on the diaphysis of certain elements indicate defleshing, which most likely represent the initial stage for bone tool manufacture.

19.5.4 Bone Implements

The Holocene layers of Braholo Cave yielded a total of 111 cercopithecid bone fragments with modifications consistent with bone tool production. Of these,

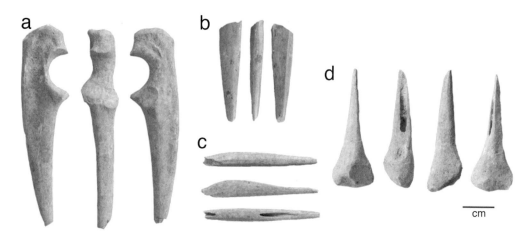

Figure 19.9 Examples of tools manufactured from cercopithecid bones in Braholo Cave: (a) ulna point (note the broken tip, G6–5524); (b). ulna point (G6–5586); (c) fibula bipoint (G6–5593); (d) fibula unipoint (G6–5586).

63.9% (NISP = 71) are finished tools and the rest are unfinished fragments and debitage. Fibula (mono and bi) points are the most common bone tool type followed by points and spatulas made from ulnae (Fig. 19.9). Several fibula (NISP = 21) and ulna fragments (NISP = 13) are in the initial stages of modification. The majority of the tools (60% of the fibula and 77.4% of the ulna points) have broken tips and probably these were discarded at the site (Fig. 19.9). The presence of numerous fibula and ulna tools provide support to the idea that the overrepresentation of these elements, and to a certain extent of distal humerus fragments, in the assemblage resulted from their retention for use in the manufacture of bone tools.

19.6   Primate Exploitation in the Regional Context

Although undeniably brought about by expansion of forests starting with the Pleistocene–Holocene transition, the predominance of arboreal taxa in the Braholo Cave assemblage, specifically of *T. auratus*, suggests that the people that utilized the cave deliberately targeted this arboreal species. Specialized targeting of arboreal leaf monkeys was also recorded in South Asia, specifically in the sites of Fa Hien-lena (Wedage et al., 2019) and Kitulgala Beli-lena (Wedage et al., 2020). In Fa Hien-lena, sedimentary layers dated to c. 45,000 years ago provide evidence for primate exploitation as a main protein source by early *Homo sapiens*. As in Braholo Cave, two cercopithecid groups were recorded, with a similar preference for the arboreal leaf monkey species. Likewise, in parallel with the findings in Braholo Cave, the hunter-gatherer communities that utilized Fa Hien-lena also manufactured implements from cercopithecid skeletal elements, of comparable morphology, and possibly use (Langley et al. 2020). Ingicco (2010) studied in detail the cercopithecid remains from the nearby Song Terus Cave (see also Ingicco et al., 2012; 2020). He also identified both T. *auratus* and M. *fascicularis* in the assemblage. The identification of T. *auratus* was supported by comparisons with the holotype. Ingicco described the differences between the cranial and dental morphologies of the two species, also in comparison with *Presbytis comata* (Javan surili), the other colobine species present in the island. He also outlined the differences in dental eruption and wear patterns between langurs and macaques (Ingicco et al., 2012). He reported that 2.4% of the identified primate remains from the Holocene layers of Song Terus as *M. fascicularis* and 97.6% as *T. auratus*.

Piper and Rabett (2014) noted that, although a wide range of taxa is represented in the zooarchaeological assemblage of numerous sites in Southeast Asia, certain animals were specifically targeted as the main protein source. This pattern is not only observed in Holocene sites. For example, a targeted emphasis on the hunting of the bearded pig (*Sus barbatus*) was observed all throughout the human habitation phases of Niah Caves (Piper and Rabett, 2014; see also Piper et al., 2008; Piper and Rabett, 2009). In Ille and Pasimbahan Caves both in Northern Palawan, the Pleistocene–Holocene faunal assemblages revealed hunting of a wide range of taxa but specific reliance on the Palawan bearded pig (*Sus ahoenobarbus*) and two extinct deer species (Lewis et al., 2008; Ochoa et al., 2014; Piper et al., 2011) as the main protein source. In Kria and Toé Caves in the Ayamaru region of the Bird's Head Peninsula, Pasveer (2004) reported the selective hunting of the brown forest wallaby (*Dorcopsis muelleri*) during the Holocene phase of site occupation. The Late Pleistocene layers of Lang Rongrien Rockshelter in Southern Thailand yielded evidence of heavy exploitation of freshwater and terrestrial turtles (Mudar and Anderson, 2007). By contrast, leaf monkeys and squirrels represent the majority of the taxa recorded in the nearby Moh Khiew Cave (Anderson, 2005). As pointed out by Piper and Rabett (2014), this hints at the difference in the subsistence economies of people living within the same geographic region. The preference for hunting specific taxa for food can still be observed in modern Southeast Asian indigenous communities. Smaller animals such as civet, birds, flying squirrels, and slow lorises and bats are exploited as supplementary protein sources when the preferred games become scarce (e.g. Chan, 2007; Dentan, 1991; Endicott & Bellwood, 1991; Wadley & Pierce-Colfer, 2004). Chan (2007) further noted that specific individuals within an arboreal group of monkeys could be targeted through the use of projectile technologies, some of which were made of plant materials including bamboo. This raises the potential of perishable tools being used by the prehistoric populations.

An emphasis on the hunting of the Javan langur is also observed in other sites in the Gunung Sewu region, aside from Song Terus, for instance in the nearby sites of Song Gupuh (Morwood et al., 2008) and Goa Tabuhan (Moigne et al., 2012). The continued exploitation of leaf monkeys by people occupying the Gunung Sewu region for millenia may suggest that populations managed to survive hunting pressures without experiencing significant decline. The age-at-death profile for *T. auratus* shows the targeting of adults, with the number of prime-aged adults three times the number of sub-adults, suggestive of a thriving population or at least one not severely affected by hunting pressures. That the leaf monkeys managed to survive continuous hunting could also be due to low human population densities or that hunter-gatherer communities moved across the landscape throughout the year.

19.7   Conclusion

Targeted hunting of monkeys for food and as source of materials for tool and ornament production has been documented in several archaeological sites in South and Southeast Asia. In this chapter we presented how monkeys were exploited and utilized by people that settled Braholo Cave, located in East Java's Gunung Sewu region, during the Early to Mid-Holocene. Similar to contemporaneous sites which produced evidence for monkey hunting in the region, we recorded deliberate targeting of the Javan langur *T. auratus* in Braholo Cave over other nonhuman primate taxa, notably the long-tailed macaque *M. fascicularis*. But unlike in other sites, we documented the presence of the Javan surili (*P. comata*) and the Javan slow loris (*N. javanicus*) in Braholo Cave. Careful examination of bone surface modifications and skeletal element composition allowed us to reconstruct how the monkeys were processed. We also noted an overrepresentation of certain skeletal elements, which together with the presence of modified bones and finished tools, suggests that the cave was used by people as site to manufacture bone implements. Overall, the evidence from Braholo Cave points to complex human and nonhuman primate relationships in Early to Mid-Holocene in East Java.

Acknowledgments

We would like to thank Dionisios Youlatos and Bernardo Urbani for inviting us to contribute to this book. This research was funded by the European Union's Erasmus Mundus International Doctorate in Quaternary and Prehistory granted to N. Amano.

References

Aimi, M. (1981). Fossil *Macaca nemestrina* (Linnaeus, 1976) from Java, Indonesia. *Primates*, **22**(3), 409–413.

Amano, N., Moigne, A. M., Ingicco, T., Sémah, F., Awe, R. D., & Simanjuntak, T. (2016). Subsistence strategies and environment in Late Pleistocene–Early Holocene Eastern Java: Evidence from Braholo Cave. *Quaternary International*, **416**(1), 46–63.

Barker, G. (2005). The archaeology of foraging and farming in Niah Cave, Sarawak. *Asian Perspectives*, **44**(1), 90–106.

Barker, G., & Farr, L. (eds.) (2016). *Archaeological Investigations in the Niah Caves, Sarawak*. McDonald Institute for Archaeological Research, Cambridge.

Barker, G., Barton, H., Bird, M., et al. (2007). The "human revolution" in lowland tropical Southeast Asia: the antiquity and behavior of anatomically modern humans at Niah Cave (Sarawak, Borneo). *Journal of Human Evolution*, **52**(3), 243–226.

Barton, H. W., Piper, P. J., Rabett, R. J., & Reeds, I. (2009). Composite hunting technologies from the Terminal Pleistocene and Early Holocene, Niah Cave, Borneo. *Journal of Archaeological Science*, **36**, 1708–1714.

Bellwood, P. (1997). *Prehistory of the Indo-Malaysian Archipelago* (revised edition). Honolulu: University of Hawai'i Press.

Bellwood, P. (2013). *First Migrants: Ancient Migration in Global Perspective*. Chichester: Wiley-Blackwell.

Birchette, M. G. (1982). The postcranial skeleton of Paracolobus chemeroni. PhD thesis, Harvard University .

Borries, C., Larney, E., Lu, A., Ossi, K., & Koenig, A. (2008). Costs of large groups: developmental and reproductive rates in wild Phayre's leaf monkeys (*Trachypithecus phayrei*). In *Proceedings of the 77th Annual Meeting of the American Journal of Physical Antropology 71*.

Botes, I.Gh. (1926). *Étude morphologique et morphogénique du squelette du bras et de l'avant-bras chez les primates*. Libraire Octave Doin, Gaston Doin & cie, éditeurs. Paris.

Dam, R. A., Fluin, J., Suparan, P., & van der Kaars, S. (2001). Palaeoenvironmental developments in the Lake Tondano area (N. Sulawesi, Indonesia) since 33,000 yr BP. *Palaeogeography, Palaeoclimatology, Palaeoecology*, **171**(3), 147–183.

Delson, E. (1973). Fossil Colobine monkeys of the Circum-Mediterranean Region and the evolutionary history of the Cercopithecidae (Primates, Mammalia). PhD thesis. Columbia University.

Détroit, F. (2006). Homo sapiens in Southeast Asian archipelagos: the Holocene fossil evidence with special reference to funerary practices in East Java. In T. Simanjuntak, M. Pojoh, & M. Hisyam, eds., *Austronesian Diaspora and the Ethnogeneses of People in Indonesian Archipelago*, Proceedings of the International Symposium. Jakarta: LIPI Press, 186–204.

Dubois, N., Oppo, D. W., Galy, V. V., et al. (2014). Indonesian vegetation response to changes in rainfall seasonality over the past 25,000 years. *Nature Geoscience*, **7**(7), 513–517.

Groves, C. P. (1971). Systematics of the genus Nycticebus. In *Taxonomy, Anatomy, Reproduction*. Proceedings of the *Third International Congress* of *Primatology* 1, 44–53.

Groves, C. P. (1998). Systematics of tarsiers and lorises. *Primates*, **39**(1), 13–27.

Groves, C., & Maryanto, I. (2008). Craniometry of slow lorises (genus *Nycticebus*) of insular Southeast Asia. In M. Shekelle, C. Groves, I. Maryanto, H. Schulze, & H. Fitch-Snyder. *Primates of the Oriental Night*. Jakarta: LIPI Press, 115–122.

Harrison, T., Krigbaum, J., & Manser, J. (2006). Primate biogeography and ecology on the Sunda Shelf Islands: a paleontological and zooarchaeological perspective. In S. N. Lehman, & J. G. Fleagle. *Primate Biogeography*. New York: Springer, 331–372.

Ingicco, T. (2010). Les primates quaternaires de Song Terus (Java Est, Indonésie) implications paléobiogéographiques et archéozoologiques pour l'Asie du Sud-Est. Ph.D. thesis, Muséum national d'Histoire naturelle, Paris.

Ingicco, T., Moigne, A.-M., & Gommery, D. 2012. A deciduous and permanent dental wear stage system for assessing the age of *Trachypithecus* sp.

specimens (Colobinae, Primates). *Journal of Archaeological Science*, **39**, 421–427.

Ingicco, T., Amano, N., Setiagama, K., et al. (2020). From food to grave good: Non-human primate exploitation in Early to Mid-Holocene Eastern Java (Indonesia). *Current Anthropology*, **61**, 264–277.

Jenkins, F. A. (1973). The functional anatomy and evolution of the mammalian humero-ulnar articulation. *American Journal of Anatomy*, **137**(3), 281–297.

Ji, X., Youlatos, D., Jablonski, N. G., et al. (2020). Oldest colobine calcaneus from East Asia (Zhaotong, Yunnan, China), *Journal of Human Evolution*, **147**, 1–13

Jolly, C. (1967). The evolution of the baboons. In H. Vartborg, ed., *The Baboon in Medical Research. Vol. II*. Austin: University of Texas Press, 427–457.

Kershaw, A. P., van der Kaars, S., & Moss, P. T. (2001). Late Quaternary Milankovitch-scale climatic change and variability and its impact on monsoonal Australasia. *Marine Geology*, **201** (1–3), 81–95.

Knussmann, R. (1967). *Humerus, ulna and radius der Simiae. Bibliotheca Primatologica*, vol. 5, Basel: Prager.

Kool, K. M. (1993). The diet and feeding behavior of the silver leaf monkey (*Trachypithecus auratus sondaicus*) in Indonesia. *International Journal of Primatology*, **14**(5), 667–700.

Ky-Kidd, K., & Piper, P. (2004). Identification of morphological variation in the humeri of Bornean primates and its application to zooarchaeology. *Archaeofauna*, **13**, 85–95.

Langley M. C., Amano N., Wedage O., et al. (2020). Bows and arrows and complex symbolic displays 48,000 years ago in the South Asian tropics. *Science Advances*, **6**, eaba3831

Larson, S. G., & Stern, J. T. (1989). Role of supraspinatus in the quadrupedal locomotion of vervets (*Cercopithecus aethiops*): implications for interpretation of humeral morphology. *American Journal of Physical Anthropology*, **79**(3), 369–377.

Lewis, H., Paz, V., Lara, M., et al. (2008). Terminal Pleistocene to mid-Holocene occupation and an early cremation burial at Ille Cave, Palawan, Philippines. *Antiquity*, **82**(316), 318–335.

Lucas, P. W., & Teaford, M. F. (1994). Functional morphology of colobine teeth. In G. Davies, & J. Oates, eds., *Colobine Monkeys: Their Ecology, Behaviour and Evolution* Cambridge: Cambridge University Press, 173–203.

Lucas, P. W., Corlett, R. T., & Luke, D. A. (1986). Postcanine tooth size and diet in anthropoid primates. *Zeitschrift für Morphologie und Anthropologie*, 76(3), 253–276.

Nekaris, K. A. I., & Jaffe, S. (2007). Unexpected diversity of slow lorises (*Nycticebus* spp.) within the Javan pet trade implications for slow loris taxonomy. *Contributions to Zoology*, 76(3), 187–196.

Nekaris, K. A. I., Moore, R. S., Rode, E. J., & Fry, B. G. (2013). Mad, bad and dangerous to know: the bio-chemistry, ecology and evolution of slow loris venom. *Journal of Venomous Animals and Toxins including Tropical Diseases*, 19(1), 21.

Newsome, J., & Flenley, J. R. (1988). Late Quaternary vegetational history of the central highlands of Sumatra. II. Palaeopalynology and vegetational history. *Journal of Biogeography*, 1, 555–578.

Nijman, V. (2000). Geographic distribution of ebony leaf monkey *Trachypithecus auratus*. *Contributions to Zoology*, 69(3), 157–177.

Nijman, V., & Van Balen, S. B. (1998). A faunal survey of the Dieng Mountains, Central Java, Indonesia: distribution and conservation of endemic primate taxa. *Oryx*, 32(02), 145–156.

Lara, M., Paz, V., Lewis, H., & Solheim, W. (2015). Bone modifications in an Early Holocene cremation burial from Palawan, Philippines. *International Journal of Osteoarchaeology*, 25(5), 637–652.

Lloyd-Smith, L. R. (2009). Chronologies of the dead: Later prehistoric burial practice at the Niah Caves, Sarawak. PhD thesis, University of Cambridge.

Maloney, B. K., & McCormac, F. G. (1995). A 30,000-year pollen and radiocarbon record from Highland Sumatra as evidence for climatic change. *Radiocarbon*, 37(02), 181–190.

Maloney, B. K., & McCormac, F. G. (1996). Palaeoenvironments of North Sumatra: a 30,000-year-old pollen record from Pea Bullok. *Bulletin of the Indo-Pacific Prehistory Association*, 14, 73–82.

Morwood, M. J., Sutikna, T., Saptomo, E. W., et al. (2008). Climate, people and faunal succession on Java, Indonesia: evidence from Song Gupuh. *Journal of Archaeological Science*, 35 (7), 1776–1789.

O'Connor, S. (2007). New evidence from East Timor contributes to our understanding of earliest modern human colonisation east of the Sunda Shelf. *Antiquity*, 81(313), 523–535.

O'Connor, S., Ono, R., & Clarkson, C. (2011). Pelagic fishing at 42,000 years before the present and the maritime skills of modern humans. *Science*, 334 (6059), 1117–1121.

Olivier, G., & Caix, M. (1959). L'humérus du Semnopithèque. *Mammalia*, 23(1), 77–90.

Olivier, G., & Fenart, R. (1956). Les os de la jambe du Semnopithèque. *Mammalia*, 20(3), 249–275.

Olivier, G., & Fontaine, M. (1957). Les os du pied du Semnopithèque. *Mammalia*, 21(4), 142–189.

Olivier, G., & Piganiol, G. (1957). Le fémur du Semnopithèque. *Mammalia*, 21(4), 430–451.

Olivier, G., & Soutoul, J. (1960). L'avant-bras du Semnopithèque. *Mammalia* 24(2), 228–258.

Olivier, G., & Soutoul, J. (1961). Les os de la main du Semnopithèque. *Mammalia*, 25, 499–527.

Pasveer, J. M. (2004). *The Djief Hunters, 26,000 years of Rainforest Exploitation on the Bird's Head of Papua, Indonesia. Modern Quaternary Research in Southeast Asia, volume 17*. Rotterdam: Balkema.

Pawlik, A. F., Piper, P. J., Paylona, M. G. P., et al. (2014). Adaptation and foraging from the Terminal Pleistocene to the Early Holocene: Excavation at Bubog on Ilin Island, *Philippines. Journal of Field Archaeology*, 39(3), 230–247.

Pawlik, A. F., Piper, P. J., Wood, R. E., et al. (2015). Shell tool technology in Island Southeast Asia: an early Middle Holocene Tridacna adze from Ilin Island, Mindoro, Philippines. *Antiquity*, 89(344), 292–308.

Piper, P. J., & Rabett, R. J. (2009). Hunting in a tropical rainforest: evidence from the Terminal Pleistocene at Lobang Hangus, Niah Caves, Sarawak. *International Journal of Osteoarchaeology*, 19(4), 551–565.

Piper, P., & Rabett, R. (2016). Vertebrate fauna from the Niah Caves, In G. Barker, & L. Farr, eds., *Archaeological Investigations in the Niah Caves, Sarawak*. Cambridge: McDonald Institute for Archaeological Research, 401–454.

Piper, P. J., Rabett, R. J., & Kurui, E. B. (2008). Using community, composition and structural variation in terminal Pleistocene vertebrate assemblages to identify human hunting behavior at Niah Caves, Borneo. *Bulletin of the Indo-Pacific Prehistory Association*, 28, 88–98.

Preuschoft, H. (1969). Statische Untersuchungen am Fuß der Primaten. *Zeitschrift für Anatomie und Entwicklungsgeschichte*, 129, 285–345

Rabett, R. J. (2005). The early exploitation of Southeast Asian mangroves: Bone technology from caves and open sites. *Asian Perspectives*, 44, 154–179.

Rabett, R. J. (2012). *Human Adaptation in the Asian Palaeolithic: Hominin Dispersal and Behaviour during the Late Quaternary.* Cambridge: Cambridge University Press.

Rabett, R. J., & Piper, P. J. (2012). The emergence of bone technologies at the end of the Pleistocene in Southeast Asia: regional and evolutionary implications. *Cambridge Archaeological Journal,* 22, 37–56.

Ravosa, M. J. (1998). Cranial allometry and geographic variation in slow lorises (*Nycticebus*). *American Journal of Primatology,* 45(3), 225–243.

Richardson, M., Mittermeier, R. A., Rylands, A. B., & Konstant, B. (2008). *Macaca nemestrina.* The IUCN Red List of Threatened Species. Version 2015.1. Available from: www.iucnredlist.org

Rose, M. D. (1983). Miocene hominoid postcranial morphology: monkey-like, ape-like, neither, or both? In R. L. Ciochon, & R. S. Corruccini, eds., *New Interpretations of Ape and Human Ancestry.* New York: Plenum Press, 405–417.

Rose, M. D. (1988). Another look at the anthropoid elbow. *Journal of Human Evolution,* 17(1–2), 193–224.

Russell, J. M., Vogel, H., Konecky, B. L., et al. (2014). Glacial forcing of central Indonesian hydroclimate since 60,000 y BP. *Proceedings of the National Academy of Sciences of the United States of America,* 111(14), 5100–5105.

Sémah, F., Sémah, A.-M., Falguères, C., et al. (2004). The significance of the Punung karst area (Eastern Java) for the chronology of the Javanese Palaeolithic, with special reference to the Song Terus cave. In S. G. Keates, & J. Pasveer, eds., *Modern Quaternary Research in Southeast Asia,* vol. 18, Rotterdam: Balkema, 45–61.

Senturia, S. J. (1995). Morphometry and allometry of the primate humerus. *Primates* 36(4), 523–547.

Senut, B. (1986). Long bones of the primate upper limb: monomorphic or dimorphic? *Human Evolution,* 1(1), 7.

Setiagama, F. K. (2006). L'industrie osseuse de l'horizon Keplek, Holocène de la grotte de Song Terus, Punung, Java Est (Indonésie). Master's thesis, Muséum national d'Histoire naturelle.

Simanjuntak T., & Asikin, I. N. (2004). Early Holocene human settlement in eastern Java. *Bulletin of the Indo-Pacific Prehistory Association,* 2, 13–19.

Supriatna, J., & Wahyono, E. H. (2000). *PanduanLapangan Primata Indonesia.* Jakarta: Yaysan Obor Indonesia.

Swindler, D. R. (2002). *Primate Dentition. An Introduction to the Teeth of Non-human Primates.* Cambridge, UK: Cambridge University Press.

Szabó, K., Brumm, A., Bellwood, P., et al. (2007). Shell artefact production at 32,000–28,000 BP in Island Southeast Asia: thinking across media? *Current Anthropology,* 48(5), 701–723.

van den Bergh, G. D., de Vos, J., & Sondaar, P. Y. (2001). The Late Quaternary palaeogeography of mammal evolution in the Indonesian Archipelago. *Palaeogeography, Palaeoclimatology, Palaeoecology,* 171(3), 385–408.

van der Kaars, W. A. (1998). Marine and terrestrial pollen records of the last glacial cycle from the Indonesian region: Bandung Basin and Banda Sea. *Palaeoclimates,* 3, 209–219.

van der Kaars, W. A., & Dam. M. A. C. (1995). A 135,000-year record of vegetational and climatic change from the Bandung area, West-Java, Indonesia. *Palaeogeography, Palaeoclimatology, Palaeoecology,* 117(1–2), 55–72.

van der Kaars, W. A., Wang, X., Kershaw, P., Guichard, F., & Setiabudi, D. A. (2000). A Late Quaternary palaeoecological record from the Banda Sea, Indonesia: Patterns of vegetation, climate and biomass burning in Indonesia and northern Australia. *Palaeogeography, Palaeoclimatology, Palaeoecology,* 155(1–2), 135–153.

Washburn, S. L. (1942). Skeletal proportions of adult langurs and macaques, *Human Biology,* 14(4), 444–472.

Wedage, O., Amano, N., Langley, M. C., et al. (2019). Specialized rainforest hunting by *Homo sapiens* ~45,000 years ago. *Nature Commications,* 10(1), 739.

Wedage, O., Roberts, P., Faulkner, P., et al. (2020). Late Pleistocene to early-Holocene rainforest foraging in Sri Lanka: Multidisciplinary analysis at Kitulgala Beli-lena. *Quaternary Science Reviews,* 231, 106200.

Willis, M. S., & Swindler, D. R. (2004). Molar size and shape variations among Asian colobines. *American Journal of Physical Anthropology,* 125 (1), 51–60.

Wirdateti, Okayama, T., & Kurniati, H. (2006). Genetic diversity of slow loris (*Nycticebus coucang*) based on mitochondrial DNA. *Tropics,* 15(4), 377–381.

Wirdateti, Dahrudin, H., & Sumadidjaya, A. (2011). Distribution and habitat of Javan Loris (*Nycticebus javanicus*) in plantations at Lebak District and Salak

Mount (West Java). *Journal Zoo Indonesia*, 20(1), 17–26.

Wurster, C. M., Bird, M. I., Bull, I. D., et al. (2010). Forest contraction in north equatorial Southeast Asia during the Last Glacial Period. *Proceedings of the National Academy of Sciences of the United States of America*, 107 (35), 15508–15511.

Yeager, C. P., & Kirkpatrick, R. C. (1998) Asian colobine social structure: ecological and evolutionary constraints. *Primates*, 39(2), 147.

Youlatos, D. (2003). Calcaneal features of the Greek Miocene primate *Mesopithecus pentelicus* (Cercopithecoidea: Colobinae). *Geobios*, 36(2), 229–239.

Dispersion, Speciation, Evolution, and Coexistence of East Asian Catarrhine Primates and Humans in Yunnan, China

Gang He, He Zhang, Haitao Wang, Xueping Ji, Songtao Guo, Baoguo Li, Rong Hou, Xiduo Hou, & Ruliang Pan

东亚狭鼻灵长类和人类在中国云南的扩散、物种形成、进化与共存

摘要

本研究对学术期刊和书籍出版物、政府档案和史册进行广泛文献综述为基础，全面回顾了中国云南自晚中新世或早上新世以来狭鼻灵长类（类人猿、长臂猿、疣猴科动物、猴科动物、古人类和中国少数民族）的分布，并在空间上展示了它们之间的关系，特别是灵长类动物与古人类和现代人之间的关系。结果表明，云南以其独特的地理位置与青藏高原东南部和喜马拉雅山东部连接，是东南亚和南亚的链通道，在促进东亚和东南亚狭鼻灵长类的分散、辐射和演化方面具有独特的作用。云南六大考古遗址（元谋、江川、唐子沟、仙仁东、小东、马鲁东）有着相同的环境和栖息地—有着强烈的共存趋势。云南还为冰川期的动植物提供了绝佳的栖息地，使得这里有着中国最多的民族(26个)和灵长类物种(15个)。少数。虽然灵长类动物在艺术、文化、社会生活和医学研究方面做出了重大贡献，但如发生在中国其他地区一样，特别是自上个世纪下半叶以来，灵长类动物及栖息地遭受了巨大的破坏—该省的两个长臂猿物种已被灭绝。

关键词

云南、灵长类动物和人类在东亚的散射和演化，青藏高原、横断山、动植物保护所

Abstract

Based on a broad literature review of journal and book publications, governmental archives, and annals, this study comprehensively examines the special contribution of Yunnan, China, to understanding East Asian catarrhines (colobines, macaques), as well as hominoids, gibbons, hominins, and modern ethnic groups since the Later Miocene or Early Pliocene. It spatially demonstrates their relationship, particularly that between primates and archaic and modern humans. The results indicate that a specific region in Yunnan, joining with the southeast Qinghai–Tibet Plateau, the end of the eastern margin of the Himalayas, and the Hengduan Mountains (SQPMH), is globally distinctive in promoting catarrhine dispersion, radiation, speciation, and evolution in East and Southeast Asia. This area forms the gateway between West, East and Southeast. Six major archaeological sites in Yunnan (Yuanmou, Jiangchuan, Tangzigou, Xianrendong, Xiaodong, and Maludong) share the same environments and habitats with primates, indicating a strong tendency for coexistence. Yunnan also offered an exclusive refugium for plants, animals, and humans during the glaciation so that it maintains the largest numbers of ethnic groups (26) and primate species (21 of 25 species) in China. Although primates inspired significant contributions to arts, culture, social life, and medical research for humans, as in other parts of China, they have suffered greatly in recent Chinese history, particularly since the second half of the last century, resulting in the extirpation of two gibbon species in the province.

Keywords East Asia, Yunnan, Qinghai Tibet Plateau, Mts. Hengduan, Refugium, Homo, Primates, Dispersion, Catarrhine Evolution

20.1   Background

This chapter is based principally on a broad literature review from academic journals and books, chronological governmental annals, and magazines, and particularly the two books by Rongsheng Wen (Wen, 2009, 2013) that historically and comprehensively integrally review the archives and annals from alternative Chinese governmental agents at county level since 1510. The records of the three primate groups, macaques, colobines (mostly the golden monkeys), and gibbons, which can easily be identified in the wild, are analyzed to illustrate their historical distribution. Fossil records of catarrhines in Yunnan, studied with historical records of extant primates and archaic *Homo* and modern ethnic groups, are mainly drawn from Jablonski (2002) and Jablonski and Chaplin (2009), as well as the recent relevant academic literature. Longitude and latitude of the counties used in this study to present the locations of archaeological sites, fossils, and historical records of the primates were worked out with Google Earth, and the related distribution maps were generated with ArcGIS.

The discovery of the earliest euprimate skulls, *Teilhardina asiatica*, from about 55 Ma in the early Eocene in Hunan Province (Bowen et al., 2002; Ni et al., 2004), and *Archicebus achilles*, dated to the Eocene, unearthed in Yangxi Formation in Jingzhou, Hubei Province (Ni et al., 2013), implies that China is likely to be one of the centres for the origin of early primitive nonhuman primates (primates thereafter). However, the significant contribution of China to primate and human evolution is its distinctive role for the dispersion, speciation, and evolution of the catarrhines migrated from Africa to Asia since the Late Miocene or Early Pliocene. This is especially remarkable when overseeing the exceptional geological structures of Yunnan and its neighboring countries of Southeast Asia, and reviewing what the catarrhines must have experienced in the region (Jablonski and Chaplin, 2009; Kelley and Gao, 2012; Roos et al., 2011; Takai et al., 2015a).

Over evolutionary time, China has experienced major changes in tectonic, climatic, and geological activities that have markedly created habitat heterogeneity and a remarkable animal and plant biodiversity (Lu et al., 2018; Qiu and Li, 2005; Zhang, 2006;). During the early Eocene (50 Ma), the collision of the Indian and Asian plates resulted in the formation of the Himalayas, the Hengduan Mountains, the Qinghai–Tibet Plateau, the Yun-Gui (Yunnan-Guizhou) Plateau in western China, and the Loess Plateau in northern China (Zhao et al., 2010). In the late Eocene, the retreat of the Tarim Sea in northwest China led to the aridification of the Asian continent and the intensification of the regional monsoon system (Bosboom et al., 2011). Such changes were further accelerated following rapid uplift of the Qinghai Tibetan

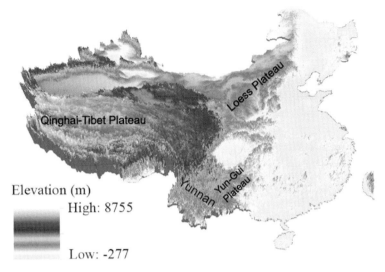

Figure 20.1 Geographic model of China.

Plateau and the Himalayas in the later Miocene or the early Pliocene (6–5 Ma), which continued throughout the Quaternary, leading to the modern configuration of China's landscape (An et al., 2001; Jablonski, 1998; Zhang et al., 2000) (Fig. 20.1).

During the processes of such significant modifications, Yunnan, particularly its Hengduan Mountains, became one of the most remarkable biodiversity hotspots (Xing and Ree, 2017), so that it currently shows four different climate patterns that have significantly improved the resilience of biodiversity to climate change (Wang et al., 2018a). Such orogenic and climate events have also created a variety of conditions favoring *in situ* speciation of plant and animal taxa, providing numerous ways for animals to extend their distribution, and promoting biodiversity following the appearance of new environments, habitats, and separation barriers, among others (Yao et al., 2012).

Consequently, Yunnan now shows a remarkable geographic profile. This is particularly evident in the area of Hengduan Mountains, connecting with the eastern Himalayans and the southeastern Qinghai–Tibet Plateau, a special region referred to as SQPMH, representing a distinctive convergence-divergence place for numerous species of plants and animals (Li et al., 2020; Yang et al., 2004). This distinctive topography is carved by numerous mountains, rivers, and gorges, and most importantly a great number of the branches of upstream of three major Asian rivers: Yangtze, Lancang (Mekong), and Nu (Salween). This makes Yunnan a province with a great number of freshwater lakes, covering an area of 9,000 km^2 and containing about 29 billion m^3 of water (Yang et al., 2004). As such, Yunnan is regarded as one of the most biologically diversified ecosystems in the world: there are over 18,000 higher plant species (51.6% of China's total) and 1,836 vertebrate species (54.8% of China's total), representing only 4.1% of China's total area (Yang et al., 2004). Furthermore, the province is crossed by five main mountain ridge systems, separated by four deep drainage systems, characterized by altitudinal and latitudinal vegetation zonation so that tropical, subtropical, temperate, and cold climates can be seen from the south to the north and from the valley floors to the tops of the mountains (Myers et al., 2000; Yao et al., 2010; Ying, 2001). In evolutionary terms, such diversity started about 500 Ma in the Cambrian, during the several "Cambrian Explosion" events resulting in early animal origin and evolution in Asia. The most famous one is the Chengjiang Biota with many invertebrates, the first fossil chordates, and the earliest vertebrates (Hou et al., 2017). It covers 34 localities that yielded 22,038 fossil specimens, resulting in numerous national and international studies that have shed light on the earliest events of marine and terrestrial animal origin and evolution (Gabbott et al., 2004; Hou, 2016; Shu et al., 2001; Zhang et al., 2001; Zhao et al., 2012).

Nevertheless, the most remarkable characteristic of Yunnan is the ways that catarrhines took advantage of the geographical, climatic, environmental, and habitat modifications to converge and diverge in the SQPMH since the Later Miocene or Early Pliocene, throughout their dispersal routes and radiation in the region (Harrison et al., 2014; Jablonski and Chaplin, 2009; Kelley and Gao, 2012; Li et al., 2020; Roos et al., 2011). As such, Yunnan is the ideal area to analyze how humans and nonhuman primates coexist by sharing the same environments and habitats, especially after the arrival of hominins (*Homo erectus* and *H. sapiens*) around ~1.7–2.1 Ma ago (Zhao et al., 2018). Both groups experienced together the significant environmental and habitat changes that followed the accelerated uplift of the Qinghai–Tibet Plateau, Himalayas, and SQPMH, and the severe monsoons – which collectively shaped their evolutionary trajectories in different ways compared to their counterparts in other parts of the world (Meldrum and Pan, 1988; Qiu, 2016; Stewart and Disotell, 1998; Zhu et al., 2018). These interactions are not only expressed in the fossil record and the alternative migration routes in and out of SQPMH, but are also recorded in the arts, culture, and social life of the area. Thus, scenes of hunting monkeys and other animals were already represented in late Neolithic rocks in southwest Yunnan, around 3,000 years ago (Ji, 2014; Ji et al., 2016a).

Unfortunately, such events, particularly those related to the dispersion, speciation, and evolution of the catarrhines in East Asia, have not been integrally reviewed and illustrated, and the association between primates and hominins has not been adequately studied. In this context, the main goals of this study are to: (a) present the integral and schematic patterns used by the catarrhines to exploit the SQPMH so as to complete their dispersion and radiation in East and Southeast Asia; (b) analyze the spatial relationship between primates and hominins, mainly referring to the six major archaeological sites of Yunnan (Yuanmou, Jiangchuan, Tangzigou, Xianrendong, Xiaodong, and Maludong); and (c) attract public attention for the protection and conservation of this part in the world.

20.2   Relationship between SQPMH and Catarrhines

The contribution of the SQPMH to dispersion, speciation, and evolution of the East Asian catarrhines since the Late Miocene is illustrated in Fig. 20.2. Some major events related to the different groups include:

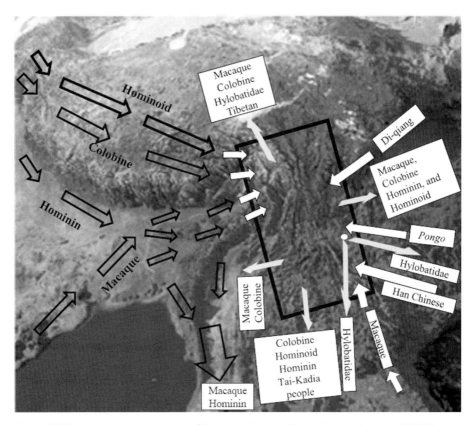

Figure 20.2 Dispersion and speciation of the catarrhines in East Asia based on the SQPMH since the Late Miocene or Early Pliocene.

20.2.1 Colobines

According to (Roos et al., 2011), colobines may have got into the SQPMH in the Late Miocene about 8.5 Ma through the Qinghai–Tibet Plateau, where related fossils, such as *Rhinopithecus, Trachypithecus* in Tangzigou (Zhang et al., 1992), and *Mesopithecus* from Zhaotong (Jablonski et al., 2020; Ji et al., 2020), were discovered. They then successfully used the geographic structures of the SQPMH to complete their dispersion to East Asia resulting in fossil *Rhinopithecus* in mainland China and Taiwan (Chang et al., 2012; Jablonski, 2002) and *Dolichopithecus* (*Kanagawapithecus*) in Japan (Nishimura et al., 2012). A western dispersion from the SQPMH is identified by the fossil *Semnopithecus* from the late Pleistocene of India (Jablonski, 2002) and the Late Pleistocene of Myanmar (Takai et al., 2015a), as well as another recently recorded species, *Myanmarcolobus yawensis*, from the Early Pliocene of Myanmar (Takai et al., 2015b). A southern dispersion of the colobines from the SQPMH can be confirmed by the fossils leading to the evolution of the existing odd-nosed monkeys and *Trachypithecus/Presbytis* in Southeast Asia, such as *Trachypithecus auratus* from the Middle Pleistocene of Java (Jablonski and Tyler, 1999; Roos et al., 2011).

20.2.2 Macaques

A detailed description of how macaques used the SQPMH has been provided and illustrated by Li et al. (2020). More precisely, macaques may have reached the SQPMH in the early Pliocene, around 5 Ma, as evidenced by the fossils discovered in China (Roos et al., 2019). They initially migrated from Africa and got into Asia along the coastlines of India. A northern dispersal of the *sinica* group, including *Macaca arctoides*, *M. assamensis*, *M. thibetana*, *M. leucogenys*, and *M. munzala*, met the Himalayas, which may have formed an unsurpassable physical barrier for their onward northern movement, and changed direction to the east getting into the SQPMH through the corridor(s) between the Himalayas and Bangladesh. On the other hand, *M. leonina* of the *silenus* group entered the SQPMH from Sundaland.

20.2.3 Gibbons

Compared to other Asian catarrhines, the phylogeny, origin, and evolution of the Hylobatidae are quite controversial due to the lack of a rich fossil record. It has been proposed that gibbons initially diverged in Africa in the early Miocene and then migrated to China (Harrison, 2005, 2016), or they monophyletically originated from Asian hominoids in the middle Miocene (Tyler, 1993) and the related descendants then spread widely to south China (Ma, 1979; Ortiz et al., 2015, 2019). The fact that the oldest true hylobatid fossils from the Late Miocene were found in Hudieliangzi and Lufeng in the SQPMH suggests that Yunnan may be the place of origin for gibbons (Chatterjee, 2009). Subsequently, some taxa moved out of the SQPMH migrating toward Southeast Asia (fossils from the Middle Pleistocene of Vietnam and Thailand), and finally reached Java and Sumatra (Indonesia) and Sarawak (Malaysia) in the Late Pleistocene (Chatterjee, 2009; Jablonski and Chaplin, 2009).

20.2.4 Hominoids

The discovery of fossil *Lufengpithecus* in Baoshan, Lufeng, Kaiyuan, Zhaotong, and Yuanmou in the deposits of 6–8 Ma (Ji et al., 2013; Kelley and Gao, 2012; Liu et al., 2002) implies that hominoids in East Asia may have arrived in the SQPMH in the Late Miocene by crossing over the Qinghai–Tibet Plateau (Grehan and Schwartz, 2009), which was relatively flatter than it is today (Wu et al., 2013). Another fossil species of the same period, *Khoratpithecus piriyai* from Thailand (Chaimanee et al., 2004) and Myanmar (Jaeger et al., 2011), indicates that hominoids crossed over the SQPMH to continue their dispersal in Southeast Asia. The geographic distribution of other hominoid fossils, such as the Pleistocene *Gigantopithecus* and *Pongo* found in Yunnan, Guangxi, Guangdong, Guizhou, Hainan, Hubei, and Chongqing in southern China (Harrison et al., 2014) suggest that they dispersed eastward crossing over the SQPMH and got into southern China. On the other hand, a recurrent dispersal of *Pongo* in the Early Pleistocene from southern China to the SQPMH provided a chance for its wide radiation in Southeast Asia. This is evidenced by the fossils unearthed from the Middle and Late Pleistocene in Vietnam (*P. weidenreichi* and *P. devosi*), Borneo (*P. pygmaeus*), Sumatra (*P. abelii*, *P. duboisi*, and *P. palaeosumatrensis*), and Java (*P. javensis*) (Grehan and Schwartz, 2009; Harrison et al., 2014).

20.2.5 Hominins

Fossils of *Homo erectus* and their associated artifacts in China imply that hominins may have arrived in East Asia by 1.7 Ma (Potts and Teague, 2010; Shunkov and Derevyanko, 2016) or 2.12 Ma in the Early Pleistocene (Zhu et al., 2018). This species approached East Asia through the Indian subcontinent or the corridors between the Himalayas and India (Mishra et al., 2010; Petraglia, 2010; Sonakia and Biswas, 1998). Fossil evidence from Yuanmou indicates that this species got into the SQPMH and moved eastward to spread to other parts of China, particularly Lantian in Shaanxi (Luo et al., 2020), and Zhoukoudian, next to Beijing (the renowned Peking man), as well as other parts of East Asia (Xing et al., 2018). On the other hand, the fact that *Homo erectus* appeared in Java by 1.5 Ma (Larick et al., 2001) implies that this species perhaps reached Flores, giving rise to the insular dwarf *Homo floresiensis* about 1 Ma (Brumm et al., 2010; van den Bergh et al., 2016). This scenario also indicates that *H. erectus* dispersed to Southeast Asia either through southern SQPMH or Myanmar, as supported by its fossil presence in Myanmar, Thailand, Laos, Cambodia, Vietnam, and Malaysia (Marwick, 2009).

20.2.6 Current Ethnic Groups

Yunnan is characterized by the largest number of ethnic groups (26) in China. In the country, a total of 56 groups, representing 8.0% of total national population size, and widely distributed in 34 provinces and autonomous prefectures, has been anthropologically and officially recognized (Wang et al., 2018b). Regarding the phylogenetic relationships among the groups in Yunnan, there have been some hot debates (Chen et al., 2007; Su et al., 1999), except for a consensus that the majority of the groups belong to the Tibeto-Burman linguistic clade (Li, 2003; Shi, 2000). They derive from the "Di-Qiang" Hain Chinese (Li et al., 2017) and originated in the upper and middle sections of the Yellow River in northern China, around 7,000 years ago (Shi, 2000; Yao et al., 2002). They entered the SQPMH through the eastern Tibet and Sichuan basin and then spread to the neighboring countries. Some groups, such as Lisu, Yi, Bai, Nakhi, and Lahu, are closely related to this migration (Cang, 1997). Alternatively, an origin from southern China has been also proposed based on genetic studies. This migration was closely associated with the T(D)ai, who are widely distributed in southern Yunnan, Thailand, Myanmar, and Laos (Sun et al., 2013). Based on their language, they are regarded as a Tai-Kadia clade and are supposed to have migrated mostly from the Han in Guangdong approximately 1,000 or 2,000 years ago (Sun et al., 2013). In general, Tibetans have more north-prevalent haplogroups (clades of the mtDNA phylogeny), while Dai and Lahu populations have high frequencies of southern-prevalent haplogroups (Yao and Zhang, 2002).

20.3   Coexistence between Primates and Humans

Fossil distribution profiles of the three primate groups (macaques, colobines, and gibbons) in Yunnan since the Oligocene and the six major archaeological sites are illustrated in Fig. 20.3. Fossil locations are always around the archaeological sites, indicating a very close relationship between humans and nonhuman primates sharing the same environments and habitats. As for the archaeological sites, Tangzigou is located on the western side of the Nujiang River and the southern edge of Mount Gaoligong. Aside from *H. sapiens*, primate remains from the early to middle Holocene (9,000 and 7,350 BP) include *Trachypithecus phayrei*, *Rhinopithecus avunculus*, *Rhinopithecus* sp., *Macaca* sp., and *M. nemestrina* (Zhang et al., 1992). The marks left on the remains of primates (Fig. 20.4) and other animals imply that humans started keeping them as pets in addition to hunting for meat (Jin, 2010; Jin et al., 2012; Zhang et al., 1992).

In Xiaodong, where the first Chinese Hoabinhian rock shelter was found in the Later Pleistocene (between 2.4 ka and 43.5 ka; Ji et al., 2016b), there are primate remains of *Macaca* and langurs (*Trachypithecus?*; Ji, unpublished data). Yuanmou, where the Late Miocene *Lufengpithecus* (*L. hudienensis*) was found (Qi et al., 2006), is

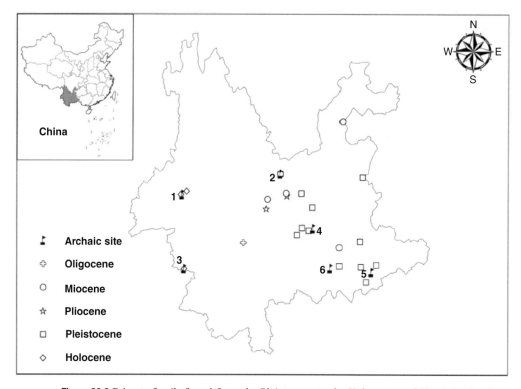

Figure 20.3 Primate fossils found from the Pleistocene to the Holocene, and Hominin sites in Yunnan. 1: Tangzigou; 2: Yuanmou; 3: Xiaodong; 4: Jiangchuan; 5: Xianrendong; and 6: Maludong.

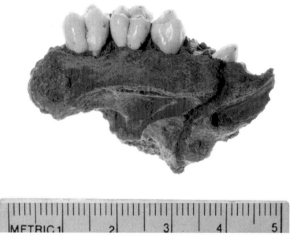

Figure 20.4 Monkey maxilla (*Macaca* sp.) unearthed in Tangzigou, Baoshan, Yunnan, dated about 8,000 years ago. (Photograph by Nina Jablonski, courtesy and with permission from Xueping Ji, Yunnan Institute of Cultural Relics and Archeology).

located at the southeastern margin of the Tibetan Plateau, and contains Early Pleistocene hominin deposits (*H. erectus*) (dated at 1.7 Ma Hyodo et al., 2002; Zhu et al., 2008). It also contains numerous Pleistocene mammalian fossils, echoing the early Pleistocene fauna of southern China (Schick and Zhuan, 2005). Yuanmou, like Gongwangling (Lantian) in Shaanxi, with the primate remains and the taxa that were located there, has provided an ideal place for the study of the evolution of foraging behavior of early *Homo* (*Homo erectus*) (Dong et al., 2013). Jiangchuan is featured because of its record of *Macaca jiangchuanensis* found in the Early Pleistocene deposit next to two lakes, Fuxin and Xinyun, home to Han and other ethnic groups (Pan et al., 1992). Xianrendong is famous for its remains of hominins and primates, including orang-utan, gibbon, and macaques (Taçon et al., 2015), as well as of another 33 fossil mammalian species from the Late Pleistocene (Zhang et al., 2004). Finally, Maludong (Red Deer Cave) is located in Mengzi, where *Homo* remains, dated between 14,500 and 13,600 years, have been found (Curnoe et al., 2012; Ji et al., 2016a).

A historical spatial distribution pattern of the primates, including macaques, colobines, and gibbons, recorded since 1510 in Yunnan is shown in Fig. 20.5. It is clear that, more than 500 years ago, primates in Yunnan were distributed almost everywhere with humans, particularly in the high mountainous regions. Unfortunately, ever since, some taxa either disappeared or have suffered severely from dwindling distribution and population reduction. A typical example is gibbons whose distribution areas in western Yunnan have been wiped out in a short period, after the second half of the last century (Fig. 20.6). This indicates that although Yunnan is characterized by its high plateau and remoteness, it was not sheltered from primate population reduction and primate extinction; nevertheless, the conservation status is relatively better compared to the coastal and central regions of China (Li

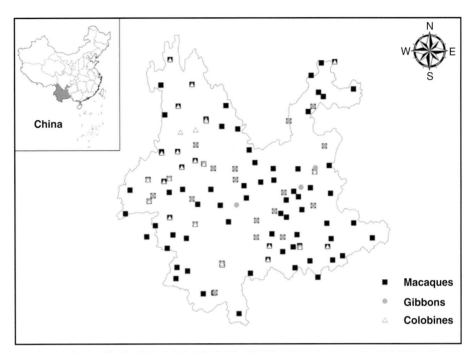

Figure 20.5 Historical locations where primates have been reported from 1510 to present in Yunnan.

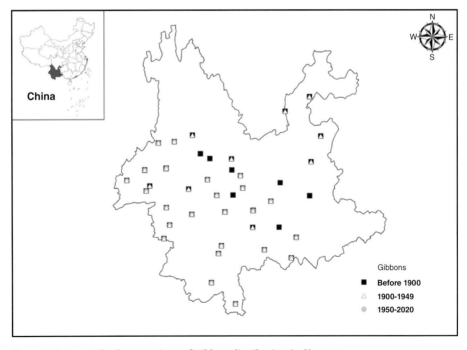

Figure 20.6 A periodical comparison of gibbon distribution in Yunnan.

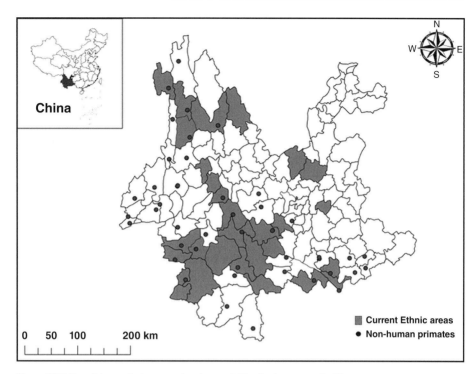

Figure 20.7 Coexistence between primates and 25 ethnic groups in Yunnan.

et al., 2018; Pan et al., 2016). Thus, a current distribution profile of the coexistence of 21 primate species and 26 ethnic groups in Yunnan (Fig. 20.7) shows that they currently coexist in the northwest and southwest of the province, but are absent in the west, a condition different from that of Fig. 20.5, which is related to the alarming situation of Yunnan: between 1950 and 1985 the forest cover of this province decreased from 63% to 34% (Zhang and Cao, 1995), principally for monoculture plantation of rubber trees. A typical example is Xishuangbanna, where the rate of plantation between 1990s to 2010 increased by 100%, covering 18% of the total surface of the area (Xu et al., 2014). This resulted in extreme biodiversity deterioration with two gibbon species, *Nomascus leucogenys* and *Hylobates lar*, recently extirpated (Li et al., 2018; Pan et al., 2016).

The coexistence between primates and humans in Yunnan, as elsewhere in China, is also reflected in the remarkable contribution of primates to Chinese culture, arts, and social life. Evidence from anthropogenic marks left on the remains (Fig. 20.4) indicate that primates were hunting targets about 8,000 years ago at Tangzigou in Baoshan, and even as back as 40,000 years ago as revealed by the newly excavated site in Xiaodong (Ji, personal communication). This is similar to the case reported in Sri Lanka dating back to 45,000 years ago (Wedage et al., 2019). Primates were also depicted on later Neolithic rock arts in the southwest of Yunnan (Figs. 20.8 and 20.9). Furthermore, primates are generally regarded as the symbols of smartness and luck in Chinese culture, as supported by numerous handicrafts depicting monkeys, dating

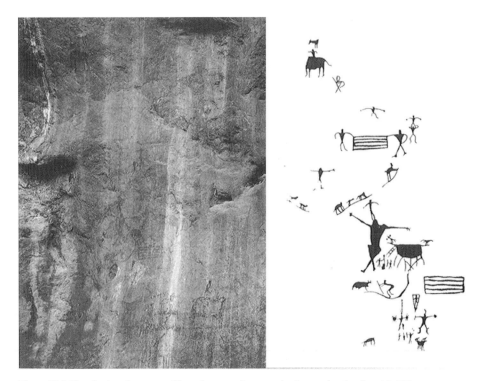

Figure 20.8 The depicted scenes of hunting monkeys and other animals about 2,220 years ago, Late Neolithic in southwest Yunnan during the Han Dynasty (see Ji, 2014). (Courtesy and with permission from Xueping Ji, Yunnan Institute of Cultural Relics and Archeology).

from as early as the Han Dynasty (206 BC to CE 220) (Xin, 2018). Monkeys are also the ninth of the zodiac animals in Chinese society and are regarded as being intelligent, sociable, amicable, very competitive, with logical thinking, and likely to be the final winners in every contest (https://chinesenewyear.net/zodiac/monkey/).

In China, symbols of primates represent about 26% for "Year of the Monkey", 19% for business logos, 12% for stamp designs, 13% for paper cutting, and 30% for other purposes (Shen, 2017). The most influential primate presence in Chinese culture is through the legendary novel *The Journey to the West*, written during the Ming Dynasty (1368–1644) (Liu and Li, 2013). It describes a team of four Buddhist monks who overcame many hardships during the journey approaching the "West" to fetch the Buddhist Scriptures. The novel was translated into English in 1943 (Arthur, 1943). In the novel, Sun Wukong, an incarnation of the macaques (*Macaca* spp.), has the character of both humans and animals, representing immortals in human forms, and is also viewed as the symbol of liberty, smartness, and revolution. Regarded as the Monkey King and a Chinese hero, Sun Wukong is deeply rooted in Chinese culture and arts, and stands for the mixture of Confucianism, Buddhism, and Taoism – the "Three-Religion-in-One" ideology (Liu and Li, 2013; Lou, 2016). Moreover, Sun Wukong is described as a trickster, just like the Greek trickster heroes of the

Figure 20.9 The depicted scenes of hunting monkeys about 3,000 years ago, Late Neolithic in southwest Yunnan (Bronze age), during the Shang Dynasty (see Wang, 1984). (Courtesy and with permission from Xueping Ji, Yunnan Institute of Cultural Relics and Archeology).

Homeric Iliad and Odyssey (Lou, 2016). The novel is also regarded as a folktale, and among the five Chinese classical masterpieces, and has been extensively and deeply embedded in Chinese culture, literature, entertainment, religions, and ideology since the sixteenth century (Ma, 1979).

Finally, primates are significantly important in scientific and biomedical research. According to Ni et al. (2018), 537,480 live primate individuals were traded in China between 1975 and 2017, mostly exported for medical and biological research. Since the 1980s some species, particularly macaques (i.e. *Macaca mulatta*, *M. arctoides*, *M. fascicularis*, *M. assemensis*, and *M. leonina*), have been legally imported into, or exported from China for biomedical research (Fan and Song, 2003). According to Hao (2007), China exports approximately 20,000 primates per year, and correspondingly, by 2008, more than 40 primate-breeding centres, hosting around 40,000 individual animals, mostly rhesus monkeys, had been established (Cyranoski, 2016; Jiang et al., 2008). Furthermore, since India's banning of primate exports in 2013 (Behal, 2014), the number of captive-bred and exported primates in China has increased, so that in 2014, about 250,000 crab-eating macaques (*M. fascicularis)* and 42,000 rhesus monkeys (*M. mulatta*) were kept. Between 2010 and 2016, China had exported more than 350,000 *M. fascicularis* and 35,000 *M. mulatta* (CITES Trade Database). Yunnan has also played a significant role. The Chinese Academy of Sciences invested about US$ 1.3 million to update the facilities of primate-breeding centers at Kunming Primate Research Center, China's arguably largest monkey center for research and export. According to Hao (2007), the center kept 1,500 rhesus macaques and several hundreds of seven other species in 2007; that number increased to 2,500 in 2010.

20.4   Conclusion

Based on an extensive literature review, this study illustrates the distinctive role of the SQPMH, a gateway between West, East, and Southeast Asia. Since the Later Miocene or Early Pliocene, it has been a special place, contributing to the dispersion, radiation, speciation, and refuge of East Asian catarrhines, including colobines, macaques, as well as gibbons, hominoids, fossil hominins, and modern human ethnic groups, besides other animals and plants. Thus, Yunnan, where SQPMH is located, is an ideal place to analyse the relationship between primates and early *Homo sapiens* as well as ethnic groups and study their co-evolutionary development that has been shaped following the accelerated geographic, climatic, environmental, and habitat modifications, particularly during the Quaternary. Primates in Yunnan have also made a significant contribution to Chinese culture, arts, social life, biological research, and medical exploration. Unfortunately, in recent Chinese history, increased deforestation, hunting, and illegal and legal trade have resulted in dwindling populations, shrinking distributions, and ultimate extinction. This is particularly evident after the second half of the last century, when two gibbon species (*Nomascus leucogenys* and *Hylobates lar*) have been extirpated. Thus, the narratives on the interactions, relationship, and association, between primates and humans in Yunnan are a typical example of requiting kindness with enmity.

Acknowledgments

This project was supported by the following research grants: Key Project of Natural Science Foundation of China (31730104), National Natural Science Foundation of China (32070450, 31672301), Strategic Priority Research Program of the Chinese Academy of Sciences (XDB31020302), Natural Science Foundation of Shaanxi Province in China (2016JZ009), the Opening Foundation of the Key Laboratory of Resource Biology and Biotechnology in Western China (Northwest University), Ministry of Education (ZSK2019006).

References

An, Z, S, Kutzbach, J. E., Prell, W. L., & Porter, S. C. (2001). Evolution of Asian monsoons and phased uplift of the Himalayan Tibetan plateau since Late Miocene times. *Nature*, **411**(6833), 62–66.

Arthur, W. (1943). *Monkey*. New York: Grove Press.

Behal, S. (2014). Primate export: Ending the monkey business. *India Today*. Available at : www.indiatoday.in/magazine/indiascope/story/19780228-government-bans-export-of-monkeys-us-forced-to-curtail-experiments-822869-2014-04-29

Bosboom, R. E., Dupont-Nivet, G., Houben, A. J. P., et al. (2011). Late Eocene sea retreat from the Tarim Basin (west China) and concomitant Asian paleoenvironmental change. *Palaeogeography, Palaeoclimatology, Palaeoecology*, **299**, 385–398.

Bowen, G. J., Clyde, W. C., Koch, P. L., et al. (2002). Mammalian dispersal at the Paleocene/Eocene boundary. *Science*, **295**, 2062–2065.

Brumm, A., Jensen, G. M., van den Bergh, G. D., et al. (2010). Hominins on Flores, Indonesia, by one million years ago. *Nature*, **464**, 748–752.

Cang, M. (1997). On the Migration Culture of the Ethnic Groups in Yunnan. *[In Chinese]*. Kunming, China: The Nationalities Publishing House of Yunnan.

Chaimanee, Y., Suteethorn, V., Jintasakul, P., et al. (2004). A new orang-utan relative from the Late Miocene of Thailand. *Nature*, **427**, 439–441.

Chang, C. H., Takai, M., & Ogino, S. (2012). First discovery of colobine fossils from the early to middle Pleistocene of southern Taiwan. *Journal of Human Evolution*, **63**, 439–451.

Chatterjee, H. (2009). Evolutionary relationships among the gibbons: A biogeographic perspective. In *The Gibbons New Perspectives on Small Ape Socioecology and Population Biology*, ed. S. Lappan, & D. J. Whittaker. Springer ScienceþBusiness Media, LLC, 25–49.

Chen, S. Q., Hu, Y., Xie, L., & Zhou, C., (2007). Origin of Tibeto-Burman speakers: evidence from HLA allele distribution in Lisu and Nu inhabiting Yunnan of China. *Human Immunology*, **68**(6), 550–559.

Curnoe, D., Xueping, J., Herries, A. I., & Kanning, B. (2012). Human remains from the Pleistocene-Holocene transition of southwest China suggest a complex evolutionary history for East Asians. *PLoS ONE*, **7**, e31918.

Cyranoski, D. (2016). Monkey kingdom. *Nature*, **532** (7599), 300–302.

Dong, W., Liu, J., & Fang, Y. (2013). The large mammals from Tuozidong (eastern China) and the Early Pleistocene environmental availability for early human settlements. *Quaternary International*, **295**, 73–82.

Fan, Z., & Song, Y. (2003). Chinese primate status and primate captive breeding for biomedical research in China. In *International Perspectives: The Future of Nonhuman Primate Resources: Proceedings of the Workshop Held April 17–19, (2002)*, ed. U.S. Institute for Laboratory Animal Research. Washington, D.C.: The National Academies Press. 36–45.

Gabbott, S. E., Hou, X. Q. Norry, M. J., & Siveter, D. J. (2004). Preservation of Early Cambrian animals of the Chengjiang biota. *Geology*, **32**(10), 901–904.

Grehan, J. R., & Schwartz, J. H. (2009). Evolution of the second orangutan: phylogeny and biogeography of hominid origins. *Journal of Biogeography*, **36**(10), 1823–1844.

Hao, X. (2007). Monkey research in China: developing a natural resource. *Cell*, **129**(6), 1033–1036.

Harrison, T. (2005). The zoogeographic and phylogenetic relationships of early catarrhine primates in Asia. *Anthropological Science*, **113**(1), 43–51.

Harrison, T. (2016). The fossil record and evolutionary history of Hylobatids. In *Evolution of Gibbons and Siamang. Developments in Primatology: Progress and Prospects.*, ed. U. H. Reichard, & C. Barelli, New York: Springer, 91–110.

Harrison, T., Jin, C., Zhang, Y., et al. (2014). Fossil *Pongo* from the Early Pleistocene *Gigantopithecus* fauna of Chongzuo, Guangxi, southern China. *Quaternary International*, **354**, 59–67.

Hou, X. G. (2016). New rare bivalved arthropods from the Lower Cambrian Chengjiang fauna, Yunnan, China. *Journal of Paleontology*, **73**(1), 102–116.

Hou, X., Siveter, D., Aldridge, R., et al. (2017). *The Cambrian Fossils of Chengjiang, China: The Flowering of Early Animal Life*, 2nd ed. Hoboken: John Wiley & Sons Ltd.

Hyodo, M., Nakaya, H., Urabe, A., et al. (2002). Paleomagnetic dates of hominid remains from Yuanmou, China, and other Asian sites. *Journal of Human Evolution*, **43**(1), 27–41.

Jablonski, N. G. (1998). The response of catarrhine primates to pleistocene environmental fluctuations in East Asia. *Primates*, **39**(1), 29–37.

Jablonski, N. G. (2002). Fossil Old World monkeys: the late Neogene radiation. In W. C. Hartwig, eds., *The Primate Fossil Record*. Cambridge: Cambridge University Press, 255–299

Jablonski, N. G., & Chaplin, G. (2009). The fossil record of gibbons. In S. Lappan, & D. L. Whittaker, ed., *The Gibbons: New Perspectives on Small Ape Socioecology and Population Biology* New York: Springer, 111–130

Jablonski, N. G., & Tyler, D. E. (1999). *Trachypithecus auratus sangiranensis*: A new fossil monkey from Sangiran, Central Java, Indonesia. *International Journal of Primatology*, 20(1), 319–326.

Jablonski, N. G., Ji, X. P., Kelley, J., et al. (2020). *Mesopithecus pentelicus* from Zhaotong, China, the easternmost representative of a widespread Miocene cercopithecoid species. *Journal of Human Evolution*, 146:102851.

Jaeger, J. J., So, A. N., Chavasseau, O., et al. (2011). First hominoid from the Late Miocene of the Irrawaddy Formation (Myanmar). *PLoS ONE*, 6, e17065.

Ji, X. (2014). *Encyclopedia of Global Archaeology*. New York: Springer Science+Business Media.

Ji, X. P., Jablonski, N. G., Su, D. F., et al. (2013). Juvenile hominoid cranium from the terminal Miocene of Yunnan, China. *Chinese Science Bulletin*, 58, 3771–3779.

Ji, X., Curnoe, D., Taço, P., et al. (2016a). Cave use and palaeoecology at Maludong (Red Deer Cave), Yunnan, China. *Journal of Archaeological Science: Reports*, 8, 277–283.

Ji, X., Kuman, K., Clarke, R. J., et al. (2016b). The oldest Hoabinhian technocomplex in Asia (43.5 ka) at Xiaodong rockshelter, Yunnan Province, southwest China. *Quaternary Internationa,l* 400, 166–174.

Ji, X. P., Youlatos, D., Jablonski, N. G., et al. (2020). Oldest colobine calcaneus from East Asia (Zhaotong, Yunnan, China). *Journal of Human Evolution*, 147, 102866.

Jiang, Z., Meng, Z., Zeng, Y., et al. (2008). CITES no-detrimental finding for exporting rhesus monkeys (*Macaca mulatta*) from China. NDF Workshop case study. *WG5-Mammals*, 6, 1–15.

Jin, J. (2010). Zooarchaeological and taphonomic analysis of the faunal assemblage from Tangzigou, Southwestern China. PhD dissertation, Pennsylvania State University.

Jin, J. H., Jablonski, N. G., Flynn, L. J., et al. (2012). Micromammals from an early Holocene archaeo-logical site in southwest China: Paleoenvironmental and taphonomic perspectives. *Quaternary International*, 281, 58–65.

Kelley, J., & Gao, F. (2012). Juvenile hominoid cranium from the late Miocene of southern China and hom-inoid diversity in Asia. *Proceedings of the National Academy of Sciences of the United States of America*, 109, 6882–6885.

Larick, R., Ciochon, R. L., Zaim, Y., et al. (2001). Early Pleistocene 40Ar/39Ar ages for Bapang Formation hominins, Central Jawa, Indonesia. *Proceedings of the National Academy of Sciences of the United States of America*, 98(9), 4866–4871.

Li, J., Zeng, W., Zhang, Y., et al. (2017). Ancient DNA reveals genetic connections between early Di-Qiang and Han Chinese. *BMC Evolutionary Biology*, 17, 239.

Li, B. G., Li, M., Li, J. H., et al. (2018). The primate extinction crisis in China: immediate challenges and a way forward. *Biodiversity and Conservation*, 27, 3301–3327.

Li, B. G., He, G., Guo, S. T., et al. (2020). Macaques in China: Evolutionary dispersion and subsequent development. *American Journal of Primatology*, 82 (7), e23142.

Li, X. (2003). The historical and cultural features of the Zang (Tibetan)-Yi Corridor. *Forum on Chinese Culture*, 45.

Liu, W., Gao, F., & Zheng, L. (2002). The diet of the Yuanmou Hominoid, Yunnan Province, China: An analysis from tooth size and morphology. *Anthropological Science*, 110, 149–163.

Liu, Y. & Li, W. (2013). A comparison of the themes of *The Journey to the West* and *The Pilgrim's Progress*. *Theory and Practice in Language Studies*, 3(7), 1243–1249.

Lou, H. (2016). A comparative study of the Chinese trickster hero Sun Wukong. Master's thesis Duke University.

Lu, H., Jiang, D., Motani, R., et al. (2018). Middle Triassic Xingyi Fauna: Showing turnover of marine reptiles from coastal to oceanic environments. *Palaeoworld*, 27(7), 107–116.

Luo, L., Granger, D. E., Tu, H., et al. (2020). The first radiometric age by isochron 26Al/10Be burial dating for the Early Pleistocene Yuanmou hominin site, southern China. *Quaternary Geochronology*, 55, 101022.

Ma, S. (1979). Probe on the Chinese origin of gibbons (*Hylobates*). *Acta Theriologica Sinica*, 17, 13– 23.

Marwick, B. (2009). Biogeography of Middle Pleistocene hominins in mainland Southeast Asia: A review of current evidence. *Quaternary International*, 202, 51–58.

Meldrum, D. J., & Pan, Y. (1988). Manual proximal phalanx of *Laccopithecus robustus* from the Latest Miocene site of Lufeng. *Journal of Human Evolution*, 17, 719–731.

Mishra, S., Gaillard, C., Hertler, C., et al. (2010). India and Java: Contrasting records, intimate connections. *Quaternary International*, **223-224**, 265–270.

Myers, N., Mittermeier, R. A., Mittermeier, C. G., et al. (2000). Biodiversity hotspots for conservation priorities. *Nature*, **403**(6772), 853–858.

Ni, X., Wang, Y., Hu, Y., & Li, C. (2004). A euprimate skull from the early Eocene of China. *Nature*, **427**, (6969), 65–68.

Ni, X., Gebo, D., Dagosto, M., et al. (2013). The oldest known primate skeleton and early haplorhine evolution. *Nature*, **498**(7452), 60–64.

Nishimura, T. D., Takai, M., Senut, B., et al. (2012). Reassessment of *Dolichopithecus* (*Kanagawapithecus*) *leptopostorbitalis*, a colobine monkey from the Late Pliocene of Japan. *Journal of Human Evolution*, **62**, 548–561.

Ni, Q., Wang, Y., Weldon, A., et al. (2018). Conservation implications of primate trade in China over 18 years based on web news reports of confiscations. *PeerJ*, **6**, e6069.

Ortiz, A., Pilbrow, V., Villamil, C., et al. (2015). The taxonomic and phylogenetic affinities of *Bunopithecus sericus*, a fossil hylobatid from the Pleistocene of China. *PLoS ONE*, **10**, e0131206.

Ortiz, A., Zhang, Y. Q., Jin, C. Z., et al. (2019). Morphometric analysis of fossil hylobatid molars from the Pleistocene of southern China. *Anthropological Science*, **127**(2), 109–121.

Pan, R., Peng, Y., Zhang, X., & Pan, R. (1992). Cercopithecid fossils discovered in Yunnan and its stratigraphical significance *Acta Anthropologica Sinica*, **11**(4), 303–311.

Pan, R. L., Oxnard, C. C., Gruete, C. C., et al. (2016). A new conservation strategy for China-A model starting with primates. *American Journal of Primatology*, **78**(11), 1137–1148.

Petraglia, M. D. (2010). The Early Paleolithic of the Indian Subcontinent: Hominin colonization, dispersals and occupation history. In J. G. Fleagle, et al., eds., *Out of Africa I: The First Hominin Colonization of Eurasia, Vertebrate Paleobiology and Paleoanthropology*, Dordrecht: Springer Science +Business Media, 165–179.

Potts, R., & Teague, R. (2010). Behavioral and environmental background to 'Out-of-Africa I' and the arrival of *Homo erectus* in East Asia. In J. G. Fleagle, et al., eds., *Out of Africa I: The First Hominin Colonization of Eurasia, Vertebrate Paleobiology and Paleoanthropology*, London and New York: Springer Science+Business Media B.V., 67–85.

Qi, G., Dong, W., Zheng, L., et al. (2006). Taxonomy, age and environment status of the Yuanmou hominoids. *Chinese Science Bulletin*, **51**, 704–712.

Qiu, J. (2016). The forgotten continent, fossil finds in China are challenging ideas about the evolution of modern humans and our closest relatives. *Nature*, **535**(7611), 218–220.

Qiu, Z., & Li, C. (2005). Evolution of Chinese mammalian faunal regions and elevation of the Qinghai-Xizang (Tibet) Plateau. *Science in China Series D*, **48**, 1246–1258.

Roos, C., Kothe, M., Alba, D. M., et al. (2019). The radiation of macaques out of Africa: Evidence from mitogenome divergence times and the fossil record. *Journal of Human Evolution*, **133**, 114–132.

Roos, C., Zinner, D., Kubatko, L. S., et al. (2011). Nuclear versus mitochondrial DNA: evidence for hybridization in colobine monkeys. *BMC Evolutionary Biology*, **11**, 77.

Schick, K., & Zhuan, D. (2005). Early paleolithic of China and eastern Asia. *Evolutionary Anthropology*, **2**(1), 22–35.

Shen, T. (2017). Recognition of symbols in different cultures: Chinese culture vs. non-Chinese culture. Master's thesis, Iowa State University.

Shi, S. (2000). The historical changes and features of the ethnic corridor in the western part of Sichuan Province. *Tian Fu New Idea*, **90**, 90–93.

Shu, D. G., Morris, S. C., Han, J., et al. (2001). Primitive deuterostomes from the Chengjiang Lagerstätte (Lower Cambrian, China). *Nature*, **414**(6862), 419–424.

Shunkov, M. V., & Derevyanko, A. R. (2016). Where has *Homo sapience* come from? In *Science First Hand*, 49, Art. 2.

Sonakia, A., & Biswas, B. (1998). Antiquity of the Narmada *Homo erectus*, the early man of India. *Current Science*, **75**(4), 391–393.

Stewart, C. B., & Disotell, T. R. (1998). Primate evolution in and out of Africa. *Current Biology*, **8**(4), 582–588.

Su, B., Xiao, J., Underhill, P., et al. (1999). Y-Chromosome evidence for a northward migration of modern humans into Eastern Asia during the last Ice Age. *American Journal of Human Genetics*, **65**(6), 1718–1724.

Sun, H., Zhou, C., Huang, X., et al. (2013). Autosomal STRs provide genetic evidence for the hypothesis that Tai people originate from southern China. *PLoS ONE*, **8**, e60822.

Taçon, P., Tan, N., O'Connor, S., et al. (2015). The global implications of the early surviving rock art of greater Southeast Asia. *Antiquity*, **88**(342), 1050–1064.

Takai, M., Nishioka, Y., Thaung, H., et al. (2015a). Late Pliocene *Semnopithecus* fossils from central Myanmar: rethinking of the evolutionary history of cercopithecid monkeys in Southeast Asia. *Historical Biology*, **28**(1–2), 172–188.

Takai, M., Thaung, H., Zin Maung Maung, T., et al. (2015b). First discovery of colobine fossils from the Late Miocene/Early Pliocene in central Myanmar. *Journal of Human Evolution*, **84**, 1–15.

Tyler, D. E. (1993). The evolutionary history of the gibbon. In *Evolving Landscapes and Evolving Biotas of East Asia since the Mid-Tertiary,*. In N. G. Jablonski, & So Chak-Lam, eds., Hong Kong: University of Hong Kong, 228–240

van den Bergh, G. D., Kaifu, Y., Kurniawan, I., et al. (2016). *Homo floresiensis*-like fossils from the early Middle Pleistocene of Flores. *Nature*, **534**(7606), 245–248.

Wang, J., Wu, R., He, D., et al. (2018a). Spatial relationship between climatic diversity and biodiversity conservation value. *Conservation Biology*, **32**(6), 1266–1277.

Wang, N. S. (1984). An introduction to rock painting in Yunnan Province. *Rock Art Research*, **1**, 75–84.

Wang, M., Wang, Z., He, G., et al. (2018b). Genetic characteristics and phylogenetic analysis of three Chinese ethnic groups using the Huaxia Platinum System. *Scientific Reports*, **8**, 2429.

Wedage, O., Amano, N., Langley, M. C., et al. (2019). Specialized rainforest hunting by *Homo sapiens* ~45,000 years ago. *Nature Communications*, **10**, 739.

Wen, R. (2009). *The Distribution and Changes of Rare Wild Animals in China.* Shandong: Academic Press of Shandong. [In Chinese]

Wen, R. (2013). *Geographical Distribution of Wild Animals in Ancient China.* Jinan: Academic Press in Shandong. [In Chinese]

Wu, Z. H., Ye, P. S., Barosh, P. J. et al. (2013). Early Cenozoic multiple thrust in the Tibetan Plateau. *Journal of Geological Research*, **2013**, 1–12.

Xin, S. (2018). The monkey in Chinese culture. *Youlin Magazine, A Culture Journal.*

Xing, S., Martinon-Torres, M., & Bermudez de Castro, J. M. (2018). The fossil teeth of the Peking Man. *Scientific Reports*, **8**, 2066.

Xing, Y., & Ree, R. H. (2017). Uplift-driven diversification in the Hengduan Mountains, a temperate biodiversity hotspot. *Proceedings of the National Academy of Sciences of the United States of America*, **114**, E3444–E3451.

Xu, J. C., Grumbine, R. E., & Beckschäfer, P. (2014). Landscape transformation through the use of ecological and socioeconomic indicators in Xishuangbanna, Southwest China, Mekong Region. *Ecological Indicators*, **36**, 749–756.

Yang, Y. M., Tian, K., Hao, J. M., et al. (2004). Biodiversity and biodiversity conservation in Yunnan, China. *Biodiversity and Conservation*, **13**, 813–826.

Yao, Y., Zhang, B., Han, F., & Pang,Y. (2010). Diversity and geographical pattern of altitudinal belts in the Hengduan Mountains in China. *Journal of Mountain Science*, **7**(2), 123–132.

Yao, Y. F., Bruch, A. A., Cheng, Y. M., et al. (2012). Monsoon versus uplift in southwestern China–Late Pliocene climate in Yuanmou Basin, Yunnan. *PLoS ONE*, **7**, e37760.

Yao, Y. G., & Zhang, Y. P. (2002). Phylogeographic analysis of mtDNA variation in four ethnic populations from Yunnan Province: new data and a reappraisal. *Journal of Human Genetics*, **47**(6), 311–318.

Yao, Y. G., Nie, L., Harpending, H., et al. (2002). Genetic relationship of Chinese ethnic populations revealed by mtDNA sequence diversity. *American Journal of Physical Anthropology*, **118**(1), 63–76.

Ying, J. (2001). Species diversity and distribution pattern of seed plants in China. *Chinese Biodiversity*, **9**(4), 393–398.

Zhang, D., Fengquan, L., & Jianmin, B. (2000). Eco-environmental effects of the Qinghai-Tibet Plateau uplift during the Quaternary in China. *Environmental Geology* **39**(12), 1352–1359.

Zhang, J., & Cao. M. (1995). Tropical forest vegetation of Xishuangbanna, SW China and its secondary changes, with special reference to some problems in local nature conservation. *Biological Conservation*, **73**(3), 229–238.

Zhang, X., Gen, D., & Liu, H. (1992). Early Holocene mammal fauna from Tangzigou. In *Baoshan Prehistoric Archaeology* Kunming, China: Yunnan Science and Technology Press. [In Chinese]

Zhang, X., Ji, X., & Shen, G. (2004). U-series dating on fossil teeth from Xianren Cave in Xichou, Yunnan Province. *Acta Anthropologica Sinica*, **23**, 88–92.

Zhang, X. L., Shu, D. G., Li, Y., & Han. J. (2001). New sites of Chengjiang fossils: crucial windows on the Cambrian explosion. *Journal of the Geological Society*, **158**, 211–218.

Zhang, Z. (2006). Chinese Late Neogene land mammals comunity and the envronmental changes of East Asia. *Vertebrata PalAsiatica*, **44**(2), 133–142.

Zhao, F. C., Hu, S. X., Caron, J. B., et al. (2012). Spatial variation in the diversity and composition of the Lower Cambrian (Series 2, Stage 3) Chengjiang Biota, Southwest China. *Palaeogeography, Palaeoclimatology, Palaeoecology*, **346–347**, 54–65.

Zhao, J., Yuan, X., Liu, H., et al. (2010). The boundary between the Indian and Asian tectonic plates below Tibet. *Proceedings of the National Academy of Sciences of the United States of America* **107**, 11229–11233.

Zhao, X., Ren, B., Garber, P. A., et al. (2018). Impacts of human activity and climate change on the distribution of snub-nosed monkeys in China during the past 2000 years. *Diversity and Distributions*, **24**(1), 92–102.

Zhu, R. X., Potts, R., Pan, Y. X., et al. (2008). Early evidence of the genus *Homo* in East Asia. *Journal of Human Evolution*, **55**, 1075–1085.

Zhu, Z., Dennell, R., Huang, W., et al. (2018). Hominin occupation of the Chinese Loess Plateau since about 2.1 million years ago. *Nature*, **559** (7715), 608–612.

21 Fossil and Archaeological Remain Records of Japanese Macaques (*Macaca fuscata*)

Yuichiro Nishioka, Masanaru Takai, Hitomi Hongo, & Tomoko Anezaki

ニホンザル（*Macaca fuscata*）の化石と考古遺骸の記録

要旨

ニホンザルの遺骸は日本本土の200箇所以上の産地から報告されている．更新世の化石記録に基づくと，ニホンザルが人類の渡来以前から日本列島に土着していたことは明らかである．後期更新世（旧石器時代）に人類がニホンザルと接触していたことを示す直接的な証拠はまだ発見されていない．一方，多くの縄文貝塚からニホンザルの遺骸や骨器が出土していることから，完新世初頭はニホンザルが食物資源の一部として利用されていたことがわかる．ニホンザルの分布域は更新世から現在まで然程変化していないが，一部の地域個体群には歯のサイズにおける形態変異が観察された．これが自然要因と人為要因のどちらによるものなのか明らかにすることが今後の課題となるだろう．

キーワード

骨器，日本 – ニホンザル – 縄文 – 旧石器 – 更新世

Abstract

Remains of Japanese macaques (*Macaca fuscata*) have been reported from more than 200 localities in the mainland of Japan. The Pleistocene fossil records of Japanese macaques clearly indicates that they had become indigenous to the Japanese islands before the arrival of Japanese Paleolithic humans, but there is no direct evidence to show the relationship between Japanese macaques and humans in the Pleistocene. Japanese macaques were one of the targets for human diets in the early Holocene, based on the records of remains and bone artifacts from many Jomon shell mounds. The habitat distribution of Japanese macaques has not changed drastically through the Holocene, while morphological variation in dental size was observed in some local populations. Future studies will focus on clarifying if the size variation of Japanese macaques is due to natural phenomena or to human actions.

Keywords: Bone tools, Japan, Japanese macaques, Jomon, Paleolithic, Pleistocene

21.1 Introduction

Japanese macaques (*Macaca fuscata*) are the only nonhuman primates endemically distributed in Japan, or strictly on three Japanese large islands (Honshu, Shikoku, and Kyushu) and their neighboring smaller islands (e.g. Yakushima) (Endo, 2009; Fig. 21.1). Particularly, the Shimokita Peninsula (41°30′N), where the average

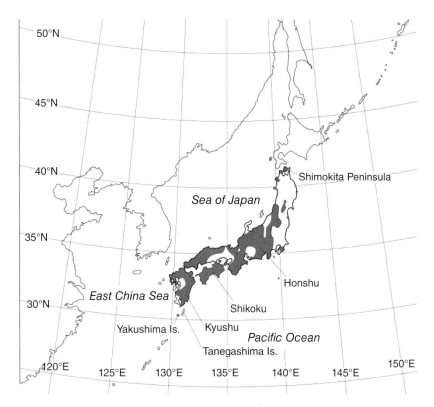

Figure 21.1 High-density area of the distribution of living Japanese macaques (in grey).

temperature of the coldest month is below -5°C, is regarded as the northern limit of all extant nonhuman primates' habitat. Japanese macaques preferably inhabit evergreen or deciduous broad-leaved forests throughout the year. Crop-raiding by Japanese macaques has been regarded as a serious problem in recent years (Ministry of the Environment, 2016; Muroyama, 2008). The coexistence of Japanese macaques and people had been maintained during the prehistoric and ancient times, but its balance started collapsing since humans stopped eating wild animals and/or initiated environmental modification (Watanabe and Mitani, 2019). The records of Japanese macaques from archaeological sites give evidence to trace chronological change of their distribution, habitat, and relationship with humans. In this chapter, we review the records of fossils and archaeological remains of Japanese macaques, in order to understand whether or not humans have impacted the distribution and morphological characters of Japanese macaques in prehistoric times.

21.2   Origin of Japanese Macaques

Macaca fuscata is a species of the genus *Macaca*, which is one of the most widely distributed nonhuman primate groups, occurring from northwestern Africa to south, southeast and far-eastern Asia, including Japan. The genus is classified into more than 20 species, and has been divided into 4 species-groups based mainly on the surface morphology such as genital morphology and tail length: *sylvanus* group, *silenus* group, *sinica* group, and *fascicularis* group (e.g. Delson, 1980; Fooden, 1980). *M. fuscata* is included in the *fascicularis* group, together with *M. fascicularis*, *M. mulatta*, and *M. cyclopis* (e.g. Delson, 1980; Fa, 1989; Fooden, 1980). Recent molecular biological studies also basically support this hypothesis (Li and Zhang, 2005; Li et al., 2009; Morales and Melnick, 1998; Tosi et al., 2000, 2003), although there are some minor differences in phylogenetic relationships probably due to the incomplete lineage sorting or ancient hybridizations between sympatrically distributed species in the Asian continent (Fan et al., 2018; Tosi et al., 2000, 2003).

Molecular biological studies indicate that *M. fuscata* is most closely related to *M. mulatta*, rhesus macaques, or to *M. cyclopis*, Taiwanese macaques, within the *fascicularis* group (e.g. Li et al., 2009; Tosi et al., 2003). The former is distributed widely in Eastern Asia, while the latter is restricted to Taiwan. Considering the geographical positional relationships among Japanese Islands and Taiwan, *M. fuscata* and *M. cyclopis* have diverged from the northeastern and southeastern populations of ancient *M. mulatta* in continental China, respectively (Osada et al., 2020). In China, numerous macaque teeth have been discovered from multiple cave deposits in the Guangxi Autonomous Region, southern China, with dates since the early Pleistocene (Takai et al., 2014). These macaque teeth likely include at least five species, suggesting the beginning of the diversification of East Asian macaques in southern China during the early Pleistocene.

Some fragmentary fossils of *M. fuscata* have been discovered from the middle Pleistocene localities of western Honshu (Table 21.1). A plausible oldest fossil is an isolated lower third molar from fissure deposits at Ando Quarry, Yamaguchi Prefecture (Fooden and Aimi, 2005; Iwamoto and Hasegawa, 1972). The associated mammalian fossil assemblage represents the middle Pleistocene fauna, including *Anourosorex japonicus*, *Palaeoloxodon naumanni*, and rhinocerotids (e.g. Hasegawa, 2009).

In the Korean Peninsula, many macaque fossils have been discovered from the late middle to late Pleistocene sites in central South Korea (Lee, 2006; Lee and Takai, 2012; Park and Lee, 1998;. Among them a zygomaxillary specimen discovered from the late Pleistocene Durubong cave, which was originally named *M. robustus*, shows a distinct similarity to *M. fuscata* (Ito et al., 2018; Lee and Takai, 2012). As mentioned above, the last common ancestor of *M. mulatta* and *M. fuscata* was distributed in Northeast Asia during the early to middle Pleistocene, and then likely dispersed to Japanese Islands through the land-bridges between Korean Peninsula and western Japan, which probably appeared at MIS (marine isotope stage) 16 (0.63 Ma) and MIS 12 (0.43 Ma) during the middle Pleistocene (Dobson and Kawamura, 1998; Kawamura, 2011).

21.3   Japanese Macaques in the Fossil and Archaeological Records

21.3.1   Paleolithic Era (Pleistocene)

Late Pleistocene localities of mainland Japan have commonly yielded fossils of Japanese macaques (Table 21.1 and Fig. 21.2). Most of the fossils are fragmentary

Table 21.1. Fossil localities of Japanese macaques in the Paleolithic Era (Pleistocene). Locality points are shown in Fig. 21.1

	Locality	Area	Geological unit	Age	Literature
1	Shiriya Quarry (Shimokita-gun, Aomori Pref.)	Northeast Honshu	Cave/fissure deposits	Late Pleistocene	Iwamoto and Hasegawa (1972)
2	Kaza-ana Cave (Hanamaki City, Iwate Pref.)	Northeast Honshu	Cave/fissure deposits	Late Pleistocene (c. 18 ka)	Shigehara et al. (2003)
3	Kuzuu Quarry (Sano City, Tochigi Pref.)	Northeast Honshu	Upper Kuzuu Formation	Late Pleistocene	Shikama (1949)
4	Yarimizu (Sodegaura City, Chiba Pref.)	Northeast Honshu	Jizodo Formation	Middle Pleistocene (> 300 ka)	Iwamoto (1991)
5	Tengakuin (Fujisawa City, Kanagawa Pref.)	Northeast Honshu	Shimosueyoshi Formation	Late Pleistocene (c. 150 ka)	Iwamoto (1991)
6	Sugiana Cave (Gifu Pref.)	Central Honshu	Cave/fissure deposits	Late Pleistocene	Kawamura and Kajiura (1980)
7	Kumaishi-do Cave (Gujo City, Gifu Pref.)	Central Honshu	Cave/fissure deposits	Late Pleistocene	Okumura et al. (1982)
8	Gansuiji (Hamamatsu City, Shizuoka Pref.)	Central Honshu	Cave/fissure deposits	Late Pleistocene	Takai and Hasegawa (1966); Iwamoto and Takai (1972)
9	Shiraiwa Mine (Hamamatsu City, Shizuoka Pref.)	Central Honshu	Cave/fissure deposits	Late Pleistocene	Hasegawa (1966)
10	Yage Quarry (Hamamatsu City, Shizuoka Pref.)	Central Honshu	Cave/fissure deposits	Late Pleistocene	Tomida (1978); Kawamura (1988)
11	Ushikawa Mine (Toyohashi City, Aichi Pref.)	Central Honshu	Cave/fissure deposits	Late Pleistocene	Iwamoto and Takai (1972)
12	Suse Quarry (Toyohashi City, Aichi Pref.)	Central Honshu	Cave/fissure deposits	Late Pleistocene	Kawamura et al. (1990)

Table 21.1. (cont.)

	Locality	Area	Geological unit	Age	Literature
13	Taishaku-Kannondo Cave Site (Jinseki-gun, Hiroshima Pref.)	Southwest Honshu	Cave deposits	Late Pleistocene (> 35 ka)	Kawamura (1988, 1992, 1995), etc.
14	Ikumo Quarry (Mine City, Yamaguchi Pref.)	Southwest Honshu	Cave/fissure deposits	Middle Pleistocene	Hasegawa (2012)
15	Akiyoshi-dai (Mine City, Yamaguchi Pref.)	Southwest Honshu	Cave deposits	Late Pleistocene/ Holocene	Iwamoto (1981)
16	Ando Quarry (Mine City, Yamaguchi Pref.)	Southwest Honshu	Cave/fissure deposits	Middle Pleistocene	Iwamoto and Hasegawa (1972)
17	Ube Quarry Locality 3 (Mine City, Yamaguchi Pref.)	Southwest Honshu	Cave/fissure deposits	Middle Pleistocene	Kawamura (1988)
18	Shikimizu Quarry (Ozu City, Ehime Pref.)	Shikoku	Cave/fissure deposits	Late Pleistocene	Hasegawa (1966); Iwamoto (1975)
19	Matsugae Cave (Kitakyushu City, Fukuoka Pref.)	Kyushu	Cave/fissure deposits	Middle Pleistocene	Ogino and Otsuka (2005)
20	Hirao-dai (Kitakyushu City, Fukuoka Pref.)	Kyushu	Cave deposits	Late Pleistocene/ Holocene	Hasegawa et al. (1968); Kawamura and Sotsuka (1984); Kawamura (1988)

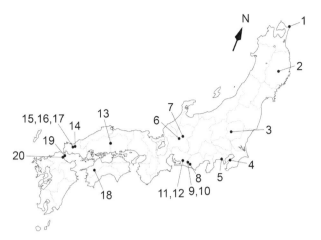

Figure 21.2 Fossil localities of Japanese macaques in the Paleolithic era (Pleistocene). Locality information is listed in Table 21.1.

teeth and bones collected from natural cave or fissure deposits, and they are undoubtedly assigned into the same species as living Japanese macaques. Exceptionally, a female skull from Shikimizu Quarry in Ehime Prefecture, Shikoku, shows unique facial characteristics, such as a broad face and well-developed zygomatic bones, so is dissimilar from living species (Iwamoto, 1975) (Fig. 21.3).

Traces suggesting that Paleolithic Mongoloid hunted animals in Japan have been found dating from 40,000 BP. Both bone cutmark and artifacts from the Paleolithic sites are rare, and if any, the bones derive from large animals, such as elephants and deer (e.g. Anthropology and Archaeology Research Group for Nojiri-ko Excavation, 1990). Thus, the remains of Japanese macaques from the late Pleistocene horizon were not directly associated with the human traces, but some were found in Paleolithic layer covered by early Holocene deposits at Jomon archaeological sites. At Kaza-ana Cave in Iwate Prefecture, northeastern Honshu 30 specimens were found that included a well-preserved Japanese macaque skull (Shigehara et al., 2003). This skull is similar morphologically to that of living female Japanese macaques, but it has a flat face relative to living species. The horizon yielding Japanese macaques contains an elephantid femur that was dated 18,140±60 yBP (19,950–19,270 calBCE) based on carbon-14 dating (Matsu'ura and Kondo, 2003). There is no direct evidence that Japanese macaques coexisted with this elephant in the area of Kaza-ana Cave, but if indeed it is true, Japanese macaques had likely survived in the boreal conifer forest that was widely distributed in northeastern Honshu during the Last Glacial Maximum (*c.* 20,000 cal BCE). Moreover, some isolated teeth of Japanese macaques were recovered above the horizon of *c.* 35,000 BP at the Taishaku-Kannondo site, Hiroshima Prefecture, southwestern Japan (Kawamura, 1992, 1995).

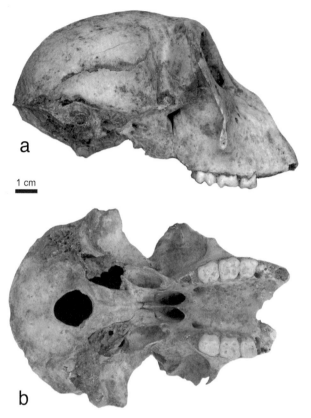

Figure 21.3 Unusual skull remain of a Japanese macaque from the Pleistocene fissure deposits of Shikimizu Quarry, Ehime Prefecture. (a) lateral view; (b) ventral view.

21.3.2 Jomon Period (Holocene)

Skeletal remains of Japanese macaques have been found commonly from archaeological sites of the Jomon Period that is the earliest history of Japan in the Holocene. The Jomon Period began about 14,000 cal BCE and continued for more than 10,000 years. There is a total of 181 Jomon Period sites where the remains of Japanese macaques are recorded (Hongo et al., 2002) (Table 21.2 and Fig. 21.4). This record is biased because the data was obtained primarily from shell mounds, and does not cover all sites recording Japanese macaques throughout Japan. The distribution of Japanese macaques in the Jomon Period is similar to that of extant populations, except for current metropolitan areas. The population density of Japanese macaques in northeastern Honshu (Tohoku area) and central Kyushu has decreased since the Jomon Period (Figs. 21.1 and 21.4). Moreover, a population on Tanegashima Island disappeared during the historic times.

The size variation of teeth is one of main study topics to understanding chronological change of Japanese macaques since the last glacial period. The body size of Japanese macaques shows geographical variation correlated with latitude and

Table 21.2. Jomon (early Holocene) archaeological sites yielding Japanese macaques (modified after Hongo et al., 2002). Locality points are shown in Fig. 21.2

	Locality		Area
1	Saibana Shell Mound	Mutsu City, Aomori	Northeast Honshu
2	Saibana D Shell Mound	Mutsu City, Aomori	Northeast Honshu
3	Shikkari-abe Cave	Shimokita-gun, Aomori	Northeast Honshu
4	Tominosawa 2 Site	Kamikita-gun, Aomori	Northeast Honshu
5	Sokeichinokami	Shimohei-gun, Iwate	Northeast Honshu
6	Anaiwa Cave Site	Shimohei-gun, Iwate	Northeast Honshu
7	Kuwagasaki Tateyama Shell Mound	Miyako City, Iwate	Northeast Honshu
8	Sakiyama Shell Mound	Miyako City, Iwate	Northeast Honshu
9	Jaoudo Cave Site	Kesen-gun, Iwate	Northeast Honshu
10	Miyano Shell Mound	Kesen-gun, Iwate	Northeast Honshu
11	Obora Shell Mound	Ofunato City, Iwate	Northeast Honshu
12	Tagara Shell Mound	Kesen-numa City, Miyagi	Northeast Honshu
13	Moniwanumahara C Site	Sendai City, Miyagi	Northeast Honshu
14	Amako Rock-shelter Sites	Higashiokitama-gun, Yamagata	Northeast Honshu
15	Hinata Cave Site	Higashiokitama-gun, Yamagata	Northeast Honshu
16	Sanganchi Shell Mound	Soma-gun, Fukushima	Northeast Honshu
17	Odaira Goseki Site	Fukushima City, Fukushima	Northeast Honshu
18	Shiobami Rock-shelter Site	Yama-gun, Fukushima	Northeast Honshu
19	Chiamigaido Site	Kiryu City, Gunma	Northeast Honshu
20	Ishihata Rock-shelter Site	Agatsuma-gun, Gunma	Northeast Honshu
21	Hasidate Rock-shelter Site	Chichibu City, Saitama	Northeast Honshu
22	Myoonji Cave Site	Chichibu-gun, Saitama	Northeast Honshu
23	Kaniwahan Cave Site	Chichibu-gun, Saitama	Northeast Honshu
24	Nakatuma Shell Mound	Toride City, Ibaraki	Northeast Honshu
25	Oyamadai Shell Mound	Inashiki-gun, Ibaraki	Northeast Honshu
26	Kannou Shell Mound	Tsukuba-gun, Ibaraki	Northeast Honshu
27	Hanawadai	Kitasoma-gun, Ibaraki	Northeast Honshu
28	Okadaira Shell Mound	Inashiki-gun, Ibaraki	Northeast Honshu
29	Okizu Shell Mound	Inashiki-gun, Ibaraki	Northeast Honshu
30	Fukuda Shell Mound	Inashiki-gun, Ibaraki	Northeast Honshu
31	Yushima Shell Mound	Bunkyo-ku, Tokyo	Northeast Honshu
32	Omori Shell Mound	Shinagawa-ku, Tokyo	Northeast Honshu
33	Shimonumabe Shell Mound	Ota-ku, Tokyo	Northeast Honshu
34	Magome Shell Mound	Ota-ku, Tokyo	Northeast Honshu
35	Toyosawa Shell Mound	Shibuya-ku, Tokyo	Northeast Honshu
36	Umesatoyamasaki	Noda City, Chiba	Northeast Honshu
37	Kamishinshuku Shell Mound	Nagareyama City, Chiba	Northeast Honshu
38	Maegasaki Shell Mound	Nagareyama City, Chiba	Northeast Honshu
39	Kainohana Shell Mound	Matsudo City, Chiba	Northeast Honshu
40	Kamagaya Nakasawa	Kamagaya City, Chiba	Northeast Honshu
41	Nakazawa Shell Mound	Kamagaya City, Chiba	Northeast Honshu
42	Horinouchi Shell Mound	Ichikawa City, Chiba	Northeast Honshu
43	Mukaidai Shell Mound	Ichikawa City, Chiba	Northeast Honshu

Table 21.2. (cont.)

	Locality		Area
44	Kasori Shell Mound	Chiba City, Chiba	Northeast Honshu
45	Kotehashi Shell Mound	Chiba City, Chiba	Northeast Honshu
46	Sonnou Shell Mound	Chiba City, Chiba	Northeast Honshu
47	Tsukiji Shell Mound	Chiba City, Chiba	Northeast Honshu
48	Tsukijidai Shell Mound	Chiba City, Chiba	Northeast Honshu
49	Noroyamada Shell Mound	Chiba City, Chiba	Northeast Honshu
50	Kamitakane Shell Mound	Ichihara City, Chiba	Northeast Honshu
51	Gionbara Shell Mound	Ichihara City, Chiba	Northeast Honshu
52	Saihiro Shell Mound	Ichihara City, Chiba	Northeast Honshu
53	Sanya Shell Mound	Sodegaura City, Chiba	Northeast Honshu
54	Gion Shell Mound	Kisarazu City, Chiba	Northeast Honshu
55	Otsubo Shell Mound	Futsu City, Chiba	Northeast Honshu
56	Fujimidai Shell Mound	Futsu City, Chiba	Northeast Honshu
57	Oderayama Cave Site	Tateyama City, Chiba	Northeast Honshu
58	Natagiri Cave Site	Tateyama City, Chiba	Northeast Honshu
59	Nishimisaki Natagiri Shrine Cave	Tateyama City, Chiba	Northeast Honshu
60	Nittano Shell Mound	Isumi-gun, Chiba	Northeast Honshu
61	Ichinomiya Shell Mound	Chosei-gun, Chiba	Northeast Honshu
62	Ishigami Shell Mound	Mohara City, Chiba	Northeast Honshu
63	Shimoota Shell Mound	Mohara City, Chiba	Northeast Honshu
64	Kuruwanouchi Shell Mound	Sakura City, Chiba	Northeast Honshu
65	Tobedai	Sakura City, Chiba	Northeast Honshu
66	Kounosu	Sanmu City, Chiba	Northeast Honshu
67	Ushikuma Shell Mound	Sanmu City, Chiba	Northeast Honshu
68	Yoyama Shell Mound	Choshi City, Chiba	Northeast Honshu
69	Uehusa Shell Mound	Katori-gun, Chiba	Northeast Honshu
70	Kohara Shell Mound	Katori-gun, Chiba	Northeast Honshu
71	Takeda Shell Mound	Katori-gun, Chiba	Northeast Honshu
72	Nado Shell Mound	Katori-gun, Chiba	Northeast Honshu
73	Adamadai Shell Mound	Katori-gun, Chiba	Northeast Honshu
74	Kinouchi Myojin Shell Mound	Katori-gun, Chiba	Northeast Honshu
75	Yoshibumi Shell Mound	Katori-gun, Chiba	Northeast Honshu
76	Okura South Shell Mound	Sahara City, Chiba	Northeast Honshu
77	Aradachi	Yokohama City, Kanagawa	Northeast Honshu
78	Hiradai Shell Mound	Yokohama City, Kanagawa	Northeast Honshu
79	Yamate-cho	Yokohama City, Kanagawa	Northeast Honshu
80	Sugita Shell Mound	Yokohama City, Kanagawa	Northeast Honshu
81	Shomyoji Shell Mound Loc.A	Yokohama City, Kanagawa	Northeast Honshu
82	Shomyoji Shell Mound Loc.□	Yokohama City, Kanagawa	Northeast Honshu
83	Shomyoji Shell Mound Loc.D	Yokohama City, Kanagawa	Northeast Honshu
84	West Aogadai	Yokohama City, Kanagawa	Northeast Honshu
85	Aoagadai Shell Mound	Yokohama City, Kanagawa	Northeast Honshu
86	Kuhiri	Yokosuka City, Kanagawa	Northeast Honshu
07	Yoshii Shell Mound	Yokosuka City, Kanagawa	Northeast Honshu

Table 21.2. (cont.)

	Locality		Area
88	Nishitomi Shell Mound	Fujisawa City, Kanagawa	Northeast Honshu
89	Tsutsumi Shell Mound	Chigasaki City, Kanagawa	Northeast Honshu
90	Choja-iwaya Rock-shelter Site	Iwafune-gun, Niigata	Central Honshu
91	Hitogaya Rock-shelter Site	Higashikanbara-gun, Niigata	Central Honshu
92	Muroya Cave Site	Higashikanbara-gun, Niigata	Central Honshu
93	Teraji Site	Nishikubiki-gun, Niigata	Central Honshu
94	Yukura Cave Site	Kamitakai-gun, Nagano	Central Honshu
95	Karasawa Rock-shelter Site	Chiisagata-gun, Nagano	Central Honshu
96	Fukamachi Site	Chiisagata-gun, Nagano	Central Honshu
97	Tochikubo Rock-shelter Site	Chino City, Nagano	Central Honshu
98	Tochihara Cave Site	Minamisaku-gun, Nagano	Central Honshu
99	Sakai A Site	Shimoniikawa-gun, Toyama	Central Honshu
100	Asahi Shell Mound	Himi City, Toyama	Central Honshu
101	Osakai Cave Site	Himi City, Toyama	Central Honshu
102	Horimatsu Shell Mound	Hakui City, Ishikawa	Central Honshu
103	Kamiyamada Shell Mound	Kahoku-gun, Ishikawa	Central Honshu
104	Iwauchi Site, Hachimanda area	Nomi-gun, Ishikawa	Central Honshu
105	Gonbo Rock-shelter Site	Ono-gun, Gifu	Central Honshu
106	Shijimi-zuka Shell Mound	Hamamatsu City, Shizuoka	Central Honshu
107	Hiraiinariyama Shell Mound	Hoi-gun, Aichi	Central Honshu
108	Ogasato Shell Mound	Toyohashi City, Aichi	Central Honshu
109	Yoshigo Shell Mound	Atsumi-gun, Aichi	Central Honshu
110	Ikawazu Shell Mound	Atsumi-gun, Aichi	Central Honshu
111	Ikawazu-satonaka	Atsumi-gun, Aichi	Central Honshu
112	Hobi Shell Mound	Atsumi-gun, Aichi	Central Honshu
113	Karekinomiya Shell Mound	Nishio City, Aichi	Central Honshu
114	Hachioji Shell Mound	Nishio City, Aichi	Central Honshu
115	Honkariya Shell Mound	Kariya City, Aichi	Central Honshu
116	Nishinomiya Shell Mound	Handa City, Aichi	Central Honshu
117	Shimizunokami Shell Mound	Chita-gun, Aichi	Central Honshu
118	Torihama Shell Mound	Mikata-gun, Fukui	Central Honshu
119	Hamazume	Takeno-gun, Kyoto	Southwest Honshu
120	Matsudasaki Site	Takeno-gun, Kyoto	Southwest Honshu
121	Shigasato Site	Otsu City, Shiga	Southwest Honshu
122	Awazu Shell Mound	Otsu City, Shiga	Southwest Honshu
123	Awazu Lake Shell Mound Loc.3	Otsu City, Shiga	Southwest Honshu
124	Ishiyama Shell Mound	Otsu City, Shiga	Southwest Honshu
125	Morinomiya Site	Osaka City, Osaka	Southwest Honshu
126	Kamotsuba Site	Gose City, Nara	Southwest Honshu
127	Kashihara Shrine, Outer Gardens	Kashihara City, Nara	Southwest Honshu
128	Narukami Shell Mound	Wakayama City, Wakayama	Southwest Honshu
129	Narukami Shell Mound Loc.5	Wakayama City, Wakayama	Southwest Honshu
130	Negi Shell Mound	Wakayama City, Wakayama	Southwest Honshu
131	Kuritani Site	Iwami-gun, Tottori	Southwest Honshu

Table 21.2. (cont.)

	Locality		Area
132	Megumi Site	Yonago City, Tottori	Southwest Honshu
133	Tatecho Site	Matsue City, Shimane	Southwest Honshu
134	Nishikawazu Site	Matsue City, Shimane	Southwest Honshu
135	Unada Shell Mound	Yatsuka-gun, Shimane	Southwest Honshu
136	Inome Cave Site	Hirata City, Shimane	Southwest Honshu
137	Hyakkennkawa-sawada Site	Okayama City, Okayama	Southwest Honshu
138	Asanebana Shell Mound	Okayama City, Okayama	Southwest Honshu
139	Hikosaki Shell Mound	Kojima-gun, Okayama	Southwest Honshu
140	Funamoto Shell Mound	Kurashiki City, Okayama	Southwest Honshu
141	Fukuda Ancient Castle Shell Mound	Kurashiki City, Okayama	Southwest Honshu
142	Funagura Shell Mound	Kurashiki City, Okayama	Southwest Honshu
143	Yabeokuda Shell Mound	Kurashiki City, Okayama	Southwest Honshu
144	Tsugumo Shell Mound	Kasaoka City, Okayama	Southwest Honshu
145	Taishaku-Anagami Rock-shelter Site	Jinseki-gun, Hiroshima	Southwest Honshu
146	Taishaku-Kannondo Cave Site	Jinseki-gun, Hiroshima	Southwest Honshu
147	Domen Cave Site	Jinseki-gun, Hiroshima	Southwest Honshu
148	West (East) Umatori Shell Mound	Fukuyama City, Hiroshima	Southwest Honshu
149	Nagai Site	Zentsuji City, Kagawa	Shikoku
150	Hoden Rock-shelter Site	Miyoshi City, Tokushima	Shikoku
151	Eguchi Shell Mound	Ochi-gun, Ehime	Shikoku
152	Kamikuroiwa Rock-shelter Site	Kamiukena-gun, Ehime	Shikoku
153	Anagami-do Cave Site	Higashiuwa-gun, Ehime	Shikoku
154	Itoku Site	Tosa Citym Kochi	Shikoku
155	Fudogaiwaya Cave Site	Takaoka-gun, Kochi	Shikoku
156	Nakamura Shell Mound	Nakamura City, Kochi	Shikoku
157	Kogetsu Shell Mound	Kurate-gun, Fukuoka	Kyushu
158	Ninobu Shell Mound	Kurate-gun, Fukuoka	Kyushu
159	Iwashita Cave Site	Sasebo City, Nagasaki	Kyushu
160	Shimomotoyama Rock-shelter Site	Sasebo City, Nagasaki	Kyushu
161	Ikiriki Site	Nishisonogi-gun, Nagasaki	Kyushu
162	Wakazono Shell Mound	Tamana-gun, Kumamoto	Kyushu
163	South Takahashi Shell Mound	Kumamoto City, Kumamoto	Kyushu
164	Kurohashi Shell Mound	Shimomashiki-gun, Kumamoto	Kyushu
165	Sobata Shell Mound	Uto City, Kumamoto	Kyushu
166	Todoroki Shell Mound	Uto City, Kumamoto	Kyushu
167	Euchi Shell Mound	Izumi-gun, Kagoshima	Kyushu
168	Muginoura Shell Mound	Sendai City, Kagoshima	Kyushu
169	Ichiki Shell Mound	Hioki-gun, Kagoshima	Kyushu
170	West Ichiki	Hioki-gun, Kagoshima	Kyushu
171	Kurokawa Cave	Hioki-gun, Kagoshima	Kyushu
172	Kusano Shell Mound	Kagoshima City, Kagoshima	Kyushu
173	Take Shell Mound	Kagoshima-gun, Kagoshima	Kyushu
174	Kunugibaru Shell Mound	Tarumizu City, Kagoshima	Kyushu
175	Katano Cave	Soo City, Kagoshima	Kyushu

Table 21.2. (cont.)

	Locality		Area
176	Nakadake Cave	Soo City, Kagoshima	Kyushu
177	Shioya-agoku Cave	Tanegashima Is., Kagoshima	Kyushu
178	Ichijin-nagasakibana Shell Mound	Tanegashima Is., Kagoshima	Kyushu
179	Hirota Site	Tanegashima Is., Kagoshima	Kyushu
180	Katayama Shell Mound	Kashiwa City, Chiba	Northeast Honshu
181	Sageto Shell Mound	Abiko City, Chiba	Northeast Honshu

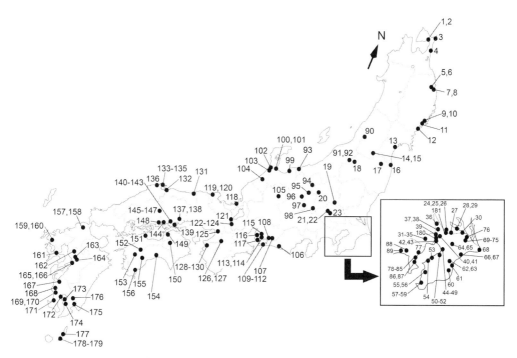

Figure 21.4 Jomon (early Holocene) archaeological sites yielding Japanese macaques. Locality information is listed in Table 21.2.

temperature, following Bergmann's rule (Hamada et al., 1996), and it affects the size of lower first molar (Asahara and Nishioka, 2017). Based on morphological comparisons using dental remains, some populations in the Jomon Period are somewhat larger than living species (Mori, 1981; Shigehara et al., 2002). Anezaki et al. (2006) indicates a difference in the degree of size reduction between male and female Japanese macaques after the early Holocene, based on the remains from Torihama shell-midden (early Jomon Period). According to their results, the size of male Torihama specimens was within the range of the living male population, whereas the size of female Torihama specimens was larger than the living female population. Nishioka et al. (2011) also recognizes that some Pleistocene and early Holocene populations have larger-sized molars than the average of living species, and suggests

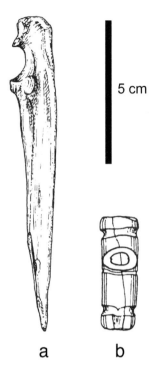

5 cm

a   b

Figure 21.5 Artificial tools made of bones of Japanese macaques (based on images from Kaneko, 1984). (a) Stabbing tool (left ulna) from Tochihara Cave Site (early Jomon), Nagano Prefecture; (b) Tubular ornament (tibia) from Kasori Shell Mound (middle Jomon), Chiba Prefecture.

such molar-size variations of Japanese macaques are correlated with geographical or genetic differentiation (e.g. Kawamoto et al., 2007) rather than chronological change.

In the later Jomon Period, Japanese macaques were eaten because a large quantity of their remains, including bone artifacts, have been found in shell mounds (refuse heaps) and among other remains (e.g. Hasebe, 1924; Kaneko, 1968, 1984, 2002). Kaneko (2002), and in his previous papers, preliminarily noted that the mandible and limb bones (especially the proximal radius) of Japanese macaques are suited to make some specific ornaments (pendants) or stabbing tools (Fig. 21.5).

21.4   Discussion

Japanese prehistoric people hunted primarily deer and wild boar from ancient times, and also used Japanese macaques as food resources and bone artifacts at least in the early Holocene, or Jomon Period (Shitara, 2008). The habitat distribution of Japanese macaques has not changed drastically since prehistoric times. However, some populations, especially around metropolitan areas and in northeastern Honshu disappeared after the Jomon Period. The populations that had lived in current metropolitan areas were certainly affected by human activities, such as developing land and cultivation, until the modern era. On the other hand, the local disappearance or habitat change in northeastern Honshu was probably due to natural factors, although it may be difficult to identify each cause because of the absence of continuous fossil records after the Jomon Period.

Tooth size variation and reduction of mammals, including Japanese macaques, are observed in many Pleistocene and Holocene remains (e.g. Anezaki et al., 2008; Fujita and Kawamura, 1997; Nishioka et al., 2011), but direct correlation with changing environmental factors has not been established yet. In general, size variation or change of mammals depends on geographical isolation (island rule), climate cline (Bergmann's rule), predatory pressure, and neutral mutation. There is little possibility of the island rule as the factor explaining the size reduction of Japanese macaques, because it was not universal throughout Japan. The result by Nishioka et al. (2011) indicates that the tooth size of Japanese macaques had decreased locally, which is possibly related to genetic differentiation between western and eastern populations. Moreover, predation by humans reduces selectively large-sized individuals, as mentioned for deer (Ohtaishi, 1983). The relationship between the size reduction of Japanese macaques and predatory pressure has not been clarified, and thus we need more accurate data with absolute ages supporting the human–Japanese macaque relationship. Further detailed morphological studies of Japanese macaques from archaeological sites of the Jomon Period might yield into that direction.

Acknowledgments

We would like to thank the late Mitsuo Iwamoto (Professor emeritus of Kyoto University) for referring his study materials and knowledge. The present study was financially supported in part by Japan Society for the Promotion of Science KAKENHI, Grant-in-Aid for Scientific Research to YN and MT [18H01327, 18K06444, 19K06863].

References

Anezaki, T., Hongo, H., & Shigehara, N. (2006). A morphometric analysis of the Japanese macaque (*Macaca fuscata*) mandibular cheek teeth from the Torihama Shell-midden, Early Jomon Period, Fukui Prefecture, Japan. *Primates*, **47**, 255–263.

Anthropology and Archaeology Research Group for Nojiri-ko Excavation (1990). Palaeolithic bone tools from the 10th excavation season at Tategahana, Lake Nojiri, Central North Japan. *The Quaternary Research*, **29**, 89–103.

Asahara, M., & Nishioka, Y. (2017). Geographic variation of absolute and relative lower sizes in the Japanese macaque (*Macaca fuscata*: Primates, Mammalia). *Zoological Science*, **34**, 35–41.

Delson, E. (1980). Fossil macaques, phyletic relationships and a scenario of deployment. In D. G. Lindberg, ed., *The Macaques: Studies in Ecology, Behavior and Evolution*. New York, NY: Van Nostrand Reinhold Company, 10–30.

Dobson, M., & Kawamura, Y. (1998). Origin of the Japanese land mammal fauna: allocation of extant species to historically-based categories. *The Quaternary Research*, **37**(5), 385–395.

Endo, H. (2009). *Macaca fuscata* Swinhoe, 1863. In S. D. Ohdachi, Y. Ishibashi, M. A. Iwasa, & T. Saitoh, eds., *The Wild Mammals of Japan*. Kyoto: Shoukadoh, 128–130.

Fa, J. E. (1989). The genus *Macaca*: a review of taxonomy and evolution. *Mammal Review*, **19**(2), 45–81.

Fan, Z., Zhou, A., Osada, N., et al. (2018). Ancient hybridization and admixture in macaques (genus *Macaca*) inferred from whole genome sequences. *Molecular Phylogenetics and Evolution*, **127**, 376–86.

Fooden, J. (1980). Classification and distribution of living macaques (*Macaca* Lacépédem 1799). In D. G. Lindberg, ed., *The Macaques: Studies in Ecology, Behavior and Evolution*. New York: Van Nostrand Reinhold Company, 1–9.

Fooden, J., & Aimi, M. (2005). Systematic review of Japanese macaques, *Macaca fuscata* (Gray, 1870). *Fieldiana Zoology (New Series)*, 104, 1–200.

Fujita, M., & Kawamura, Y. (1997). Preliminary report on the size changes in Late Pleistocene to Holocene middle and large mammals from the Taishaku kyo sites, Hiroshima Prefecture, west Japan. *Annual Bulletin of Hiroshima University Taishaku-Kyo Sites Research Centre*, 12, 143–154. [In Japanese]

Hamada, Y., Watanabe, T., & Iwamoto, M. (1996). Morphological variations among local populations of Japanese macaque (*Macaca fuscata*). In T. Shotake, & K. Wada, eds., *Variations in the Asian Macaques*. Tokyo: Tokai University Press, 97–115.

Hasebe, K. (1924). Japanese monkeys in the Stone Age of Japan. *The Journal of the Anthropological Society of Nippon*, 39, 217–218. [In Japanese]

Hasegawa, Y. (1966). Quaternary smaller mammalian fauna from Japan. *Fossils*, 11, 31–40. [In Japanese]

Hasegawa, Y. (2009). Fauna of Quaternary mammals based on mammalian fossils found in limestone caves and fissure deposits of the Akiyoshi-dai Plateau. *Mammalian Science*, 49, 97–100. [In Japanese]

Hasegawa, Y., Yamauti, H., & Okafuji, G. (1968). A fossil assemblage of *Macaca* and *Homo* from Ojikado-Cave of Hiraodai Karst Plateau, northern Kyushu, Japan. *Transactions and Proceedings of the Palaeontological Society of Japan, New Series*, 69, 218–229.

Hongo, H., Fujita, M., & Matsui, A. (2002). Change of distribution of Japanese macaques from archaeological sites in Japan. *Asian Paleoprimatology*, 2, 1–12. [In Japanese]

Ito, T., Lee, Y., Nishimura, T. D., Tanaka, M., Woo, J., & Takai, M. (2018). Phylogenetic relationship of a fossil macaque (*Macaca* cf. *robusta*) from the Korean Peninsula to extant species of macaques based on zygomaxillary morphology. *Journal of Human Evolution*, 119, 1–13.

Iwamoto, M. (1975). On a skull of a fossil macaque from the Shikimizu Limestone Quarry in the Shikoku District, *Japan. Primates*, 16(1), 83–94.

Iwamoto, M. (1981). Remains of the Japanese monkey (*Macaca fuscata*) from Takaga-ana Limestone Cave in Akiyoshi-dai District, Japan. *Bulletin of Nishi Akiyosi-dai Takaga-ana Limestone Cave Research 1981*, 159–66. [In Japanese with English summary]

Iwamoto, M. (1991). Fossil macaques from Fujisawa and Kisarazu, Kanto district, Japan. *Primate Research*, 7, 96–102. [In Japanese with English abstract]

Iwamoto, M., & Hasegawa, Y. (1972). Two macaque fossil teeth from the Japanese Pleistocene. *Primates*, 13(1), 77–81.

Iwamoto, M., & Takai, F. (1972). The Pleistocene macaque from the Tokai District, Japan—morphological consideration mainly from the tooth-size–. *Journal of the Anthropological Society of Nippon*, 80 (1), 1–10. [In Japanese with English abstract]

Kaneko, H. (1968). Animal remains from Shomyoji D Shell Mound. *Musashino*, 47(2, 3), 51–61. [In Japanese].

Kaneko, H. (1984). *Archaeology Series 10. Knowledge about Animal Bones in a Shell Mound: A Relationship between Humans and Animals*. Tokyo: Tokyo Bijutsu. [In Japanese]

Kaneko, H. (2002). Outline on archaeology of Japanese macaques. *Asian Paleoprimatology*, 2, 35–36. [In Japanese]

Kawamoto, Y., Shotake, T., Nozawa, K., et al. (2007). Postglacial population expansion of Japanese macaques (*Macaca fuscata*) inferred from mitochondrial DNA phylogeography. *Primates*, 48(1), 27–40.

Kawamura, Y. (1988). Quaternary rodent faunas in the Japanese Islands (Part 1). *Memoirs of the Faculty of Science, Kyoto University, Series of Geology & Mineralogy*, 53(1, 2), 31–348.

Kawamura, Y. (1992). Stratigraphic distribution of mammals in the Taishaku-kyo sites, Hiroshima Prefecture, west Japan. *The Quaternary Research*, 31 (1), 1–12. [In Japanese with English abstract]

Kawamura, Y. (1995). Mammalian remains of the Pre-Jomon Period from Taishaku-Kannondo Cave Site (Part 4): Mammalian remains obtained by the excavation of 1979. *Annual Bulletin of Hiroshima University Taishaku-kyo Sites Research Centre*, 10, 118–26, [In Japanese]

Kawamura, Y. (2011). Immigration of mammals into Japan during the Pleistocene: land and ice bridge formation, immigration, and extinction. *Palaeolithic Archaeology*, 75, 3–9. [In Japanese with English abstract]

Kawamura, Y., & Kajiura, K. (1980). Mammalian fossils from Sugi-ana Cave, Gifu Prefecture, Central Japan. *Journal of the Speleological Society of Japan*, 5, 50–65. [In Japanese with English abstract]

Kawamura, Y., & Sotsuka, T. (1984). Preliminary report on the Quaternary mammalian remains from several caves on the Hiraodai Plateau, Fukuoka Prefecture, northern Kyushu, Japan. *Bulletin of the Kitakyushu Museum of Natural History*, 5, 163–88. [In Japanese with English abstract]

Kawamura, Y., Matsuhashi, Y., & Matsu'ura, S. (1990). Late Quaternary mammalian faunas at Suse Quarry, Toyohashi, Central Japan, and their implications for the reconstruction of the faunal succession. *The Quaternary Research*, 29(4), 307–317. [In Japanese with English abstract]

Lee, Y. (ed) (2006). *The Paleolithic Culture of Jungwon Region, Korea.* Cheongju: Institute for Jungwon Culture, Chungbuk National University. [In Korean with English abstract]

Lee, Y., & Takai, M. (2012). The Middle to Late Pleistocene macaque fossils from central Korea. In N. I. Drozdov, Y. Lee, & J. Woo, eds., *The 17th International Symposium: Suyanggae and Her Neighbors in Kurtak.* Cheongju: Institute of Korean Prehistory and Krasnoyarsk State Pedagogical University, 116–119.

Li, Q., & Zhang, Y. (2005). Phylogenetic relationships of the macaques (Cercopithecidae: *Macaca*), inferred from mitochondrial DNA sequences. *Biochemical Genetics*, 43(7–8), 375–386.

Li, J., Han, K., Xing, J., et al. (2009). Phylogeny of the macaques (Cercopithecidae: *Macaca*) based on Alu elements. *Gene*, 448(2), 242–249.

Matsu'ura, S., & Kondo, M. (2003). Preliminary analysis on the age of sediments of Layer 4 on Kaza-ana Cave. In Y. Dodo, W. Takigawa, & J. Sawada, eds., *Search of Pleistocene Hominid Fossils from the Kitakami Mountain Area in Iwate, Japan.* Sendai: Tohoku University Press, 281–283. [In Japanese]

Ministry of the Environment (2016). Guidelines for Specified Wildlife Conservation and Management Plan: Japanese Macaques, 2015. *Tokyo: Office for Wildlife Management*, Wildlife Division, Nature Conservation Bureau, Ministry of the Environment. [In Japanese]

Morales, J. C., & Melnick, D. J. (1998). Phylogenetic relationships of the macaques (Cercopithecidae: *Macaca*), as revealed by high resolution restriction site mapping of mitochondrial ribosomal genes. *Journal of Human Evolution*, 34, 1–23.

Mori, T. (1981). Japanese macaques from Torihama Shell Mounds. *Monkey*, 25(1), 16–18. [In Japanese]

Muroyama, Y. (2008). Conservation of Satoyama and damage management: Japanese macaques. In S.

Takatsuki, & J. Yamagiwa, eds., *Mammalogy in Japan 2: Middle-, and Large-sized Mammals including Primates.* Tokyo: University of Tokyo Press, 427–452. [In Japanese]

Nishioka, Y., Anezaki, T., Iwamoto, M., & Takai, M. (2011). Chronological and geographical variations of Late Pleistocene/Holocene Japanese macaques (*Macaca fuscata*) based on molar measurements. *Mammalian Science*, 51(1), 1–17. [In Japanese with English abstract]

Ogino, S., & Otsuka, H. (2005). Morphological study of fossil *Macaca* cf. *fuscata* detected in the middle Pleistocene Matsugae fauna excavated from the cave deposits in northeastern Kyushu, Japan. *Primate Research*, 21(1), 1–9. [In Japanese with English summary]

Ohtaishi, N. (1983). Sika deer. In S. Kato, T. Kobayashi, & T. Fujimoto, eds., *Studies on Jomon Culture 2.* Tokyo: Yuzankaku Press, 122–135. [In Japanese]

Okumura, K., Ishida, S., Kawamura, Y., Kumada, M., & Tamiya, S. (1982). Latest Pleistocene mammalian assemblage of Kumaishi-do Cave, Gifu prefecture and the significance of its ^{14}C age. *Earth Science (= Chikyu Kagaku)*, 36(4), 214–218. [In Japanese with English abstract]

Osada, N., Matsudaira, K., Hamada, Y., & Malaivijitnond, S. (2020). Sex-biased migration and admixture in macaque species revealed by comparison between autosomal and X-chromosomal genomic sequences. *bioRxiv*, 2020.05.26.115915, Available from: https://doi.org/10.1101/2020.05.26.115915

Park, S., & Lee, Y. (1998). Pleistocene faunal remains from Saekul/Chonyokul at Turupong cave complex with special emphasis on the large mammalian fossils. In Q. Xu, & Y. Lee, eds., *International Symposium for the Celebration of Chinese Academician Jia Lanpo's 90th Birthday: Suyanggae and Her Neighbours.* Beijing: Science Press, 55–70.

Shigehara, N., Kaneko, H., & Iwamoto, M. (2002). Teeth of Japanese macaques (*Macaca fuscata*) from archaeological sites in Japan. *Asian Paleoprimatology*, 2(3), 21–34.

Shigehara, N., Hongo, H., & Takai, M. (2003). Pleistocene Japanese macaques and wolves from Kaza-ana Cave. In Y. Dodo, W. Takigawa, & J. Sawada, eds., *Search of Pleistocene Hominid Fossils from the Kitakami Mountain Area in Iwate, Japan.* Sendai: Tohoku University Press, 387–396. (in Japanese)

Shikama, T. (1949). The Kuzuü Ossuaries: Geological and palaeontological studies of the limestone fissure deposits, in Kuzuü, Totigi Prefecture. *Science Reports of the Tohoku University, 2nd Series, Geology*, **23**, 1–201.

Shitara, H. (2008). Sense of Jomon people towards the animals. In T. Nishimoto, ed., *Japanese History of Human and Animals 1: Archaeology of Animals*. Tokyo: Yoshikawa Kobunkan, 10–34. [in Japanese]

Takai, F., & Hasegawa, Y. (1966). Vertebrate fossils from the Gansuiji Formation. *Journal of the Anthropological Society of Nippon*, **74**(3/4), 155–67. [In Japanese]

Takai, M., Zhang, Y., Kono, R. T., & Jin, C. (2014). Changes in the composition of the Pleistocene primate fauna in southern China. *Quaternary International*, **354**, 75–85.

Tomida, S. (1978). On the Quaternary cave and fissure deposits and vertebrate fossils from Yagé Quarry, near Lake Hamana, Central Japan. *Bulletin of the Mizunami Fossil Museum*, **5**, 113–141. [In Japanese with English abstract]

Tosi, A. J., Morales, J. C., & Melnick, D. J. (2000). Comparison of Y chromosome and mtDNA phylogenies leads to unique inferences of macaque evolutionary history. *Molecular Phylogenetics and Evolution*, **17**(2), 133–144.

Tosi, A. J., Morales, J. C., & Melnick, D. J. (2003). Paternal, maternal, and biparental molecular markers provide unique windows onto the evolutionary history of macaque monkeys. *Evolution*, **57**(6), 1419–35.

Watanabe, K., & Mitani, M. (2019). *Human and Nature*, **30**, 49–68. [In Japanese with English summary]

Index